FLORENTINE CODEX

Florentine Codex

General History of the Things of New Spain

FRAY BERNARDINO DE SAHAGÚN

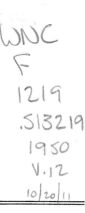

Book 11 – Earthly Things

Translated from the Aztec into English, with notes and illustrations

By

CHARLES E. DIBBLE

UNIVERSITY OF UTAH

ARTHUR J. O. ANDERSON

SCHOOL OF AMERICAN RESEARCH

IN THIRTEEN PARTS

PART XII

Chapter heading designs are from the Codex

Published by

The School of American Research and The University of Utah

Monographs of The School of American Research and The Museum of New Mexico

Santa Fe, New Mexico

Number 14, Part XII   1963

ISBN-10: 0-87480-008-0 (Book 11)
ISBN-13: 978-0-87480-008-1

ISBN-10: 0-87480-082-X (Set)
ISBN-13: 978-0-87480-082-1

Published and distributed by
The University of Utah Press
Salt Lake City, Utah 84112

Preparation of the *Florentine Codex* has been greatly aided by grants made the translators and editors.

A National Science Foundation grant to Charles E. Dibble permitted the necessary time for research and writing. The cooperation of the Foundation and of all those connected with it is gratefully acknowledged.

A Fellowship and awards to Arthur J. O. Anderson by the John Simon Guggenheim Memorial Foundation permitted the necessary time and funds for travel and studies in Europe and for research and writing. In their personal interest and courtesies, Dr. Henry Allen Moe and Dr. James F. Mathias, and all connected with the Foundation, have always been unusually helpful.

CONTENTS

ELEVENTH BOOK, WHICH TELLETH OF THE DIFFERENT
ANIMALS, THE BIRDS, THE FISHES; AND THE TREES
AND THE HERBS; THE METALS RESTING IN THE
EARTH — TIN, LEAD, AND STILL OTHERS;
AND THE DIFFERENT STONES

LIST OF ILLUSTRATIONS

BOOK XI

following page 220

Identifications of the illustrations are provisional

Page from *Florentine Codex* (Chapter 5)

342. Chiancuetla
343. Nextecuili
344. (a) Cinocuili,
     (b) tlaçolocuili
345. Citlalocuili
346. Temoli
347. Cuitlatemoli
348. Ayoxochquiltemoli
349. Quauhtemoli
350. Quauhocuili
351–355. Icpitl
356. Mayatl
357. Tecmilotl
358. Çayoli
359. Miccaçayoli
360. Xopan çayoli
361. Tzonuatzalton
362. Chilton
363. Cuitlaçayoli
364. Çayolton
365. Xiuhçayoli
366. Moyotl
367. Xalmoyotl
368. Forest
369. Mountainous forest
370. Forest animals
371. Wood-gathering
372. Wild beasts
373, 374. Tlatzcan
375. Oyametl
376. Ayauhquauitl
377. Ocotl
378. Ilin
379. Aueuetl
380. Pochotl
381. Auaquauitl
382. Auatetzmoli
383. Tepetomatl
384. Pocquauitl
385. Uexotl
386. Quetzalhuexotl
387. Icçotl
388. Tlacuilolquauitl

389. Tlacalhuazquauitl
390. (a) Uitzquauitl,
     (b) quappotzalli,
     (c) quauhcayactli
391. Tree planting
392. Tree
393. Tree trunk
394, 395. Tree shape
396. Branch
397. Tree top
398. Tender shoot
399. Tree bark
400. Wood chopping
401. Wood for sieve rims
402. Small beams
403. Beams
404. Plank
405. Binding wall beams
406. Wooden door
407. Joist
408. Pillars
409. Wood fragments
410. Tree planting
411. Tzapotl
412. Cochiztzapotl
413. Tlacaçoltzapotl
414. Atzapotl
415. Xicotzapotl
416. Totolcuitlatzapotl
417. Maçaxocotl
418. Atoyaxocotl
419. Xalxocotl
420. Teonacaztli
421, 422. Uaxi
423. Mizquitl
424. Quetzalmizquitl
425. Capoli
426. Elocapoli
427. Tlaolcapoli
428. Quauhcamotli
429. Nopalli
430. Iztac nochnopalli
431. Coznochnopalli

432–439. Nopalli
440. Quauhcamotli
441. Camotli
442. Xicamoxiuitl
443. Cimatl
444. Tolcimatl
445. Cacapxon
446. Acaxilotl
447. (a) Çacateztli
448. (c) Atzatzamolli
449. Coatl xoxouhqui
450, 451. Tlapatl
452. (a) Tzitzintlapatl,
     (b) mixitl
453. (a) Nanacatl,
     (b) tochtetepon
454. Atlepatli
455. Haquiztli
456. (a) Tenxoxoli,
     (b) quimichpatli
457. (a) Nanacatl,
     (b) tzontecomanana-
         catl,
     (c) xelhoaznanacatl
458. (a) Chimalnanacatl,
     (b) menanacatl
459. (a) Çacananacatl,
     (b) quauhnanacatl
460. (a) Cimatl,
     (b) hamolli
461. (a) Tecpatli,
     (b) yiamoli
462. Vauhquilitl
463. Petzicatl
464. (a) Itzmiquilitl,
     (b) quiltonilli,
     (c) ayoxochquilitl
465. (a) Ayoyacaquilitl,
     (b) axoxoco,
     (c) mizquiquilitl
466. (a) Acuitlacpalli,
     (b) tziuinquilitl,
     (c) tacanalquilitl,
     (d) mamaxtla

467. (a) Uei uauhquilitl,
     (b) tzitzicazquilitl,
     (c) etenquilitl,
     (d) tlalayoquilitl
468. (a) Xaltomaquilitl,
     (b) tzitziquilitl,
     (c) eloquilitl
469. (a) Quauheloquilitl,
     (b) moçoquilitl,
     (c) tzayanalquilitl
470. (a) Achochoquilitl,
     (b) auexocaquilitl,
     (c) tehtzonquilitl
471. (a) Iztaquilitl,
     (b) tepicquilitl,
     (c) eçoquilitl
472. (a) Uitzquilitl,
     (b) quauitzquilitl,
     (c) chichicaquilitl,
     (d) coyocuexi
473. Popoyauh
474. Mexixin
475. Xoxocoyoli
476. Xoxocoyolpapatla
477. (a) Xoxocoyolcue-
         cuepoc,
     (b) xoxocoyolhui-
         uila,
     (c) miccaxoxocoyoli
478. (a, b) Quauhxoxo-
          coyoli,
     (c) quanacaquilitl
479. (a) Xonacatl,
     (b) tepexonacatl,
     (c) maxten
480. (a) Papaloquilitl,
     (b) ayauhtona,
     (c) xiuitl xochi-
         quallo
481. (a) Xicama,
     (b) tolcimaquilitl
482. Acaxilotl
483. Atzatzamolli
484. Çacateztli
485. Xaltomatl
486. Coyototomatl

487 (a) Atlitliliatl,
    (b) tlalxilotl
488 (a) Tlalayotli,
    (b) iztac patli
489 (a) Cuicuitlapile,
    (b) iztac çaçalic
490. Centli ina
491. Tlatlauhcapatli
492. Tlanoquiloni
493. Eloxochineluatl
494. Naui iuipil
495. Tlalcacauatl
496. Tetzmitl
497. Eloquiltic
498. Chichipiltic
499. Coyotomatl
500. Tlalchichic
501. Coatli
502, 503. Tzipipatli
504. Nanauaxiuitl
505. Necutic
506. Coayielli
507 (a) Tememetla,
    (b) texochitl
508 (a) Yiauhtli,
    (b) xonecuilpatli
509. Xoxouhcapatli
510. Tzitzicaztli
511. Tecomaxochitl
512. Picietl
513. Itzietl
514. Hecapatli
515. Tlapatl
516. Nanacatl
517. Peyotl
518. Toloa
519. Çoçoyatic
520. Pipitzauac
521. Iztac quauitl
522. Coanenepilli
523. Ilacatziuhqui
524. Macoztic metl
525. Chapolxiuitl

526. Totonacaxiuitl
527. Uei patli
528. Ixyayaual
529. Eeloquiltic
530. Toçancuitlaxcolli
531. Coztomatl
532. Çacacili
533. Iztac palancapatli
534. Cototzauhqui xiuitl
535. Chichientic
536. Cococ xiuitl
537. Xaltomatl
538. Ixnexton
539. Tecanalxiuitl
540. Xoxocoyoltic
541. Iceleua tlacotl
542. Chilpanton
543. Chichilquiltic
544. Tlatlalayotli
545. Tepeamalacotl
546. Iztaquiltic
547. Tlalmizquitl
548. Poçauizpatli
549. Uauauhtzin
550. Tlacoxiuitl
551. Tlalchipili
552. Acaxilotl
553. Chichilquiltic quauitl
554. Uauauhtzin
555. Iztaquiltic
556. Memeya
557. Tetzmitic
558. Tzatzayanalquiltic
559. Ichcayo
560. Tlalyetl
561. Mexiuitl
562. Uitzocuitlapilxiuitl
563. Iztac patli
564. Quachtlacalhuaztli
565. Haauaton
566. Ololiuhqui
567. Iztauhyatl

568. Quauhyayaual
569. Mamaxtla
570. Xaltomatl
571. Quapopultzin
572. Tlalamatl
573. Xoxotlatzin
574. Tonalxiuitl
575. Tlacoxochitl
576. Ocopiaztli
577. Topoçan
578. Quetzalhuexotl
579. Tlayapaloni xiuitl
580. Uei patli
581. Ololiuhqui
582. Aitztolin
583. Use of coaxoxouhqui
584. Acocoxiuitl
585. Tepetomatl
586. Tlatlacotic
587. Texoxocoioli
588. Tlatlanquaie
589. Use of tlatlanquaie
590. Tonacaxochitl
591. Tlacoxochitl
592. Quetzalmizquitl
593. Youalxochitl
594 (a) Cozcaquauh-
        xiuitl,
    (b) tzopelic xiuitl
595. Tlatlalpaltic
596. Metl
597. Use of metl
598. Ciuapatli
599. Nopalli
600. Use of nopalli
601. Chía
602. Use of chía
603. Haacxoyatic
604. Maticeuac
605. Iztac patli
606. Oquichpatli
607. Tlamacazqui ipapa
608. Cicimatic

609. Tzompoton
610. Cuitlapatli
611. Oquichpatli
612. Use of oquichpatli
613. Chichic patli
614 (a) Cocopaltic,
    (b) cocopi
615. Quiauhteocuitlatl
616. Lightning flash and
    the quiauhteocuitlatl
617 (a) Xiuhtomoltetl,
    (b) eztetl
618. Atl chipin
619. Quinametli
620. Flesh of the ocelotl
621. Coyayaual
622. Temazcalli
623, 624. Axocopac
625. Mecaxuchitl
626. Ayauhtonan
627. Tlalpoyomatli
628. Yiauhtli
629. Epaçotl
630. Azpan xiuitl
631. Tlalquequetzal
632. Itzcuinpatli
633. Çacayaman
634. Tequixquiçacatl
635 (a) Uauhçacatl,
    (b) çacamamaztli
636. Xiuhtecuçacatl
637. Çacateteztli
638. Haxalli
639 (a) Caltoli,
    (b) itztolin
640. Tolpatlactli
641. Tolmimilli
642. Petlatolli
643. Toliaman
644. Tolnacochtli
645. Atetetzon
646. Xomali
647. Amamalacotl

BOOK ELEVEN -- EARTHLY THINGS

LIBRO VNDE
cimo que es Bos
que, jardin, ver
gel de lengua
Mexicana.

De las propríedades de los anímales

ELEVENTH BOOK, WHICH TELLETH OF THE DIFFERENT ANIMALS, THE BIRDS, THE FISHES; AND THE TREES AND THE HERBS; THE METALS RESTING IN THE EARTH — TIN, LEAD, AND STILL OTHERS; AND THE DIFFERENT STONES.

JNJC MATLACTLI OCE AMOXTLI, INTECHPA TLATOA, IN NEPAPĀ IOLQUE: IN TOTOME, IN MJMJCHTIN: YOAN IN QUAVITL, YOAN IN XIHUJTL: IN TLALLAN ONOC TEPUZTLI, AMOCHITL, TEMETZTLI, YOĀ OC CEQUJ, YOAN IN NEPAPĀ TETL.

First Chapter, which telleth of the four-footed animals.[1]

Injc ce capitulo: intechpa tlatoa in iolque, in manenemj.

FIRST PARAGRAPH, which telleth of the wild beasts.

INJC CE PARRAPHO: intechpa tlatoa in tequanjme.

OCELOT[2]

It is a dweller of the forests, of crags, of water; noble, princely, it is said. It is the lord, the ruler of the animals. It is cautious, wise, proud. It is not a scavenger. It is one which detests, which is nauseated by [dirty things]. It is noble, proud.

It is long: long bodied, straight, round like a pillar; squat, not tall; thick, corpulent; hard-fleshed, very hard-fleshed; long-tailed; of gopher-like paws, very thick; wide-padded — of very wide pads; thick, fat of neck; of pot-like head, very pot-headed, great-headed; of droplet-shaped ears; of thick, stubby, spongy, soft muzzle with a fatty, oily nose; of wide face with eyes like live coals; toothy, with small, pointed front teeth, with molars like pestles; wide-mouthed, open-mouthed; clawed, with sharp, curved claws, with dewclaws.[3] It is varicolored, quite varicolored, spotted with black, blotched with black; white-chested, smooth, sleek.

Like ocelots, it becomes varicolored; it is variously colored, variously marked; it becomes varicolored, it is variously colored, like an ocelot. Claws emerge.

OCELUTL:

quauhtla chane, texcalco chane, atlan chane: tecpilli, tlaçopilli: qujl inpillo, intlatocauh in iolque: mjmati, moiecîmati, mocenmatinj hamo tzopiloanj, tlayîianj, motlaeltianj: pilli, tlaçotli.

Veiac tlacveiac, melactic, temjmjltic, pachtic, amo uecapan: tomaoac, tlaque, nacatetic, nacatepul, cujtlapilhujiac, matôtoçantic, matôtomactic, macpalhueuei, macpalpapatlactic, quechtomaoac, quechnanatztic, quatecontic, quateconpul, quatenamaztic, nacazchîchipichtic, tentomaoac, tentetepontic, tenpochectic, tenpochichitic, iacatzolchiactic, iacatzolchiaoac: ixpechtic, ixtletlexochtic; tlancujcujtztic, tlācujnene, tlancoiolomjtic, tlācochtexolotl, camaxacaltic, camaxacal: izte, iztiujujtztic, izticucultic, chôchole. Cujcujltic, cujcujlpatic: moholchapanj, motlilchachapatz, eliztac, tetzictic, alaztic,

ocelotic, cujcujlivi, mocujcujloa, cujcujltic, cujcujltia, mocelocujcujloa, iztiqujça, tlamotzoloa, tlamomotzoa, tlāqujça tlancochqujça, coatlanqujça, tlancuj-

1. The identification of mammals is based upon Rafael Martín del Campo: "Ensayo de interpretación del libro undécimo de la Historia General de las Cosas de Nueva España, de Fray Bernardino de Sahagún," III, "Los mamíferos," *Anales del Instituto de Biología,* Vol. XII, No. 1, pp. 489–506 (Mexico, 1941), and Bernardo Villa R.: "Mamíferos silvestres del Valle de México," *Anales del Instituto de Biología,* Vol. XXIII, Nos. 1 and 2, pp. 269–492 (Mexico, 1952). Changes due to current taxonomy, as well as the English names, are the result of consultation with Dr. Stephen D. Durrant, Professor of Zoölogy, University of Utah.

2. *Ocelotl:* in earlier publications we have translated *ocelotl* as ocelot. Martín del Campo (*op. cit.,* p. 491) identifies it as *Felis hernandesii hernandesii* or ocelot; Durrant identifies it as *Felis onca hernandesii* (Gray) or jaguar.

3. *Chocholli* is translated as talon or as *pie de venado,* depending upon whether the term applies to the *Felidae* or *Cervidae* family. Corresponding Spanish text: *"tiene pescuños en los braços, y en las piernas."*

They grasp, they clutch. Teeth, molars, canines emerge. It bares its teeth, gnaws, bites, tears. It growls, snarls, howls, roars like the blowing of trumpets.

WHITE OCELOT[4]

It is said to be the leader of the ocelots. It is white, very white. Some are only whitish, varicolored, painted — blotched with black, spotted.

RUDDY OCELOT[5]

It is reddish, ruddy, blotched with chili-red, blotched as with rubber. It is varicolored, variously hued, ruddy.

The nature, the ways of this ocelot

It goes about eating the small animals, the deer, the rabbit, etc. And it is very reserved; no eater of offal;[6] very well kept. It bathes, washes, cleans itself; it washes its face by licking, with its saliva. It prepares itself; it cares for itself.

And by night it watches; it seeks out what it hunts, what it eats. Very good, clear is its vision. In truth, it sees very well; it can see far. Even if it is very dark, even if it is misty, it sees.

When it sees one, when it meets, when it comes upon a huntsman, a hunter, it does not run, it does not flee. It just settles down to face him. It places itself well; it hides itself not at all, this ocelot. Then it begins to hiss, so that by its breath it may make faint, may terrify the hunter. And then the hunter begins to shoot arrows at it. The first reed, the arrow, *which he shoots*, the ocelot just catches with its paws; it shatters it with its teeth. It seats itself upon it growling, snarling, rumbling in its throat. When [the hunter] shoots more, it is just the same; howsoever many he shoots at it, to all [the ocelot] does the same.

And the hunters have their reckoning (as well as their custom) that they shoot only four times. If he shoots four [arrows], the hunter is [as good as] dead. Thereupon the ocelot prepares itself; it stretches, it yawns, it stirs, it shakes itself; it cleans itself, it licks itself. Then indeed it crouches, springs, flies through the air. Whether the hunter stands ten spans — even

tzoa, tlatetexoa, tlanquetzoma, tlatlācotona, qujqujnaca, nanalca, choca, tzâtzi, iuhqujn tlapitza.

IZTAC OCELOTL:

qujl imachcauh in ocelome, iztac, iztacpatic: cequjntin, çan ticeoaque, cujcujltic, mocujlo, motlilchachapatz, moholchapanj.

TLATLAUHQUJ OCELUTL:

tlatlactic, tlatlauhquj, mochilchachapatz, molchachapatz, mocujcujlo, mocujcujloa, tlatlavia.

In jeliz in jnemjliz, inin ocelutl:

qujquaquatinemj, in iolcatzitzinti, in maçatl, in tochin. etc. Auh cenca momalhujanj: amo tzopoctic, cēca mocenmati, maltia, mopapâca, moiectia, mjxamja iztlactica, ichichitica; mocencaoa, mocenmati.

Auh in ioaltica: vellachia, qujmjtta, in tlein qujntemoa, in qujnqua: cenca qualli, in jtlachializ, chipactic: ça nelli, cenca vellachia, vel veca tlachia: in manel tzontic, in manel aiauhtic: qujtta.

Ca in iquac qujtta: in iquac qujnamiquj, in qujmjxnamjctia: Anquj, in tlamjquj: amo motlaloa, amo choloa: çan qujxnamjctimotlalia, Vel motlalia, hatle qujmotoctia: inin ocelutl. Niman peoa: in mjpotza, injc ihiiotica qujçotlaoaz, qujiolmjctiz, in tlamjnquj. Auh njmã peoa: in tlamjnquj, qujmjna: in ce qujtlaxilia acatl, in mjtl, çan qujmacuj, in ocelutl: qujtlanxaxamanja, conmocpaltia, qujqujnacatica, nanalcatica, hizoloca, in jtozcac: in oc ce qujtlaxilia çan no iuj, in quezquj qujtlaxilia: çan moch iuhquj chioa.

Auh intlapoal: in tlamjnque, (no inneteumanjlilton) çan navi: injc tlamjna: intla otlan nauj, ie omjc, in tlamjquj: njman, ie ic mochichioa, in ocelutl: mahana, cochcamachaloa, movîvixoa, motzetzeloa, moîeiectia, mopapaloa. Nimã vel motapaiollalia: tlacxotla, patlani: intla matlacmapan, hicac, tlamjnquj: intla nel noço, caxtolmapan: vmpa canatiuh, çã çepa

---

4. *Iztac ocelotl*: Martín del Campo (*loc. cit.*) suggests *Felis glaucula glaucula*. Durrant suggests *Felis wiedii glaucula* (Thomas) or the margay.

5. *Tlatlauhqui ocelotl*: Martín del Campo (*loc. cit.*) writes, "*Supongo que se trata de los individuos jóvenes de Felis hernandesii hernandesii, cuyo color es más rojizo que el de los adultos.*" Hence, young ocelot; or young jaguar, according to Durrant.

6. Bernardino de Sahagún: *Historia General de las Cosas de Nueva España*, Vol. VIII, *Códice matritense de la Real Academia de la Historia* (ed. Francisco del Paso y Troncoso; Madrid: Hauser y Menet, 1907; henceforth referred to as *Acad. Hist. MS*) — *amo tzopiltic*.

fifteen spans — away, there it goes to seize him. Only once does it leap — fly — swish — bristling, its hair ruffled. There dies the hunter; there he is eaten.

But the skilled hunter, when he shoots the first arrow, if [the ocelot] seizes it with its paws, then takes an oak leaf [or] the petal of a tree flower. At the tip of the arrow he places it; with its tip he pierces it. Then he shoots it. The reed with the leaf goes fluttering; like a locust it goes perhaps half way, perhaps by [the ocelot]. When it flies, when the oak leaf falls, [the ocelot] is thus distracted. Thus the hunter succeeds in shooting it with an arrow; thus he can reach it.

When the ocelot is shot, it leaps up. And when it comes to fall on the ground, it sits up like a man; it sits up; it sits upright. It sits up as it first was. It fixes its eyes upwards; it does not close them as it dies. It just remains looking; it seems to be alive.

Wherever the ocelot eats, first it hisses at one in order to terrify one — to make him swoon away. And its flesh burns like pepper.

The conjurers went about carrying its hide — the hide of its forehead and of its chest, and its tail, its nose, and its claws, and its heart, and its fangs, and its snout. It is said that they went about their tasks with them — that with them they did daring deeds, that because of them they were feared; that with them they were daring. Truly they went about restored. The names of these are conjurers, guardians of tradition, debasers of people.

Ocelot[7]

Also they name it *tlacomiztli*. It is small, squat, rather long, the same as a Castilian cat; ashen, whitish, varicolored — varicolored like an ocelot, blotched with black.[8]

Tapir[9]

It is very large, bigger than a cow. Its head is very large, the muzzle long, its ears very wide, its molars, its teeth also very large, like the teeth of us human beings. Its neck is very thick, very fleshy. Its fore [and] hind legs are very thick; its hooves like a bull's, very large. Its dewclaws are only callosities, not of bone; its haunches are very large, its tail very thick, long, quite smooth. Its hair is everywhere completely

choloa: patlanj, hicoioca, moçoneoa, mopaçoloa: vncan mjqui, in tlamjnqui: vncan qualo.

Auh in mozcalia tlamjnquj, in ce qujtlaxilia, acatl, intla oqujmacujc: njman concuj, in quaoacazoatl, in quauhxioatlapalli: yiacac qujtlalia, yiacac qujço, in acatl: njmã qujtlaxilia, papatlacatiuh: in acazoatl. Iuhqujn chapolin: ic iauh, aço tlatlaco, aço ie itlan: in patlanj, in vetzi, in quaoacazoatl, ic qujxpatilia; ic vel qujmjna, in tlamjnquj: ic vel câci:

in omjnoc, ocelutl: mâcotonvitzoa. Auh in ouetzico tlalpan: meoatitlalia, moqujchtlalia, motlamelauhcatlalia: iuh motlalia, in juh achto catca: vel panj qujtlatlalia, in jxtelolo: amo mjxpiquj, injc mjquj; çan iîtztica, iuhqujnma ioltica ic neci.

In canjn tlaqua ocelutl: achtopa, tehipotza, ic teiolmjctia, ic teçotlaoa. Auh in jnacaio cococ.

In nonotzaleque: qujtqujtinemj, in jeoaio; iehoatl, in jxquaceoa, yoan in jelpaneoa, yoan in jcujtlapil, yiac, yoan yizti, yoã in jiollo, yoan in jcoatlan, yoã yiacatzol: qujl ic ihiiooatinemj, qujl ic tlaixmauhtia, qujl ic imacaxo: ic acan ixmauj, ca nel paiotinemj: iehoantin in intoca, nonotzaleque, pixeque, teiolpachoanj.

Tlacoocelutl:

yoan qujtocaiotia, tlacomjztli, tepiton, pachtontli, melacpil: vel ixqujch, in castillan mjzton, nexeoac, ticeoac, cujcujltic, ocelocujcujltic. molchachapatz

Tlacaxolutl,

cenca vei qujpanavia in vaca; in jtzontecon cenca vei, tenvilaxtic: in jnacaz cenca papatlaoac; in jtlancoch, in jtlan cenca no vevei; iuhqujn titlaca totlã, in jquech cenca tomaoac, cenca nacaio: in jma, in jcxi, cenca totomaoac, in izti iuhqujn quaquave cenca vevei, in jchochol çan chachacaioltic, amo omjo: in jtzintamal cenca vevei, in jcujtlapil cenca tomaoac, viac çan vel xipetztic: in jtomjo in novian çan muchi

---

7. *Tlacoocelotl: Felis pardalis pardalis* in Martín del Campo, *loc. cit.; Felis pardalis pardalis* (Linnaeus) or ocelot, according to Durrant.

8. The *Acad. Hist.* MS skips from *tlacoocelotl* to *cuitlachtli.*

9. *Tlacaxolotl: Tapirella bairdii* and *Tapirella dowii* in Martín del Campo, *op. cit.*, p. 492; *Tapirus bairdii* (Gill), according to Durrant.

yellow, not very long — like a deer's hair. Its hide is very thick.

This tapir is edible. But not of only one flavor is its flesh; all the various meats are in it: human flesh, wild beast flesh — deer, bird, dog, etc.

This tapir is quite rare. It lives there at Atzaccan, Tepoztzotlan, Tlanquilapan, there in the great forests, among the crags which no one reaches. It eats tender shoots of *tochquiquiztli* and tender shoots of *tlacalhuazquauitl* when it finds no other food. When wild cacao grows — which no one plants — called *teocacauatl* and *quappatlachtli*, [it eats these] and maize. When it comes upon a maize field, it finishes it all. When it defecates, it heaps up [voided whole] cacao beans, almost a carrier's load. The common folk hunt for these in the forest, in order there to find the cacao beans.

It is not frightening. It cannot be slain with an arrow, even if shot with an arrow. In order to take it, they make it fall into a pit, a hole which they dig deep—three arm spans deep. Such is its depth. When they have dug it, they spread tree branches over it, they cover it with grass. And it gives way. Later the tapir falls into the pit; there they spear it, so that there it dies. Later they draw it forth with heavy ropes.

Tzoniztac[10]

It is a wild animal which lives in Toztlan [and] Caseapan, almost by the ocean shore. As for its being named *tzoniztac*, its head is a pure white which extends to its neck. It is rather large, something like an ocelot, thick-bodied, squat. It goes about hunting [other] wild animals. When it sees one, then it growls much, it bares its teeth; then it pounces upon it. Its fore [and] hind feet are like an ocelot's; it is a very high jumper which seemingly flies into the trees. All its body — its forelegs, its hind legs — all are glistening black. Its tail is long, just like an ocelot's.

No one can easily find this *tzoniztac*. Whosoever comes upon it, if he sees that its head is yellow, he who sees it will then die. But to whosoever sees that its head has not yellowed, it comes to pass that he will grow very old; and its meaning is that he will be poor even if he lives still longer, even if he still works hard for his living. If two, if perhaps three [men see it], all die; sometimes only one man is spared. They take

coztic, amo cenca viac, iuhqujn maçatl itomjo: in jeoaio cenca tilaoac.

Inin tlacaxolotl qualonj: auh amo çan centlamantli injc velic in jnacaio mochi itech catqui in nepapan nacatl in tlacanacatl, in tequannacatl in maçatl, in totolin in chichi. etc.

Inin tlacaxolotl, çan tlaçonemj vmpa nemj Atzaccan, tepuztzõtlan, Tlanqujlapan, vmpan vei quauhtla in aiac onaci in texcalla. In qujqua tochqujqujztli yiacacelica yoan tlacalhoazquavitl yiacacelica: iquac in amo tle qujtta itlaqual. In jquac muchioa quauhtlacacaoatl in aiac qujtoca: itoca, teucacaoatl, yoan quappatlachtli, yoan in tonacaiotl: in cana ipan qujça centetl mjlli, vel qujtlamja: injc moxixa qujtepeuhtitlalia in cacaoatl, achi vel centlamamalpan. In macevaltin qujtemotinemj in quauhtla, injc vncan qujcnopilhujzque in cacaoatl:

amo, momauhtianj, amo ic mjquj in mitl, in manel momjna: injc maci çan qujtlacomolhuja, cenca vecatlan in qujtataca in tlaxapuchtli, emapan injc tlanj, injc vecatlan; in jquac oqujtatacaque, in pani quavitl qujteteca, quiçacatlapachoa yoan papatla: çatepan vncan motlacomolhuja in tlacaxolutl, vncan qujxixili, ic vncan mjquj: çatepã quãmecatica qujoalqujxtia.

Tzoniztac:

tequanj, vmpa nemj in Toztlan Caseapan, achi itlan in vei atenco: Injc mjtoa tzoniztac, çanjo in jtzontecõ cenca iztac, iquechtlan tlantica, achi veitontli; ach iuhqujn ocelutl tomactontli, pachtontli: cenca qujntemotinemj in manenemj: in iquac qujmjtta, njman cenca qujqujnaca, tlancujtzoa: njmã qujcujtivetzi: injma, in icxi çan iuhqujn in ocelutl, cenca acocholoanj iuhqujn patlanj in itech quavitl, in ie muchi itlac in jcxi, in jma muchi tliltic, pepetzca: in jcujtlapil viac, çan no iuhquj in ocelutl.

In iehoatl tzõiztac, aiac vel qujtta: in aqujn qujnamjquj, intla qujttaz, in ie coztic in jtzontecon, ca ie mjqujz in aqujn qujtta. Auh in aqujn qujtta in amo coçavia in jtzontecon: ic neci, ca cenca vecaoaz yoã inezca, cenca motolinjz in manel oc vecaoaz, in manel cenca oc motlaiecultiz: intla vmentin, intla noço eintin, muchintin mjquj, in quẽmanjã ça ce tlacatl, in mocaoa, iuhqujn tetzavitl ipan qujmati: injc maci,

---

10. *Tzoniztac: Tayra barbara senex* in Martín del Campo, *loc. cit.; Eira barbara senex* (Thomas) according to Durrant.

[the animal] as an omen of evil. In hunting it, they just shoot it with arrows.[11]

CUITLACHTLI OR CUETLACHTLI[12]

It is of woolly, tangled, snarled fur, of dark, bushy tail. When it is already old, its tail is tangled. Everywhere its fur is matted. It is droplet-eared; round, broad of face, as if man-faced; thick, short of muzzle. Much does it wheeze; a great hisser is it. When it hisses to terrify one, it is as if a rainbow comes from its mouth. Very clever is it—a great stalker, a crouching spy. It stalks one; preys, hisses at one.

MOUNTAIN LION[13]

It is just like all the ocelots, [but] nowhere are there [any spots] on it. It is completely smooth, very smooth. However, it is very long-clawed, very hook-clawed. Quite large are its dewclaws. It is dark yellow. [Some] are called ruddy mountain lions, yellow, blond mountain lions. The fur of some is whitish; they are called white mountain lions.

JAGUARUNDI[14]

It is the same as the mountain lion, but always lives in trees, among tree-tops, where it gets its food. Seldom does it walk on the ground.

MAÇAMIZTLI[15]

It is the same as the mountain lion. For this reason it is called *maçamiztli*: its fur is quite like deerskin. And quite similar [to the deer's] is its body, quite similar are its head [and] its face. The male has horns; the female is like a doe. Quite similar [to the deer's] are its tail, its ears, its feet; quite similar [to the deer's hoof] are its claws. Nowhere else do they resemble, nowhere else are they like a deer. In all, it differs from [the deer], for it has teeth like a jaguarundi's: it has the front teeth, the fangs, the molars. In short, it is a wild beast.

çã qujmjna.

ceoac, cujcujltic, ocelocujcujltic, molchachapatz.

CUJTLACHTLI: ANOÇO CUETLACHTLI,

paçotic, pâçoltic, pâçolpul, cujtlapilpoiaoac, cujtla-pilcueiaoac: in ie veue cujtlapilpaçoltic: noujan papa-paqujzquj in jtômjo: nacazchichipichtic, ixtemama-lacachtic ixpechtic iuhqujn achi tlacaxaiaque tento-maoac, tentetepontic: cenca ihiio: cenca mjpotzanj. Injc mjpotza, inic teçotlaoa: iuhqujn aiauhcoçama-lotl icamacpa qujça. vel mjmati: vel motepachiujanj, motenevillavianj: motepachivia motenevillavia, tehi-potza.

MIZTLI:

Vel iuh iuhquj, vel ixqujch in Ocelutl: hacan tle qujmotlalili, çan vel centetzictic, tetzicpatic, çan ix-qujch, cenca iztiviviiac, cenca izticultic: vel vei in jchochol, poccoztic: mjtoa tlatlauhquj mjztli, coztic, coçauhqui miztli. in cequintin ticeoac in intomjo: motocaiotia, iztac mjztli.

QUAMMJZTLI:

çan ie no ie in mjztli, çan ieh mochipa, quauhti-tech, quauhticpac in nemj, in tlaquaqua: çan quen-man in tlalpan nemj.

MAÇAMJZTLI:

çan ie no ie in mjztli, injc motocaiotia, maçamjztli: vel iuhquj in jtomjo, maçatl itomjo. Auh vel iuhquj in jtlac: vel iuhquj in jtzontecon, in jxaiac: in oqujch-tli, quaquaquave: in cioatl, iuhqujn cioamaçatl: vel iuhquj in jcujtlapil ic ca, njmã ie ieh, in jnacaz, nimã ie ieh in jicxi: vel iuhquj in jizti ic ca, njmã acan quj-neuh, njman acan qujtlaneuj in maçatl. Ça ixqujch injc qujcaoa: ca tlane, in juhquj Quãmjztli: tlanjx-quaie, coatlane, tlancoche: ça çe ca tequanj.

---

11. Four words follow in the Nahuatl text which appear to have been crossed out; they repeat a part of the description of the ocelot.

12. *Cuitlachtli*: Martín del Campo, *loc. cit.*, suggests *Ursus horriaeus* or *Euarctos machetes*. Durrant suggests *Ursus horriaeus* (Baird) — grizzly bear, or *Ursus americanus machetes* (Elliott) — black bear. The term has also been translated as *lobo* (wolf); cf. Alonso de Molina: *Vocabulario de la Lengua Mexicana* (ed. Julio Platzmann; Leipzig: B. G. Teubner, 1880).

13. *Miztli*: *Felis azteca azteca* or puma in Martín del Campo, *op. cit.*, p. 493; *Felis concolor azteca* (Merriam) or mountain lion, according to Durrant.

14. *Quammizztli*: *Felis cacomitli* or *Felis yaguaroundi* in Martín del Campo (*loc. cit.*). Durrant gives *Felis yagouaroundi cacomitli* (Berlandier) or jaguarundi.

15. *Maçamiztli*: "El mazamiztli es, a todas luces, un animal imaginario" — Martín del Campo, *loc. cit.*

And its mouth, its jaws, especially its place of devouring, are very large, very thick. Its dewclaws stand at its ankle joints like metal hooks. Whatsoever it seizes, whatsoever it catches, it rips open from belly to neck with them. Especially does it go imitating, mimicking these deer; it goes as one of them, among, in the midst of them. And when in need of food, when hungry, it pounces upon one; it suddenly rips open its belly, it strews its entrails on the ground with its claws, its dewclaws. But nevertheless there is a sign by which the deer recognize it: it is of sickly odor.

CUITLAMIZTLI

It lives in the forests. It is the same as a mountain lion. As for its being named *cuitlamiztli*: when it reaches a deer, it attacks it. When it seizes it,[16] it eats it, eats it gluttonously, eats it as it lies; indeed it consumes it all. For two days, for three days, it eats nothing [else]. It eats absolutely the whole of it; it lies down, lies digesting it. Hence it is called *cuitlamiztli*; because it is a glutton, and because it does not hide itself away. During the night it eats up the turkeys; it finishes them up if there are even twenty. When filled, it just kills them and the sheep.

RINGTAIL[17]

It is the same as the *cuitlamiztli*. As for its being named [*itzcuinquani*], at night it goes forth to the settlements. It cries out. And when it has cried out, then all the dogs answer it. All howl. All hear its howl. Then they go toward it. And when they have gathered around it, when they have circled about it, then it seizes as many as it can to eat them. Its favorite food is dogs. It preys especially on them; they are choice; it prefers them.

¶

SECOND PARAGRAPH, which telleth of all the animals, the four-footed forest-dwellers.

COYOTE[1]

It is long-furred, shaggy, bushy, woolly; bushy-tailed, pointed-eared; large-muzzled, a rather slender, blackish, soft one; spindle-legged; curved of claw. Very black are its claws. It is cunning, astute.

Auh in jtlamaia: in jtlâtlamaia, in mache itequaia: cenca vei: cenca tomaoac: in jchochol, in jxoquechtlan hicac: iuhq'nma tepuzchicolli, in tlein cana, in tlein câci: ic qujtixotla, qujquechxotla. Oc cenca iehoan in mamaça; inca maviltitinemj, in inca mocaiauhtinemj: intzalan innepantla, hicatinemj. Auh in ie maiana, in ie teucivi, ce qujcujtivetzi, qujtixotlateoa, qujcujtlaxcoltepeoa, ica imjzti, in jchochol. Auh tel vnca inezca injc qujximati, mamaça: ca cocoiac.

CUJTLAMJZTLI:

quauhtla nemj, ca çan ie no ieh in mjztli: injc motocaiotia, cujtlamjztli, in ocacic centetl maçatl, qujpeoaltia in qujqua: qujqua, qujtequjqua: qujquatoc, vel qujtlamja: omjlhujtl, eilhujtl injc âmo tlaqua, çan qujcenqua, çã vetztoc, tlatemovitoc, ic mjtoa cujtlamjztli: ipampa xixicujn yvan ipampa in amo motlatia in iooaltica qujnoalqua in totolme qujntlamja intlanel centecpantli in oixuic ça qujnmjctia yoan in ichcame.

ITZCUJNQUANI

ca çan ie no ieh in cujtlamjztli: injc motocaiotia cujtlamjztli: in iooaltica oallauh in câcalla: choca. Auh in ochocac njmã mochintin qujnanqujlia in chichime mochintin tzatzi in jxqujchtī qujcaqujlia itzatziliz: njman ivicpa vih. Auh in oitlan mocentlalique: in ocololhujque, vncan cana in quezqujtetl velitiz qujnqua, cenca vel itlaqualhoan in chichime: vel qujnmoiautia tleoia ipan qujnmati.

¶

INJC VME PARRAPHO: intechpa tlatoa, in jxqujchtin iolque, manenenque: in quauhtla in nemjã.

COIOTL:

tomjo, veiac, paçoltic, paçol, paçotic, cujtlapilpaçol: nacazvivitztic, temmetlapiltic, achi tempitzaoac, tempochectic, tempochichitic, xotlatlacotic, izticocoltic: tlitliltic in jzti, iolizmatquj mjmati.

---

16. Read *q'ana,* as in the *Acad. Hist. MS.*

17. *Itzcuinquani: Bassariscus astutus astutus* (Lichtenstein) in Villa R., *op. cit.,* p. 454; ringtail, according to Durrant.

1. *Coyotl:* probably several species of coyote. Martín del Campo, *op. cit.,* p. 494, has *Canis cagottis;* Durrant suggests *C. latrans cagottis* (Hanneton-Smith).

It hunts in this way: it is a stalker, an ambusher. It creeps; it crouches on the ground; it crouches spying; it hides its feet [and] its ears; it looks with caution; it looks from one side to another. As a stalker it is quite as astute as a man. And first it hisses, whether at birds, whether at sheep. Whatsoever it wishes to catch it terrifies.

And it is in every way diabolical. If I take from it, if I make it drop its catch, it will take vengeance, it will repay me in kind. It also goes to take my animals, which I raise. And if I [should have] no animals, it will await me on the road, confront me, bark at me as if it wished to eat me, to menace me. And it will engage two [or] three of its companions to mangle me, perhaps by night, perhaps by day.

But also this animal is grateful and appreciative. A short time ago, in our time, a man came upon a coyote sitting on the grassy plain; the warrior was going along his way. And the coyote then beckoned to him with its paw. And the warrior was much frightened and took it as an omen.[2] He went toward it, and when he came to reach it, he saw a serpent which was coiled around [the coyote]. The serpent protruded from its neck, from under its front legs. [The serpent,] called a *cincoatl,* was thus well coiled. And the warrior said within himself, "Which shall I help?" Then the warrior went up, taking a stick, a club, a green branch. Then he repeatedly beat the serpent with them; for the serpent abhorred the stick. Then the serpent fell to the ground; whereupon the coyote staggered off.

And when it had revived, then it ran off. In perhaps a couple of hours, farther on in the maize field, the coyote went to look for the warrior who had rescued it. It brought him two turkey cocks, went on to throw them down, proceeded to push them on with its muzzle almost as if to say to him, "Take them." Once again the coyote went. When the warrior was going to his house, once more he met the coyote on the road. It gave him another one, a turkey hen. And when the warrior had gone to his house, again, a little later, it came to throw down another turkey cock in his courtyard.

The foods of this coyote are meat, raw meat, ripe maize ears, green maize ears, green maize stalks, tomatoes, tunas, American cherries, tamales, tortillas, honey.

Injc tlama: vel motlapachivianj, vel motepachivianj: movillana, tlaltech moteca, motlatlachteca: qujmototoctia in jma, in jnacaz: vel motlatlachialia, havic tlachia: vel iuhquinma tlacatl ic mjmati injc motlapachivianj. Auh achtopa qujmjpotza: in at totolme, in at ichcame: in çâço tlein caciznequj qujçotlaoa.

Auh çan njman vel atlacatl: intla onjccujli, intla onjctlaçalti, y imal motzoncujz, nopan qujcuepaz: no canatiuh in tlein noiolcauh njcnemjtia. Auh intlacaiac noiolcauh nechôchiaz, nechiaiacatzacujliz, nechoaoaltzaz. iuhqujn nechquaznequjz, inic nechmamauhtiz: yoã vntetl, etetl, qujnmotlaqueviz in jicnjoan, nechmomotzozque at iooaltica, at noço tlaca.

Auh yoan inin iolquj, tlatlaçocamatinj mocnelilmatinj: qujn izquj iqujn ie topan. Ce tlacatl ipã qujçato: çacatla eoatica, in coiotl: vtli qujtocatiuh, in tiiacauh. Auh in coiotl; njman ie qujoalmanotza: auh vel tlamaviço, yoã vel motetzavi, in tiacauh: ca ivic iatia. Auh in oitech acito: qujttac cooatl, in jtech omotetecujs: iquechtlan qujztoc, in cooatl iciiacacpa qujztoc, vel ic omotetecujs: in jtoca cincooatl. Auh yitic: qujto; in tiacauh. Ac ieh in njctlaoculiz, y: njmã concujto in tiacauh in tlacutl, in tetlacutl, in ollacutl: njman ieh ic qujvivitequj, in cooatl: ca aiel qujttaz, in tlacutl, in cooatl: njman oalchapantivetz, in cooatl, njma ie iaiatica, in coiotl.

Auh in omozcali njmã ie motlaloa, aço ome horatica, in nepa milpan, ipan acito in coiotl, in tiacauh, in oquimomaqujxtili: vnteme in totolme, vexolome in qujnvica, iixpan qujmõtlaçato, qujntentopeuhtinemj ach iuhqujnma qujlhujznequj xiccuj. Oc ceppa ia in coiotl, in ie iauh, ichan tiâcauh: oc ceppa vtlica qujnamjc, in coiotl: oc no centetl qujmacac cioatotolin auh in oia ichan tiacauh: oc no ceppa iquezqujioc, no centetl qujtlaçato, yitoalco vexolotl.

In jtlaqual, y, coiotl: nacatl, nacaxoxouhquj: cintli, elutl, ooatl, xaltomatl, nochtli, capolin, tamalli, tlaxcalli, necutli.

---

2. The Acad. Hist. *MS* here adds *vel q'motetzavi.*

And thus is the coyote hunted: it is snared, snares are set for its feet, [other] traps are set, it is forced into a pitfall, it is shot with arrows. At its place of drinking raw maguey syrup, there it is noosed, it is caught with a wild chicle bait.

Auh injc mâci coiotl: motlahpeoalhuja, momovia, motlâpevia, motlaxapochvia, momjna, in jnequayia, vncan motlahçalhuja motepetzicvia.

CUITLACHCOYOTL OR ÇUETLACHCOYOTL

It is just the same as a coyote, but its fur resembles that of the *cuitlachtli;* it is *cuitlachtli*-like, dark where its belly is.

CUJTLACHCOIOTL: ANOÇO CUETLACHCOIOTL,

çan ie no ieh in coiotl: ieceh in itomjo, mocujtlach-nênequj: cujtlachtic, chichintic vnca itoxi.

AZCALCOYOTL

It is just the same as a coyote. For this reason is it called *azcalcoyotl:*[3] when it howls, it howls like many coyotes—some in a full voice, some in a high-pitched one, some in a wail.

AZCALCOIOTL:

çan ie no ieh in coiotl, injc motocaiotia azcalcoiotl: in jquac choca: iuhqujn centzõtli coiotl, choca, cequj tlatomaoa, cequj tlapitzaoa, cequj pipitzca.

BADGER[4]

Its name is "ground coyote." It runs about the villages, on the plains. It is not born among the crags, but just somewhere underground. *Tlalcoyotl* means the not distant coyote, which only emerges among house settlements, among us. It goes about eating turkeys, tunas, green maize ears, dried maize ears, American cherries. It eats all that has died; it eats all the salamanders, serpents, etc.

TLALCOIOTL:

itoca tlalcoiotl in callah, in jxtlaoacan nênemj, in amo texcalco tlacati, in çan cana tlalla: qujtoznequj, in tlalcoiotl: amo veca coiotl çan calla, çan totlan in qujqujztinemj, totôtolquatinemj, nochquatinemj, elo-quatinemj, cinquatinemj, capulquatinemj: mochi quj-qua in mjcquj, mochi qujqua in tapaiaxin, in cooatl. etc.

BOBCAT[5]

The bobcat is of smoky yellow, dark yellow back, with blackish tips to its fur; of white belly; it is white-bellied, like flecks of cotton, like carded cotton. Its belly is spotted with black, marked like an ocelot, blotched like an ocelot. [Its fur is] soft, soft, very soft; dark, blended here and there, much blended, with brown. It is small and squat, small and round [of body], massive, heavily fleshed. It is large-headed, with droplet-shaped ears, round-faced, snubbed of muzzle, spiny of tongue. Very high-pitched is its voice when it howls. Very agile is it, a true flyer. It bounces, it flies. Its food is flesh.

OCOTOCHTLI: OCOTUCHIN,

poccoztic, coziaiactic, in jcujtlapan: quachichintic in jtomjo, in jelpan, iztac eliztac, ichcatetic, ichcatla-pochintic: in jelpan tlilcujcujltic, ocelocujcultic, oce-locujcujliuhquj, iamanquj, iamaztic, iamazpatic, po-iaoac, popoiactic, popoiacpatic pachtontli, mimjlton-tli, tomaltontli: nacateton quateconton, nacazchichi-pichton: ixiaoalton, tenteteponton, nenepilaoaio, cenca pitzaoac in jtozquj injc choca: vel tzicujctic, nel pa-tlanjnj tzicujnj, patlanj In jtlaqual nacatl:

And this bobcat is absolutely uncanny in its service to [other] wild animals.[6] And thus it performs its task. If it sees any living thing, perhaps a deer or a man, then it quickly hides itself behind any tree or tangle of shrubs. There it crouches. And if [the

auh inin ocotuchtli, njmã âcemelle, intlamacauh in tequanjme. Auh injc qujchioa itequjuh: intla oquit-tac, itla iolquj: in at maçatl, in at noço tlacatl njman itla quavitl, aço quappaçoltontli, qujmotocatiuetzi: vncã qujmopachivitoc. Auh intla oitech acico çã ic

---

3. The corresponding Spanish text of the *Florentine Codex* suggests that some of the Nahuatl text may have been omitted: *"se sienta sobre los hormigueros, y por esto se llamã azcatl coyotl."* Martín del Campo's suggested identification (*loc. cit.*) is *Tamandua tetradactyla mexicana.*

4. *Tlalcoyotl: Taxidea taxus berlandieri (ibid.,* p. 495).

5. *Ocotochtli:* in *loc. cit.,* *Lynx rufus texensis* (bobcat); the term may also apply to the *Potos flavus aztecus* (kinkajou).

6. Wording in the *Acad. Hist. MS* varies slightly here.

victim] comes to it, it quickly attacks. It passes its tongue over the eyes [of the victim] — flicks it over its eyes. And the deer, or the man, is at once blinded, so that he can no more help himself. And then it breaks [the victim's] neck.

And the brute then howls, screams, and sounds out loudly. Thus it informs the [other] wild animals that it has made a catch. Then the wild animals come to eat it. And when they have come, then they drink [the victim's] blood. And when they have finished its blood, they suck at its flesh. But some only suck its blood; afterwards they eat its flesh; they tear it to pieces.

GREY FOX[7]

It is called a cave-dweller because it goes about looking for caves. There it makes its home, there it hunts for things, there [the females] bear their young. Like a coati, it is long- and narrow-muzzled. And its fur is dark, a little rough, a little soft. And its food is mice, kangaroo rats, and small birds,[8] if one of them somewhere passes by it. It eats all of them.

RACCOON[9]

Also its name is "priestess," and its name is "little old woman." It is named *mapachitli* because its hands are quite like our hands; likewise, its feet are quite like our feet. It destroys maize in summer, as if it ground it up and ate it all. Since it has really human hands, it climbs trees, it climbs the *nopal*. It eats up American cherries, fruit, tunas, honey.

A cave is its dwelling; in forests, crags, the water, among reeds, everywhere it lives. Wherever it feels comfortable, there it lives. In the winter it eats mice, salamanders, [small] animals. Since it has really human hands [and] feet, sometimes it goes upright when it walks. And since it is a great thief, since it takes everything that it sees, and since it has human hands, a thief is also called *mapachitli*.

It is wide, broad-footed; it has feet with soles — soles like a man's [and] hands like a man's. It is small, squat, cylindrical; tangle-haired; it has a dark tail, arched, long; it is large-headed, with pointed ears, with large muzzle, [or] a thin, thinnish one, a soft one.

qujmachititiqujça, in qujxpalotiqujça, yixpan qujztiqujça. Auh in maçatl: in anoço tlacatl, njmã ic ixpopoioti, ic aoc vel mopalevia: yoã njmã ic concocoxamanja.

Auh in tlapalpul: njman ie ic choca cenca tlapitzaoa: auh cenca caqujzti, injc q'nmachitia, in tequanjme in ca otlama: njman ie ic vitze in tequanjme, in tlaquazque. Auh in ooallaque: niman ie ic catli, in jezço: auh in ie tlantiuh in jezço ça qujpapachichina, in jnacaio, auh in cequjntin, ça qujchichina in jezço: çatepan qujqua in jnacaio, qujtzatzaiana.

OZTOOA:

injc mjtoa oztooa, vel qujtemotinemj, in oztotl: in vncã mochantia, vncan tlatemoa, vncan mopilhoatia: iuhqujn peçotli tenpitzactic. Auh in itomjo, chichintic: achi chamaoac, achi iamanquj: auh in jtlaqual iehoatl in qujmjchin, in veçacotl, in at cana ipan qujça, totzintli: mochi qujqua.

MAPACHITLI:

yoan itoca cioatlamacazquj, yoan itoca Ilamaton: injc mapachitli motocaiotia, in jma: vel iuhqujn titlaca, tomacpal: no iehoatl in jicxi, vel iuhqujn toxocpal. njmã haqujtlamachvia in tonacaiotl, in xopan vel iuhqujn qujteci, mochi qujqua: ca nellacamaie, vel quauhtleco, nupalleco: conquaqua in capolin, in xocotl, in nochtli, in necutli:

oztoc inentla, quauhtla, texcalla, atlan, tulla, noujan nemj: in canjn movelmati, vmpa nemj: in tonalco, qujmjchme, tapaiaxti, iolcame in qujnqua. ca nel noço tlacamaie; tlacaicxe in quẽman moquetztiuh, in nenemj. Auh injc cenca ichtequjnj inic mochi qujcujnj, in tlein qujtta, yoan injc tlacamaie: no motocaiotia. Mapachitli in jchtecquj

xopapachtic, xopapatlactic, xocpale, tlacaxocpale, tlacamacpale: pachtontli, mjmjltontli, paçotic cujtlapilpopoiaoac, cujtlapilxexeltic, cujtlapilhueiac quatecontic, nacazvivitztic, tẽmetlapiltic, tempitzaoac, tempitzapil, tempochichitic.

---

7. *Oztoa* refers to several sub-species of *Urocyon cinereoargenteus* or grey fox, according to Martín del Campo, *loc. cit.*

8. *Tototzintli* in *Acad. Hist. MS.*

9. *Mapachitli: Procyon lotor hernandezii* in Martín del Campo, *loc. cit.*

COATI[10]

It is just like the raccoon, but it does not have human hands. It is also dark, black. As for its being named *peçotli*, it is because its food is everything — maize, fruit; because it is a great eater. And anyone who is a great eater, intemperate, is called *peçotli*. "I am a *peçotli*" means "I eat a great deal," or "I gorge myself," or "I eat hurriedly," or "I am intemperate."

PECCARY OR FOREST PECCARY[11]

The name is also coati. It is quite like [yet at the same time] unlike, dissimilar to, the pig,[12] and in size it does not equal the pig which comes from Castile. It is bristly, stiff-haired, of coarse bristles. Its bristles are like awls, rough, tough, sparse, strong, wiry, sinewy. This one is called "the cloven one."

Its food is acorns, American cherries, maize, roots, fruit, just like what a pig eats. Hence they call the peccary a pig. And hence is a pig called *pitzotl*, because when it eats it makes a smacking sound, as if it sucks.

¶

THIRD PARAGRAPH, which telleth of the habits of still other four-footed animals.

SQUIRREL[1]

It is small and cylindrical, small and long, blackish, brown: somewhat dark; soft-furred; soft, small, pointed of ear; slender of muzzle; long, arched, very dark of tail. The tips of its fur are blackish. Its tail is somewhat thick.

Its food is all maize and fruit, tunas, American cherries, etc. And it plunders the maize; even if [the maize] is guarded, it is not thereby frightened, it does not therefore leave it alone. It appears in full view as it eats, as it steals. And a thief is also called *techalotl*. A shrill whistler, it whistles shrilly.

TREE SQUIRREL

This is a tree-dwelling squirrel which breeds in the treetops. It always lives[2] in trees. And as for its being called *quauhtechalotl*, it eats everything — pine nuts, the tender ends of tree [branches], and tree worms.

PEÇOTLI:

çan no iuhquj in mapachitli, çan amo tlacamacpale no tlilchichintic: injc motocaiotia peçotli, ipampã moch itlaqual, in tonacaiutl, in xochiqualli ipampan cenca tlaquanj. Auh in aqujn cenca tlaquanj in amoxvicama itoca peçotli: njpeçoti, qujtoznequj; cenca mjec in nicqua, anoço njxixicujnti, anoço njtlaquativetzi, anoço ânjnoxvicamati.

COIAMETL: ANOÇO QUAUHCOIAMETL,

no yoan itoca peçotli, vel iuhquj njman hacan contlaz, hacan qujtlanevi in puerco: auh injc quauhtic, amo qujnevivilia in puerco, in castillan vitz: paçotic, paçopol, tomjo chamaoac; in jtomjo iuhqujn coiolomjtl, oapaoac, chicaoac, atic, pipinquj, tlalichtic, tlalhoatic: iehoatl in motocaiotia, xeloaztli.

In jtlaqual: haoatl, quauhcapolin, tonacaiotl, tlanelhoatl, xochiqualli: vel iuhquj injc tlaqua in puerco, ic oqujtocaiotiq̃: coiametl in puerco. Auh injc motocaiotia pitzotl: in puerco, ipãpa injc tlaqua in motencacapatza, in juhquj mopitzoa.

¶

INJC EI PARRAPHO: intechpa tlatoa in oc cequjntin, in quenamjque iolque, in manenenque.

TECHALUTL:

mjmjlpil, veiacapil, iaiactontli, camjltic, poiactontli, tomjiopoiactic, iamãquj nacazvivitzton, tempitzaoac, cujtlapilhujac, cujtlapilxexeltic, cujtlapilpopoiactic, quachichintic: in jcujtlapil, tomactontli.

In jtlaqual mochi in tonacaiutl yoan in xochiqualli, nochtli in capolin. etc. Auh çan njman haqujtlamachhuja: in tonacaiutl, manel mopia, amo ic momauhtia, amo ic qujcaoa: vellatetlachielti injc tlaqua, injc ichtequj auh in jchtecquj, no motocaiotia techalutl, mapipitzoanj, mapipitzoa.

QUAUHTECHALUTL:

iehoatl in quauhtla nemj techalutl, quauhticpac in tlaqua: çan mochipa quauhtitech in nemj. Auh injc motocaiotia quauhtechalutl: mochi qujqua in ococintli, in quavitl yiacacelica, yoan in quauhocujltin

---

10. *Peçotli: Nasua narica narica* (ibid., p. 496).

11. *Coyametl:* in *loc. cit.* it is *Pecari angulatus crassus*. Durrant suggests *Tayassu tajacu crassus* (Merriam) or collared peccary.

12. In the *Acad. Hist.* MS this phrase reads: *amo quinevili ỹ puerco in castillã vitz.*

1. *Techalotl* refers to various species of the genus *Sciurus* (Martín del Campo, *op. cit.*, p. 497).

2. *Acad. Hist.* MS: *tlacati.*

It goes about barking the trees there where the tree worms are. It whistles shrilly.

GROUND SQUIRREL[3]

It is the same as the squirrel. This one lives in house settlements, in maize fields. As for its being called ground squirrel, its burrow is underground, in an opening in the rocks, in holes. And like the gopher, it bears its young underground. It completely destroys maize [fields].

CHIPMUNK[4]

It is small, little, blackish, dark. The tail is somewhat dark, somewhat long; a little whitish. All food for the chipmunk is the same as the food for the squirrel.

BROWN CHIPMUNK

It is the same chipmunk, though very dark, very blackish, very brown. Like the gopher, like the mouse, its burrow is underground, just the same [as theirs].

¶

FOURTH PARAGRAPH, which telleth of the habits of a four-legged animal called opossum.

OPOSSUM[1]

The *tlaquaton* or *tlatlaquaton* is fleecy, quite like a skunk, but when it ages, as an old male, as an old female, it becomes chalky. Rather long and thin-muzzled, its face is [as if] painted; the hollows of its eyes are black. It is of small, pointed ears, of long, hairless tail. Its tail is all flesh; nowhere is there hair, though there is a fine down.

And as to its habits: it brings forth its young underground, in burrows, somewhere under ledges of rocks. And when it bears its young, when it goes out somewhere, it carries its young with it. There is a pouch at its belly; there it places, there it inserts its young. It takes them with it when it goes out to eat; there they are suckled. It is quite harmless, not vicious; it does not bite one, it does not nip one when it is taken, when it is seized. And when it is caught,

qujxixipeuhtinemj in quavitl, vncan qujmana in quauhocujltin: mapipitzoa.

TLALTECHALUTL:

çan ie no iehoatl in techalutl, iehoatl in cacalla, in mjlla nemj: injc mjtoa tlaltechalutl, tlallan in jchan, tecamac, tlacoiocco. Auh iuhqujn toça: tlallā in mopilhoatia, vel qujxpoloa in tonacaiutl.

MOTHOTLI:

çan qualton, çan tepiton, iaiactontli, popoiacpil: cujtlapilpoiactontli, cujtlapilveiacatontli: iuhqujn achi ticeoacatontli. In jxqujch itlaqual techalutl: no ixqujch in jtlaqual, in Mothotli.

MOTOIAVITL

ça ie ieh in mothotli, iece vel poiactic: vel tlilpoiaoac, vel camjltic, in juhquj toçan, in juhquj qujmjchin, tlallan ichā: çan vel no iuhquj.

¶

INJC NAVI PARRAPHO intechpa tlatoa in quenamj yieliz, in iolquj manenenquj; in jtoca tlaquatl.

TLAQUATL:

tlaquaton, anoço tlatlaquaton: paçoltontli, vel iuhqujn epatl. Auh in ie vecaoa: in ie veve, in ie ilama: teteçauj tempitzaton, mjhichiuh mjhixtetlilcomolo, nacazvivitzpil, cujtlapilhujac, cujtlapilxixipetztic: çā vel nacatl in jcujtlapil: hacan ca tzontli, in manei tomjtl.

Auh in jeliz: tlallā tlacoiocco, cana tepancamac in mopilhoatia: auh in omopilhoati, in canapa iauh, qujnvica in jpilhoan ca xillanxiqujpile, vncan qujmōtema, vncan qujmonaaquja, in jpilhoan: qujnvica in tlaquaquaz, vmpa chichitivi, njman hamo iellele, amo tlavele, amo tequa, amo tetetexoa: In jquac ano, in jquac tzitzqujlo. Auh in jquac axioa: choca, pipitzca, vel qujça imjxaio: oc cēca iquac in ano, yoan in jpilhoā: cēca qujnpipitzqujlia, in jpilhoan: qujnchoquj-

---

3. *Tlaltechalotl*: Martín del Campo (*loc. cit.*) gives *Citellus mexicanus mexicanus* and *Otospermophilus variegatus variegatus*. Durrant identifies these as *Citellus mexicanus mexicanus* (Erxleben) or rock squirrel.

4. *Mothotli*: Villa R., *op. cit.*, pp. 372–73, gives *Citellus mexicanus mexicanus* (Erxleben). Martín del Campo, *loc. cit.*, suggests a species of the *Eutamias* genus — chipmunk.

1. *Tlaquatl*: *Didelphis mesamericana mesamericana* (*ibid.*, p. 498); *Didelphis marsupialis californica* (Bennett) according to Villa R., *op. cit.*, p. 308.

it cries, it squeals; true tears come forth, especially when it is taken with its young. Much does it squeal for its young. Much does it weep for them; true tears come forth. It places each in its pouch; it takes them out.

And its food is maize, maguey scrapings, and honey. And its flesh is edible, savory, like rabbit, like hare.

But its bones, especially its tail, are in no wise edible. If one eats of them, especially if one eats many of them, all the intestines which are within him come forth. Once a dog and a cat secretly ate the flesh of an opossum; they chewed, they gnawed all its bones. Really it was the dog. At dawn, it had scattered out its intestines; it went about dragging them behind it.

But its tail is a medicine which expels, which extracts, wherever something has gotten in, especially in an opening in a bone, which cannot come out. [Salve of] opossum tail is spread on thickly; it is spread on many times. Even if it is very well lodged, this draws it out; it gradually removes it. And [women] who have difficulty in childbirth, who cannot deliver the child, drink [the infusion]. Thus the little child is born quickly. And whoever can no longer defecate, who has a stoppage of the bowels, drinks it to open the passages, the tubes, to clean them, to purify them, to sweep out obstructions.

Likewise one who has a cough also drinks opossum-tail [infusion]; with it he gathers, he sends down the phlegm. Also one drinks chocolate with *uey nacaztli*, with *tlilxochitl*, with *mecaxochitl*. One who can no longer digest food eats [opossum tail] for constipation, when there are obstructions.

¶

FIFTH PARAGRAPH, which telleth of the habits of still other four-footed animals.

HARE[1]

It is of long, well-formed legs; clawed; of long body, of rather long neck; of pointed, very long, wide, concave ears; of rounded, snubbed muzzle. Its fur is grey, a little darkened at the tips; it is soft, dark, blackish; quite dark; not long, not short; moderately smooth. It is an easy runner, a runner which darts, which goes like the wind; which is agile, very agile. It has a stubby, small tail, a white breast. And its

lia, vel qujça in jixaio qujmõtetema in jxiqujpilco, qujnoalqujqujxtia.

Auh in jtlaqual tonacaiutl: metzalli, yoan necutli: Auh in jnacaio qualonj: velic, iuhqujn tochin iuhqujn citli:

auh in jiomjo oc cenca ieh, in jcujtlapil, çan njmã amo qualonj. In aqujn qujquaz oc cenca ieh, intla mjec qujquaz, mochi qujça in jitic ca, in jcujtlaxcol. Ceppa qujchtacaqua in chichi: yoan mjzton in jnacaio tlaquatl: çan mochi qujteteitz, qujtotopotz in omitl: ca nel noço chichi, in tlatvic: omochi motepeoaco in jcujtlaxcol ça qujvilantinemj.

Auh inin icujtlapil, ca patli ca tlatepeoanj, tlaqujxtianj: in canjn tlein calaquj, oc cenca ieh in omjcamac in havelqujça, õmopapalteuhteca in tlaqua cujtlapilli mjecpa õmoteca, in manel vel tzitzicaticac, qujqujxtia çan jvian qujq'xtitiuh. Auh in iehoantin in havellacachioa: in auel mjxivi ca conj ic hiciuhca tlacati in conetzintli. Auh in aqujn aoc vel maxixa in maxixtzaqua, ca conj qujtlapoa in piaztli in cocotli, qujpopooa, qujiectia, cochpana in jtextenca

No iehoatl in tlatlaci: no conj, in jcujtlapil tlaquatl: ca qujcxotla qujtemovia in alaoac. No iehoatl conj in cacaoatl ipan vei nacaztli, ipan tlilxochitl, mecaxochitl ipan: in aq'n aoc temo qujqua in ocujtlaxcol itlacauh in omotexten.

¶

INJC MACUJLLI PARRAPHO: oc no cequjntin in iolque, manenenque itechpa tlatoa in quenamjque.

CÎTLI:

tetepon viviiac, tetepõcocoztic, izte, tlacviac quechviacatontli, nacazvivitztic, nacazvivitlatztic, nacazpapatlactic, nacazcôcopichtic, tenololton, tentetepontic, ticeoac in jtomjo, çan achi in iacachichintic: iamanquj, poiactic, popoiactic, popoiaoac amo no viac, amo no teteztic çan vel ipan, alaztic, painanj, totocanj, motlamjnanj, hecatoconj, tzicujctic tzicujcpatic: cujtlapilteteponton, eliztac: auh in jcujtl, ololpipil: iuh-

1. *Citli*: a species of the genus *Lepus,* in Bernardino de Sahagún: *Historia General de las Cosas de Nueva España* (Angel Ma. Garibay K., ed.; Mexico: Editorial Porrúa, S.A., 1956; henceforth referred to as Sahagún [Garibay ed.]), Vol. IV, p. 327. Durrant suggests jack rabbit.

excrement is small and round, like kernels of maize, indeed [like] sheep's dung. It runs, it springs up, it leaps, it sits up, it flies.

Rabbit[2]

It is just like the hare, except that it is quite small. It bears its young underground; it goes down, burrows, makes a nest; or else somewhere among maguey plants [it lives] in dark, inaccessible places. It is good-tasting, savory, healthful, the best.

Weasel[3]

It is slender, rather squat, rather long-tailed, rather thin and long of snout. Its face is painted, blotched. It is rather ruddy; it is white-breasted. Its food is mice, *nextecuillin* worms, *tlalomitl* worms. It also eats turkeys; it sucks them from below. Its offal is unpleasant — very salty, very sickening. It preys especially on newly-hatched turkeys and bird eggs. It comes creeping up to spy on, indeed forces itself among, the sitting hens.

Skunk[4]

It has fleecy, straggly, woolly [fur]: black, dark; arched tail; a rather squat build; pointed ears; slender muzzle. It bears its young, it dwells underground, in burrows, in openings in the wall, in openings in the rocks.

Its food is black beetles, maguey worms, *nextecuillin* worms, small cockroaches. And it preys especially on turkeys, on bird eggs; like the weasel, it also sucks the turkeys from below. And when it is full, it bites their heads off; it eats only their heads. And when it is really full, furthermore, [it continues to strangle them];[5] it throws them away. Frightful is its spray, truly stinking, a deathly stench, a bad stench. When it sprays, [the stench] is spread all over the land; it pervades the whole countryside.

And if anyone tries to catch it, it no more than sees him than it quickly raises its tail so that it spreads its spray over him. If perhaps it sprays one, it yellows his cape; it completely takes everything over; such is its stench. Its spray consists of small globules which are within it. If it falls, flies in one's face, it blinds

qujn tlaolli, vel iehoatl in jchcacujtlatl: motlaloa, motompitzoa choloa, macoquetza, patlanj.

Tochin: anoço tochtli,

çan vel no iuhquj in Cîtli, iece çã tepiton tlallan in tlacachioa, in tlatema, motlatataquja, motapaçoltia: anoço cana metitlã, in tlatlaiooaian, in ovicatonco: velic, aviac vel patic, vel tzõpatic.

Coçama: anoço coçatli,

pitzatõ pachtontli, cujtlapilhujacapil tẽpitzaton mjhichiuh in jxtecujcujlo, tlatlactic, tlatlactontli, eliztac. In jtlaqual: qujmjchin, nextecujlin, tlalomitl: no qujqua in totolin, çan qujntzinpachichina: temamauhti in jiel, cenca poiec, cenca cocoiac: vel qujnmoiautia, in totolcocone, yoan in totoltetl: vel qujnmonevilavitinemj, vel qujnmopipiznauja, in tlapacho.

Epatl:

paçoltic, paçoltontli, papaçoltic, tliltic, catzaoac, cujtlapilxexeltic: pachtontli, nacazvivitztic, tempitzaton: tlallan tlacoiocco, tepancamac, tecamac in mopilhoatia, in mochantia.

In jtlaqual: pinacatl, metzonocujlin, nextecujlin, caltatapach. Auh vel qujnmoiautia: in totolme, in totoltetl, in iuhquj coçama: no qujtzinpachichina, in totolme. Auh in oixvic: qujnquequechcotona, çan yio in qujnqualia, intzontecõ: auh in ovel ixvic, ça iequene qujntlaça, qujntetema: vel temamauhti in jiel: vel hiiac, mjqujzhiialtic, hiialpatic: in mjexi centlalli moteca, centlalli mantiuh.

Auh in aca canaznequj; in çã nel qujtta niman motzinquetztivetzi ic tetoca in jiel: in aço itilma qujiexilia coçavia vel cenqujcuj injc hiaia. In jiel ololotonti: yitic caca: in aqujn yixco vetzi, in jixco chitonj, in jiel Epatl: ixpopoioti, ixitlacavi. In nanaoati: çã cõpetztoloa, in jiel epatl, qujl ic pati, in nanaoatl.

---

2. *Tochtli: tochtli* and *tochin* are alternative forms. The term includes species of *Sylvilagus*. Durrant suggests cottontail.

3. *Coçama* (*coçatli* is an alternative form): *Mustela frenata frenata* (*Lichtenstein*) or long-tailed weasel, in Villa R., *op. cit.*, p. 457.

4. *Epatl:* Martín del Campo, *op. cit.*, p. 499, states that, on the basis of Sahagún's description, the term refers to nearly all species of the subfamily *Mephitinae*, genera *Mephitis, Conepatus, Spilogale.* These are striped skunk, hognosed skunk, and spotted skunk, respectively, according to Durrant.

5. For *quintlaça*, the *Acad. Hist. MS* has *quinquequechmatiloa.* We have preferred the latter.

one, it damages his eyes. Those who have pustules merely swallow skunk spray; it is said that with it the pustules heal.

MONKEY[6]

Its name is also *quauhchimal*. It is a forest-dweller in Anahuac, toward the east. It has a small back — minute; it is round-backed; it is of rounded back; it has a long, curled tail. It has human hands, human feet, nails, real nails — long nails.

And as to its actions: it is a shouter, a shrill whistler, making gestures toward one. It stones one, it hurls sticks at one. It has a face which is a little human. It is shaggy . . . , round-backed, of rounded back. It bears its young in the crags; it produces only one.

And all the maize, fruit, meat become its food; it eats like a human being. Also it eats pine nuts, acorns, and also tender shoots of trees.

And to capture them, a large fire is built; ears or kernels of maize are put around the edge, and in the blaze is buried a very large [stone called] *cacalotetl*. And the trappers, the hunters, take cover. And when [the fire] smokes, these monkeys, wherever they are, smell the fire, the smoke. Then they come; they carry their young on their backs; they seat themselves about the fire. They begin to warm themselves; the ears of maize begin to roast [and] they eat roasted maize. They walk about as they warm themselves; they change their children about as they warm and heat them. And when the *cacalotetl* stone has been heated (for it can in no way endure fire) it then cracks, bursts open, explodes, blows up just like the firing of a gun. And the embers, the ashes, scatter all over; the embers spread all over these monkeys; the ashes get into their eyes. So they run, they flee as if someone pursued them. They quickly abandon, throw aside, their young; although they still hunt for them, they can no longer see them. So there the hunters quickly seize them with their hands; there quickly are taken the young monkeys. Later they are raised, tamed.

The monkey is a rather tame [animal] which sits like a man. Also it teases the young women; it begs from them, extends the hand, continually offers its hand in their presence. To speak, it whistles shrilly.

OÇOMATLI:

yoan itoca quauhchimal, quauhtla chane, anaoac, tonalixco: cujtlapicic, cujtlapicictic, cujtlaolol, cujtla-ololtic: cujtlapilhujac, cujtlapilcocoltic, tlacamaie, tlacaicxe: izte, vel izte, iztiviviac.

Auh in jtlatlachioal motenpapavianj, mapipitzoanj: tevic momamamananj, tetepachoa, tequauhtlaxonecujlhuja. Achi tlacaxaiaque: paçotic, popoltic, cujtla-ololtic, cujtlaolol: texcalco in mopilhoatia ça centetl in qujchioa.

Auh in jtlaqual mochioa ixqujch in tonacaiutl, in xochiqualli, in nacatl vellacatlaqua, no qujqua in ococintli, no qujqua in aoaquauhtomatl, in aoato-matl, no yoan in quauhcelutl.

Auh injc maci: vei tletl motlalia, cintli moiaoaloch-tia, anoço tlaolli: auh in tleco motoca, cenca vei in cacalotetl. Auh in tlamanj, in anque, motlaltoca: auh in ie popoca, in manel canjn cate, in iehoãtin oçomati: qujoalinecuj in tletl, in poctli: njman oalhuj qujnmamama in inpilhoan, cololhujtimoteca in tletl. Peoa in mozcooa: peoa in mocinixquja in mocalhuja, mocuecuepa in mozcooa, qujncuecuepa in inpilhoan, in qujmozcooa, in qujntotonja. Auh in oicucic caca-lutetl (ca nel noço aqujttaz in tletl) njman cueponj, vellatzcueponj, xitoncueponj: vel ivi in tlequjqujztli vetzi. Auh in tlexochtli in nextli moiaoa cenmanj: in tlexochtli, inpan cenmanj, in iehoantĩ oçomati: in nextli imjxco calaquj, ic motlaloa, choloa: iuhqujn aca qujntoca: qujntlazteoa, qujnmamaiauhteoa, in inpilhoan: in manel noço oc qujntemoa, aocmo qujmjtta: ic vncan temamacujtivetzi, in anque: vncan ano in oçomacocone, çatepan oapaoalo, tlacacivitilo.

In oçomatli: achi tlacaciuhquj, moqujchtlalianj, no qujncamanalhuja, in cioatzitzinti: tetlatlaitlanjlia, mamaçoa teixpan teixtlan qujmamana in jma: injc tlatoa pipitzca.

---

6. *Oçomatli*: on the basis of the illustrations of the *Florentine Codex*, Martín del Campo, *op. cit.*, p. 500, suggests *Alouatta palliata mexicana* and *Ateles neglectus*. Durrant suggests *Alouatta villosa mexicana* (Merriam) or howler monkey, and *Ateles geoffroyi* or *A. vellerosus* (Gray), or spider monkey.

SIXTH PARAGRAPH, which telleth of four-footed animals like the deer, and of others like it; then of dogs which they bred in times past.

INJC CHIQUACEN PARRAPHO: intechpa tlatoa in maneneque, in juhquj iehoatl Maçatl: yoā in oc cequjntin, çan no iuhque: njmā iehoantin in chichime, in qujnnemjtiaia ie vecauh.

DEER[1]

Its name is also *acaxoch* and forest deer. It is a forest dweller, tall, with sinewy, well-formed legs. Large-bodied, thick-bodied, it has a belly. It is broad of back, long of neck, large of muzzle, thin, slender of muzzle; of long, pointed, concave ears; greasy, oily of nose; hoofed. Its nails are called hooves. It is rounded of rump, stubby of tail. It is good to the taste, savory, edible. Its fur is ashen.

And when it is born, it at once stands up; it is born like a sheep, like a horse — strong, fleet.

Its food is maize, kernels of maize, dried maize ears, green maize ears, beans, bean plants; and tender shoots of trees, and rotten wood, and tree worms, and green maize stalks, and leaves of shrubs.

The deer with antlers is a buck. [The antlers] are whitish, like wood, like tree forks. When its antlers are loose, they are shed. It inserts its antlers in the fork of a tree; then it backs up; it breaks off the antlers in the tree. Thus it becomes young again.

The deer without antlers is a doe. Still immature, a fawn, it is spotted, spotted white like a mountain goat.

WHITE DEER

It is said to be the ruler of the deer. It appears only rarely. The [other] deer go gathered around it. [Its color is] not really like carded cotton but only whitish, ashen.

ANTELOPE[2]

It is very big, very tall. Its face is painted, darkened in the hollows of its eyes. It also is ashen.

DOG[3]

Its pet names are *xochcocoyotl*, and *tetlami*, and *teuitzotl*. Some are black, some white, some ashen, some smoky, some dark yellow, some dark, some spotted, some spotted like ocelots. Some are high, tall, towering; some medium. Some are smooth,

MAÇATL:

no yoan itoca Acaxoch quauhtlamaçatl, quauhtla chane, quauhcholtic, teteponmemecatic, teteponcocoztic: tlaque, tlactomaoac hite, cuitlatomactic, quechviac, temmetlapiltic, tempitzaoac, tempitzaton, nacazviviac, nacazvivitztic, nacazcôcopichtic: iacatzolchiac, iacatzolchiaoac, chochole in jjzti, itoca chôcholli, tzintopoltic, tzintopantic, cujtlapiltetepontic, velic, haviac, qualonj in jtomjo nexeoac.

Auh injc tlacati: çan njman moquetztivetzi, iuhqujn ichcatl ic tlacati, iuhqujn cavallo: tzomoctic, tzicujctic.

In jtlaqual: tonacaiutl, tlaolli, cintli, elotl, etl, eçoqujlitl: yoā in quauhcellotl, yoan quappalā, yoan quauhocuilin, yoan eloçacatl yoan tlacoxivitl.

In maçatl quaquave: ca oqujchtli, quaquauhtiticectic, quaquāmatzoltic. In otlatziuh iquaquauh, moquaquauhtlaça: quāmaxac caquja, in jquaquauh: njman tzintlacça, vncā qujquappoztequj in jquaquauh: ic qujpilqujxtitiuh.

In maçatl: in amo quaquave, ca cioatl: in oc piltontli, in maçaconetl: cujcujltic, iztacacujcujltic, iuhqujn temaçatl.

IZTAC MAÇATL:

qujl intlatocauh in mamaça, çan tlaçonemj: colôlhujtinemj in mamaça: amo nelli in ma vel ichcatlapochintic: çan ticeoac, nexiaiactic.

TLAMACAZCAMAÇATL:

vel veiac vel quauhtic: mjhichiuh, mjhixtetlilcomolo, no nexeoac.

CHICHI: ITZCUJNTLI,

itlaçotoca xochcôcoiotl yoan tetlamj yoā tevitzotl. Cequj tliltique, cequj iztaque, cequj nextique cequj poctique, cequj poccoztique, cequj iaiactique, cequj cujcujltique, cequj ocelocujcujltique, cequj vecapan, quauhtic, quauhcholtic: cequj çan vel ipan qualton,

---

1. *Maçatl: Odocoileus virginianus mexicanus,* according to Villa R., *op. cit.,* p. 306.

2. *Tlamacazcamaçatl: Antilocapra americana mexicana* or pronghorn (Martín del Campo, *op. cit.,* p. 501).

3. *Chichi, itzcuintli:* mentioning the illustrations of the *Florentine Codex,* Martín del Campo (*loc. cit.*) observes: *"se encuentran representados cuatro perros domésticos, diferentes por la longitud de su pelo y de su cola, por su coloración y por la posición de sus orejas."*

some shaggy, woolly. . . . The muzzles are large,[4] with large teeth, with small, pointed teeth. The ears are pointed, concave, hairy, shaggy. The head is round, bowl-shaped. It has a body — fat, thick. It has claws, long claws. It is domesticated, a house-dweller, a favorite companion, a constant companion, which follows running. It is happy, amusing; a tail-wagger, a barker, which lays its ears back. It barks, it is happy, it lays its ears back, it wags its tail.

Its food is maize, raw meat, cooked meat. It eats all: the flesh of the dead, the spoiled; it eats the revolting, the stinking, the rotting.

Teuih

This means dog. It is shiny, hairless, fat, smooth.

Xoloitzcuintli[5]

It is a dog with no hair at all; it goes about completely naked. It sleeps upon a cape, which covers it. Thus do they produce a *xoloitzcuintli*: when it is still a puppy, they cover it with turpentine unguent, so that its hair falls out absolutely everywhere. Thus its body becomes bare.

Tlalchichi[6]

This means a rather small dog, squat, small and round.

Otter[7]

It is like the *tlalchichi,* [but] a water-dweller. It inhabits the water, it lives within the water. Its fur is like the gopher's fur — dark, dark hued, soft. And it can in no wise become wet; the water merely flows off of it, as if it were greased. Its food is fish — all which is in the water.

Gopher[8]

It is small and yellowish, fleshy, corpulent, fat, squat; tailed; long-clawed, with curved claws; provided with front teeth, with bent, curved front teeth; with ears like droplets — round ears. It is edible, good-tasting, savory; it is greasy, fat. It is blinded by light. It is a maker of earth ridges, of small earth

cequj tetzictic, cequj paçotic, paço, popoltic, temmetlapil: tlãcujtztic, tlancujnene: nacazvivitztic, nacazcocopichtic, nacazpapaiatic, nacaztlan papaçoltic: quatecontic, quatetecontic: tlaq̄. cujtlatolontic, cujtlatomactic izte, iztivivitztic: tlacaciuhquj, techannemjnj, tevicalxoch, tevîvicanj, tetlalochtocanj: papaqujnj, teahavilianj, mocujtlapilaiacachoanj, pipitzcanj, inacaz qujmototoctianj pipitzca, pâpaquj, inacaz quimototoctia mocujtlapilahaiacachoa.

In jtlaqual tonacaiutl: nacaxoxouhquj, nacatl hicucic: mochi qujqua, in tlein mjcquj nacatl: vellahelli, qujqua in jhiiac, in xoqujac in palanquj.

Tevih:

qujtoznequj, chichi, tetzictic, amo tomio, chamaoac, alaztic.

Xoloitzcujntli:

chichi, çan njmã hatle in jtomjo: çan vel petlauhtinemj, tilmatli in jtlan cochi in qujmoquẽtia Injc qujchioa xoloitzcujntli: in oc piltontli, oxitica qujpepechoa: vel novian ic tepevi in jtomjo, ic xipetzivi in jnacaio.

Tlalchichi:

qujtoznequj, itzcujntli, pachtontli: tlalpanton, tolonpil.

Aitzcuintli:

iuhqujn tlalchichi, atlan chane: atlan nemj: atl yitic in nemj. In jtomjo iuhqujn toçan itomjo: poiactic, poiaoac, iamanquj. Auh çan njman amo vel palti çan peiaoa in atl: iuhqujnma mantecaio. In jtlaqual mjchin: in jxqujch atlan onoc.

Toçan:

coztontli, nacateton, nanatztontli, nanatztic, pachtic cujtlapile, iztiviviac, izticôcoltic tlanixquaie: tlanjxquatepoztic, tlanjxquacocoltic, nacazchichipichtic, nacaziaiaoaltic. Qualoni, velic, haviac: chiaoa, ceceio, ixmjmjqujnj, mopotzanj, mopotzaltianj: tlallan in jchan, tlallan in tlacati: aic tlalticpac qujça, cemjcac

4. The *Acad. Hist. MS* adds *tempetlapiltic.*

5. *Xoloitzcuintli* and *tlalchichi:* identification is uncertain; Martín del Campo, *op. cit.,* p. 502, suggests *Canis americanus* and *C. caribaeus* for the hairless dogs.

6. See n. 5.

7. *Aitzcuintli: Lutra annectens* (*ibid.,* p. 503); *Lutra annectens annectens* (Major), or southern river otter, according to Durrant.

8. *Toçan:* from Sahagún's description, Martín del Campo (*loc. cit.*) identifies the terms as representing "various species of the genus *Blarina*" or short-tailed shrew. Villa R., *op. cit.,* pp. 376 *sqq.,* identifies the *tuza* as various species of the genera *Thomomys* and *Cratogeomys.*

hills. Its home is underground; it is born underground. Never does it come out on the earth's surface; it always lives underground. When it comes out on the earth's surface, it no longer recognizes its hole; its house is lost. It digs; it makes earth ridges.

Its food is of all kinds. It eats roots — tree roots, maguey roots, herb roots. It eats ears of maize, beans, green ears of maize. It buries all the rubbish, the dried maize stalks, the green maize stalks, the bean leaves; it gnaws all the roots; it takes all underground.

I dig out a gopher.

¶

SEVENTH PARRAGRAPH, which telleth of the small animals, like the mouse, and of others like it.

MOUSE[1]

Its names are also *tepanchichi*, and *tepanmamal*, and *calxoch*. This mouse is a little ashen, blackish, a little dark, rather yielding, a little soft. It is small and long; it has a tail, a long, little tail. It has a slender little muzzle.

It is called *tepanchichi* because it lives in the walls [and] by the walls. It is called *tepanmamal* because it bores holes in, it penetrates walls — the house walls. It is called *calxoch* because it always lives in the house.

Its food is maize. It eats ripe ears of maize, it eats chili, gourds, gourd seeds, and *chía*, and wrinkled *chía*; it eats chocolate [and] cacao beans. It indeed eats like a human being. It eats tunas, American cherries, etc. It eats tamales, tortillas; it eats raw meat, cooked meat, fish; it eats all that which is fetid. It grinds it up.

It makes nests of grass, of soft grass. Also it hunts out articles of value. It gnaws, it shreds the capes, the precious feathers. Whatsoever is guarded as precious, it gnaws all; it damages all. No matter where it is, no matter if it is carefully guarded as precious, no matter how inaccessible the place, it enters, it damages the precious things. Hence also the eavesdropper is also called mouse, because no matter where, he continually enters the house, he hears and acquires the information and inquires into one's affairs. Hence is said the saying, "I mouse him"; that is to say, "I

---

tlallan nemj. In tlalticpac quiça: aocmo ommati in jtlacoiocco, mocalpoloa: tlatataca, mopotza.

In jtlaqual: yixqujch qujqua in tlanelhoatl in quauhnelhoatl, in menelhoatl, in xiuhnelhoatl: qujqua in cintli, in hetl, in elutl: muchi caquja in tlaçolli, in ooaquavitl, in toctli, in eçoquilitl: muchi quitotopotza in tlanelhoatl, muchi tlallampa qujoallana:

njtoçantataca.

¶

INIC CHICOME PARRAPHO: itechpa tlatoa in ioiolitoton, in juhquj iehoatl, qujmjchin: yoan in oc cequjntin, çan no iuhque

QUJMJCHIN:

yoan itoca tepanchichi, yoan itoca tepanmamal, yoan itoca calxoch. Inin qujmjchin: nextontli, chichintontli, poiactontli, iaiamazpil, iaiamaztontli: viacapil, cujtlapile, cujtlapilviacatontli, tempitzaton.

Inic motocaiotia tepanchichi: ipampa in tepamjtl yitic, in jtech nemj. Inic motocaiotia tepanmamal: ipãpa in qujcôcoionja, in qujqujqujçoa tepamjtl, in caltechtli. Inic motocaiotia calxoch: ipãpa in çan mochipa calitic nemj.

In jtlaqual tonacaiutl: qujqua cintli, qujquã chilli, aiotli, aiooachtli: yoan in chien, yoã in chientzotzol: qujquã cacaoatl, in cacaoatetl: vel tlacatlaqua, qujquã nochtli, in capolin. etc. qujquã tamalli: tlaxcalli, qujquã nacaxoxouhquj, in jcucic nacatl in mjchin muchi qujqua, in xoqujac: vel iuhqujn tlateci

In jtapaçol qujchioa ca çacatl: çacaiamã, no qujtemoa in tlaçotli: qujtoponia, qujtetequj in tilmatli, in quetzalli: in tlein tlaçopialonj, mochi qujtotoponja, muchi qujtlacoa: in manel cenca canjn ca, in manel cenca motlaçopia, in manel ovican, calaquj: cõhitlacoa in tlaçotli. Ic no motocaiotia qujmjchin: in tetlânenquj, ipampa in manel canjn: cacalaquj ca concaquj, ca concuj in tlatolli: yoan ontlanemilia, ic mjtoa in tlatolli Niqujmjchti: qujtoznequj, njtetlanencati: tlatetequj, tlatotopotza.

---

1. *Quimichin: Mus musculus jalapae* (J. A. Allen and Chapman), according to Durrant.

eavesdrop on one." [The eavesdropper] gnaws, frays [the information].

Thus is a mouse caught: the cat kills it; it is snared, it is trapped; it is poisoned with *quimichpatli*.

Injc maci qujmjchin: mjzton, gaton qujnmjctia: momõvia, motlapevia: moqujmjchpavia.

WATER MOUSE[2]

Also its name is water gopher. It is the same as the mouse. It is a water-dweller, a paddler, a swimmer. It is small and fleshy, corpulent; long-tailed.

AQUJMJCHIN:

yoan itoca Atoçã, çan ie ieh in qujmjchin: atlã nemjnj, tlamaneloanj: panonj, tomactontli, nacateton: cujtlapilhujac.

FOREST MOUSE

It is a mouse which lives in the forest; it is long, thick.

QUAUHQUJMJCHIN:

in quauhtla nemj qujmjchin, viac, tomaoac.

FIELD MOUSE

It is a mouse which lives in the maize fields, on the plains.

TLALQUJMJCHIN:

in mjlpan in jxtlaoacan nemj, qujmjchin.

HOUSE MOUSE

It is a mouse which lives in one's house.

CALQUJMJCHIN:

in techan nemj qujmjchin.

TECOCON, TECOCONTON

It is the same as the mouse, [small, small and round].

TECOCON: TECOCONTON

çan ie no ieh in qujmjchin, [tepiton. ololtõtli.]

[TETLAQUECHILILLI]

[It is the same as the mouse.][3] Its muzzle is small and long, small and slender. It is blind.

[TETLAQUECHILILLI.]

[çã ye no yeh ỹ quimichĩ.] tenviacapil, tẽpitzaton, ixpôpoyotic.

KANGAROO RAT OR LONG-TAIL[4]

It is long-bodied, small and thin. Its tail is long.

VEÇACOTL: ANOÇO CUETLAPILHUJAC,

tlacviac, pitzaton, viac in jcujtlapil.

POCKET GOPHER[5]

It is the cheek-bagged one; or the cheek-bags. Like the gopher, it is thick, with small, thick back. It eats all the maize; it attacks beans especially. As for its being named *camaxixiqui*, even if it is a bushel of beans, it takes all of it, it carries off all of it. Its pouches are like two bags. There it places, there it puts in whatever it carries off, and it makes storage places underground; it fills them there, so that later it can continue eating it.

CHACHAOATL:

camaxiqujpile, anoço camaxixiquj: iuhqujn toçan, tomavac, cujtlatomactontli, muchi qujqua in tonacaiutl: oc cenca qujmoiautia in hetl. Inic motocaiotia camaxîxiquj: in manel çe hanega hetl, mochi qujtqujz, muchi qujçacaz. In jcamaxitecujl: ontlamantli xixiqujpilteuhca: vmpa qujtema, vmpa qujcalaquja, in tlein qujçaca: yoan motlallancuezcontia, vmpa qujtentiquetza: injc çatepan qujquatinemj.

2. *Aquimichin: Sigmodon hispidus berlandieri*, according to Martín del Campo, *loc. cit.* Durrant suggests *Sigmodon hispidus berlandieri* (Baird) or hispid cotton rat.

3. Omission in the Nahuatl text of the *Florentine Codex* is supplied (in brackets) from *Acad. Hist. MS.*

4. *Veçacotl: Dipodomys phillipsii phillipsii* (Gray), according to Villa R., *op. cit.*, p. 401.

5. *Chachaoatl: Cratogeomys merriami merriami* (*ibid.*, p. 377).

Second Chapter, which telleth of all the different kinds of birds.

First paragraph, which telleth of the many different kinds of birds, of whatever sort.

RESPLENDENT TROGON[1]

Its bill is pointed, yellow; its legs yellow. It has a crest, wings, a tail. It is of medium size, the same as the slender-billed grackle.[2] The tail feathers are streaked. On [the tail], the feathers which grow on it are called *quetzalli*. Those which are on its tail are green, herb-green, very green, fresh green, turquoise-colored. They are like wide reeds: the ones which glisten, which bend. They become green, they become turquoise. They bend, they constantly bend; they glisten.

The tail of this one is black, dark. [These feathers] cover [and] underlie [the *quetzalli* feathers]. These are also green, glistening. [These feathers are] only on the interior side.[3] They are [rather] long, wide, smoky, blackish, sooty. They cover, they protect [the *quetzalli* feathers]; they become smoky, dark, green, glistening.

This bird is crested; of quetzal spines, of quetzal thread feathers is its crest, very resplendent, very glistening. They are called *tzinitzcan*. A crest is formed; a crest develops, emerges, grows.

About its neck, its throat, and its breast, [the feathers] are reddish — well colored, even colored, well textured, chili-red, resplendent, wonderful, precious. The name of the feathers is *tzinitzcan*. They are chili-red. They become chili-red, reddish, resplendent, glistening, well textured.

About its neck and back are those called *tzinitzcan*, *tzinitzcan* feathers of the resplendent trogon, which are green, resplendent, glistening.

On its belly are [those] called *olincayotl*; they are yielding, not stiff; green, herb-green. They yield, they are soft; they become glistening green.

Injc vme capitulo: intechpa tlatoa in jxqujchtin, in jzqujtlamantin: in nepapan totome.

Injc ce parrapho: itechpa tlatoa, in jzqujtlamantin nepapan totome: in çaço quenamjque.

Quetzaltototl:

tenvitztic, tencoztic, xococoztic, quachichiqujle, amatlapale, cujtlapile, çan ipan qualton, ixqujch in vei tzanatl, in cujtlapiltzatzapal hiviio. In jtech ca: in qujxoaltia hivitl, itoca quetzalli, icuitlapiltitech in manj, xoxoctic, qujltic, xoxocpatic, xiuhcaltic, ximmaltic: iuhqujn tolpatlactic, cuecueiaoanj, vivitolivinj, xoxovia, ximmalivi, vitolivi, vivitolivi, cuecueiaoa.

Injn iciujtlapil tliltic catzaoac: injc qujtlapachoa, yoan qujpechtia: no xoxoxoctic, no xoxotla: in jiomjo, çan centlapal viiac, patlaoac, pochectic, cujchectic, cujcheoac: tlatlapachoa, tlamalhuja: pocheoa, cujcheoa, xoxoxovia, xoxotla.

Inin tototl quachichiqujle; quetzalomjtl, quetzaltomjtl in jquachichiqujl: cēca pepetlaca, xoxotla: itoca tzinitzcan, moquachichiqujltia, quachichiqujlloa, quachichiqujlqujça, quachichiqujlhixoa.

In iquechtlan: in jtozcac, yoā in jelpan: tlatlavic, vel paltic, vel qujzquj, vel icucic, chichiltic, pepetzca: maviztic, tlaçotli: itoca tzinitzcan chichil, chichilivi, tlatlavia, pepetlaca, xoxotla, icuci.

In jquechquauhiotitech onoc: yoan in jcujtlapan, iehoatl in mjtoa tzinitzcan, quetzaltzinitzcan, xoxoctic, pepetzca, pepetlaca.

In jtzintenpan manj: jtoca olincaiotl, çotlaoac, amo chicaoac, xoxoctia, qujltic, çotlaoa, çoçotlaoa; xoxoxovia.

---

1. *Quetzaltototl*: *Pharomachrus mocino* de la Llave. Herbert Friedmann, Ludlow Griscom, and Robert T. Moore: "Distributional Check-List of the Birds of Mexico," *Pacific Coast Avifauna*, Nos. 29, 33 (Berkeley, Calif.: Cooper Ornithological Club, 1950, 1957; henceforth referred to as Friedmann *et al.*), Pt. II, p. 11.

2. *Tzanatl*: *Cassidix palustris* (Swainson), *ibid.*, p. 280.

3. Corresponding Spanish text: *"Estas plumas negras, de la parte de fuera sõ muy negras, y de la parte de dentro, que es lo que esta junto con las plumas ricas, es algo verde escuro. . . ."*

On its wing, one kind which grows at the very point of the wing-bend is called *tzicoliuhqui*. They are of average size, black at the base, flesh-colored,[4] somewhat curved. And those which follow, which come forth at its wing-bend, are called *tecpatic*.[5] They are a little wide, pointed at the end.

Those which cover the bases of its flight feathers are called *quetzalhuitztli* and *chilchotic, piaztontli, yacauitztic*. They are green, very green, resplendent; they glisten, they become very green.

The breeding place of these birds is [the province of] Tecolotlan; and in the trees they make their homes and raise their young.

MEXICAN TROGON[6]

It lives in the water. Its feathers are black, dark. And for this reason is it called *teotzinitzcan*:[7] on its breast and its underwing it is varicolored, half black, half green. It is glistening green, resplendent.

ROSEATE SPOONBILL[8]

Also its name is *teoquechol*. It is a waterfowl, like the duck: wide-footed, chili-red footed. It is wide-billed; its bill is like a palette knife. It is crested. Its head — as well as on its breast, on its belly — and its tail, and its wings are pale, pink, whitish, light-colored. Its back and its wing-bend are chili-red, a well-textured, dried chili-red; the bill becomes yellow. The bill is yellow, the bill becomes wide; the legs become yellow, the legs become very yellow, chili-red. [Its plumage] becomes pale, pink, chili-red, well textured.

XIUHQUECHOL[9]

Its feathers are herb-green; its wings and tail are blue. It lives in Anahuac.

TROUPIAL[10]

It is pointed of bill; the feathers over the nose are chili-red. Everywhere [over the body] its feathers are tawny. And for this reason is it called *çaquan*; its tail is yellow, very yellow, intense yellow, colored yellow,

In jatlapaltitech onoc: injc centlamãtli, in vel yiacol iacac ixoa: itoca tzicoliuhquj: çan qualton, tzintliltic, xoxovic, achi tzicoltic. Auh in qujoaltoqujlia: in jiacolpan eoa, itoca: tecpatic, patlactontli, iacavitztic.

In qujtzinpachoa yiahaz: itoca, quetzalhujtztli, yoan itoca chilchotic, piaztontli, iacavitztic, xoxoctic, xoxocpatic: pepetzca, xoxotla, xoxoccaltia.

Inin tototl vel itlacachan, in tecolotlan: auh quavitl yitic, in mochantia, yoã in mopilhoatia.

TZINITZCAN TOTOTL: TEUTZINITZCÃ,

atlan in nemj: tliltic, catzaoac in jviio. Auh injc mjtoa teutzinitzcan: hielpan, yoan iciiacac in manj, chictlapanquj, centlacotl tliltic, centlacotl xoxoctic: xoxotla, pepepetzca.

TLAUHQUECHOL:

yoan itoca teuquechol, atlan chane, iuhqujn canauhtli, xopapatlactic, xochichiltic, tempatlaoac, mactepoztic in jten: quachichiqujle. In jtzontecon; yoan in jelpan, in jitipan, yoan in jcujtlapil, yoã in jiahaz, in jatlapal: iztaleoac, tlaztaleoaltic, iztalectic, pineoac. In jcujtlapan: yoan in jiacol, chichiltic, vel icucic, chilpatzcaltic tencoçavia: tencoztia, tempatlaoa, xocoçavia, xocôcoçavia: xochichilivi, iztaleoa tlaztaleoalti, chichilivi, icuci.

XIUHQUECHOL:

qujltic in jivio, texotic in jahaz, yoan in jcujtlapil: anaoac nemj.

ÇAQUAN:

tenvitztic, iacachichiltic: in novian ihiviio, quappachtic. Auh inj moteneoa çaquã icujtlapil in; coztic, vel cozpatic, cozpiltic, cozpalalatic. Auh tliltic injc qujtlapachoa: no ic qujpechia, in jquac qujçoa.

---

4. Corresponding Spanish text: *"color de vña."*

5. Lit. flint-knife-like.

6. *Tzinitzcan: Trogon mexicanus* Swainson (Friedmann *et al., op. cit.,* p. 12). *Teutzinitzcan* is an alternative name.

7. Fig., really precious.

8. *Tlauhquechol: Ajaia ajaja* (Linnaeus) in *ibid.,* Pt. I, p. 35. *Teoquechol* is an alternative name.

9. *Xiuhquechol: Momotus lessoni goldmani* in Rafael Martín del Campo, "Ensayo de interpretación del Libro undécimo de la Historia General de las Cosas de Nueva España de Fray Bernardino de Sahagún," II, "Las Aves," *Anales del Instituto de Biología,* Vol. XI, No. 1. (Mexico, 1940), p. 388. *Cotinga* sp. according to Sahagún (Garibay ed.), Vol. IV, p. 369.

10. *Çaquan: Gymnostinops montezuma* (Lesson) in Friedmann et al., *op. cit.,* Pt. II, p. 276.

but there are black [feathers] which cover it, which also underlie it. When it spreads its tail, then the yellow shows through. The black ones show splendor, radiate like a flame; like embers, like gold they show through.

AYOQUAN[11]

It is a forest-dweller; especially is it a dweller there [in the province of] Cuextlan and in Michoacan. The bill is pointed, black: everywhere [over the body] its feathers are black, but its tail is mixed white [and black],[12] so that it is called *ayoquan*.

AYOQUAN

It is a water bird. Thus does it live: accompanying it go all the water birds. And wheresoever it lights, there settle, there land the [other] birds. It is yellow-billed, green of wing-bend;[13] its flight feathers, its tail are [as if] shot with mirror-stones — mingled with white. Everywhere [over its body] its feathers are ruddy. The bill is pointed; [the feathers] are ruddy; they are [as if] shot with mirror-stones.

BLUE HONEYCREEPER[14]

It is a forest-dweller; small, pointed and small of bill. Its head and tail are herb-green, and its wings, on the outer surfaces, are also herb-green, somewhat dark green. And the under part of its wings and all its body are light blue, turquoise, very light blue, the color of fine turquoise. It is light blue; it becomes light blue; it turns turquoise-colored.

LOVELY COTINGA[15]

It is an inhabitant of Anahuac, a dweller in Anahuac. It is like all the slender-billed grackles. The bill is pointed, black. Its breast is purple, its back a really light blue, a very light blue, its wings pale, and its tail mixed, part blue-green, part black.[16]

TURQUOISE-BROWED MOTMOT[17]

Its name is also *tziuhtli*. The bill is long. The legs are black. Its head, and its back, and its wings,[18] and its tail are light blue; its belly and its wing-bend

AIOQUAN:

icujtlapil: iquac in oalneci coztic; vel qujtlanexmaca, qujtonameiotia in tliltic: iuhqujn tletl, iuhqujn tlexochtli, iuhqujn teucujtlatl oalneci.

AIOQUAN:

quauhtla chane, oc cenca tlaquauh vmpa chane; in cuextlan, yoan in mjchoacã. tenvitztic, tentliltic, noviã tliltic in jhiviio. Auh in jcujtlapil iztac ic viviltecquj: ic mjtoa Aioquan.

AIOQUAN:

atlan chane, inic nemj: cololhujtinemj, in jxqujch tototl, atlan nemj. Auh in canjn moquetza: vncan moteca, vnca pachivi in totome. Tencoztic: acolxoxouhquj, in jahaz, in jcujtlapil: tecpacâcalqui, iztacaviviltecquj, in novian ihiviio, tlatlauhquj, tenvitzavi; tlatlavia, motecpacacali.

CHALCHIUHTOTOTL:

quauhtlacatl, tepiton, tenvitzton. In jtzontecon: yoan in jcujtlapil qujltic, yoan in jatlapal: in tonalli qujtztinemj, no qujltic achi yiauhtic. Auh in tlanj ca yiatlapal: yoan in ie mochi itlac, texotic, xiuhtic, texocaltic, teuxiuhtic: texoti, texotia, xippopoca.

XIUHTOTOTL:

anaoac in nemjnj, anaoac chane: iuhquj, ixqujch in tzanatl. tenvitztic, tentliltic: in jielpan aiopaltic, in jcujtlapan vel xoxoctic, texocaltic, ticeoa in jatlapal, yoan in jcujtlapil: chictlapanquj, centlapal xoxoctic, texotic; centlapal tliltic, chictlapanquj.

XIOAPALQUECHOL;

yoan itoca tziuhtli, tenviac, xotlitliltic: in jtzõtecon, yoan in jcujtlapan, yoan in jatlapal, anoço iamatlapal, yoã in jcujtlapil: texotic, quappachtic, in ijtic, yoan

---

11. *Aioquan:* Mexican Cacique, *Cassiculus melanicterus,* in Martín del Campo, *op. cit.,* p. 388. See, however, Friedmann *et al., op. cit.,* p. 277.
12. Corresponding Spanish text: *"eceto la cola que tiene las plumas, las medias blancas, y las medias negras."*
13. *Ibid.: "los codillos de las alas."*
14. *Chalchiuhtototl: Cyanerpes cyaneus* (Linnaeus) in Friedmann *et al., op. cit.,* p. 235.
15. *Xiuhtototl: Cotinga amabilis* Gould (*ibid.,* p. 59).
16. Corresponding Spanish text: *"la cola tiene de plumas ametaladas, de verde y açul y negro."*
17. *Xioapalquechol: Eumomota superciliosa* (Sandbach) in Friedmann *et al., op. cit.,* p. 18.
18. *Jatlapal anoço iamatlapal* — alternative terms for wing.

tawny. It becomes green, it is green; it becomes tawny, it is tawny.

EMERALD TOUCANET[19]

The forest is its abode, the forest is its home. It breeds especially there in Totonaca country [and] in Cuextlan; it raises its young in the trees. It merely builds a bag-like nest for its young [and] suspends them.

The bill is long, concave, yellow, very yellow, colored yellow. For this reason it is called *xochitenacal*: about its throat [and] neck [the feathers] are very yellow, yellow, well textured, flower-yellow. And its head and its body are dark, dark green. And its wings and its tail are tawny and black mingled with white.[20] The bill widens; it becomes concave; it becomes yellow; there are marks as of hawk scratches; [colors] are mingled.

SQUIRREL CUCKOO[21]

It is tawny, completely tawny: smoky, even-colored, well textured. It is smoked; it is smoky; it turns smoky.

BLUE GROSBEAK[22]

Its wings and its bill are of dull colors. It is [the color of] the lovely cotinga — light blue. It looks dull; it turns dull.

¶

SECOND PARAGRAPH, which telleth of birds like the young yellow-headed parrot and the scarlet macaw, and still others.

YOUNG YELLOW-HEADED PARROT[1]

It has a yellow, curved bill, like that of the white-fronted parrot; the head is crested. Its breeding place is especially [the province of] Cuextlan. These are its chick feathers — herb-green, dark, dark green on its back, and about its neck, and its tail, and its wings. And those at the tip of its wing-bend are green [and] yellow; they cover its flight feathers. And on its breast, on its belly, its feathers are yellow, dark yellow. They are called *xollotl*. And its tail and its wings are ruddy.[2]

in jacol: xoxovia, xoxoctia, quappachivi, quappachti.

XOCHITENACAL:

quauhtla inentla, quauhtla ichan: oc cenca vmpa tlacanemj in totonacapan, in cuextlan, quauhtitech in mopilhoatia: çan qujnxiqujpilquetza in jpilhoan qujmpiloa.

Tenviac: tenacaltic, tencoztic, tencozpiltic, tencozpalalatic. Injc mjtoa xochitenacal: in jtozcatlan, in jquechtlan cozpatic, toztic: vel icucic, xochitic, in jtzontecon, in joan itlac yiauhtic, yiappaltic. Auh in jatlapal yoan in jcujtlapil, quappachtic auh tliltic, iztac ic viviltecquj tempatlaoa, tenacalivi, tencoçavia, motlotlovitequj, moviviltequj.

QUAPPACHTOTOTL:

quappachtic, motqujtica quappachtli: poctic, vel qujzquj, vel icucic pocheoa, poctia, pocti.

ELUTOTOTL:

tlaceviltic in jatlapal, yoan in jten, xiuhtototic, texotic: tlacevilneci, tlacevilti.

¶

INJC VME PARRAPHO: intechpa tlatoa in totome, in juhquj iehoatl Toznene, in Alo: yoã in oc cequintin.

TOZNENE:

tencoztic, tencoltic, tencochotic, quachichiquiltic, vel tlaquauh itlacachan in cuextlan. Izcatquj in jpilhiviio: qujltic, yiauhtic, yiapaltic, in jcujtlapan, yoã in jquechtlan, yoan in jcujtlapil, yoan in jatlapal. Auh in jacoliac: xoxoctic, coztic: qujtzimpachoa in jahaz. Auh in jelpan in jitipã. coceoac, coziaiactic; inin hiviio, itoca xollotl. Auh in jcujtlapil: yoã in jatlapal, matlatlauhquj:

---

19. *Xochitenacal: Aulacorhynchus prasinus* (Gould) in Friedmann *et al., op. cit.,* p. 23.

20. Corresponding Spanish text: *"las alas y la cola leonado, y ametalados de negro y blanço."*

21. *Quappachtototl: Piaya cayana* (Linnaeus) Friedmann *et al., op. cit.,* Pt. I, p. 133.

22. *Elototl: Guiraca caerulea* (Linnaeus) in *ibid.,* Pt. II, p. 333.

1. *Toznene: Amazona ochrocephala* (Gmelin) in *ibid.,* Pt. I, p. 131.

2. *Matlatlauhqui* — read *tlatlauhqui.*

In crags, in tree-tops, on water plants it nests, lays eggs, sits, hatches its young. There it is captured [to be] tamed.

ADULT YELLOW-HEADED PARROT[3]

When the young yellow-headed parrot is already developed, it turns yellow, it becomes very yellow. It develops fluffy feathers. When completely feathered, then it is called *toztli*.

SCARLET MACAW[4]

It lives especially in [the province of] Cuextlan, in crags and in the dense forest. It is tamable. Yellow, curved is its bill; rough are its feet, with callosities. The tongue is covered with callosities; it is round, black. Flaming red are its eyes; yellow are its breast [and] belly.

Its back is dark; its tail, its wing [feathers] are ruddy, reddish, a well-textured, even color. They are called *cueçalin*. The wing coverts and tail coverts are blue, becoming ruddy, reddish, bright reddish, orange.

WHITE-FRONTED PARROT[5]

It resembles the young yellow-headed parrot. It has a yellow, curved bill; it is crested. Everywhere [over its body] its feathers are dark green; its coverts are dark red [and] dark yellow. Its feathers named *xollotl*, the small feathers of its tail [and] its wing, are ruddy. It is a singer, a constant singer, a talker, a speaker, a mimic, an answerer, an imitator, a word-repeater. It repeats one's words, imitates one, sings, constantly sings, chatters, talks.

AZTEC PARAKEET[6]

It resembles the young yellow-headed parrot and the white-fronted parrot. It is small, tiny; the small head is chili-red. Everywhere [the body is] herb-green, dark green. The wing coverts are dark red. Its food is maize. It eats grains of dried maize.

I give it grains of dried maize to eat.

RED-CROWNED PARROT[7]

It is a forest-dweller with curved, yellow bill, a chili-red head, purple-brown wing-bend, dark yellow

texcalco, quauhticpac, apachiticpac in motapaçoltia, in tlatlaça, in tlapachoa, in tlatlapana: vncan ano, tlacacivitilo.

TOZTLI:

in ie chicaoac toznene, coçavia, cozpiltia, tomjolti: in novian yhiviio, ic mjtoa toztli.

ALO:

tlaquauh vmpa nemj, in cuextlan, texcalco, quauh-ovican in tlacatinj: tlacacivitilonj. tencoztic, tēcoltic, xoteteçontic, xochacaioltic, nenepilchacaioltic, nenepilololtic, nenepilliltic: ixtletlexochtic, elcoçauhquj, hiticoçauhquj.

In jcujtlapan yiauhtic: in jcujtlapil, yoan in jatlapal: tlatlactic, tlatlauhquj, icucic, vel qujzquj: itoca cueçali. In jacol quauhio: yoã in qujtzinpachotoc, icujtlapil: texotli, tlatlavia, tlatlactia, tlatlacti, cozcamjlivi.

COCHO:

qujnenevili in toznene, tencoztic, tencoltic, quachichiqujltic in novian yhiviio, yiappaltic, in jacol quauhio: tlappoiaoac, coziaiactic. In jiviio: itoca xollotl, pilivitl: in jcujtlapil, yoan in jatlapal, matlatlauhquj: cujcani, cujcujcanj, tlacatlatoanj tlatoanj, tetlaehecalhujanj, tetlananãquilianj, tetlamachcujnj, tetencopinanj. Tetencopina, tetlamachcuj, cujca, cujcujca, tlatlatoa, tlacatlatoa.

QUJLITON:

qujnenevili in toznene, yoan in cocho: tepiton, tetzoton, quachichilton, qujltic: novian yiappaltic. In jacol quauhio: tlapalpoiaoac: tonacaiutl in jtlaqual, tlaolqua,

njctlaolqualtia.

TLALACUEÇALI:

quauhtla chane, tencoltic, tencoztic, quachichiltic, acolcamopalpoiaoac, elcoziaiactic, in jcujtlapan, in

3. See Friedmann *et al., loc. cit.*

4. *Alo: Ara macao* (Linnaeus) in *ibid.,* p. 125.

5. *Cocho: Amazona albifrons* (Sparrmann) in *ibid.,* p. 129.

6. *Quiliton: Aratinga astec* (Souancé) in *ibid.,* p. 126. Olive-throated parakeet in E. R. Blake, *Birds of Mexico* (Chicago: University of Chicago Press, 1953), p. 192.

7. *Tlalacueçali: Amazona viridigenalis* (Cassin) in Friedmann *et al., op. cit.,* p. 130.

breast. Its back, wings, tail are dark green, seemingly dark green. Its tail and wings are leaf-colored.

HUMMINGBIRD[8]

The bill is black, slender, small and pointed, needle-pointed, needle-like. In shrubs, in trees it makes itself a nest, it lays eggs, sits, hatches its young. It has only two eggs; its young are rare. Its food is flower honey, flower nectar.[9] It is whirring, active [in flight]; ashen in color. It rejuvenates itself. It sucks, sucks honey; it builds itself a nest, lays eggs, sits, hatches its young, raises its young; it flies, darts, chirps.

In the winter, it hibernates. It inserts its bill in a tree; [hanging] there it shrinks, shrivels, molts.[10] And when [the tree] rejuvenates, when the sun warms, when the tree sprouts, when it leafs out, at this time [the hummingbird] also grows feathers once again. And when it thunders for rain, at that time it awakens, moves, comes to life.

This one is medicine for pustules. One who wishes never to have pustules eats often of its flesh. But they say it makes one sterile.

BROAD-TAILED HUMMINGBIRD[11]

Its throat is chili-red, its wing-bend ruddy. Its breast is green. Its wings and its tail [feathers] resemble quetzal feathers.

COSTA HUMMINGBIRD[12]

It is entirely, completely light blue like a cotinga, pale like fine turquoise. It is resplendent like turquoise, like fine turquoise.

THE BROAD-BILLED HUMMINGBIRD[13] is light green; a turquoise shade; herb-green.

THE YIAUHTIC UITZILIN is dark green.

THE RUFOUS HUMMINGBIRD[14] is red and black.

THE HELOISE HUMMINGBIRD[15] is light brown, the color of tunas.

jatlapal, in jcujtlapil: yiappaltic, mjiappalnenequj: xioapaltic in jcujtlapil: yvan in jatlapal.

VITZITZILI:

vitzili, tentliltic, tempitzaoac, tenvitzaponatic, tentzaptic, tenvitzmalotic. Tlacotitech: quauhtitech in motapaçoltia, in tlatlaça, in tlapachoa, in tlatlapana: çan vntetl in jteuh, tlaçopilhoa: xochinecutli, xochimeiallotl in jtlaqual. çoloctic, tzomoctic, nexeoac, mopilqujxtianj, tlachichina, necuchichina, motapaçoltia: tlatlaça, tlapachoa, tlatlapana, mopilhoatia; patlanj, çoloni, pipitzca.

In tonalco: mooatza, quauhtitechcaquja in jten: vncan quauhvaquj, tetzolhoacquj, mjhujiotepeoa. Auh in jquac izcalli in ie tlatotonja, in ie tlatzmolinj, in ie tlacelia: no iquac oc ceppa mopiliviiotia. Auh in jquac: quaqualaca qujiavitl, iquac iça, iquac moholinja, iquac mozcalia.

Inin nanaoapatli: in qujnequj aic nanaoatiz, mjecpa qujqua in jnacaio: iece qujtoa, tetetzacatili.

QUETZALHUJTZILIN:

tozcachichiltic, acollalauhqui: xoxoctic in jelpan, yoan in jatlapal, yoan in jcujtlapil: moquetzalnenequj.

XIHUJTZILLI:

macitica, motqujtica texotic: xiuhtototic, ticeoac teuhxiuhtic, xippopoca, teuxippopoca.

CHALCHIHUJTZILI: xoxoxocpatic ximmaltic, qujltic.

YIAUHTIC VITZILI: yiappaltic.

TLAPALHUJTZILI: tlapalpoiaoac.

AIOPALHUJTZILI, tlapalcamjltic nochtic.

---

8. *Vitzitzili*: Fam. *Trochilidae* (Martín del Campo, *op. cit.*, p. 391).

9. *Acad. Hist. MS*: xochimeneyallotl.

10. "... *en este caso es incontrovertible que se hace intervenir a los capullos de ciertas mariposas*" (Martín del Campo, *loc. cit.*).

11. *Quetzalhuitzilin: Selasphorus platycercus* (*loc. cit.*); *S. platycercus* (Swainson) in Friedmann *et al.*, *op. cit.*, p. 182.

12. *Xihujtzilli: Calypte costae* (Martín del Campo, *loc. cit.*); *C. costae* (Bourcier) in Friedmann *et al.*, *op. cit.*, p. 181.

13. *Chalchihuitzili: Cynanthus latirostris* (Martín del Campo, *op. cit.*, p. 392); *C. latirostris* Swainson (Friedmann *et al.*, *op. cit.*, p. 166).

14. *Tlapalhuitzilin: Selasphorus rufus* (Martín del Campo, *loc. cit.*); *S. rufus* (Gmelin) in Friedmann *et al.*, *op. cit.*, p. 183.

15. *Aiopalhujtzili: Atthis heloisa heloisa* (Martín del Campo, *loc. cit.*); *Atthis heloisa heloisa* (Lesson and De Lattre) in Friedmann *et al.*, *op. cit.*, p. 182. Bumblebee Hummingbird in Blake, *op. cit.*, p. 266.

THE ALLEN HUMMINGBIRD:[16] its feathers are glistening, resplendent.

THE CINNAMOMEOUS HUMMINGBIRD[17] is smoky, dark yellow, tawny.

HECAUITZILIN[18]

It is small and long. Some are ashen, some black. The ashen ones have a black stripe across the eyes. Thus are they painted. And the black ones are painted on the face with white; they are striped across the eyes with a wind painting.[19]

RUBY-THROATED HUMMINGBIRD[20]

It is ashen, ash-colored. At the top of its head and the throat, its feathers are flaming, like fire. They glisten, they glow.[21]

TELOLOUITZILIN

It is small and round, small and ashen, small and chalky. It becomes round, chalky, ashen.[22]

YOLLOTOTOTL[23]

It lives there in [the province of] Teotlixco, toward the southern sea. It is quite small, the same as a quail. As for its being called *yollototl*, the people there say thus: that when we die, our hearts turn into [these birds]. And when it speaks, when it sings, it makes its voice pleading; it indeed gladdens one's heart, it consoles one. [On] its head, on its breast, on its back it is rather ashen, rather yellow. Its tail is black, only at the tips of the feathers, white [and black] are mixed. The wing-tips are white. It is edible.

RAIL[24]

Its home is in the forest. As for its being called *popocales*, it speaks so. Always in the twilight and at dawn, it says *popocales*. And it frequents the canyons; it lives there in [the provinces of] Toztlan [and] Catemahco. It eats fish. It is the size of a duck, only a little taller.

TLEVITZILI: xoxotla, in jhiviio pepepetzca.

QUAPPACHVITZILIN: poctic, poccoztic, quappachtic.

HECAVITZILI:

viacatontli, ceq'n nexeoaque, cequj tliltique. In nexeoac: tliltic in jixtlan caan: injc mjhchiuh. Auh in tliltic: iztac injc mjhchiuh, mjhchioa, mecahichioa, ixtlan tlaana.

TOTOZCATLETON: TOZCATLETON, TOZCATLE,

nextic, nexeoac, in jquanepantla, yoan in jtozcac: vel xoxotla in jhiviio, iuhqujn tletl, pepepetzca, xoxotla.

TELOLOVITZILI:

ololtontli, nextontli, ticectontli: ololivi, tiçeoa, nexeoa.

YOLLOTOTOTL:

Vmpa nemj teutlixco, ivicpa in vitzilatenco: çan tepiton ixqujch in çolin. Injc mjtoa iollototl: iuh qujtoa, in vmpa tlaca. Ca in jquac timjquj: qujmjxiptlatia in toiollo. Auh injc tlatoa: injc cujca qujcnotlalia in jtozquj: vel teiolcemelti, teiollali. In jtzontecon: in jelpan, in jcujtlapan: achi ixnexcoztic. In jcujtlapil: tliltic, çanjo in jahavitz, iztacaviviltecquj. In jahavitz: iztac, qualonj.

PÔPOCALES:

quauhtla ichan. Injc motocaiotia, pohpocales, iuh tlatoa: muchipa iquac, in ie oncalaquj tonatiuh, yoan in aiamo valqujça tonatiuh: in qujtoa pohpocales. Auh çan atlauhtli qujtocatinemj: vmpa nemj toztlan, catemahco: mjchin in qujqua. Ixqujch in patos: çan ie achi quauhtic.

16. *Tlevitzilli: Selasphorus alleni* (Martín del Campo, *loc. cit.*); probably *S. sasin* (Lesson) as in Friedmann *et al.*, p. 183.

17. *Quappachvitzilin: Amazilia rutila rutila* (Martín del Campo, *loc. cit.*); *A. rutila rutila* (De Lattre) in Friedmann *et al.*, *op. cit.*, p. 171.

18. *Hecauitzilin:* probably *Phaeoptila sordida* and female *Cyanolaemus clemenciae* (Martín del Campo, *loc. cit.*); see also n. 19.

19. Corresponding Spanish text: *"vnos dellos son cenjcientos, otros son negros: estos cenjcientos, tienen vna Raya blancagro [sic] por los ojos, y los negros tienen vna Raya blanca por los ojos."* In Sahagún (Garibay ed.) Vol. III, p. 238, *"estas cenicientas tienen una raya de negro."*
The terms used in the Nahuatl also describe the face painting of Tezcatlipoca.

20. *Totozcatleton: Archilochus colubris* (Martín del Campo, *loc. cit.*); *A. colubris* (Linnaeus) in Friedmann *et al.*, *op. cit.*, p. 180.

21. Corresponding Spanish text: *"tienen la garganta colorada, y resplandeciente, como vna brasa."*

22. The *Acad. Hist.* MS omits *yollotl, pôpocales, tecuciltototl*, and *ixmatlatototl*.

23. Martín del Campo, *loc. cit.*, suggests *Hedymeles ludovicianus*.

24. *Popocales:* *"probablemente de la familia* Rallidae" (*loc. cit.*).

Its bill is pointed, rather round, chili-red. Its eyes are chili-red. Its head is dark yellow. Its neck, its back, its breast, its tail are ashen. The undertail coverts are white, but are slightly ashen. Its legs are chili-red. It is edible.

TECUCILTOTOTL

It is so named [because] it always so speaks; it indeed pronounces [the sound] *tecucilton, tecucilton.* Its voice is thin. It is the same [size] as a quail,[25] and its feathers are the same. It is edible. It lives in the same place, [the provinces of] Teutlixco [and] Toztlan.

IXMATLATOTOTL

Its home is in the forest. It lives there in Anahuac. It is called *ixmatlatototl* because [its song] is almost like our own speech. When it sings, it says *campa uee,* as if it imitated those who live there.

Its bill is silvery. Its head, its breast, its back, its tail are completely ashen; its feet are ashen. It is edible.

¶

THIRD PARAGRAPH, which telleth of the waterfowl.

DUCK

It lives on the water; it feeds on fish, water flies, worms, water snails.

GOOSE[1]

It is ashen, large, squat. It is wide-billed, broad-billed, broad-footed, wide-footed. It is ashen; its feet are wide. It is a dweller in the lagoon here, and here it raises its young, builds its nests, lays eggs, sits, hatches its young.

MEXICAN DUCK[2]

It is white-breasted; [otherwise] ashen; of average size, not too large. Its breast — on its breast, on its belly, it is white. It has a wide, black bill, quill feathers, wing feathers, neck feathers, downy feathers.[3]

MALLARD[4]

The head [feathers] are dark green. The head is black. Its head feathers are resplendent, shimmering.

In jtē vitztic: mjmjltontli, chichiltic. In jxtelolo chichiltic. In jtzontecon poccoztic. In jquech; in jcujtlapan, in jelpan, in jcujtlapil nextic: in tlanjpa onoc iztac, auh in tlanj onoc achi ixcujchectic: in jicxi chichiltic. Qualonj.

TECUÇILTOTOTL:

injc motocaiotia, muchipa iuh tlatoa, vel qujtenqujxtia. tecuçilton, tecucilto: pitzaoac in jtlatol, ixqujch in çoli: auh çan no iuhquj in jhivio. Qualoni. çan no vmpa nemj teutlixco, toztlan

IXMATLATOTOTL:

quauhtla ichan, vmpa nemj in anaoac. Injc motocaiotia ixmatlatototl: achi vel iuhquj in totlatol titlaca, injc tzatzi: qujtoa Campa vee: iuhqujnma qujntlaieiecalhuja, in vmpa chaneque.

In jten: cujtlatexotic. In jtzontecon: in jelpan, in jcujtlapan, in jcujtlapil: çan mocemaquj nextic: in jicxi nextic. Qualonj.

¶

INJC EI PARRAPHO: itechpa tlatoa in iehoantin totome, atlan nemj.

CANAUHTLI:

atlan nemj, mjchī, axaxaiacatl, ocujlin, atecocolin in qujqua.

CONCANAUHTLI:

nextic vei, cujtlapachtic, tempatlaoac, tempatlactic, xopapatlactic, xopapachtic. Nexeoac; xopapatlaoa, çã njcan atlan in nemj in; yoã in mopilhoatia, motapaçoltia; tlatlaça, tlapachoa, tlatlapana.

CANAUHTLI:

eliztac, nexeoac, çan qualli, çan vel ipan: in jel, in jelpan, in jitipan iztac, tempatlaoac, tentliltic, ahavitze, ahaçe, tapalcaio, tlachcaioio.

CANAUHTLI

tzoniaiauhquj: quatliltic, pepepetzca, pepetlanj in jqua ihiviio.

---

25. Corresponding Spanish text: *"es del tamaño de vna codorniz."*

1. *Concanauhtli:* probably *Anser albifrons gambeli* (Martín del Campo, *op. cit.,* p. 393).

2. *Canauhtli: Anas diazi* (?) in *loc. cit.*

3. *Acad. Hist. MS: alapachyo* follows *tapalcaio.*

Corresponding Spanish text: *"tienē cañones en las alas, tienen plumas a manera de cōchas, tienen debaxo pluma delicada como algodon."* See also § 10, *infra.*

4. *Anas platyrhyncha platyrhyncha* (Martín del Campo, *loc. cit.*).

WHITE-FRONTED GOOSE[5]

Also they call it "water bird." It is large. The legs are chili-red, red. [The bill] is ashen; the back is rounded. It is good-tasting, savory. It has downy feathers; its down is used for capes. It has breast feathers.

BROWN CRANE[6]

The bill is long, like a nail, dart-shaped; the head is chili-red, [the body] ashen, the neck long. It is tall, high, towering. The legs are stringy, very long, black, like stilts. It is edible, savory, of good taste.

XOMOTL[7]

It is crested, short-legged, squat. The feet are wide, black, dark, blackish. It is a water-dweller, a fish-eater.

THE TEÇOLOCTLI is small, one which whirs [as it flies].

AMERICAN WHITE PELICAN[8]

It is large, broad-billed. It has a net-like throat. It is white like the turkey-cock.

The goose, the brown crane, the American white pelican, the Mexican duck are white-breasted. The mallard, the *xomotl*, the *teçoloctli* are sea-dwellers. They hatch on the seashore, on the sand, especially there to the west. And when frost comes, they come here to feed.

AMERICAN COOT[9]

It lives on the water; it belongs with the ducks. Its head is chili-red, its bill pointed. It lives, it is hatched only here, among the reeds.

THE YACACINTLI is the same as the American coot.

BLACK-CROWNED NIGHT HERON[10]

Its legs are long, dark green. Its bill is pointed, long and pointed, green. It forms a point; it is pointed. The head becomes chili-red; its legs become long, rope-like. Its legs are stringy.

TLALALACATL:

yoan qujtoa Atototl, vei: xochichiltic, xotlatlauhquj, nexeoac, cujtlaololtic; velic, aviac: tlachcaioio, hivitilmatli mochioa in jtlachcaio, alapachio.

TOCUJLCOIOTL:

tenviac, tentepuztic, tentlaxichtic, quachichiltic, nexeoac, quechviac, quauhtic, quauhtitinpol, quauhcholpol, xomemecapol, xovivitlatzpol, xotlitliltic, xotlacotic. qualonj: velic, veltic.

XOMOTL:

quachichiqujle, xopapachtic, cujtlapachtic, xotlitliltic, xopapatlactic, catzaoac, tlilectic. Atlan chane. mjchquanj.

TEÇOLOCTLI: tepiton, çolonjnj.

ATOTOLIN:

vei, tempatlaoac: quechmatle. Iztac: iuhqujn vexolotl.

In tlalalacatl: in tocujlcoiotl, in atotolin, in canauhtli eliztac. In tzoniaiauhquj: in xomutl, in teçoloctli: vei, atlan chaneque; vei atenco, xaltitlan in tlapanj: tlaquauh vmpa in tonatiuh icalaqujan. Auh çan iquac in oalhuj çevetzi, oallaquaqua.

QUACHILTON:

atlan nemj, cempouj in canauhtli, quachichiltic, tenvitztic, çan njcan novian tulla in nemj in tlacati.

IACACINTLI: çã no iehoatl in quachil.

VEXOCANAUHTLI:

xoviviac, xoiaiauhquj, tenvitztic, tenvitzaponatic, tenxoxouhquj, tenvitzavi, tenvitzti: quachichilivi, xoveveiaquja, xomemecatia, xomemecati.

---

5. *Tlalalacatl: Anser albifrons gambeli* (*loc. cit.*); *A. albifrons* (Scopoli) in Friedmann *et al., op. cit.*, Pt. I, p. 37.

6. *Tocujlcoiotl: Grus canadensis* (Linnaeus) in *ibid.*, p. 81.

7. *Xomotl: cierto pato* in Molina, *op. cit.* (*xumutl*). Martín del Campo believes this term and *teçoloctli* include a number of species. Since Francisco J. Santamaría: *Diccionario de Mejicanismos* (Mexico: Editorial Porrúa, S.A., 1959), p. 1125, says that *xomote* is a Valley of Mexico term for *pato triguero*, which is the Mexican duck (*Anas diazi* Ridgway in Friedmann *et al., op. cit.*, p. 40; see n. 2 *supra*), it would seem that Martín del Campo is correct.

8. *Atotolin: Pelecanus erythrorhynchus* Gmelin (Friedmann *et al., op. cit.*, p. 20).

9. *Quachilton: Fulica americana* Gmelin (*ibid.*, p. 87).

10. *Vexocanauhtli: Nycticorax nycticorax* (Linnaeus). See Martín del Campo, *op. cit.*, p. 394, and Friedmann *et al., op. cit.*, p. 31.

WILSON SNIPE[11]

Also it is called *çoquiaçolin*. It is long-billed, long-legged. It is varicolored like a quail. It becomes varicolored like a quail; varicolored. Its home is in the water, among the reeds. It is varicolored like a quail.

NORTHERN PHALAROPE[12]

It is round-backed. The bill is long and pointed, needle-like, pointed, very pointed, black. The legs are long, very long, stilt-like, like stilts, broom-like, slender. Its dwelling place is [the province of] Anahuac. It is white-breasted. The large northern phalarope is heavily fleshed, fat, greasy. It is greasy; it makes itself greasy; it is fat.

CLIFF SWALLOW[13]

It nests in the crags and house roofs, house fronts. It is a mud nest builder which plasters with its bill. Its nest is of tattered cloths. It is [dark] ashen, like a barn swallow. It builds itself a nest; it builds itself a nest of mud, it plasters its nest with its bill.

BARN SWALLOW[14]

It is small and black, with small, pointed bill, with small, short legs. It is charcoal-colored, very black, like the American cherry. It is a warbler, a crier, a constant warbler, an awakener of the sleeping. It is a builder of mud nests in house roofs, in house fronts. It is a traveler, a disappearer; later it comes, in [the month of] Atemoztli. It awakens sleepers, it brings them from their sleep; it warbles, it cries out; it flutters; it cleans itself, beautifies itself; it hurls itself into the water, it bathes itself.

SNOWY EGRET[15]

It is [also] called *teoaztatl*. It is white, very white, intensely white, snow-white. The back is rounded; dry, old looking. It is long-necked, stringy, curved. The bill is pointed, long and pointed, black. The legs are very long, stringy, stilt-like, black. The tail is stubby.

LITTLE BLUE HERON[16]

It resembles the brown crane [in color]: it is ashen, grey. It smells like fish, rotten fish, stinking fish. It smells of fish, rotten fish.

AÇOLIN:

yoan itoca çoqujaçolin, tenviac, xoviviac, çolcujcujltic, moçolcujcujloa, cujcujltic: atlan, tulla ichan: moçolcujcujloa.

ATZITZICUJLOTL:

cujtlaololtic, tēvitzaponatic, tenvitzmallotic, tenvitztic, tenvitzpatic, tentliltic, xovitlatztic, xovivitlatztic, xotlacotic, xotlatlacotic, xoihizqujztic, xopitzactic. Anaoac chane: eliztac, vei atzitzicujlotl nacateton, chiaoac, vel ceceio, ceceiooa: moceceiotia, chiaoa.

ACUJCUJALOTL:

texcalco chane, yoan calquac, calixquac, moçoqujcaltianj: tempitzqujqujztic in jcal. mehtollo: cujcujtzcatic, nexeoac; mocaltia, moçoqujcaltia, qujtempitzqujqujçoa in jcal.

CUJCUJTZCATL:

tliltontli, tenvitzpil, xopapachton; tecoltic, tlilpatic, cacapoltic, tlatlatole, tzatzatzinj, tlatlatoanj, cochhiçanj: tecalquac, calixquac moçoqujcaltianj: ianj polivinj: q'n hiquac oallauh, in atemuztli cochhiça: tehixitia, tlatlatoa, tzatzatzi, papatlaca, moiectia, moiêiectia, mapantlaça, maltia.

AZTATL:

mjtoa teuaztatl. iztac, iztacpatic, aztapiltic, cehpaiauhtic, cujtlaololtic, oacçoltic, quechveiac, quechmecatic, quechcocoltic; tenvitztic, tenvitzaponatic, tentliltic: xovivitlatztic, xomemecatic, xotlâtlacotic, xotliltic: cujtlapiltetepontic.

AXOQUEN:

motocujlcoionenequj, nextic, nexeoac: xoqujhiac, xoqujpototl, xoqujhialtic, xoqujhiaia; xoqujpotoivi.

---

11. *Açolin: Capella gallinago* (Linnaeus); *ibid.,* p. 98.

12. *Atzitzicujlotl: Lobipes lobatus,* according to Martín del Campo, *loc. cit.; Crocethia alba* (Pallas) or sanderling, according to Friedmann *et al., op. cit.,* p. 99.

13. *Acuicuialotl: Petrochelidon pyrrhonota melanogaster* (Swainson); *ibid.,* Pt. II, p. 109.

14. *Cuicuitzcatl: Hirundo rustica* Linnaeus; *ibid.,* p. 113.

15. *Aztatl: Leucophoyx thula* (Molina); *ibid.,* Pt. I, p. 30.

16. *Axoquen: Florida caerulea* (Linnaeus); *ibid.,* p. 29.

WILD TURKEY

It is like the domesticated turkey, though a little smoke-colored. The wing-bend is white. It is edible —savory, good-tasting, fat. It is a gobbler. The turkey cock [and] the turkey hen.... They gobble, they cough....[17]

PELICAN

It is the ruler, the leader of all the water birds, the ducks. When the various birds come, this is when it comes; it brings them here at the time of the Feast of Santiago, in the month of July.

And the head of this pelican is rather large, black. Its bill is yellow, round, a span long.[18] Its breast, its back are all white; its tail is not long; only average. Its legs have no long bones at all; its feet are at its body. They are about a span long, very wide. Its body is long, very thick. Its wings are not very large; its wing feathers are not very long.

This pelican does not nest anywhere in the reeds; it always lives there in the middle of the water, and it is said that it is the heart of the lagoon because it lives in the middle.

Also it sinks people. To sink them it only summons the wind; it sings, it cries out. It sinks them only when they try to catch it. To catch it they stalk it two, three, or four days. But if they fail to catch it by the third day, on the fourth day the water folk prepare themselves and then assemble and steel themselves to go forth to die. For this is the custom of the water folk.

For this pelican, after four days, sits awaiting the water folk; it rests on the water's surface; it sits looking at them. For if they fail to catch it in four days, by sunset, when the fifth sounds, the water folk thus know it as a sign that they will die; for they who have failed to catch it have been tried.

And this pelican, when they have failed to shoot it by sunset of the fourth day, then calls out, cries out like a crane; it summons the wind to sink the people. Thereupon the water foams; thereupon the water birds cry out exceedingly; they arrange themselves as it were in rows on the surface of the water: they beat [their wings]. All the fish well up. And the water folk can no longer help themselves, although they try hard to pole [their boats]. Their arms are

QUAUHTOTOLI:

çan vel iuhqujn totolin, tel achi poctic, hacolihiztac. qualonj; velic, aviiac, chiaoac: tlacocoloanj. In vexolotl: in cioatotolin, tlatotocujcuj quaquavianj, tlatoxixivianj: tlacohcoloa: totolca. tlatotocujcuj, quaquavia, tlatoxixivia.

ATOTOLIN:

intlatocauh, imachcauh, in jxqujchtin totome: atlan nemj. In cacanauhti: in jquac oalhuj, nepapan totome: çan no iquac oallauh, quinoalhujca: iquac sanctiago ilhujtzin, ipã metztli Julio.

Auh in iehoatl Atotolin: in jtzontecon, achi vei, tliltic. In jten coztic: çan mjmjltic, viac: cemjztitl. In jelpã: in jcujtlapan, cemjztac. In jcujtlapil amo viac: çan qualton. In jicxi: amo tle itlanjtz, çan njman itech catquj in jnacaio: in jxocpal, achi vel cemjztitl injc viac: cêca patlaoac. In jnacaio tlacviac cenca tomaoac. In jatlapal amo vehvei: in jahaz, in jahavitz: amo viviac.

In iehoatl in Atotolin: amo ma cana mochantia, In tultitlan: çan muchipa vmpã nemj, in jiolloco atl: yoan mjtoa: ca iiolloan in vei atl; ca çã tlaçonemj.

No teilaquja: injc teilaquja, çan qujnotza in ehecatl: tzatzi, choca: çan iquac in teilaquja: in jquac ie caciznequj. Inic caci: omjlhujtl, eilhujtl qujmopachivia: anoço navilhujtl. Auh intlacamo vel cana: injc eilhujtl, injc navilhujtl: mocêcaoa in atlaca, ica mocentlalia yoã ic motlapaloa in mjqujtivi: ic momjcatlaça. Iehica: ca oncatquj innaoatil in atlaca.

Ipampa in iehoatl in Atotoli, in jpan navilhujtl: ca muchipa qujnoalmochieltitoc in atlaca: atlixco moteca, qujnoalitztoc. Iehica: intlacamo vel canazque, in ie navilhujtl: ie teutlac, in jquac macujlli tzilinj: ic qujmati, inezca omjcque in atlaca: ca nel omoiehiecoque, in amo vel caci.

Auh in iehoatl Atotoli: in jquac amo vel oqujmjnque, injc navilhujtl: in ie teutlac. Nimã tzatzi, choca, tocujleoa: qujnotza in heecatl: injc teilaqujz. Nimã ie ic poçoni in atl: njman ie ic çenca tzatzi in totome, iuhqujn atl ixco moçoçoa: motzetzeloa. In mjmjchtin: mochintin panj oalmotetema. Auh in iehoantin atlaca: aocmo vel mopalevia, in manel çenca tlaneloznequj: ça in mamjmjquj, iuhqujnma aca qujntzintilinja: ic vncã mjquj in atlaca: vncan polaquj in acalli.

---

17. The *Acad. Hist. MS* skips descriptions from this point to § 4.

18. Corresponding Spanish text: *"el pico amarillo, redondo, y largo, como vm palmo."*

simply numbed; it is as if someone pulls them down. So there the water folk die; there the boat sinks.

And when the pelican can be caught, when it can be shot, perhaps they can shoot it, they can take it in two or three days. When the water folk shoot it, at once they seize it. They quickly, firmly grasp its bill; then they cast it into the boat. There they quickly disembowel it [while] it still lives. They disembowel it with a dart [with] three points at its head, called *minacachalli.*

They seize it quickly, they grasp its bill firmly and quickly, so that it cannot regurgitate what is within it. For if they do not do so, it will at once regurgitate what is within it. Then they take it, whereupon they cut open its gizzard. Within is a precious green stone; and if not a green stone, various precious feathers are there within, in its gizzard. And if they do not find a precious green stone or a feather, [but] only a piece of charcoal appears there, this becomes a sign that the hunter will die. But for him who finds, who takes from it, a precious green stone or feather, it becomes a sign that he always will be able to take, to capture, the various birds or fish; he will prosper. Although, as has been said, all which he will eat will be at hand — the various birds which he will capture — his grandsons will be in debt; they will indeed be poor.

And thus is the flesh of the pelican eaten: all the water folk assemble. They eat it only as a choice food; only a very little is offered one. For it is verily the heart of the water.

This pelican also takes with it the different water birds, when it goes. It goes there toward the west, where the sun sets.

These water folk consider it as their mirror. For there they see what each is to merit in their profession as water folk.

WATER-TURKEY[19]

It comes after the pelican [as a waterfowl]. It is also the heart of the water; it also is the leader of the [water] birds. It also appears at the time that the water birds come, on the Feast Day of Santiago.

Its head is as large as the turkey hen's. The bill is pointed, black, quite cylindrical; the outer edge of the tip is yellow. Its breast is rather white. Its back, its wings are all ashen, blackish, like duck feathers. It

Auh in jquac: in vel maci, in vel momjna in Atotoli: aço çan vmjlhujtl, anoço eilhujtl, in vel qujmjna: in vel caci. In jquac oquimjnque: çan njmã iciuhca qujcujtivetzi, in atlaca; qujtentzitzqujtivetzi, njmã qujoallaça in acalco, vncan iciuhca qujtitzaiana, çan ioioltoc: tlachichtli, ei manj in jquac acatl itoca mjnacachalli, inic qujtitzaiana.

Injc iciuhca qujcujtivetzi: qujtentzitzqujtivetzi, injc amo qujçotlaz, in jtic catquj. Iehica intlacamo iuh qujchioa in: ca njmã iciuhca qujçotlaz, in jitic catquj. Qujn iquac conana: in jquac qujtitzaiana in jmemetl, yitic catquj chalchivitl. Auh intlacatle chalchivitl: nepapan tlaçohivitl, in vncan catquj yitic imemetl. Auh intlacatle qujttazque: chalchivitl, anoço hivitl: çan teculli, in vncan neciz. Inezca mochioaz: in aqujn tlamjnquj, ca ie mjqujz. Auh in aqujn qujttaz in caniliz chalchivitl, anoço hivitl; inezca muchioa, muchipa vel qujmanaz, qujmaciz, in nepapã totome, anoço mjmjchtin: mocujltonoz. Macivi in omjto: in mochi neciz in qujquaz, in caciz, nepapan totome: in ixvivan, iehoantin tlaxtlaoazque: vel motolinjzque.

Auh injc moquaia: in jnacaio Atotoli, mocentlalia in jxqujchtin atlaca: çã qujtlaçoquaia, çan tepitoton in temacoia: ca nel yiollo in atl.

In iehoatl Atotoli: çan no qujnvica in jxqujchtin, nepapã totome, in jquac vi: vmpa itztivi in Cioatlampa, in vmpa calaquj tonatiuh.

In iehoantin atlaca iuhqujnma intezcauh, ipan qujmatia. Ca vncan qujtta: in cecenme tlein in maceoaltiz: in jpã atlacaiotl.

ACOIOTL:

qujtoqujlia in atotoli, no yiollo in atl, no imachcauh in totome: çan no iquac neci, in jquac oalhuj totome: atlan nemj, in jpã ilhujtzin Sanctiago.

In jtzontecõ ixqujch in jtzontecon, Cioatotolin: tenvitztic, tliltic: çan mjmjltontli: in jtenco iatoc coztic. In jelpan achi iztac. In jcujtlapan: in jhaaz, in jatlapal: çã muchi nextic, ixcujchectic: iuhqujn

19. *Acoiotl: Anhinga anhinga* (Linnaeus), Friedmann *et al., op. cit.,* p. 25.

is long-bodied. Its legs are thick, not long; they are at its rump, almost at its tail. Its feet are very wide, like our hands. It also is rare; it also can sink one.

All told of the pelican also [applies] similarly to the water turkey.

WESTERN GREBE[20]

It is also rare. Likewise, it comes when the various [water] birds come.

Its head is quite small, black, with a pointed, chili-red bill. Its eyes are like fire. It is long-necked. Its body is small and straight, small and thick: its breast very white, its back black, its flight feathers white, its wing-bend tips black, its legs black: they are also somewhat toward its rump, like a duck's legs.

It lives there in the lagoon and is caught in nets.

This western grebe does not fly very high; sometimes the water folk only chase it in boats; they spear it. And when they chase it, when they harass it exceedingly, when they are about to spear it, then it ruffles up, cries out, summons the wind. The lagoon foams much, it breaks into waves. So before the eyes of the water folk it vanishes, it suddenly enters the depths of the water. Occasionally they hit their mark; [the bird] is successfully speared. Also it brings forth no young [here]; it also migrates.

BLACK SKIMMER[21]

It flies high always at night there over the lagoon. It is the same size as a dove. Its head is quite small, black. Its breast is somewhat white, somewhat dark. Its back is black; its wings quite small. Its body is all small and round, its tail small, and its legs are like a dove's.

For this reason is it called "obsidian bill": it has three bills in all. Its food enters in two places, [though] there is only one throat by which it swallows it. It has also two tongues. Its [three] bills are one over the other.

And if one captures this black skimmer, it is a sign that he is about to die. And they say that his house will be destroyed; his house folk will perish. For this reason it is named a bird of ill omen.

The food of the black skimmer is water flies, flying ants which fly high.

canauhtli hiviio. tlacviiac: tomaoac, amo viac in jcxi: çan itzintenpan in mamanj, achi vel itlan in jcujtlapil: çeca papatlaoac in jxocpal: ixqujch in tomacpal. çan no tlaçonemj: no teilaquja.

In jxqujch omjto in jpan Atotoli: çan no iuhquj in acoiotl.

ACITLI:

çan no tlaçonemj, çan no iquac in oalhuj; in jquac oalhuj, nepapan totome.

In jtzontecon: çan tepiton: quatliltic, tenvitztic, chichiltic. In ixtelolo: iuhqujn tletl, quechviac. In jtlac: melactontli, tomactontli, in jelpan vel iztac, in jcujtlapan, tliltic: in jahavitz iztac: in jacoliacac tliltic. In icxitlan tliltic. Çan no achi itzintenpan in mamanj: iuhquj in canauhtli icxi.

Vmpa nemj in vei atlan: auh inic maci momatlavia.

In iehoatl Acitli: amo cenca vel acopatlanj, in quẽmanjan, çan qujtotoca acaltica: qujmjna. Auh in jquac ie qujtotoca: in cẽca ie qujtolinja, in qujmjnaznequj. Niman moçoneoa: tzatzi, qujnotza in heecatl: cenca poçoni, mocueiotia in vei atl. Ic imjxpan polivi in atlaca: atl yitic, calactivetzi: çan quẽmanjan ipanti, in vel momjna: amo no vel mopilhoatia, çan no iauh.

TENITZTLI:

çan mochipa iooaltica, acopatlantinemj, in vmpa in vei apan: ixqujch in paloma. In jtzontecon: çan tepiton, tliltic. In jelpan: achi iztac, achi cujchectic. In jcujtlapan tliltic, in jaztlacapal, in jahaz çã tepitoton. In ie muchi itlac: çan tapaioltontli: in jcujtlapil, çan tepiton: in jicxi, çã iuhqujn paloma ixomatzal.

Injc motocaiotia Tenitztli: eitemj in jten. In jtlaqual: occã in calaquj, ça oçeti in jtozcac, injc tlatoloa: no vme, in jnenepil, cecen qujtocaticac in jten.

Auh in iehoatl Tenjtztli: in aqujn caci, inezca ca ie mjqujz. Yoan qujtoa: tlaliooaz in jchan, tlamjzque in jchan tlaca. Ipampa in qujtocaiotiaia, tetzauhtototl.

In jtlaqual Tenitztli: amoiome azcapatlan; in âcopatlantinemj.

---

20. *Acitli: Aechmophorus occidentalis* (Lawrence); *ibid.*, p. 13.
21. *Tenitztli: Rynchops nigra* Linnaeus; *ibid.*, p. 112.

WOOD IBIS[22]

It is a bald-head — big, tall, the same as the little blue heron. Its head is large, like that of our native turkey cock;[23] its head is featherless, bald, bare to the back of its head. The sides of its head are chili-red, reaching to its neck. It is long-necked. Its bill is very thick as well as cylindrical, long, like a bow. Its breast is black. Its back, its wings are completely ashen, except that the wing-bends are very black. Its tail is short, black.

This wood ibis also comes when [water] birds come. It is quite rare.

And when it is caught, it is considered an evil omen. Either some of the lords will die, or war [will come]. If somewhere war breaks out, warriors will go off to die. Thus did the water folk verify it: as often as they took wood ibis, so often the city suffered some harm, and so they died. In times of old, as many lords died, one by one, as the number of wood ibis which they had first taken, perhaps three, perhaps two.

Its food is fish and all which lives in the mud. Its flesh is very good to the taste.

PURPLE GALLINULE[24]

It likewise is rare. Also it comes when [the other water] birds come. It is of average size, like a dove. For this reason is it called "mirror-head": on its head is something like a mirror, a round [patch] on the crown of its head.[25] There we appear. On the front of its head is a thin row of feathers, somewhat ashen. Its bill is quite small, cylindrical. Its breast, its back are completely light blue; its wings, its tail are likewise light blue. All its feathers are a little white.[26] Its legs are yellow. And when it swims, when it paddles with its feet in the water, it looks like an ember; it goes glowing, glistening.

And the appearance of this purple gallinule was [a sign of] war. Whoever captured one looked at himself in the mirror. If he were to go, to go forth to battle, he saw that he was carried off, taken captive; they dragged him away. But if he were to have

QUAPETLAOAC:

quapetlanquj, vei, quauhtic: ixqujch in axoquẽ. In jtzontecon: vei, ixqujch in njcan tovexolouh, in jtzontecon amo hiviio: quapetlanquj, xixipetztic, icuexcochtlan ontlantica: in jcanaoacan chichiltic, iquechtlan tlantica: quechviac In jten: cenca tomaoac, çan no mjmjltic: viac, iuhqujn tlavitolli ic catqui, tliltic: in jelpan, in jcujtlapan, in jahaz, in jamatlapal cenqujztica nextic: çan iquac in jahaz, cenca tliltic: in jcujtlapil amo viac, tliltic.

Inin quapetlaoac: çan no iquac oallauh, in jquac oalhuj totome: çan tlaçonemj.

Auh in jquac maçia tetzavitl ipan machoia. Anoço iehoãtin in tlatoque: ceme ie momiqujlizque, anoço iauiotl: intla cana iauqujxoaz, mjqujtivi in iaoqujzque. Injc qujneltilia in atlaca: in jzqujpa oqujmãque, in quapetlaoaque: izqujpa, itla ic itlacavi in altepetl, yoan injc omjcque: ie vecauh tlatoque, in cecenme mjquja: no izqujpa achtopa qujmanaia: aço etetl, anoço vntetl in quapetlaoaque.

In intlaqual mjchin: yoan ixqujch, in çoqujtitlan nemj: cenca velic in jnacaio.

QUATEZCATL:

çan no tlaçonemj, nò iquac oallauh, in jquac oalhuj totome: çan qualton ixqujch in paloma. Injc mjtoa quatezcatl: in jcpac, iuhqujn tezcatl manj: in jquanepantla, iaoaltic: vmpa tonneci. çan cenpãtontli: in vel ixquac onoc hiviio achi nextic: in jten çan tepiton mjmjltontli: in jelpan, in jcujtlapan, çan moçemaquj texotli: injahaz, in jcujtlapil, çan no texotli: in ie mochi hiviio, achitzin iztac: in jicxi coztic. Auh in jquac atlan nemj in tlacxinelotinemj, in atlan oalneci iuhqujn tlexochtli tlatlatiuh petlantiuh.

Auh in iehoatl i: in quatezcatl, inezca catca in iauiotl. In aqujn cacia: vmpa vmmotta, intla iaz, iauqujçatiuh: in conjttaz, vico, omaltic, qujvilana. Auh intla tlacnopilhujz; intla itla imaceoal, in conjttaz: tevilana.

---

22. *Quapetlaoac: Mycteria americana* Linnaeus; *ibid.*, p. 34. *Quapetlanqui* is an alternative name.

23. Corresponding Spanish text: *como la de vn gallo de papaga* [*sic*].

24. *Quatezcatl: Porphyrula martinica* (Linnaeus); Friedmann *et al., op. cit.*, p. 87.

25. See illus. Corresponding Spanish text: *"tiene vn espejo redondo en medio de la cabeça. Representa la cara como espejo: tiene las plumas al rededor del espejo pequeñas y cortas como vn perfil cenjciento."*

26. *Ibid.*: *"tiene las espaldas y el pecho açul: las alas, y la cola tambien açul hazia la carne, tiene blancas las plumas."*

good fortune, if he [were to] attain his reward, he saw that he dragged [the foe] off.

AMERICAN BITTERN[27]

Also its name is *atoncuepotli* and *ateponaztli*. It is rather large, the same size as the Castilian chicken, the capon. Its head is dark yellow; its bill yellowish, small, and cylindrical, about a span in length.[28] Its breast, its back, its tail, its wings are all dark yellow, slightly blackened; its legs, its shanks, are dark.

And for this reason is it called *tolcomoctli*: as it sings, it resounds. For this reason is it called *atoncuepotli*: when it sings, it is clearly heard to explode; it is very loud. And it is called *ateponaztli* because it sounds from a distance like a two-toned drum, so loud is it.

This American bittern always lives here in the reeds; here it raises its young. It sits on only five, or four eggs.

For these water folk this American bittern is always a portent. When it sings a great deal, always all night, they know thereby that rains will come, it will rain much, and there will be many fish — all manner of water life. But if it will not rain much, if there will not be many fish, it does not sing much. Only perhaps every third day, after much time, does it sing.

ACUITLACHTLI

It is much like the forest-dwelling wild beasts.[29] It is as small as a small dog. Its head, ears, muzzle, belly, back, front feet, hind feet, claws are just like [those of] the forest-dwelling wild beasts, except that its tail is a cubit long, but broad, like the tail of the alligator;[30] not divided but quite pointed at the end. No one has been able to take hold of it. He who lays hold of its tail with difficulty disengages his hands.

The water folk used to hunt the *acuitlachtli*. Also they said that this *acuitlachtli* was the heart of the lagoon. It lived there in Santa Cruz Quauhacalco, where there is a spring [whose water] comes to Santiago [Tlatelolco]. When the *acuitlachtli* dwelt there, because of it the water overflowed foaming, and the fish welled up to the surface. And when [the animal] entered the mud, the ground was agitated as if there were an earthquake. So the water folk can

TOLCOMOCTLI:

yoan itoca Atoncuepotli, yoan Ateponaztli: veitontli, ixqujch in castillan totolin: capon. In jtzontecon: poccoztic, in jten: achi coztic, mjmjltontli: injc viac achi uel cemjztitl: in jelpan, in jcujtlapan, in icujtlapil, in jahaz, in jatlapal, mochi poccoztic: çan achi injc tliltic. In jcxi: in jtlanjtz tlilpoiaoac.

Auh injc motocaiotia tolcomoctli; injc tlatoa, iuhqujn oncomonj. Injc motocaiotia Atoncuepotli: injc tlatoa çan cen, in oalcacaqujzti; xittõcueponj, cenca caqujzti. Auh injc mjtoa Ateponaztli: injc tlatoa, in veca iuhqujn teponaztli, ic caqujzti.

In iehoatl tolcomoctli: çan muchipa njcan nemj tulla, njcan mopilhoatia: çan macujltetl, anoço nauhtetl in qujpachoa.

In iehoatl in tolcomoctli: in iehoantin atlaca, muchipa inneixcujtil muchioa: in jquac cêca tlatoa, in muchipa ceniooal: ic qujmati, ca ie vitz in qujiavitl, cenca qujiaviz: yoan cenca oniezque in mjmjchtin, in ie mochintin atlan nemj. Auh in jquac amo cenca qujaviz: in amo çenca oniezque mjmjchtin, amo cenca tlatoa: çan aço viptlatica, vecauhtica, in tlatoa.

ACUJTLACHTLI:

vel iuhquj in quauhtla nemj, tequanj: çan ic tepiton ixqujch in perro tepiton in jtzontecon, in jnacaz, in jten, in jelpan, in jcujtlapan, in jma, in jicxi, in jizti: çan vel iuhquj in quauhtla nemj, tequanj: çanjo in jcujtlapil, çen molicpitl injc viac, çan patlachtic, iuhqujn icujtlapil acuetzpalin: amo quaxexeltic, çan vel iacavitztic: aiac vel qujtzitzqujaia. In aqujn: itech onaci in icujtlapil, aiaxcã canaia in imma in atlaca. In jquac cacique Acuetlachtli: in iehoatl acuetlachtli, no qujtoa: yiollo in veiatl. vmpa nemja in sancta cruz quavacalco, in vmpa catquj ameialli, in oallaticac Sanctiago. In jquac vmpa nêca Acujtlachtli: injc oalqujçaia, poçonja in atl: yoan in mjmjchtin, panj oalmotetemaia. Auh in jquac: çoqujtitlan calaquja, vel macomanaia in tlalli: iuhqujnma tlallolinja. Injc vel qujneltilia: in atlaca, ca iehoantin qujttaia: no iehoãtin cacique: oc ce tlacatl õnemj,

---

27. *Tolcomoctli: Botaurus lentiginosus* (Montagu). Friedmann *et al., op. cit.,* p. 34.
28. Molina, *op. cit.: vn xeme.* A *jeme* is the distance between the extended thumb and the extended index finger.
29. Corresponding Spanish text: *"es semejante en todas sus facciones al cujtlachtli que anda en los montes...."*
30. *Ibid.: "la cola tiene como anguila."*

testify, for they saw it and they also captured it. One man still lives, called Pedro Daniel, [who saw it]. He is sixty-two years [of age].[31] When Don Juan Auelittoc ruled [in Tlatelolco and] saw the *acuitlachtli*, he regarded it with terror and then commanded that they go off to bury the body of the *acuitlachtli* there at Tetepetzinco.

BLACK-BELLIED PLOVER[32]

It is a waterfowl. It is called *couixin* because when it speaks it says *couix, couix.* It is quite small; it is a little larger than a dove. Its head is quite small; its bill is chili-red, black at the end, small and cylindrical. Its back, its wings, its tail are all like quail feathers; its breast alone is tawny. Its legs are chalky, very long. And when it is old, when [the feathers] are already about to go, all its feathers go, they emerge [again] tawny.[33]

This bird also rears no young here; it also comes and it also goes. It eats fish. Its flesh is edible.

AMERICAN AVOCET[34]

It is a waterfowl. It is named *icxixoxouhqui* because its legs are green. Its bill is small and cylindrical, small and slender, black, curved upward. Its head is quite small, white; it is rather long-necked. Its breast, its back are white; its tail is also white. Quite small are its wings; the upper surfaces are black, and the under surfaces quite white; its wing-bends have black placed on both surfaces. And when it has shed, its head and neck are almost chili-red, reaching to its wing-bends. It raises its young here, two or four young, when the rains come. It is also edible. And it also leaves when [the other water] birds migrate.

COMMON TEAL[35]

It is a duck called *quetzalteçolocton* because its head is ornamented as if with quetzal feathers. On the crown of its head its feathers are yellow. Its bill is black, small, and wide. Its neck is yellow, its wings resplendent [green]. But otherwise its wings are all ashen. Its back, its tail are likewise ashen. Its breast is white, its legs ashen though a little chili-red, small,

COVIXIN:

atlan nemj, injc motocaiotia Covixi: injc tlatoa qujtoa: covix, covix: çan tepiton, achi qujpanavia in paloma. In jtzõtecon: çan tepiton, in jten chichiltic: in jquac tliltic, çan mjmjltontli; in jcujtlapan, in jahaz, in jcujtlapil çan muchiuhquj, in çoli hivio çanjo in jelpan quappachtic, in jcxi tenextic; viviac. Auh in jquac ie veue: in ie iaz, çenqujça in hiviio, quappachqujça.

Inin tototl: amo no njcan mopilhoatia, çã no vallauh, auh çan no iauh. In qujqujquanj mjchi: qualonj in jnacaio.

ICXIXOXOUHQUJ:

atlan nemj, injc motocaiotia icxixoxouhquj: ipampa in icxi xoxoctic. In jten mjmjltontli, pitzaton, tliltic, acopa itzticac: in jtzõtecon, çan tepiton, iztac, achi quechviac, in jelpan, in jcujtlapan iztac: in jcujtlapil, no iztac: çan tepiton in jahaz, in jatlapal: in pani onoc tliltic, auh in tlani onoc vel iztac: in jacolpa nenecoc tliltic, in qujmotlatlalili. Auh in jquac ie iazque: in intzontecon, yoan in jquech: achi vel chichilivi, yiacolpan õtlamj. Nican mopilhoatia: ontetl, anoço nauhtetl, in jpilhoã, in iquac oallauh qujavitl: no qualonj. Auh çan no iauh: in jquac vi totome.

QUETZALTEÇOLOCTON:

canauhtli, injc motocaiotia quetzalteçolocton: in jtzontecon, iuhqujn quetzalli in hiviio, injc mjchiuh: In jquanepantla, coztic in hiviio in jten tliltic, patlactontli: in jquech coztic, in jahaz pepetzca auh in ie muchi iamatlapal nextic: in jcujtlapan, in jcujtlapil çan no nextic: in jelpan iztac, in jcxi nextic: çan achi ixchichiltic, papatlactotonti: amo njcã mopilhoatia.

31. *Ibid.:* "*a cuarenta y tres años.*"

32. *Covixin: Squatarola squatarola* (Linnaeus); Friedmann *et al., op. cit.,* p. 90.

33. Corresponding Spanish text: "*Muda las plumas cada año, bueluese leonado todo el cuerpo, y poco a poco se buelue, como de antes de color de codornjz.*"

34. *Icxixoxouhqui: Recurvirostra americana* Gmelin; Friedmann *et al., op. cit.,* p. 101.

35. *Quetzalteçolocton: Anas crecca* Linnaeus; *ibid.,* p. 41.

and wide. It does not rear its young here. Its flesh is edible.

BLUE-WINGED TEAL[36]

For this reason is it called *metzcanauhtli*: on its face it is decorated with white feathers like the [crescent] moon. On the crown of its head its feathers are ashen; its breast, back, tail are all ashen, resembling a quail. Its wing feathers are of three kinds. The upper coverts are pale blue; those lying in second place white; those lying in third place green, resembling quetzal feathers. The tips of its wings are black; its axilla white; its legs yellow, small and wide. It does not rear its young here; it also migrates. Its flesh is edible.

CANVAS-BACK[37]

It is a duck, called *quacoztli* because its head and its neck are tawny to its shoulder. It is as large as a female Peru [duck].[38] Its eyes are chili-red; its breast white; its back ashen, a little yellow; its tail likewise somewhat yellow, quite small. The feathers of its under wings are mingled white and ashen; its legs ashen tending to chili-red, small, and wide. Of its down are made capes. It does not rear its young here, but also migrates. Its flesh is very savory.

HOODED MERGANSER[39]

It is called *ecatototl* because its black feathers adorn the face [in the manner of the wind god].[40] It is the size of a duck. Its head is quite small; it is crested. Its feathers are tawny, ashen, somewhat dark. Its breast is white interspersed with black. Its legs are black, small, and wide. It does not rear its young here; it also migrates. It is edible. Many of them come.

BUFFLE-HEAD[41]

It is called *amanacoche* because of its white feathers placed on both sides of its head. It is the size of the common teal. The crown of its head is ashen; its neck is also ashen. Its breast is white; its back black: its tail black with two white [feathers], one on one side, one on the other. Its wing-bends have white

Qualonj in jnacaio.

METZCANAUHTLI

ipampa in motocaiotia metzcanauhtli, in ixco injc mjchiuh: iztac in jhiviio, iuhqujn metztli ic catquj. In jquanepantla onoc hivio nextic, in jelpan, in jcujtlapã in jcujtlapil: çan muchi nextic, moçolnenequj: in jaztlacapal etlamantli in jhivio. In iacatoc: cujtlatexotli. Injc ompãtitoc: iztac. In jquepãtitoc in jahaz: xoxoctic, moquetzalnenequj: in jquac iahavitz, tliltic; iztac in jciacatzon, in jcxi coztic: papatlactotonti. Amo njcã mopilhoatia, çan no iauh. in jnacaio, qualonj.

QUACOZTLI:

canauhtli, injc mjtoa, quacoztli: in jtzontecõ, yoan in jquech: quappachtic, yiacolpan tlantica: Injc vei, ixqujch in peru tototl, cioatl, in ixtelolo, vel chichiltic: in jelpã iztac, in jcujtlapan nextic, achi ixcoztic: in jcujtlapil çã no achi ixcoztic, çan tepiton: in jciacatzon hivio, iztacaviviltecquj, nextic: in jcxi nextic, çan achi injc ixchichiltic, papatlactotonti: in jtlachcaio, hivitilmatli muchioa, amo njcã mopilhoatia: çan no iauh, cenca velic in jnacaio.

HECATOTOTL:

injc motocaiotia hecatotl, tliltic in hivio, injc mjchiuh: Ixqujch in canauhtli: in jtzontecon çan tepitõ: quachichiqujle, ixquappachtic, nextic, achi ixtliltic: in jelpan iztac, tliltic injc viviltectoc: in jcxi tliltic, papatlactotonti, amo no njcan mopilhoatia, çã oallauh, yoan ça no iauh: qualonj, mjequjntin in oalhuj.

AMANACOCHE:

injc motocaiotia amanacoche, iztac in hiviio, nenecoc icanaoacan qujmotlalili: ixqujch in quetzalteçoloctõ. In jquanepantla nextic: in jquech çan no nextic: in jelpã iztac, in jcujtlapan tliltic, in jcujtlapil tliltic, iztac qujtzatzacutimanj, in jacoliacac iztac, in nenecoc qujmotlatlalili in jahaz iztac ic tlacocoton-

36. *Metzcanauhtli: Anas discors* Linnaeus; *loc. cit.*
37. *Quacoztli: Aythya valisineria* (Wilson); *ibid.*, p. 43.
38. Corresponding Spanish text: *"es del tamaño de vn pato de los del peru."*
39. *Hecatototl: Lophodytes cucullatus* (Linnaeus); Friedmann *et al., op. cit.*, p. 46.
40. Corresponding Spanish text: *"llamase desta manera, porque tiene vnas rayas negras por la cara, a manera de los que se componjan con rayas negras por la cara a honrra del ayre."*
41. *Amanacoche: Bucephala albeola* (Linnaeus); Friedmann *et al., op. cit.*, p. 44.

placed on both surfaces; its wings half white, half black, the tips black. Its legs are black. It also migrates; it does not rear its young here. Many come. They are edible.

RUDDY DUCK[42]

Also [it is called] *yacatexotli*. It is a duck. It comes here in the vanguard, before [other water] birds have come. It is named *atapalcatl* because if it is to rain on the next day, in the evening it begins, and all night [continues], to beat the water [with its wings]. Thus the water folk know that it will rain much when dawn breaks. It is named *yacatexotli* because its bill is light blue, small, wide. And near its head [the bill] is white. Its head is tawny; its wings, breast, back, tail are all tawny; only its belly is white [and] blackish. Its feet are black, wide, and small. It rears its young here; [it has] ten, fifteen, twenty young. Sometimes not all leave; some remain. They are edible.

PINTAIL[43]

It is a duck. It is named *tzitziua* because of the feathers growing from its rump; among its tail feathers are two very white ones, located one above the other. A third, a small [white] one, stands between them. Their points are curved; they turn upward. Its head is ashen; its neck, its throat white. Following down the back of its neck,[44] it is ashen. Its breast is white, its tail ashen; its feet black, wide, and small. It does not rear its young here; it also migrates. Neither does it come singly; there are many. Their flesh is edible, good-tasting, savory, [and] not fishy.

BALDPATE[45]

It is named *xalquani* because it always eats sand, though sometimes it eats *atatapalacatl* [water plants]. It is the size of the goose. [On] its head, its feathers are white on the crown; the sides of its head green, resplendent. Its neck is like a quail's;[46] its back ashen; its breast white; its tail dark ashen, [but] on each side is placed a white [feather]. Its wings are silvery, not long; its wings glisten; the ends are white, the wing tips black. On both sides [of the bird] are placed tawny [feathers]. Its legs are black, short, and

ATAPALCATL:

tica tliltic, in jahavitz tliltic, in jcxi tliltic çan no iauh amo njcã mopilhoatia, mjequjntin in oalhuj. qualonj.

yoan iacatexotli, canauhtli; oaliacattivi, in aiamo oalhuj totome. Injc motocaiotia, Atapalcatl: intla muztla, qujiaviz; teutlacpa in peoaz, yoan ceioal in acocomotza: ic qujmati in atlaca, ca cenca qujiaviz, in vallatviz. Auh injc motocaiotia iacatexotli: in jten texotic, patlactontli: auh in vel itech itzõtecon iztac, in jtzontecon quappachtic, in jatlapal, in jelpan in jcujtlapan, in jcujtlapil mochi quappachtic: çanjo in jxillan, iztac ixcujchectic: in jcxi tliltic, papatlacto-tonti. nican mopilhoatia: matlactetl, caxtoltetl, cen-tecpantli, in inpilhoan; quẽmanjan amo moch vi, ce-qujntin mocauhtivi: qualonj.

TZITZIOA:

canauhtli, injc motocaiotia tzitzioa: in jtzintenpan ixoatimanj, in jhivio: in jnepantla in jcujtlapil, çẽca iztac, ome manj, çã monepanotimanj, iquei çan te-pitõ yitic icac, achi quacoltic, acopa itzticac: in jtzon-tecon nextic, in jquechtlan, in jtozcatlã iztac: in jquechquauhio qujtocaticac, nextic; in jelpã iztac, in jcujtlapil nextic, in jcxi tliltic, papatlactotonti: amo njcã mopilhoatia, çan no iauh Amono çan cen-tetl in oallauh ca mjequjntin qualonj in innacaio: velic, aviac, amo xoqujiac.

XALQUANI:

injc motocaiotia xalquanj, çan muchipa xalli in qujqua: çan quẽmanjan atatapalacatl, in qujqua: ix-qujch in cõcanauhtli. In jtzõtecõ: in jquanepantla, iztac in hivio: in jcanaoacã xoxoctic, pepetzca: in jquech cultic, in jcujtlapan nextic: in jelpan iztac, in jcujtlapil tlilnextic, iztac nenecoc qujmotlatlalili: in jatlapal cujtlatexotic, amo viac: in jahaz pepetzca, in jquac iztac: in jahavitz tliltic, in jiomotlan, nene-coc qujmotlatlalili quappachtic: in jcxi tliltic, papa-tlactotonti. Amo no njcan mopilhoatia: çan no oal-

---

42. *Atapalcatl: Oxyura jamaicensis* (Gmelin); *ibid., p.* 45.

43. *Tzitzioa: Anas acuta* Linnaeus; *ibid.,* p. 41.

44. Corresponding Spanish text: *"el lomo del pescueço."*

45. *Xalquani: Mareca americana* (Gmelin); Friedmann *et al., op. cit.,* p. 42. It is also known as American Widgeon (Blake, *op. cit.,* p. 51).

46. Read *çultic.*

small. It does not rear its young here; it also comes, it also migrates. Many come. They are edible, savory.

EARED GREBE[47]

Also [it is called] *nacaztzone*. It is called *yacapitzauac* because its bill is small and pointed, something like a small nail, and it pierces one sharply. And it swims under water; it always feeds under water. And it is named *nacaztzone* because its feathers which are over its ears, inclined toward the back of its neck, are somewhat long, tawny. Those at the crown of its head are dark ashen, slightly white. Its eyes are like fire, chili-red. Its neck, its back are dark ashen; its breast somewhat white. Its tail is also dark ashen, quite small; its wings black; white [feathers] lie underneath. Its feet are like the claws of a turkey, [but] very flat. It does not rear its young here; it also migrates. Its food is its [own] feathers, only sometimes it eats fish. It is not fishy, its flesh is savory.

TZONYAYAUHQUI[48]

It is named *tzonyayauhqui* because its head is very black, much like charcoal, reaching to its neck. Its eyes are yellow; its neck, its breast very white; its back dark ashen. Its tail is quite small, also dark ashen; its belly black, [but two] white [feathers] are placed on both sides near its tail. Its feet are black and broad. It does not rear its young here; it just comes [and] goes. Many come. They eat what is in the water, [as well as] the sand from the rocks and water plant seeds. Good-tasting is their flesh; it is fat, like bacon.

MALLARD[49]

It is named *çolcanauhtli* because its feathers are all like quail feathers. It is rather large, the same size as a Peru [duck]. White [feathers] are set only on the point of each wing-bend. Its bill is small and wide; its legs black, wide, small. It is an eater of *atatapalcatl* [water plant] and *achichilacachtli* [gibbous duckweed]. It also comes, it also migrates with the others. Also it does not rear its young here. Many come here. Good-tasting is their flesh.

CINNAMON TEAL[50]

It is named *chilcanauhtli* because its head, breast, back, tail are all like tawny chili: likewise its eyes.

lauh, no iauh: mjequjntin oalhuj. Qualonj, velique.

YACAPITZAOAC:

yoã nacaztzone, injc motocaiotia iacapitzaoac: in jten, vitztontli, achi teputzmjmjltontli: yoã cenca techopinjanj, yoã apopotli: muchipa çan atlitic in ontlaqua. Auh injc motocaiotia nacaztzone: achi viac in jvio, in jnacaztlan mãnj, icuexcochtlampa itztimanj: quappachtic, in jquanepantla, tlilpoiauhquj, achi iztac: in jxtelolo iuhqujn tletl, chichiltic: in jquech, in jcujtlapan, tlilpopoiauhquj: in jelpan achi iztac, in jcujtlapil çan no tlilpopoiauhquj, çã tepiton: in jamatlapal tliltic, iztac in tlanj onoc: in jcxi iuhqujn totolin, ixomatzal, papalachtic. Amo no njcan mopilhoatia: çan no iauh, in jtlaqual, çan no iehoatl in hivio, çã quẽmanjan, in qujqua mjchin amo xoqujac, in jnacaio, velic.

TZONIAIAUHQUJ:

injc motocaiotia tzoniaiauhquj, in jtzõtecõ cenca tliltic, vel iuhqujn tecolli, iquechtlan ontlantica: in jxtelolo coztic, in jquech, in jelpan cenca iztac. in jcujtlapan, tlilpopoiauhquj: in cujtlapil çã tepiton, çan no tlilpopoiauhquj: in jxillan tliltic, iztac nenecoc qujmotlatlalili achi itlã in jcujtlapil, in jcxi, tliltic papalactic. Amo no njcã mopilhoatia: çan oallauh, çan no iauh: mjequjntin in oalhuj, in qujqua: ie in atlan onoc: tepetlaxalli, acpatlaolli, velic in jnnacaio: chiaoa, iuhqujn tocino.

ÇOLCANAUHTLI:

injc motocaiotia çolcanauhtli, in hivio, çan muchiuhquj, in çolin hivio, achi veitontli: ixqujch in Peru tototl: çanjo in jacoliacac iztac, in nenecoc qujmotlatlalili: in jten patlactontli, in jcxi tliltic, papatlactotonti. In qujquanj: atatapalacatl, achichilacachtli. çan no oallauh, no tehoan iauh. Amo no njcã mopilhoatia; mjequjntin oalhuj. velic, in innacaio.

CHILCANAUHTLI:

injc mjtoa chilcanauhtli, in itzõtecõ, in jelpan, in jcujtlapan, in jcujtlapil, çan muchiuhquj, in chilli,

47. *Yacapitzaoac: Colymbus nigricollis* (Brehm); Friedmann *et al., op. cit.*, p. 13.
48. *Tzonyayauhqui:* unident. spec. of duck — Sahagún (Garibay ed.), Vol. IV, p. 366.
49. *Çolcanauhtli: Anas platyrhynchos* Linnaeus; Friedmann *et al., op. cit.*, p. 39.
50. *Chilcanauhtli: Anas cyanoptera* Vieillot; *ibid.*, p. 40.

Its wings are silvery, its flight feathers black, its wing tips also black. On its axilla they are mingled silver and yellow. Its belly is black; its feet chili-red, somewhat wide. It eats fish. Also it does not rear its young here; it also goes, comes with the others. Many come. They are edible.

ACHALALACTLI[51]

It is a duck. It is named *achalalactli* because it sings thus: *cha, chacha, chuchu, chala chala chala.* It is the size of a *teçolocton.* But this bird does not live in the brackish lagoon; rather it lives in the fresh water. It frequents the crags. Also it does not settle upon the water but always goes to alight upon the tops of willows, on treetops. And when it wishes to feed, from there it descends, suddenly dives into the water, it takes what it hunts, perhaps a fish, perhaps a frog. And when it has gone to take it, then it also calmly goes to the treetop there to eat it.

Its head is crested; ashen are its feathers. White ones are placed on the sides of its head. Its bill is black, small, pointed, cylindrical. It is rather long-necked; [black and] white mixed are its feathers. Its breast is white, its back dark grey, its tail small [and] dark grey. Its wing-bend tip is white on both surfaces. Its flight feathers, the flight feather tips are dark ashen. Its legs are black, its claws like those of the northern phalarope, wide and small. It always lives here; [there are] not very many; they are somewhat rare. It is not known where they rear their young. They are edible.

SHOVELLER[52]

It is a duck. It is named *yacapatlauac* because its bill is somewhat long and very wide at the end. It is the size of a goose. When it comes here, its feathers are still completely ashen: but when it lives here, it molts twice. First it sheds its downy feathers; and the second time is when it is about to leave. Its head is a very resplendent black as far as its shoulders. Its eyes are yellow, its breast whitish, its back ashen. Its tail is white at the base, ashen at its ends. Its wings are silvery; its flight feathers green, glistening, black at the ends. Its wing tips are ashen; its belly shows tawny; its legs are chili-red. Also it does not rear its young here; it also migrates. It is edible. Many come here.

quappachtic: çan no iuhquj, in jxtelolo: in jamatlapal, cujtlatexotic: in jahaz tliltic, in jahavitz no tliltic: iciacac mamanj, cujtlatexotic, coztic ic viviltequj: in ixillan tliltic, in jcxi chichiltic, papatlactotonti: in qujqua, mjchi: amo no njcã mopilhoatia, çan no tehoan iauh, no tehoa vallauh: miequjntin in oalhuj: qualonj.

ACHALALACTLI:

canauhtli, injc motocaiotia achalalactli, iuh tlatoa: cha, cha cha, chuchu, chala chala, chala: ixqujch in toçolocton. Auh inin tototl: amo vmpa nemj in tequjxquiapã çã acellopan in nemj, qujnamjctinemj in tepexitl: amo no atlixco motlalia, çan muchipa: vexoticpac, quauhticpac in motlalitinemj. Auh in jquac ie tlaquaznequj: vmpa oaleoa, in atlan calactivetzi: conana in tlein caci, aço mjchi, aço cueiatl. Auh in oconanato: njmã, no vmpa tlamattiuh, in quauhticpac: vmpa qujqua.

In jtzontecon: quachichiqujle, nextic, in hivio: iztac in jcanaoacan, qujmotlatlalili: in jtẽ tliltic, vitztontli, mjmjltontli, achi quechviac, iztacacujcujltic in hivio: in jelpan iztac, in jcujtlapan tlilnextic: in jcujtlapil çan tepiton, tlilnextic: in jacoliacac, iztac nenecoc: in jahaz, in jahavitz tlilnextic; in jcxi tliltic, iuhqujn ixomatzal, atzitzicujlotl, patlachpipil: çan muchipa njcan nemj, amo cenca mjequjntin, achi tlaçonemj: amo no macho, in campa mopilhoatia: qualonj.

IACAPATLAOAC:

canauhtli, injc mjtoa iacapatlaoac: in jten achi viac, yoan cenca quapatlaoac: ixqujch, in cõcanauhtli. In jquac oallauh: çan oc mocemaquj nextic, in hivio. auh in jquac, njcã nemj: vppa in qujtepeoa in hivio: in achtopa, qujtepeoa in jpilhivio: auh injc vppa, iquac in ie iaz: in jtzõtecon cenca tlilivi, pepetzca, yiacoltitech ontlamj: in jxtelolo coztic, in jelpan iztaia, in jcujtlapan nextic, in jcujtlapil tzitziniztaia, in jquac nextic: in jamatlapal, cujtlatexoti: in jahaz xoxovia, pepetzca, quaquatlilihuj: in jahavitz nextic, in jxillan quappachqujça: in jcxi chichiltic. Amo no njcan mopilhoatia: çan no iauh, qualonj: mjequjntin in oalhuj.

---

51. *Achalalactli:* Martín del Campo, *op. cit.,* p. 400, identifies it as *Stroptoceryle alcyon alcyon.*
52. *Iacapatlaoac: Spatula clypeata* Linnaeus; Friedmann *et al., op. cit.,* p. 42.

BLACK-CROWNED NIGHT HERON[53]

It is a duck. It is named *uactli* because its song is like *uactli*: it makes [the sound] *uac, uac*. It is the size of a rooster. The crown of its head is black, [but] white [feathers] are placed on each side of its head, and at its crown lie three plumes inclined toward the back of its neck—white, well curved. Its bill is black, rounded: a yellow band follows the base of the bill.[54] The neck is white, reaching to the wing-bends. The neck is somewhat long. Its breast is also white; on its back it is ashen. Its wings, its wing tips are ashen; its feet yellow, with claws — long claws. It eats fish and frogs. It always lives here; it rears its young here. Its eggs are four or five; they are a mottled green. It is edible, savory. What is told of this black-crowned night heron [applies to] the hen. But the male black-crowned night heron is not very large — only of average size, and all of its feathers are ashen.

PIPITZTLI[55]

It also lives in the water. Its head is black; its eyes are also black; white [feathers] are set on the eyelids [so that these] appear to be its eyes. It is somewhat long-necked. The throat and breast are white. Down the back of its neck, on its back, its tail, wings, wing tips, it is black. The tips of both wing-bends are white. Its legs are quite long, chili-red, slender. There is really not very much to its body, but it is quite tall. Some migrate, some remain and rear their young here. Four are its eggs; only on the ground, on dried mud, on the plain, or somewhere on the top of a clod it lays its eggs; not on grass nor feathers. It is edible.

WESTERN GREBE[56]

It lives on the water. It is named *acachichictli* because it is as if it sings *achichichic*. And it lives only among the canes, the reeds. And this bird is also an omen for the water folk: always when it sings it is about to dawn. First it begins to cry out; then the various [other] waterfowl answer it.

Its head is quite small; its bill is pointed and small. All of its feathers are yellow, slightly ashen. Its legs are yellow, greenish. It always lives here; it rears its young here. Four are its eggs; like a dove's are its eggs. It is edible.

OACTLI:

canauhtli, injc motocaiotia oactli: iuhquj in oactli itlatol, qujchioa: *oac, oac*: ixqujch in quanaca, in jquanepantla tliltic, iztac nenecoc qujmotlatlalili: in jcanoacan, yoan iquanepantla, iquetzal ie manj, icuexcochtlanpa itztimanj, iztac, vel vivitolivi: in jten tliltic, mjmjltontli, coztic qujtetentocatoc: quechiztac, yiacolpan tlantica, achi quechviac: in jelpan çan no iztac; in jcujtlapan, nextic: in jamatlapal, in jahaz, in jahavitz nextic: coztic in jcxi, xomatzale, viviac in jzti: in qujqua mjchi, yoan cujatl: muchipa njcan nemj, njcan mopilhoatia: nauhtetl anoço macujltetl in jteuh, achi ixxoxoxoctic qualonj, velic. Injn oactli: in omoteneuh cioatl. Auh in oqujchtli oactli: amo cenca vei, çan qualton yoan çan muchi ixnextic in hivio.

PIPITZTLI:

çã no atlan nemj, in jtzontecon tliltic: no tliltic in ixtelolo, iztac ixquatoltitech qujmotlatlalili, iuhqujn ixtelolo ic neci, achi quechujac: in jtozcatlan, yoan ielpan iztac: in jquechquauhio, in icujtlapan, in jcujtlapil, in jamatlapal, in jahaz, in jahavitz tliltic: in jacoliacac, iztac nenecoc: in jcxi vel viviac, chichiltic, pitzatotõ, amo cenca vel in ie muchi inacaio; çan ie cenca quauhtic. cequjtin vi, cequjntin mocauhtivi: auh njcan mopilhoatia, nauhtetl in jteuh, çan tlalpan aoatzalpan ixtlaoacan, anoço cana tlachcujticpac in motetia amo çacapan, amo no tle hivitl: qualonj.

ACACHICHICTLI:

atlan nemj, inic mjtoa acachichictli, iuh tlatoa: achichichic, yoan çan acatzalan, toltzalan in nemj. Auh inin tototl: no immachiouh in atlaca: muchipa iquac tlatoa in ie tlatviz; achtopa qujpeoaltia in tzatzi, njmã qujnãqujlia in nepapan totome, atlan nemj.

In jtzontecon: çan tepitõ, tenvitzton: in ie muchi hivio, coztic, achi ixnextic: in jcxi coztic, ixxoxoctic: muchipa njcã nemj, njcã mopilhoatia in jteuh nauhtetl, iuhqujn paloma iteuh: qualonj.

---

53. *Oactli: Nycticorax nycticorax* (Linnaeus); *ibid.*, p. 31.
54. Corresponding Spanish text: *"tiene el pico negro, tiene vna lista de amarillo, por la juntura del pico."*
55. *Pipitztli*: probably *Larus jranklini*, according to Sahagún (Garibay ed.), Vol. IV, p. 349.
56. *Acachichictli*: Martín del Campo, *loc. cit.*, suggests *Aechomophorus occidentalis*. See also Friedmann, *et al., op. cit.*, p. 13.

Fourth paragraph, which telleth of all the birds [of prey].

Eagle[1]

The eagle is yellow-billed — very yellow; the bill is yellow, very yellow. The bill is thick, curved, humped, hard. The legs are yellow, an intense yellow, very yellow, exceedingly yellow. They are thick. The claws are curved, hooked. The eyes are like coals of fire. It is large, big. On its head, and neck, and on its wings, on its wing-bends, and on its back lie feathers called *quauhtapalcatl*.[2] [Those on] its wings are called *ahaztli*, and *apalli*, and *mamaztli*. Its tail [feathers] are called *quauhquetzalli*; [the feathers] which cover its tail are called *quammoloctli*[3] [and] *quappoyaualli*, and those which lie next to [its skin] are called *tlachcayotl*; so one calls them *quauhtlachcayotl*.[4]

The eagle is fearless, a brave one; it can gaze into, it can face the sun. It is brave, daring, a screamer, a wing-beater. It is ashen, brown. It beats its wings, constantly beats its wings; it grooms itself; it constantly grooms itself.

Golden eagle:[5] the one which is still young is of average size.

The crab-hawk[6] is dark; its face is adorned.

White eagle

It has scant, ashen [feathers]; it lacks down; it is very chalky. The bill is yellow, the legs are yellow.[7]

Nocturnal eagle

It is the same as the white eagle. It is called "nocturnal eagle" because it appears nowhere much by day, but at night it eats, it preys on [its victims].

Marsh hawk[8]

Also it is called *chienquauhtli*. It resembles a black-bellied plover. It has a yellow beak, it has yellow legs.

Injc navi parrapho intechpa tlatoa in ixqujchtin totome.

Quauhtli:

in quauhtli tecoztic, tencozpiltic, tencoçauhquj, tencozpatic; tentomaoac, tencoltic, tencoliuhquj, tentepoztic: xocoztic, xocôcoztic, xocohcozpatic, xocohcozpiltic: xototomactic, izticultic, izticoliuhquj: ixtletlexochtic, veipol, veitepol: in jcpac onoc hivitl, yoan in jquechtlan, yõ in jatlapaltitech, in jacol ipan, yoan in jcujtlapan, itoca: quauhtapalcatl, in jatlapal: itoca ahaztli, yoan hapalli, yoan mamaztli: in jcujtlapil, itoca: quauhquetzalli, in qujtzinpachoa icujtlapil, itoca: quãmoloctli, quappoiaoalli: auh in vel itech onoc ihivio itoca: tlachcaiotl, ic mjtoa: quauhtlachcaiotl.

In quauhtli: aixmauhquj, amjxmauhtianj: vel qujxnamjquj, vel qujtztimoquetza in tonatiuh: ixchicaoac, ixtlapalivi: pipitzcanj, motzetzeloanj, nexeoac, camjltic: motzetzeloa, motzêtzetzeloa, moiectia, moiehiectia.

Itzquauhtli: çan qualli, iehoatl in oc telpochtli.

Mixcoaquauhtli: cuichectic mjhichiuh.

Iztac quauhtli:

nexcacaiactic, amo tlachcaiotic, cenca vel ticeoac, tencoztic, xocoztic.

Iooalquauhtli:

çan no iehoatl, in jztac quauhtli: ic mjtoa iooalquauhtli, acan cenca neci: auh iooaltica in tlaquaqua, in tlavitequj.

Tlacoquauhtli:

yoan itoca chienquauhtli, mocujxnenequj: tencoztic, xocoztic.

---

1. *Quauhtli*: *Aquila chrysaëtos*, according to Sahagún (Garibay ed.), Vol. IV, p. 330. In the Nahuatl text it appears to be a general term for eagle. The corresponding Spanish text states: *"Ay agujlas en esta tierra de muchas maneras, las mayores dellas tienen el pico amarillo gruesso, y coruado, y rescio. . . ."*

2. The Spanish text in Chap. II, § 10, *infra*, states: *"las plumas del pescueço se llaman, tapalcaiotl, o quauhtapalcatl. La pluma de todas las aves, assi de la barriga, como la de las espaldas, se llama alapachtli, y itapalcaio."*

3. *Quammoloctli*: in *ibid.*, *"la pluma que tienen las aues cerca de la cola, que estan* [sic] *sobre las plumas de la cola se llama olincaiotl, poiaoallotl, o quammoloctli."*

4. *Quauhtlachcaiotl*: in *ibid.*, *"la pluma blanda, que esta cerca de la carne se llama tlachcaiotl, o quauhtlachcaiotl."*

5. *Itzquauhtli*: *Aquila chrysaëtos* (Linnaeus); Friedmann *et al.*, *op. cit.*, Pt. I, p. 61.

6. *Mixcoaquauhtli*: *Buteogallus anthracinus* (Lichtenstein); *ibid.*, p. 59.

7. *Iztac quauhtli*: Corresponding Spanish text: *"es cenjcienta, tiene el pico amarillo, y los pies."*

8. *Tlacoquauhtli*: *Circus cyaneus* (Linnaeus); Friedmann *et al.*, *op. cit.*, p. 61.

WATER EAGLE

It is of average size, not very large. The water is its habitat. It preys upon, it eats the waterfowl.[9]

GOLDEN EAGLE[10]

It is large, the same size as those first mentioned. The bill is yellow; its legs are yellow. It is called *itzquauhtli* because the feathers of its breast, of its back are very beautiful; they glisten as if blotched with gold, and they are called *quauhxilotl*. Its wings, its tail are blotched with white; they are somewhat golden like the feathers of the falcon. And it is called *itzquauhtli* because it is a great bird of prey. It preys on, it slays the deer, the wild beasts.

To kill them, it beats them in the face with its wings and then pecks out their eyes. It can slay very thick snakes, and can kill whatever kind of bird flies in the air. It carries them off wherever it wishes to go to eat them.

OSPREY[11]

It is like the golden eagle. Its head is a little golden, a little more black. Its bill is a little blackish, somewhat yellow. On its breast, its back, its wings it is completely black [and] gold. Its tail is only flecked with white; it is long, a cubit long. Its legs are slightly green, [slightly] yellow.

It is named *aitzquauhtli* because when it goes flying high, if it wishes to eat, from there it streaks down. When it descends, it goes whirring, it suddenly dives into the water; it seizes whatever it wishes to eat, perhaps a fish. The lagoon water does not damage its eyes.

CRAB-HAWK[12]

It is not very large; average in size, somewhat the same as the turkey hen living here. It is named *mixcoaquauhtli* because at the back of its head are its feathers, paired feathers forming its head pendant. It is white across the eyes, joined, touching the black; so is the face adorned.[13] Its bill is yellow, curved. All its feathers are somewhat black [trimmed with] yellow. Its legs are yellow. It lives everywhere and is also a bird of prey.

AQUAUHTLI:

çan qualton, amo cenca vei: atlan inentla, qujnmo-iautia qujnqua in atlan nemj totome.

ITZQUAUHTLI:

vei, çan no ixqujch in achto ommoteneuh: tencoz-tic, xocoztic: injc mjtoa itzquauhtli, in jelpan, in jcuj-tlapan hivio: cenca maviztic, pepetlaca, ixcoztic injc cujcujltic: yoã itoca quauhxilotl: in jahaz, in jcujtla-pil iztacacujcujltic, achi ixcoztic, iuhqujn tlotli hivio, yoan injc mjtoa: itzquauhtli, cenca tlavitequjnj, q'n-vitequj, qujnmjctia in mamaça, in tequanjme.

injc qujnmjctia, qujmjxtlatzinja, ica in jaztlacapal: yoan njman qujmjxtelolo chopinja. In cocoa cenca tomaoaque, vel q'nmjctia: yoan vel qujnmjctia, in çaço tleique patlãtinemj, ehecaticpac: qujnvica in çaço canjn qujnquatiuh.

AITZQUAUHTLI:

çan no iuhquj in Itzquauhtli, in jtzontecõ, achi ixcoztic, achio cenca tliltic. In jten achi tlilnextic, çan achiton injc coztic: in jelpã, in jcujtlapã, in jahaz: cenqujztica tliltic, ixcoztic. In jcujtlapil: çanjo izta-caviviltecquj: viac, cemmolicpitl injc viac. In jcxi: achi xoxoxoctic, ixcoztic.

Injc motocaiotia Aitzquauhtli: in jquac aco patlan-tinemj, intla ie tlaquaznequj: vmpa oalleoa in oal-temo, oalicoiocatiuh; atlan calactivetzi, conana in tlein qujjquaznequj, in aço mjchin: amo qujtlacoa in jxtelo vei atl.

MIXCOAQUAUHTLI:

amo cenca vei, çan qualton, çan achi ixqujch in njcan nemj cioatotolin: injc mjtoa Mixcoaquauhtli, in jcuexcochtlan manj hivio vme manj in hivitl, iquappilol: in jxco, iztac, injc viltectoc, qujnamjq' tliltic ic mjchichiuh: in jten coztic tencoltic. In ie muchi hivio achi tliltic: ixcoztic, in jcxi coztic: çan novian nemj, no tlavitequjnj.

---

9. *Itzquauhtli, aitzquauhtli,* and *mixcoaquauhtli* are not described in *Acad. Hist. MS.*

10. See n. 5.

11. *Aitzquauhtli: Pandion haliaëtus carolinensis* (Gmelin); Friedman *et al., op. cit.,* p. 62; and Martín del Campo, *op. cit.* p. 401.

12. See n. 6.

13. Corresponding Spanish text: *"tiene la cabeça negra, y vna raya blanca atrauesada por los ojos."*

The different eagles mentioned inhabit inaccessible places, among the crags; [there] they nest, lay eggs, hatch their young.

And they hunt them in this way: so that their young may be taken, the hunter places a palm-leaf or solid reed basket on his head. When the eagle becomes angry, it sets out to seize the palm-leaf basket; it carries it off. Very high it carries it. From there it drops it, thinking it is the hunter. When [the eagle] has released it, then it comes thundering down on it. But the hunter has meanwhile removed its young far away.

The eagle's food is flesh.

KING VULTURE[14]

It is smoky. The wings are curved, resembling an eagle's. The bill is curved.

LAUGHING FALCON[15]

It resembles the king vulture. It sings in this manner: sometimes it laughs like some man; like a man speaking it can pronounce these words: *yeccan, yeccan, yeccan*. When it laughs, it says *ha ha ha ha ha, ha hay, ha hay, hay hay, ay*. Especially when it finds its food it really laughs.

BLACK VULTURE[16]

It is black, dirty black, chili-red-headed, chalky-legged. All its food is what has died — stinking, filthy.

OWL[17]

It is round, like a ball. The back is rounded. The eyes are like spindle whorls; shiny. It has horns of feathers. The head is ball-like, round; the feathers thick, heavy. It is blinded during the day. It is born in crags, in trees. It feeds by night, because it sees especially well in the dark. It has a deep voice when it hoots; it says, *tecolo, tecolo, o, o.*

BURROWING OWL[18]

It is small, blotched like a quail, only it is also like the *tecolotl*. It is called *çacatecolotl* because it is born in the grasslands.

In nepapan quauhtli: omjtoq̃, ovican texcalco in mochantia in motapaçoltia, in tlatlaça, in tlatlapana:

auh injc qujmana, injc ano inpilhoan: tõpiatli, anoço otlachiqujvitl in icpac qujquetza in anquj. In iquac qualanj in quauhtli qujmotzoloteoa in tompiatli, qujvica vel huecapan in qujvica, vmpa qujoallaca in momati aço ieh in tlamanj in oqujoalcauh: njman oallalatzcatitemo ipã. auh in anquj: ie cuele ueca qujmonaxitia in jpilhoan:

nacatl in jtlaqual quauhtli.

COZCAQUAUHTLI:

pocheoac amatlapal cocoltic moquauhnenequj, tencoltic.

OACTLI:

mocozcaquauhneneq', injc tlatoa: in quenmã, iuhqujnma aca tlacatl vevetzca: iuhq'nma tlacatlatoa, vel qujtenqujxtia, inin tlatolli: ieccan, ieccan ieccan. Injc vetzca qujtoa: hahahahaha, hahay, hahai, hahai, ai. oc cenca iquac in qujtta itlaqual vel vevetzca.

TZOPILOTL:

tliltic, catzaoac, quachichiltic, xothiticectic, much itlaqual in tlein mjcquj, in hiiac, yoan in tlaelli.

TECOLOTL:

ololtic, tapaioltic cujtlalololtic, ixtemamalacachtic, ixpechtic, quaquave hivitica: quateololtic, quatecontic, hivitilaoac, hiviotilaoac, ixmjmjqujni in tlaca, texcalco, quavitl itic in tlacati iooaltica, in tlaquaqua: ipampa oc cenca vellachia in iooan, tlatomaoa injc tlatoa: qujtoa tecolo, tecolo, o. o.

ÇACATECOLUTL:

tepiton, çolcujcujltic. çan vel no iuhqujn in tecolutl: injc mjtoa çacatecolutl, çacatla in tlacati.

---

14. *Cozcaquauhtli: Sarcoramphus papa* (Linnaeus); Friedmann *et al., op. cit.*, p. 46.

15. *Oactli: Herpetotheres cachinnans* (Linnaeus); *ibid.*, p. 63.

16. *Tzopilotl*: black vulture, *Coragyps atratus* (Bechstein), or turkey vulture, *Cathartes aura* (Linnaeus); *ibid.*, p. 47. See also Martín del Campo, *op. cit.*, p. 402.

17. Apparently generic term for owl. See Santamaría, *op. cit.*, p. 1018 (*tecolote*).

18. *Çacatecolutl: Speotyto cunicularia* (Molina); Friedmann *et al., op. cit.*, p. 146.

COMMON RAVEN[19]

Also it is called *calli* and *cacalli*. It is really black, really charcoal-colored, a well-textured black: very black. Its feathers glisten. It is an eater of ripe maize ears, of tunas, of mice, of flesh. It stores things. It eats ripe maize ears, it stores ripe maize ears — it piles the ripe maize ears up within [the hollows of] trees. It eats tunas, it eats flesh.

JABIRU[20]

It is black — a waterfowl, an eater of water life. The legs are long, very long, black; it has a sharp, curved bill.

FRANKLIN GULL[21]

It is white, like a dove; its head is adorned [black and white]. It is a sea dweller, an ocean dweller. It is called *pipixcan* because when it is about to freeze, when the maize is about to be harvested, it comes here.

PRAIRIE FALCON[22]

Also its name is *totli*. It is ashen. It is a hunter, a bird of prey; a whirrer; a flesh-eater. Its bill is pointed, curved; green, dark green. Its legs are dark green.

MARSH HAWK[23]

Also it is called *tlacotlotli*. It is large, ashen. It hunts rabbits.[24]

QUAUHTLOTLI

Likewise [it is called] *tloquauhtli*.[25] The hen is somewhat large, and the cock somewhat small. The hen is a great hunter. It is called a falcon. It has a yellow bill; its feathers are all dark grey; there are twelve [feathers] on its tail. Its legs are yellow. When it hunts, [it does so] only with its talons. When it goes flying over birds, even when it flies above them, it does not strike them with its wings; it only tries to seize them with its talons. And these birds can no longer fly; if they try to fly, they can no longer go, [but] only suddenly fall. And if [the *quauhtlotli*] succeeds in catching one, it at once clutches [the victim] by the breast; then it pierces its throat. It

CACALOTL:

yoan itoca calli, yõ cacalli, vel tliltic, vel tecoltic, vel icucic injc tliltic: tlilpatic, tzotzotlanj in hivio: cinquanj, nochquanj, qujmjchquanj, nacaquanj: motlatlatilianj, cinqua cintlatlatia, quavitl iitic qujtentiquetza in cintli, nochqua, nacaqua.

ACACALOTL:

tliltic, atlan nemjnj atlan tlaquaquanj, xovivitla xovivitlatz, xotlitliltic tenvitztic, tencoltic.

PIPIXCAN:

iztac, iuhqujn paloma, mjhichiuh: vei apan chane, ilhujcaapan chane. Injc mjtoa pipixcan: iquac in ie cevetziz oalqujça, in jquac in ie pixcoz.

TLHOTLI:

yoan itoca, thotli, nexeoac, tlatlamanj, tlavitequjnj, tlatlatzcanj, nacaquanj: tẽvitztic, tencoltic, tenxoxoctic, tenyiauhtic, xoihiiauhtic.

TLHOQUAUHTLI:

yoan itoca tlacotlhotli, vei nexeoac: caçin tochin.

QUAUHTLOTLI:

yoan tloquauhtli, achi vei in cioatl: auh in oqujchtli çan achi tepiton. In cioatl cenca ie tlamanj: itoca Alcon: tecoztic, in jhivio muchi tlilnextic; in jcujtlapil, matlactli omume: icxi coztic. Inic tlama: çan ica injzti. In jquac impã mocacanauhtiuh totome macivi in impan mocacanaoa amo ic qujnvitequj in jamatlapal: çan iztitica qujnmotzoloznequj. Auh in iehoantin totome aocmo vel patlanj, in patlaniznequj aocmo vel vi, ça chachapantivetzi. Auh intla centetl vel caci: çan njman ielpã, qujmotzoltzitzquja: njmã qujquechcoionja, catli in jezço, vel qujtlamja: amo tle cana itla qujchipinja, in eztli. Auh in iquac vel tlaqua: achtopa qujvivitla, in hivio tototl.

---

19. *Cacalotl: Corvus corax sinuatus;* Martín del Campo, *op. cit.,* p. 402; Blake, *op. cit.,* p. 375.

20. *Acacalotl: Jabiru mycteria* (Lichtenstein), of the Ciconiidae or stork and wood ibis family (Friedmann *et al., op. cit.,* p. 35). According to Santamaría, *op. cit.,* p. 13, the term *acacalote* is applied to *Plegadis guarauna* L. of the *Threskiornithidae* or ibis and spoonbill family.

21. *Pipixcan: Larus pipixcan* Wagler (Friedmann *et al., op. cit.,* p. 105).

22. *Tlhotli: Falco mexicanus* Schlegel; *ibid.,* p. 65.

23. *Tlhoquauhtli: Circus cyaneus* (Linnaeus); *ibid.,* p. 61.

24. *Quauhtlotli, coztlotli, hecatlotli,* and *itztlotli* are not found in *Acad. Hist. MS.*

25. See n. 23, *supra.*

drinks its blood, consumes it all. It does not spill a drop of the blood. And when it can eat it, first it plucks out the bird's feathers.

It eats three times a day: first, before the sun has risen; second, at midday; third, when the sun has set. It brings forth its young in inaccessible places; it nests in the openings of the crags. It has only two young.

And this falcon gives life to Uitzilopochtli because, they said, these falcons, when they eat three times a day, as it were give drink to the sun; because when they drink blood, they consume it all.

Its flesh is not edible. But thus are the falcons hunted: before one of them they place a duck, and in its breast, in its breast cage, they conceal a snare, though some only wrap the snare around it.

Yellow falcon[26]

It is quite small. And the cock is called *turcuello*. It is named "yellow falcon" because its feathers are yellow. It also feeds three times [a day]; it hunts in the same way [as previously related].

Ecatlotli

It is the same as the falcon. It is named *ecatlotli* because the face is shot across with white. Its feathers are somewhat dark. It hunts in the same way as has been told.

Ayauhtlotli

Its name is [also] *moralo*. This one is named *ayauhtlotli* because it hunts and strikes in the clouds. It also feeds three times [a day]. All said of the falcon is the same [as to the *ayauhtlotli*] except that its feathers are quite ashen, like the brown crane's feathers.

White falcon

Its name is [also] *sacre*. It is large and tall, very strong. It does not hunt ducks much; it wars upon hares, rabbits, turkeys, and chickens. It is called "white falcon" because its feathers are pale striped with white. It always hunts [its prey] by day, perhaps four or five times. Its legs are yellow.

Obsidian falcon

Or else [it is called] "reed falcon." Its name is [also] *gavilán*. It is named "reed falcon" or "obsidian

in cemjlhujtl expan tlaqua. Injc ceppa iquac in aiamo valqujça, tonatiuh. Injc vppa: nepantla tonatiuh. Injc expa: iquac in oncalac tonatiuh, mopilhoatia: vel ovican, texcalcamac in mochãtia: çan vnteme in ipilhoan.

Yoan in iehoatl tlootli: qujiollotiaia in vitzilobuchtli. Ipãpa ca qujtoaia: in iehoantin tlotlhotin, injc espa tlaqua in cemjlhujtl: iuhqujnma catlitia in tonatiuh, yoan ipãpa: in jquac catli eztli, moch qujtlamja:

amo qualonj in jnacaio. Auh injc maci tlhotlotin ixpan qujtlalilia canauhtli, yoã ielpan, ielchiqujpan qujtlalilia tzoaztli: auh in cequjntin, çan qujiaoalochtia in tzõoaztli.

Coztlhotli:

çan tepiton, auh oqujchtli: itoca turcuello. Injc motocaiotia coztlhotli: ipãpa, ixcoztic in hivio: no expa in tlaqua, çan no ivi in tlama.

Hecatlhotli:

çan no iehoatl in Alcon. Injc motocaiotia hecatlhotli: ipampa in jxaiac, ic mjixtlã mjti iztac, in hivio: achi tencujchectic. çan no ivi in tlama in ommoteneuh.

Aiauhtlhotli:

itoca moralo. Inin motocaiotia Aiauhtlhotli: aiauhtitlan, in tlama, yoã tlavitequj: no expa in tlaqua. In ixqujch omjto ipan Alcon: çan no iuhquj. çanjo in hivio. vel nextic, iuhqujn tocujlcoiotl hivio.

Iztac tlhotli:

itoca Sacre, vei; yoan quauhtic, cenca chicaoac amo cenca qujmaci in cacanauhtin, iehoantin qujnmoiautia in cicitin, in totochtin, totolme, yoan in quanacame. Injc mjtoa iztac tlhotli: in hivio ixtenextic, vel iztac injc mjxtlãmjti: çã mochipa tlâtlama, in cemjlhujtl: aço nappa, anoço macujlpa: coztic in jcxi.

Itztlhotli:

anoço Acatlhotli, in jtoca cavillan. Injc motocaiotia Acatlhotli: anoço itztlhotli, ipampa çan piaztontli:

---

26. The Spanish text corresponding to the Nahuatl descriptions of *coztlotli, ecatlotli, ayauhtlotli* and *iztac tlotli* reads:
"*Ay tambien cernjcales como los de españa, y la color dellos es como la color de los de españa.*"
"*Ay tambien cavillanes como los de españa de la mjsma color, y del mjsmo tamaño y de las mjsmas costumbres.*"
"*Alcon açor cavillan.*"

44

falcon" because its bill is quite long and narrow, like an obsidian point. Its feathers are quite smoky, dark. And its tail is somewhat long, white mingled [with black].

And these obsidian falcons and reed falcons hunt only birds which go flying up—quail, dove, Peru dove, etc. Only from time to time do they hunt ducks, and only for the purpose of eating them. Wherever they find the birds, there they hunt them.

Also their legs are yellow.

THE OBSIDIAN FALCON: its name is also *tletleuhtzin*. It is small, bold; a whirrer; a bird of prey.

YOUALTLOTLI[27]

It is the same as a falcon. It is named *youaltlotli* because it sees in the dark: it can hunt, it can strike its prey.

NECUILICTLI

— or *necuiloctli*, or *ecachichinqui*; and they name it *cenotzqui* and *tletleuhton*.[28] It is of average size. The bill is pointed, small and pointed. It is an eater of mice, of lizards, of *çacacilin* [birds]. It is an air-sucker. It is [spotted] yellow and black. When it has eaten, then it sucks in air; it is said that thus it gets water. And from the wind it knows when the frost is about to come. Then it begins to sing.

LOGGERHEAD SHRIKE[29]

Its wings are mingled white [and black]. Its bill is pointed, like a metal awl. It is called *tetzompa* because, when it has fed, when it is satiated, it impales its catch — mice, lizards — on trees [and] on maguey leaves.

¶

FIFTH PARAGRAPH, which telleth of still other kinds of birds, of whatever sort.

BULLOCK ORIOLE[1]

Its throat, breast, belly are yellow: flower-like, well textured. It has a face-band. Its head, back, wings, tail are [black] mingled with white, in wavy lines. Its legs are black.

in jtē iuhqujn itztli, çan ixpoctic, ixcujchectic in hivio. Auh in jcujtlapil achi viac: izatc injc viviltecquj.

Auh in iehoatl itztlôtli: yoan acatlhotli, çan iehoantin in qujmana totome, acopatlantinemj: in çulin, in vilotl, in cocotin. etc. cā quēmanjan in qujmaci cacanauhti: yoan çan ic nemj in tlaqua, in campa qujmjtta totome, vel ompa qujmonaci:

çã no icxicoztic.

ITZTLHOTLI: yoan itoca tlehtleuhtzin, tepiton, âtlamati, tlatlatzcanj: tlavitequjnj,

IOOALTLHOTLI:

çan ie no ieh in tlhotli. Injc mjtoa: iooaltlhotli, tlachia in iooaltica: vel tlama vellavitequj.

NECUJLICTLI:

anoço necujloctli, anoço hecachichinquj: yoan qujtocaiotia, cenotzquj, yoan tlehtleuhton: çan qualton, tēvitzton, tenvitzpil: qujmjchquanj, cuetzpalquanj, çacatzilquanj: hecachichinanj, coziaiactôtli: In otlaqua: njmā hecachichina, qujl ic tlaapachoa. Auh in quenjn qujmati ehecatl: in ie vitz çetl, njman peoa in tzatzi.

TÊTZOMPA, TETZOMPÃ MÂMANA:

amatlapalhujviltecquj, iztacatica: tenvitztic, tentepoçomjtic: injc mjtoa tetzompa, in otlaqua in oixvic: quauhtitech, metitech qujnçoço in jmalhoan: in qujmjchin, in cuetzpalin.

¶

INJC MACUJLLI PARRAPHO: oc centlamantin intechpa tlatoa, in jxqujchtin totome, in çaço quenamjque.

XOCHITOTOTL:

in jtozcac, in jelpã, in jitipan coztic, xochitic, vel icucic, mjhichiuh: in jtzontecon, in icujtlapan, in jatlapal, in jcujtlapil, iztacaviviltecquj, motlôtlovitec: xotlitliltic

27. *Youaltlotli:* gavilán nocturno, *Nauclero furcatus,* or *Chordeiles acutipennis texensis,* according to Sahagún (Garibay ed.), Vol. IV, p. 372.

28. *Necuilictli:* as *ecachichinqui,* it is *Falco columbarius* in *ibid.,* p. 335, and Martín del Campo, *op. cit.,* p. 403; *ecachichinqui* is whip-poor-will or *Caprimulgus vociferus* Wilson in Friedmann *et al.,* I, p. 156; as *tletleton* or *cenotzqui* it is *Falco columbarius* subspecies in Martín del Campo, *loc. cit.,* and Friedmann *et al., op. cit.,* p. 66.

29. *Tetzompa: Lanius ludovicianus* Linnaeus; *ibid.,* Pt. II, p. 214.

1. *Xochitototl: Icterus abeillei* (Martín del Campo, *loc. cit.*).

BANDED-BACKED WREN[2]

It is tawny. It is called *ayacachtototl* because its call, which it makes when it sings, is *cha cha cha cha, shi shi shi shi, charechi, charechi, cho cho cho cho.*

TACHITOUYA

It is small and green, small and round; a companion of the woodsman. It is named *tachitouya* because of its song, because its song says *tachitouya.* Whomever it sees, it comes along with him, singing as it goes; it goes along making [the sound] *tachitouya.*

GOLDEN-FRONTED WOODPECKER[3]

Also its name is *quauhchochopitli*, and its name is *quauhtatala.*[4] The bill is pointed, pointed like a nail, strong, rugged, like obsidian.[5] It is light ashen; agile; a tree-climber; a hopper up trees: a borer of holes in trees, a tree borer. Its food is worms; it destroys insects in trees when it bores them. There it nests.

WHIP-POOR-WILL[6]

It is like the barn owl; it looks like the barn owl. It is small, fluffy. As it flies, it only goes about flying erratically. Hence it is called *poxaquatl*. Dark yellow, dark yellow on the surface are its feathers.

CRESTED GUAN[7]

It lives in the forest, like the wild turkey. It is smoky, blackened. It is crested, but its crest is only of feathers.

BARN OWL[8]

It has thick feathers, eyes like spindle whorls, a curved bill. It is unkempt, fluffy. Its feathers are ashen, blotched like a quail's. It is round-headed, stubby-tailed, round-winged. The eyes shine by night; they are weak by day. It is a night traveler which sees at night; it feeds, it lives by hunting. By day it is blinded by light; it sees little. It eats mice [and] lizards. It claws one.

AIACACHTOTOTL:

quappachtic, Injc motocaiotia aiacachtototl: iê in jtlatol, ca qujchioa injc tlatoa: cha cha cha cha, xi xi xi xi, charechi, charechi, cho cho cho cho.

TACHITOVIA:

xoxoctontli, ololpil, quauhtlacatl, tevîvicanj. Injc motocaiotia tachitouja: ca itlatol ca qujtoa inin tlatolli: tachitovia. In aqujn qujtta itloc iatiuh, tlatotiuh: qujchiuhtiuh tachitovia.

QUAUHTOTOPOTLI:

yoan itoca quauhchochopitli, yoan itoca quauhtatala: tenvitztic, tentepuztic, tenchicaoac, tentlapalivi, tenitztic: nexeoacaticectic, tzicujctic: quauhtleconj, quauhtitech chichitonjnj, quavitl qujcoionjanj, quauhcoionjanj: ocujlin in jtlaqual, quavitl qujiolcapeoaltia, in qujcoionja: in vncan mochantia.

POXAQUATL:

chiquatic, chiquanezquj: tepiton, çonectontli, injc patlanj, çan chichipatlantiuh: ic mjtoa poxaquatl, coziaiactic, ixcoziaiactic in hivio.

VITLALOTL:

quauhtlanemj, iuhqujn quauhtotolin, pochectic tlileoac, quachichiqujle: çan hivitl in jquachichiqujl.

CHIQUATLI:

hiviotilaoac, ixtemamalacachtic, tencoltic, paçotic, çonectic: in hivio nexeoac, çolcujcujltic; quatecontic, cujtlapiltetepontic: amatlapaliaoaltic, iooalixpetztetl, tonalixvitzal; iooaian nemjnj, in iooaltica tlachia, tlaquaqua, tlâtlama. nemj in tlhaca: ixmjmjquj, amo cenca tlachia: qujmjchin, cuetzpalin in qujqua, temomotzoa.

---

2. *Aiacachtototl: Campylorhynchus zonatus* (Lesson); Friedmann *et al., op. cit.,* p. 149.

3. *Quauhtotopotli: Centurus aurifrons* (Wagler); *ibid.,* p. 33.

4. Corresponding Spanish text: *"se llama quauhtatala, que qujere dezir, que golpea en los arboles."*

5. *Acad. Hist. MS: tenychtic.*

6. *Poxaquatl:* questionable; Martín del Campo, *op. cit.,* p. 404, suggests *Anthrostomus vociferus.* See also n. 28, *supra.*

7. *Vitlalotl:* Martín del Campo, *loc. cit.,* suggests *Penelope purpurescens.* See, however, Friedmann *et al., op. cit.,* Pt. I, p. 68.

8. *Chiquatli: Tyto alba pratincola* (Bonaparte); *ibid.,* p. 137; Martín del Campo, *loc. cit.*

TAPALCATZOTZONQUI

It is the same as the barn owl. It is named *tapalca-tzotzonqui* because its call is as if one struck potsherds, or rattled them. Thus does it sound.

CHICHTLI is the same as barn owl.

TLALCHIQUATLI

It is the same as the barn owl. It is small. For this reason is it called *tlalchiquatli*: its nest is in a hole, underground, where it lays eggs, sits, hatches its young. Only in a hole does it live; it is not a tree-climber, only a ground-dweller. It goes over the surface of the ground when it flies.

BROWN TOWHEE[9]

It is ashen, chalky; ashen-backed. It is roundish, blunt-billed. It has a small crest. Its home is everywhere in settlements.

WREN[10]

It is the same as the brown towhee. It is named *tlatuicicitli* because of its song. When it is still dark, long before dawn, it begins to sing. As it sounds its song, it is as if it says *tlatuicicitli*. It lives in one's roof, in one's wall. It awakens one.

MEADOWLARK[11]

The bill is pointed, the breast yellow. Its back, wings, tail are ashen, blotched like a quail, as well as its head.

SPARROW[12]

The little sparrow is small and round, smoky. It is called *çacatlatli* because it lives in grasslands. Amaranth [seed] is its food.

VERMILLION FLYCATCHER[13]

Its body, its feathers are an over-all chili-red, but its wings, its tail are ashen, well colored, well textured. It is very chili-red, the color of dried chili. It is a night-singer. It becomes chili-red, it becomes ashen. Four times, five times at night does it sing. It is not fat.

TAPALCATZOTZONQUJ:

çan ie no ieh in chiquatli. Ic motocaiotia tapalca-tzotzonquj: in jtlatol, ca iuhqujnma haca tapalcatl, qujtzotzona: in manoçe qujcacalatza, injc tlatoa.

CHICHTLI: çan no ieh, qujtoznequj in chiquatli.

TLALCHIQUATLI:

çan in no ie in chiquatli, tepiton: injc mjtoa tlalchiquatli, tlallan tlacoiocco in jchan, in tlatlaça, in tlapachoa, in tlatlapana: çan tlacoiocco in nemj, amo quauhtleconj, çã tlalpan in nemjnj, tlalli ixco onotiuh injc patlanj.

ILAMATOTOTL:

nexeoac, tiçeoac, cujtlanextic, ololtic: tenteepontic, quachichiqujlecapil: cahcalla, novian inentla.

TLATVICICITLI:

çan no ieh in jlamatototl. Injc motocaiotia tlatvici-citli: itlatol. ca in vel oc iooã, in oc veca vitz, iooalli: peoã tlatoa, injc caqujzti itlatol: iuhq'nma qujtoa. tlatvicicitli: tetlapanco, tetepanticpac in nemj, tehixitia.

CHIQUÂTOTOTL:

tenvitztic, elcoztic: in jcujtlapan, in jatlapal, in jcujtlapil: nexeoac, çolcujcujltic; yoan in jtzontecon.

ÇACATLATLI:

çacatlaton, ololtontli, pochectontli injc mjtoa çaca-tlatli, ca çacatla in nemj, oauhtli in jtlaqual.

TLAPALTOTOTL:

novian chichiltic in jnacaio, in hivio. Auh in jatlapal: yoan in jcujtlapil, nexeoac, vellapalqujzqui, vel icucic, chichilpatic, chilpatzcaltic, iooallatoanj, chichilivi, nexeoa: nappa, macujlpa in tlatoa ceiooal: amo chiaoa.

---

9. *Ilamatototl: Pipilo fuscus* Swainson; Friedmann *et al.*, *op. cit.*, Pt. II, p. 356.

10. *Tlatuicicitli:* the genus *Thryothorus;* see Martín del Campo, *loc. cit.*, and Friedmann, *et al.*, *op. cit.*, p. 153.

11. *Chiquatototl: Sturnella magna mexicana* Sclater (*ibid.*, p. 295); Martín del Campo, *loc. cit.*

12. *Çacatlatli:* Martín del Campo, *op. cit.*, p. 405, suggests the genera *Melospiza, Spizella, Passerculus, Plagiospiza.*

13. *Tlapaltototl: Pyrocephalus rubinus mexicanus* Sclater; Friedmann *et al.*, *op. cit.*, p. 69; Martín del Campo, *loc. cit.*

Red warbler[14]

It is the same as the vermilion flycatcher. Its flesh is inedible. It has no blood; its blood is only like serous fluid.

Common house finch[15]

It is chalky, ashen, dark ashen; short-billed; medium sized, small; agile, a hopper; a singer. It is a warbler, a talker. It is capable of domestication; it is teachable; it can be bred. It is a molting bird which turns yellow, turns brown. The completely ashen one is the hen, and the chili-red-headed one is the cock. They domesticate it. I domesticate it; I teach it. It sings, it sings constantly. It hops about, it hops about constantly. It is agile; it moves with agility.

Quachichil[16]

It is the same as the common house finch, but because it is chili-red-headed it is named *quachichil*. It becomes chili-red; its head becomes chili-red.

Nochtototl

It is the same as the common house finch or *quachichil*. It is named *nochtototl* because the head is chili-red and its rump is bordered with chili-red; especially because its real food is tuna. It eats amaranth [seed], *chia*, ground maize, ground maize treated with lime.

Inca dove[17]

It is small and squat, near the ground. The wings are spotted like *chia*, like quail, smooth. The legs are chili-red, short. And it is from its song that it is called *cocotli*; its song says, *coco, coco*. Its food is seed of *argemone, chia, lepidium*. It has only one mate. When [its mate] dies,[18] it always goes about as if weeping, saying, *coco, coco*. And it is said that it destroys one's grief, that its flesh destroys one's torment and affliction. They make the jealous eat of its flesh; thus they will forget [their] jealousy.[19]

Chiltotopil:

çan ie no ie in tlapaltototl, amo qualonj in jnacaio: amo ezço, çan iuhqujn chiaviçatl yiezço.

Molotl:

ticeoac, nexeoac, nexiaiactic, tentetepontic, qualtŏ, qualtepil, tzicujctic; chôcholoanj, cujcanj, tlatlhatole; tlatole, tlacacivitilonj, machtilonj, nemjtilonj, mocuepanj: coçavianj, camjlivinj; in çan cemacquj nexeoac, ca cioatl. Auh in quachichiltic: ca oqujchtli, tlacaçivi: njctlacacivitia, njcmachtia, cujca, cujcujca: chocholoa, chochocholoa, tzitzicujnj, tzitzicujcatinemj.

Quachichil:

çan ie iehoatl in Molotl, çan ipampa in quachichiltic in motocaiotia, quachichil: chichilivi, quachichilivi

Nochtototl:

çan ie no ie in molotl, manoço quachichil: ic motocaiotia nochtototl, in quachichiltic; yoan jtzintenpan chichiltic. Oc cenca ipampa; in vel itlaqual nochtli. In qujqua: oauhtli, chien, tlaoltextli, nextamaltextli.

Cocotli:

pachtontli, tlalpanton: amatlapalalactic, chiencujcujltic, çolcujcujltic, tetzictontli: xochichiltic, xopapachton. auh itlatoltitech tlaantli: injc mjtoa cocotli, in jtlatol qujtoa: coco, coco. In jtlaqual: chicalutl, chien, mexixin ixinacho çan ce in jnamjc: in jquac mjquj, muchipa iuhqujn chocatica: qujtoa coco, coco. auh qujl tetlaoaculpolo: qujl qujpoloa in netequjpacholli, in jnacaio: in chaoazqujme qujn qualtia in jnacaio: injc qujl caoazque chaoaiotl.

---

14. *Chiltotopil: Ergaticus ruber* (Swainson); Friedmann *et al., op. cit.*, p. 270; Martín del Campo, *loc. cit.*

15. *Molotl: Carpodacus* sp.; see n. 16.

16. *Quachichil* and *nochtototl: Carpodacus mexicanus mexicanus* (Martín del Campo, *loc. cit.*). In Friedmann *et al., op. cit.*, p. 315, *nochtototl* is identified as *C. mexicanus* (P. L. S. Müller).

17. *Cocotli: Scardafella inca* (Lesson); *ibid.*, Pt. I, p. 118.

18. *Acad. Hist. MS* adds *ynamic.*

19. Corresponding Spanish text: *"dizen que la carne destas aues comjda, es contra la tristeza: a las mujeres celosas dan las a comer la carne destas aues, para que olujden los celos, y tambien los hombres."*

SIXTH PARAGRAPH, which telleth of still other kinds of birds.

MONTEZUMA QUAIL[1]

Its bill is pointed, ashen-green. Its breast is spotted with white; its wings are called *chía*-spotted. It is a runner. It is edible, savory, good-tasting; savory, very good-tasting, exceedingly good-tasting. It has eggs. When it lays eggs, when it hatches its young, it lays forty eggs. It hatches indeed fifty young. Its food is dried grains of maize, *chía*, and *xoxocoyolteuilotl*.

TECUÇOLIN

It is the same as the Montezuma quail; it is the cock. It is large, smoky-breasted, well spotted, much spotted, crested.

OUATON[2]

It is the same as the Montezuma quail. It is small, quite ashen, only a little spotted. This is the hen. Thus they nest: some make them wide; some cylindrical, so that they can sit on their eggs. And if they make them wide, she allows the companion to sit [with her].

They can be bred, they can be domesticated. I breed them, I domesticate them.

Thus do they travel; they travel only in bevies. And if someone scatters them, by just a cry, a call, they all reassemble, for [the sound] is very clear. He who first scatters them and puts them to flight there spreads out his net or his snare. Then one of them comes. Then it cries out, it whistles. A number of them hear. Then they come; they come running. There they fall into the snare [or] the net.

And in order to protect her young, when someone sees them, when someone tries to catch them, she then flutters as if she can no longer fly. Sometimes she attacks one while her young hide. Then she flies up — she flies away. And in a while she settles there where they went off, where her young scattered. There she calls out, she whistles; there all reassemble. Thus also they are sometimes caught there.

¶

SEVENTH PARAGRAPH, which telleth of still other birds, of their habits.

INJC CHIQUACEN PARRAPHO: itechpa tlatoa, in oc centlamãtin totome.

ÇOLIN: ANOÇO ÇOLLI,

tenvitztic, tenxoxoctic, nexeoac, iztacacujcujltic in jelpan, in jatlapal mjtoa chiencujcujltic, mocxitlaloanj: qualonj, velic, haviac, veltic, vel tzompatic, vel tzompalalatic: teteoa. Injc tlatlaça: injc mopilhoatia, ontecpantli in jteuh, qujtlaça: in vel mopilhoatia, ontecpantli õmatlactli. In jtlaqual: tlaolli, chiẽ, xoxocoioltevilotl.

TECUÇOLI:

çan ie no ie in çoli, ca oqujchtli: vei, elpoctic, vel cujcujltic, cujcujlpatic, quachichiqujle.

OOATON:

çan ie no ieh in çoli, çan tepiton, vel nexeoac, çan achi in cujcujltic: inin ca cioatl. Injc motapaçoltia: cequj pechtic in qujchioa, cequj mjmjltic: injc vel qujpachoa in jteuh. Auh in qujchioa pechtic; concavia in qujnpachoa, in teoan:

nemjtilonj, tlacacivitilonj: njcnemjtia, njctlacacivitia.

Injc nemj: çan ololiuhtinemj auh in aca qujncenmana: çan in tlatoltica, in tozqujtica in nechicavi: ca cenca naoa. In aqujn achto qujncẽmana: auh in vncã qujmevitia, vncã qujteca in jmatl, anoço itzonoaz. njmã ie vitz in centetl, njmã ie ic tzatzi, tlanqujqujci, qujoalcaquj, in cequjntin: njmã ie vitze, icxinenentivitze vncã oalhuevetzi, in tzonoazco, in matlac.

Auh injc qujmpie ipilhoã: in aca qujtta, in qujmanaznequj: njmã tlapapatlatza: momoiavi, iuhqujma ca oc vel patlanj: in quẽman teca momotla, oc ommotlatia in pipiltotonti: çatepan eoa, patlanj. Auh in achitonca, in vncan oieoacque, in vncã ocenmãque ipilhoan; vncã moquetza, vncã tzatzi, vntlanqujqujci: vncan nechicauj, ic no vncan ano, in quenmanjan.

¶

INJC CHICOME PARRAPHO: itechpa tlatoa in oc centlamãtin totome, in quenamjq̃.

---

1. *Çolin: Callipepla squamata* (Vigors); Friedmann *et al., op. cit.,* p. 72. Martín del Campo, *loc. cit.,* has *Cyrtonyx montezumae.*

2. Corresponding Spanish text: *"Las codornjçes hembras llamalas* [sic] *ooaton, y son mas pequeñas que los machos."*

SLENDER-BILLED GRACKLE[1]

It is black. Its bill is curved. It is a well-textured [black].

BOAT-TAILED GRACKLE[2]

It has a long, nail-like bill; it has a streaked tail; the tail is streaked, as if streaked. It has a good voice; it speaks well, it speaks pleasantly. The one which is not very black, but a little sooty, is the hen; the very black one, very curved of bill, glistening, is the cockerel and is called *teotzanatl*.

It is named *teotzanatl* because it did not live here in Mexico in times of old.[3] Later, in the time of the ruler Auitzotl it appeared here in Mexico. For he commanded that they be brought here from [the provinces of] Cuextlan [and] Totonacapan. It was made known especially that those which came here were to be fed. But when they multiplied, they scattered, they traveled everywhere, they ate everywhere. They eat lizards.

And when they were still esteemed, no one might throw stones at them. If anyone stoned them, they chided one another; the common folk said to one another, "What are you doing over there? Do not shout at, do not stone the lord's birds!"

ACATZANATL OR ACATZUNATL[4]

Some are quite black, some only smoky. They dwell among the reeds; among the reeds they hatch. They prey especially upon maize, and worms, and the small insects which fly.

COYOLTOTOTL[5]

It is the same as the *acatzanatl*, though some have a chili-red throat, breast, wings, rump. Some are yellow-breasted, very yellow-breasted, with white wing-bends. And very good, very clear, is its song — much like a bell, pleasing, sweet. Hence is it named *coyoltototl*. In the reeds, in the midst of reeds it sits, it hatches.

MOURNING DOVE[6]

It has a slender, pointed bill. It is chalky-ashen. Its legs are like sticks, long, extending [back] toward the tail; the tail is long. It is somewhat tall, long-

TZANATL:

tliltic, tencoltic, icucic.

TEUTZANATL:

tenviac, tentepuztic, cujtlapiltzatzapal, cujtlapiltzatzapaltic, cujtlapiltzatzapaliuhquj, iectozque, iectlatole, tlatolhuelic. In amo cenca tliltic çã achi cujcheoac cioatl, in vel tliltic, in vel tencoltic, in tzotzotlanj oqujchtli: yoan itoca teutzanatl.

Injc motocaiotia teutzanatl: ca amo njcan mexico nenca, in ie vecauh: qujn ipan, in tlatoanj Avitzotl, in nezque njcan mexico: ca tlanaoati, injc ompa oalhujcoque cuextlan, totonacapan: oc cemmachoa, tlaqualtiloia, in njcã ic oallaque. Auh in ie mjequja: cenmanque, noviã qujzque, novian tlaquaquaia: conqua in cuetzpalin.

Auh oc maviztia, aiac vel qujnmotlaia, nepanotl ic neaioia: in aquj qujnmotlaia, nepanotl qujmolhujaia in maceoaltin: tle tay, o, maca xicnotza, maca xicmotla, itotouh in tlacatl.

ACATZANATL: ANOÇO ACATZUNATL,

cequj vel tliltique, cequj çan pochectique: tullâ chaneque, tullâ in tlapanj, vel qujmoiautia in tonacaiutl: yõa in ocujli, yoan in tlein iolcatontli, patlantinemj.

COIOLTOTOTL:

çan ie no ieh in Acatzanatl, iece cequj, tozcachichiltic, ielchichiltic, amatlapalchîchichiltic, tzintetenpan chichiltic, cequj elcoztic, elcoçauhquj: acoliztac. Auh cenca qualli: cenca iectli in itlâtol, vel coioltic, velic, tzopelic, ic motocaiotia coioltototl: tulla, tulitic in tlapachoa, in tlatlapana.

VILOTL:

tempitzaoac, tenvitztic, nexeoacaticectic, xotlacotic, xoviac, cujtlapillanquj, cujtlapilhujac, achi quauhticatontli, quechancatontli. In jtlaqual: tlaolli, chien,

---

1. *Tzanatl: Cassidix palustris* (Swainson); Friedmann *et al., op. cit.,* Pt. II, p. 280; Martín del Campo, *op. cit.,* p. 406.
2. *Teotzanatl: Cassidix mexicanus* (Gmelin); Friedmann *et al., op. cit.,* p. 279. See also Martín del Campo, *loc. cit.*
3. Corresponding Spanish text: *"llamanse teutzanatl que qujere dezir aue rara, o tzanatl preciosa."*
4. Corresponding text ref. to *"otras maneras de estas aues que se llaman tzanatl"* agrees with Martín del Campo, *loc. cit.,* and Santamaría, *op. cit.,* p. 18 (*acazanate*).
5. *Coyoltototl:* Martín del Campo, *loc. cit.,* suggests *Agelaius gubernator grandis.*
6. *Uilotl: Zenaidura macroura* Linnaeus (Friedmann *et al., op. cit.,* Pt. I, p. 116; Martín del Campo, *loc. cit.*).

necked. Its food is grains of maize, *chia*, amaranth, *argemone, lepidium* seed.

It is lazy. Its nest is only sticks which it places together; it piles a little grass on the surface. And it is so lazy that it does not drink by day; only later, when night has fallen, when darkness has come, at night, it runs back and forth seeking water.

And its habits are much like those of the *cocotli*. They are very attentive to their mates, to their hens. And if one dies, the one [remaining] always lives in mourning. And it seems constantly to weep; it makes [the sound] *uilo-o-o*. And its name, *uilotl*, is taken from its song, which says *uilo*.

And of the *uilotl* it is said that the rest of the birds said to it, "Come on, let us scratch for water so that we may drink there." It is said that [*uilotl*] wished much to be first, but was very lazy; it only lay down. When they called to it, it said to them, "Let all go. Really, all do not go." And when they had found water, then all deserved to drink water in peace and quiet. But the priest [*tlamacazqui*], because it really did not dig for water with the others, it is said, they abandoned there, so that it did not drink with the others. So only at night, secretly, it drinks water. And *uilotl* was named — his derisive named became — *tlamacazqui*, because he only said, "Let all go."

GROUND DOVE[7]

It is large, round, ball-like. Some are ashen, some chalky, some dark green, some smoky, some tawny. It is really much like the Castilian *uilotl*.

¶

EIGHTH PARAGRAPH, which telleth of the birds which are good singers.

CURVE-BILLED THRASHER[1]

It has long legs, stick-like legs, very black; it has a pointed, slender, curved bill. It is ashen, ash-colored, dark ashen. It has a song, a varied song.

It is named *cuitlacochtototl*, which is taken from its song, because it says *cuitlacoch, cuitlacoch, tarati, tarat, tatatati, tatatati, titiriti, tiriti*.

It is capable of domestication; it is teachable. It breeds everywhere, in treetops, in openings in walls. Wherever it is inaccessible, there it breeds. Its food is insects, flies, water flies, flesh, ground maize.

oauhtli, chicalutl, mexixin ixinachio:

tlatziuhquj, in jtapaçol çan tlacotl in connepanoa: quezquj çacatontli ixco contema. Auh injc cēca tlatziuhquj: amo atli in tlâca; ça qujn tlapoiaoa, tlaixcuecuetzivi, tlaixmjmjquj, in avic motlaloa: qujtemoa in atl.

Auh çan vel no iuhquj in jieliz: cocotli yieliz, çan tlatlaixcavia in innamjcoan, in incioaoan: auh in ocetica mjcq̃, muchipa tlaocuxtinemj in centetl. Auh iuhqujn muchipa chochoca: qujchioa, vilo. o. o. Auh injc vilotl itoca; çan itech tlaantli in jtlatol, in qujtoa: vilo.

Auh injc vilotl: qujl qujlhujque, in oc çequjntin totome: ma tivian, tatatacazque, in vncan tatlizque: qujl cenca motachcauhnequja, yoã cenca tlatzivia; çan vetztoc in qujoalnotza, qujmjlhuja. Ma viloa; amo nel ie viloa. Auh in oqujnextique atl: ic mochi tlacatl qujmaceuh, in jvian atlioaz, in iocoxca atlioaz. Auh in tlamacazquj: ca nel noço, amo oteoan atatacac: qujl oncan cōmocavili, injc amo tehoan atliz: ic çan iooaltica, in qujchtacai atl. Auh motocaiotia: yiaviltoca mochiuh in iehoatl, tlamacazquj in vilotl. ipampa: çan qujtoaia ma viloa.

TLACAVILOTL:

vei, ololtic, tapaioltic, cequj nexeoac, cequj ticeoac, çequj mamatlaltic, cequj poctic, cequj quappachtic çan vel nelli iuhquj in castillã vilotl.

¶

INJC CHICUEI PARRAPHO: itechpa tlatoa in totome, vel cujcanj.

CUJTLACOCHIN: ANOÇO CUJTLACOCHTOTOTL,

xoviviac, xotlacotic xotlitliltic, tenvitztic, tempitzaoac, tencoltic, tencoliuhquj, nextic, nexeoac, nexcamjltic: tlatole, tlatlatole.

Injc motocaiotia cujtlacochtototl: itech tlaantli in jtlatol, in qujtoa cujtlacoch, cujtlacoch, tarati, tarat, tatatati, tatatati, titiriti, tiriti:

tlacacivitilonj, machtilonj: çan novian in tlacati, quauhticpac, tepancamac: in canj̃ ovican oncan tlachioa. In jtlaqual: ioioli, çaioli, axaxaiacatl, nacatl, tlaoltextli.

---

7. *Tlacauilotl: Chamaepelia passerina pallescens* (*loc. cit.*; Friedmann *et al., op. cit.*, p. 119).

1. *Cuitlacochin: Toxostoma curvirostre* (Swainson); Friedmann *et al., op. cit.*, Pt. II, p. 176; Martín del Campo, *op. cit.*, p. 407.

And in winter it does not sing, it does not cry out, it does not produce songs. When the rains come, when they threaten, when it becomes warm, then it begins to sing. Toward whence the wind comes, there it settles facing it, continuing to call, to sing.

NORTHERN MOCKINGBIRD[2]

It is ashen, a little dusky. The breast is white, the wings white mingled with red. There is a [white] bar over the eyes. [The body] is small and long. Its dwelling place, where it breeds, is in the forest, in inaccessible places. It does not sing in the winter, only during the summer.

It is named *centzontlatole* because it mocks all the birds; it also mocks the turkeys — the cocks, the hens. It also mocks the dogs. When it still lives in its habitat, it sings all night.

MIAUATOTOTL

Also its name is *xopan tototl*. It is small, round, dark yellow. It has a song, a soft song; it is a singer. It gladdens one; it makes one rejoice. It is small, tiny, minute.

LADDER-BACKED WOODPECKER[3]

It is large as a *tzanatl*. It is crested. Dark colored is its crest;[4] white its bill; black spotted with ashen are its feathers. Its throat is yellow. Its legs are somewhat like those of the *tzanatl*. Its food is tree worms; it extracts the worms from the trees. And it nests, it breeds within the tree; it makes a hole in the tree.

And when it sings, it cries out much, it warbles, sometimes like whistling with the fingers; and it sings as if there were many birds.

But when it seems to shriek,[5] it is angry. So, it is said, this was taken as an omen. Whoever heard it said, "It is shrieking at us. Take care; something may befall us." But when it whistled, they said it was happy. And the travelers or merchants said, "It whistles. Perhaps something will be our reward." And where there is contention, one is called *chiquimolin* for this reason. When he whom they distrust shouts at one or contends with one, where perhaps they sit rejoicing, they say, "Go — leave! Like a *chiquimolin* you come sowing discord among us." Espe-

Auh in tonalco: amo tlatoa, amo tzatzi, amo cujca: in ie vitz, in ie oallaznequj qujavitl, in ie tlatotonja: iquac peoa, in tlatoa; in campa oallauh ehecatl ompa itztimotlalia, tzatzitica, tlatotica.

ÇENTZONTLATOLE:

nexeoac, achi cujcheoac, eliztac, amatlapaliztac, amatlapalhujviltecquj, mjhichiuh, melactontli; quauhtla, ovican in jnentla, in tlacati. Amo tlâtoa in tonalco, çan iquac in xopan.

Injc mjtoa centzontlatole: muchi qujtlaeiecalhuja in tototl, no qujtlaeiecalhuja in totolin, in vexolotl, in cioatotolin: no qujtlaeiecalhuja in chichi: in oc ichã nemj ceiooal in tlatoa.

MIAOATOTOTL:

yoan itoca xopã tototl, ololtontli, coziaiactic; tlâtole, iamanca tlatole, cujcanj, teiolpaqujlti, teiolavielti: qualton, qualtepil, qualteton.

CHIQUJMOLI:

iuhqujn tzanatl ic vei: quachichiqujle, tlappoiaoac in jquachichiqujl: iztac in jtẽ, tliltic, in jvio, nextic ic mocujcujlo: in jtozcac coztic: in jcxi ach iuhq'n tzanatl: in jtlaqual quauhocujli itech qujqujxtia quavitl in ocujltin. Auh in mochãtia, in vncã tlacati, quavitl iitic, qujcoionja in quavitl.

Auh injc tlatoa cenca tzatzi, chachalaca: in quẽman iuhqujn mapipitzoa: yoã iuhqujnma, mjequjntin totome ic tlatoa:

Auh in jquac iuhquj pipitzcatica: qualanj, in juh mjtoa: inin no tetzãmachoa, in aqujñ, qujcaquja: qujtoaia, ie topan pipitzca, xõmjmattivia tlein topã muchioaz: auh in jquac mapipitzoa qujl pactica: auh qujtoaia in nenẽque in anoço pochteca. Mapipitzoa aço itla tomaçeoaltiz. Auh vncã aio ic tocaiotilo, chiqujmoli: in aqujn amo qujteimachiltia teaoa, anoço itla ic techalanja, in aço vncã pacoatoc qujlhuja xiauh, xiqujça iuhqujn tichiqujmoli otonepantla tommotecaco. oc cenca ie itechpa mjtoa, in tenetechalanja. in jtla ic tenepantla moteca.

---

2. *Centzontlatole: Mimlus polyglottos* (Linnaeus); Friedmann *et al., op. cit.,* p. 171; Martín del Campo, *loc. cit.*

3. *Chiqujmoli: Dryobates scalaris bairdi* (*loc. cit.*). See Friedmann *et al., op. cit.,* p. 40, under *Dendrocopos scalaris* (Wagler).

4. Corresponding Spanish text: *"colorado deslabado."*

5. *Ibid.*: *"quãdo gruñe como raton."*

cially is this said when one arouses contentions, when one arouses bad feeling among others.

COMMON CHACHALACA[6]

It is the same size as the *teotzanatl*. It is somewhat yellow all over; its tail is mixed [black and] white. Its food is fruit; also maize kernels, ground maize. It nests in inaccessible parts of trees. And it sings in winter. It is called *chachalacametl* because if a number of them settle together, only one begins to sing; then all sing. And the neck is like a turkey's neck, only very small. And it sings three times during the night, like a Castilian rooster. It is said that it awakens one.

¶

NINTH PARAGRAPH, which telleth of the native turkeys.

TURKEY[1]

Its name is also *iuiquen, iuiquentzin,* and *xiuhcozca* is [also] its name. It is a dweller in one's home, which can be raised in one's home, which lives near and by one. The feathers are thick, the tail rounded. It has wings; it is heavy, not a flyer. It is edible. It leads the meats; it is the master. It is tasty, fat, savory. It molts.

When still a poult, its food is said to be ground maize, roasted maize, cooked greens. It eats *tonalchichicaquilitl, quanacaquilitl, coyocuexi, tetzitzili* herbs. It hatches, breaks through with its bill, takes on color, grows, molts, sheds the chick-feathers, becomes bare.

Some turkeys are smoky, some quite black, some like crow feathers, glistening, some white, some ashen, ash-colored, some tawny, some smoky.

The cockerel, the male turkey, is big, big and coarse. It has air-sacs,[2] a big belly, wattles, a chest, breasts, a long neck. The stalky neck has a necklace, a neck-coral. The head is blue; it is dewlapped; it has a dewlap. The eyelids are cylindrical, swollen. It has a rounded protuberance, an erectile process. It is a tail-feather-spreader, a bristler, an attacker. It spreads its tail feathers, bristles, sounds its air-sacs. It treads upon others, tramples others underfoot, attacks others.

Its rounded protuberance is pliant, leathery, like leather, soft, very soft. One who hates another feeds

CHACHALACAMETL,

ixqujch in teutzanatl, achi ixcoztic, noviã iuhquj, in jcujtlapil iztacaviviltecquj: in itlaqual suchiqualli: no ie tlaolli, textli: quauhovicã in motapaçoltia: auh tonalco in tlatoa: injc mjtoa chachalacametl intla quexqujchtin omotlaliq̃, çã cẽ cõpeoaltia tlatoa, mec moch tlatoa. auh cozq̃, iuhqujn totolin icozquj çã tepitotõ: auh in ioaltica, expã tlatoa: in juhquj caxtillã vexolotl: mitoa teixitia.

¶

INJC CHICUNAVI PARRAPHO: intechpa tlatoa, in njcã totolme.

TOTOLI:

yoan itoca hiviquẽ, hiviquentzin, yoan itoca xiuhcozca: techan nemjnj, techan oapaoalonj, tetloc, tenaoac nemjnj, hiviotilaoac, cujtlapiliaoaltic, amatlapale, ahaze, hetic: amo patlanjnj, qualonj, qujiacati nacatl, tlacâoa, velic, chiaoa, haviac, moxima.

In jtlaqual in oc piltontli, qujl textli, izqujo; in qujpaoaci qujlitl, in qujqua: tonalchichicaqujlitl, quanacaqujlitl, coiocuexi, tetzitzili; tlapanj, motencopina, mopoiaoa, mozcaltia, moxima, mopilhiuiotlaça, mopetlaoa.

In totoli: cequj pochectic, cequj vel tliltic, cequj iuhqujn cacalotl hivio: tzotlanj, cequj iztac, cequj nextic, nexeoac: çequj quappachtic, cequj poctic.

Vexolotl: oqujchtotoli, vei, veitepol, acome, xixiaoa, xelhoaçe, elmetze, ciciotcaio, quechveiac quechooaio, cozque, quechtatapachtic, quaxoxoctic, quãtoltic, quatole, ixquatolmjmjltic, ixquatolpopoçactic: iacatole, iacacujtle: moxittomonjanj, motomonjanj, tepanchol: moxittomonja, motomonja: qujtetecujtza, qujcocomotza in jacõ: tequequeça, teicça, tepancholoa:

in jiacatol, atultic, cuetlaxtic, cuetlaxiuhquj, iamãquj, iaiamaztic. In tecocolianj: cacaoatl, molli ipan

---

6. *Chachalacametl: Ortalis vetula* (Wagler). Friedmann *et al., op. cit.,* Pt. I, p. 69.

1. *Totoli; Huexolotl* (male): *Meleagris gallopavo* Linnaeus (*ibid.* p. 80).

2. Problematical; Roger M. Latham, *Complete Book of the Wild Turkey* (Harrisburg, Penn., 1956), p. 29, suggests a possible interpretation. The nearby crop may be meant.

[the protuberance] to him in chocolate, in sauce; he causes him to swallow it. It is said that he thereby makes one impotent.

I pluck it. I remove its wings. I pluck its tail. I remove the callosities from its feet. I extract the bill. The erectile process of the turkey makes one impotent. I strike, I break open the air-sacs....

Its food is maize, tortillas, tamales, shelled maize, grains of maize, cooked grains of maize, ground maize, chili, greens. It quickly dies from salt; not one hour can it last.

The turkey hen is of average size, of medium size, low, low-backed. She has a necklace; she is coral-headed, with a coral[-colored] head. She is the one which takes the cock, the one which is mounted. She is the one which lays the eggs; she is the egg-layer, the sitter. She sits. She is tasty, healthful, fat, full of fat, fleshy, fleshy-breasted, heavy-fleshed. She takes the cock, lays the eggs, makes her nest; she gathers her eggs, she lays eggs, she sits. She hatches, she rears [her young]. She gathers her poults under her wings. And each one enters under her, inserts itself under her. She warms them; she apportions them [food]; she gives food to her poults.

The development of the turkey, or its nature: a drop forms; it thickens; a covering forms, a shell forms. The egg is laid. When it falls, [the shell] is still soft; then it quickly hardens in the air. It is settled over; it is warmed. It breaks open, hatches, becomes colored. The little poult, the poult is a molted one; it becomes round. The young turkey cocks, the young turkey hens mature, form air-sacs, develop wattles.

¶

TENTH PARAGRAPH, which telleth of the parts of the different birds.

The names of [the feathers] of all the different birds are *çaquan, quechol, tzinitzcan*: and of them it is understood that they are the precious ones. The proverb speaks of "the precious feathers of the lord."

The property, the possession, which belongs to all the different birds and to turkeys is feathers. And those which appear on their heads, even the not precious, are called *tzinitzcan*. Those which appear on the head of a resplendent trogon are called *que-tzaltzinitzcan*. And those which appear on the neck are called *tapalcayotl*; its *tapalcayotl* feathers. So one refers to the eagle's *tapalcatl* feathers. Those which

qujtequaltia, qujtetololtia: qujl ic tetlamjctilia:

njcvivitla, njcahavitzana, njccujtlapilhujvitla, njc-cacçollaça, njctencopina. tetlamjctilia in totoli yiaca-cujtl: njcaconvitequj, njcacontlapana, njcxixiapachoa.

In jtlaqual tonacaiutl; tlaxcalli, tamalli, tlaoio, tla-olli, tlaolpaoaxtli, textli, chilli, qujlitl: in iztatl hi-ciuhca ic mjquj, amo vel ce hora.

Çioatotoli, çan qualli, çan qualton: pachtic, cujtla-pachtic, cozque, quatatapachtic, quatatapachiuhquj; moquequeçanj, mocçanj, motetianj, tlatlaçanj, tlapa-choanj, tlapacho: velic velpatic, chiaoa, ceceio, na-natztic, elnanatztic, nacatetic: moquequeça, motetia, mopepechia, motlapepechia, tlatlaça, tlapachoa, tla-tlapana; tlacaoapaoa, yiahaztitlan qujmaquja in jpil-hoã. Auh itlan cacalaquj; itlan mocacalaquja, qujn-totonjlia, q'ntlaxexelhuja, qujntlaquaqualtia in jpil-hoan.

In jneoapaoaliz in totolin: in anoço yieliz, chipinj, tetzaoa, peioioa cacallooa; tlaçalo totoltetl, in oalhue-tzi: çan oc atic: qujn hiciuhca hecatetzaoa: pacholo, totonjlilo: tlapanj, tlacati, mopoiaoa, poiaoa: totol-conetontli, totolconetl, moxinquj: momjmjloa, tel-pochtotolin, ichpochtotolin: maci, macontia, xelhoaz-qujça.

¶

INJC MATLACTLI PARRAPHO: itechpa tlatoa, in intla-tlamantiliz, nepapan totome.

In jxqujch nepapan tototl: itoca. çaquan: quechol, tzinitzcan: yoan impan mocaquj in tlaçoti, qujtoa in tlatolli, Içaquaoã, itotooan, iquecholhoan in totecujo.

In ixqujch nepapan tototl: yoan in totolin, in jtech ca, in jtlatquj, in jaxca: hivitl. Auh in jcpac eoa ma-civi in amo tlaçotli, itoca tzinitzcan. In quetzaltototl icpac eoa, itoca: quetzaltzinitzcan. Auh in jquech-tlan eoa: itoca, tapalcaiotl, itapalcaio; iuh mjtoa, quauhtapalcatl. In jitipan eoa: yoan in jcujtlapã itoca: alapachtli, yoan itapalcaio: in vel inacaio itech onoc itoca tlachcaiotl, iuh mjtoa: quauhtlachcaiotl,

54

appear on its belly and on its back are called *alapach-tli* and its *tapalcayotl* feathers. Those which are right on its skin are called *tlachcayotl*. So one refers to the *tlachcayotl* feathers of the eagle, the scarlet macaw, the *xomotl*. And those which are at the edge of its rump, which cover the base of the tail, are called *olincayotl, poyaualli, poyauallotl. Imaxtli,* so it is said, are the eagle's *moloctli* feathers, the resplendent trogon's *olincayotl* feathers, the *tzinpoyauacayotl* feathers of a turkey, of a bird, the *imaxtli* feathers of a heron.

WINGS: those on the wing-bend are called *tzinitz-can* [lesser coverts]. Those which follow are called *tzicoliuhqui* [middle coverts]. Those which follow next, which cover the flight feathers, are called *chilchotic* [or] *tecpatic* [greater coverts]. They are pointed feathers.

FLIGHT FEATHERS: the flight feathers are long, hollow, shaft-like. They have fluff; they are fluffy feathers. One refers to the flight feathers of the eagle, of the turkey, of a bird; the wings.

PRIMARIES: these appear at the very tip of its wing. It is the real place of its flight. I pluck the primaries. I draw out the primaries. The *ahauitztli* — and they are [also] called *nacatl* — are the very pointed tips of the wings.

AHAZTLI is the general term for the wing, the organ for flying. It is so called when the turkey hen covers its young under its wing.

Especially does this also mean the wing when extended. It is said, "The bird has not yet its wings" — "There are its primaries."

TAIL: it may be straight, wide, long, stubby, small.

[The parts] of which all the feathers are formed are the end or its tip, the fluff, the shaft, the thread-feather, the barrel.

And of this same bird the names of what is of the flesh [follow].

BILL: the pointed bill, the wide bill, the curved bill; the bird's bill, the bill of a bird; the turkey hen's pointed bill; the duck's wide bill, the wide bill of a duck; the eagle's curved bill. The bird's bill: with it, it picks, it pecks; it devours, it feeds.

EYE: the eye, the bird's eye, the eye of a bird; the turkey's eye, the eye of a turkey. With it, it looks, it looks in different directions, it becomes blind.

alotlachcaiotl, xomotlachcaiotl. Auh in itzintenpan manj: in qujtzinpachoa icujtlapil, olincaiotl, poiaoalli, poiaoallotl. Imaxtli: iuh mjtoa, quammoloctli: yiolicaio in quetzaltototl, itzinpoiaoaca in totolin in tototl, aztaimaxtli.

HATLAPALLI: aztlacapalli, in jtech ca, in jacolpan onoc; tzinitzcan; in qujoaltoqujlia itoca, tzicoliuhquj: in oc ceppa qujoaltoqujlia, in ie qujtzinpachoa, mamaztli itoca; chilchotic, tecpatic, hivivitztli.

MAMÂZTLI: mamaztli, viac, acaio, quauhio, tomjo, hivitomjo, mjtoa: quammamaztli: totolmamâztli, totolacatl ahaztli.

AHAVITZTLI: in jvel yiacac eoa in jatlapal, vel ie in jpatlanja: njcaâvitzana, njcahavitzcopina: ahavitztli, yoan itoca in nacatl, in vel yiacavitzauhca in jatlapal.

AHAZTLI: ic mocemjtoa in atlapalli, in patlanjoanj; ic mjtoa. In totolin yiahaztitlan qujmaquja in jpilhoan:

oc cenca no iehoatl qujtoznequj, in jatlapal in viac, mjtoa, aoc tle in jahaz tototl: ie onca in jahavitz.

CUJTLAPILLI, melaoac, patlaoac, viac, tetepontic, tepiton

In ixqujch hivitl, in jtech ca, injc tlachioalli: mamaztli, anoço yiacaio: tzinhivitl: hiviquavitl, hiviquauhiotl, hivitlacotl; hivitomjtl, hiviomjtl.

Auh in ie iehoatl tototl: in nacatl in jtech ca in jtotoca

TENTLI: tenvitztli, tempatlactli, tencolli, tototentli, tototl iten, totolin itenvitz: canauhtenpatlactli, canauhtli itenpatlac: quauhtencolli. In tototl in jten: ic tlachoponja, tlachopinja, tlachochopotza, tlaquâqua.

IXTLI: ixtelolotli, totoixtli, tototl iix, totolixtli, totolin yix: ic tlachia, tlatlachia, ixpopoioti,

55

I blind one; I smash it in the eye; I smash it in the eyeball. I put fear in its eye. It opens its eye. I remove its eyeball.

EYELID: with it, it covers [the eye]; with it, it opens, it covers its eye; it blinks. With the eye covering it sees in the water.

HEAD: one refers to a bird's head, an eagle's head, a turkey's head, a duck's head, etc.

BRAIN, BRAINS: the brain of a turkey, of a bird.

SKULL: the skull of a bird.

NECK, neck skin, neck joints, cervical vertebrae: one speaks of the cervical vertebrae, the neck skin, the neck joints of a turkey, of a bird.

TONGUE: bird's tongue; the tongue of a bird.

THROAT: a turkey's throat; the throat of a turkey.

GULLET: the gullet of a bird.
The body is round. On the body are the wings. On it are the wings, the shoulder, the shoulder joint; the shoulder joint of a turkey. *Aztlacapalli* is also the name of the two joints of the wing. It is said, "A turkey wing is given to me."

Ahauitztli is the very tip of the wing. They say[1] it is desired. I eat the wing tips of a turkey; I am given them. They are fleshless, thin-fleshed, good-tasting, very good-tasting.

BELLY: the belly of a bird, of a turkey.

INTESTINES: a bird's intestines, a turkey's intestines.

CROP: the depository, the food bag, the refuse jar, the refuse net.

GIZZARD: the gizzard grinds, it pulverizes, . . .

INTESTINES: a turkey's intestines; the ovary.

RUMP GLAND: it is on its rump. It is odorous, smelly. One refers to a turkey's rump gland.

TOE WITH ITS FOOT: by it is understood also all its lower leg. They say of merchants, vanguard merchants, those who departed, those who went, those who entered — because, it is said, they are travelers — their lot is the turkey leg, the toes.

njqujxpopoiotilia, njqujxpitzinja, njqujxtelolopitzinja, njqujxmauhtia, mjxcueionja, njqujxteloloqujxtia.

IXQUEMPALLI: ic hicopi, ic mjxcueionja, mjxpeionja, mjxpepeiotza, ixpeiotl, ic atlan tlachia.

TZONTECOMATL: mjtoa tototzontecomatl; quauhtzontecomatl, totoltzontecomatl, canauhtzontecomatl. etc.

QUATEXTLI: QUATETEXTLI, totolin, tototl iquatexio:

QUAXICALLI, tototl iquaxical.

QUECHTLI: quechooatl, quechtetepontli, quechquauhiotl: mjtoa totolin, tototl iquechquauhio, iquechooaio, iquechtetepon.

NENEPILLI: totonenepilli, tototl inenepil:

COCOTL, totolin icocouh, totolcocotl:

TLATOLHOAZTLI, tototl itlatolhoaz.

Tlactli: ololtic. In jtech ca tlactli: hatlapalli, aztlacapalli: In jtech ca aztlacapalli: hatlapalli, hacolli, hacoltetl; totolin yiacolteuh, haztlacapalli: no itoca injc omjxtli tlatlapalli; mjtoa totoli yiaztlacapal in njmaco.

Ahavitztli: in vel yiacavitzauh ca hatlapalli: qujtoa in moxicoa. totolin yiahavitz in njcqua in njmaco: hanacaio, nacaio totochtic: velic, vel patic.

HITITL: tototl, totoli yiti.

CUJTLAXCOLLI: totocujtlaxcolli, totolcujtlaxcolli.

TLATLALILLI: tlatlalilonj, tlaquaxiqujpilli: cujtlatecomatl, cujtlamatlatl.

MEMETLATL: tememetlatl, tlateci, tlacuecho, tlaaxtilia tlaaxooa

CUJTLAXCOLLI, totolcujtlaxcolli: conexiqujpilli.

TLETL, itzintempan ca, chipaiac, qujpiac: mjtoa totolin itleuh.

XOMATZALLI: ie in jxocpal no ipan mocaquj in mochi itlanitz: qujtoa in pochteca, in oztomeca, in jiaque, in ianj, in calaquj qujl ipampa nenemjnj, intonal in totolicxitl, in xomatzalli.

---

1. *Acad. Hist.* MS adds ȳ ça.

Third Chapter, which telleth of all the animals which dwell in the water.

FIRST PARAGRAPH, which telleth of some kinds of birds which always dwell in the water.

THE GOOSE, or *atlatlalacatl,*[1] or *atototl,* comes from the west. It has been mentioned among the birds.

DUCK is the collective name for the white-breast, the mallard, the *teçoloctli.* All also come from the west. They have been mentioned among the birds.

THE GOOSE breeds here among the reeds. It has been mentioned among the birds.

THE ÇOQUICANAUHTLI is the same as the goose. It also breeds among the reeds. However, its feathers are smoky, sooty.

THE YACACINTLI[2] has been mentioned among the birds.

THE NORTHERN PHALAROPE has been mentioned among the birds.

THE RUDDY DUCK is just like the duck. It is of average size.

THE ATONCUEPOTLI is also called *atapalcatl.* It is small, smoky, white-breasted. Its head feathers glisten. It is named *atoncuepotli* because, when it sings, it is as if someone beat the two-toned drum.

THE AMERICAN BITTERN,[3] also called *acoyotl* and *atotolin,* is large, long-necked, pointed-billed, cylindrical-billed, dark yellow. It is called *ateponaztli* because, when it talks, it puts its bill in the water. It sounds as if someone beat the two-toned drum. It is called *atotolin* or *acoyotl* because it is a drowner of people.

THE XOMOTL has been mentioned among the birds.

THE ACACALOTL has been mentioned among the birds.

Inic ei capitulo: itechpa tlatoa in jxqujch iolque atlan nemj.

INJC CE PARRAPHO: intechpa tlatoa in centlamantin totome, muchipa atlã nemj.

TLALALACATL: anoço atlatlalacatl, anoço atototl: tonatiuh icallaqujampa vitz. omjto in impan totome.

CANAUHTLI: çan incentoca, in eliztac, in tzoniaiauhquj, in teçoloctli: no mochintin vmpa vitze, in tonatiuh icallaqujampa. omjto in impan totome.

CONCANAUHTLI: njcan tulla tlacati: omjto in impan totome.

ÇOQUJCANAUHTLI: çan ie no ieh in concanauhtli, çan no tûlla in tlacati; iece pochectic, cujcheoac in jhivio.

IACACINTLI: omjto in impan totome.

ATZITZICUJLOTL: omjto in impan totome.

ATAPALCATL: çan no iuhqujn canauhtli, çan qualton.

ATONCUEPOTLI: no itoca atapalcatl, tepiton, pochectontli, eliztac, xoxotla, in jquahivio. Inic motocaiotia Atoncuepotli: injc tlatoa, iuhqujn aca teponaçoa.

ATEPONAZTLI: yoan itoca acoiotl, yoan atotolin: vei, quechviac, tenvitztic, temmjmjltic, coziaiactic. Injc mjtoa ateponaztli: injc tlatoa, atlã conaquja in jten: iuhqujn aca teponaçoa ic caqujzti. Injc mjtoa Atotolin: anoço Acoiotl, teilaqujani.

XOMOTL: omjto in impã totome.

ACACALOTL: omjto in impã totome.

---

1. *Atlatlalacatl, atototl:* see n. 5, Chap. II, § 3.

2. *Yacacintli:* desc. in Francisco Hernández, *Historia Natural de Nueva España* (Mexico: Universidad Nacional de México, 1959), Vol. II, p. 354; he notes it as a coot or scoter (*foja*).

3. *Ateponaztli: Botaurus lentiginosus* (Montagu) in Friedmann *et al., op. cit.,* Pt. I, p. 34.

THE SNOWY EGRET has been mentioned among the birds.

THE ACUICUIYALOTL or *acuecueyalotl* has been mentioned.

These birds are thus hunted, thus caught: they are netted, they are noosed, they are caught by a cord about the feet, they are snared.

¶

SECOND PARAGRAPH, which telleth of all the fishes.

FISH

All kinds of fish are cylindrical, wide, tailed, with a forked tail; finned; covered with tile-shaped scales, scaled, scaly. They are corpulent, thick-bodied, compact, thick-necked. Water is their habitat; they are water-dwellers; they live in the water; they enter the water. They are flyers, darters. They are slippery, slick. *Nitlâtlama* means "I catch fish." I eat fish.

TLACAMICHIN[4]

That is, a large fish, a dweller of the sea, the ocean: savory, good to the taste, edible, rare, wonderful. And its food is small fish, baby fish.

COAMICHIN[5]

Its head is like that of a serpent. But its tail, its fins, its scales are the same as those of a fish. It is quite oily.

CHIMALMICHIN[6]

It lives in the sea. It is round, like a shield. It has a tail, fins; its head is the head of a fish.

TOTOMICHIN

This so-called *totomichin* is a real fish, with fins a little long. It is called *totomichin* because its head is just like a bird's head. The beak is well pointed, cylindrical. It is a pecker. It pecks; it swallows things whole.

UITZITZILMICHIN[7]

It is a real fish. It is named *uitzitzilmichin*, because its fins, its swimmers, its rowers, are somewhat long. And its beak is very pointed, long, just like a hummingbird's bill; spine-like, needle-like; a needle-bill.

AZTATL: omjto in impã totome.

ACUJCUJIALOTL: anoço acuecueialotl omjto.

Injque in totome ic axioa, injc ano: matlavilo, tzonvilo, xomecavilo, tlâçalhujlo.

¶

INJC VME PARRAPHO: intechpa tlatoa in ixqujchtin mjmjchtin.

MICHI:

in çaço tlein mjchi, mjmjltic, patlachtic, cujtlapile, cujtlapilmaxaltic, amatlapale: tapalcaio, xoneoaio, xincaio; tlaque, tlactomaoac, cujtlapechtic, quechtomaoac, atlan chane, atlan nemjnj, atl yitic nemjnj, atlan calaqujnj, patlanjnj, çolonjnj: atlactic, petzcauhquj, njtlâtlama: qujtoznequj, mjchin njcaci; njmjchqua.

TLACAMJCHI.

q. n. vei mjchi, vei apan, ilhujcaapan nemjnj: velic, haviac, qualonj, tlaçotli maviztic. Auh in jtlaqual: mjchtepitzitzin, mjchcocone.

COAMJCHI:

iuhqujn cooatl itzõtecon. Auh in jcujtlapil, in jatlapal, in jxincaio, çan ie ie in mjchi, vel chiaoa.

CHIMALMJCHI:

vei apan in nemj, iaoaltic, iuhqujn chimalli: cujtlapile, amatlapale: mjchtzontecomatl in jtzontecon.

TOTOMJCHI:

inj moteneoa totomjchin, vel mjchi, achi amatlapalviac. Injc mjtoa totomjchi: in jtzontecon vel iuhqujn tototl itzontecon ic ca: vel tenvitztic, temmjmjltic, tlachoponjanj, tlachoponja, tlapetztoloa.

VITZITZILMJCHI:

vel mjchi, injc mjtoa vitzitzilmjchi. achi viviac in jatlapal, in jpatlanja, in jtlanelooaia. Auh in jten vel vitztic; viac, vel iuhqujn vitzitziltentli in jten: tenvitzaponatic, tenvitzmalotic, tenvitzmallotl.

---

4. *Tlacamichin*: Described in Hernández, *op. cit.*, p. 398. See also Cecilio A. Robelo: *Diccionario de Mitología Náhuatl* (Mexico: Ediciones Fuente Cultural, 1951), p. 340.

5. *Coamichin*: *Anguila* cuv. (Sahagún, Garibay ed., Vol. IV, p. 327). See also Hernández, *op. cit.*, p. 400.

6. *Chimalmichin*: *Chelonia imbricata*. Rafael Martín del Campo, "Ensayo de interpretación del Libro Undécimo de la Historia de Sahagún," *Anales del Instituto de Biología*, Vol. IX, Nos. 3 and 4 (Mexico, 1938), p. 390.

7. *Uitzitzilmichi*: desc. in Hernández, *op. cit.*, pp. 397, 399.

PAPALOMICHIN[8]

It is a sea-dweller; for this same is a fish. But it is so, it is formed so as to be just like a butterfly — flat, with antennae. Like a butterfly, it has wings; its fins are like butterfly wings. It lives within the water; it seems to fly, to dart.

OCELOMICHIN

It also lives in the sea. Its body is that of a fish, only its head is like that of an ocelot: just like one in being round-headed, stubby-muzzled, thick-muzzled. It is spotted in the same manner. But its body is that of a fish — smooth, slick, slimy.

QUAUHXOUILI

It is a fish; the sea is its dwelling-place. And it is named *quauhxouili* because its head is just like that of an eagle, with curved, yellow bill. Like gold is its bill.

[AXOLOMICHIN][9]

It is just like an *axolotl*; it is oily, slick. Its head is much like it, only it is long, thick; and it is very similar in being boneless. Good is its flesh; it is completely flesh.

¶

THIRD PARAGRAPH, which telleth of all the small water animals.

TECUICITLI OR ATECUICITLI[10]

It is good-tasting, savory, somewhat like a shrimp. It is big, very large. And that which is eaten is only its shoulders; but its body is inedible. And its intestines are very black, like *tecuitlatl* — very good-tasting, edible.[11]

CHACALI[12]

It is a sea-dweller; its habitat is the sea, or the river, or a spring among crags. It is like the shrimp, a little large, ruddy, smelly, edible, good-tasting.

TURTLE[13]

Like the frog, it is edible, good-tasting, very good. It has a shell; it gets into its shell, a strong bone. On

PAPALOMJCHI:

vei apan chane, ca çan ie mjchi: auh injc ca, injc tlachioalli: vel iuhq'n papalotl, patlachtic, iacatzone: in juhquj papalotl, amatlapale; in jatlapal vel iuhq'n papalotl yiatlapal: in atl yitic ic nemj, iuhqujn patlanj, çolonj.

OCELOMJCHI:

no vei apã in nemj. In jtlac ca mjchin; çanjo in jtzontecon; in juhq' ocelutl: vel iuhquj injc quatecontic, injc tentetepontic, injc tentomaoac: vel iuhquj injc mocujcujlo. Auh in jtlac ca mjchin; alactic, alaztic, alaoac.

QUAUHXOVILI:

ca mjchi, vei atlã in jchan. Auh injc mjtoa quauhxovili: in jtzontecon vel iuhqujn quauhtli; tencoltic, tencoztic, iuhqujn teucujtlatl iten:

[AXOLOMICHI]

vel iuhqujn axolotl ic tzotlanj, injc alactic; vel iuhqujn ic ca itzontecon. ieçe ca viac, tomaoac: auh vel iuhqujn injc amo omjo, vel iectli nacatl, vel nacaio.

¶

INJC EI PARRAPHO: intechpa tlatoa in jxqujch atlan nemj iolcapipil.

TECUJCITLI: ANOÇO ATECUJCITLI,

velic, haviac, achiuhquj in acocilin ic ca: ca vei, veipol. Auh in qualilo; çan ie in jacolteuh. auh in jtlac amo qualonj; auh in jitic ca, vel tliltic, iuhqujn tecujtlatl, vel velic, qualonj.

CHACALI:

vei apan nemjnj, vei apan chane, anoço atoiac, texcallapan: iuhqujn acocili, achi veitontli, tlatlactic, xoqujac; qualonj, velic.

AIOTL:

iuhqujnma cueiatl, qualonj, velic, vel patic, tapalcaio: in jtapalcaio conmaquja, chicaoac, omjtl: in

---

8. *Papalomichi*: desc. in *ibid.*, p. 399.

9. *Acad. Hist. MS* supplies omitted heading.

10. *Tecuicitli*: cangrejo de mar. Sahagún, Garibay ed., Vol. IV, p. 353.

11. Corresponding Spanish text: *"lo comestible dellos es los hombros; y el cuerpo, no es de comer, y los intestinos dellos son negros, no son de comer."*

12. *Chacali*: camarón grande. . . . llamado también langostín y acocil (Cambarellus montezuma Sauss). Santamaría, *op. cit.*, p. 343.

13. *Ayotl*: Kinosternon hirtipes (Martín del Campo, *op. cit.*, pp. 390–391).

its back it is somewhat chalky.[14] And it hurries along on its stomach. The bone is white. When it walks, when it feeds, it extends its hands, its feet, its head. And when frightened it enters into its shell. I break open the turtle.

Thus does it bring forth its young: it lays its eggs on the sand; it buries them in the sand. In some way they go on to be hatched; they hatch. And when it is time to hatch, they are edible; they taste better than turkey eggs.

Thus are they hunted, thus are turtles captured: only at night when they come out of the sea. And on the sand the fishermen lie in wait as the turtles come out arranged in order. When they have emerged, the fishermen quickly pounce upon them to throw one on its back. There it lies. They run; they go to seize another; they run to throw another upon its back. They do nothing but throw each one on its back. Later they gather them without haste, for once they have fallen upon their backs, no longer can they right themselves again. The good fisherman, one who holds night vigil, takes ten, fifteen, twenty of them.

Snail[15]

The flesh is like a small snake; it has horns like something large, like the *tlalmaçacoatl*, [like] the *tzompilacauaztli*. Its shell is a white bone — very white; smooth — very smooth; spiral — spiral within, as if spiral within. What we speak of as at the lips of the snail shell is at its tail. What we say has become its tail has become its mouth. For from there it comes out; there it enters. As it enters, it only retreats.

Tapachtli[16]

Also its name is *atzcalli*.[17] It is the flesh [and shell] of all which dwell in the water. Also the shell named *atzcalli* is called a "physician's bowl."[18] They are varicolored — violet, white, crimson; concave, flat, flattish. The bone [center] is hard.

Pearl

It is the same as the oyster. This shell is [like] bone. It shines, it glistens.

---

jcujtlapampa achi ticeoac, auh injc tlacçatinemj, in jelpan: iztac in omjtl. In jquac nenemj: in jquac tlaquaqua, qujoalqujqujxtia in jma, in jcxi, in jtzontecon. Auh in momauhtia, yitic calaquj in jtapalcaio: naiotlapana.

Injc mopilhoatia: xaltitlan in qujtema iteoã, qujnxaltoca: çaço ic tlapanjtivi, tlapanj in ie in tlacatizpan: qualonj, oc qujpanavia in totoltetl ic velic.

Injc mana: injc maci Aiotl, çan iooaltica in oalqujça vei atlã. Auh xaltitlan qujnchixtoq̃ in tlatlamaque: injc oalqujça motecpana, in oqujçaco: qujncujtivetzi in tlatlamaque, caquetztitlaça, vncan vetztoc: oc ce motlaloa cânatiuh, oc ce motlaloa, caquetztitlaçatiuh: çan oc tequjtl qujmahaquetztitlaça, qujn ivian qujmahana. Ipampa: in oçeppa haquetztivetz, aocmo ceppa vel meoaz: in vellama, in cochiçanj: matlactli, caxtolli, centecpantli in cana.

Tecciztli:

in nacatl iuhqujn coatontli, quaquaquave: iuhquj, intla vei: in tlalmaçacooatl, in tzompilacaoaztli. In itapalcaio: omjtl iztac, iztacpatic, tetzcaltic, tetzcalpatic, ilacatztic: hitiilacatztic, hitiilacatziuhquj. In tiqujtoa tecciztli itenco: ie hicujtlapilco; in tiqujtoa, icujtlapil mochioa: ieh icamacpa mochioa. Ca ieh vmpa oalqujztiuh, ieh vmpa in calaquj: injc calaquj, çan tzinjloti.

Tapachtli:

yoan itoca atzcalli, in jxqujch atlan nemj tapachnacatl: no itoca atzcalli, in jtapalcaio: in mjtoa ticicaxitl, nepapan tlapaltic, aiopaltic, iztac, xoxotla, caxtic pechtic, pechiuhquj: omjtl tlaquaoac.

Eptli:

çan no iehoatl in atzcalli, iehoatl in tapalcaiotl in omjtl, in petlanj, in pepetlaca.

---

14. Corresponding Spanish text: *"tienen conchas gruessas, y pardillas, y la concha de debaxo es blanca."*

15. *Tecciztli:* corresponding Spanish text: *"caracoles de la mar"*; in Ignacio Ancona H. y Rafael Martín del Campo, "Malacología Precortesiana," *Memoria del Congreso Científico Mexicano*, Vol. VII (Mexico, 1953), p. 16, *Strombus gigas.*

16. *Tapachtli: Spondylus* sp. (*ibid.*, p. 12). Corresponding Spanish text: *"las conchas del agua . . . las de los rios, como las de la mar."*

17. *Atzcalli:* in *loc. cit.*, synonym for *tapachtli*, and also *las avaneras de los rios*; in Molina (*Vocabulario*), *ostia de la mar*; in Ancona H. and Martín del Campo, *loc. cit.*, *las conchas Unionidas de los géneros* Unio y Anodonta.

18. Corresponding Spanish text: *"la concha llamase tambien ticicaxitl, porque la usan las medicas para agorear."*

OYSTER

The little oyster just occurs in water, not in the sea. It is small — small and black, dark, smoky, edible.

BITUMEN

It falls out on the ocean shore; it falls out like mud.

¶

FOURTH PARAGRAPH, which telleth of the animals, of the name of each kind, and of the fishes which live in the rivers or in the lagoons.

ARMADILLO[1]

It lives in the forest; it is a forest inhabitant. [The name] is as if to say "gourd-rabbit." It is called *ayotochtli* because its head is just like a rabbit's; the ears are pointed, long; the muzzle stubby. And its hands, its feet are just like a rabbit's. It has a shell; like the turtle it goes enveloped in its shell [in which it goes protecting itself].[2] Its shell is not bone, but rather like scales, very strong, very firm, solid, hard.

IGUANA[3]

It is a forest-dweller, just like a lizard: thick, long — a cubit long, with coarse scales, with rough scales; black, dark, long-tailed. Its food is insects, flies, earth. It is called "tree-lizard" because it lives only on trees. This one is a robust breather: even if for two, three, or even five days it is shut in somewhere, if it eats nothing, it remains alive. For it lies open-mouthed, inhaling air. Thus it remains alive. It is edible.

TEXIXINCOYOTL[4]

Its dwelling is in the crags. It is edible.

TECOUIXIN[5]

It is somewhat like a lizard — thick, full-bodied, thick-bellied, coarse-scaled, thick-scaled, hissing. It hisses; thus it speaks.

MILQUAXOCH[6]

It is like a lizard — long, slender, long-tailed. It is varicolored: green [and yellow stripes] stand along

ATZCALLI:

atzcaltontli, çan cana atlan mochioa, in amo vei apan: tepiton, tliltontli, catzactontli, pochectontli: qualonj.

CHAPOPOTLI:

vei atenco oalhuetzi: iuhqujn çoqujtl oalhuetzi.

¶

INJC NAUJ PARRAPHO: itechpa tlatoa in iolque, in cecentlamantli intoca, yoan mjmjchti: in atoiapan, in anoço atezcapãnemj.

AIOTOCHTLI:

quauhtlanemj, quauhtla chane: iuhqujn qujtoznequj. Aiotl tochin. Injc mjtoa Aiotochi: vel iuhqujn tochin itzontecon, nacazvivitztic, nacazpapatlactic, tentetepontic. Auh in jma, in jicxi: vel iuhqujn tochin, tapalcaio: in jtapalcaio, iuhqujn aiotl itapalcaio onactinemj: amo ma omjtl in jtapalcaio, çan iuhqujn xinacaiotl; çenca chicaoac, çenca oapaoac, tlaquaoac, tepitztic.

QUAUHCUETZPALI:

quauhtla chane, vel iuhqujn cuetzpali: tomaoac, viac, cēmatzopaztli; xincaio chamaoac, xincaio oapaoac, catzaoac, cujcheoac, cuitlapilviac: ioioli, çaiolli, tlalli in jtlaqual. Injc mjtoa quauhcuetzpali: çan quauhtitech in nemj. Inj vel ihio tlapalivi; in manel omjlhujtl, eilhujtl, anoço nel macujlilhujtl, cana tzaqualoz. in atle qujquaz, ca ioltoz: camachalotoc, qujhiioantoc in ehecatl ic ioltoc: qualonj.

TEXÎXINCOIOTL:

texcalco in ichan qualonj.

TECOVIXI:

ach iuhqujn cuetzpalin, tomaoac, tlaque, cujtlatomactic, xincaio chamaoac, xincaio tilaoac, tlanqujqujcini: tlanqujqujci injc tlatoa.

MILQUAXOCH:

iuhqujn cuetzpali, viac, pitzaoac, cujtlapilhujac: mocujcujlo, in jcujtlapan qujquequetz xoxoctic: pai-

---

1. *Ayotochtli*: *Dasypus novemcinctus mexicanus* Peters, in Villa R. ("Mamíferos silvestres"), p. 349.

2. *Acad. Hist. MS* adds *yc momalhuitinemi.*

3. *Quauhcuetzpali*: Martín del Campo, *op. cit.*, p. 380, suggests *ciertas especies de Ctenosaura* or *Iguana iguana rhinolopha.*

4. *Texixincoyotl*: "una lagartija perteneciente a las especies del tecuetzpallin, pero con el cuerpo más delgado y escamoso" (Hernández, *op. cit.*, p. 379). For *texincoyote*, Santamaría, *op. cit.*, p. 1041, has "lagartija más conocida por tecomate (Sceloorus torquatus), reptil saurio."

5. *Tecouixi*: *Sceloporus spinosus* (Martín del Campo, *op. cit.*, p. 381).

6. *Milquaxoch*: *Cnemidophorus sexlineatus gularis* (*loc. cit.*).

its back. It runs lightly; it is a runner. Flies are its food.

TOPOTLI[7]

It is a fish, wide-bellied, big-bellied, dark-bellied. It is a fish of the crags; good-tasting, perfect.

AMILOTL[8]

Also its name is *xouilin*. It is called white *amilotl* [and] white *xouilin*. The *amilotl* is especially understood to be the white *xouilin*; *amilotl* is also especially understood to be the thick fish. The *xouilin* is especially understood to be the thick fish, the dark one. The one called *amilotl* they sell; they eat the especially fattened white *amilotl*.

The *amilotl*, the *xouilin* have eggs. Their food is waterflies and those which are small insects, and *tlalcuitlaxcolli*, and mud. Pools are their homes; underwater caverns, caves, sink holes are their dwelling places. *Amilotonti* are small; they are white. *Xouilton* are small; they are dark.

XALMICHIN:[9] it is small; it is white.

CUITLAPETOTL[10]

It is a big-bellied fish, small and round, stiff-necked, like the *topotli*. Its head is bitter, dark.

MICHÇAQUAN

It means "baby fish." It is a small fish which goes in schools. It is a darter, an agile one. It is agile, it darts, it swims in schools.

THE YAYAUHQUI MICHIN[11] or dark fish lives everywhere.[12]

THE WHITE FISH is small; it breeds in saline water.

MICHTEUHTLI

It means "very small fish," either white or dark. Especially it means "small dried fish."

MICHPICTLI

These are fish cooked on a griddle. They are [wrapped] in [maize] husks.

na, mocxitlaloanj: çaiolin in jtlaqual.

TOPOTLI:

mjchi, cujtlapatlachtic, cujtlatolontic, hite iaiauhquj, texcalmjchi: velic vel tzompatic.

AMJLOTL:

yoan itoca xovili, mjtoa iztac amjlotl, iztac xovili. In amjlotl: oc cenca ipã mocaquj, in iztac xovili: in amjlotl oc no cenca ipan mocaquj in tomaoac mjchi. In xovili oc cenca ipan mocaquj: in tomaoac mjchi, in iaiauhquj: in iuh mjtoa amjlotl in qujnamaca in qujqua in oc cenca conchamaoa. iztac amjlotl in qujqua.

Amjlotl: xovili teteoa. In jtlaqual: axaxaiacatl, yoã in tlein iolcatontli: yoan tlalcujtlaxcolli, yoan çoqujtl: amanalco in innentla, aoztoc, oztoc, acuezcomac in jchan. Amilotontli: tepiton, iztac, xoviltõ, tepiton, iaiauhquj.

XALMJCHI: tepiton, iztac,

CUJTLAPETOTL:

mjchi, cujtlatolontic, ololtontli, quechacquj, iuhqujn topotli: tzonteconchichic, iaiauhquj.

MICHÇAQUAN:

qujtoznequj. mjchconetl; in tepiton mjchi, cuecueionjnj, motlamjnanj, tzitzicujcanj, tzitzicujca, motlamjna, cuecueionj.

IAIAUHQUJ MJCHI: anoço mjchiaiauhquj, can novian in nemj.

IZTAC MJCHI: tepiton, tequjxqujapan in mochioa.

MICHTEUHTLI:

qujtoznequj. mjchin tepitoton: in aço iztac, in aço iaiauhquj: oc tlaquauh qujtoznequj, tepitoton mjchi tlaoatzalli.

MICHPICTLI:

in mjchin comalco tlacuxitl, in izoac catquj.

---

7. *Topotli:* small freshwater fish common in southern Mexico; unident. (Santamaría, *op. cit.,* p. 1073 — *topota, topote*).

8. *Amilotl, xouilin:* Sahagún (Garibay ed.), Vol. IV, pp. 321, 370, has *Chirostoma humboldtianum* for *amilotl,* and *Cyprinus americanus* or *Algansae tincella* C. for *xouilin.*

9. *Xalmichi: Chirostoma humboldtianum* (*ibid.,* p. 368). See also Santamaría, *op. cit.,* p. 627 (*jalmichi*).

10. *Cuitlapetotl:* Sahagún, *op. cit.,* p. 332, reads *cuitlapetlatl,* identified as *Girardinichthys innominatus.* See also Hernández, *op. cit.,* p. 402.

11. *Iaiauhqui:* "la menor de las especies llamadas xohuilin, un pececillo de lago escamoso y negruzco, de donde el nombre" (Hernández, *op. cit.,* p. 395).

12. Read *çan* as in *Acad. Hist. MS.*

MICHTLACECTLI are small fish cooked on a griddle.

MICHTLAXQUITL are *xouilin, amilotl, xalmichin* roasted, cooked on a griddle.

TENTZONMICHIN

— or bearded fish; its name is *texcalmichin*. In rivers, about crags are where it lives — its habitat. It is small and thick, thick-scaled, coarse-scaled, large mouthed, full of bones, savory.

¶

FIFTH PARAGRAPH, which telleth of all the small animals which live in the water: the edible ones.

TADPOLE

It lives in fresh water, among the reeds, the algae, the ducks, the waterlilies. In these algae and among still other things which are in the water, it protects itself. But in places like ponds it dies, dies of cold. Its food is mud and very small water-living insects. It is black, big-bellied, thick-bellied, stiff-necked, streaky-tailed, flat-tailed. It is good-tasting, edible; what one deserves.

FROG[1]

It is black, dark; it has hands, it has feet. It is big-bellied. It is edible. It can be skinned.

TECALATL

This is the very large frog, the mature frog, the old female. It is good, it is edible. The eggs, the off-spring of the frog, of the *tecalatl,* are very many — countless. Black are their eggs, glistening. It is a croaker; it croaks.

ACACUEYATL

It is green, black-spotted, blotched black, speckled. It is long-legged, a jumper, a constant jumper. It jumps; it jumps constantly.

ÇOQUICUEYATL

It is black. When in water which is drying up, it does not go elsewhere; it just enters into the mud. Even if the earth cracks, it does not die; where it is, it is absorbing [moisture]. It is edible.

MICHTLACECTLI: in mjchin tepitoton, in comalco tlacuxitilli.

MICHTLAXQUJTL: in xovili, amilotl, xalmjchi, comalco tlaxqujtl tlacuxitilli.

TENTZONMJCHI:

anoço tentzone mjchi, yoan itoca texcalmjchi: atoiac, texcalla in nemj in jchan, tomactontli, xincaio tilaoac, xincaio oapaoac, camacoiaoac: moca omjtl, velic.

¶

INJC MACUJLLI PARRAPHO: intechpa tlatoa in jxqujch iolcatontli atlan nemj, in qualonjme.

ATEPOCATL:

iec apan in nemj, tulla, acpatitlan, atapalcatitlan, atlacueçonantitlan; itlan momalhuja inin acpatl, yoan in oc cequj atlan onoc. Auh in çan juh ca in atezcapã mjquj; cioapaoa.

In jtlaqual çoqujtl: yoan in tlein ioiolitoton atlan nemj: tliltic, cujtlatolontic, cujtlatomactic, quechacquj, quechtepi, cujtlapiltzatzapal, cujtlapilpatlach: velic, qualonj, tetonal.

CUEIATL:

tliltic, iaiactic, mâmaie, iicxe, cujtlatolontic. qualonj, xipeoalonj.

TECALATL:

in cenca vei cueiatl, in omacic cueiatl, in oilamatic: qualpol, qualtepol. In cueiatl in tecalatl iteuh in ipilhoa cenca mjec, amo çan tlapoalli: tliltique in jteoan, cuecueiochauhticate, cotaloanj, cotaloa.

ACACUEIATL:

xoxoctic, moholcapanj, molchachapatz mocujcujcujlo: xoujujac, choloanj, chôcholoanj: cholooa, chocholooa.

ÇOQUJCUEIATL:

tliltic, in jquac ipan oaquj atl, amo campa iauh: çan çoqujtitlã calaquj, in manel tzatzaianj tlalli, amo mjquj: in vncã ca, tlachiaoatica, qualonj.

---

1. *Cueiatl: Rana esculenta, R. temporaria* (Sahagún, *op. cit.,* p. 331).

AXOLOTL[2]

Like the lizard, it has legs, it has a tail, a wide tail. It is large-mouthed, bearded. It is glistening, well-fleshed, heavily fleshed, meaty. It is boneless — not very bony; good, fine, edible, savory: what one deserves.

ACOCILIN[3]

It is like the shrimp. Its head is like a grasshopper's. It is small, dark; it has legs. But when cooked, it is red, ruddy, hard, firm. It is edible; it can be toasted, it can be cooked. I toast, I cook, I sell *acocilin*.

ANENEZTLI[4]

It is long and small, cylindrical, glistening. It has legs. The head is broad, wide. It is dark, swarthy. It is edible. It is an insect which transforms itself. It turns itself into a *cincocopi*; it becomes a *cincocopi*.

AXAXAYACATL[5] OR QUATECOMATL

It is small and round, small and wide. The mouth is pointed, the head is round. It has legs, it has wings. It is a little ashen. It is a water traveler, a flyer, a swimmer, a diver. It dives, it swims, it flies.

AMOYOTL

It is like a fly, small and round. It has legs, it has wings; it is dry. It goes on the surface of the water; it is a flyer. It buzzes, it sings.

OCUILIZTAC[6]

It is long, small and long, cylindrical, white. It becomes cylindrical, long, white. It darts; it is agile, agitated.

MICHPILI

It is as if to say, "baby fish." It is a very small fish, round, like an *açauatl*. It has legs; it is dark green — red when cooked. It is good-tasting, savory, of good, pleasing odor.
I catch *michpili* in a net, I catch *michpili*; I bake *michpili*, I cook *michpili* in an olla, I eat *michpili*.
Michpili eggs or *amilotl* eggs are round, roundish, like amaranth or *Argemone mexicana* [seed]: white,

AXOLOTL:

iuhqujnma cuetzpali, mamae, cujtlapile, cujtlapil-patlachtic, camacoiaoac, papaoa, tzotlactic, vel nacaio, nacatetic, nanacaio: haomjo, amo cenca omjo; qualli, iectli, qualonj, aviac, tetonal.

ACOCILI:

iuhqujn chacali. In jtzontecon: iuhqujn chapoltzontecomatl, tepiton, iaiactontli, mâmaie. Auh in oicucic tlatlavic: tlatlauhquj, oapaoac, oapactic: qualonj, hiceconj, paoaxonj. Nacocilicequj; nacocilpaoaci, nacocilnamaca.

ANENEZTLI:

melactontli, mjmjltontli, cuêcueio, mamaie: quapatlachtic, quapatlachiuhquj, iaiactic, iaiauhquj: qualonj, mocuepanj; cincocopi mocuepa, cincocopiti.

AXAXAIACATL: ANOÇO QUATECOMATL,

ololtontli, patlachtontli: tenvitzton, quatecontic, mamaie, hatlapale: nextontli, atlan nemjnj, patlanjnj: tlamaneloanj, polaqujnj, polaquj: tlamaneloa, patlanj.

AMOIOTL:

iuhqujn çaioli, ololtontli, mamaie, hatlapale, oacçoltic: atl yixco ietinemj, patlanjnj: qujqujnaca hicaoaca.

OCUJLIZTAC:

melaoac, melactontli, mjmjltic, iztac: mjmjlivi, melaoa, iztaia: motlamjna, molinja, mocuecuetzooa.

MICHPILI:

iuhqujn qujtoznequj, mjchin piltontli, michin cenca tepiton, ololtontli, açaoatic, mâmaie; iaiactõtli in xoxouhquj, tlatlauhquj in icucic: velic, haviac, havixtic, havixpatic.
Nimjchpilmatlavia: nimjchpilaçi, njmjchpilixca, nimjchpilpaoaci, nimjchpilqua.
Michpiltetei: anoço amjlotetl, ololtic, ololauhquj iuhqujn oauhtli, chicalotl, iztac ichio, teteicanj, tetei-

---

2. *Axolotl: Amblystoma tigrinum* L., *Proteus mexicanus, Sideron humboldti* (*ibid.*, p. 323).

3. *Acocili: Cambarellus montezumae* (Santamaría, *op. cit.*, p. 21).

4. *Aneneztli: Larva de libélula* (dragonfly) — Sahagún, *op. cit.*, p. 321.

5. *Axaxayacatl:* defined in Santamaría, *op. cit.*, as *Ephidra californica* Torrey or possibly *Corixa* sp.: see *aguaucle* (p. 42) and *axayacate* (p. 100).

6. *Ocuiliztac:* "gusano de las tierras húmedas, que al tostarse se pone blanco" (*ibid.*, p. 769 — *oculiste*); "*Larva de varios insectos*" (Sahagún, *op. cit.*, p. 347).

like maguey fiber; crunchable, crushable. They become round; they become like maguey fibers. They crush. These are *amilotl* eggs.

Izcauitl[7]

It is slender, small and slender, pointed at both ends; ruddy; alive.

I gather *izcauitl*; I take *izcauitl*; I roast, I cook, I sell *izcauitl*.

Tecuitlatl,[8] acuitlatl, açoquitl, [or] amomoxtli

It is green. It coagulates. When the *açoquitl* wells up, spreads over the surface of the water, congeals there, the water folk take it there. They ball it together, throw it into the canoes, spread it upon ashes.

I am a *tecuitlatl* gatherer; I spread *tecuitlatl*; I pick up, I sell, I roast *tecuitlatl*.

njnj, ololavi, mjchiotia anoço mochiotia, teteinj: inin iteoan in amjlotl.

Izcavitli:

pitzaoac, pitzactontli, necoc iacavitztic, tlatlauhquj, ioioli.

Nizcavicuj, njzcaviana, njzcaviixca, njzcavipaoaci, njzcavinamaca.

Tecujtlatl, acujtlatl, açoqujtl, amomoxtli:

xoxoctic, papachca. In jquac momoloca açoqujtl: atl yixco oalmoteca, vncan tetzaoa: vncã qujcuj, cololoa in atlaca: cacaltema, nexpan qujtoiaoa.

njtecujtlacujnj, njtecujtlatoiaoa, njtecujtlaeoa: njtecujtlanamaca, njtecujtlaixca.

---

7. *Izcauitli: "masa de pequeñisimas lombrices que, capturadas con redes en el lago mexicano y guardadas en amplios recipientes, se venden en los mercados"* (Hernández, *op. cit.*, p. 395).

8. *Tecuitlatl: "Brota el TECUITLATL, que es muy parecido a limo, en algunos sitios del vaso del lago mexicano, y gana al punto la superficie de las aguas de donde se saca o barre con redes o se apila con palas"* (*ibid.*, p. 408). Waterfly eggs adhering to rocks, according to Santamaría, *op. cit.*, p. 1020 (*tecuitate*).

Fourth Chapter, which telleth of still other animals which live in the water, which are inedible.

First paragraph, which telleth of inedible water-living animals.

Crocodile[1]

It is large, thick, high, long, very long, fat-backed. It has arms, legs, tail, a divided tail. Just like a lizard's are its body, its head. It is really big-mouthed, open-mouthed. It is a swallower of things, of people whole, one which attracts people with its breath. It is black, dirty-colored, with a shell. Its shell, its scales are like stones — strong, solid, hard, rubbery, strong, firm, tough. Its flesh is bad, stinking. It attracts things, it attracts people with its breath; it swallows things whole; it puts them in all in one piece. It has not arrived in the sea; it lives only in the rivers.

Acipaquitli[2]

It really lives in the seas; it lives in the ocean, in the midst of the ocean. It is long, thick, thick-bodied. It has arms, it has feet, it has nails; and it has wings, it has a tail. Its tail is jagged, long. Its organ for eating serves as its sword. With it, it strikes. Whatsoever it strikes, it splits, beheads, chops to pieces.

Its food is all the related fish. It strikes things, it strikes people, it cuts things. It swallows things; it swallows people. It fills its mouth, it gorges, it swallows things whole, it constantly swallows things whole. It swallows things whole, grinds them up, pulverizes them.

The otter has been mentioned among the dogs.

Acoyotl

It is a water-dweller, one that really enters the water; a diver. Its dwelling-place is in the water. It appears just like a dog, a coyote, though tawny. Its fur is slippery, smooth, water-repellent, impermeable, not absorbent. It is white-breasted. Still another account of it has been given under the coyote.

Injc nauj capitulo: intechpa tlatoa in oc cequjntin iolque, in atlan nemj in amo qualonj.

Injc ce parrapho: intechpa tlatoa iolque, in amo qualonj atlan nemj.

Acuetzpali:

vei, tomaoac, vecapan, viac, viacapol, cujtlatomacpol, mâmae ihicxe, cujtlapile, cujtlapilxexeltic: vel iuhqujn cuetzpali in jtlac, in jtzontecon: ieh vel camacoiaoac, camaxacaltic, tlapetztoloanj, tepetztoloanj, teihiioananj: tliltic, catzaoac, tapalcaio. In jtapalcaio in jxincaio iuhqujn tetl; chicaoac, tlaquaoac, tepitztic, oltic: chicaoac, tlapaltic, tlalichtic: in jnacaio cocôiac, toquaiac, tlaihiioana, teihiioana, tlapetztoloa, tlacēcalaquja. Amo onaci in vei atl yitic: çã amapan in nemj.

Acipaqujtli:

vel veiapan in nemj, ilhujcaapan, ilhuicaatl yitic in nemj: viac tomaoac, tlactomaoac, mamae, ihicxe, izte; yoan amatlapale, cujtlapile: in jcujtlapil tzitziqujltic, viac, iehoatl itequaia muchioa, imaquauh ipan povi, ic tlavitequj: in tlein qujvitequj, xelivi, tzontequj, tlâcocotonj.

In jtlaqual: mochintin in mjchteiccaoan: tlavitequj, tevitequj, tlatequj, tlatoloa, tetoloa, tlacamatema, tlatlāchiquivia, tlapetztoloa, tlapepetztoloa; tlapetztoloa tlateci, tlacuechooa.

Aitzcujntli: oipan mjto in chichi.

Acoiotl:

atlan chane, vel atlan calaqujni, polaqujnj, atlan inentla: vel iuhqujn chichi, coiotl, injc tlachia, iece quappachtic; in jtomjo alaoac, pepetzca, haqujmatinj in atl, âpaltinj, hâacujnj, eliztac: in oc cequi itlatollo, omjto in jpan coiotl.

---

1. *Acuetzpali: Crocodylus acutus, C. moreletti* in Martín del Campo ("Ensayo," *Anales del Instituto de Biología,* IX, 3–4), p. 391.

2. *Acipaquitli:* Sahagún, Garibay ed., Vol. IV, p. 319: *"Mala lectura de Cipactli"* (*Crocodylus* sp.). In Hernández, *Hist. Natural,* Vol. II, p. 398, it is *"pez que los latinos llaman* serra *y que vive en ambos océanos."*

SECOND PARAGRAPH, which telleth of an animal named *auitzotl,* like a monster as to its body and as to its habits. It lives, makes its home in the water, either in a river or somewhere in a spring.

AUITZOTL[1]

It is very like the *teui,* the small *teui* dog; small and smooth, shiny. It has small, pointed ears, just like a small dog. It is black, like rubber; smooth, slippery, very smooth, long-tailed. And its tail is provided with a hand at the end; just like a human hand is the point of its tail. And its hands are like a raccoon's hands or like a monkey's hands. It lives, it is a dweller in watery caverns, in watery depths.

And if anyone arrives there at its entrance, or there in the water where it is, it then grabs him there. It is said that it sinks him, it plunges him into the water; it carries him to its home, it introduces him to the depths; so its tail goes holding him, so it goes seizing him.

And when it grabs one, so that no one will fall upon it, so that there be fear, it then stirs the water; a tempest spreads; water is tossed up; it foams; it reaches far up; it overflows; large drops form; the foam spreads.

And the fish, the *xoxouilin,* the *amilotl,* and the frogs all emerge. The fish scatter; the frogs, the big frogs go jumping. The drowned one disappears forever.

But sometimes the *auitzotl* or the *tlilcoatl* raises him to the surface. The one it has drowned no longer has his eyes, his teeth, and his nails; it has taken them all from him. But his body is completely unblemished, his skin uninjured. Only his body comes out slippery-wet; as if one had pounded it with a stone; as if it had inflicted small bruises.

And no single other person used to come to take what was there, the drowned one. The priests, the guardians of the gods, took personal charge. It is said that they were clean; for that reason they themselves took hold of him.

For thus were they deluded: they said this drowned one went there to heaven, the place named Tlalocan. There the Tlaloc gods sent him.

Hence they accorded the dead one much honor as they took him. They bore him away upon a litter to bury him at *Ayauhcalco.* They went blowing their flutes for him; they built him a covering of reeds.

AVITZOTL:

vel iuhqujn tevi, in chichiteviton, xixipetztontli, tetzictontli, nacavivitzpil, vel iuhqujn chichiton: tliltic, iuhqujn olli, alaztic, alactic, alazpatic, cujtlapilhueiac. Auh in jcujtlapil quamacpallo: vel iuhqujn tlacamaitl ic ca, icujtlapiliac. Auh in jma: iuhqujn mapachitli ima, anoçe iuhqujn oçomatli ima. Aoztoc, axoxovilco in nemj, in chane:

auh in aqujn vmpa aci in jqujiaoac, in anoço in oncan ca in atlan njman vmpa qujoalana, mjtoa: qujlaquja, qujpolactia, qujvica in jchan: centlani qujcalaquja, ic cantiuh in jcujtlapil ic qujtzitzqujtiuh.

Auh in jcoac qujoalana: injc aiac ipan onvetziz, injc motlamauhtilia: njmã colinja in atl, cocoxontimomana, motompitzoa, poçonj veca ahaci, nonoquj-vi: in jpoçonallo, chachapanj, motlatlalia in poçonallotl.

Auh in mjmjchti: in xoxovilti, in amilome, in cuecueia: vel mjec in oalqujça, tlapapatlaca in mjmjchti, tlachocholivi in cuecueia, in tetecala: iccen iauh in elaqujlo.

Auh inquẽmanian: pani qujoalquetza in avitzotl, in anoço tlilcooatl: in quelaquja aoc tle in ixtelolo, in jtlan, yoan in jzti, omochiqujcujlique: auh njman acã quenami in jnacaio, in ma tlaxoleoalli: çan ie iuhqujn tlatlaqujlatequjli mochioa in jnacaio, iuhquj on in ma aca oqujtetevi in oqujˆqujlpaltix

Auh aiac oc ce tlacatl canatiuh in vmpa icac, in oilaqujloc: vel cõnomaviaia in tlamacazque, in teupixque: qujl amo teuhioque, amo tlaçolloque: ipampa in in noma conana.

Auh injc moztlacaviaia: qujtoaia Inin oelaqujloc: vmpã via in ilhujcac, in jtocaiocan tlalocã vmpa qujtititlanj, in teteu tlaloque.

Ic cenca qujmaviztiliaia injc conanaia, in mjquj: tlapechtica in qujvica qujtocazque, in aiauhcalco: qujtlapichilitivi, qujtolcaltia.

---

1. *Auitzotl: Lutra felina* (Sahagún, *op. cit.,* p. 320; also characterized as *Animal legendario, que reviste caracteres fantásticos*).

But if someone were to dare to try to take the drowned one — perhaps someone of vicious life — it is said that [the *auitzotl*] would also carry him off there; or else a great ailment called the gout would there seize him.

And it was said that the drowned one was good of heart, wherefore they bore him to Tlalocan: or he had cherished a precious green stone, wherefore, it was said, the Tlalocs were angered. For it was said also that precious green stones were their bodies, or their spirits. So for this reason he had been drowned. Yet it was said also that he had gone there to Tlalocan, whither he had been summoned. So once again it was a joy for his kinfolk. They said, "His son hath received favor, for he is gone there to Tlalocan." And these, it was said, would become rich; they gained as reward maize, amaranth, *chia*, etc.

But still behold in what manner they were befuddled. It was said that if one had been drowned, the same would yet also befall still others of his kinfolk. Either they would also be drowned, or a thunder-bolt would strike them, so that they would also go there to heaven, the place called Tlalocan. Hence they were careful not to bathe much.

And the villainy of this little animal! When no one fell into its hands, when it drowned no one, then it drove the fish, the *xoxouilin*, the *amilotl*, the frogs up to the surface. The frogs scattered; they went jumping. And indeed some of the fish, the white fish, cast themselves on dry land. Also the *tlilcoatl* did the same.

And he who possessed a net seemed to become covetous. Thereupon he saw the fish; he fished, he fished contentedly. Then he continued placing the fish in the fold of his cape. This was just the little beast's way of hunting people. Thereupon the water foamed over one; thus one there died, drowned, perished. There it became his memorial — the whirlpool, the torrent.

And behold still another example of the trickery, the method of hunting people, of the *auitzotl*. When it was annoyed — had caught no one, had drowned none of us commoners — then was heard as if a small child wept. And he who heard it thought perhaps a child wept, perhaps a baby, perhaps an abandoned one. Moved by this, he went there to look for it. So there he fell into the hands of the *auitzotl*; there it drowned him.

Auh intla aca tlapalivi: canaznequjz in oelaqujloc, in anoço aca teuhio, tlaçollo: qujl no vmpa qujoalanazque, anoce vmpa qujcujz, vei cocoliztli, in jtoca; cooaciviztli.

Auh in elaqujlo: qujl qualli in jiollo. ic ipampa in vmpa qujvica tlallocan. Auh anoçe qujpia chalchivitl: qujl ic qualanj in tlaloque. Ca qujl noço innacaio, manoçe intonal in chalchivitl: ic ipampa in elaqujlo: tel qujl no vmpa iauh in tlalocan. vmpa tititlano: ic oc ceppa impapaqujliz catca, in teoaniolque: qujtoaia. Ca otlacnopilhuj in jpiltzin: ca vmpa oia in tlalocan. Auh in iehoantin: qujl mocujltonozque, qujl qujmaceoa in tonacaiotl, in oauhtli, in chiẽ. etc.

Auh oc izca: injc motlapololtiaia, qujlmach intla oce oelaqujloc: oc no iuhquj impan mochioaz, in oc cequjntin in joaiolque: aço no elaqujlozque, anoço impã tlatlatzinjz: injc no vmpa iazque in jlhujcac, in jtocaiocan tlalocan: ic çan mjmatcanenca, amo cenca maltiaia.

Auh in jtlavelilocaio: in ioioliton: in jquac aiac imac vetzi, in aiac qujlaquja; njman qujoalpantlaça in mjmjchtin, in xoxovilti, in amjlome, in cuecueia: tlapatlaca, tlachocholivi in cuecueia. Auh nel cequjn tlalhoacpan in motlatlamotlatinemj mjmjchti, in jztac mjchtin: no iuh qujchioa in tlilcooatl.

Auh in aqujn matlaoa: iuhqujn mjhicoltia qujmjtta mjmjchti, njmã ie ic tlatlama: momati, paqujn tlatlama, qujn mocujcujxãtia in mjmjchtin: inin ca çã itetlacaanaia in iolcapil, njmã ie ic ipan poçonj in atl ic vncã mjquj, vncan elaqujlo, vncan popolivi, vncã ipoctlan, yiaiauhtlan mochioa in popoviztli in âtlanonotzalli

Auh izca occentlamãtli: in jtecanecacaiaoaliz, in jtetlacaanaliz in avitzotl: in omoxiuhtlati aiac cana, in aiac qujlaquja timaceoalti, in caco: iuhqujn conetontli choca. Auh in aqujn qujcaquj: in momati aço piltzintli in choca, aço conetzintli: aço netlatlaxililli: ic tlaocoia, vmpa iauh qujttaz: ic vmpa imac onvetzi in avitzotl, vmpa qujlaquja.

He who only saw it, who did nothing to it, the one [the *auitzotl*] did not drown, took it as an omen of evil; it was said he would die. It did not throw him into terror as in the fable; it was only that he was sore afraid, and it blew a little upon him, that he died.

A little old woman seized one; she covered it with her shift. Then she cast it into a water jar; she covered it with water. She carried it before the lords; they looked at it well. Indeed they took the little animal to be a god: it was said it was Tlaloc; it was said it was the priest. Then they commanded the little old woman to leave it there where she had gone to take it. They told the little old woman she had done evil. She said, "In some way it will destroy me. I took only one; I have damaged its spirit; I have taken its power. It drowns people; there are drownings."

¶

THIRD PARAGRAPH, which telleth of a very thick serpent which is in the water.

ACOATL, TLILCOATL[1]

It is a water-dweller; it lies in the mud: cylindrical, thick — a fathom in girth; long, very long, exceedingly long. It is large-headed, big-headed; bearded; black, very black; glistening; fiery-eyed; fork-tailed. In craggy waters, in water caverns [it makes] its dwelling-place. Its food is fish. It is one which attracts people with its breath; it drowns people.

And when it has caught no one, when it has drowned no one, it also hunts people. It digs a small pit at the water's edge; it forms it like a basin. And there in the watery cavern it catches crag fish, the bearded ones, any kind of fish. It removes all; it quickly brings them up in its teeth; it places them in the sandy basin which has been dug. There submerge the fish which it has caught. When first it emerges, bringing them up in its teeth, at the very first it raises itself up perhaps a fathom or two fathoms high. When it comes to the surface, it looks all around, turns about repeatedly, twists its neck repeatedly, looks to one side and the other, looks all around. Then it deposits the fish in the earth basin. Once again it enters the water; once again it submerges; and for a little while it remains submerged.

And someone daring, someone drunk, while the serpent has submerged, then runs up. He takes, he

In aqujn çan qujtta: in amo tle ipan qujchioa, in amo quelaquja; qujmotetzavia, qujl mjqujz. Amo qujtetzavia, in iuhca nenonotzalli: çan ipãpa in cenca momauhtia, yoã achi qujpitza: ic mjquj.

Ca ce tlacatl ilamaton: qujcujtivetz, ivipil ic qujtlapacho: njman apilolco cõtlaz, atl contecac: imjxpan qujvicac in tlatoque, vel qujttaque: ca nel noço qujteumatia in iolcapil, qujlmach tlaloc, qujl tlamacazquj: njman tlanaoatique, oc ceppa vmpa qujcaoato, in vmpa canato ilamatzin: qujlhujque in jlamatzin, in ca otlatlaco, çã qujto: çaço quẽ nechpoloz, ça çe onjcacic onocõtonalitlaco, onocontleiocujli. teelaquja: nelaqujlo.

¶

INJC EI PARRAPHO: itechpa tlatoa, in ce coatl, in atlan ca, cenca tomaoac.

ACOOATL: TLILCOOATL,

atlan chane, çoqujtitlan onoc, mjmjltic, tomaoac, centlacujtlanaoatectli: viac, vitlatztic, vitlatzpatic: quatecõtic, quatenamaztic: papaoa tliltic, tlilpatic, tzotlactic: istletle, cujtlapilmaxaltic: atexcalco, aoztoc in jnẽtla in jtlaqual mjchi, teihioananj, teelaqujanj.

Auh in jquac: aiac cana, in aiac quelaquja; no tetlacaana. tlatataca in atenco, atlacomoltontli qujtlalia, iuhquj apaztli: auh in aoztoc, vmpa qujmonana in texcalmjchtin, in tentzoneque, in çaço tlein mjchi, mochi qujoalqujxtia, q'ntlatlanquativitz: vncan qujnoaltetema in xalapazco, in tlatataco, vmpa polaquj in qujmonaana mjmjchti: in ceppa oalqujça qujntlanquativitz, oc achtopa moquetza; aço cenmatl, anoço vmmatl ipã, in panvetzi, novian tlatlachia momamalacachoa, quequechnecujloa, avic tlachia, nouian tlatlachia: njmã qujmõtema in mjmjchtin in tlalapazco, oc ceppa calaquj in atlã oc ceppa polaqui: auh achi õvecaoa in polaquj.

Auh in aqujn motlapaloanj: in mjvintianj, in opolac cooatl: njmã õmotlaloa qujmonana, qujmocuex-

---

1. *Acoatl, tlilcoatl: Drymarchon corais melanurus* (?) in Martín del Campo, *op. cit.*, p. 382.

gathers up the fish; he puts them in the folds of his cape. As many as he can, so many does he place in the folds of his cape. He loads all upon his back. In a brief moment, during a favorable moment, he will run. Then he takes off with them.

And when the serpent has emerged, then it can see that its fish have indeed been taken. It raises itself up; it rises to run on its tail. It looks about, twists its neck about repeatedly, looks to one side and the other. No matter where this man goes, it can see him. And it smells his footprints, wherever he is headed, wherever he has carried away his fish.

Then it begins to run; it follows him as if flying; it comes out sliding on the grass, on the shrubs. When it goes to reach the one bearing fish on his back, then it coils itself around him; it coils many times about him. And its tail, since it is really forked, it inserts in each of his nostrils, or in his anus. Then the *tlilcoatl* moves;[2] it squeezes the one who had robbed him. He then dies.

But a discreet one, a foresighted one,[3] first digs a hole at the base of a tree. When the serpent pursues him, he quickly hides himself in the tree, and quickly enters, inserts himself into the hole there. And this *tlilcoatl* then wraps itself about the tree; it coils itself many times, it stretches itself well. It stretches so much that it becomes very thin; its spine is broken up. Thus this serpent dies there.

And if someone just finds it or reaches the place where the *tlilcoatl* lies, in order to seize him, this *tlilcoatl* first strikes him. It coils itself well. Then like the shooting of an arrow it extends itself; it quickly straightens itself. And thus its venom comes out; thus it casts it forth: like a rainbow it rises up from its mouth. By it, he whom it hunts is dulled; he becomes just as if drunk. Then it attracts him with its breath. This same man goes toward the poisonous [serpent] — he goes violently dragged, struggling from side to side like a drunkard. He enters the mouth of the poisonous [serpent]. It carries him off; it drowns him.

It follows one, runs, slithers, goes like the wind, flies, coils itself, hisses, blows; it strikes one, attracts one with its breath, drowns one; it swallows things; it swallows one whole; it coils itself.

anoa in mjmjchti: in quexquich veliti, ixqujch qujmocuexanaltia, ixqujch qujmomamaltia: çan tel ixqujch in vel ipan motlaloz, njmā qujmotlalochtia.

Auh in ovalqujz cooatl; njman vel qujtta in caoanoque imjchoan, moquetza, vel icujtlapil ic tlacçatimoquetza: tlatlachia, quequechnecujloa, avic tlachia: in manel canjn ie iauh, vel qujtta: yoan qujnecuj in jcxi, in campa oitztia, in campa oqujvicac imjchoan.

Nimā vmpeoa motlaloa qujtoca iuhqujn patlanj, çacaticpac, tlacoticpac in qujça, in mopetzcoa; in oitechacito in michmama, njmā itech motecuja, vel itech motetecuja. Auh in jcujtlapil: ca nel noço maxaltic, yiacac conahaqujlia, anoço itzinco: njman ie ic molinja in tlilcooatl, qujmecapatzca in oqujchtequjli, oncan mjquj.

Auh in mozcalianj: in tlanemjlianj; achtopa tlatataca in quavitl itzintlan: in ie qujtoca cooatl, qujmotoctitivetzi in quavitl: auh vncan calactivetzi, vncan ōmaqujtivetzi in tlacoiocco. Auh in iehoatl tlilcooatl: njman itech mjcuja in quavitl, vel motetecuja, vel motilinja: injc cenca motilinja vel pitzaoa, cocotoca in jcujtlatetepon; ic oncā mjquj in iehoatl cooatl.

Auh in aca çan qujpantilia: in aço vmpa aci, in oncan canjn onoc tlilcooatl: injc vel cana achtopa qujztlacmjna, in iehoatl tlilcooatl, vel moiaoallalia: njmā iuhqujn tlamjna injc motilinja: melaoatiuetzi. auh in jztlac ic qujça: injc qujtlaça, iuhqujn aiauhcoçamalotl, icamacpa oalmoquetza: ic iolmjquj in aqujn cana, ça iuhqujn tlaoanquj mochioa: njmā qujhiioana, yioma ivicpa iauh in tequanj; mochichicanauhtiuh, chichicoieoatiuh, iuhqujn tlaoanquj icamac calaquj in tequanj; qujvica, qujlaquja:

tetoca, motlaloa, mopetzcoa, hecatoca, patlanj, mocuecueloa, hicoioca, moiehecaiotia, teiztlacmjna, teihiioana, teelaquja: tlatoloa, tepetztoloa, motêcuja.

---

2. *Motolinia* in *Acad. Hist. MS.*
3. *Ibid.* adds *tlâtlama.*

FOURTH PARAGRAPH, which telleth of still other water-dwelling serpents.

ACOATL[1]

It is a water-dweller; the water is its habitat. It is cylindrical, cord-like, slender-tailed, thick-headed, wide-headed. It has scales; it is scaly — thin scaled. Its belly is dark yellow; it is striped in many hues, some yellow, some green, some black, some chili-red.

It is [a serpent] which swallows things whole, which coils, which winds. It winds, it shoots like a dart. Its food, its sustenance, is frogs, reed frogs, green frogs, toads, small frogs, and fish. Whatever small creatures it finds, it swallows.

CITLALAXOLOTL

It is just like the *axolotl*, but the belly is green; only[2] it is flecked with white, it is white-spotted. It frightens one, it terrifies one. It is very slimy. And it has much flesh, like mucus, very slippery, stinking, smelly, evil smelling.

This one's dwelling-place is everywhere; its breeding-place is there where it is damp, and in the mud. And it also lives in water — in the midst of the water. Like the *axolotl* it is spotted, spotted white. On the back, it becomes black; on the belly, green.

CACATL

It is a water-dweller, just like the toad. It is very long-handed, very long-footed; dried out, very dried out; very wrinkled; a loud croaker which makes one's head ache, makes one's ears ring, molests one. Its name is taken from its croak; its croak is endless. It says, *cacaca*. It is a river-dweller. In the forests, the craggy waters, the river pebbles it makes its home.

TOAD[3]

It is round, dirty, dark. Its voice is coarse, rough. It is very fat, very corpulent, big-headed; it has hands, it has feet. It is a jumper. It is lazy. When it travels, it does not go walking on its feet, it only jumps. And as it jumps it does not make a continuous [movement] but only goes by jumps, or jumps only once, remains sitting there, looking, croaking.

From this has come the saying by which is shamed, by which is chidden, one who does not carry a mes-

ACOOATL:

atlan chane, atlã inentla: mjmjltic, mecatic, tzinpitzaoac, quatomaoac, quatepatlachtic: xincaio, xoneoaio, xoneoaio canaoac, helcoziaiactic, tlatlatlapalpovalli injc oaoanquj, cequj coztic, cequj xoxoctic, cequj tliltic, cequj chichiltic in qujmoquequechili:

tlapetztoloanj, motecujanj, mocuecueloanj, mocuecuelova, motlamjna. In jtlaqual: in jnenca, in jiolca cueiatl, acacueiatl, xochcatl, tamaçoli, milcalatl: yoan in mjchi, in tlein iolcatzintli qujtta qujtoloa.

CITLALAXOLOTL:

çan ie vel iehoatl in axolotl, tel hitixoxoctic, can ie iztacacujcujltic, moztacacujcujlo: temamauhti, tecuecuechauh, cenca alaoac auh mjiec nacaio, tzonqualactic, alacpatic, xoqujiac, xoqujialtic, xoqujpototl.

Inin moch novian inentla: in jtlacatia, vncan in tlacuechaoa, yoan in çoqujtitlan: auh no atlan, aitic in nemj: in iuhquj axolotl mocujcujlooa, moztacachachapatza, cujtlapan tlilivi, hitixoxovia.

CACATL:

atlan chane, çan vel no iuhquj in tamaçoli, mavivitlapol, xovivitlapol: oacçolli oacçolpol quapitzpol: vel naoatl tetzõteconeuh, tenacaztititz, teahaman: in jtoca, itlatol itech tlaantli, atlamjnj in jtlatol cacaca, qujtoa: atoiac in nemjnj, quauhtla, texcalapan: atoiatetl in jtlan chãchioa.

TAMAÇOLI:

ololpol, catzacpol, iaiacpol, chachaquachtic, teçontic, in jtlatol: cujtlatolpol, cujtlatolompol, quatecõtic, mamaie, ihicxe, choloanj, tlatziuhquj: in jquac nenemj, amo mamanenemj, çan choloa. Auh injc choloa: amo çan concenquetza, çan chocholotiuh; anoço çã ceppa choloa, vncan eoatica itztica, cujcatica.

Itech oqujz in tlatolli: injc pinavilo inic aio, in avel motititlanj: qujlhuja. Xommotlalo, çã xommotlalo

---

1. *Acoatl: Thamnophis* sp. (Martín del Campo, *loc. cit.*).

2. *Acad. Hist. MS:* çã.

3. *Tamaçoli: Bufo* sp. (Sahagún, *op. cit.*, p. 352).

72

sage. They say to him, "Run, just run! He is like the toad carrying the ruler's message. It jumps once — it remains looking."

Its food is flies, insects, ants, and all the small insects it finds.

MILCALATL[4]

It is something like the toad, but quite small, of average size. As it is rough, so it is called *milcalatl*. It is slender-legged; it is very thin [or] very fat. Its eyes are like jewels.

ivin tamaçoli motecutitlanj: ceppa choloa itztica.

In itlaqual çaioli, ioioli, azcatl: yoan mochi in tlein qujtta ioiolitzin.

MILCALATL:

çan no ach iuhquj in tamaçoli, iece çan tepiton, çan qualli injc chachaquachtic: injc mjtoa mjlcalatl, xopipitzactic, cujtlapicictic, cujtlatolontic: ixmacuex.

---

4. *Milcalatl: see milacatl* (*Bufo* sp.) in *ibid.*, p. 343.

Fifth Chapter, which telleth of the various serpents, and of still other creatures which live on the ground.

Fɪʀsᴛ ᴘᴀʀᴀɢʀᴀᴘʜ, which telleth of a large serpent with rattles.

Tecutlacoçauhqui[1]

It is thick, broad, long. It has rattles, a head, a wide head, a broad head. It is big-mouthed, big-lipped; it has teeth,[2] it has a tongue, a forked, divided tongue. It has scales, thick scales. It is yellow, very yellow, a little yellow, the color of yellow ochre, gourd-blossom yellow; but it is spotted, spotted black, spotted like an ocelot. It has ashen rattles, separated one from another; they are hard. It is a hisser.

Its food is rabbit, hare, bird. It pursues whatever little animal it sees, and although it has teeth, it does not chew it. When it is said that it eats it, it only swallows it whole; later it grinds it up within.

And thus does it hunt: when it finds some little thing, it then swallows it; and if what it wishes to eat is in a difficult place, such as on top of a *nopal,* first it shoots its venom at it. Twice, thrice it casts it at it. Of itself it tumbles down.

A huntsman sees that a squirrel which is on top of a *nopal* chatters much. Then he watches what happens. He sees that twenty spans away lies a *tecutlacoçauhqui.*[3] It coils itself. Then it rears up; it becomes rigid, and something like a rainbow comes forth from its mouth. Then the little animal chatters; when [the serpent] has made the little animal swoon, it falls head first. Then [the serpent] shoots like an arrow; thus it goes to devour the little animal, which lies fallen. Thus [the serpent] there swallows it whole.

And at what it wishes to eat, or when it sees someone, then it rattles its rattles, its sign that it is angry, or glad.

Injc macujlli capitulo: itech tlatoa in nepapan cocoa, yoan oc cequjnti iolque tlalpan nemj.

Iɴᴊᴄ ᴄᴇ ᴘᴀʀʀᴀᴘʜᴏ: itechpa tlatoa çe cooatl, cueche, vei.

Tecutlacoçauhquj:

tomaoac, tomactic, viac, cueche, tzontecome, quapatlachtic, quatepatlachtic, camaxacaltic, tenxacaltic, tlane, nenepile, nenepilmaxaltic, nenepilmaxaliuhquj: xincaio, xincaiochamaoac, coztic cozpatic cozpil tecoçauhtic, aioxochqujltic: auh mocujcujlo. motlilchachapatz, mocelocujcujlo, cuechnexeoac tlatlamantitica, tetecpichtic, tlanqujqujcinj.

In jtlaqual: tochi, citli, tototl, in tlein qujtta iolcatzintli qujcentoca: auh macivi in tlane amo qujquaqua: in mjtoa qujqua. çan qujpetztoloa, qujn hitic qujteci.

Auh injc tlama: in oqujpantili tleintzin niman qujtoloa: auh intla ovican ca, in tlein qujquaznequj: in juhquj nopalticpac, achtopa qujztlacmjna: ontetl etetl qujtlaxilia inoma oalhuetzi.

Ce tlacatl tlamjnquj qujttac: cenca pipitzca in techalotl, nopalticpac in ca: njman qujtemo in tlein muchioa, qujttac cempoalmapan in onoc tecutlacocauhquj moiaiaoallalia: njman ie ic motlamjna, moquappitzoa: auh iuhqujn aiauhcoçamalotl, icamacpa oalqujça: njmã pipitzca in iolcatontli, in oqujçotlauh valmotzonjquetz in iolcatzintli, njman iuhqujn tlamjna: ic iâ injc qujquativetzito, ça movetzititoc in ioiolitzin ic oncan competztolo.

Auh in tlein qujquaznequj; anoço in jquac aca qujtta, njman caiacachoa in jcuech: inezca qualanj anoço papaquj.

---

1. *Tecutlacoçauhqui: Crotalus* sp. (Martín del Campo, "Ensayo," *Anales del Instituto de Biología,* IX, 3–4, p. 383).
2. *Acad. Hist.* MS adds *tlanuitztic, covatlane.*
3. Without cedilla in *Florentine Codex.*

And thus does it live: not just by itself does it live; its mate is there. But they are not in pairs; they stretch out separately. And to speak to each other, they hiss. And when one is killed, although one is dead, the other pursues [the killer]; it goes to strike him.

And its birth date is noted from its rattles; each year, one erupts. And thus it advances, thus it travels: it cannot go on bare ground; it can fly on grass, on shrubs, on anything rough. And it is called *tecutlacoçauhqui* for this reason: it comes from "lord" and "yellow." It is called "yellow lord" because it is said to be the leader of the serpents. And so it is called lord.

It is not one to attack people; it is not an aggressive one. Wherever it is seen, it does not pursue one. When it has been seized, then it becomes angry; then it pursues one.

And when it is taken, in order to be caught, it is beaten with a stick,[4] a willow. And to be speedy, it is caught with fine tobacco. He who wishes to take it rubs fine tobacco in his hands; then also he throws it at [the serpent]. Especially if the fine tobacco enters its mouth, this serpent then stretches out stupefied; it moves no more. Thus he simply takes it up with his hand. This happens with all serpents; they are stupefied by fine tobacco.

He at whom the *tecutlacoçauhqui* or some serpent hisses, it harms; he swells up. And sometimes his neck swells; what is called a cyst appears on his neck.

The fat of the *tecutlacoçauhqui* is a remedy for the gout. Wherever the gout is, there it is anointed with its fat. Its skin is a remedy for a fever; the feverish patient drinks it [ground in water].

Iztac coatl[5]

It is white, long, cylindrical, slender-tailed, thick-headed. It has teeth, it has fangs. The tongue is forked. It is venomous, poisonous. It has rattles, scales, hard scales. It is a slippery one, a flyer — a furious, violent, raging one which flies at one, which chokes one. This *iztac coatl* produces young of not just one sort; many kinds of serpents does it produce. This one is quite rare; in few places, seldom, does it appear.

Tleuacoatl[6]

Its name is *tleua*; it is thick, long; its nature is that of the *iztac coatl*. On its back, it is ashen; its belly is

Auh injc nemj: amo çan icel nemj, onca inamjc: auh amo imomextin onoque, nononqua in temj: auh injc monotza tlanqujqujci auh in jquac ce mjctilo in manel vel omjc ce, in oc ce tetoca, techoponjtiuh.

Auh in jtlacatiliz: itech motta in jcuech, in ce xivitl cētetl qujça; auh injc otlatoca, injc nenemj amo vel iauh in tlalnemjuhian: veli patlanja in çacatl, in tlacotl, in tlein oapaoac. Auh injc mjtoa tecutlacoçauhquj: itech qujça in tecutli, yoan coçauhquj: injc mjtoa tecutlacoçauhquj, quil imachcauh in cocooa: yoan injc mjtoa tecutli,

amo tepeoaltianj, ieh peoaltilonj: in campa itto amo tetoca, in jquac analo: iquac qualanj iquac tetoca.

Auh in jquac mana: injc maci, iehoatl in tlacotl, in ollacotl ic movitequj: auh in çã içiuhca ic maci, iehoatl in picietl: in aqujn canaznequj ic momatiloa in picietl: njmã no ic qujmotla, oc cenca intla icamac calaquj picietl: in iehoatl cooatl njman çotlaoatimoteca, aocmo molinja ic ça imatica conana: mochiuhque in jxqujchti cocoa injc çotlacmjquj in picietl:

in aqujn qujĵpotza in tecutlacoçauhquj in anoço tlein cooatl: qujtlacoa, popoçaoa: yoan quēmanjan ic quechpoçaoa, mjtoa cooatetl iquechtlan qujça:

In jxochio in tecutlacoçauhquj, cooacivizpatli; in canjn onoc cooaciviztli, õcan ommalaoa in jxochio. In jieoaio atonavizpatli, conjz in atonauhquj

Iztac Cooatl:

iztac, viac mjmjltic, tzinpitzaoac quatomaoac tlane, cooatlane, nenepilmaxaltic: iztlaque, tenqualaque, cueche, xincaio, tapalcaio, mopetzcooanj, patlanjnj, tlavele, qualane, iellele, tepan patlanjnj, tequechmatiloanj. Inin iztac coatl: amo ça ceccan icac in qujnchioa, mjec tlamantin in cocooa qujnchioa. Inin çan tlaçonemj, çan canjn, çan quēman in neci.

Tleoâcooatl:

itoca tleoâ, tomaoac, melactic, çan no iuhquj in jeliz iztac cooatl, in jhiio, nexeoac, in jcujtlapan elchi-

---

4. *Acad. Hist.* MS adds *tetlacotl.*
5. *Iztac coatl: Crotalus* sp. (Martín del Campo, *loc. cit.*).
6. *Tleoâcoatl: Crotalus* sp. (*ibid.*, p. 384).

chili-red, ruddy; its tail is ruddy. It is a slitherer; wherever it slithers, it flies[7] over the grass, it goes erect, it just goes erect on its tail. It blows much. It is uncontrollable. It is named *tleua* because whomever it bites, his body feels as if it burns. There is no longer any escape; he dies.

¶

SECOND PARAGRAPH, which telleth of a very large serpent with rattles.

CHIAUITL OR CHIAUHCOATL[1]

It is thick, long; it has a [large] head, a tail, rattles, scales, thick scales; venom, poison. It is ashen, ash-colored; on its back it is spotted with black; spotted. It is a terrifying one, a poisonous one; one that strikes one,[2] spies on one, watches one on the road. Especially it spies upon one early in the morning, stretched out by the side of the road. But first it tests how far it must spring, how far it must slither; that far it departs from the road. And it makes a test on some small stone, shrub, small tree; it strikes it. Twice, thrice it flies at it, as it quickly strikes it. As if on a man it does this practicing, before a traveler comes, so that it no longer misses when it strikes him, for there has already been a time of testing.

In summer this *chiauitl* bites one. Especially in the early morning is it deadly, because it is especially filled with venom. But when it is already daytime, or already afternoon, it is said, its pain is less.

And when it bites one, one swells up, one becomes very hot. Something like water comes out where it has bitten one. It is called *chiauitl* because [where it bites one][3] it produces matter; it drips like a spray. And when it has swelled, if his snake bite is not somehow treated, he dies of it. But if his hand or foot is bitten, even if it is yet cured, it dries up, it shrivels; it sometimes falls off, breaks off.

And the cure for snakebite is to suck it at once. And many lines are slashed on the surface of the snake bite where it has proceeded to swell. And where he has been bitten is spread over, wrapped with a thin maguey fiber cloth. [Then] it is stretched over live coals and rubbed with fine tobacco.

The *chiauitl* serpent slithers, coils, shakes its rattles, rattles its rattles, buzzes, whistles, bites one, strikes

chiltic, eltlatlauhquj, tzintlatlauhquj: mopetzcoanj, in campa mopetzcoa çacaticpac, patlanj, moquetztiuh çan jcujtlapil inic tlacçatiuh, cenca iehecaio: njmã atlamati. Injc moteneoa tleoa: in aquin qujqua iuhqujn tlatla inacaio, in qujmati: njman aocmo qujçaz mjquj.

¶

INJC VME PARRAPHO: itechpa tlatoa ce cooatl, cenca vei, cueche

CHIAVITL: ANOÇO CHIAUHCOOATL,

tomaoac, viac, tzontecome, cujtlapile: cueche, xincaio, xincaio chamaoac, iztlaque, tenqualaque: nextic, nexeoac, molchachapatz: in jcujtlapan mocujcujlo, temauhti, tequanj, techopinjanj, motepachivianj, tehuchianj: oc cenca iquac in iooatzinco, injc motepachivia: otenco in moteca. Auh achtopa moieiecoa in quexqujch ic choloz, in quexqujch ic mopetzcoz: ixqujch ic qujtlalcavia in vtli. Auh itla tetontli: tlacotl, quauhtontli in jtech moieiecoa qujchoponja: vppa, expa ipan oalpatlanj, in qujchoponjtivetzi: iuhqujnma tlacatl ipã qujchioa, aoc tleica in ie vitz nenenquj ic aocmo qujneoa in qujchoponja, ca ie tlaieiecolpã:

In xopantla tequa inj chiavitl, oc cenca iquac in iooatzĩco: mjcoanj, ipampa oc cenca iztlactentica: auh in ie tlaca, anoço ie teutlac qujl ie elelçeuhquj.

Auh injc tequa: poçaoa, vel mjtonja: iuhqujn atl qujça, in canjn tequa: ic mjtoa in chiavitl, cenca chiaoa, vel chichipica iuhqujn aoachiaoa: auh in opoçaoac, intlaca quemmacho in jcooaqualocauh ic mjquj: auh intla ça oc pati, intla ima, anoço icxiqualo: oaquj, totopochvaquj, in quẽman valvetzi, cotonj.

Auh in jpaio tecooaqualiztli: njman iciuhca mochichina, yoan moxoxotla in pani poçaoatiuh, tecoaqualli: yoã motemjlia, meciotica moqujmjlhuia in jcooaqualocauh, tlexochpan moteca: yoan picietica momatiloa.

In cooatl chiavitl: mopetzcoa, mocuecueloa, mocuechichaiatza, mocuechaiacachoa: çaçaoaca, tlanquj-

7. *Acad. Hist. MS* adds ỹ *tlalnemiuhya patlani.*
1. *Chiauitl: Crotalus triseriatus triseriatus* (Martín del Campo, *loc. cit.*).
2. *Acad. Hist. MS: techoponiani.*
3. *Ibid.: yn canĩ tequa* is added.

things, strikes one; it uses venom, it uses venom on one, it forces venom out. It swallows, it swallows whole. Whatever it eats — perhaps it swallows a rabbit — it first strikes, it first wounds, so that it will no more resist, so that it will no more struggle. [Thereupon it calmly lies swallowing it.] [4]

This one lives, breeds everywhere. In the forest, in craggy mountains, in grassy mountains, among reeds it makes its nest, bears its young, lays [eggs].

Olcoatl[5]

Also it is called *tlilcoatl*. It is as thick as the *tecutlacoçauhqui*; ruddy-mouthed, black — very black, like rubber; yellow-bellied; a poisonous one, deadly when it bites one. This one lives in forests, among the crags.

Tlilcoatl

It lives in the water. It has been told of in the Eighth Paragraph.

Çolcoatl[6]

It is of average size, of moderate size, not very thick, not very long. It is spotted just like a quail. The belly is white, the mouth yellow. And it is really harmful, a deadly one when it bites one, extremely treacherous. And it is indeed a mocker; it mocks some people, also the quail, for it is really called "quail serpent."

When it is hungry, it calls the quail; it sings like a quail; it sings very softly. Then the quail go toward it — they think it is a friend who calls them. There they continue falling into its mouth.

And the indiscreet one, when he hears a quail which lies singing, goes there toward it. It bites him, strikes him. He dies of it.

But when the discreet one hears it, if just one whistles, if no [quail] answers it, and if it whistles only in one place, if it is not moving, he [knows] it is the *çolcoatl*. Therefore he avoids it.

It hisses, sings like a quail, flies, becomes spotted, is spotted like a quail.

¶

Third paragraph, which telleth of a two-headed serpent.

---

qujci, tequa, tlachoponja, techoponja: tetenqualacvia, tetech motenqualacvia, motenqualacqujxtia: tlatoloa, tlapetztoloa, in tlein qujqua, in aço tochin in qujtoloa: injc aocmo momapatla, injc aocmo mocuecuetzoa; achtopa qujchoponja, achtopa qujcocoltia.

Inj: çan novian in nemj, in tlacati: quauhtla tepetla texcalla, tepepa, çacatla, tulla motapaçoltia: mjxivi tlatema.

Vlcooatl:

yoan mjtoa tlilcooatl, injc tomaoac iuhqujn tecutlacoçauhquj: tentlatlauhquj, tliltic, vel tliltic iuhqujn olli, elcoztic: tequanj, mjcoanj injc tequa: inin quauhtla, texcalla in nemj.

Tlilcooatl:

in atlan nemj, omjto in jpan ic chicuei parrapho.

Çolcooatl:

çan qualton, çã vel ipan, amo cenca tomaoac, amo no cenca veiac: vel çolcujcujltic, eliztac, tencoztic. Auh vel ihiio: mjcoanj injc tequa, njman atequjxti: auh vel teca mocaiaoanj, inca mocaiaoa in aqujque, yoã in çoçolti; ca nel noço mjtoa çolcooatl.

In jquac maiana: qujnnotza in çoçolti in iuh tlatoa çoçolti vel ivin tlatoa: njman ivicpa vitze in çoçolti, in momati ca icnjuh in qujnotza vmpa icamac onvetztimanj.

Auh in amozcalianj: in oqujcac çolin in tlatotoc, ivicpa iauh vmpa qujqua qujchoponja ic mjquj.

Auh in mozcalia qujcaquj: intla çan ie cen tlanqujqujci, intlacaiac can qujnãqujlia. yoã intla çan ie cecnj tlanqujqujci, intlacamo hutlatoca: ca iehoatl in çolcooatl, ic qujtlalcavia:

tlãqujqujci, çollatoa, patlanj, cujcujlivi, moçolcujcujloa.

¶

Injc ei parrapho: itechpa tlatoa ce cooatl vntetl itzontecon.

---

4. *Ibid.: inic ça yvian quitolotoc* is added.

5. *Olcoatl:* Sahagún (Garibay ed.), Vol. IV, p. 367 — *ulcoatl;* Santamaría, *op. cit.,* p. 1099 — *ulcoate:* unident.

6. *Çolcoatl: Trymorphodon biscutatus* or *Agkistrodon bilineatus* (Martín del Campo, *loc. cit.*).

MAQUIZCOATL

[Its name] comes from *maquiztli*, which is to say *macuextli*, and *coatl*. It is as if to say "bracelet snake." This serpent is also named *tetzauhcoatl*.

This snake has a head at each end, and also a mouth at each end. It has teeth, it has eyes, it has tongues at each end. It is not apparent [if these are really in its mouth (or)]¹ in its tail. And it is not long; it is of average size. And it is painted: four black [stripes] are on its back. And [the stripes] are chili-red on its left side, and yellow on its right side.

And since it is really provided with a head at each end, it can go nowhere when it is seen. To travel, it just stretches itself out; to go along its way, it just runs on both ends.

And it is called *tetzauhcoatl* because it rarely appears — only once in awhile; and it appears in few places.

And thus did they delude themselves when they regarded it as an omen; for this reason was it called a serpent of omen. Then one who saw it made an armlet of it for himself. It was said that if he were about to die it would very peaceably be content on his arm. That is, he had come to reach his time to die; his time had come to an end. But it is said that no one would die when he made of it an armlet for himself [and] it was not content on his arm; it was not enough, as if it were not long [enough]; it is a little serpent. So they called it a serpent of omen. It is not poisonous. This is all about the so-called *tetzauhcoatl*.

Hence, those who go stirring up trouble, who gossip, are named *maquizcoatl*; because it is as if he spoke falsely, was a tale-bearer, like an evil omen.

MAÇACOATL²

It is very big, very thick, dark. It has rattles, it has horns. Its horns are just like the horns of a forest deer. It lies in inaccessible places, in the crags. When mature, it only lies somewhere, where they travel the road. When it eats the rabbit, the deer, the bird, it just lies attracting them with its breath.

MAÇACOATL³

It is black, thick, without rattles, toothless. It is one which can be tamed, raised, bred — bred for its flesh; it is edible. It is bred for its flesh; it is eaten.

MAQUJZCOOATL:

itech qujça maqujztli, qujtoznequj: macuextli, yoan cooatl: iuhqujn qujtoznequj, macuexcooatl: inin cooatl no itoca tetzauhcooatl.

Inin cooatl necoc tzontecome, auh no necoc camaie. tlatlane, ihixtelolooa necoc campa: necoc nenepile, amo neci in cãpa icujtlapilco: auh amo veiac, çan tepiton: auh injc mochichiuh, navi in jcujtlapan tliltic: auh in jopochcopa chichiltic, auh in jieccan coztic.

Auh ca nel noço necoc tzontecome: acampa vel iauh in jquac itto. injc nenemj çan motitioana, injc vtlatoca çan necoc motlaloa.

Auh injc mjtoa tetzauhcooatl: ca aic cenca neci, çã quenmanja: auh çan canjn neci.

Auh injc moztlacaviaia: in qujmotetzaviaia, injc mjtoa tetzauhcooatl: njmã conanaia in aqujn qujtta, cõmomacuextia: qujlmach intla ie mjqujz, cẽcan tlamach ommonamjquj in ima: qujtoznequj, oacico in jmjqujzpan, otlan in jcaviuh. Auh in qujlmach aiac uel mjqujz: in cõmomacuextia, amo õmonamjquj in jma, amo oneoa iuhqujn macamo veiac: cooatontli; ic qujtocaiotia tetzauhcooatl, amo tequanj çaçan ie ixqujch in qujlmach tetzauhcooatl.

Ic motocaiotia: in tetzalan; in tenepantla motecatinemj in tetlatolçaçaca: maqujzcooatl, ipampa iuhqujnma necoc tlatoa, necoc tene, iuhqujn tetzavitl.

MAÇACOOOATL:

cenca vei, cenca tomaoac, cujcheoac, cueche; quaquave: in jquaquauh, vel iuhqujn quauhtla maçatl iquaquauh: ovican, texcalco in onoc. In jquac omacic, ça onoc acampa vtlatoca: in qujqua tochin, maçatl, tototl çan qujhioantoc.

MAÇACOOATL

tliltic, tomaoac, amo cueche, amo tlane: tlacaciuhquj, nemjtilonj, vapaoalonj, nacaoapaoalonj, qualonj, monacaoapaoa qualo.

---

1. *Acad. Hist. MS* adds *ye nelli camac.*
2. *Maçacoatl: Crotalus cerastes,* or other *Crotalus* sp., suggested by Martín del Campo, *op. cit.,* p. 385.
3. *Maçacoatl: Constrictor constrictor mexicana* (*loc. cit.*).

FOURTH PARAGRAPH, which telleth of still other serpents; of the names of still other kinds.

MAÇACOATL

It is small, horned, blackish; not poisonous; without rattles. They who are much given to women, in order to produce semen, just scrape and drink it [in water]; they just capture the eye of two [or] three women they are about to meet. He who drinks too much continually erects his virile member and constantly ejects his semen, and dies of lasciviousness.

TLALMAÇACOATL

It lives in the hot lands. It is called *tzompilacauaztli*. It is small and black, small and glistening, slippery. It has a shell, a sea-shell. It is called *tlalmaçacoatl* because it dwells everywhere in the maize fields; and from deer, because it has small horns. This one appears when it rains. As it goes about, when it emerges, there it goes exuding as it were a varnish liquid, like glue. He who drinks this [in an infusion], if he drinks much of it, also dies of lasciviousness, and his moisture ends. So he will die; he will finally sicken because of it.

TETZAUHCOATL[1]

It is not very large, not very thick nor very long.[2] And on its belly and neck it is very ruddy, like a live coal.

And it is named, it is called *tetzauhcoatl* because in few places is it seen, and also few people see it. He who sees it is much terrified; because of it he dies of fright, or he becomes very sick. For that reason they give it the name *tetzauhcoatl*.

TLAPAPALCOATL[3]

It is not very large, only of average size. And it is named *tlapapalcoatl* because on it are indeed all colors; it is striped with them; they run from one end to the other. It is somewhat like [the one] called *miauacoatl*. It is rare.

COAPETLATL OR PETLACOATL[4]

This is not a single one; serpents are assembled, gathered, much as if they were made into a reed mat, on which is a serpent seat — or else it is separate. And

MAÇACOOATL:

tepiton quaquave, catzactontli: amo tequanj, amo cueche: iehoatl injc momeialtia in aqujque cenca cioanequjnj, çan conjchiquj in conj, çan imjxtlama in vme ei cioatl qujnamjqujz in aq'n ommotototza in conj, çan çẽ tlaquauhtilia, yoan çan cenqujzticac in jxinach, yoã ioiommjquj.

TLALMAÇACOOATL:

in tonaian nemj, itoca: tzumpilacaoaztli, tliltontli, tzotlactontli, alactontli cacallo atecocollo. Injc mjtoa tlalmaçacooatl: ca çan novian, in mjlpan nemj: auh injc maçatl itech onca, ca quaquauhtone. Inin iquac neci in qujavi. injc nenemj, in vncan qujça iuhqujn tiçaaiotl, iuhqujnma tzacutli qujnoqujtiuh. In aqujn qujz y: intla mjec quj, no ioiommjquj, yoan aiotlamj: ic mjqujz, iccẽ ic cocolizqujz.

TETZAUHCOOATL:

amo cenca vei, amo cenca tomaoac, amo no cenca viac: auh in jelpan, yoan in jquechtlan, cenca tlatlauhquj; iuhqujn tlexochtli.

Auh ic mjtoa: ic motocaiotia tetzauhcooatl, cenca çã canjn neci: auh cenca çan no aca in qujtta. In aqujn qujtta: cenca momauhtia, ic mauhcamjquj; anoce cenca cocoia: ic contocaiotique tetzauhcooatl.

TLAPAPALCOOATL:

amo cenca vei, çan qualton. Auh injc mjtoa tlapapalcooatl: vel ixqujch itech ca in tlapalli, ic movavavan. qujmoquequechili: ach iuhqujn mjtoa, mjiaoacooatl, çan tlaçonemi.

COOAPETLATL: ANOÇO PETLACOOATL.

Inin amo çan ce: mocẽtlalia, monechicoa in cocooa: vel iuhqujn mopetlachioa, ipan ca cooaicpalli, anoço nonqua ca. Auh injc iauh: injc nenemj, çan avic

---

1. *Tetzauhcoatl: Diadophis regalis (loc. cit.)*.
2. *Acad. Hist. MS* adds: *auh tliltic in icuitlapan* — and black on its back.
3. *Tlapapalcoatl*: Martín del Campo suggests various *Lampropeltis* sp. (*op. cit.*, p. 386).
4. Possibly *un acoplamiento colectivo* (*loc. cit.*).

it goes, it travels, in this way: it runs back and forth; it runs in all directions, because the serpents' heads lie in all directions making the border of the serpent mat. Thus it runs in all directions; it goes back and forth. And on it goes the serpent seat; it goes rocking.

Whoever sees it, if ingenious, if advised, has no fear; he quickly seats himself on it; as if on a reed mat he seats himself. And the serpent seat upon which he seats himself is as if it were a seat belonging to him. Either the serpent mat still remains flat or he bends it a little. He rides upon the seat; he goes making the serpent seat his seat. Then the serpents break apart; there is flight; they travel in every direction.

When he did this, two things came to mind. First, it was said it was his omen that already he would die or something dangerous would befall him. Second, it was said that he would then merit, then attain lordship, rulership as a reward. It was said he would be a lord, he would become a ruler: this because he had quickly seated himself upon the serpent mat.

Coapetlatl[5]

It is of average size, not large nor wide. It is a little like a [sheet of] paper. Its head is as if at one corner of the mat, and at the other end is its tail. As it travels, it is as if someone dragged a mat. It just runs back and forth. It lives in few places; and only few see it.

Chimalcoatl or coachimalli[6]

This is really a serpent — long, thick. It has head, tail, rattles. And for this reason is it called, is it named *chimalcoatl*: on its back its very body is round, painted to look like a shield. This one is rare.

When the foolish one sees it, they say, it is his omen that he is about to die or that some danger will befall him. But the one who is advised is glad when he sees it. It is said that then he gains merit: he merits the eagle mat, the ocelot mat; it is said that he merits the estate of ruling general, of general.

Citlalcoatl[7]

Its name, alternatively, is *citlalin imiuh*. It is green and painted like a star. In few places and very seldom does it appear — is it seen. Nevertheless, it is poison-

motlaloa, çan noviampa motlaloa: ipampa ca in jtzontecon cocooa noviampa iten mochiuhtoc in cooapetlatl: ic çan noviampa motlaloa aviccampa iauh: auh in jpã ietiuh cooaicpalli, momjmjlotiuh.

In aqujn qujtta: in iolizmatquj, in nenonotzale: amo qujmacaci, ipã ommotlalitivetzi, iuhqujnma petlapan ommotlalia: auh in cooaicpalli, ipã ommotlalia, iuhqujnma icpalli ipan qujpoa: aço oc moteca in cooapetlatl, anoço achi qujtoctia: ipan ietiuh, qujmocpaltitiuh in cooaicpalli: njman xitinj in cocooa netlatlalolo, çaço ac ie cãpa itztiuh.

In juh qujchioaia y, vntlamantli in qujlnamjquja. Injc centlamantli: qujl itetzauh ie mjqujz, anoçe itla ovi ipan mochioaz. Injc ontlamantli: qujl vncan qujmomacevia, vncã qujcnopilhuja in tecuiotl in tlatocaiotl: qujl tecutiz: tlatocatiz: ic ipampa, in jpã ommotlalitivetzi in cooapetlatl.

Cooapetlatl:

çan qualton amo vei, amo no patlaoac, ach iuhqujn ce amatl. In jtzontecon: centlapal petlanacazcon ca, auh oc no centlapal in jcujtlapil: injc nenemj, iuhqujnma aca petlatl qujvilana, çan avic motlaloa: inin çan canjn nemj, auh çã aca in qujtta.

Chimalcooatl: anoço cooachimalli

inin nelli cooatl, viac, tomaoac, tzontecome, cujtlapile, cueche. Auh injc mjtoa: injc moteneoa chimalcooatl, in jcujtlapan manj iaoaltic, vel inacaio, tlatlacujlolli: vel iuh neci in chimalli. Inin çan tlaçonemj: in aqujnmamatcaoa qujtta, qujtoa: ca itetzauh, ca ie mjqujz, anoço itla ovi ipan mochioaz. Auh in nonotzale: qujcnelilmati in qujtta, qujlmach vncan tlamaçeoa, qujlmach qujmaceoa in quappetlatl, in ocelopetlatl; qujl qujmaceoa in tlacatecaiotl in tlacochcalcaiotl.

Citlalcooatl:

anoço itoca citlalin imjuh, xoxoctic, auh citlalcujcujltic: cencan canjn, yoan çan cencã quemã in neci, in jtto: auh tel tequanj, vel temamauhti: in aquj̄ quj-

---

5. *Coapetlatl*: "puede tratarse de las culebras que, aplanando su cuerpo, lo extienden lateralmente aplicándolo contra el suelo, o que ensanchan su región cervical del mismo modo que se observa en las Naja" (*loc. cit.*).

6. *Chimalcoatl*: Crotalus sp. (*loc. cit.*).

7. *Citlalcoatl, citlalin imjuh*: Drymobius margaritiferus (*loc. cit.*)

ous,[8] truly terrifying. He whom it bites, [whenever it bites him,][9] then always goes off to die as dawn nears, when the morning star appears. It is said that it shoots an arrow into him; really, the *citlalcoatl* has bitten him.

And especially do the Chichimeca watch for the *citlalcoatl*, because it lies in dangerous places in the crags. And the snake-bitten one they surround with medicine. The Chichimeca encircle him with arrows, and they expect that when the morning star appears, that is when he will die or will improve. But if he follows the star a little, if it goes still farther, the snake-bitten one will not die; he will recover. Especially if it has dawned, if the light shines on him, the patient will recover.

METLAPILCOATL[10]

It is thick, cylindrical; when seen from afar it is not apparent where its mouth is. At both ends it is like a mano; at both ends it is pointed; it is just like something smoky,[11] dark. As it travels, it slithers, and sometimes it only rolls like a mano. Yet it is not poisonous, not harmful. It lives especially there in the Totonac region.

¶

FIFTH PARAGRAPH, which telleth of a thick serpent.

AUEYACTLI[1]

It is very big, thick, like a beam perhaps ten cubits long. It has rattles, teeth, fangs. It is slick, smooth, slippery, smoky, dark like the *tlilcoatl*. The belly is smoky-yellow, the nose-tip ruddy. It is poisonous. There is no cure for it if it bites one; it is fatal. It lives in the hot lands. In very many places and often is it seen in Totonac country.

It bites one, it strikes one; it completely envelops things, it swallows them whole. It awaits one on the road, it blocks the road to one. Wherever there is a single opening, there it stretches out — it stretches out blocking the road. It stretches out along it, or diagonally across it; it stretches out crossing the way so that none may pass, or so that there it may bite one. And if there is flight, if there is departure from its presence, it pursues one, it flies at one.

quâ, qujn çen iquac mjqujtiuh in ie tlatvinaoac, in jquac oalcholoa citlalin: qujl qujmjna, canoço citlalcooatl in oqujqua.

Auh ca tlaquauh iehoan qujtta: in chichimeca in citlalcooatl: ipampa ca ovican, texcalla in onoc. Auh injc qujpaiaoalochtia in ocooaqualoc: in iehoantin chichimeca, qujiaoalochtia in mjtl: auh tlatemachia in jquac oalcholova citlalin, ca oncã in mjqujz, in anoço caxaoaz. Auh intla ie achi qujtoca citlali: intla ie veca iauh, patiz amo mjqujz in tlacooaqualli: oc cenca intla oc otlatvili, intla oipan tlanez: ca patiz in cocoxquj.

METLAPILCOOATL:

tomaoac, mjmjltic: in veca motta amo neci in campa ie icamac, çan necoc iuhqujn metlapilli, in çan necoc vitztic. Vel iuhqujn pechtic, iaiactic: injc vtlatoca mopetzcoa, auh in quẽman çan momjmjloa iuhqujnma metlapilli: tel amo tequanj, atle itlatlacul: oc cenca vmpa nemj in totonacapan.

¶

INJC MACUJLLI PARRAPHO: ce cooatl itechpa tlatoa. tomaoac.

AVEIACTLI:

cenca vei tomaoac iuhqujn ce vepantli, aço quen matlacmatl injc viac, cueche, tlane, cooatlane: alaoac, alactic, petzcauhquj, pochectic, iaiauhquj, motlilcooanenequj, elpoccoztic, iacatzollatlauhquj, tequanj: aoc tle ipaio inic tequa, mjcoanj: tonaiã tlalpan in nemj, oc cenca mjeccã, yoan mjecpa itto in totonacapan:

tequa, techoponja, tlacẽcalaquja, tlapetztoloa, tevchia tevtzaqua: in canjn çan yiocan vel qujxova, vncan oalmoteca, qujtzacutimoteca in hutli, qujtocatimoteca, anoce ixtlapal moteca, qujviltectimoteca, injc aocac vel qujça: anoço injc vncan tequatoz. Auh intla netlalolo: intla ixpampa eoalo, tetoca, tepã patlanj:

---

8. *Acad. Hist. MS: vel.*

9. *Ibid.: In çaçe quẽmã quiqua is added.*

10. *Metlapilcoatl: Bothrops nummifera* (or possibly *Dermophis mexicanus*); Martín del Campo, *op. cit.,* p. 387.

11. *Acad. Hist. MS: pochectic.*

1. *Aueiactli: Crotalus durissus durissus* (Martín del Campo, *loc. cit.*).

But in order that it will not fly at one, in order that it will not destroy, he wraps up fine tobacco in paper; he throws it at [the serpent]. Or else he fills small jars [with fine tobacco] to throw the small jars at it so that the small jars suddenly burst, and the fine tobacco suddenly scatters. Thus [the serpent] stretches out enfeebled. Then he puts on the end of a stick a paper, a rag, well provided with fine tobacco; he inserts it in its mouth, so that it then does nothing more. He there captures it; he kills it.

And it lies in water caverns, in crags, in canyons. There it lies eating, enjoying, swallowing, swallowing whole the small animals.

PALANCACOATL[2]

It is of average size, about like the *tecutlacoçauhqui*. It is smoky. And it is called *palancacoatl* because it stinks, and its body looks as if it were full of sores, as if it lay mouldering. On it lie flies swarming. And wherever it travels the road, there it goes stinking; with it the flies go swarming, they go along buzzing. And it is indeed a *palancacoatl*: whomever it bites no more escapes; it has no cure, so that he dies, he is consumed by the suppuration.

HECACOATL OR HECAUA[3]

It is of average size, not very[4] thick. It is long; when mature it is four [or] three fathoms. It is yellow, chili-red, green, white, which run along its back; it is striped with them. It is not poisonous; only when it is made angry, or when it hunts, it just coils itself about one, crushes one, or chokes one.

It is called *hecacoatl* because when it travels it raises itself erect. On level land, it goes standing on the end of its tail; it is as if it went flying along. And when it emerges on grasses, on bushes, when it goes there, it is as if a narrow current of air emerged.

TZOALCOATL

It is of average size and not very long. It has no rattles, no teeth. It is smoky, dark. One really names it *tzoalcoatl* [because] it is as black as amaranth seed dough. Also it is inoffensive, not poisonous; an ordinary serpent, a stupid little snake, a very useless little snake — harmless, ...

auh injc amo tepan patlanjz, injc amo tlaixpoloz: amatica qujqujmjloa in picietl, ic qujmomotla: anoço contotõco qujtema, ic cõmotla in cõtontli, injc njmã tlapantivetzi in contontli. auh no cemmantivetzi in picietl, ic çotlaoatimoteca: njman quavitl iquac qujtlalia, amatl, tzotzomatli vel picieio, icamac caquja, ic çan njman aoc tle qujchioa: vncan conana qujmjctia.

Auh aoztoc: texcalco, axoxovilco in onoc: vncan qujquatoc, qujpalotoc, qujntotolotoc, qujnpetztolotoc in iolcatzitzinti.

PALANCACOOATL:

çan ipan qualli, achi ixqujch in tecutlacoçauhquj pochectic. Auh inic mjtoa palancacooatl hiiac: auh injc neci, in jnacaio, vel iuhqujnma papalanj, iuhqujnma xoxolocatoc, vncan onoc çaiolooatoc: auh in campa otlatoca vmpa hiiaxtiuh, cololhujtivi in çaiolti, qujcaoatztivi: auh ca nel noço palancacooatl, in aqujn qujqua, aocmo qujça, ça aoc tle ipaio: injc mjquj vellantiuh in palanj.

IECACOOATL: ANOÇO IECAOA

çan ipan qualli, amo cen tomaoac, ie viac, in omacic nãmatl, ematl: coztic, chichiltic, xoxoctic, iztac in qujmoquequechili icujtlapan, injc movavavã, amo tequani: çan in jquac qualanjlo, anoço in tlama, çã tetech motecuja, temecapatzca, anoço tequechmateloa.

Inic mjtoa hecacooatl: in jquac otlatoca moquetzteoa, in tlalnemjuhian moquetztiuh, çã icujtlapil injc tlacçatiuh; iuhqujnma patlantiuh. Auh in çacatla, in tlacutla, çan icpac in qujça, in iauh: auh in vncã iauh, iuhqujn hecapitzactli qujça.

TZOOALCOOATL:

çan qualton, amo no cenca viac, amo cueche, amo no tlane: pochtic, iaiactic; ac mach noço qujtocaioti in tzooalcooatl, iuhqujn tzooalli ic tliltic: ano tle itlatlacul, amo tequanj çaça ie cooatl: cooaxolopitzintli, çaçan molhuj cooatzintli: aiellele, aieltzoio.

---

2. *Palancacoatl*: Bothrops atrox (*ibid.*, p. 388).

3. *Hecacoatl*: probably *Masticophis taeniatus taeniatus* (*loc. cit.*).

4. *Acad. Hist. MS: cēca.*

SIXTH PARAGRAPH, which telleth of all the large serpents; of the names of each one.

CINCOATL OR CENCOATL[1]

It is of average size. It is like the poisonous serpent, the *chiauitl*. It has no rattles, nor is it poisonous. It is painted yellow, ruddy, dark; it resembles the *tecutlacoçauhqui*. It is broad-headed, big-mouthed, large-mouthed; not a bearer of young but an egg-layer, an egg-producer, a hatcher, a nest-maker. It is one which coils about one; not poisonous, just a striker; one which swallows things whole. It has no poison, no venom. It strikes, swallows, swallows whole, coils itself about one.

Thus does it kill: once a coyote was seen seated on the grass by the edge of the road, its face very much swollen; it had protruded its eyes. And a traveler came upon it. It was beckoning to him with its paw; like a man was this coyote. Then the traveler went toward it and saw that a *cincoatl* was coiled about its neck and its legs; it protruded from its flank. Thus [the serpent] could kill it. Then the traveler took a stick; he repeatedly beat the serpent with it. Then the *cincoatl* uncoiled and fell to the ground, whereupon the coyote fled. Later the coyote paid its debt well, for it gave many birds to this warrior who had saved it.

QUATZONCOATL

It is quite slender, just like a hair.[2] And it travels in this manner: it just goes forming itself into a bracelet, forming itself into a ball. Like a discarded hair, like one which is pulled out, it travels little by little. And this one is rare; seldom and in few places is it seen.

MECACOATL[3]

The *mecacoatl* is as thick as our thumb, but it is not known how long, because where it is seen it cannot be followed to where it ends. It is seen there in the hot lands. No one can follow it to where it ends, because it lies emerging from the crags, the narrow places, the forests; it really emerges from underground.

TETZMOLCOATL[4]

It is as large as the *cincoatl*. It is herb-green; also spotted. It is really hateful, furious; one which pur-

SIXTH PARAGRAPH: INJC CHIQUACEN PARRAPHO: intechpa tlatoa, in ixqujchtin cocoa veveintin, in cecentetl intoca

CINCOOATL: ANOÇO CENCOOATL

çã ipan qualli ixquich in tequanj cooatl in chiauitl, amo cueche, amo no tequanj: coztic, tlatlactic, iaiactic injc mocujcujcujlo, motecutlacoçauhcanenequj: quatepatlachtic, camaxacal, camaxacaltic: amo mjxivinj, çan tlatlaçanj, motetianj, tlatlapananj, motapaçoltianj: tetech motecujanj, amo tequanj, çan tlachoponjanj, tlapetztoloanj, amo tẽqualaque, amo iztlaque: tlachoponja, tlatoloa, tlapetztoloa, tetech motecuja.

Injc tlamjctia: ceppa ittoc çacatla, vtenco ieoatica in coiotl; omach ixtomaoac, opanj qujtlatlali in jxtelo. Auh in nenenquj ipan qujçato: qujoalmanotztica, iuhqujnma tlacatl in iehoatl coiotl: njman ivicpa ia in nenequj. Auh qujttac oiquechtlan motecujx in cincooatl, yoan imapan. oiciacacpa qujqujz, ic vel conmjctia: niman tlacotl qujcujc in nenenquj, ic qujvivitec in cooatl: njman oalchapantivẽtz in cincooatl, ic motlalo in coiotl: çatepan vel tlaxtlauh in coiotl, ca mjec in qujmacac totoli in iehoatl tiacauh in qujmomaqujxtili.

QUATZONCOOATL:

vel pitzaoac, vel iuhqujnma tzontli: auh injc nenemj çan momacujxtinemi, çan molollalitinemj: in juh tlalilo quatzontli, in iuh mopia; ivin nenemj. Auh inin çan tlaçonemj; çan iqujn auh çan canjn itto.

MECACOOATL:

injc tomaoac mecacooatl, ixqujch in toveimapil: auh amo vel macho in quexqujch veiac. Ipampa in canjn itto: ca amo vel icxitoco in canjn tlantoc. vmpa in itto: tonaian tlalpan, ca aiac vel qujcxitoca in canjn tlamj: ipampa ca texcalla ca cujllotla, ca quauhtla in qujztoc: nel tlallan in qujça.

TETZMOLCOOATL:

injc vei ixqujch in cincooatl, qujltic, no cujcujltic: vel iellele, tlavele, tetocanj, tepan patlanj, tequechma-

---

1. *Cincoatl: Pituophis deppei* (Martín del Campo, *op. cit.,* p. 388).
2. *Acad. Hist. MS: quatzõtli.*
3. *Mecacoatl: Leptophis mexicanus* (Martín del Campo, *op. cit.,* p. 389).
4. *Tetzmolcoatl: tesmulcoate* (unident.) — Santamaría, *op. cit.,* p. 1039.

sues people, which flies at one, which chokes one. It is named *tetzmolcoatl* because the person or thing about which it coils itself, it never more lets go until it kills it. And it is very strong, very wiry.

QUETZALCOATL

Often it is seen in the Totonac country. It is of average size, about the size of the water serpent, or only an arm, some a cubit [long]. It is called, it is given the name *quetzalcoatl* because the flesh on its back is just like precious feathers. Also the base [of the feather] is blackish, and that which forms its shaft is just like the shaft of a quetzal feather, blackish. These protrude along its spine. And what forms the quill is quite green. It lies already along its side as if heaped up or colored. And on its neck they are like Mexican trogon feathers, and its tail, its rattles, are like lovely cotinga feathers; and on its belly they are quite chili-red.

But nowhere can it be seen where it is, nor what it eats. As soon as it appears, it bites one, it strikes one. And he whom it strikes dies suddenly; it is not an hour when he dies — only a very little time. And in order to bite one, first it flies, quite high up; well up it goes; and it just descends upon whom or what it bites. And when it flies or descends, a great wind blows. Wherever it goes, it flies. And when it bites one, it also dies at the same time, it is said, because all at once its poison, its venom, is used up; for in truth its seat of life is wherewith it strikes one. No longer can it bury its fangs; and also this little serpent falls there.

¶

SEVENTH PARAGRAPH, which telleth of the large serpents and of the names of each kind.

XICALCOATL[1]

It is named for *xicalli* and *coatl*. Some are large, some small; they are water-dwellers. They say of the large serpent that something like a large gourd bowl lies upon its back; and of the still small one that something like a small gourd bowl lies upon its back. And this gourd bowl: the coloring with which it is painted is part of it. It is well painted; it is intricately designed,[2] like ear pendants.

This serpent's organ for hunting people is like a gourd bowl. When it wishes to hunt, it extends itself

teloanj. Injc mjtoa tetzmolcooatl in aqujn, anoço in tlein itech motecuja, nimã aoc vel qujcaoa; ixqujchica in qujmjctiz, yoan çenca chicaoac, çẽca ichtic.

QUETZALCOOATL:

mjecpa vmpa itto in totonacapan, çan qualton, çan ixqujch in acooatl, anoço çan çen ciacatl, cequj çemmitl. Injc mjtoa: in motocaiotia quetzalcooatl, in inacaio, in jcujtlapan vel iuhquj in quetzalli, no tzintlileoac: auh in jquauhio mochioa, vel iuhquj in jquauhio quetzalli, in tlilectic, icujtlatetepon qujtocaticac. Auh in quetzalomjtl mochioa: vel xoxouhquj: ie cuel yiomotlã in onoc, in ma iuhquj peiaoatoc, in manoçe poiaoatoc. Auh in jquechtlan: iuhqujn tzinitzcan: auh in jcujtlapil: in jcuech, iuhqujn xiuhtototl; auh in jelpan: vel chichiltic;

auh acan vel itto, in canjn onoc: auh no tlein qujqua, çã iquac neci in tequa, in jquac techoponja. Auh in aqujn qujchoponja: çan njmã mjctivetzi, amo vel ce ora in mjquj. çan vel achitonca: auh injc tequa. achtopa palanj, vel tlacpac, vel aco in iauh: auh çan ipan oaltemo in aqujn in noço tlein qujqua. Auh inic patlanj: in manoçe ic oaltemo, cenca ieheca: in quexquich ic nemj, injc patlantinemj. Auh in jquac tequa: njmã no iquac mjquj, qujl ipãpa: çan njmã mochi tlamj in itenqualac, in jztlac: ca nel noço iehoatl in jiolca, in canjn techoponja, aocmo achi contoca in choponjlonj: auh no vncan vetzi inin cooatontli

¶

INJC CHICOME PARRAPHO: intechpa tlatoa cooame, veveintin: auh cecẽtlamãtli intoca.

XICALCOOATL:

xicalli itech mjtoa, yoan cooatl cequj vei, cequj tepiton; atlan chane; qujtoa: inic vei cooatl, iuhqujn vei xicalpechtli icujtlapan manj. Auh in oc piltontli: iuhqujn xicaltontli, icujtlapan manj. Auh inin xicalli: vel itech cenqujzca ca in tlapalli, injc tlacujcujlolli, vel cujcujltic, tlamomoxôtolti cujcujlchampochtic.

Inin cooatl: vel itetlacaanaia, iuhqujn xicalli: in jquac tlamaznequj, pani valmoteca, iece amo monex-

---

1. *Xicalcoatl:* unident. watersnake (Santamaría, *op. cit.,* p. 633; *jicalcoate*).
2. *Acad. Hist. MS: tlamomoxoltic.*

along the surface [of the water]; however, it shows nothing of itself except the gourd bowl which is upon its back, which it places on the surface. Indeed it makes it desirable, as if it were going carried by the water, intricately designed. And an ignorant one with avarice, with covetousness, considers that it has been shown to him, and that he merits a very good gourd bowl; then he descends into the water. When he wishes to take it, it only goes drifting away; he goes to follow it there; little by little it makes him reach for it in the depths of the water. Thereupon the water churns up; it foams over him so that there he dies.

Some say the serpent is black; only its back is intricately designed like a gourd vessel; it is its body.

Miauacoatl[3]

It is somewhat like the *hecacoatl*, though of average size; but it is also similarly striped. It has no special attributes; it is not venomous, not harmful.

Petzcoatl

It is small and black; an ordinary little snake, small and slick, scaleless, like the *tzoalcoatl*. It has no special attributes; it is harmless; it just travels about.

Coaatatapayolli

One kind is only a massing together of serpents. Sometimes all are massed together, rounded together, gathered into a ball. Nowhere does its tail appear; only its head goes showing. They become rounded. And when this *coatatapayolli* goes, it just goes rolling. These[4] serpents are, however, frequent.

And when someone pursues them, or strikes them, or startles them, they take fright, they scatter, they take cover. For they are serpents.

Another kind of *coatatapayolli* is of such a nature, is so born as to be round. And they call it *olcoatl*. [Its name] comes from *olli* because it is round, [and black]; then *coatl*, because it has its head and its tail. From its middle come its head and its tail. And serpent-like are its head and its tail.

Petlaçolcoatl[5]

Its name comes from *petlaçolli* and *coatl*, because it is almost like a serpent. And it is called *petlaçolli*

tia çannjo in xicalli in jcujtlapan mani in panj qujoalmana: nelli vel tetlanecti, iuhqujn aatocotinemj, vellamomoxoltic. Auh in aqujmamatcaoa: in jicol in jztlaccomoc, in momati ca oqujmottili: auh ca oqujcnopilhuj, in cenca qualli xicalli, njman ontemo in atlan: in qujcujznequj çan mjquanjtiuh, vmpa qujtocatiuh, çan iuh nenti, in avecatlan caxitia: njman ie ic ipan poçonj in atl, quaqualaca; ic vncã mjquj.

cequjntin qujtoa: in cooatl tliltic, çanjo in tlamomoxoltic in jcujtlapan, iuhqujn xicalli, ca inacaio.

Miaoacooatl:

achi iuhqujn hecacooatl; iece çan qualton iece no ivin movavan: atle itequjuh, aellele, aeltzoio.

Petzcooatl:

tliltontli, çaçã ie cooatontli, xixipetzpil, amo xincaio, iuhqujn tzooalcooatl atle itequjuh, ano tle itlatlacul çan monenemjtia.

Cooatatapaiolli:

injc centlamantli, çan innecentlalil in cocoa, in quenmanjan mocentlalia, vel molollalia, motatapaiollalia: acan neci in jcujtlapil, çanio in jtzontecon vel neztiuh: vel ololtique in mochioa. Auh in jquac iauh y, cooatapaiolli, çan momjmjlotiuh: achca tel noço iehoantin in cocooa.

Auh in aqujn qujntoca anoço qujnvitequj, anoço qujnmauhtia: cenca mavi, momoiaoa, tlacacalaquj ca nel noço cocooa.

In oc centlamantli cooatapaiolli: çan iuh iol, çã iuh tlacat, çan ololtic: yoan qujtocaiotia olcooatl, itech qujztica olli: ipampa ololtic, njmã ie cooatl: ipampa vnca itzontecon, yoan icujtlapil, çan itlacotia in qujzquj itzontecon, yoã icujtlapil: auh iuhqujn cooatl itzontecon yoan icujtlapil.

Petlaçolcooatl:

itech qujça in itoca petlaçolli, yoan cooatl: ipãpa ca achiuhquj in cooatl. Auh injc mjtoa petlaçolli: ipam-

---

3. *Miauacoatl: miaguacual* (unident.) in Santamaría, *op. cit.*, p. 723.

4. *Acad. Hist. MS* appears to add *y vih* after *iehoantin*.

5. *Petlaçolcoatl*: centipede (Santamaría, *op. cit.*, p. 839: *petaçolcoate*).

because it is wide and very many are its legs — 400, they say — like a straw mat, one whose edges are frayed; which has many of its rolled edges coming out. They are taken for its legs. Also it is called *petlaçolcoatl* because it breeds very prolifically there in the rubbish, in the dried maize stalks, in the roots of dried maize stalks; also especially there where it becomes wet, in the humid places.

This *petlaçolcoatl* is wide, wide-headed; it has teeth; it has antennae. And it is not very large; it is said to be a span in size. And some are white, some yellow, some ruddy, some black or dark, some herb-green, etc. And as it bites someone, it is also an inflicter of pain, though not deadly. Nevertheless, it is said that their poison implants suppuration. In order to alleviate, when a *petlaçolcoatl* bites one, there is sucking, there is pricking with an obsidian point.

———

All serpents, [if] we still omit the *coatapayolli* and the *coapetlatl*, are cylindrical, straight, long; they have tails, they have heads; they are broad-headed, open-mouthed, deep-mouthed. They are biters, swallowers of things whole, slitherers, twisters, winders . . . , rattlers, hissers. Some have rattles, some not; they have scales, hard scales; a few have no scales. They coil themselves about one, they frighten one; they have venom, they have poison. The serpent is one that shoots venom into one; it bites one, envenoms one, poisons one, slays one, strangles one, coils itself about one. The remedy for serpent bite: it is sucked, it is pricked with an obsidian point; a sweat bath is taken; fine tobacco is applied, etc.

¶

EIGHTH PARAGRAPH, which telleth of the manner of life of a number of small insects.

SCORPION

It is stubby. Some are ashen, some whitish, some green; there are various scorpions. Four are its arms, four are its feet. It has small horns; the tail is forked. The one which lives in the hot country hurts one a good deal when it bites one; in two days, in three days [the pain] abates. The one which lives in the cool country, the one called *tlaçolcolotl*, is of no great moment when it bites one; quickly [the pain] abates. In order to abate [the pain of] a scorpion bite, it is sucked, it is rubbed with fine tobacco.

pa in patlachtic, yoan cenca mjec in jma: qujtoa, centzontli: in juhquj petlatl, petlaçolli tēxitinj, ca cenca mjec in qujqujztiuh, itenpapaçoliuhca: ipan ommota in jma, oc no ic motocaiotia petlaçolcooatl: ca cenca tlaquauh vncã tlacati in tlaçoltitlan, in ovaquauhtitlan, in ooaquauhtetepõtitlan: oc cenca no vncan in canjn tlaciava, in tlacuechaoaian.

Inin petlaçolcooatl; patlachtic, quapatlachtic, tlane, quaquauhtone: auh amo cenca vei, in vei mjtoa cemjztitl: auh cequj iztac, cequj coztic, cequj tlatlauhquj, cequj tliltic, anoçe tlilectic, cequj quiltic. etc. Auh injc tequa: no toneoanj, tel amo mjcoanj: iece qujl palanaliztli qujtlalia in jtēqualac: injc pati injc tequa, in petlaçolcooatl, mochichina, mjtzavavia.

———

In jxqujch cooatl: oc ticcaoa in cooatapaiolli, yoã in cooapetlatl, ca mjmjltic, melaoac, viac cujtlapile, tzontecome, quapatlachtic, camaxacaltic, camacoiaoac: tlachoponjanj, tlapetztoloanj, mopetzcoanj, mocuelooanj, mocuecuelooanj, moxtlananj hizaoacanj, çaçaoacanj: cequjntin cuecheque, cequj amo: xincaioque, tapalcaioque, çan quezqujn in amo xincaioque: motecujianj, temauhti, iztlaque, tenqualaque: in cooatl teiztlacmjnanj, tequa, teiztlacvia, tetenqualacvia, temjctia, tequechmateloa, tetech motecuja: In jpaio tecooaqualiztli: mochichina, mjtzaoavia, motema, mopicievia. etc.

¶

INJC CHICUEI PARRAPHO: intechpa tlatoa in cequjntin ioiolitoton in quenamj in jieliz.

COLOTL:

tetepontontli, cequj nextic, cequj iztaleoac, cequj xoxouhquj: nepapan in colotl, navi in jma, navi in jcxi, quaquauhtone, cujtlapilmaxaltic: in tlatotonian nemj, vel tecoco injc tequa: omjlhujtl, eilhujtl in cevi: in tlaitztiaian nemj, in motocaiotia tlaçolcolotl: çan qualli injc tequa, can iciuhca cevi: injc cevi in tecoloqualiztli, mochichina, mopiciexaqualova.

Poisonous spider

Also they call it *tzintlatlauhqui*. It is small and round, black, quite black. It is called *tzintlatlauhqui* because it is chili-red on its abdomen. And its web is very white, very soft, like feather down. It is an egg-layer; it envelops its eggs in spider-web; it suspends them. They are very many, much like *corixa* water-fly eggs.

The venom of some which live in the hot country is fatal. But some are not fatal. But the bite of the spider which lives in the cool country is worse than [that of] the *chiauhcoatl*. When it bites one, it hurts one much; it makes one suffer much. In two days, in three days it abates a little. But so much does it hurt that it increases [pain] even of the blow we gave our head somewhere long ago. It increases the stumbling where we struck ourselves, where we tripped. It increases; all rises. The spider-bitten one indeed thrashes, hurls himself about; his body becomes all covered with matter,[1] so much does the spider's poison rise [to the surface]. Indeed, one's heart burns, one suffers pain. In order to alleviate, they massage him, they repeatedly press and quickly suck [the spider bite], and they bathe him. And many drink wine if breathing is difficult. In three days, in four days it leaves him, it will abate a little.

The venom of this spider really makes us suffer. However, those afflicted by pustules place it there wherever their pustules are, thereby curing, although only on the surface. Then the gouty one anoints himself with it, with *axin*, with lampblack; for it alleviates it.

This spider dwells there in the hot country like the so-called *tlalomitl* [worm]. He whom it stings [will no longer escape; he will die].[2] And [the bite] will just fill up with matter, it will just go on oozing from where it stung him. And much do his heart, his body burn. He will go about crying out, as if continually burned. There is no cure for it.

Tocamaxaqualli

It is round, with long arms. It is hairy; it has an ugly, round head. It is an ordinary insect, harmless. Only in the summer does it go about, and when it goes about, as it goes on its way, it just wanders aimlessly; it keeps running here and there.

Tequanj Tocatl:

yoan qujtocaiotia tzintlatlauhquj, ololtontli, vel capotztic, vel tliltic. Auh injc mjtoa tzintlatlauhquj: chichiltic in jtzintlan, auh in jtzaoal vel iztac, vel iamāquj: iuhqujn tlachcaiotl. Motetianj: in jteoan qujntocatzaoalqujmjloa, qujmpiloa: vel iuhqujn aoauhtetl, vel mjec.

In tlatotoian nemj: cequj mjcoanj in jtenqualac, auh in cequj amo mjcooanj: yoan in tlaitztiaian nemj tocatl, injc tequa qujpanavia in chiauhcooatl: ic tequa cenca tecoco, cenca teihiioti: omjlhujtl, eilhujtl in achi cevi: Auh injc cenca tecoco: mochi queoa, intlanel ie vecauh, cana titoquatzotzonque; mochi queoa in netepotlamjlli, in canjn titovitecque, in titotecujnjque: mochi queeoa mochi panvetzi: vel motlatlamotla, momamaiavi in tocaqualo, vel mochi chiaoa in jnacaio, injc panvetzi in tocatenqualactli: vel tlatla in jiollo, vel toneoa. Injc mopalevia: qujpapachoa, ipan motlatlalia: yoan iciuhca qujchichinjlia, yoan qujtema, yoan mjec in quj octli: in cēca ihiio eilhujtl, navilhujtl in qujcaoaz, in achi ceviz.

Inin tocatl: vel teihiioti in jtēqualac, iece in nanaoati; ca vncā contlatlalilia, in canjn ca inanaoauh, ic pati, iece çan panj: njman ie iehoatl in cooaciviztli, axio, tlillo, ic momatiloa: ca qujcevia.

Inin tocatl: vmpā nemj in tlatotonia, iuhqujn mjtoa tlalomjtl: in aqujn qujmjnaz, auh çan chiavaca tlamjz, çan ixicatoz in vncā qujmjna: auh cenca tlatlaz in jiollo, in jnacaio: vel tzatzitoz, vel iuhqujnma tlecujcujlolo: aoc tle ipaio.

Tocamaxaqualli:

ololtic, mavivitlapol, totomjo, quatecōpol: çacan ie ioioli, atle itequjuh: çan yio xopan in nemj, auh injc nemj, injc vtlatoca çan ixtotomaoa, avic motlatlaloa.

---

1. *Acad. Hist. MS: iuhq'n mitonia, iuhqui auahpixavi in inacayo* is added.

2. *Ibid.: aocmo quiçaz miquiz* is added.

BEDBUG

It is small and flat; the head is small and flat. It has arms, it has legs. It is a biter of people, with a mouth which produces itching. It raises welts on one; it annoys one; it bites one, sucks one, raises welts on one.

CALTATAPACH

It is a little ashen, small and flat, winged. Of two kinds are its wings: the part above is like sherds; below, it is soft. This is its flying part.

When it bites one, its mouth makes one itch; it raises welts on one. Its dwelling places, its breeding places are in house cracks, in rubbishy places, in damp places. It comes out especially when it is already the hot season, when the rains have already come. When it sees a torch, when it sees a fire, there it casts itself.

PINAUIZTLI

[Its name] comes from "I am ashamed," or "I shame someone." It means "the shaming of one." Thus the people of olden times named it when they saw it. They said, "I have seen that the insect reveals to me that something shameful, afflicting will befall me. Now I must act carefully." Some said, "Dost thou know what will happen, thou little insect? Shall I perhaps in some way perish?" He killed it. If one were appreciative of it, he said to it, "Thou hast shown me favor. Hast thou made thyself humane?" Then it buzzed him.

This little insect is ruddy; also it has a slight bite, but is not poisonous; it is not venomous.

¶

NINTH PARAGRAPH, in which the ways of the ants are told.

ANT

The ant of whatsoever kind has a small, reed-like neck;[1] a small, round abdomen; arms, legs, antennae. It is a stinger. It is, as we say, a biter; it has poison, it has venom. It is one which builds a nest for itself, builds a home for itself, makes an underground house for itself, hunts its food. It is a carrier, a transporter, a storer of things. It is a wood-dragger, a dragger of things. It carries, it drags wood; it hides things for itself; it hides things, hunts food, gnaws things, makes itself a nest, forms itself a mound, forms itself a sandy

---

TEXCAN:

patlachpil, quapatlachpil, mâmae, ihicxe, tequanj, tenquequexqujc, tetapalo teaman: tequa, tepachichina, tetapaloa.

CALTATAPACH:

nextontli, patlachtontli, amatlapale: ontlamantli in jatlapal, cecnj panj ca tapalcatic, in tlanj ca iamanquj; iehoatl ipatlanja.

Injc tequa: tenquequexqujc, tetapalo: calcamac, tlaçoltitlan, tlacuechaoaian in inentla, in jtlacatian: oc cēca iquac panvetzi in ie tlatotonja, in ie vitz qujavitl: in qujtta ocutl, in qujtta tletl vmpa ommotlaça.

PINAVIZTLI:

itech qujça in njpinaoa, anoço njtepinauhtia: qujtoznequj, tepinauhtiliztli: injc qujtocaiotique, in jquac qujttaia ie vecauh tlaca: qujtovaia. Onjqujttac in ioioliton ca nechtlalvia itla nopan mochioaz tepinauhti, tetolinj in axcan ma oc nõnjmattinemj, In aca qujtoaia. Cujx teticmati in tiioioliton: ma çaço quē njpoliviz, conmjctia, in aca qujtlaçocamati: qujlhuja. otinechmocnelili: cujx timotlacaiocoia, njmā cõquatlatzinja.

Inin ioioliton: tlatlactontli, no tequacapil, tel amo iztlaque, amo tēqualaque.

¶

INJC CHICUNAVI PARRAPHO: itechpa mjtoa in quēamjque azcame.

AZCATL:

in çaço tlein azcatl quechtacapitzpil, cujtlaololpil, mamae, iicxe, quaquave, temjnanj: in tiqujtoa tequa, tenqualaque, iztlaque, mocaltiani, mochantianj, motlalancaltianj, motlaiecultianj, tlaçacanj, tlaçaçacanj, motlatlatilianj: vepananj, tlavilananj, tlaçaca, vepana, motlatlatilia, tlatlatia, motlaiecultia; tlaquaqua, mocaltia, motlatiltia moxaltiloltia, mopotzaltia, mazcapotzaltia: mopotza, tequa: azcatl tequa, tetoneoa, teiztlacvia, tetenqualacvia: motetia mopilhoatia.

---

1. *Acad. Hist. MS: tzintacapitzpil* is added.

mound, forms itself a hill, forms itself an anthill; it makes a hill; it bites one. The ant which bites one torments one, injects one with poison, injects one with venom. It lays eggs, it produces young.

RED ANT OR ANT OF RED ABDOMEN

It is somewhat average in size, a little firm, a little hard, ruddy. It has a heap of sand, a mound of sand, a hill. It sweeps, makes itself sand heaps, makes wide roads, makes roads, makes itself a home. It is the worst one to bite. If it bites the foot, [the effect] extends to the groin; if it bites the hand, it extends to the armpit; it swells.

LONE ANT

It is a little large. It exceeds the red [ant in redness]. It is of very intense color, a little chili-red. And it is as if ruddy-fuzzed. It is without special qualities; it just goes about. It is called "lone ant" because it goes about only alone; it does not go about in pairs, nor in threes, like the other ants. Yet many, in many places, are seen, are met traveling separately.

TREE ANT

It is named from *quauitl* [tree] and *azcatl* [ant] because it lives on trees, on rotten wood, where it breeds. And in size it exceeds, it compares with the red ant. It is very long and straight; the arms are very long. It is thin. Some are black, some pale, some a little ruddy. When mature, they are also stingers, also venomous, also like the red ant, also something like the lone ant.

DUNG ANT

It is named from *cuitlatl* [dung] and *azcatl* [ant] because it smells of dung. Some of these are a little ashen, [some] brown, some dark yellow. They breed there in maguey pith, in dung, in rubbish. Also they cling when they bite one; also they torment one. And not just a few travel; very many travel; they travel in a swarm. And as they travel along their way, they go in good order, in procession, in a wide stream, or only in single file.

BLACK ANT

It is also called *tzicatl*. These live in cold lands. They are very small; they breed underground, in maguey pith. And also they are rather inclined to bite one. And when it is summer, its young are dug

TLATLAUHQUJ AZCATL, ANOÇO TZINTLATLAUHQUJ AZCATL,

achi qualton, chicactontli, vapactontli, tlatlauhquj, xaltilole, xallatile, potzale: motlachpanja, moxallatiltia, mochpantia, moôquechilia, mochãtlalia. tachcauh injc tequa: in tocxic tequa, toquexilco maanalotia; in tomac tequa tociacac mahallotia, tlatlaolloloa.

ICEL AZCATL:

achi vei, qujpanavia in tlatlauhquj, cenca icucic, achi chichiltic: auh iuhqujn tlatlactomjo, atle itequjuh, çan monenemjtia: inic mjtoa icel azcatl, çan icel in nenemj, amo vntemãtinemj, amo no ieheteietinemj, iuhqujn oc cequjn azcame, tel mjequjn, mjeccan itto, namjco, cenmãtinemj.

QUAUHAZCATL:

itech mjtoa quavitl, yoan azcatl: ipãpa quauhtitech, quauhpalanitech ioli, in tlacati: auh inic vei qujpanavi, qujnenevili in tlatlavic azcatl, melacpol, mavivitlapol, cocolopol: cequj tliltique, cequj iztaleoaque, cequj achi tlatlauhque, in ochicaoaque: no tequanj, no iztlaque, no iuhqujn tlatlavic azcatl, çan vel no iuhquj in jcel azcatl.

CUJTLAAZCATL:

itech mjtoa in cujtlatl, yoan azcatl: ipampan cujtlaiac, inj cequj achi nextique, camiltique, cequj coziaiactique: vncan tlacati in metzonco, in cujtlatitlan, in tlaçoltitlan: no tequapipiloa, no tetoneuhque. Auh amo çan quezqujn nemj: cenca mjequjntin nemj, ololiuhtinemj: auh injc vtlatoca, çan motecpana, movipana, patlavativi: anoço çan cenpanti.

TLILAZCATL:

no itoca tzicatl iehoantin in tlaitztiaiã nemj tepitoton; tlallan, metzonco in tlacati: auh no tequanjpipil. Auh in jquac xopã: motataca, manjlia in jpilhoã, iztaque iuhqujn iztac ocujlton: qualo, velique, mje-

90

out; they are gathered. They are white, like white worms. They are eaten; they are savory. Many are cooked in an olla. Their name is really *tzicame*, or else they are called *azcamolli*.

TZICATL

It is similar to the dung ant. It lives there in damp places; and wherever anything edible or fat falls,[2] quickly they swarm there. And in hot lands absolutely nowhere may anything fall or be placed, nor anything remain long, [for] then the *tzicatl* ants form a mass; they eat it.

TZICANANTLI[3]

It is a thick serpent which lives in the anthills. Wherever there are *tzicatl* or *azcatl* ants, there it lives underground. It is varicolored, spotted with various colors. It terrifies, it frightens one much.

TZICATANA

Also it is called *tepeuani*. It is like the red ant. It lives in the cold lands. It is ruddy. And thus does it live: it cannot travel alone, but in a swarm. It is called "the conqueror" because it eats everything that is tender. Whatever it clings to it no more releases; it consumes it, it sucks it dry. When they follow their path, they go in a wide stream. So it is said they draw up for battle; so it is that they are conquerors.

NEQUAZCATL[4]

It settles mainly underground; there it lives, there it breeds. And it is called "honey ant" because its abdomen, its stomach, is sweet like wild bee honey. It is eaten.

¶

TENTH PARAGRAPH, which telleth of the small insects whose dwelling place is on the ground.

TLALXIQUIPILLI

The back is rounded, ball-like; the neck slender, constricted; the nose has hair, or horns. The jaws are pointed. It has long legs. It is black, like bitumen. And this small insect lives only in the summer; it is not rare. And this insect is very bad. Whomever it bites then dies; his intestines are cut to pieces; his tongue swells as if it burned; his lips blister. And if it

qujn mopaoaci: vel intoca tzicame, anoço mjtoa azcamolli.

TZICATL:

itloc in cujtlaazcatl, vncan ioli in tlacuechaoaian, yoan in canjn tlein vetzi qualonj, anoço chiaoa, hiciuhca vncan molonj. Auh in tlatotonian tlalpan: çã njmã acan tle vel huetzi, acan tle vel motlalia, ano tle vel vecaoa: njman cololhuja, qujqua in tzicame.

TZICANANTLI:

cooatl tomaoac, azcapotzalco in onoc: in canjn cate tzicame, anoço azcame, vncan tlallan in onoc, vel cujcujltic: nepapan tlapalli injc mocujcujlo, vel temauhti, teiçavi.

TZICATANA:

yoan mjtoa tepeoanj, iuhqujn tlatlavic azcatl: in tlaitztiaian nemj tlatlactic. Auh injc nemj: amo vel icel nemj, çan ololiuhtinemj: injc mjtoa tepeoanj, ca mochi qujqua in tlein celic, in tlein ceppa itech mopiloa, aocmo qujcaoa, qujtlamja, qujoatza. Injc vtlatoca, patlavativi: ca noço qujl iauqujzque, ca noço tepeoanjme.

NEQUAZCATL:

in tlallan vei injc motlalia, vmpa ioli, vmpa tlacati. Auh injc mjtoa nequazcatl: in jtzintlan, ixillã aciticac in necutic, iuhq'n quauhnecutli, qualo.

¶

INJC MATLACTLI PARRAPHO: intechpa tlatoa in iolcatotonti in tlalpan innemjan.

TLALXIQUJPILLI:

cujtlatolõtic, cujtlaololtic, quechpitzaoac, tacapitztic, iacatzone, manoço quaquaquave, tenvitztic, mavivitlatic, tliltic, chapopotic. Auh inin ioioliton: çan yio iquac in xopantla nemj, amo tlaçotin. Auh inin ioioli: cenca amo qualli, in aqujn qujqua: njmã mjquj, cocotoca in jcujtlaxcol, valpotzavi in jnenepil, iuhqujn tlatla: xixitomonj in jtenxipal. Auh in canjn

---

2. *Ibid.: hiciuhca cololvia* is added.
3. *Tzicanantli: Lampropeltis polyzona* (Martín del Campo, *op. cit.*, p. 390).
4. *Acad. Hist. MS: necuazcatl.*

settles on the surface of our body, it boils up as if it were burned. The cure for this is [as for] skin sores.[1] It keeps blistering; it putrefies.

TLALACATL

It is small and smooth. It has arms, it has legs. Some are ruddy, some very white, some pale. Their dwelling-place is in damp ground, among rubbish. It is harmless; it only goes about. It cannot make a pleasant sound. In desolate places it only puts its head into the ground; there is as it were a kicking din underground. Thus does it speak.

TAPAXI OR TAPAYAXI[2]

It is broad-backed — broad. It has arms, it has legs, it has a tail. It is thorny, spiny, like metal awls extending along the back of its head. And thus they act in a worldly way: they mount, they mate, or they stretch out; one lies below, on its back; one lies above. Also they move lasciviously. It is very notorious that they act in a worldly way.

And it reproduces in this manner; it gives birth in this manner — not like the other little insects. It only scratches its abdomen; it bursts; it perforates its abdomen. There its young are born. Then they each run off; there is entering among the herbs. Especially they seek out the plants called *memeyal*; they penetrate among them. Still in it they grow, still eating only earth. But when they already go on to mature, they eat the small flies.

CONYAYAUAL

It is a worm. Some are dark yellow, some ruddy, some pale, some dark. For this reason is it called *conyayaual*: when someone looks at it or molests it, it then quickly forms a circle. And very many are its arms. This one is deadly. One who drinks it dies. It is like the *tlalxiquipilli*, and as is known, it causes suffering. And this one is a remedy for toothache. It is spread on the surface of the palate, in order to abate the pain. And it is spread on where there is gout.

TLALOMITL

It is a small worm. Its name comes from *tlalli* [earth] and *omitl* [bone], because it is really a creature in the ground, and always remains there. And as for "bone," because it is white and firm, really

panj tonacaiopan ommoteca, aquaqualaca iuhqujn motlatia. Inin ipaio in xiotl ca quaqualatza, qujpalanaltia.

TLALACATL.

xixipetzpil, mamae, ihicxe: cequj tlatlauhquj, cequj vel iztaque, cequj iztaleoac: vel innentla in tlacuechaoaian, in tlaçoltitlan atle itlachioal, çan monenemjtia, amo vellatoa: in nemjuhian, çan tlallan caqujа in jtzontecon, iuhqujn tlatetecujtztica tlallan, injc tlatoa

TAPAXI: ANOÇO TAPAIAXI

cujtlapatlachtic, patlachtic mamae, ihicxe, cujtlapile: vitzio, aoaio: iuhqujn tepoçomjtotonti, icuexcochtlan manj. Auh injc tlalticpac tlamati: moquetztimanj, mjxnamjctimanj, anoço moteca, ce tlanj onoc, aquetztoc, ce panj onoc no moioma cenca caqujzti injc tlalticpac tlamati.

Auh injc tlacachioa; injc mjxivi, amo ivi in oc cequjntin ioiolitzitzi: çan mjtichichiquj, vmpeti, qujcoionja in jiti: vncã tlacati in impilhoan, njmã motlatlaloa, xiuhtitlan calacooa: oc cenca iehoatl qujtemoa in xivitl, in jtoca memeial: intlan calaquj, oc itlan chicaoa, çan oc tlalli in qujqua: auh in ie ixtlamattivi, qujnqua in çaioltzitzin.

CONIAIAOAL:

ca ocujli cequj coziaiactic, cequj tlatlactic, cequj iztaleoac, cequj iaiauhquj: injc mjtoa coniaiaoal, in jquac aca qujtta anoço aca colinja: njman moiaoallalitivetzi, auh cenca mjec in jma. Inin mjcoanj: in aqujn qujz mjqujz, iuhqujn tlalxiqujpilli: auh injc machoz cocoiac. Auh inin, in tlanqualiztli ipaio: panj tocamatapalpan õmoteca: ic cevi in cocoli, yoan oncan ommoteca in canjn onoc cooaciviztli.

TLALOMJTL:

ocujlton, itech qujça in jtoca tlalli, yoan omjtl: ipampa in çan vel tlallan ioli, yoan mochipa vmpa onoc: auh injc omjtl, ipampa in iztac, yoan chicaoac, vel oapactontli: aic mocollalia ça cẽ quapitztic, iuh-

---

1. *Acad. Hist. MS:* ỹ *xixiotl* is added.
2. *Tapaxi, Tapayaxin: Phrynosoma asio, Ph. cornutum, Ph. orbiculare* (Sahagún, Garibay ed. Vol. IV, p. 352).

hard. It never contracts itself, but is completely rigid, like a small metal awl. Well pointed at the end is its tail. It is harmless. And because it is a little rigid, he who is feeble hunts it, eats it. It is said that thus he makes the member rigid. He eats or drinks it only uncooked.

UEUETLANEUHQUI

It is a small insect, whitish. Its outside is like skin, like a sherd. It has horns; they are small. It has no functions; it only goes about.

TECUITLAOLOLO

Its name comes from *cuitlatl* [dung] and *cololoa* [it makes it into a ball], because wherever it sees dung, it makes it into a ball, it forms it into a ball, and goes rolling it along; it transports it. And not alone does it go, not only one travels; they always travel in twos; they go sharing it as they go rolling it together. And as they go, they each take hold of the sphere. And this little round insect, together with the *temolin*, is a little dark. Its wings glow a little. It has no other particular function.

PINACATL[3]

It is blackish, dark, small and flat, with pointed jaws. It is sherd-like; rigid is its sherd. And when anyone molests it, then it breaks wind; it frightens one with its stink, its flatulence. It lives, it dwells, in damp places, in rubbish.

TZONTLI IMA

It is small and round, tiny, small and black. Its name comes from *tzontli* [hair] then *ima* [its arms], because its arms are very long, black, small and slender, just like hair. On them it travels, it goes scampering; its small body goes high up. And this little creature is harmless; only[4] it is completely evil-smelling; it has a strong smell. Its breeding-place, its dwelling-place, is especially among magueys, in maguey roots.[5]

¶

ELEVENTH PARAGRAPH, which telleth of the bees which produce honey.

XICOTLI[1]

It is round, small and round, yellow-legged, winged. It is a flyer, a buzzer, a sucker, a maker of

qujnma tepoçomjtõtli, vel iacavitztic in jcujtlapil; atle itequjton. Auh injc chicactontli: qujtemoa, qujqua in tlacuetlaxoa: qujl ic tlaiolitia, çan xoxouhquj in qujqua anoço quj.

VEVETLANEUHQUJ:

ioioliton, ticeoac in jpanj eoaio, iuhq'n tapalcatl, quaquavecatontli, amo tle itlachioal, çan monenemjtia.

TECUJTLAOLOLO:

in jtoca itech qujça in cujtlatl, yoã cololoa: ipampa ca in canjn qujtta cujtlatl cololoa, qujteololalia: auh qujmjmjlotiuh qujvica. Auh amo çan içel in nemj, amo çan centeietinemj: mochipa onteme ietinemj, cõcavitinemj in qujmjmjlotinemj. Auh injc nemj qujmocujcujlitinemj in jntlalololol: auh inin ololtontli, itloc in temoli, pochectontli, achi xoxotla in jatlapal, atle oc centlamãtli in jtequjuh.

PINACATL:

pochectic, pocheoac patlachtontli, tenvitztic, tapalcaio, vapaoac in jtapalcaio. Auh in jquac aca colinja: njman mjexi, temamauhti injc hiiac yiel: tlacuechaoaian, tlaçoltitlan in nemj, in ioli.

TZONTLI IMA:

ololtontli, piciltontli, tliltontli: in jtoca itech qujça tzontli, njmã ie ima: ipampa in jma cenca viviac, tliltic, pitzatoton vel iuhqujn tzontli ic nenemj ic tlatlaçatiuh, vecapã in ietiuh itlacton. Auh inin ioioliton atle itequjuh çan ixqujch çenyiac, cenca qujpiiac; oc cenca itlacatian, oc cẽca inentla in mec, in metzõco.

¶

INJC MATLACTLI OCE PARRAPHO: itechpa tlatoa pipiolti, in qujtlacatilia necutli.

XICOTLI:

ololtic, ololtontli, xococoztic, amatlapale, patlanjnj, qujqujnacanj, tlachichinanj, motapaçoltianj, motlata-

---

3. *Pinacatl:* "Insecto áptero; escarabajo grande y negro que se cría en los lugares húmedos" (Santamaría, *op. cit.,* p. 852: pinacate).

4. *Acad. Hist. MS* has cenca in place of çan.

5. *Ibid.:* ỹ memac is added.

1. *Xicotli: Bombus* sp. (Sahagún, *op. cit.,* p. 368).

hives, an earth excavator, a honey producer, a stinger. When it stings one, it is a producer of swellings, a producer of much pain. Only in summer does it breed. It builds hives, excavates earth, sucks, produces honey, produces beeswax. It stings one; its sting swells up.

PIPIOLIN[2]

It is small, similar to the *xicotli*, it is small and round, dark yellowish. Its hive is underground, where it breeds. It produces honey underground. Its honey is yellow, like *tomiolin*, or like yellow ochre. It is a buzzer, a flyer; it flies, sucks, produces honey; it stores [honey] underground. It flies, flies constantly, flies rapidly.

MIMIAUATL

It is slender, small and constricted. It lives especially there in the hot lands and in the forests. It has wings, it has arms; it is a stinger of people; it is a producer of honey. Its hive [has holes] going clear through. But nevertheless, it is a producer of honey like the *xicotli*, also like the *pipiolin*.

When it makes its honey, it is the so-called wild honey. And as they hatch, as they breed, they do not fertilize one another, like the small insects. The very honey is alive, if it is not taken away, if the honey is not poured out. When still aqueous, it thickens. This insect changes into a worm; later it flies.

BUTTERFLY

Whatever the kind of butterfly, it is long and straight, the abdomen is slender, the neck is constricted. It is fuzzy, like fat; winged. Its wings are twofold. It has arms, it has legs, it has antennae. It is a flyer, a constant flyer, a flutterer, a sucker of the different flowers, and a sucker of liquid. It is fuzzy. It trembles, it beats its wings together, it constantly flies. It sucks, it sucks liquid. It is not solid. There are many kinds of butterflies.

XICALPAPALOTL OR XICALTECONPAPALOTL
OR XICALTECON

It is somewhat large. Its name comes from *xicalli* [gourd bowl] and *papalotl* [butterfly], because it is yellow, it is quite yellow, it is fuzzy. And it is painted with black; it is varicolored. So it is very beautiful, coveted, desirable, constantly desirable, constantly required. It is fragile. It yellows, it becomes painted,

taqujanj, monenecutianj, temjnanj: injc temjna poçaoanj, cenca toneoanj, çã yio xopan in tlacati, motapaçoltia, motlatataquja, tlachichina, monecutia, moxicocujtlatia, temjna; poçaoa in jtlaminal.

PIPIIOLI:

tepiton, itloc in xicotli, ololtontli, coziaiacpil, tlallan in jchan in tlacati, tlallan monecutia: in jnecu coztic, iuhqujn tomjioli, anoço tecuçavitl: qujqujnacanj, patlanjnj, patlanj: tlachîchina, monecutia, motlallancuezcontia; patlanj, papatlanj, patlantinemj.

MIMJAOATL:

pitzaoac, tacapitztontli; oc cenca vmpã nemj in tonaian, yoan quauhtla: amatlapale, mamae, temjnanj, monecutianj, mocaltianj: in jcal qujqujztic. Auh çan ie, in tlacatinj necutli: no iuhqujn xicotli, no iuhqujn pipiioli.

In qujchioa inecu: iehoatl in mjtoa quauhnecutli. Auh injc motlapana: injc moxinachoa, amo moquequeça, in juh ioiolitzitzin: çan ie in necutli ioli, intlacamo cujva, intlacamo oalnoqujlo in jnecu. In oc atic, tetzaoa; iehoatl ioli, ocujlin mocuepa, çatepan patlanj.

PAPALOTL:

in çaço tlein ipapaloio, melactic, tzimpitzaoac, quechtacapitztic, tomjo, iuhqujn pochqujo, amatlapale, ohomemanj in jiamatlapal, mamaie, iicxe, iacatzone, patlanjnj, papatlanjnj, papatlacanj: qujchichinanj in nepapan xochitl, yoan achichinanj, tomjollo, âtevivi momatlaxcaloa, papatlanj, tlachichina, achichina, amo chicaoac: mjec tlamantli in papalotl.

XICALPAPALOTL, ANOÇO XICALTECONPAPALOTL,
ANOÇO XICALTECON;

achi vei, itech qujça in itoca xicalli yoan papalotl: ipampa ca coztic, vel coztic, tomjollo: auh mocujcujlo tliltica, cujcujltic: ic cenca qualnezquj, teicolti, tetlanecti: nequîtli, nenequjztli, ieheleviliztli, amo iollotlapalivi, coçavia, mocujcujlova, cujcujlivi, tlacati tetzaoa, vapaoa, patlantinemj.

---

2. *Pipiolin: abeja silvestre* (Santamaría, *op. cit.*, p. 858: *pipiol*).

it becomes varicolored. It breeds, it becomes firm, it develops; it flies constantly.

TLILPAPALOTL

It is similar to — also just the same as — the *xicalpapalotl*, but black flecked with white. Thus its wings are varicolored.

TLECOCOZPAPALOTL

Its name is also *quappachpapalotl*. It is called "fire-yellow" because it glows, it glistens a little. Its body is a little fiery, but it is smoky, tawny. It glows, glistens, glistens constantly. It is tawny, smoky, smoky yellow. It becomes smoky yellow; it turns smoky yellow.

IZTAC PAPALOTL

Some are a little large, some average, some quite small. They are not really white, only as whitish, only as pale as they are yellow.

CHIAN PAPALOTL

It is somewhat similar to the *xicalpapalotl*, because it is painted as if sprinkled with *chia*, flecked everywhere on its body; and its wings are painted, painted with a *chia* design.

TEXOPAPALOTL

Some are large, some tiny; they are not uniform. Its name comes from *texotli* [light blue]. But it is not really a blue; it is just so rather pale, just so pallid, just so yellow as to be livid. It is just a light blue hue. It takes on a light blue hue;[3] it becomes blue-brown.

XOCHIPAPALOTL

Some are large, some small. Many kinds of colors are on them, so that they are varicolored, much like flowers, of very intricate design, and truly sought after, truly wonderful. They are of intricate design, sought after, flower-like.

UAPPAPALOTL

It is of average size; its wings are painted chili-red. It is also beautiful, also wonderful. Amaranth leaves or foliage are also called *uappapalotl* when the amaranth leaves already become mature, ripe. Then they are named *uappapalotl*, because they become yellow or chili-red.

TLILPAPALOTL:

çan no iuhquj, çan no ixqujch, in xicalpapalotl: iece tliltic, iztac qujmotzitzicujchili, ic cujcujltic in jatlapal.

TLECÔCOZPAPALOTL:

no yoã itoca quappachpapalotl. Injc mjtoa tlecocoz; ipampa achi xoxotla pepetzca: in jnacaio achi tletic, çan poctic, quappachtic, xoxotla, pepetzca, pepepetzca, quappachtic, poctic, poccoztic pocoztia, poccoçavia.

IZTAC PAPALOTL:

cequj achi vei, cequj çan qualton, cequj cenca çan vel tepitoton, amo vel iztac, çan iztaleoac, çã pineoac injc coztic.

CHIAN PAPALOTL:

achi itloc in xicalpapalotl, ipampa mocujcujlo, iuhqujn chien tzitzicujcatoc in novian inacaio itech, yoan in jatlapalpã mocujcujloa, mochiancujcujloa.

TEXOPAPALOTL:

cequj vei, cequj tepitoton, acan cenqujzquj: itech qujça in jtoca texotli. amo tel vel texotic, çan achi iztaleoac, çan pineoac, çã camaoac: injc xoxoctic, çan texopoiaoac: texopoiaoac, texocamjlivi.

XOCHIPAPALOTL:

cequj vei, cequj tepiton, mjec tlamantli tlapalli itech ca injc cujcujltic: vel xochitic, vellamomoxoltic: auh vel moxtic, vel maviztic, tlamomoxolti, moxti, xochiti.

VAPPAPALOTL:

çan qualton, chichiltic injc cujcujltic, yiatlapal: no qualnezquj, no mavizticapil. No itoca vappapalotl: in jamatlapal vauhtli, in manoço iqujllo: in jquac ie chicaoa, in ie icuci vauhtli iiatlapal: iquac motocaiotia vappalotl, ipãpa ixcoçavia anoço chichilivi.

---

3. For *texopoiaoac, Acad. Hist. MS* has *texopoya*.

TWELFTH PARAGRAPH, which telleth of the locusts and how they are subdivided.

THE LOCUST of whatever kind is straight, with slender abdomen, with stubby head. It has spittle, it has saliva; it has wings, arms, legs. Some are large, some small; some fly, some just crawl, just go about on four legs; some just go hopping.

And as to its nature, its manner of life: it reproduces underground; it lays eggs underground. When it lays eggs, it inserts its abdomen underground; there it deposits its eggs.

And there they hatch. These know that they will sometime hatch. When they come forth, they are already small locusts; already they go hopping. And they eat plants. Whatever appeals to them they eat, cut up, destroy. They hop, support themselves, fly; they fly, they are constantly flying, whirring.

ACACHAPOLIN

It is large, a little tall, rough; the upper leg is long, smooth; its lower leg is jagged. It is a flyer, a buzzer, a hummer. It is pale. Its name comes from *acatl* [reed], that is, "arrow," because when it flies, it is as if one shot an arrow. It flies, hums, buzzes, flies constantly; it goes constantly flying. It becomes pale, ashen.

YECTLI CHAPOLIN

It is of average size. Its lower legs are chili-red, its breast chili-red. It appears when it is harvest time. It is edible. It becomes chili-red, ruddy.

XOPAN CHAPOLIN

It is large, round, round-backed, heavy, slow-moving. It only travels about on its legs; it only crawls. It eats things, cuts things up, attacks the beans, etc. Some are black, some green, some painted — nowhere uniform, but mixed.

TLALCHAPOLIN

It is also known as *ixpopoyochapolin*. It is quite small, a small locust. It is *tlalchapolin* because it lives continually and everywhere; it is *ixpopoyochapolin* because it is stupid; it does not take fright, it just completely stops. And on the road, in the middle of the road, it begets its young. And when it is sitting somewhere on the road, it does not move out of the way of passers-by, even though they are to pass over them, even if they are to jump on them. They just remain sitting, as if they saw not.

INJC MATLACTLI OMOME PARRAPHO: itechpa tlatoa in chapoli, yoan injc moxexeloa.

IN ÇAÇO TLEIN CHAPOLI: melaoac, tzimpitzaoac, quatepõtic, chichale, tenqualaque, hatlapale, amatlapale, mamae ihicxe: cequj vei, cequj tepiton; cequj patlanj, cequj çan movilana, çã manenemj; çequj çan cholotivi.

Auh in jeliz, in jnemjliz: tlallan in mopilhoatia, tlallan in motetia: injc tlatlaça tlallan caquia in jcujtlapil, vncan qujntema in jteoan.

Auh vncan tlacati: in çaço iqujn tlacatizque, iehoantin qujmati: in oalqujça ie chapoltoton, ie tlachocholivi. Auh xivitl in qujqua: in tlein qujvelmati, tlaqua, tlatetequj, tlatepoloa, cholooa, tlacxotla, patlanj, chipatlanj, chipapatlaca, çoçoloca.

ACACHAPOLI:

vei, veicatõtli çan quappitztic, teteponviviac, teteponahatlatic: in jtlanjtz tzitziqujltic, patlanjnj, çoçolocanj, çolonj, ticeoac: in itoca itech qujça in acatl: qujtoznequj mjtl: ipampa inic patlanj, iuhqujn tlamjna: patlanj, çolonj, çoçoloca, chipapatlaca, chipapatlacatiuh ticeoa, nexeoa.

IECTLI CHAPOLI:

çan qualton chichiltic in jtlanjtz, elchichiltic: iquac in pixqujzpã valneci, qualonj, chichilivi tlatlavia.

XOPAN CHAPOLIN:

veipol, ololpo, cujtlaololpol, eticapol hameuhcapol, çan manenẽtinemj, çan movilana: tlaqua, tlatetequj, qujmoiaotia in hetl. etc. cequj tliltique, cequj xoxoctique, cequj cujcujcujltique, acan cenqujzque çan tlanenel.

TLALCHAPOLI:

yoan moteneoa ixpopoiochapoli, çan tepiton chapulton: injc tlalchapoli, çan muchipa, yoan çan novian in nemj: injc ixpopoiochapoli, amo mozcalia, amo momauhtianj, çan vel mana. Auh vtlica, vnepantla in mopilhoatia auh in jquac: cana vtlica ieoatica, amo qujntlalcavia in nenenque: maço ipan qujçazq̃, manoço ipan cholozque, çan eoatica, iuhqujn amo tlachia.

ÇOLACACHAPOLIN

It is not much like the *acachapolin*, just similar to it. It is named *çolacachapolin* because its wings are painted like a quail's. But the under part of its wings and its body are ruddy.

ÇACATECUILICHTLI

It is of average size, a little ashen, ruddy on the under part of its wings. It is called *çacatecuilichtli* because it always settles on the grass, singing, making a *chi-i, chichi, chi, chi, chi*. But the one which lives in the hot lands is called *touacaletl*. When it sings, it makes a *touacale, touacale, touacale, chi chi chi chi chi*.

CAPOLOCUILIN

Also its name is *auatl*. It hatches on American cherry trees. First it makes a web about the cherry leaves. Then countless numbers of the *capolocuilin* hatch there. They eat, they dry up the cherry tree; they wither it so that the cherry tree produces nothing. Later the *capolocuilin* become pupas and finally [vanish];[1] they change into butterflies.

AUATECOLOTL

It is a worm something like the *paçotl*. It is fuzzy; it has coarse fuzz. And the fuzz of this one is stinging; it torments one like fire. Some of the *auatecolotl* occur on cherry trees, some on fruit, some on the grass; and many breed, but only when it is summer. And when mature, then they form cocoons, they turn yellow; then they become pupas; then they become butterflies. They occur in the salt grass. They are eaten, especially when they already enter the cocoon, especially furthermore when they become pupas. They are savory, good to the taste.

PAÇOTL

In times of old they called it "the *paçotl* of the god." Some named it *payatl*. It is similar to the *auatecolotl*. This one has coarse spines, coarse fuzz; like awls is its fuzz. And it also makes one throb, burn; its fuzz also molests one, like that of the *auatecolotl*. It is called *paçotl* because it is always bristling; its fuzz never hangs, is never smooth. It always goes spiky. It is bristling, fuzzy, spiky, spiny. It pricks one; it goes about spiky, bristly.

ÇOLACACHAPOLI:

amo cenca ixqujch in acachapoli, çan itloc; injc mitoa çolacachapoli, çolcujcujltic in jatlapal: auh in tlanj iiatlapal, yoan in jnacaio tlatlavic.

ÇACATECUJLICHTLI:

çan qualton, nextontli: tlatlavic, in tlanj yiatlapal. Injc mjtoa çacatecujlichtli: mochipa çacatitech in motlalia, tlatotica, qujchiuhtica chij, chichi, chi, chi, chi: auh in tlatotonian nemj, itoca tovacaletl: inic tlatoa qujchioa, tovacale, tovacale, tovacale, chichichichichi.

CAPOLOCUJLI:

yoan itoca havatl, itech tlacati in capuli: achtopa tocatzavalloa, in capulxivitl: njman vncan tlacati, in amo tlapoalli capulocujli: qujqua, qujoatza in capuli, qujoaoaçoa: ic atle muchioa in capuli. çatepan tzontetezcame muchioa in capulocujlti: auh iequene ic papalome mocuepa

AVATECOLOTL:

ocujli, achiuhquj in paçotl, tomio, tomjochamaoac. Auh inin itomjo tequanj, tetoneuh, iuhqujn tletl. In cequj aoateculotl: capultitech in muchioa, cequj xocotitech, cequj çacatla: auh amo çã quexqujch in tlacati, çã nel yio iquac in xopan. Auh in omacique: njman chipichavi, coçavia: auh njmã tzontetezcati, njmã papaloti: in tequjxqujçacatla muchioa qualo oc cenca iquac in ie mochipichaquja, oc cenca iequene iquac in tzontetezcatl mochioa: ca velic, ca haviac.

PAÇOTL:

qujtoaia in ie vecauh, teutl ipaçouh, cequjntin qujtocaiotia paiatl, itloc in aoateculotl. Inin vel havaiochamaoac, tomjochamaoac, coiolomjtic in jtomjo: auh no tecuecueiotz, no tetlati, no teama in jtomjo, in juhquj aoatecolutl. Injc mjtoa paçotl: çã cen paçoliuhtinemj, aic mopiloa, aic qujpechteca in jtomjo, çan çen çoneoatinemj: çoneoac, paçoltic, tomjo, çonectic, havaio, teâvavia: çoneoatinemj, paçoliuhtinemj.

---

1. *Acad. Hist. MS: popolivi* is added.

THIRTEENTH PARAGRAPH, which telleth of the different ways of the worms.

TETATAMACHIUHQUI

Its name comes from *tetamachiua* [it measures one], because the little worm is a little long. And its arms are eight; they are on its neck or chest; and also an equal number of feet are at its tail [end]. And as it travels, as it goes its way, it goes by doubling itself, by looping itself, as if measuring something. This one lives, hatches on the *topoçan* tree. And thus is it adorned: part black, part green, running in stripes along its back. It contracts itself, it doubles itself.

MEOCUILIN[1]

It is like the *cinocuilin* — white, very white, exceedingly white. It occurs within the maguey plant. It presents itself in this manner: wherever it rests, it bores a hole into the maguey leaf; it makes an exit opening in it. There it lies excreting, and it lies eating the maguey. It is a cutter, a chewer, a borer, a doubler. [It is edible, savory, good-tasting. It doubles itself,][2] cuts, eats, bores things.

CHICHILOCUILIN[3]

It is just like the *tlalomitl*; it is purple, it is chili-red. It occurs, it lives within maguey roots. Very many abound where they lie. They are savory.

METZONOCUILIN

This one occurs in maguey roots. It is white, slender on the end, small.

TZINOCUILIN

This one lives in ordure, in filth. Some die right there. They turn into flies.

TZINOCUILIN[4]

These are worms which are within one. He in whom they are appears thus: the face has spots, blotches, blisters. [The worms] are white, small, and slender.

TZONCOATL

Worms well out of the anuses of us people:[5] also *tzoncoatl* worms well out of the anuses of dogs.[6] Also

INJC MATLACTLI OMEI PARRAPHO: itechpa tlatoa in intlatlamantiliz ocujlme.

TETATAMACHIUHQUJ:

in jtoca itech qujça tetatamachioa: ipampa ca viacatontli in ocujlton. Auh in jma chicuei: in jquechtlan, manoço yielpan manj: auh no izquj in jicxi, in jcujtlapilco manj. Auh injc nenemj, injc vtlatoca mocuecuelpachotiuh, mococototztlalia, iuhqujnma itla qujtamachioa. Inin vel itech ioli, itech tlacati in topoçan: auh injc mochichiuh çequj tliltic, cequj xoxoctic in qujmoquequechili, injc mooaoavan: mococototztlalia mocuelpachoa.

MEOCULI:

iuhqujn cinocujli, iztac, iztacpatic, aztapiltic: metl iitic in mochioa. Inic neci: in canjn onoc, qujcoionja in mematl, qujtlecallotia, vncã oalmoxixtoc, auh qujquatoc in metl: tlatequjnj, tlaquaquanj, tlacoionjanj, mocuecueloanj, tlatetequj, tlaquaqua, tlacoionja.

CHICHILOCULI:

vel iuhqujn tlalomjtl, camopaltic, chichiltic metzontetl iitic in mochioa in nemj, cenca mjec in temj in onoque, vel huelique.

METZONOCUJLI:

iehoatl in metzontetl mochioa, iztac, tzinpitzaoac, tepiton.

TZINOCUJLIN:

iehoatl in cujtlatl, in tlailli itlan ioli: cequj çan vncan mjquj, çaiolme mocuepa.

TZINOCUJLI:

in teitic cate ocujlti: injc neci in aqujn yitic cate, ixihicuci, ixiaiapaleoa, ixahatemj: iztaque, pitzactotonti.

TZONCOOATL:

in titlaca itzinco oalpotzavi, ocujlti: no tzõcooatl, in chichi itzinco oalpotzavi ocujlti: no tzoncooatl, in

---

1. *Meocuil: Acentrocneme hesperiaris* Kiby (Santamaría, *op. cit.*, p. 716).
2. *Acad. Hist. MS* adds *qualoni velic avixtic mocuecueloa.*
3. *Chichilocuilin: chilocuil* or *tecal* (Santamaría, *op. cit.*, p. 387).
4. *Tzinocuilin:* Enrique G. Vogelsang and Rafael Martín del Campo, "Parasitología de los Nahoas," *Revista de Med. Vet. y Paras.* (Caracas, 1947), Vol. VI, Nos. 1–4, p. 4, think these may be *Necator americanus.*
5. *Ascaris lumbricoides* L. (*ibid.*, p. 3).
6. *Toxcara canis* or *T. felis* (*loc. cit.*).

tzoncoatl worms are like [the medicinal plant] *tlalcuitlaxcolli*. Those which are in the common folk, which well out of their anuses, are small white worms like the worms in meat when it starts to putrefy. Only when one sleeps do they come forth, and [among] dogs they appear when they defecate.

All are called worms, in whatever putrefaction they live.

CHIANCUETLAN OR CHIENCUETLAN

Also they call them *tetepolchichic*. They are thick, pale, a little green; they have antennae. They are a span long; they really frighten one. They are called *chiancuetlan* because the *chienquauitl* tree is really their mother; right in it they are, they develop.

NEXTECUILIN[7]

It is like all the *cinocuilin,* ashen, chalky, green-backed. Its dwelling is in the earth; in the earth it hatches, it lives. It eats earth. When it does not rain, it attacks the maize stalks; it cuts them at the root. And although there are its legs, it sometimes travels only by going on its back. So for that reason one who is not discreet is called *nextecuilin*: because he does not live as everyone [else] lives.

CINOCUILIN

Also its name is *cenocuilin*. This one is ashen, like the *nextecuilin*. This one lives right on, hatches on the green maize ears. It eats it, cuts it up, until it is a mature green ear, a dried, already dried maize ear. It is an eater of things, a cutter, a spoiler, a destroyer. It destroys, cuts up, chews up.

TLAÇOLOCUILIN

It is of average size, a little ashen. It hatches right in rubbish; it lives right in it. It is an ordinary little worm, harmless.

CITLALOCUILIN

It is the same as the *tlalomitl* — painted like a star. It lives, it breeds especially on the fruit of the *nopal*.

CITLALOCUILIN[8]

They are on, they form on mice, rabbits, etc. They are like the *nextecuilin,* or a little like the *paçotl*: fuzzy. The back is somewhat thick. Perhaps the mice, or whatever creature the worm lives on, flees.

juhquj tlalcujtlaxcolli. In maceoalli itech ca, in jtzinco oalpotzavi iztacatotonti, in ocujltoton; iuhquj, in q'n ie peoa nacatl palanj yiocujllo, çan iquac in cochi oalqujça: auh in chichi, iquac in momanavia valneci.

Ça mochi oculin itoca, in çaço tlein palanquj itech ioli.

CHIANCUETLA: ANOÇO CHIĒCUETLA,

yoan qujtocaiotia tetepolchichic tomaoac, iztaleoac, achi xoxoctic, quaquaquave, cemjztitl injc viac, vel temauhti. Injc mjtoa chiancuetla: vel inã in chienquavitl, vel itech in onoc in mochioa.

NEXTECUJLI:

iuhquj, ixqujch in cinocujli, nextic, ticeoac cujtlaxoxoctic, tlallan in jchan, tlallan in tlacati, in nemj: tlalli in qujqua. In jquac amo qujavi: qujmoiautia in toctli, qujtzintetequj: auh macivi in onca ima, in quēman çan aquetztiuh in nenemj: ic ipampa in jtechpa mjtoa in aqujn amo mozcalia nextecujli: ipampa in juh nemoa amo iuh nemj.

CINOCUJLI:

yoan itoca cenocujli, inin nexeoac, iuhq'n nextecujli: inin çan vel itech ioli, itech tlacati in elotl, qujqua, qujtetequj, ixqujchica in omacic elotl, in vaquj, in ie cintli: tlaquanj, tlatetequjnj, atlamalhujanj, tlaixpoloanj: tlaixpoloa, tlatetequj, tlatoponja.

TLAÇOLOCUJLI:

çan qualtõ nexectontli, çan vel iitic tlacati in tlaçolli, çan vel itech ioli: çaçan ie ocujlitzintli, atle itequjuh.

CITLALOCUJLI:

isqujch in tlalomjtl, citlalcujcujltic: tlaquauh itech nemj, itech tlacati in nochtli

CITLALOCUJLI:

in jtech ca in jtech mochioa qujmjchi, tochi. etc. iuhqujn nextecujli manoçe ach iuhqujn paçotl totomjo, cujtlatomactontli aço motlatlaloa in qujmjchi, in anoço tlein iolcatl itech ietinemj in ocujli valitzti-

---

7. *Nextecuilin: nesticuil, nisticuil,* etc. (Santamaría, *op. cit.,* p. 757).

8. *Citlalocuilin:* probably *Pupipara (Oestridae)* larvae, according to Vogelsang and Martín del Campo, *op. cit.,* p. 4.

The worm continues to look out from [the flesh of the animal]. It is said they are named "star arrow," and what they are on is called "shot by a star."

TEMOLIN[9]

It is tawny, small and round. The neck is round. It has arms, legs, wings, a shell. Underneath its shell, from there are its wings, its place of flight. The time when it appears is when it is already rainy; then it emerges; then it spreads out.

CUITLATEMOLIN

They live in ordure, in dung. They are just like the *temolin*.

AYOXOCHQUILTEMOLIN

This one, which sucks the squash blossoms, is a little yellow. It is harmless.

QUAUHTEMOLIN

This one hatches in the trees, on the trees. It is ruddy; it is a little large.

QUAUHOCUILIN

This one hatches in wood;[10] it lives in it. It is white. It is white, as nowhere does it see the sun. Some are a little large, some very small. This one has a firm mouth, a tough mouth, a strong mouth, a mouth like metal. It is a cutter, a gnawer, a carver. It gnaws, cuts, carves things.

¶

FOURTEENTH PARAGRAPH, which telleth of the little insects called fireflies, and of others like them.

ICPITL

It is whatever kind of insect shines at night.

One kind of *icpitl* is called *coquitl*. It is like a locust, a little long. When it rains, it travels at night. There are very many of them. And its light is a little large, somewhat like a candle. Its light is on its tail —almost one-half of its body. For that reason its light is rather large.

And sometimes it shines like a pine torch, because of the dark. And sometimes they just form a line as they travel along. And the uninformed name them *tlauipochtin* [sorcerers].

nemj, mjtoa motocaiotia citlalmjtl auh in tlein itech ca, citlalmjnquj itoca.

TEMOLI:

quappachticatontli, ololtontli, cujtlaololoton mamae, ihicxe, amatlapale, tapalcaio: in jtlanjoc itapalcaio vmpa ca in vel yiamatlapal, in jpatlanja: hiquac neci in ie qujiavi, iquac pãvetzi, iquac molonj.

CUJTLATEMOLI:

in cujtlatitlan, in axixtitlan ioli, ça vel iuhquj in temoli.

AIOXOCHQUJLTEMOLI:

iehoatl in aioxochqujlitl qujchichina coztontli, atle itlatlacolpil.

QUAUHTEMOLI:

iehoatl in quavitl yiti, in quavitl itech tlacati: tlatlactic achi vei.

QUAUHOCUJLI:

iehoatl in quavitl itech tlacati, in jtech ioli, iztac: injc iztac ca noz acan qujtta tonalli, cequj veveinti, cequj tepitoton. Inin tentlapalivi, tenjchtic tenchicaoac, tentepoztic, tlatequjnj, tlatotopotzanj, tlacujcujloanj: tlatotopotza, tlatetequj, tlacujcujloa.

¶

INJC MATLACTLI ONNAVI PARRAPHO: itechpa tlatoa in ioiolitoton in mitoa xoxotlame, yoã in juhque oc cequjn.

ICPITL:

in çaço tlein ioioli, in tlanextia iovaltica.

Injc centlamantli icpitl: itoca, coqujtl, iuhqujn chapoli, achi viac: in jquac qujavi, iooaltica in nemj, cenca mjeq'ntin: auh achi vei in jtlanex ach iuhqujnma candela. icujtlapiltitech inca itlanex achi centlacotl in jtlac: ipãpã achi vei itlanex.

Auh in quẽman iuhqujn ocopilli ic tlanextia, ipampã iooalli: auh in quẽman çan motecpana injc vtlatoca. Auh in aqujmamatcaoaque qujntocaiotia tlavipochtin.

---

9. *Temolin: Hallorina duguesi* (Sahagún, *op. cit.*, p. 354).

10. The Nahuatl text favors "on the wood"; corresponding Spanish and the context, "in the wood."

A second kind of *icpitl* is [like] a small butterfly; its small light is also on its tail.

A third kind of *icpitl* is a small worm; its light is also on its tail.

A fourth kind is an ant, a butterfly-ant. Likewise its little fire is on its tail. It is a light, a lighting; it glows.

A fifth kind is called *copitl*, which comes from *nicopi* [I close my eyes], because it goes shining, it goes with light extinguished. Black are its wings. When it flies,[1] when it appears, it glows.

Mayatl[2]

It lives in the hot countries. It is green; it glistens much. Very beautiful are its shell, its wings. It is harmless. It glows, it glistens; it appears beautiful.

Tecmilotl[3]

It is the same as a large fly. It is a little ashen, small, and flat. It has arms, legs, wings. It has excellent eyes; it sees well. And it is very agile; it is a buzzer, a biter, with a small, fiery mouth. Especially it attacks horses. It is one with a really fiery mouth. It is a sucker of people; it sucks one, it sucks one like a mosquito; it torments one, it burns one.

Whatever the kind of fly, it has wings, antennae, arms, legs. It is a flyer, it is lively.

Miccaçayolin[4]

It is round, just like the *temolin* or like the *tecuitla-ololo*; its body is somewhat green. It is a flyer, a buzzer. It travels with great violence when it flies; it goes buzzing, constantly striking the walls, the ground, ever restless. It is called *miccaçayolin* because it is said it is the lot of corpses. It buzzes, it flies violently, it hurls itself.

Xopan çayolin

It is small and round, green; it glistens, it glows. Only in the summer does it appear. It is very active. As it travels, it flies constantly, it buzzes constantly, it constantly throws itself about violently. It is active; it flits, it goes fleeing.

Injc vntlamantli icpitl: papalotontli, no itzintlan in ca itlanexton.

Injc etlamantli icpitl ocujlton no itzintlan ca in jtlanex.

Injc nauhtlamantli azcatl: azcapapalotl, çan no itzintlā in ca itleton: tlanextli, tlanextianj, xoxotla.

Injc macujllamantli, itoca copitl: itech qujçā njcopi, ipāpa vallanextitiuh oceuhtiuh: tliltic yiatlapal in itlapatlanja iquac in neci in cueponj.

Maiatl:

tonaian in nemj, xoxoctic, cenca pepetlaca, cenca qualli in jtapalcaio iiatlapal. atle itlatlacul, xoxotla, pepetzca, qualneci.

Tecmjlotl

ixqujch in vei çaioli, nextontli, patlachtontli, mamae, ihicxe, amatlapale, ixpapāton cenca tlachia: auh cenca tzicujctic, qujqujnacanj, tequanj, tentleton: oc cenca qujmoiautia in cavallo, vel tentleton, tepachichinanj, tepachichina, techichina, in iuhquj moiotl, tetoneoa, tetletlequechia.

In çaço tlein çaioli: amatlapale, iacatzone, mamae, iicxe, patlanjnj tzomoctic.

Miccaçaioli:

ololtic, vel iuhqujn temoli, manoce iuhq'n tecujtlaololo, achi xoxoctic in jnacaio: patlanjnj, qujqujnacanj, çan mochichiccanauhtinemj injc patlanj, qujqujnacatinemj: caltechtli, tlalli ic movivitectinemj, çan açemelle: injc mjtoa mjccaçaioli qujl intonal in tomjccaoan: qujqujnaca mochichicanaoa, motlatlamotla.

Xopan çaioli:

ololtontli, xoxoctic, pepepetzca, xoxotla çan iio xopan in oalneci cenca tzicujctic: injc nemj in papatlantinemj qujqujqujnacatinemja, motlatlalotiqujça, tzitzicujnj, qujqujztivetzi, motlatlalotinemj.

1. *Acad. Hist. MS: yn iquac tlapatlania.*
2. *Mayatl: Hallorina duguesi* (Sahagún, *op. cit.*, p. 341; also Santamaría, *op. cit.*, p. 707).
3. *Tecmilotl: moscardón* (Span. text and Sahagún, *op. cit.*, p. 353); *tábano* (Vogelsang and Martín del Campo, *op. cit.*, p. 3).
4. *Miccaçaioli: Musa* sp. (Sahagún, *op. cit.*, p. 342).

Tzonuatzalton[5]

It is a small fly, completely black, [like] a small twig, a little long. It is called *tzonuatzalton* because it is not fleshed, just small and lean, really small and active. It is never visible as it goes. It is a stinger.

Chilton[6]

It is a little fly — very small. It is called *chilton* because it just goes about seeking out the eyes; it is an enterer of one's eyes. And it hurts much, just like chili dropped into one's eyes. It is a damager of one's eyes. One's eyes are harmed, galled. Its secretion galls, harms, scratches one's eyes.

Çayolin

Also its name is *cuitlaçayolin*. It is small and round, a little smoky, a little black. It is called *cuitlaçayolin* because it lives in ordure, that in which the *tzinocuilin* worms live. And wherever there is a fetid odor, or food, it goes following the odor; it swarms about on the drink, the food, the sauce. It lives everywhere; it drops everywhere; there it dies. It is called *cuitlaçayolin* because it smells of excrement. If anyone swallows one, he thereupon vomits it up. He hates it, he abhors it. Wheresoever it settles, it sucks; on the same place it also rubs its rump; there it quickly lays eggs; soon little worms live there.

Çayolton

This small, slender fly lives everywhere it is shady. And when it lives in the cool lands, it is harmless. The one which lives in the hot lands is a biter. Its bite causes an itching.

Xiuhçayolin

It is small and green, like an herb. It is of average size. It does nothing but use its arms [as if] drilling a fire; however, all of them are like [ordinary] flies.

Moyotl[7]

It is a little ashen, lean, thin. The *tollamoyotl*, the *quammoyotl* are somewhat large. It has long legs, a pointed mouth. It is a sucker, a flyer. And when it flies, at the same time it goes buzzing; it continues buzzing. When it does not fly, it does not buzz. When it sucks one, it does so to excess; it fills well with

Tzonvatzalton:

çaiolton, çã cenqujztica tliltic, tlacopitzaton, viacatontli. Injc mjtoa tzonvatzalton, amo nacaio, çan oaccatontli vel tzicujctontli, njman amo nezquj injc iauh temjnanj.

Chilton,

çaiolton: cencan tepiton. Injc mjtoa chilton çã qujtemotinemj in ixtelolotli, teixco calaqujnj: auh çẽca toneoa, vel iuhqujn chilli onvetzi tixco: teixitlacoanj teixitlaco, teixoaoaço: teixoaoaçoa, teixitlacoa, teichichiticoa in jaxix

Çaioli:

yoan itoca cujtlaçaioli, ololtontli, pochectõtli, tliltontli. Injc mjtoa cujtlaçaioli, cujtlatitlan in ioli: iehoatl ioli in tzinocujli. Auh in campa ca xoqujiac, anoço qualonj, vmpa qujnecutiuh, cololhuja, apan tlaqualpan, molpan: noviã nemj, novian onvetzi, vmpa mjquj. Injc mjtoa cujtlaçaioli; ca cujtlaiac, in aqujn qujtoloa ic mjçotla, qujiolitlacoa, qujtlaelitta. In campa tlein itech motlalia, in qujchichina: çan no yoã itech motzĩchichiquj, vncan hiciuhca motetia, iciuhca ocujltotõ vncan ioli.

Çaiolton:

in tepiton pitzaoac çaioli, çan noviã in nemj in canjn çeçeoaian. Auh in tlaitztiaia nemj, atle intlatlacul: in tlatotoniã nemj tequanjme, tenquequexqujque.

Xiuhçaioli:

xoxoctontli, iuhqujn xivitl, qualton; çan ic nemj in momatlemamali, tel ie mochiuhque in çaiolti.

Moiotl:

nextontli, vacçolpil, quappitzpil. In tollamoiotl, in quammoiotl, oc achi vei, mavivitlatic, tenvitztic, tenvitzaponatic, techichinanj, patlanjnj: auh in jquac patlanj, çã çen qujqujnacatiuh, qujqujnacatinemj: in jquac amo patlanj, amo qujqujnaca. Injc tepachichina: pipicicavi, vel eztemj, vel chichilivi: in cequj

---

5. *Tzonuatzalton: moscardón* (Sahagún, *op. cit.*, p. 366).

6. *Chilton:* prob. *simúlidos* in Vogelsang and Martín del Campo, *op. cit.*, p. 2.

7. *Moyotl: Anopheles* sp. (Sahagún, *op. cit.*, p. 344).

blood, it really turns chili-red. Some, as they die, become dried blood; some yet escape.

ic mjquj ezquaoaquj, in cequj oc maqujça

Xalmoyotl

It is very small, very minute; all live there on the coast. They are really great biters. Although they enter some [other] places, their habitat is in the sand. Nevertheless, they enter the ground.

Xalmoiotl:

vel pitzaoac, vel piciltic, vmpa moch in nemj in anaoac, cenca tequanjme in manel canjn calaquj: ca xaltitlan in cate in inchã in manel tlallan calaquj.

Sixth Chapter, which telleth of the various trees, and of the various properties which correspond to them, such as their strength.

FIRST PARAGRAPH, in which are told the names of the different trees.

FOREST

It is a place of verdure, of fresh green; of wind — windy places, in wind, windy; a place of cold: it becomes cold; there is much frost; it is a place which freezes. It is a place whence misery comes, where it exists; a place where there is affliction — a place of affliction, of lamentation, a place of affliction, of weeping; a place where there is sadness, a place of compassion, of sighing; a place which arouses sorrow, which spreads misery.

It is a place of gorges, gorge places; a place of crags, craggy places; a place of stony soil, stony-soiled places; in hard soil, in clayey soil, in moist and fertile soil. It is a place among moist and fertile lands, a place of moist and fertile soil, in yellow soil.

It is a place with cuestas, cuesta places; a place with peaks, peaked places; a place which is grassy, with grassy places; a place of forests, forested places; a place of thin forest, thinly forested places; a place of thick forest, thickly forested places; a place of jungle, of dry tree stumps, of underbrush, of dense forest.

It is a place of stony soil, stony-soiled places; a place of round stones, round-stoned places; a place of sharp stones, of rough stones; a place of crags, craggy places; a place of *tepetate*; a place with clearings, cleared places; a place of valleys, of coves, of places with coves, of cove places; a place of boulders, bouldered places; a place of hollows.

It is a disturbing place, fearful, frightful; home of the savage beast, dwelling-place of the serpent, the rabbit, the deer; a place whence nothing departs, nothing leaves, nothing emerges. It is a place of dry rocks, of boulders; bouldered places; boulder land, a land of bouldered places. It is a place of caves, cave places, having caves — a place having caves.

It is a place of wild beasts; a place of wild beasts — of the ocelot, the *cuitlachtli*, the bobcat; the serpent,

Injc chiquacen capitulo: itechpa tlatoa in nepapã quavitl, yoan in izqujtlamantli itech ca, iuhqujnma ichicaoalizo.

INJC CE PARRAPHO ipã mjtoa in jtoca in izqujtlamantli quavitl.

QUAUHTLA:

tlatzmolinja, tlaceliaian, ehecaia, ehecaiocã, ehecatlan, ehecaio, tlaceceiaia, tlaceceia, çetla, cevetziia; icnoiotl iqujztoia, yieoaian, nentlamachooaia, tenentlamachtican, techoctican, tenentlamachticã chocovaian tlaocuialoia, tetlaocultican, elciciovaiã, teellelaxitican, tlacnomamãcan:

atlauhtla, ahatlauhtla, texcalla, tetexcalla, tetla, tetetla, tlaltepitzpã, teçoqujpan, atocpan, atoctitlã atoctla, tlalcozpã,

tlamjmjlolla, tlâtlamjmjlolla tlachichiqujlla, tlâtlachichiqujlla, çacatla, çaçacatla, quauhtla quaquauhtla, quauhcaiactla, quâquauhcaiactla, quautilactla, quâquauhtilactla: quapotzalla, quâvatzalla, quauhiacacatla, quauhiooaiatla:

tetla, tetetla, teololla, teteololla, techachalla, techachaquachtla, texcalla, tetexcalla, tepetlatla; tlachipaoaia, tlachichipaoaia, tlavelmaia, qualcã quaqualcã quâqualcan: tlaltepexitla tlâtlaltepexitla, tlatlaacaliuhian,

hacemellecan, temauhtican, temamauhticã: tequanj ichan cooatl, tochin, maçatl inemja, atle iievacã, atle iieoaian, atle iqujztocã, tetl vavaccan, tepexitla, tetepexitla, tlaltepexitla, tlâtlaltepexitla, oztotla, ohoztotla, ohoztoio, ohoztoiocan,

tequãtla, tequanjtla, ocelotla, cujtlachtla, ocotochtla, coatla, tocatla, tochtla, maçatla, tlacotla, çacatla,

the spider, the rabbit, the deer; of stalks, grass, prickly shrubs; of the *nequametl,* the *netzollin,* the *uitztecolotl,* the *teonochtli*: of the mesquite, of the pine. It is a place where wood is owned. Trees are felled. It is a place where trees are cut, where wood is gathered,[1] where there is chopping, where there is logging: a place of beams.

It becomes verdant, a fresh green. It becomes cold, icy. Ice forms and spreads; ice lies forming a surface. There is wind, a crashing wind; the wind crashes, spreads whistling, forms whirlwinds. Ice is blown by the wind; the wind glides.

There is no one; there are no people. It is desolate; it lies desolate. There is nothing edible. Misery abounds, misery emerges, misery spreads. There is no joy, no pleasure. It lies sprouting; herbs lie sprouting; nothing lies emerging; the earth is pressed down. All die of thirst. The grasses lie sprouting. Nothing lies cast about. There is hunger; all hunger. It is the home of hunger; there is death from hunger. All die of cold; there is freezing; there is trembling; there is the clattering, the chattering of teeth. There are cramps, the stiffening of the body, the constant stiffening, the stretching out prone.

There is fright, there is constant fright. One is devoured; one is slain by stealth; one is abused; one is brutally put to death; one is tormented. Misery abounds. There is calm, constant calm, continuing calm.

¶

Second paragraph, which telleth of the different trees.

Tlatzcan[1]

The *tlatzcan* is high, slender; it has branches. It is not forked; it is like a stone column. Its leaves cast a shadow. They are straight, slender, light blue, herb green, the color of the lovely cotinga. It has a terminal bud, a terminal growth. It has a blossom, it has blossoms, it has seeds. It is of pleasant, fragrant odor. It is a long-lived one, which does not become dormant, which does not rot, which is not eaten by worms nor gnawed. It is fine-textured, smooth, soft, compact. It has roots, a base, a trunk, a top. The trunk is thick, slender at the top. It has a bark; it can be barked. It has wood, a center, leaves; leaves, foliage, knots, leaves. It has a trunk, terminal growth, terminal buds, a summit, suckers.

tzioactla; nequametla, netzolla, vitztecolla, teunochtla, mjzqujtla, teucotla, quaovaian, quauhtlaçaloa, quauhtecoia, quaquauhcujvaian, tlatepozviloian, vepanoia, vepãtla.

tlatzmolinj, tlacelia, tlaceceia, ceoa, cetl ixoatoc, cetl pavetztoc, eheca, tlatlatzca ehecatl, ehecatlatlatzca, ehecapipitzcatoc, ehecatl motetevilacachoa, cetl êcatoco, ehecatl mopetzcoa:

aiac tlacatl, aiac tlatlacatl, cactimanj, cactzinvetztoc, atle qualonj, tlacnomamanj, icnoiotl qujztoc, icnoiotl vetztoc, aaviialo, avellamacho: tlaxoatoc, tlaxiuhixoatoc, atle qujqujztoc, tlalli tzitzica, amjcoa, çacaxoatoc, atle vevetztoc, maianalo, teuciova, apiztli ichã, apizmjcoa, cecmjcoa, cioapaoalo, cuecuechco, netlantzitzilolo, netlantzitzilitzalo, cequappitzoa, nequappitzolo, nequaquapitzolo, necatzmelaoalo,

nemauhtilo, nemamauhtilo; tequalo, teichtacamjctilo, temjctilo, texoxouhcamjctilo, teixnenpeoaltilo, tlacnomamanj, pacoa pâpacoa, papacoa.

¶

Injc vme parrapho: itechpa tlatoa in nepapan quavitl.

Tlatzcan,

tlatzca, veiac, piaztic, mamaie, hamaxallo, temjmjltic, ceoallo, hecauhio in jacazvaio, ixmelactic, ixpipitzaoac, texotic, qujltic, xiuhtototic, izcallo, mjiaoaio, xochio, xoxochio, xinachio, velic, aviac, vecaoanj, hatlatzivinj, hapalanjnj, haocujlqualonj, haquaqualonj; cuechtic, xipetztic, iamanquj, picquj, nelhoaio, tzine, tlaque, quaie, tlactomaoac, quapitzaoac, xincaio, xipeoalo, nacaio, iollo, acazoaio, avazoaio, qujllo, ixe, atlapale, tetepone, izcallo, mjaoaio, tzone, pilhoa.

---

1. *Acad. Hist. MS: quâquacovaya.*
1. *Tlatzcan: Cupressus benthannii* Endl., *C. thurifera* H.B.K. (Santamaría, *Diccionario de Mejicanismos,* p. 1061 — *tlaxcal*).

[A tree] sprouts, grows, enlarges, develops, forms terminal growth, forms branches, forms branches in different places, forms foliage, leaves. The buds burst open; it forms blossoms; it blossoms; [the blossoms] swell. It sheds its blossoms, it drops them. It sheds its leaves, sheds leaves; it drops its foliage. It grows dormant; it dries, it becomes a dried tree. Branches are removed; branches break off; they fall. [The tree] rises above us; it is torn up by the roots; it falls with a crash. It falls to the ground[2] — broken, broken to pieces, shattered to pieces.

It is chopped, it is topped, broken up, straightened, formed into a beam, cut. It is required; it is used for constructing houses. It is planed, hollowed, hollowed in many places.

It produces suckers; suckers emerge. It forms a root; it takes root. It is transplanted, it is planted. Seeds scatter; they are sown; they swell, they swell up, they produce shoots.

Fir[3]

It is slender, straight; suitable for being broken up, for being cut for beams, for being split, for being divided, for making houses. The branches are slender. They are like turquoise. It has bark; it can be barked. There are saplings, old trees, strong trees, tender trees, mature trees. It is chopped, broken up, formed into a beam, worked by a carpenter, burned, cut, felled, chopped, broken up, straightened.

Ayauhquauitl[4]

It is tall, thick, compact. It has branches; it has a ruddy bark. It has knots — many knots; the tree is knotty. It has a trunk, roots — thick roots, slender roots. It takes root, forms roots. It grows, sends out a shoot, forms a shoot, sets a node, develops, grows, lengthens, becomes high, stands casting a shadow, stands shading, stands [spreading] branches; stands towering — highest of all.

Pine[5]

The pine tree is tender, verdant, very verdant. It has particles of [dried] pine [resin]. It has cones — pine cones; it has a bark, a thick skin. It has pine resin, a resin. [The wood] can be broken, shattered.

Ixoa: mozcaltia, mana, mooapaoa, izcalloa, momatia, momamatia, moqujllotia, amatlapaloa, xotla, moxochiotia, xochiova, totomolivi, moxochiotlaça, moxochiotepeoa, mozoaiotlaça, macazoaiotlaça, moqujllotepeoa: tlatzivi, vaquj, quauhvatzalti, momatlaça, matzaianj, vetzi, motopaneoa, motzineoa, tlacomonjtivetzi, quauhtevetzi, poztectivetzi, popoztectivetzi, tlaxaxamatztivetzi:

motepozvia, motzontequj, motlapana, movelteca, mooapalteca, moxima; neco, necaltilo, mochichiquj, mooacaloa, mooaoacaloa,

mopilqujxtia, pilqujça, monelhoaiotia, nelhoaiooa, maquja, motoca moxinachoa, mopixoa, poçonj, oalpoçonj, achichilacachtia.

Oiametl:

piaztic, melaoac, tlapanonj, oapalteconj, tzaianonj, xelolonj, necaltiloni: mapipitzaoac, ximmaltic, eoaio, tlaxipeoallo: quauhpilli, vevequavitl, quauhchicaoac, quauhcelic, omacic quavitl, motepuzvia motlapana, mooapalteca, moquaquavi, tlatilo, motequj, motlaça, motepozvia, motlapana, movelteca.

Aiauhquavitl:

veiac, tcmaoac, picquj, mamae, evaio tlauhtic, ixe, iixe, quauhixio, tetepone, nelhoaio, nelhoaiotomaoac, nelhoaiopitzaoac, nelhoaiooa, monelhoaiotia, ixoa, itzmjqujltia, achichilacachtia, ce iix qujoalquetza mana mozcaltia, veiaquja, vecapanjvi, cevalloticac, hecauhioticac, mamaeticac, panqujzticac, panvetzticac.

Ocotl,

ocoquavitl, celic, cecelic, ocoxallo, cinio, ococinio, xincaio, eoaiotilaoac, ocotzoio, oxio, tzomonquj, tzotzomonquj, oconapallo: netlavililonj, tlachialonj, oxitlatilonj, çonectic, poxaoac: açotic mocotzoiotia, ixi-

---

2. *Acad. Hist. MS: quauhteuhvetzi.*

3. *Oyametl: Abies religiosa* (H.B.K.) Schlecht and Cham.; Paul C. Standley, "Trees and Shrubs of Mexico," *Contributions from the United States National Herbarium*, Vol. 23, Pt. 1 (Washington: Government Printing Office, 1920), p. 59.

4. *Ayauhquauitl:* possibly *Pinus ayacahuite* (Santamaría, *op. cit.*, p. 101 — ayacahuite).

5. *Ocotl: Pinus* sp. (Standley, *op. cit.*, p. 55).

The pine is embracing. It is a provider of light, a means of seeing, a resinous torch. It is spongy, porous, soft. It forms a resin; drops stand formed; they stand sputtering. They sputter. It burns, it illuminates things, it makes a resin; a resin exudes. It turns into a resin. Resin is required.

Ash[6]

It is verdant, shiny — shiny on the surface; smooth, smooth on all parts, round on all parts like a stone column. It is a dye — a ruddy color, a tawny dyeing medium. It has branches; it is average in height, in thickness. It dyes things, makes things brown, makes things beautiful.

Cypress[7]

It is of dark yellow surface, without blemishes. It has branches, spindle-whorl-shaped ones, like spindle whorls. It has a crotch: many crotches; it is crotched. It is fragrant, of pleasant odor. It is large, high, thick, shady, shadowy. There is constant entering into its shade; under it one is shaded. It is said that a mother, a father become the silk cotton tree, the cypress. It shades things, it forms a shadow; it gives shade, it gives shadow. It takes the form of a spindle whorl. It thickens, extends its branches, extends branches everywhere, forms foliage. It sheds foliage, it sheds butterfly-like leaves. It towers above, it excels.

Silk cotton tree[8]

It is smooth, smooth in all parts; dense; quite circular, well rounded, quite rounded; shady, shadowy. It shades; it gives shade, it gives shadow; it shades one. Under it, one is shaded. Hence, for this reason, it is called "the governor"; for he becomes [as] a silk cotton tree, a cypress. It bears fruit, it produces fruit; nowhere is its fruit needed. When shriveled, it is cast off. Therefore it is said of the proud, to whom later great misery comes, "The fruit comes to earth. This one has ripened; already it falls to the ground."

Auaquauitl, auatl, teoquauitl[9]

It is hard, tough, resilient, compact, firm; a rounded tree, round. It has branches — many-forked, bifurcated branches, branches which are crotched. It has leaves, it has Spanish moss. It is a tree which is bifur-

caticac icoiocaticac, icoioca, tlatla, tlatlanextia, oxiti, oxiqujça, oxitl mocuepa: monequj in oxitl.

Ilin,

cecelic, tzotzotlaca, ixtzotzotlaca, xipetztic, xixipetztic, ipanoca temjmjltic, tlapalonj, tlatlauhquj, tlaquappachpalonj, mamae, çan ipan qualli injc veiac, injc tomaoac: tlapa, tlacamjloa, tlaqualnextia.

Avevetl:

ixcoziaiactic, tlatlacanezquj, mamae, malacachtic, maiacachiuhquj, maxallo, mamaxaliuhquj, mamaxaltic, aviac, velic, vei, vecapan, tomaoac, cevallo, hecauhio, itlan necacalaqujlo, itlã neçeoalhujlo: mjtoa pochotl, avevetl mochiuhtica, in nantli in tatli: tlaceoalhuja, tlaehecalhuja, moceoallotia, moiacauhiotia, momalacaiotia: tomaoa, moçooa, mamaçoa, moqujllotia, moqujllotlaça, mopapalotlaça, tlapanavia, tlacaoa.

Pochotl:

xipetztic, xixipetztic, tlatztic, vel tevilacachtic vel iaoaltic, vel iaoalivhquj, cevallo, hecauhio, ceoalloa, moceoallotia, moiacauhiotia, teceoalhuja, itlan neceoalhujlo: ic ipãpa mjtoa in tepachoanj. Ca pochotl, avevetl mochiuhticac: xocoiooa, tlaaqujlloa, acan monequj in jtlaaqujlo in oontlatziuh, valmotepeoa: ic impã mjtoa in mopoanj, in çatepã cenca icnoiotl itech iauh, valxoxocotioã tlalticpac, onjcucic, o, ie valchapantivetzi.

Avaquavitl: avatl, teuquavitl

tepitztic, tlaquaoac, oltic, picquj, tlaquactic, quauhiaoaliuhquj, iaoaltic, mamae, mamaxaltic, mamatzocoltic, mamatzocollo, avazvaio, pachio, quauhtzotzocoltic, quauhtzotzocolli; atlacacemelle, acemelle, tê-

---

6. *Ilin:* Corresponding Spanish text: *"Ay fresnos en esta tierra, a llamanse ylin."* See Standley, *op. cit.,* Pt. 4, p. 1133.

7. *Aueuetl: Taxodium mucronatum (ibid.,* Pt. 1, p. 60).

8. *Pochotl: Ceiba pentandra* Gaertn. (Santamaría, *op. cit.,* p. 873).

9. *Avaquauitl: Quercus* L. sp. (Standley, *op. cit.,* Pt. 2, p. 171).

cated, a bifurcated tree. It is monstrous, restless, creaking, crackling. Wheels are made, cartwheels are cut; digging sticks are cut. It is topped, trimmed, split, broken up, broken to pieces. It is a firewood tree; it provides firewood. It has Spanish moss, it produces Spanish moss, it forms a tree of Spanish moss.

Auatetzmolin[10]

It is drooping,[11] matted, small and round, with tapering branches. It becomes round; it becomes matted. The branch tapers, the branches taper.

¶

Third paragraph, which telleth of trees which are not very large, which are considered as herbs.

Manzanita[1]

It is ruddy. It has berries; it has a berry. It is a round tree of average size. It becomes ruddy; it produces berries; it produces a berry.

Tomazquitl[2]

It has blossoms; it has a blossom. It is ruddy. It has tapering branches. It is a round tree, a rounded tree.

Quauhtepoztli[3]

It is thick barked. It is a dye. It is barked.

Uicquauitl

It is a hard tree, a rock-like tree. It stands in rocks, in crags. It sprouts in the rocks, it grows in rocky places.

Necalizquauitl

It is a flaring one, one which shoots forth. In the fire it flares, it shoots forth.

Pocquauitl

It is smoky; a smoker; an encaser, a carrier of smoke. It smokes; it produces smoke. It makes one weep;[4] it makes one weep constantly; it brings out one's tears, it makes one's tears fall, it makes one's eyes sore.

tecujtztic, tetecujtztic, moquauhtemalacachioa, moquauhtemalacaxima, movicxima, motzontequj, motzotzontequj, motzaiana motlapana, motlatlapana, tlatlatilquavitl, tlatlatilquauhti, pachiova, mopachiotia, moquappachiotia.

Avatetzmoli,

chachapatic, pâçoltic, iaoaltontli, mamatzoltic, iaoalivi, paçolivi, matzolivi, mamatzolivi.

¶

Injc ei parrapho itechpa tlatoa in quavitl in amo cenca vevei in çan iuhquj xivitl ipam povi.

Tepetomatl,

tlatlactic, cacapollo, capollo, quauhiaoalli ipan qualli, tlatlavia, cacapoloa, capolloa.

Tomazqujtl,

xoxochio, xochio tlatlauhquj, mamatzoltic, quauhiavalli, quauhiaoaltic.

Quauhtepuztli

eoaiotilaoac tlapalonj, moxipeoa.

Vicquavitl,

quauhtepitztli, tequavitl, tepan, texcalpan ihicac tetla ixoa, tetetla mooapaoa.

Necalizquavitl,

tlatlatzcanj cuecuepocanj, in tleco tlatlatzca, cuecuepoca.

Pocquavitl,

pocio, popocanj, tlapoccaloanj, tlapocmamanj, popoca, mopociotia, techoctia, techochoctican, teixaioqujxtia, teixaiotepeoa, teichichitictia.

---

10. *Auatetzmoli:* also identified as *Quercus* L. sp. in Standley, *loc. cit.*

11. Read *chachapactic,* as in *Acad. Hist. MS.*

1. *Tepetomatl: Arctostaphylos tomentosa.* See Santamaría, *op. cit.,* p. 1034, and Standley, *op. cit.,* Pt. 4, p. 1098.

2. *Tomazquitl: especie de madroño* (Hernández, *Hist. Natural,* Vol. I, p. 232).

3. *Quauhtepoztli:* probably same as *tepozcauil* (Santamaría, *op. cit.,* p. 1036) — *Copaifera himenifolia.*

4. *Acad. Hist. MS: techóchoctia.*

TEOCOTL[5]

It is smokeless. Its odor is pleasing, fragrant to smell. It is the wood of noblemen; their lot. It is made their lot; it is appropriated as, it is taken as their lot; it is reckoned as their own.

COATLI[6]

It is a carrying-frame tree, cordlike, slender, slender and thin; compact, yielding, sparse. It is medicine and [a wood] from which water can be extracted. Its sap is blue. It is a urine medicine. It twists, bends, forms into a circle. Water is extracted which is drunk.

THE ÇAYOLITZCAN[7] is the same as the *coatli*. It is scaly.

TOPOÇAN[8]

It is also scaly. It is thin-skinned. It has branches. It is a round tree. The leaves are wide, the leaves are broad, blue on their upper surfaces, ashen, white on their back surfaces, like the *cocoyatic* [and] *coayelli* herbs. It is medicine; the essence of its root is to be drunk.[9] It cleans one's urine, it purifies it; it aids one's digestion, lessens one's fever, benefits one, cures one. It benefits.

WILLOW[10]

It is thick-skinned, rough. It has tapering branches. It has branches. It is a grower, one which shoots up, enlarges. It is a large tree, soft, spongy, porous. It is a large tree; it thickens, shoots up, lengthens, whispers, forks, forms crotches, becomes like a spindle whorl, forms branches.

QUETZALUEXOTL, QUETZALAUEXOTL[11]

It is slender, a little smooth, slender-branched. Its foliage is slender. It is bitter. An average-sized tree, it is tough, yielding, compact, tough. It forms a crotch, it forms suckers. Suckers emerge, suckers are produced. It is transplanted.

ICÇOTL[12]

It is thick, black. It has a blossom; it is a blossoming one. It is rough, spongy within, with a fatty material. It swells, enlarges, bursts, blossoms.

TEOCUTL,

apocio, velic, aviac in jiaca: tecpilquavitl, tetonal tetonaltilo, netechtilo, netonaltilo, tetechpoalo.

COATLI

vacalquavitl memecatic pipitzaoac, piaztic, pipiaztic, pipinquj, oltic, atic: patli, yoan aqujxtilonj, matlaltic in jaio, axixpatli. Nolivi, colivi, tevilacachivi maqujxtia, mjh.

ÇAIOLITZCAN çan no iuhquj in coatli, xincaio.

TOPOÇAN

no xincaio, eoaiocanaoac, mamae, quauhiaoalli, amatlapalpatlaoac, aoazoapatlaoac: in jamatlapal in jixco texotic in jtepotzco cujtlanextic, ticeoac cocoiac, coaieltic, patli, yoanj, in jnelhoaio ihiyo, teaxixiectia, teaxixchipaoa, tetlatemovilia, tetlecevia, tepalevia, tepatia, tlapalevia.

VEXOTL, AVEXOTL, MJCCAAVEXOTL

eoaiotilaoac, chachaquachtic mamatzoltic, mamae, mozcaltianj, motlamjnanj, mananj, vei quavitl, poxaoac, çonectic açotic vei quavitl, tomaoa motlamjna, veca iauh, cacapaca, mâxaloa, mamaxalloa, malacachivi, momatia.

QUETZALHUEXOTL; QUETZALAVEXOTL,

piaztic, achi xipetztic, mapipitzaoac, in jqujllo pipitzaoac chichic çan vel ipan quavitl, tlaquaoac, oltic, picquj, pipinquj momaxallotia, mopilqujxtia pilqujça, mopilhoatia maquja.

ICÇOTL

tomaoac, catzaoac, xochio, cueponcaio, chachaquachtic, hitipochinquj, pochqujo, totomolivi, mjmjlivi, xotla, cueponj.

---

5. *Teocotl: Pinus teocote* (Sahagún, Garibay ed., Vol. IV, p. 355).
6. *Coatli: Eysenhardtia polystachya* (Standley, *op. cit.,* Pt. 2, p. 443).
7. *Çayolitzcan:* same as *topoçan* (*tepozán*), says Santamaría (*op. cit.,* p. 1150 — *zayoliscán*): *Buddleia americana.*
8. See n. 7.
9. *Acad. Hist.* MS adds *yua mih.*
10. *Uexotl: Salix* L. sp. (Standley, *op. cit.,* Pt. 1, p. 160).
11. *Quetzalhuexotl: Salix lasiopelis* (Sahagún, *op. cit.,* p. 351).
12. *Icçotl: Yucca albifolia* Y. (*ibid.,* p. 337).

ÇOTOLIN[13]

It is drooping, spiny; it has breast-like leaves. It stands drooping. It is spiny. It does not lie growing; it lies flat; it lies sprouting.

ÇOYATL[14]

It has branches; it is spreading, thick. It has no Spanish moss, no production of Spanish moss. It has blossoms, it has edible fruit — good, fine, sweet. It stands alone; it is especially preferred. The lone ant breeds, runs [on it].

TLACUILOLQUAUITL[15]

It is varicolored, glistening, thick,[16] smooth, dense. It is varicolored; it is painted, lined with black, designed. Two-toned drums are made; ground drums, guitars are made. They have a good sound like a bell. Their voices are soft, their song beautiful. It is coveted, desirable, desired, required. It sounds clear, it sounds well, it resounds; it is beautiful. One is made to desire it, to covet it.

TLACALHUAZQUAUITL

It is slender, reed-like; slender in all parts; hollow, [the hole] going clear through. It serves as a throwing device, as a blow-gun, a device for hunting, for killing. It is hollow; its interior is hollow; it serves as a blow-gun; it hurls things; it is for hunting.

THE AYOTENTLI is chili-red.

CHICHIC QUAUITL,[17] CHICHIC PATLI

[An infusion of its bark] is potable; it aids one's digestion, soothes one's intestines, serves as a laxative, purges one; it soothes one's intestines; it clears, fortifies the intestines, the stomach. It is a remedy for the urine; it opens [the passages for] urine. If much is drunk, it causes blood to appear. Only an average amount is drunk; not much.

AMAQUAUITL[18]

It is smooth, smooth overall; its leaves, foliage, verdure gleam; its bark is herb-green. It is made into paper; it becomes paper. It is beaten.

ÇOTOLI,

chapactic, vitzio, chichioale. &c. chachapacaticac vitzio, amochiuhtoc, onoc ixoatoc.

ÇOIATL,

mamae, chachaiactic, tomaoac, apachiio, apachiqujzio, xochio, xochiquallo, qualonj, iectli, qualli, necutic icelicac, mocecocamati, icecelazcati, mozcaltia, motlamjna.

TLACUJLOLQUAVITL,

cujcujltic cuecueioca, tomactic, xipetztic tlatztic, cujcujlivi, mocujcujloa motlitlilanja, motlatlamachia: teponaztli mochioa, vevetl, mecavevetl mochioa, vel naoatl coioltic, in jtozquj iamanquj in jtlatol, qualneci, teiculti, tetlanecti, eleviliztli, nequjztli, naoati, caqujzti, tzilinj, qualneci, tetlanectia, teicultia.

TLACALHOAZQUAVITL,

pitzaoac, acatic, pipitzaoac, iticoionquj qujqujztic, tlamotlalonj, tlatlacalhoazvilonj, tlamalonj, tlamjctilonj, coionj, iticoionj: tlatlacalhoazvia, tlamotla, tlama.

AIOTENTLI, chichiltic.

CHICHIC QUAVITL: CHICHIC PATLI

ioanj, tetlatemovili, tecujtlaxcoliecti, tetlanoqujli, tetlanoqujlia, tecujtlaxcoliectia, qujpopoa, qujtlachicazvia, in cujtlaxcolli: in totlatlaliaia, teaxixpatia, teaxixtlapoa: in mjec mj eztli qujnextia; çan ipan qualli in mj amo quexqujch.

AMAQUAVITL,

xipetztic, xixipetztic in jatlapal, in jxiuhio, in jqujllo, tzotzotlaca, qujltic in jeoaio: mamachioa, amatl mocuepa, movitequj.

---

13. *Çotoli: Dasylirion* sp. (Santamaría, *op. cit.,* p. 985; Standley, *op. cit.,* Pt. 1, p. 99).

14. *Çoyatl: Brahea dulcis (ibid.,* p. 75).

15. *Tlacuilolquauitl:* also called *oceloquauitl;* described in Hernández, *op. cit.,* Vol. I, p. 40 and *passim.*

16. *Acad. Hist. MS: tomatic.*

17. *Chichic quauitl: Coutarea latiflora* Moc. (Sahagún, *op. cit.,* p. 333).

18. *Amaquauitl: Ficus benjamina, F. involuta (ibid.,* p. 321; Standley, *op. cit.,* pp. 205–213).

THE COPALQUAUITL has a liquid; it exudes a liquid.

OCOTZOQUAUITL,[19] XOCHIOCOTZOQUAUITL

It is rough, thick, round. It has a liquid, it exudes a liquid. Its bark is chopped; from there the resin, the liquidambar, comes out.

OLQUAUITL[20]

It is thick, like a spindle-whorl, like the silk cotton tree. It has a liquid. Its bark is chopped; there comes out, there exudes the rubber. It is a medicine, a remedy for all ailments — a remedy for eye ailments, for festering. It is potable. With chocolate, it relieves our stomach, our intestines. It restores our internal organs; it cures where there is infection. The rubber exudes,[21] it thickens; it is fibrous, nerve-like, tough; it jumps. It is soft, spongy, flesh-like.

UITZQUAUITL[22]

It is chili-red, a dye, a chili-red dye. It releases a color; it makes things chili-red; it dyes, stains things.

———

Matted trees are thick; they make much darkness. They are crowded together, interlaced. They are shading things; they are matted together. They are rounded, bushing out; they are each one bushing out.

Sparse trees are sparse. There is light. They are sparse, spaced out, each one far apart. It is a desolate place.

"Tree" is the name of that which stands verdant, that which is developed, can be transplanted, can be put in the ground; [it is the name of] the tree become firm, the matured tree, the old one.

"Tree" is the name of that which can be planted, that which can be transplanted, that which sprouts, which forms a shoot, which sends up a shoot, which sets a node; that which grows, develops,[23] enlarges; the sapling, the young tree, the tender tree, the tree become firm. It is planted, sown; it matures; it is wetted, moistened; it forms roots; it takes root, bursts, germinates, sprouts,[24] pushes up, emerges at the surface, forms a shoot, sends out a shoot, sets a node, grows, develops, extends, continues a little,

COPALQUAVITL: memeiallo, memeia.

OCUTZOQUAVITL: XOCHIOCUTZOQUAVITL,

tetecujtztic, tomaoac, iaoaltic, memeiallo, memeia; motepozvia in jeoaio, vncan oalqujça in ocutzotl in xochiocutzotl.

OLQUAVITL,

tomaoac, malacachtic, pochotic, memeiallo; motepozvia in jxipeoallo, vncã oalqujça, vncan oalmeia in olli. Patli, mochi inamjc in cocoliztli: ixcocoliztli inamjc, palanaliztli inamjc: yoanj, cacaoatl ipan, qujpatia in totlatlaliaia, in tocujtlaxcol; tlapatia in titic, tlapatia in canjn tlapalanj; in olli mea, tetzaoa, tlalichtic, tlalhoatic, tlaquaoac, choloa, papatztic, patztic nacatic.

VITZQUAVITL:

chichiltic, tlapalonj, tlachichilolonj, tlatlapalqujxtia, tlachichiloa, tlapa, tlamaoa.

———

Quappotzalli, tilaoac, mjec tlatlaiooa, tepeuhtimanj, moquequetztimanj, tlaiooatimanj, potzauhtimanj, iaoaliuhtimanj, poçontimanj, popoçõtimanj.

Quauhcaiactli: caiaoac, tlatlaneztica, caiaoatimanj, cacaiaoatimanj, vevecamamanj nemjuhian.

Quavitl itoca, in xoxovixticac: vapaoalonj, aqujlonj, tlalhujlonj: yiolloquavitl, omacic quavitl, ovevetic.

Quavitl itoca, in toconj in aqujlonj, in ixoanj in achichilacachtianj, in itzmjqujltia, in ce yix, qujoalquetzanj, in moxoaltianj, in oapaoalonj in mananj, in quauhconetl, in quauhpilli, in quauhcelic in jiollocoquavitl: motoca, mopixoa, camaoa, ciaoa, poxcavi, monelhoaiotia, nelhoaiova, tlapanj, tlacati, iacaomj, oallaxiponoa, oallalticpacqujça, achichilacachti, itzmjqujltia, ce yix qujoalquetza mozcaltia, mana, motitioana, achi qujtoca, tetzaoa, chicaoac, otlatoca, mantiuh, mozcallotia, moqujllotia, maoazoaiotia, moma-

19. *Ocotzoquauitl: Liquidambar styraciflua* L. sp. (Standley, *op. cit.*, Pt. 2, p. 317).
20. *Olquauitl: Castilla elastica* (ibid., pp. 214–216).
21. *Acad. Hist. MS: meya.*
22. *Uitzquauitl: Caesalpina echinata* (Sahagún, *op. cit.*, p. 367).
23. *Acad. Hist. MS: mozcaltiani.*
24. *Ibid.: yacaomiti.*

grows firm, strengthens, grows bigger, enlarges, puts on terminal growth; forms foliage, leaves, branches, forms a crotch; forms crotches; forms branches in different places; puts on terminal growth, forms terminal growth, puts on terminal buds, forms terminal buds.

It becomes a sapling, a young tree, a tender tree, a firm tree. It becomes strong, matured, well matured. It sheds its foliage, drops its foliage, sheds its butterfly-like leaves; it drops leaves, sheds leaves.

It buds, it forms buds; the buds swell; they enlarge, burst, bloom, form blossoms. It sheds blossoms. Droplets form; it forms fruit; it develops fruit; fruit remains.

¶

FOURTH PARAGRAPH, which telleth of the parts of each tree; such as the branch; then the root.

On the tree, so that it stands upright, is the root, the tree root, pointed at the end, cylindrical, strong, nerve-like. It enters into the ground; it runs in all directions; it grasps, it takes hold; it causes development; it nourishes; it takes water, it takes food.

The base of the tree, the tree's thick base, is ball-like, scabrous, asperous, rough; of matted roots, of tapering roots; hard, firm, tough, strong. It is what grips the earth well, what grips twisting, what grips binding. It is fibrous. It is what carries, supports, bears [the tree]. It carries, supports, bears, completely carries, supports [the tree].

The trunk of the tree, the tree trunk: this rises from the base; it reaches to the slender part [above]. It is thick, cylindrical, a cylindrical trunk, like a stone column, thick of base, slender of top. It has knots, tree knots; it has branches, tapering branches; it has bark. It has concavities; it is torn, forked, bifurcated, divided, straight. [There are] curved trees, matted trees, tree fibers, damaged trees, asperous, bumpy, scabrous. It enlarges, it thickens, it grows large, it becomes cylindrical, it widens, it becomes concave. Its base thickens, its top becomes slender. It becomes thin, it grows long; it goes straight; it twists, curves, forms knobs, forms knots, forms tree knots; it produces suckers; it forms a crotch, it forks: a tree fork, a tree bifurcation, a division.

[The term "tree trunk"] is derived from a person; it resembles one. One has a crotch. It derives from one, resembles one, follows one, comes later.

Branches are curved, doubled over, matted. [There are] matted trees, tapering branches, outstretched

tia, momaxallotia, momamaxallotia, momamatia, mozcallotia, izcalloa, momjiaoaiotia, mjaoaioa,

quauhconeti, quappilti, quauhcelti, yiolloquauhti, chicaoa maci, vel maci, moqujllotlaça, moqujllotepeoa, mopapalotlaça maoazoaiotepeoa, maoazoaiotlaça,

celia, itzmolinj, totomolivi, mjmjlivi, xotla, cueponj, moxochiotia, moxochiotlaça, chipini, moxocoiotia, xocoioa, xocottoc.

¶

INJC NAVI PARRAPHO: itechpa tlatoa in jviviltecca, in ceceiaca quavitl: in juhquj quammaitl, njman ie iehoatl tlanelhoatl.

In quavitl in jtechca injc hicac, tlanelhoatl, quauhnelhoatl, iacaomjtic, mjmjltic chicaoac, tlalhoatic, tlallan calaquj, motlatlamjna, tlatzitzquja. tlamotzoloa, tlaoapaoa, tlazcaltia, atli tlaqua.

Quauhtzontetl, quavitl itzintomaoaca, tapaioltic cocomotztic tetêcujtztic chachaquachtic, tzinpaçoltic, tzimmamatzoltic, tepitztic, tlaquactic, tlaquaoac, chicaoac, vellalpitl, tlatetzilpitl, tlacacatzilpitl, ichtic, tlanapaloanj, tlatqujnj, tlamamanj, tlanapaloa, tlatquj, tlamama tlacennapaloa, tlacemjtquj.

Quauhtlactli; in jtlac quavitl: iehoatl in jtech oaleoa in quauhtzontetl in jtech onaçi iquapitzaoaia, tomaoac, mjmjltic, tlacmjmjltic, temjmjliuhquj, tzintomaoac, quapitzaoac, ixe, quauhixio, maiê, matzocole, eoaio, vacaltic, quaquatacaltic, maxaltic, maxaliuhquj, mâxallo, melaoac, quauhcocolli, quauhpapaçolli, quauhichtli, quauhtlailli, tetecujtztic, xixipochtic, cocomotztic, motoma, motomaoa veia, mjmjlivi, patlachivi, oacalivi, tzintomaoa, quapitzaoa, piacivi, piaztia, melaoa, cuelivi, colivi, xixipochavi, mjxtia, moquauhixtia, quauhixioa, momâxallotia, mâxaloa, quammaxalli, quãmaxallotl, maxallotl,

tetech qujzquj, teneneuhca, temaxallo, tetech qujça, tenenevilia, tetoqujlia, tlatoqujlia.

Quammaitl, coltic, cueltic, paçoltic, quappaçoltic, quãmatzoltic, mamaçouhquj, mamaxaltic, mamaxal-

113

branches, forked branches, bifurcated branches, dried trees, desiccated trees. The branches fork; they taper, stretch out, fall, crackle.

The tree top is matted, entangled, with tapering branches — with tapered branches. The branches taper. They become matted; they mat all over; they are matted, entangled; they become dry; they break, break in different places, snap, crackle.

The terminal bud, the tree's terminal bud, is tender — a nascent, delicate thing. It buds, develops, shoots out, extends; it becomes delicate.

The terminal growth, the terminal growths, are pointed, pointed at the end. They are pointed at the end, slender at the end, soft, spongy. They become soft, slender, pointed at the end.

The tree's crotch is tapering. It comes together. It becomes narrow, thin.

The bark, the tree's bark, that which is barked, the barking, is thick, thin, narrow, wide, smooth, slick, scaly, tile-like, like thick scales, like thin scales, hard, strong, leathery, hide-like, leather-like, wrinkled, loose, thick. It thins, it hardens, becomes scaly, is made tile-like, wrinkles, loosens.

The wood of the tree,[1] the tree's wood, the tree's good wood, is soft; it is soft, spongy, porous, light, weightless. It becomes long. [There is] spoiled wood, fluffed, fibrous wood; compact, resilient, tough, hard. It becomes long, thick.

The tree's center, the center of the tree, is thin, yellow, dark, black. It takes water, it takes food.

¶

Fifth paragraph, which telleth of the dried tree which is no longer verdant, which is well dried, which just lies dried.

"Tree" is the name of dried wood which stands or lies felled. It is that which can be chopped, can be topped, can be trimmed, can be broken, made into kindling wood, split, split into pieces.

I chop it, I top it; I top it in various places. From it comes the beam, that which can be well cut, that which can be carpentered. I carpenter it, I dress it, I hew it; I cut it wide, I trim it wide; I bore a hole in the end of it.

That which is broken up, the tree which is broken up, that which is broken up is cylindrical, wide; it is wide, thick and wide. I break it up, I part it; it is that which is split.

iuhquj quavavaztic, quavavaciuhquj. mamaxilivi, matzolivi, mamatzolivi, mamaçoa, vevetzi, hicoioca.

Quauhtzontli, paçoltic, paçoliuhquj, mamatzoltic, mamatzoliuhquj, matzolivi, paçolivi, papaçolivi, paçoltia, paçolti, vavacivi, poztequj, popoztequj, teinj, teteica.

Izcallotl, quavizcallotl, celic chinequjztli, chonequjztli, celia, mana, motlamjna, motitivana chinequjzti.
Miaoaiotl mjmjaoaiotl, iaq̃, iacavitzauhquj, iacavitztic, iacapitzaoac, poxaoac, poxactic. poxaoa, pitzaoa, iacapitzaoa.

Quãmaxac, tzoltic, picquj, tlatzolivi, tlapitzaoa.

Quauheoatl, quauheoaiotl, quauhtlaxipeoalli, xipeoallotl, tilaoac, canaoac, pitzaoac, patlaoac, alaoac, alactic, xincaio, tapalcaio, xincaiotilaoac, xincaiocanaoac, capaoac, chicaoac, cuetlaxtic, cuecuetlaxtic, cuetlaxiuhquj, noltic, atic, tilaoac, canaoa, vapaoa, xincaiova, motapalcaiotia, nolivi, atia.
Quauhnacaiotl: quavitl inacaio, quavitl iiecnacaio, iamanquj, poxaoac, çonectic açotic, acovetzquj, hecauhtic, melaoa, quauhtlaelli, quauhpapaçolli, quavichtli, picquj, oltic, tlaquaoac, tepitztic, melaoa, tomaoa,
quauhiollotl, quauhiollotli, piaoac, coztic, tlilectic, tlileoac, atli, tlaqua.

¶

Injc macujlli parrapho: itechpa tlatoa in quavitl vacquj, in acmo celia, in ovelhoac, in ça oactoc.

Quavitl itoca in quauhvatzalli, in icac, in anoço vetztoc tepozvilonj, tzonteconj, tzotzonteconj tlapanonj, tlatlapanonj, tzaianonj, tzatzaianonj,

nictepuzvia, njctzontequj, njctzotzontequj: itech qujça in vepantli, vel teconj, quâquaovanj, njcquaquavi, njcvelteca, njctepuzxima, njcpatlachxima njcpatlachteca, njciacacoionja.

Tlatlapantli, tlatlapanquavitl, tlatlapanalli, mjmjltic, patlachtic, patlachiuhquj, patlachtilaoac: njctlapana, njcxeloa, tlatzaiantli.

---

1. Literally, "the flesh of the tree"; corresponding Spanish text, "meullo."

The beam is thick, thin, concave, hollowed. I trim the beam, I shape the beam.

The foundation beam—*xopetlatl*—is a thick beam: thick, wide, thin, slender, long, small, each one short, each one small and short, concave, scooped out, hollowed out.

I shape it thick, I trim it thick; I trim it into short pieces; I widen it, I prune it wide; I make it slender, I make it long, I make it concave, I scoop it out.

The wood for sieve rims is thin, small and thin; a thin thing, little and thin. It trembles; it is weak; [as if] fevered, it keeps giving way. I split it, I break it.

The small plank is thick, thin, wide; it is wide, long, small, in short pieces, in small short pieces, in pieces which are short.

I dress it, I trim it wide, I dress it wide. I provide it with a cord. I color it vermilion; I place a design on it.

The log, the pole, is round, cylindrical. It has bark; it is scaly; it is girded. The base is thick, the top thin. It is one that has been topped. I top it, I carpenter it.

Joists, small beams, [are] of average size. I straighten the edges; I smooth them, I plane them.

The binding wall beams [are] thick [and] strong. They bear.

Ilhuicatl means the same as binding wall beam. It bears; it bears everything.

The plate is that on which the wood is placed. It rests upon the wall. It either caps its edge or [serves as] scaffolding.

The floor joist is that which rests upon the foundation, and upon it wood is laid. It is what covers. It covers it.

The façade is also called *ilhuicatl*. It is sturdy, thick, wide; slender; planed. It carries — it completely carries — [the superstructure].

The pillar, the round pillar, the prop, the support, is thick, sturdy, strong. It carries the façade; it completely supports, completely bears, completely carries, grasps [what is above].

The pillar is wide; it is wide, thick, very thick, strong, sturdy, very sturdy. It bears, it supports.

The wooden door is something fashioned like paper. I close the door.

Uapaltzacayotl: and also [the term] means the wooden columns [with which the courtyard] is surrounded.[1]

Vapalli, tilaoac, canaoac, vacaltic, vacaliuhquj, njvapalteca, njoapallapana.

Tlapechoapalli, xopetlatl, vapaltilaoac, tilaoac, patlaoac canaoac, pitzaoac, viac, tepiton, tetepontic, tetepontontli vacaltic, copichtic, copichauhquj:

njctilaoacatlapana, njctilaoacateca, njcteteponoa, njcpatlaoa, njcpatlaoacatlaça, njcpitzaoa, njcviaqujlia, njcoacaloa, njccopichoa.

Vapalçoiatl, canaoac, canactontli, chicanactli, canacpil, atevivi, atetlapalo. atonaviztli, iâiaquj: njctzaiana, njctlapana.

Quauhacatl, tilaoac, canaoac, patlachtic, patlachivhquj, viac, tepiton, tetepontic, tetepontõtli, teteponauhquj:

njcvelteca, njcpatlachxima, njcpatlachteca, njcmecanja, njctlauhtlalia, njctlilanja.

Quauhtectli, quammjmjlli mjmjltic, mjmjliuhquj, eoaio, xincaio, tlaquaquechtli, tzintomaoac, quapitzaoac, tlatzontectli: nictzontequj njcquaquavi.

Vevetzquj, vepantontli, ipan qualli, çan ipan qualli, nictẽmelaoa, njcxipetzoa, njcchichiquj.

Elquauhiotl, tomaoac, chicaoac, tlananapaloa

Ilhujcatl: çan no iehoatl qujtoznequj, in elquauhiotl, tlanapaloa, tlacennapaloa.

Quauhtentli: iehoatl in jpã quauhtemalo, in tepampan onoc, anoço tlapechtli iten, anoço tanatli.

Quauhtepanjtl, iehoatl in caltetzontli ipan onoc, yoan in jpan quauhtemalo, tlaquapachoanj, tlaquapachoa.

Calixquatl, no motocaiotia ilhujcatl: chicaoac, tilaoac, patlaoac, pitzaoac, tlachichictli tlanapaloa, tlacennapaloa.

Tlaquetzalli, tlaquetzalmjmjlli, tlaxillotl, quauhteçacatl, tomaoac, chicaoac, tlâpaltic, ilhujcanapaloa, tlacemjtquj, tlacenmana, tlacẽnapaloa tlatzitzquja.

Tlaquetzalli, patlaoac, patlactic, tilactic, tilacpatic, tlâpaltic, chicaoac, chicacpatic, tlatquj, tlamama.

Quauhtzacaiotl, tlaamateuhtlalili, njquauhtzatzaqua.

Vapaltzacaiotl. No yoan qujtoznequj, in quauhtlaiavalo.

---

1. Corresponding Spanish text: "*A las puertas, llaman quauhtzaccaiotl, o vapaltzaccaiotl. A las colũnas de madero, que estan al rededor del patio llaman, quauhtlaiaoalo.*"

The tree trunk, the trunk of the tree, is that from which the beams or logs come. They are round; they are round, they are short.

The door sill: on it stands resting the door.

The shavings, the wood shavings, the shavings of wood, the planings are broken up, fine, twisted, contracted, crimped. I carve out the shavings; I carpenter shavings.

Fragments, wood fragments, are trunk-like, short pieces. I break them up; I break something up.

The wooden lever is thick, strong, hard wood.[2] I pry something.

The stake is pointed at the end. The end is pointed. I drive it in something; I stake it.

Sawdust is fine, like *pinole*. I make it *pinole*-like; I make it fine.

Rotten wood is fluffy, spongy, moldy. It becomes fluffy, moldy.

¶

SIXTH PARAGRAPH, which telleth how trees are planted.

The tree is that which is planted, sown, covered; that which is planted and covered, that which is transplanted, transplanted in the ground.

I plant it, I sow it. I plant and cover it. I transplant it.

It softens. It is wet, it is moistened. It sprouts, it breaks its hull, forms a shoot, bursts forth. The dormant tree swells, buds, forms a bud, produces foliage. It produces leaves, forms a crotch, divides. [It becomes] a fruit tree.

SAPODILLA[1]

The sapodilla tree is smooth, thick, shiny on the surface. Its leaves are each rounded on the surface: round. Its wood is white, soft, light, buoyant. It comes up. Each bud swells; they swell, they enlarge, break, open, burst, blossom, form small fruit. It forms fruit; they extend, growing larger, enlarging. They are tender. They extend, becoming tender. They mature, they ripen; they extend, ripening. They become overripe, very soft; they fall to the ground; they fall down. Thus is it said of one who has excelled, when once again he falls down, "The fruit comes to earth; ripened, it falls to the ground."

I pick, I gather [the fruit]; I shake [the tree].

Quauhtzontli, quauhtzontetl: in tlein vepantli, anoço quauhtectli itech vetzi; iaoaltic, ololtic, tetepontic.

Quauhpepechtli: in jpan tlacçaticac tlatzacujllotl.

Tlaximalli, tlaximalquavitl, quauhtlaximalli, tlaximalutl: textic, cuechtic, çeçepoctic, çeçepouhquj, vavapaltic: njtlaximalcujcuj, njtlaximalquaquavi.

Tzicuevallotl, quauhtzicueoalli: tlaque, tetepontic, njctzicueoa, njtlatzicueoa.

Quammjtl; tomaoac, chicaoac, quauhtepitztli, quauhtetl, njtlaquammjvia.

Tlaxichtli: iacavitztic, iacavitzauhquj, njtlaquammjna njctlaxichtoca.

Quauhtextli: cuechtic, pinoltic, njcpinoltilia, njccuechoa.

Quappalan: nanaltic, çonectic, poxcauhquj, nanalivi, poxcavi.

¶

INJC CHIQUACEN PARRAPHO itechpa tlatoa in quenjn quavitl maquja.

Quavitl. toconj, pixolonj pacholonj, tlapacholteconj aqujlonj, tlalaqujlonj:

njctoca, njcpixoa, njctlapacholteca, njcaquja,

camaoa, ciaoa, poxcavi, ixoa, calixoa, iacaomjti, valhujtonj: in quavaqujlli pochqujiova, celia, itzmolinj, moqujllotia qujlloa, momaxallotia, maxaloa, xochiqualquavitl.

TZAPOTL:

tzapoquavitl: xipetztic, tomaoac, ixtzotzotlaca: in jatlapal ixiaiaoaltic, iaoaltic: in jnacaio iztac, iamanquj, acovetzquj, hecauhtic, âcovetzi: totomolivi, tomolivi, mjmjlivi, tlatzinj, tlapouj, xotla, cueponj, chipinj: xocoti, xocottoc, tomaoa, tomaoatoc, piltic, piltitoc, mâci, icuci, icucitoc, cujtlacuci, atolivi, chapanj, valchapanj: ic ipã mjtoa in panvetzinj, in oc ceppa ie tlanj vetzi. Valxoxocotioan tlalticpac: icuçic oalchapanteoa:

njctequj, njctetequj, njctzetzeloa.

---

2. *Ibid.*: "*A los maderos rollizos que echan debaxo de las vigas, quãdo las arrastran, llamã, quammjtl.*"

1. *Tzapotl: Lucuma mammosa, Achras sapota* (Sahagún, *op. cit.*, p. 365).

The fruit of the sapodilla[2] is round, sweet, soft, mushy, fine-textured. It has a center. Its skin is harsh; it burns the throat. If much is eaten, it passes through one, it loosens the bowels, it gives one indigestion, it gives one diarrhea.

My bowels are loosened; I have diarrhea.

COCHIZTZAPOTL[3]

It is just the same. It relaxes one; it makes one lazy — puts one to sleep, calms one. It brings, it lowers the star of the night.[4]

TLACAÇOLTZAPOTL

It is just the same. It is very big, large, massive, round, very round, exceedingly round, like a large ball, like a very large ball.

ATZAPOTL[5]

The *atzapotl* tree is a smooth one, smooth in all parts; a slick one.

The fruit of the *atzapotl* is edible, good, fine, sweet, very sweet; pleasantly, agreeably sweet; fiery, fiery like bees. It makes one swoon. It is yellow, like a child's excrement; of fine texture, very fine texture — most surpassingly fine, surpassingly fine texture. It is watery. It has a center.[6] And the center of this one is a medicine for infections.

I eat the *atzapotl*; I bite it; I dissolve it, masticate it in my mouth. I swallow it, swallow it whole, take it in one bite. It grows in the east; its habitat is in the east, in hot lands.

XICOTZAPOTL[7]

The *xicotzapotl* tree: the fruit is small and round, of average size, yellowish,[8] a little yellow. It is fine-grained, very fine-grained — sweet, pleasantly sweet, completely sweet. It grows in the east; the place where it grows is Totonac country.

TOTOLCUITLATZAPOTL[9]

The *totolcuitlatzapotl* tree is one which grows in Totonac country; the hot lands are its proper place.

In tzaputl, in xochiqualli: ololtic, tzopelic, iamanquj, atoltic, texio, iollo: in ieoaio tetelqujc, tozcacococ. In mjec moqua tenalqujxti, teapitzalti, tetlavitomjli; teamj,

njnapitza, njnamjna.

COCHIZTZAPUTL;

çan vel no iuhquj: teçotlauh, tecujtlaçotlauh, tecochtlaça, teiamanj, qujoalhujca qujtemovia in iacaotztli

TLACAÇOLTZAPUTL;

çan vel no iuhquj, cenca vei, veitepul, ixachipul, tolontic, tolonpul, tolompatic, ololpul, ololtepul.

ATZAPUTL,

atzapoquavitl, xipetztli, xixipetztli, tlatztli.

Atzaputl xochiqualli, qualonj, iectli, qualli, necutic, necutzopatic, necutzopiltic, necutzocaltic, tletic, tlepipioltic, teiolmjcti, coztic, conecujtlatic, cuechtic, cuechpatic, cuechtzompatic, cuechtzontic, axtic, iollo. Auh inin ca pallancapatli in jollo;

atzaputl njcqua, njquetzoma, njccamapatla, njccamaneloa, njctoloa, njcpetztoloa, njccencamatilia: tonaiã mochioa, tonaian tlatotonian ichan.

XICOTZAPUTL,

xicotzapoquavitl: in xochiqualli ololtontli qualton, copilcoztontli, texio, tetexio, necutic, necutzopâtic necutzocaltic: tonaiã mochioa totoncatlalpan imochiuhian.

TOTOLCUJTLATZAPUTL,

totolcujtlatzapuquavitl: totoncatlalpan mochioanj, tlatotonian inematian: in xochiqualli tliltic, cuechtic,

---

2. *Acad. Hist. MS: quacaxtic qualoni necutic* is added.

3. *Cochiztzapotl: Cuepia polyandra* Rose (Sahagún, *op. cit.*, p. 328).

4. *Acad. Hist. MS: yacaviztli.*

5. *Atzapotl: Lucuma salicifolia* K. (Sahagún, *op. cit.*, p. 323).

6. *Acad. Hist. MS: yn iyollo oc ceppa nepa yollo* is added.

7. *Xicotzapotl: Achras sapota* L. sp. (Standley, *op. cit.*, Pt. 4, p. 1119).

8. *Acad. Hist. MS: cozpil.*

9. *Totolcuitlatzapotl: Dyospiros ebenaster* Rotz (Sahagún, *op. cit.*, p. 360).

The fruit is black, fine-textured, very fine-textured. It is like birds' excrement; hence it is called — hence it is named — *totolcuitlatzapotl.* Its skin is green on the surface.

TEÇONTZAPOTL[10]

The *teçontzapotl* tree: the fruit of the *teçontzapotl* is like volcanic rock: rough, glistening brown on the surface, white within. Its center is black.

THE ETZAPOTL[11] is the same; the *eeyotzapotl* is the same.

QUAUHTZAPOTL[12]

It is the same. I pick them; I separate out from them; I select the best from them; I choose from them; I choose the better ones from them; I harvest them.

AUACATL[13]

The leaves, the foliage of the avocado tree are brown. Its fruit is black, dark; it shines. Within, it is herb-green. Its base is thin, the top rounded, round. It is oily; it has moisture; it has a center.

TLACAÇOLAUACATL

It is thick, large, big. Nursing mothers do not eat it; it physics their children.

QUILAUACATL

It is green, small, choice, good: the avocado of noblemen.

¶

SEVENTH PARAGRAPH, which telleth of the various kinds of trees on which fruit grows.

The fruit tree, the fruit of whatever kind growing on it: the quite sour, the slightly sour.

TEXOCOTL[1]

The *texocotl* tree is a round tree of tapering branches. It has branches. It is thorny; it has thorns. It is of sparse foliage. It is resilient — a twister. It is nerve-like, compact. The base roots are thin. Its fruit is yellow, rounded — round. It sets one's teeth on edge, deadens one's teeth, causes one to salivate,

cuechpatic, iuhqujn totolin icujtl: ic mjtoa, ic motocaiotia in totolcujtlatzaputl xoxoctic in panj in jeoaio.

TEÇONTZAPUTL,

teçontzapuquavitl: in xochiqualli, teçontzaputl, teçontic, chachaquachtic, ixcamjllalactic, iztac in jitic; tliltic in jiollo.

HETZAPUTL çan no iehoatl, heeiotzaputl, çan no iehoatl.

QUAUHTZAPUTL

çan no iehoatl: njctequj, njctlaanja yiacac njctlaana, njctlapepenja, njctzonana, njctlapixavia.

AOACATL,

aoacaquavitl: ixcamiltic in jatlapal, in jqujllo: in jtlaaqujllo tliltic, iaiactic tzotlanj: in jitic qujltic, tzimpitzaoac, quatolontic, quaololtic, chiaoac, memeiallo, iollo.

TLACAÇOLAOACATL:

tomaoac, vei, veipol: amo qujqua in chichioame, qujnnalqujxtia in jpilhoan.

QUJLAOACATL,

xoxoctic, tepiton tlaçotli, qualli, tecpilaoacatl.

¶

INJC CHICOME PARRAPHO: itechpa mjtoa in çaço quenamj quavitl itech mochioa xochiqualli

Xocoquavitl, in çaço tlein xocotl itech mochioa in vel xococ, in çan achi xococ.

TEXOCOTL,

texocoquavitl, quauhiaoalli, mamatzoltic, mamae, vitzio, vivitzio, atic, oltic, nolivinj, tlalhoatic, pipinquj, xonehoaiocanaoac: in jtlaaqujllo coztic, ololtic, ololauhquj tetlancecepouh, tetlanmjmjcti, teiztlacmeialti, teitipoçauh: iztac in jxochio, teitipoçaoa teiztlacmeialtia, tetlanmjmjctia, tetlançeçepoa,

---

10. *Teçontzapotl: Calocarpum mammosum* (L.) Pierre (Robert L. Dressler, "The Pre-Columbian Cultivated Plants of Mexico," *Botanical Museum Leaflets,* Harvard University, Vol. 16, No. 6, 1953, p. 125).

11. *Etzapotl: Annona* sp. (Sahagún, *op. cit.,* p. 335).

12. *Quauhtzapotl: Annona Cherimolia* Mill. (Dressler, *op. cit.,* p. 123).

13. *Auacatl: Persea americana* Mill. Gard. (Standley, *op. cit.,* Pt. 2, p. 290).

1. *Texocotl: Crataegus mexicana (tejocote);* cf. Charles E. Dibble and Arthur J. O. Anderson, tr., ed.: *Florentine Codex,* Book X, "The People" (Santa Fe: School of American Research and University of Utah, 1961), p. 79, n. 11.

swells one's stomach. Its blossom is white. It swells one's stomach, causes one to salivate, deadens one's teeth, sets one's teeth on edge.

I shake [the tree]. I pick [the fruit]. With stones I cause it to be shaken down.

PLUM[2]

It grows in the east, in Totonac country. Its fruit is chili-red, yellow, small, juicy. Its flesh is yellow within.

ATOYAXOCOTL[3]

It is the same. It is thick, dense. The *maçaxocotl,* the *atoyaxocotl* are sweet, honeyed, acid to the taste; of pleasing, fragrant smell. It has a center. It is thin-fleshed. It is edible uncooked; it can be cooked in an olla. It is made into wine; it turns into wine. It can be juiced. It makes one acid.

I mash it. I mash it in the hand. I mash it in the mouth. It makes one acid. It is stinking-sweet.

XALXOCOTL[4]

The *xalxocotl* tree is of thin foliage, of sparse foliage. Its wood is brown-red on the surface. Its limbs shed. Its fruit is pale, dark yellow, fine-textured, very fine-textured, grainy. Its center is like sand. It is round; it is sweet-sour. It causes one to belch, sets one's teeth on edge, makes one salivate.

My teeth are set on edge. I salivate. I become acid. My teeth are set on edge.

CACAO TREE[5]

It has broad branches. It is just a round tree. Its fruit is like an ear of dried maize, like an ear of green maize. Its name is "cacao ear." Some are reddish brown, some whitish brown, some bluish brown. Its center, that which is its interior, its filled interior, is like a kernel of maize. The name of this when growing is "cacao." This is edible, potable.

This cacao, when much is drunk, when much is consumed, especially that which is green, which is tender, makes one drunk, takes effect on one, makes one dizzy, confuses one, makes one sick, deranges one. When an ordinary amount is drunk, it gladdens one, refreshes one, consoles one, invigorates one. Thus

njctzetzeloa, njctequj, njctetzelhoatza.

MAÇAXOCOTL,

tonaian, totōcatlalpan mochioa: in jtlaaqujllo chichiltic, coztic, pitzaoac, aio in jnacaio, in jtic coztic.

ATOIAXOCOTL,

çan no iehoatl: tomaoac, chamaoac, in maçaxocotl, in atoiaxocotl, tzopelic, necutic, cacamaxococ, velic aviac in jiaca, iollo, nacaiototochtic, xoxouhcaqualonj paoaxonj: octli mochioa, octli mocuepa, patzconj, texoxocoli:

njcpatzca, njcmapatzca njccamapatzca; texoxocolia, tzopelicayiaia.

XALXOCOTL,

xalxocoquavitl: qujllo caiaztic, qujllo caiaoac ixtlatlaccamjltic in jnacaio, cocopeoa in jquauhio: in jtlaaqujllo iztaleoac, coziaiactic, texio, tetexio, xallo: in jiollo iuhqujn xalli, ololtic, tzopelicaxocoiac, tehipotzalti, texocociviti teiztlacmeialti,

njxococivi noztlacmeia, noxocolia, njxococivi.

CACAOAQUAVITL,

mapapatlaoac, çan quauhiaoalli: in jtlaaqujllo iuhqujn cintli, iuhq'n elotl: motocaiotia cacaoacintli, cequj tlapalcamjltic, cequj azcamjltic, cequi tetexocamjltic: in jiollo in jitic ca, in jitic tenticac, iuhqujn tlaolli; ieieh in nemj, in jtoca cacaoatl: inin qualonj, yoanj.

Inin cacaoatl in mjec mj, in mjec ioa oc cenca ieh in xoxouhquj, in amaneoa teivinti, tetech qujz, tequaivinti, teixmalacacho, teiollopolo, teiollotlavelilotili: in çan vel ipan mjh tecelti, tececelti, teiollali, teacotlaz: ic mjtoa njnocacaoavia, njnotenciaoa, njnocecelia.

---

2. *Maçaxocotl: Spondias mombin* sp. (Sahagún, *op. cit.,* p. 341).
3. *Atoyaxocotl: Spondias purpurea* L. (Santamaría, *op. cit.,* p. 96: *atoyajocote, jobo*). See also Standley, *op. cit.,* Pt. 3, pp. 656 *sqq.*
4. *Xalxocotl: Psidium Guajava* L. (Dressler, *op. cit.,* p. 145).
5. *Cacaoaquauitl: Theobroma cacao* L. sp. (Standley, *op. cit.,* Pt. 3, p. 805).

it is said: "I take cacao. I wet my lips. I refresh myself."

TEONACAZTLI[6]

The fruit of the *teonacaztli* tree,[7] the *uei nacaztli*, is of pleasing odor, fragrant. Its scent is dense; it pierces one's nose; it is strong. It is yellow; it has fuzz; it is fuzzy like cotton bolls. It is potable; the juice is extracted when it is drunk, or it is ground in cacao. Roasted first, it is drunk uncooked.

A medicine, it lessens the fever. It is drunk not many times and not much;[8] for it takes effect on one; it makes one drunk as if it were mushrooms.

I plant the *teonacaztli*. I transplant the *teonacaztli*. I plant the *uei nacaztli*. I transplant the *uei nacaztli*. I pick the *teonacaztli*. I put *teonacaztli* in the cacao. I add blossoms to it. With blossoms added, I drink the cacao. I smell the *teonacaztli*.

UAXIN[9]

The *uaxin* tree is smooth. It is smooth; its foliage is green like the mesquite, everywhere thin, broken in many sections, sparse, thin. . . . It is swaying. Its fruit is like string beans — wide, long. It has a center; it is bean-like; it is chili-red. Its center is edible, although it is a little bad smelling.

I pick *uaxin*. I bear the *uaxin* on my shoulders. I sell *uaxin*. I pick, I cut *uaxin* — a bunch, a cluster.

MESQUITE[10]

The crust of the mesquite tree is sooty, smoky, rough. Its [interior] skin, its bark, is white. It is nerve-like, fibrous, compact, strong, resilient, transparent. It is a medicine; it is potable. It bends.

I bend it. I form it into a circle. I make it round. This tree, the mesquite, is very hard, resilient; it is hard, strong. It is a firm tree, a hard tree. It has a nodule; it has nodules; the top sways. It has branches, tapering branches. It is forked. It is bushy, a matted tree, a round tree, etc.

The leaves of the mesquite tree are herb-green, straight, slender, serrated, spreading. They spread. They are spread, spreading, radiating. Its foliage and its tender shoots are an eye medicine; it is applied to the eye in drops. [Its foliage] scatters, extends, spreads, goes in all directions.

TEUNACAZTLI,

teunacazquavitl, vei nacaztli: in jtlaaqujllo, velic, aviac: in jiaca motetzaoaca inecuj, teiacaxelo, chicaoac: coztic, tomjiollo, tomjlollo, ichcacacallotic yoanj, maqujxtia in mjh, anoço moteci cacaoatl ipan: achtopa mjcequj, moxoxouhcaih:

patli, qujpevia in totonquj: amo mjecpa in mj, yoan amo mjc, ca tetech qujz, teivinti, iuhqujn nanacatl;

njteunacaztoca, njteunacazaquja, njveinacaztoca, njveinacazaquja, njteunacaztequj, njcteunacazvia in cacaoatl, njcxochiotia, xochio njquj in cacaoatl, njqujnecuj in teunacaztli.

VAXI,

vaxquavitl: xixipetztic, xipetziuhquj: in jqujllo mjzqujqujltic, pipitzaoac, matzatzaianquj, caiaztic, caiaoac, caciltic, câcaciltic, caciliuhquj, vivichtic, exoio: in jtlaaqujllo patlachtic, veveiac, iollo, eio chichiltic: ieh in jiollo qualonj, quecinamj, achiton chipaiac:

njoaxtequj, njoaxmama, njoaxnamaca: njoaxqua, njctequj, njccotona in oaxin çentlapilolli, cemocholli.

MIZQUJTL,

mjzqujquavitl, in ixincaio, cujchectic, cujcheoac, chachaquachtic, in jeoaio, in jxipeoallo iztac, tlalhoatic, tlalichtic, pipinquj, chicaoac, oltic, atic: pâtli, ioanj, nolivi:

nicnoloa, njciaoallalia, njctevilacachoa.

Inin quavitl, in mjzqujtl, vellaquaoac, oltic, tepitztic, chicaoac, quauhtetl, quauhtepitztli, ixe ihixe, quavichtli, mamae, mamatzoltic, maxaltic, tapaçoltic, quauhpaçoltic, quauhiaoalli. etc.

In jatlapal mjzqujtl, qujltic, memelactic, pipitzaoac, tzatzaianquj, chachaiactic, xexeltic, xexelivi, xexeliuhquj, momoiaoac. Ixpatli in jqujllo, yoan in jiacacelica: ommochipinja in tixco, momoiaoa, xexelivi, cuecueiaoa, totoiaoa.

---

6. *Teonacaztli: Cymbopetalum penduliflorum;* cf., however, Dibble and Anderson, *op. cit.,* p. 77, n. 6.

7. Corresponding Spanish text: *"las flores deste arbol."*

8. *Acad. Hist. MS: mjec.*

9. *Uaxin: Leucaena esculenta* Moc. and Sessé (Standley, *op. cit.,* Pt. 2, p. 368).

10. *Mizquitl: Prosopis juliflora* (ibid., p. 351).

Its fruit is bean-like, in handfuls, like clusters. It is called a cluster, two clusters, a bunch. It is edible. It is honey-like, sweet; it is very fine-textured. It has a center. It is long, wide, like a lock of hair. It is harsh to the throat; it irritates the throat. When much is eaten, it swells one's stomach. It makes one's teeth smell unpleasant.

I pick the mesquite. I cook the mesquite in an olla. I make tamales of the mesquite. I eat the mesquite. I suck the mesquite.

QUETZALMIZQUITL is the same as this [mesquite].

MULBERRY[11]

The mulberry tree is smoothed, smooth. It has foliage, much foliage, thick foliage. Its foliage is herb-green, fuzzy, slick on its under surface. Its fruit is chili-red, sweet, very sweet.

I pick it. I shake it. I eat mulberries.

CAPULIN[12]

The trunk and the bark and the foliage of the *capulin* tree are harsh, bitter. Its foliage and its tender shoots are eye medicine; [the sap] is dropped into our eyes when our eyes are inflamed.

The name of the fruit of this tree is *capulin*. It is round, shining. It has a center. [The buds] swell, form flower buds, burst, blossom. It sheds blossoms, drops blossoms, takes form; it spreads, taking form; it forms a small fruit; it enlarges; it becomes brown, chili-red, black. It becomes black. It blackens water.

I pick *capulin*. I shake the *capulin* tree. I sell *capulin*. I eat *capulin*.

When many of these are eaten, they physic one, they give one diarrhea. They physic one; they cause one to have diarrhea. The name of the center of the *capulin* is *capuliollotli*. Also the center is hard, tough; this is rejected. Its center is edible roasted. When much is eaten, one's stomach swells.

ELOCAPULIN

It is the same; however, the tree is tall, thick, high, very broad. Its foliage, its leaves, its fruit are broad, thick, fat, ball-like; each one ball-like, large, pulpy, breakable into small pieces, watery.... They fill one's mouth, satisfy one, taste good to one, make one covet

In jtlaaqujllo, exotic, mamapichtic, ohocholteuhca: mjtoa cemocholli, omocholli, centlapilolli, qualonj, necutic, tzopelic, tetexio, iollo, viviac, patlachtic, pâpachtic, tetelqujc, tetetelqujc: in mjec moqua, teitipoçauh, tetlanjali:

njmjzqujtequj, njmjzqujpaoaci, njmjzqujtamaloa, njmjzqujqua, njcpachichina.

QUETZALMJZQUJTL: çan no iuhquj, çan no iehoatl.

AMACAPULI,

amacapulquavitl, xipetztic, xipetziuhquj, qujllo, qujqujllo, qujllotilaoac: in jqujllo, qujlpaltic, tomjo, tetetztic in jcujtlapan. In jtlaaqujllo, chichiltic, necutic, necutzopiltic:

njctequj, njctzetzeloa, namacapulqua.

CAPULI,

capulquavitl: in jtlac, yoan in jeoaio, yoan in jqujllo, tetelqujc, chichic. In jqujllo, yoan in jacacelica ixpatli, ommochipinja in tixco, in jquac titixtlevia.

In jtlaaqujllo inin quavitl; itoca capuli, ololtic, cuecueiochauhquj, iollo: totomolivi, xochio tatapachivi: xotla, cueponj; moxochiotlaça, moxochiotepeoa; tlacati, tlacattoc, chipinj, tomaoa, camjlivi, chichilivi, tlileoa, tlilivi, atlitliliati:

njcapultequj, njcapultzetzeloa, njcapulnamaca, njcapulqua:

in mjec moqua i, tenalqujxti, teamj, tenalqujxtia, teamjna: in jiollo in capuli itoca capuliollotli, oc no iollo tepitztic, tlaquaoac, iê cauhio: in jiollo qualonj mjcequj: in mjec moqua teitipoçauh.

ELOCAPULI:

çan no iehoatl, iece vecapan in quavitl, tomaoac, viac, ixpapatlaoac in jqujllo in jatlapal, in jtlaaqujllo, tomaoac, chamaoac tolontic, tôtolontic, vevei, papatztic, xixitzaianquj, aio temachpul, temachpopol, tecamate, teiolpachiviti, teiolqujma, teiculti, tetlanecti,

---

11. *Amacapulin: Morus celtidifolia (ibid.*, p. 204).
12. *Capulin: Prunus capuli (ibid.*, p. 340).

them, make one want them, are constantly required. The center is fat; they fill one's mouth; they satisfy one.

TLAOLCAPULIN[13]

The *tlaolcapulin* tree is a trembler, not [well] trunked. It is just a small, round tree. It is thin, dried. It has tapering branches. The name of its fruit is *tlaolcapulin*. It is called *tlaolcapulin* because it is small, tiny. It disappoints one, it constantly disappoints one. It is thin-fleshed, harsh, bitter to the taste, nowhere a desired thing, nowhere one's friend. It offends one. It is not regarded by anyone; it is not respected.

XITOMACAPULIN

It is the same as the *elocapulin*. However, the center is small. Nowhere does it gladden one. But the skin of this same one is thick, well fleshed. It is juicy, spurting juice. It is one of which little is eaten. It shatters one's stomach; it enlarges, rounds it. It shatters one's stomach.

QUAUHCAMOTLI[14]

The branches are wide. It is a small, round tree. Its foliage, its leaves, are brown-colored on the surface, dark-colored on the surface. Its root is edible; this is called *quauhcamotli*. It is white, long, slender; it can be cooked in an olla.

I plant the *quauhcamotli*. I grub up the *quauhcamotli*. I cook the *quauhcamotli* in an olla.

¶

EIGHTH PARAGRAPH, in which are told the sorts of *nopal* and the tunas on them.

NOPALLI is the collective name of all the *nopal*. The branches are wide, thick, green, thorny, smooth, like a smooth reed. It has an excretion; it has tunas, fruit, tubes. It is stringy; it becomes nerve-like; it becomes like nerves.[1] It forms a branch, it forms branches, it produces leaves. This *nopal* is edible; it is edible uncooked, it is cookable in an olla. It is eaten in moderation.

The name of the fruit of this *nopal* is tuna. It is round, with a top like a spindle whorl, the top filled out,[2] round, slender-based. It is prickly, full of thorns.

nenequjztli, iollochamaoac, tecamatema, teiolpachivitia.

TLAOLCAPULI,

tlaolcapulquavitl, amo tevivi, amo tlaque, çan quauhiaoaltontli, vavaztic, vavazpil, mamatzoltic. in jtlaaqujllo itoca tlaolcapuli: injc mjtoa tlaolcapuli piciltic, piciliuhquj, tenenco, tenenenco nacaiototochtic, tetelqujc, tozcachichic, acan eleviliztli, acã teicnjuh, teiolitlaco, aiac ica, atle ipan itto.

XITOMACAPULI

çan no iuhquj in elocapuli, iece iollopiciltic acã teavialti in jiollo, auh ie vel ieoaio tilaoac, vel nacaio, [ayo] aiopipitzictic, amo momjeccaquanj, teitixaxamatz, tomaoa, tolonavi, teitixaxamatza.

QUAUHCAMOTLI,

mapapatlaoac, quauhiaoalton: in jxiuhio in jatlapal, ixtlapalcamjltic, ixtlapaliaiactic: in jnelhoaio qualonj, iehoatl in motocaiotia quauhcamotli, iztac, viac, pitzaoac, paoaxonj:

njquauhcamotoca, njquauhcamotataca, njquauhcamopaoaci.

¶

INIC CHICUEI PARRAPHO itechpa mjtoa in quenamj nopalli itech ca nochtli.

NOPALLI icentoca in jxqujch nopalli mapapatlaoac, matilaoac, xoxoctic, âoaio, alaoac, alaoacaio, iacacujtle, nochio, xochiquallo, tlaaccaio, ichio tlalhoaioa tlatlalhoaioa, momatia, momamatia, mamatlapaltia. Inin nopalli qualonj, xoxouhcaqualonj, paoaxonj, çan vel ipan in moqua.

Inin nopalli in jtlaaqujllo itoca nochtli, ololtic, quamalacachtic, quateque, tolontic, tzinpitzaoac, âoaio, moca aoatl, eoaio, iollo, in jnacaio texio, aio, in jiollo

---

13. *Tlaolcapulin: Prunus* sp. (Sahagún, *op. cit.*, p. 363).

14. *Quauhcamotli: Manihot esculenta* Crantz (Standley, *op. cit.*, Pt. 3, p. 643).

1. *Acad. Hist. MS: tlalvayo, tlatlalvayo* is added.

2. *Ibid.: quatēq'.*

It has a skin; it has a center. Its flesh is fine-textured, juicy. A sandy [substance] comes out of its center. [The fruit] spreads enlarging[3] — growing; it thickens; the top fills out. It ripens; it becomes overripe.

I pick the tuna. I eat the tuna. I tear the inside of it apart. I break up the inside of it. I peel it.

There are many kinds of *nopal*. They stand in many places; they emerge in many places.

IZTAC NOCHNOPALLI[4]

Its tuna is white, sweet. Sometimes its name is "white tuna."

COZNOCHNOPALLI[5]

The branches are long; its leaves are long. This *nopal* is sour. And the name of its fruit is "yellow tuna." It is fat; each one is fat, long. It is very yellow, very sweet.

TLATOCNOCHNOPALLI[6]

The branches are somewhat thick. [The tuna] is dark yellow; thence comes its name, *tlatocnochtli*. Brown-colored, it only seems to be chili-red. It is of average size, not very large.

CUICUILNOCHNOPALLI

From it come [the tunas] named *cuicuilnochtli*. [Its leaves] are striped with color, varicolored, rose colored. They are striped with color,[7] painted, varicolored, rose colored.

ANOCHNOPALLI

From it come [the tunas] named *anochtli*. They are big, fat, large. They are somewhat disagreeable to the taste, unpleasant tasting.

TLAÇOLNOCHNOPALLI is the same as *anochtli*.

TZOOALNOCHNOPALLI

From it comes its fruit named *tzooalnochtli*. It is chili-red,[8] ashen red, fat, long.

TLAPALNOCHNOPALLI[9] is the same as *tzooalnochtli*.

xaltic qujça, mjmjliuhtoc, mochiuhtoc tomaoa, quatemi, icuci, cujtlacuci:

njnochtequj, njnochqua njqujtitzaiana, njqujtitlapana, njcxipeoa.

In nupalli mjec tlamantli, mjeccan icac, mjeccan qujzquj.

IZTAC NOCHNOPALLI

iztac in jnochio, necutic, aquenamj itoca, iztac nochtli

COZNOCHNOPALLI,

maviviac, in jatlapal viviac xoxococ inin nopalli. Auh in jtlaaqujllo itoca coznochtli, coztic, tomaoac, totomactic, viviac, cozpiltic, necutzopatic.

TLATOCNOCHNOPALLI,

achi matitilaoac, çacatlaxcaliaiactic: in jtech qujqujça, itoca tlatocnochtli, tlapalcamjltic, çã mjximati injc chichiltic, çã ipan qualli, amo cenca vevei.

CUJCUJLNOCHNOPALLI:

in jtech qujça, itoca cujcujlnochtli, motlatlapalhoaoan, mocujcujcujlo, motlatlapalpoiauh, motlatlapalhoaoan, mocujcujloa, mocujcujcujloa, motlatlapalpoiaoa.

ANOCHNOPALLI,

in jtech qujça itoca anochtli, vevei, totomaoac, totomactic, achi acecec, aceceiac.

TLAÇOLNOCHNOPALLI: çan no iehoatl in anochtli.

TZOOALNOCHNOPALLI:

in jtech qujça, in jtlaaqujllo itoca, tzooalnochtli, chichiltic, tlapalnextic, totomaoac viviac.

TLAPALNOCHNOPALLI: çan no iehoatl in tzooalnochtli.

---

3. *Ibid.: mimiliviuhtoc* (possibly a misspelling).

4. *Iztac nochnopalli: Opuntia* sp.; Rafael Martín del Campo, "Las Cactáceas Entre los Mexica," *Cactáceas y Suculentas Mexicanas,* Vol. II, No. 2 (Mexico, 1957), p. 28.

5. *Coznochnopalli: Opuntia* sp. (*loc. cit*).

6. *Tlatocnochnopalli: Opuntia* sp. (*ibid.,* p. 30).

7. *Acad. Hist. MS: motlapalvavana.*

8. *Ibid.: chichictic.*

9. *Tlapalnochnopalli: Opuntia* sp. (Martín del Campo, *loc. cit.*).

TZAPONOCHNOPALLI[10]

The branch is thick, round. Its leaf is like ashes, ashen. It is not one to extend far, not one to put out a stalk; it is a creeper. The name of its fruit is *tzaponochtli*. It is fat, round, like the *ayocomolli*. It becomes fat, corpulent.

TLANEXNOPALLI

The name of its fruit is also *tlanexnochtli*.[11] It is ripe brown, dark brown, dark red, the color of gourd blossoms. It is fat.

CAMAXTLE

The name of its fruit is also *camaxtle*. It is white. It is thick-skinned, sour-skinned. Its center is sweet, grainy; its center is [as if] cooked.

XOCONOCHNOPALLI[12]

It is coarse-spined, thick-spined. The name of its fruit is *xoconochtli*. It is white, sour. Its exterior, its skin, gives one a sour taste; it sets one's teeth on edge, deadens one's teeth; it causes one to salivate. It can be cooked in an olla. It gives one a sour taste; it causes one to salivate.

I cook it in an olla.

Its center, its good flesh, is honey-like, flaming, sweet, granular. It breaks up.

TENOPALLI[13]

It is a *nopal* which occurs in the forest, the mountains, the grasslands. The name of what grows on it is *çacanochtli*. It is sour, harsh, small — small and round. It can be cooked in an olla. It is edible uncooked.

AZCANOCHNOPALLI

It is coarse-spined. It also grows in the mountains, the desert, the plains.

The name of its fruit is *azcanochtli*. It is of different colors; white, chili-red, purple, brown. It is sweet, very sweet; it is small and round; it is round. The centers are tiny like tomato [seeds].

TECOLONOCHNOPALLI

It is long. The branches are slender. Its fruit is ashen-red, and its name is *tecolonochtli*. The skin is thick.

TZAPONOCHNOPALLI:

matilaoac, iaiaoaltic: in jatlapal nextic, nexeoac, amo veiaqujanj, amo izcalloanj, movilananj: in jxochiquallo itoca tzaponochtli, cujtlaiaoaltic, ololtic iuhqujn aiocomolli cujtlaiaoallivi, nanatzivi.

TLANEXNOPALLI:

in jtlaaqujllo çan no itoca tlanexnochtli, camopalcamjltic, camopaliaiactic, tlapaliaiactic aiopaltic, cujtlaiaoaltic.

CAMAXTLE:

in jxochiquallo, çan no itoca camaxtle, iztac eoaiotilaoac, eoaioxococ, tzopelic: in jiollo xaxallo, totopoca in jiollo.

XOCONOCHNOPALLI,

aoaiochamaoac, aoaiotilaoac, in jtlaaqujllo, itoca xoconochtli, iztac, xococ: in jpan jeoaio, texoxocoli, tetlancecepouh, tetlanmjmicti, teiztlacmeialti, paoaxonj, texoxocolia, teiztlacmealti:

njcpaoaci.

In jiollo in jiecnacaio necutic, tletic, tzopelic, xaxallo, teteinj.

TENOPALLI:

in quauhtla, in tepetla, in çacatla onoc nopalli: in jtech mochioa itoca çacanochtli, xococ, tetelqujc, tepiton ololtontli, paoaxonj xoxouhcaqualonj.

AZCANOCHNOPALLI,

aoaiochamaoac, no tepetla, ixtlaoacã teutlalpan in mochioa.

In jtlaaqujllo: itoca azcanochtli nepapan tlapaltic, iztac, chichiltic, camopaltic, camjltic, tzopeltic, tzopelpatic, ololtontli ololpil iollopiciltic iuhqujn xitomatl.

TECOLONOCHNOPALLI,

veiac, mapipitzaoac, tlapalnextic in jxochiquallo: auh itoca tecolonochtli, eoaiotilaoac.

---

10. *Tzaponochnopalli: Opuntia ficus-indica* (*loc. cit.*).
11. *Acad. Hist. MS: tlanexi.*
12. *Xoconochnopalli: Opuntia imbricata* (Martín del Campo, *loc. cit.*).
13. *Tenopalli: Epiphyllum* sp. (*ibid.*, p. 31).

NINTH PARAGRAPH, which telleth of all the edible fruits which are within the earth.

QUAUHCAMOTLI[1]

It is a root, a tree root. It can be cooked in an olla. It is fine-textured. It is cylindrical. It becomes cylindrical, it becomes fine-textured.[2]

CAMOTLI[3]

It is a root, cylindrical, round, ball-like, twisted. The *camoxalli* is the small *camotli*. Its foliage just creeps like the bean, like the *caxtlatlapan* herb. And as for transplanting, to be propagated, only its foliage, its vine is transplanted. It can be cooked in an olla; it is edible raw. The *camotli* is planted here. Here the foliage is transplanted; here it is grubbed up. Here it is cooked in an olla, here it is baked.[4]

I eat it raw.

XICAMOXIUITL

It creeps, forms vines, has foliage — much foliage. The root of this is edible; its name is *xicama*.[5] It is round, fat, soft. It has a taproot; it has a skin, a thin skin. Its flesh is white, very white, like snow, like wood ashes. It is juicy; it is edible uncooked. It breaks up.

I plant the *xicama*. I grub up, glean, gather the *xicama*.

CIMATL[6]

[The name] comes from its root. The name of its foliage is *quaueco*. [The root] is thick. It is cookable in an olla. It is really something to be cooked, not to be eaten raw: it causes vomiting, it causes diarrhea; it is fatal. Thus it is said of one a little feeble, a little pale: "This one has only *cimatl'd* himself." When well cooked, it is good, edible, chewable. It is fine-textured, very fine-textured.

I grub up the *cimatl*. I eat the *cimatl*. I cook the *cimatl* in an olla. I chew the *cimatl*. I take the *cimatl*. I vomit. I get diarrhea. I am purged.

INIC CHICUNAVI PARRAPHO: itechpa mjtoa in jxqujch tlalli yitic onoc xochiqualli qualonj.

QUAUHCAMOTLI

tlanelhoatl quauhnelhoatl; paoaxonj, texio, mjmjltic, mjmjltia motexotia.

CAMOTLI

tlanelhoatl, mjmjltic, ololtic, tapaioltic, cueltic; camoxalli, in tepitoton camotli: in jqujllo çan movillana iuhqujn etl, iuhqujn caxtlatlapan. Auh injc maquja, injc moxinachoa çan ie in jxiuhio, in jmemecaio maquja: paoaxonj, xoxouhcaqualonj: in camotli njcan motoca, njcan moxiuhaquja, njcan motataca, njcan mopaoaci, njcan moxca;

njcxoxouhcaqua.

XICAMOXIVITL:

movilana, memecatia, qujllo, qujqujllo: in jnelhoaio iehoatl in qualonj: in jtoca xicama ololtic, cujtlaiaoaltic, papatztic, cujtlapille, eoaio, eoaiocanaoac, iztac in jnacaio, iztacpatic, iuhqujn cepaiavitl, iuhqujn quauhnextli, aio, xoxouhcaqualonj, teteinj:

njxicamatoca njxicamatataca, njnoxicamatitixia, njxicamacujcuj.

CIMATL;

itech qujça inelhoaio in xivitl in jtoca quaveco: tomaoac, paoaxonj, vel icuxitilonj, amo xoxouhcaqualonj, teiçotlalti, teapitzalti, mjcoanj: ic ipan mjtoa in iaiacapil, in jztalecpil ie on çã omocimavi: in vel icucic qualli, iectli, qualonj, quaqualo, texio, tetexio.

njcimatataca, njcimaqua, njcimapaoaci, njcimaquaqua, njnocimavia, njnjçotla, njnapitza, njcnoquja.

---

1. *Quauhcamotli: Manihot esculenta* Cr. (§ 7, n. 14, *supra*).

2. *Acad. Hist. MS: motexyotia.*

3. *Camotli: Ipomoea batatas* Poir or *Convolvulus batata* Lam. (Sahagún, *op. cit.*, p. 326).

4. *Acad. Hist. MS:* after *in camotli,* the passage reads *nicamotoca. nicamoxiuhaquia. nicamotataca nicamopavaxi. nicamoyxca*—I plant *camotli,* etc.

5. *Xicama: Pachyrrhizus erosus* (L.) Urban (Dressler, *op. cit.*, p. 140).

6. *Cimatl: Phaesolus coccineus* Linn., or *Canavalia villosa* Benth., or *Desmodium amplifolium;* cf. Dibble and Anderson, *op. cit.*, p. 145.

TOLCIMATL[7]

It is cylindrical. It is edible uncooked or can be eaten raw.[8] It can be cooked in an olla; it is chewable. It is fine-textured, very fine-textured. Its foliage is cord-like, its blossoms chili-red.

I eat the *tolcimatl*. I grub up the *tolcimatl*. I cook the *tolcimatl* in an olla. I chew the *tolcimatl*.

CACAPXON

[The root] is round, small and round, it breaks up. It resembles the *xicama*.

CACOMITL[9]

[The root] can be cooked in an olla, can be eaten. It is fine-textured; it is satisfying. Its shell is sweet; its foliage, its leaves, are a little like the *tolpatlactli*.

ACAXILOTL[10]

It is cylindrical, cord-like, long, like the *tolpatlactli*. Its root can be eaten uncooked.[11] It is cookable in an olla. It is quite fine-textured. It grows in the water.

ATZATZAMOLLI[12]

Like volcanic rock, it is rough. It can be cooked in an olla. Its skin is gourd-like, tough, black. The center of this is what is edible; it is white, *tamal*-like. Its leaves are wide, round; it is called *atlacueçonan*. Its blossom is white, white; its name is *atzatzamolxochitl*. Its stalk is slender, hollow. It grows in water,[13] forms a droplet, grows large, becomes like a volcanic rock, roughens, forms leaves [which] become broad. It opens on the surface of the water, it opens spreading on the surface of the water; it blossoms, it produces blossoms; it flowers.

ÇACATEZTLI[14]

[The root] is small and round like a maize kernel: small and cylindrical, white, fine-textured. It can be cooked in an olla; it is tasty, savory, pleasing, insipid, ... small. Its foliage is straight, its blossom white like

TOLCIMATL

mjmjltic xoxouhcaqualonj, anoço xoxouhcaqualonj, paoaxonj, quaqualonj, texio, tetexio; in jqujllo memecatic in jxochio chichiltic,

njtolcimaqua, njtolcimatataca, njtolcimapaoaci, njtolcimaquaqua.

CACAPXON:

ololtic, ololtontli iztac, teteinj, qujnenevilia in xicama.

CACOMJTL

paoaxonj, qualonj texio, papachiuhtica in jtapalcaio, tzopelic: in jqujllo in jxiuhio tolpatlacticapil.

ACAXILOTL:

mjmjltic, mecatic viac, tolpatlactic: in jnelhoaio xoxocaqualonj, paoaxonj, vel texio, atlan mochioa.

ATZATZAMOLLI,

teçontic, chachaquachtic, paoaxonj: in jeoaio xicaltic tlaquaoac, tliltic: in jiollo ie in qualonj, iztac, tamaltic: in jqujllo papatlactic, iaiaoaltic, itoca atlacueçona, in jxochio iztac, aztic, itoca atzatzamolxochitl: in jquauhio, pipiaztic iticoionquj: Atlan in mochioa chipinj, veia, teçonavi, chachaquachivi, moqujllotia, papatlaoa, atlixco çouj, atlixco çoçouhtoc, cueponj, moxochiotia, xochiova.

ÇACATEZTLI

ololtontli, tlaoltic, mjmjlpil, iztac, texio, paoaxonj, velic aviac, avixtic, acecec achochotic, piciltic: in jxiuhio memelactic, in jcueponca iztac izqujxochitic: in jquauhio acatic, mjmjltic, hiticoionquj, atlan in

---

7. *Tolcimatl:* "reed roots" (*ibid.*, p. 79).
8. *Acad. Hist. MS* appears to read *xoxouhcaqualoni anoço xoxouhcaquaqualoni.*
9. *Cacomitl: Tigridia pavonia* Ker.; cf. Dibble and Anderson, *loc. cit.*
10. *Acaxilotl:* desc. in Hernández, *op. cit.*, Vol. II, p. 224.
11. *Acad. Hist. MS: xoxouhcaqualoni.*
12. *Atzatzamolli:* probably *Castalia gracilis* (Sahagún, *op. cit.*, p. 323).
13. *Acad. Hist. MS: atlan ymochiuhya* is added.
14. *Çacateztli:* probably *Panicum* sp. (Sahagún, *op. cit.*, p. 372).

the *izquixochitl*. Its stalk is reed-like, cylindrical, hollow. It grows in the water; it is grubbed up in the mud.

mochioa, çoqujtitlã motataca.

QUEQUEXQUI[15] [OR] QUEQUEXQUIC

It is [a root which] grows in the east. It is thick, white, cookable in an olla, edible.

QUEQUEXQUJ, QUEQUEXQUJC:

tonaian mochioa, tomaoac, iztac, paoaxonj, qualonj.

XALTOMATL[16]

Its root is cylindrical, edible uncooked. It can be cooked in an olla, it can be baked on a griddle. It is sweet, ever sweet; it is harsh to the throat.

XALTOMATL

inelhoaio, mjmjltic, xoxouhcaqualonj, paoaxonj, ixconj, necutic, nenecutic, tetelqujc.

UITZOCUITLAPILLI[17]

Its root is cylindrical; its name is *uitzocuitlapilli*. It can be baked on a griddle. It burns the throat.

VITZOCUJTLAPILLI

inelhoaio: mjmjltic: in jtoca vitzocujtlapilli ixconj, tozcacococ.

---

15. *Quequexqui:* possibly *quequeste* (Santamaría, *op. cit.,* p. 904) — *Colocasia antiquorum* Schl. *Xanthosoma violaceum, X. robustum* Schott.

16. *Xaltomatl: Saracha jaltomata* Schlecht; Emily Wolcott Emmart, *The Badianus Manuscript* (Baltimore: The Johns Hopkins Press, 1940), p. 219.

17. *Uitzocuitlapilli: Aporocactus flagelliformis* (L.); Francisco Hernández, *Historia de las Plantas de Nueva España* (Mexico: Imprenta Universitaria, 1946), Vol. III, p. 936).

Seventh Chapter, which telleth of all the different herbs.

FIRST PARAGRAPH, in which are told the names of the many different herbs which perturb one, madden one.

COATL XOXOUHQUI OR OLOLIUHQUI[1]

Its leaves are slender, cord-like, small. Its name is *ololiuhqui*. It makes one besotted; it deranges one, troubles one, maddens one, makes one possessed. He who eats it, who drinks it, sees many things which greatly terrify him. He is really frightened [by the] poisonous serpent which he sees for that reason.

He who hates people causes one to swallow it in drink [and] food to madden him. However, it smells sour; it burns the throat a little. For gout, it is only spread on the surface.

PEYOTE[2]

This peyote is white and grows only there in the north region called Mictlan. On him who eats it or drinks it, it takes effect like mushrooms. Also he sees many things which frighten one, or make one laugh. It affects him perhaps one day, perhaps two days, but likewise it abates. However, it harms one, troubles one, makes one besotted, takes effect on one.

I take peyote; I am troubled.

TLAPATL[3]

It is small and round, blue, green-skinned, broad-leafed, white-blossomed. Its fruit is smooth, its seed black, stinking. It harms one, takes away one's appetite, maddens one, makes one besotted.

He who eats it will no longer desire food until he shall die. And if he eats it moderately, he will forever be disturbed, maddened; he will always be possessed, no longer tranquil.

And where there is gout, it is spread on thin as an ointment in order to cure. Nor is it to be sniffed, for

Inic chicome capitulo: itechpa tlatoa, in jxqujch in nepapan xivitl.

INJC CE PARRAPHO: ipã mjtoa in jzqujtlamantli, in jtoca in xivitl, in tequaivinti, teiollotlavelilocatili.

COATL XOXOUHQUJ, ANOÇO OLOLIUHQUJ,

pitzaoac, memecatic ixpitzaoac in jatlapalio: itoca ololiuhquj, teivinti, teiollomalacacho, teiolpolo, teiollotlavelilocatili, tetech qujneuh: in aqujn qujqua, in quj, mjec tlamantli qujtta in cenca temamauhti, vel mjhiçavia, coatl tequanj, tlein mach qujtta.

In tecocoliani: atl tlaqualli ipã qujtetololtia, injc teiollotlavelilotilia: iece xoiac, achi tozcacococ. Cooacivizpatli çan panj in ommoteca.

PEIOTL:

inin peiotl iztac: auh çan yio vmpa in mochioa in tlacochcalcopa, in teutlalpã in mjtoa mjctlanpa. In aqujn qujqua in, in anoço quj: itech qujça, iuhqujn nanacatl: no mjec tlamantli qujtta in temamauhti, anoço tevetzqujti aço cemjlhujtl, anoço omjlhujtl in jtech qujça, tel çan no concaoa: iece ca qujtlacoa in jiollo, tetlapololtia, teivintia, tetech qujça:
njnopeiovia, njciovia.

TLAPATL,

iaoaltontli, movitic: in jeoaio xoxoctic, in jxiuhio papatlaoac iztac, in jxochio xixipetztic: in jxocoio tliltic, in jachio hiac teiolitlaco, tetlaqualizcaoalti, teiollotlavelilotili, teivinti.

In aqujn qujquaz, aocmo queleviz in tlaqualli, ixqujchica in mjqujz: auh intla çan veli qujqua cemjcac iollochicotiz, iollotlavelilotiz, cemjcac itech qujneoaz aoc tlacacemelle iez.

Auh in canj onoc coaciviztli, cenca nauhtic ommalaoa ic pati, amo no mjnecujz, ca teiollitlaco, tetla-

1. *Coatl xoxouhqui: Rivea corymbosa;* Sahagún (Garibay ed.), Vol. IV, p. 328; *ololiuhqui: Ipomoea sidaefolia, Rivea corymbosa, Datura metaloides (ibid.,* p. 347). Corresponding Spanish text: *"Ay vna ierva que se llama Coatl xoxouhqui, y crian vna semjlla que se llama ololiuhquj, o coatl xoxouhquj."*

2. *Peyotl: Lophophora williamsii* (Lem.) (Standley, "Trees and Shrubs," Pt. 4, p. 932).

3. *Tlapatl: Datura stramonium* (Sahagún, *op. cit.,* p. 364).

it harms one; it takes away one's appetite. It harms one, deranges one, takes away one's appetite.

I take *tlapatl;* I eat, I go about eating *tlapatl.*

So it is said of him who goes about belittling, who goes about haughtily, presumptuously, [that] he goes about eating the *mixitl* [and] *tlapatl* herbs; he goes about taking *mixitl* [and] *tlapatl* to himself.

TZITZINTLAPATL

It is just like *tlapatl.* However, the bud is spiny. Its smell is also the same.

MIXITL[4]

It is of average size, round, green-leafed. It has seeds. Where there is gout, there [the ground seeds] are spread on. It is not edible, not drinkable. It paralyzes one, closes one's eyes, tightens the throat, stops off the voice, makes one thirsty, deadens the testicles, splits the tongue.

It is not noticeable that it has been drunk, when it is drunk. He whom it paralyzes, if his eyes are closed, remains forever with closed eyes. That which he is looking at, he looks at forever. One becomes rigid, mute. It is alleviated a little with wine.

I take *mixitl.* I give one *mixitl.*

NANACATL[5]

It is called *teonanacatl.* It grows on the plains, in the grass. The head is small and round, the stem long and slender. It is bitter and burns; it burns the throat. It makes one besotted; it deranges one, troubles one. It is a remedy for fever, for gout. Only two [or] three can be eaten. It saddens, depresses, troubles one; it makes one flee, frightens one, makes one hide.

He who eats many of them sees many things which make him afraid, or make him laugh. He flees, hangs himself, hurls himself from a cliff, cries out, takes fright. One eats it in honey.

I eat mushrooms; I take mushrooms.

Of one who is haughty, presumptuous, vain, of him it is said: "He mushrooms himself."

TOCHTETEPON

It is a small herb. It has leaves which are slender.[6] The branch is serrated. Its root is white. It is deadly; it paralyzes one.

qualizcaoalti teiolitlacoa, teiollotlavelilotilia, tetlaqualizcaoaltia:

njnotlapavi, njtlapaqua, njtlapaquatinemj.

Ic ipan mjtoa in aqujn atle ipan tlachia, in mopouhtinemj, in atlamattinemj mixitl, tlapatl qujquatinemj: momjxivitinemj, motlapavitinemj.

TZITZINTLAPATL:

çan no ie in tlapatl, iece vivitzio: in jxocoio çan ie no iuhquj injc ihio.

MIXITL

çan qualton, iaiaoaltic: in jatlapal xoxoctic, xinachio: in canjn onoc coaciviztli, oncã ommoteca, amo qualonj, amo ivanj, teçotlacmjcti, tetentzacu, tetozcailpi, tetlatoltzacu, teamjcti, teatetzocomjcti, tenenepiltzatzaian,

amo machiztli injc omj, in mjh In aqujn qujçotlacmjquj intla icopi, cemjcopi, in tlatlachia ça çen tlachia quapitzavi, nõti: in achi ic mopalevia iehoatl in vino:

njnomjxivia, njtemjxivia.

NANACATL:

mjtoa teunanacatl, ixtlaoacan, çacatzontitlan in mochioa, quamalacachton, xopiazton, chichicacococ, tozcacococ: teivinti teiollomalacacho, tetlapololti: atonaviztli, coaciviztli ipaio, çan ontetl, etetl in qualonj, teiolpatzmjcti, tetequjpacho, teamã, techololti: temamauhti, tetlatiti.

In aqujn mjec qujqua mjec tlamãtli qujtta temamauhti, anoço tevetzqujti: choloa, momecanja motepexivia, tzatzi, momauhtia. Injc qujqua necutli ipan

njnanacaqua, njnonanacavia
In mopoanj, in atlamatinj in cuecuenotl: ipan mjtoa monanacavia.

TOCHTETEPON:

xiuhtontli, qujllo, pipitzaoac, matzatzaianquj: in jnelhoaio iztac, mjcoanj, teçotlacmjcti.

---

4. *Mixitl: Datura stramonium* (*ibid.,* p. 343).

5. *Nanacatl, teonanacatl:* R. Gordon Wasson, in "The Hallucinogenic Fungi of Mexico," *Botanical Museum Leaflets,* Vol. 19, No. 7 (Harvard Univ., 1961), pp. 159 *sqq.,* lists species of *Conocybe, Panaeolus, Psathyrella, Psilocybe,* and *Stropharia.* In Sahagún, *op. cit.,* p. 356, *teonanacatl* is *Panaeolus campanulatus, P. sphinctrinus.*

6. Corresponding Spanish text: *"tiene las hoias menudas como las del arbol del peru."*

One who drinks it, one who eats it, it burns up; it breaks his intestines. One drinks it in maguey wine; some remove it from the liquid after a short time. It paralyzes one, deadens one's hands [and] feet: no longer can they be stirred, no longer can they be moved.

Thus it is said of the sorcerer, "He is one who gives one *tochtetepon*."

I give him *tochtetepon*.

ATLEPATLI[7]

It is a small herb which lies along the ground. It grows by the water, in the mud. It is deadly. He who eats it dies of it; the animals which eat it die of it. It blisters, it burns wherever it is placed on the surface of our body. It is a remedy for skin sores. It burns one, it causes blisters.

I apply *atlepatli* to skin sores.

AQUIZTLI[8]

It is cord-like, stalky, blue. Its foliage burns one, causes swellings on one. It is a producer of swellings, of inflations. It blisters, burns one. It raises blisters on one. He who urinates on it has blisters all over his body. Where it touches on the skin, it there blisters; it burns it; it festers. He who has blisters drinks [an infusion of] a handful of its foliage.

This *aquiztli* is drunk uncooked during fasting; it brings the blisters to the surface, it draws all the blisters to the surface.

I treat the sores with *aquiztli*.

TENXOXOLI

Its leaves are long like reeds; they are slender. Its bottom, its root, has caused one to vomit, to expel blood. It causes one to vomit, to expel blood.

QUIMICHPATLI[9]

It is small and stalky, stemmed, podded. It burns one, kills one. It is an irritant; it burns, it bites.

It is called *quimichpatli* for this reason: it is food [for] mice, because, it is asserted, if they eat it, they die of it; their intestines break up. If it is placed there where there is festering, it eats it; it burns the festering, it exposes the sound flesh.

I take *quimichpatli*.

In aqujn quj, in aqujn qujqua: qujtlatia, qujcocototza in jcujtlaxcol: in octli ipan quj çequjntin, çan achitonca maqujxtia: teçotlacmjctia, qujmjmjctia in toma, tocxi, aocmo vel necuecuetzolo, aocmo vel neolinjlo.

Ic itechcopa mjtoa in moteieiecoltianj: tetochtetepovianj,

njctochtetepovia.

ATLEPATLI:

xiuhtontli, tlalli ixcomanj, atlan çoqujtitlan in mochioa, mjcoanj: in aqujn qujqua ic mjquj: in iolque qujqua ic mjquj, in canin topan jnacaiocan motlalia aquaqualaca, tlatla: xiopatli, tetlatia, tlaaquaquaqualatza:

njcatlepavia in xiutl.

HAQUJZTLI:

memecatic, tlatlacotic, texotic. In jqujllo tetlati, tetech mjhioti: mjhiiotianj, ihiio, tetotomonalti, tetlatia, tetotomonaltia. In aqujn caxixa totomoca in jnacaio, vel novian: in cana motlalia in topaneoaio ipan, njman aquaqualaca, qujtlatia palanj: in aqujn totomonj, centlamatzololi in conj, in jxiuhio.

Inin âqujztli: çan xoxouhquj in mj, aia tle moqua: qujoalpantlaça, mochi panj qujoalteca in totomoctli:

njcaqujzvia in xixiutl.

TENXOXOLI,

tolpatlactic in jqujllo, pipitzaoac in jtzinteio in jnelhoaio tehiçotlalti, teezviton: tehiçotlaltia, teezvitoma.

QUJMICHPATLI,

tlacotontli, qujioio, cueche tetlati, temjcti, tlaaquaqualatzanj, tlatlatianj, tlaquaquanj.

Injc mjtoa qujmjchpatli: in qujqujmjchti, tlaqualli qujn nelhuja, intla qujqua ic mjmjquj, tlatlacocotoca in incujtlaxcol. In canjn palanj intla vncan ommotema, qujqua, qujtlatia in palãquj, qujoalnextia in iectli nacatl;

njqujmjchpavia.

---

7. *Atlepatli*: possibly *Ranunculus stoloniferus* (cf. Dibble and Anderson, *Florentine Codex*, Book X, p. 157, n. 11).

8. *Aquiztli*: *Paullinia fuscecens* or *Anacardium* sp. (Sahagún, *op. cit.*, p. 322).

9. *Quimichpatli*: *Buddleia sessiliflora* H.B.K.; *Sebadilla officinarum* Gray (cf. Dibble and Anderson, *op. cit.*, p. 77, n. 9).

SECOND PARAGRAPH, which telleth of the mushrooms.

Mushrooms, mushrooms of the forest, are not edible uncooked: they are to be well cooked. They are healthful. Those which are eaten uncooked, and not well cooked, cause one to vomit, to have diarrhea, to be thirsty. They are fatal. In order to be abated, in order to stop the diarrhea which the mushrooms cause, *axin* — boiled, softened — goes in the rectum.

TZONTECOMANANACATL[1]

It is round, large, like a severed head.

XELHUAZNANACATL

It is divided, cylindrical, scarified, like something split.

CHIMALNANACATL

It is round; it is like the *atlacueçonan*. Verily it becomes like a shield; it is like a tortilla. These are all edible; they grow in the forest. And all are tough, firm; and to be eaten they are well cooked. They are healthful.

MENANACATL

It is round, white like oysters, tender, quickly cooked. It is a remedy. It can be baked — baked on the griddle. It is edible, tasty, savory.

ÇACANANACATL

The stem is long and thin; it is dark. The head is whorl-shaped, flat. It is not tough; it is like greens. It is a remedy. It is edible, tasty. The growing place is in the grass; it grows only when it rains anew. All these mushrooms are inedible raw.

QUAUHNANACATL

Its growing place is by the forest. It is edible; it can be cooked in an olla, it can be baked on a griddle. All these mushrooms are inedible raw. They can be cooked in an olla, they can be baked on a griddle.

I gather mushrooms; I pick mushrooms.[2]

CIMATL[3]

It is a root. The name of its foliage is *quaueco*, but also its name is *cimaquilitl*. [Its seed] is just like fat beans; they say that it is some sort of fat bean. It is

1. *Tzontecomananacatl:* prob. *Amonita muscaria* (Sahagún, *op. cit.*, p. 366).

2. *Acad. Hist. MS: ninanacacuicui.*

3. *Cimatl: Desmodium amplifolium* Hemsl., *D. parviflorum* Mart. & Gal. (Hernández, *Hist. de las Plantas*, Vol. II, pp. 659, 661); *Phaseolus coccineus* L. (*P. multiflorus* Willd.), in Dressler, "Pre-Columbian Cultivated Plants," p. 143.

INIC VME PARRAPHO itechpa tlatoa in nanacatl.

Nanacatl, quauhtla nanacatl: amo xoxouhcaqualonj, vel icucinj, vel pati: in qualo in çan xoxouhquj yoan in amo vel icucic teiçotlalti, teapitzalti, teamj, mjcoanj: injc palevilo, injc motzaqua in apitzalli in qujchioa in nanacatl: axin moquaqualatza, iamanquj tecujtlapanpa iauh.

TZONTECOMANANACATL,

ololtic, veipol iuhqujn tzontecomatl ic ca.

XELHOAZNANACATL,

xexeltic, mjmjltic, tzitziqujltic, iuhqujn xelhoaztli ic ca.

CHIMALNANACATL:

iaoaltic, iuhqujn atlacueçona ic ca. iuhqujn manoçe chimalli ic motlali, iuhqujn tlaxcalli ic ca. Inin qualonj: mochi quauhtla in mochioa. auh mochiuhquj injc iollotlapalivi injc chicaoac: auh injc moqua vel icuci, vel pati.

MENANACATL:

iaoaltic, iztac atzcalteuhca, amo iollotlapalivi, hiciuhca icucinj, patinj, ixconj, comalco ixconj, qualonj, velic, âviac.

ÇACANANACATL,

xopiazton xoiaiauhquj, quamalacachtic, quamanquj, amo iollotlapalivi, iuhqujn qujlitl, patinj, qualonj, velic, çaçacatla in mochiuhian: çanjo iquac in iancujcan qujavi mochioa: inin mochi nanacatl, amo xoxouhcaqualonj.

QUAUHNANACATL,

quauhtitech imochiuhian: qualonj, paoaxonj, ixconj. Inin mochi nanacatl amo xoxouhcaqualonj, paoaxonj, ixconj:

njnanacaheeoa njnacanacacujcuj:

CIMATL

tlanelhoatl: in jxiuhio itoca, quaveco, tel no itoca cimaqujlitl: vel iuhqujn aiecotli. qujtoa: qujl itlatla in aiecotli, motlatlamjnanj, movivilananj, xochio,

one that sends out runners, a creeper. It has flowers, green beans, beans.

Its root, when green or not well cooked, causes vomiting, causes diarrhea. It is fatal. In order to relieve[4] one who has taken *cimatl, axin* is cooked soft; it goes in the rectum. And to be eaten, this root is heated two days in order that it be well cooked. But first the water with saltpeter cooks, boils. Also they place it in hot water.

I take *cimatl*; I feed him *cimatl*.

AMOLLI[5]

It is long and narrow like reeds. It has a shoot; its flower is white. It is a cleanser. The large, the thick [roots] remove one's hair, make one bald; the small, the slender ones are cleansers, a soap. They wash, they cleanse, they remove the filth.

I use *amolli*; I soap myself.

The animals which are not strong, such as small fish, die from it; for therewith are the small fish taken. He who swallows a leech, this one drinks [an infusion of] *amolli* to kill the leech which is within.

TECPATLI,[6] TECPALOTL

It is sticky and also just like *amolli*. It is a medicine for broken bones. When one fractures his bones, when they have set them, splints are pressed on; they are covered with *tecpatli*. Also it is a snare, a trap; birds are taken with it. It is hung on the grass at the drinking place, the eating place of the birds. They creep there; so they are caught, stuck on. Hence it is called, given the name, "bird-catcher"; for it is very sticky, and the birds are stuck to it. It becomes glued to one.

I apply *tecpatli* to something. I catch something with *tecpatli*. I hunt [with *tecpatli*].

YIAMOLLI[7]

It is dark. Its stem is long and slender, herb-green. Its leaves glisten. They are slender. It has berries; its berries are purple. Its berries are medicine for dandruff.

ACOCOTLI[8]

exoio, eio.

In jnelhoaio in xoxouhquj, in noce amo vel icucic tehiçotlalti, teapitzalti: mjcoanj. Injc mopalevia mocimavi: iehoatl motzoionja in axin, iamanquj icujtlapampa iauh. Auh injc moqua inin tlanelhoatl: omjlhujtl in tlatla, injc vel icuci. auh achtopa tzoionj, quaqualaca in atl, tequjxqujo: atotonjltitlan in no contema:

njnocimavia, njccimavia.

HAMOLLI,

tolpatlactic, qujioio; iztac in jxochio. tlapaconj: in vevei in totomaoac tetzontepeuh, tequaxipetzo in tepito in pitzaoac tlapaconj, neamovilonj: tlapaca, tlachipaoa, tlatzoqujxtia:

njcamolhuja, njnamovia:

in iolloque, in amo iollotlapalivi, ic mjquj: in juhquj mjmjchti, ca ic maci in mjmjchti. Auh in aqujn acujcujiachin qujtoloa iehoatl conj in amolli ic mjquj in jitic onoc acujcujiachi.

TECPATLI, TECPAOLOTL,

çaçalic: auh çan no iuhquj in amolli poztequjzpatli. In aquin mopoztequj in oqujçaloque moquappachoa ic mopepechoa in tecpatli: yoã tlamalonj, tlatlamalonj ic maci in totome: çacatitech mopiloa in canjn imatlian, intlaquaian totome: oncan momamana ic mahci, ic moçaloa: ic mjtoa motocaiotia: tlahçalli: ca cenca çaçaltic yoã ic moçaloa in totome: tetech mochioa çaçalivi.

nitlatecpavia, nictecpavia, njtlatlaçalhuja.

YIAMOLI,

catzaoac: in jquauhio pipiaztic, qujltic: in jxiuhio tzotzotlaca, ixpipitzaoac, cacapollo, camopaltic; in jcacapollo: quatequjxicivizpatli in jcacapollo.

ACOCOTLI

---

4. *Acad. Hist. MS: palevilo.*

5. *Amolli: Sapindus saponarius, Stegnosperma halimifolium* (Sahagún, *op. cit.,* p. 321).

6. *Tecpatli:* unident.; desc. in Emmart, *Badianus MS,* p. 246; Santamaría, *Diccionario de Mejicanismos,* p. 1031 (*tepacle*), etc.

7. *Yiamoli: Phytolacca octandra* Linn.: cf. Dibble and Anderson, *op. cit.,* p. 139, n. 9.

8. *Acocotli: Arracacia atropurpurea, Dahlia variabilis, Euphorbia hypreicifolia, Lagenaria vulgaris, Pentacripta purpurea* (*ibid.,* p. 161, n. 1).

THIRD PARAGRAPH, which telleth of the herbs which are edible cooked.

UAUHQUILITL,[1] AN EDIBLE HERB

It is herb-green; it is tall. Its stem, its stalk, has branches. It has foliage like butterflies; it has hairs. The name of its foliage is *uauhtzontli*: the name of its seed is *uauhtli*. They are like a small whorl, or small whorls. [The herb] is cookable in an olla; it tastes of ashes; water can be drained [from the cooked herb]; it can be used with *epazote;* it can be compressed. Tamales can be made — their name is *quiltamalli.* Grains of maize can be added — the name of [this mixture] is *quillaxcalli.*

I cook [*uauh*]*quilitl* in an olla. I compress [*uauh*]-*quilitl.* I eat [*uauh*]*quilitl.* I make [*uauh*]*quilitl* tamales. I make [*uauh*]*quilitl* tortillas. I gather the [*uauh*]*quilitl.*

UAUHTZONTLI

It is the prickly, the hairy part of the *uauhquilitl.* It is spreading, radiating, pestle-shaped, green, cookable in an olla, compressible. It is edible as greens. When mature, when ripe, it is no longer cookable in an olla, no longer edible as greens; it is already seed.

QUILTONILLI[2]

The [leaf] surface is wide. When still small, it is edible; when larger its name is *petzicatl* or *pitzicatl.* It can be cooked in an olla, it can be treated with salt-peter; water can be pressed out, water can be squeezed out. This *quiltonilli* has black seeds. The name of its seeds is *petzicatl* or *pitzicatl.*

ITZMIQUITL[3]

It is a creeper, very tender. The branches are thick, small but thick. The leaves are small and round. It can be cooked in an olla.

AYOXOCHQUILITL[4]

It is the flower, the blossom of the gourd. It is cylindrical, green. When it has blossomed, it is yellow. Its center is hairy, fuzzy; it has a center. This *ayoxochquilitl* is prickly; it has thorns. These can be peeled, husked; the centers can be removed. They

INIC EI PARRAPHO: itechpa tlatoa in qualonj qujlitl icucinj.

QUALONJ XIVITL: VAUHQUJLITL

qujltic, melaoac: in jquauhio in jtlacoio mamae, qujllo, papaloio, tzone: in jqujioio, itoca vauhtzontli, in jxinachio itoca vauhtli, malacachtontli, anoço malacachtotonti: paoaxonj nexcococ, aqujxtilonj, mopaçoiotianj, papatzconj, tamalolonj itoca qujltamalli, tlatlaoiotilonj: itoca qujllaxcalli:

njqujlpaoaci, njqujlpatzca, njqujlqua, njqujltamaloa, njqujllaxcaloa, njqujqujlpi.

VAUHTZONTLI:

im jaoaio, itzon in vauhqujlitl, chachaiactic, chachaiaoac, texaltic, xoxoctic, paoaxonj, patzconj, qujlqualonj. In ie icucic, in ie moxaoa: aocmo paoaxonj, aocmo qujlqualonj, ca ie xinachtli.

QUILTONJLLI,

ixpatlaoac: iquac in oc tepiton qualonj; in ie vei itoca petzicatl, anoço pitzicatl paoaxonj, tequjxqujvilonj, patzconj, papatzconj. Inin qujltonjlli vauhio; tliltic in joauhio itoca petzicatl anoço pitzicatl.

ITZMIQUJLITL,

movivilananj, celpatic matitilactic, matitilacton, ixiaiaoaltoton paoaxonj.

AIOXOCHQUJLITL

ixochio icuepõca: in aiotli mjmjltic, xoxoctic in cueponquj coztic, tomjlollo, tomjiollo, iollo. Inin aioxochqujlitl, aoaio, quaquave: xipeoalonj, iectilonj, iolloqujxtilonj, paoaxonj: mjmjlivi, cueponj:

---

1. *Uauhquilitl, uauhtli;* the latter is *Amaranthus paniculathus* (Santamaría, *op. cit.,* p. 603); *uauhtli* is *A. leucocarpus* S. Wats., *A. cruentus* L., and *uauhtzontli* is *Chenopodium Nuttalliae* Safford, according to Dressler, *op. cit.,* pp. 121, 128.

2. *Quiltonilli: Amaranthus hypocondriacus* (Sahagún, *op. cit.,* p. 352

3. *Itzmiquilitl:* sp. of purslane (Dibble and Anderson, *op. cit.,* p. 92); *Portulaca rubra* in Rémi Siméon: *Dictionnaire de la langue nahuatl ou mexicaine* (Paris: Imprimerie Nationale, 1885).

4. *Ayoxochquilitl: Cucurbita* sp. (Sahagún, *op. cit.,* p. 324).

can be cooked in an olla. It becomes cylindrical; it blossoms.

I pick, I gather gourd blossoms. I cook gourd blossoms in an olla.

GOURD VINE TIPS

Gourd tips: these are the tips, the tender tips of the gourd vine. They are tender, edible, savory.

AXOXOCO[5]

Its leaves are wide, long; its stalk is rope-like. It is cookable in an olla; it is savory.

MIZQUIQUILITL

Its stalk is rope-like; its leaves are herb-green. The branches are serrated, toothed. It is cookable in an olla; water can be pressed out. It is tasty, savory.

I pick *mizquiquilitl*. I eat *mizquiquilitl*.

ACUITLACPALLI

[Its leaves] are straight, broad. Its growing place is at the water's edge, in the water. It is cookable in an olla.

TZIUINQUILITL OR ATZIUENQUILITL

Its habitat is in the water, at the water's edge. [Its leaves] are serrated, blue. It is cookable in an olla.

TACANALQUILITL

Its leaves are *tacanalli*.[6] Its habitat is in the mountains. It is ash-colored, faded to an ash color. It can be cooked in an olla, it can be baked on a griddle.

MAMAXTLA[7] OR MAMAXTLAQUILITL

It resembles the *acuitlacpalli* herb. Its habitat is in the water, at the water's edge. It is cookable in an olla; it is savory.

TZITZICAZQUILITL[8]

It is prickly; it bites. Its growing place is in the water, at the water's edge. It can be cooked in an olla.

UEI UAUHQUILITL OR TEOUAUHQUILITL

It is bitter. It is young, small amaranth.[9] When mature, it is very bitter. It can be cooked in an olla.

naioxochqujlpi, naioxochqujqujlpi, naioxochqujlpaoaci.

AIOIACAQUJLITL:

aioiacatl, iehoatl in jiac, in jiacacelica: aiomecatl, celic, qualonj, velic.

AXOXOCO

papatlaoac, melactic: in jqujllo memecatic, in jquauhio paoaxonj velic.

MIZQUJQUJLITL,

memecatic; in jquauhio qujltic, in jxiuhio matzatzaianquj, tzitziqujltic paoaxonj, patzconj, velic, aviac:

njmjzqujqujlpi, njmjzqujqujlqua.

ACUJTLACPALLI,

memelactic, papatlaoac, atenco, atlan imochiuhian, paoaxonj.

TZIVINQUJLITL, ANOÇO ATZIVĒQUJLITL,

atlan atenco ichan tzitziqujltic: texotic, paoaxoni.

TACANALQUJLITL,

tacanalli ixiuhio, tepepan chane nextic, cujtlanextic, paoaxonj ixconj.

MAMAXTLA, ANOÇO MAMAXTLAQUJLITL:

qujnenevilia in acujtlacpalli, atlan atenco chane, paoaxonj, velic.

TZITZICAZQUJLITL,

aoaio, tequaqua, atlan atenco imochiuhian, paoaxonj.

VEI VAUHQUJLITL, ANOÇO TEUVAUHQUJLITL,

chichic: vauhtli piltontli, tepiton: in ie vei vel chichic, paoaxonj.

---

5. *Axoxoco: Gaulteria acuminata* Schl. (*ibid.*, p. 323).
6. See, however, corresponding Spanish text: *"la rrayz desta yerua se llama, tacanalli."*
7. *Mamaxtla: Iresine* sp. (Sahagún, *op. cit.*, p. 340).
8. *Tzitzicazquilitl (tzitzicaztli): Jatropha urens;* Dibble and Anderson, *op. cit.*, p. 149, n. 5.
9. Corresponding Spanish text: *"son bledos siluestres."*

Etenquilitl

This is the tip of the bean, its foliage, its dross. It can be cooked in an olla.

I gather *etenquilitl*, I gather *etenquilitl* greens. I cook *etenquilitl* in an olla. I eat *etenquilitl*.

Tlalayoquilitl[10]

Xaltomaquilitl

¶

FOURTH PARAGRAPH, which telleth of all the edible herbs.

Tzitziquilitl[1]

It is tender, very tender. It is tender; it has a blossom, it has blossoms; it has seeds. It is tasty. It is dark green.

Eloquilitl[2]

It is herb-green, exceedingly fresh, very fresh. It is blossomed, a producer of blossoms. It is pleasing, very pleasing.

Quauheloquilitl

It is a rather large reed.[3] It grows in the forest, among the tuna cactus. It becomes tender, fresh; it freshens greatly; it is exceedingly fresh.

Moçoquilitl[4]

It is a faded ashen color, hairy, rough, tasty, savory.

Tzayanalquilitl

Its growing place is in the water. Its branches are hollow, like reeds. It is called *tzayanalquilitl* for this reason: the center of [the stem] is split.

Achochoquilitl[5]

It is light green, like turquoise. It causes one to belch. Its growing place is at the water's edge.

AUEXOCAQUILITL is the same as *achochoquilitl*.

Tetzonquilitl

It is herb-green, cylindrical, like the *axalli* herb. It is salty. [When chewed] it crackles, it crunches.

Etenqujlitl,

etentli: in jqujllo, ieçoqujllo: paoaxonj,

netēqujlpi, netenqujqujlpi, netenqujlpaoaci, netenqujlqua.

Tlalaioqujlitl.

Xaltomaqujlitl.

¶

INIC NAUI PARRAPHO: itechpa tlatoa, in jxqujch qujlitl qualonj.

Tzitziqujlitl,

celic, celpatic, celtic, xochio, xoxochio, xinachio, haviac, qujliaiactic.

Eloqujlitl,

qujltic, cecelpatic, cecelic, xochiovanj, moxochiotianj, avixtic, avixpatic.

Quauheloqujlitl,

veacatontli: quauhtla, nupalla in mochioa: celia, cecelia, cecelpatia, cecelpati.

Moçoqujlitl,

cujtlanextic, cujtlanexeoac, tômjo vapaoac velic aviac.

Tzaianalqujlitl;

atlan imochiuhian. iticoionquj, acatic: injc mjtoa, tzaianalqujlitl: tzatzaianquj in jiollo.

Achochoqujlitl,

texotic, ximmaltic, teipotzalti; atenco imochiuhian.

AVEXOCAQUJLITL çan no ie in achochoqujlitl.

Tehtzonqujlitl:

qujltic, mjmjltic, haxaltic, popoiec, xaxamanj, xaxamaca:

---

10. *Ibid.*: "*son calabaças siluestres comense cozidas.*"

1. *Tzitziquilitl: Erigeron pusillus* Nutt. (Dibble and Anderson, *op. cit.*, p. 92, n. 12).

2. *Eloquilitl: Bidens pilosa* (*ibid.*, p. 92, n. 10).

3. *Acad. Hist. MS: veyacatōtli.*

4. *Moçoquilitl: Eupatorium deltoideum* Jacq. (Dibble and Anderson, *op. cit.*, p. 92, n. 11).

5. *Achochoquilitl: Bidens chrysanthemoides, B. pilosa, B. tetragona* (Hernández, *op. cit.*, Vol. II, p. 361). Corresponding Spanish text: "*Dizen desta yerua q̃ si los muchachos o muchachas la comē hazense impotētes pa engēdrar, pero despues de grādes todos la comen seguramente.*"

I make it crunch; I make it crackle.

njcxaxamatza, njcxaxamanja.

Iztaquilitl

It is drooping, small and drooping. It is edible raw and cookable in an olla. It is salty, very salty.

Iztaqujlitl,

chapactic, chapactontli, xoxouhcaqualonj yoan paoaxonj, poec, poelpatiç.

Tepicquilitl[6]

Its leaves are long, pointed, pointed at the end. It is not to be eaten frequently; it goes through one.

Tepicqujlitl:

ixmemelaoac in jqujllo, iacavitztic, iacavitzauhquj; amo mjecca qualonj, tenalqujxti.

Eçoquilitl

It is the foliage of the bean. The leaves are round, downy, rough-backed. It causes flatulence in one.
I pick, I gather *eçoquilitl*. I eat, I chew *eçoquilitl*.[7]

Eçoqujlitl,

etl iqujllo, ixiaiaoaltic, tomjo, teçontic in jicampa, teipotzalti:
neçoqujlpi, nequjqujlpi, neçoqujlqua, neçoqujlquaqua.

Uitzquilitl[8]

It is prickly, thorny, ashen; a rustler. It is stringy, fibrous. It has blossoms, it is blossoming. It grows at the water's edge.

Vitzqujlitl,

âoaio, vivitzio, ticeoac, xaxamanjnj, ichio, iichio, xochio, cueponcaio atẽco in mochioa.

Quauitzquilitl

This one is the same as *uitzquilitl*. However, this *uitzquilitl* grows in the dry lands, in the forests;[9] they give it the name *quauitzquilitl*. "It eats me [as] I eat it," because it first pricks one as it is eaten.

Quavitzqujlitl

çan ie no iehoatl in vitzqujlitl: iece iehoatl in tlalhoacpan, in quauhtla mochioa vitzqujlitl: quavitzqujlitl qujtocaiotia. nechonqua noconqua: ipampa in achto tetzoponja ic moqua.

Chichicaquilitl[10]

It grows in the water, at the water's edge, in the reeds, on good lands, on cultivated lands. It is very tender. The roots are white. It is only a little bitter.

Chichicaqujlitl:

in atlã in atenco, in tolla, in qualcan, in tlaelimjcpan, mochioa: cecelpatic, tzitziniztac: çan achi in camatetelqujc.

Tonalchichicaquilitl[11]

It grows in dry lands, in the grasslands, in the forest. It is a faded ashen color, ashen; very bitter. It is especially the remedy of one who has an internal fever. It aids the digestion; it soothes the intestines, especially when one fasts, when the intestines are irritated.

Tonalchichicaqujlitl,

in tlalhoacpan, in çaçacatla in quauhtla mochioa, cuetlanextic nexeoac, tlaquauhchichic oc cenca inamjc in teiticnemj totonquj, tetlatemovili, tecujtlaxcoliecti: oc cenca iquac in aiatle moqua, tecujtlaxcolichic.

Coyocuexi[12]

It resembles *uitzquilitl*. It is soft, stalky; it has blossoms. Its blossoms are fragrant. It is not to be eaten

Coiocuexi,

qujnenevilia in vitzqujlitl: iamanquj, qujioio, xochio: in jxochio pochqujo. Amo pipilqualonj, tetoz-

---

6. *Tepicquilitl: Mesembryanthemum blandum* L. (Dibble and Anderson, *op. cit.*, p. 92, n. 13).

7. *Acad. Hist.* MS: *neçoquilpipi.*

8. *Uitzquilitl: Circium mexicanum* (Sahagún, *op. cit.*, p. 367).

9. Corresponding Spanish text: *"se crian en las montañas."*

10. *Chichicaquilitl: Carraja mexicana, Sonchus siliatus, Mimulus glabratus* (Dibble and Anderson, *op. cit.*, p. 144, n. 70). In the *Acad. Hist.* MS, this text corresponds to *tolchichicaquilitl*, an herb not found in the *Florentine Codex*. For *chichicaquilitl* the *Acad. Hist.* MS text reads: *quicevia ỹ tletl ỹ totõqui tehitic nemi. yvani. qualoni. teaxixyecti. teaxixtlapo.* It alleviates internal fire, internal fever. It is potable, edible. It cleanses one's urine; it is a diuretic.

11. *Tonalchichicaquilitl:* prob. *Oenothera lacinata* Hill (Sahagún, *op. cit.*, p. 359).

12. *Coyocuexi:* Possibly *coyocuechtli* (unident.); Hernández, *op. cit.*, Vol. III, p. 794.

by children. One is made hoarse; it irritates the throat.

POPOYAUH[13]

It is like a small stick, like a small tree. It is called *popoyauh* because its foliage is very black [and green]. It is edible raw, and it is cookable in an olla, and it can be ground — made into tortillas on the griddle.

MEXIXIN[14]

It burns. Its leaves are small. It is edible uncooked. When much is eaten, it burns one, blisters one. It is cookable in an olla; it can be ground. It can be made into tortillas [or] into tamales called *mexixquillax-calli* [or] *mexixquiltamalli*. Its seeds are yellow, small but broad, very hard. It is really the food of the servants, and it is a medicine for the flux. It expels the flux. They make an *atole* from its seeds, which cleans out, moves out the flux which is in the intestines. It soothes one's intestines.

XOXOCOYOLI[15]

It is sour, edible; edible raw, cookable in an olla. *Xocoyoli* is the same as *xoxocoyoli*.

XOXOCOYOLPAPATLA

The stem is long, cylindrical. Its leaves are only on its top.[16] [They are] broad; for this reason is it called *xoxocoyolpapatla*. [They are] very tasty, savory, when cooked.

XOXOCOYOLCUECUEPOC[17]

The stem is cylindrical, long. It has blossoms, it is a blossomer, so it is called *xoxocoyolcuecuepoc*. It is very tasty; it is like the tomato. It grows only when the rains set in anew.

XOXOCOYOLHUIUILA[18]

It is cord-like, a creeper. [The leaves] are small and round; they are savory.

MICCAXOXOCOYOLI

It is like the *xoxocoyolpatlac*; however, the stalk is stubby, thick, hairy. The leaf is broad. It is very sour,

cananalo, tetelqujc.

POPOIAUH:

iuhqujn tlacotontli, iuhqujnma quauhtontli. Injc mjtoa popoiauh: vel poiactic in jqujllo: xoxouhca-qualonj, yvan paoaxonj, yoan texvilonj, comalco ma-nalonj.

MEXIXIN,

cococ in jqujllo, tepiton: xoxouhcaqualonj. In mjec moqua, tetlati, teaquaqualatz, paoaxonj, texvilonj, tlaxcalolonj, tamalolonj: ic mjtoa. mexixqujltamalli, mexixqujllaxcalli. In jxinachio, coztic, patlachpipil, vellaquaoac: vel intlaqual in cocoti. Yoan tlaelpatli: in tlaelli qujtlaça, catolhuja in jxinachio, cochpana, cololoa in tlaelli, in cujtlaxcolli itech onoc, tecujtlax-coliecti.

XOXOCOIOLI,

xococ: qualonj, xoxouhcaqualonj, paoaxonj, xoco-ioli, çan no iehoatl in xoxocoioli.

XOXOCOIOLPAPATLA,

xoveiac, xomjmjltic: çan iquac in manj yiatlapal, papatlaoac. Injc mjtoa xoxocoiolpapatla: vel velic, aviac in jquac oicucic.

XOXOCOIOLCUECUEPOC,

mjmjltic, xoviac: aqujllo, xochio cueponquj. Injc mjtoa xoxocoiolcuecuepoc: vel velic, qujnenevilia in xitomatl: çanjo iquac in mochioa, in jquac iancujcan qujavi.

XOXOCOIOLHUJVILA,

memecatic, vivilanquj ixiaiaoaltoton, velic.

MICCAXOXOCOIOLI:

iuhqujn xoxocoiolpatlac, iece tetepontomaoac. toto-mjo, amatlapalpatlaoac, xocopatic, xocopalalatic, xo-

---

13. *Popoyauh: Ustilago maidis* DC. (Sahagún, *op. cit.*, p. 349); *Raphanus rhaphanistrum* in Bernardino de Sahagún, *Historia General de las Cosas de Nueva* España (Mexico: Pedro Robredo, 1938), Vol. III, p. 339.

14. *Mexixin:* watercress (Dibble and Anderson, *op. cit.*, p. 92, n. 21).

15. *Xoxocoyoli: Oxalis* sp. (Sahagún, *op. cit.*, p. 370).

16. *Acad. Hist. MS: icpac.*

17. *Oxalis* sp. (Sahagún, *loc. cit.*).

18. *Oxalis* sp. (*loc. cit.*).

extremely sour, surpassingly sour. It sets one's teeth on edge; it deadens one's teeth.

Quauhxoxocoyoli[19]

It is perhaps broad-leafed or creeping. It is thick like the *miccaxoxocoyoli*; however, it is tasty, savory, good.

I pick, I gather the *xoxocoyoli*.

Quanacaquilitl

When it appeared, it was like the *coyocuechi* herb. They say it is some form of lettuce. The seeds of the lettuce are borne by the wind,[20] and where they fall, there they sprout. They named this *quanacaquilitl*, because the fowls are nourished by it. It is edible; it travels.

Xonacatl[21]

It is slender like reeds. It glistens. The bottoms are white. It has a beard. It stinks; it burns. It aids the digestion; it throws off, rids one, of a cough.

Tepexonacatl

Wherever it grows is not very well known. It probably belongs among the herbs. They say it is some kind of onion. It burns much.

Maxten

It resembles the onion. It is stalky, blooming. It is a little like the onion, a little acrid smelling. Its roots are cookable in an olla. The roots of this are well diffused; there are many. Thus it is said of him who engenders many, whose many children live, "He has offspring like the *maxten*."

Papaloquilitl[22]

It is fragrant, tasty. [The leaves] are small and round. It grows in the east.

Ayauhtona[23]

Its growing place is in the mountains, in the grasslands. It is [colored] like the lovely cotinga. It is dwarfed, like something small and bushy. It has many blossoms.

copetzquavitl: tetlancecepouh, tetlanmjmjcti.

Quauhxoxocoioli,

aço papatla, anoço vivilan: chamaoac iuhqujn mjccaxoxocoioli, iece velic, aviac, qualli,

nixoxocoiolpi, njxoxocoiolpipi

Quanacaqujlitl:

qujn onez, iuhqujn coiocuechi, qujl itlatla in lechugas: in jxinachio lechugas in ecato. Auh in campa vetzi in vmpa ixoa iehoatl oqujtocaiotique quanacaqujlitl: ipampa ic oapaoa in totolme, qualonj, tlaotlatoctia.

Xonacatl.

tolpatlactic, cuecueiaoac, tzitziniztac, tentzone. hiiac, cococ, tetlatemovili, qujtopeoa, qujquanja in tlatlaciztli.

Tepexonacatl,

in çan canjn mochichioa, in amo tlacenmachtli in çaçan xivitl pouj: qujl itlatla in xonacatl, vel cococ.

Maxten:

moxonacanenequj, qujioio, cuecueponquj achi quecinamj, achi chipaiac: In itzinteio, paoaxonj. Inin itzinteio vel cuecueiochauhtica, vel mjec: ic ipan mjtoa in aqujn cenca mopilhoatianj, in mjequjntin onnemj ipilhoan. Maxtenpilhoa.

Papaloqujlitl:

yiiac, velic, malacachtontli tonaian mochioa.

Aiauhtona,

tepepan çacatla imochiuhia: xixiuhtototic, tlalpãton, iuhqujn quamalacachtontli, xoxochio.

---

19. *Quauhxoxocoyoli*: Oxalis angustifolia, O. corniculata (*ibid.*, p. 350).
20. *Acad. Hist. MS: hecatoco.*
21. *Xonacatl*: in corresponding Spanish text, *çebollas pequeñitas*.
22. *Papaloquilitl*: Porophyllum seemanii Sch. (Sahagún, *op. cit.*, p. 348).
23. *Ayauhtona*: Cuphea jorullensis H. B. K., Porophyllum coloratum D. C. (Dibble and Anderson, *op. cit.*, p. 92, n. 19).

A fruit-producing herb, camoxiuitl

It is cord-like, a creeper, a blossomer, a bloomer. [The leaves are] round. Its roots are cylindrical. Some are round; those which follow are forked.

The name of this root is *camotli*.[24] Some are white; their name is *iztac camotli* [or] *poxcauhcamotli*. Some are yellow; their name is *xochicamotli*. Some are blue; their name is *tlapalcamotli*. And the name of those mentioned above is *camoxalli*. They are cookable in an olla; they are edible uncooked.

Xicama[25]

It is an herb. [The leaves are] broad, round. [It is] blossoming, flowering. The name of its root is *xicama*. It is round, broad, constricted, sweet, tasty, savory, honey-like. It crackles, crunches as it is eaten.

Tolcimaquilitl

It is cord-like, a creeper, a bloomer. Its blossom is very chili-red; it is longed for, a coveted thing, craved, desirable, tender. The name of its root is *tolcimatl*. In an olla it may be cooked in a water and ash solution. It is fine-textured — very fine-textured. *Ichcatolcimatl* is of very fine texture [and] a little large.

I eat *tolcimatl*; I chew *tolcimatl*.

Acaxilotl

It is a broad reed. Its root can be eaten uncooked; it is cookable in an olla.

I grub up, I chew the *acaxilotl* [root].

Atzatzamolli[26]

Its root is [like that of] the *atlacueçonan*. It is pitted, rough, black; the center [of the root] can be cooked in an olla. [It is] like maize leached in wood ashes.

Çacateztli[27]

The root is round and small. It can be cooked in an olla. It is fine-textured, savory, tasty.

Xaltomatl [or] xaltotomatl[28]

It is the fruit of the *xaltomatl* herb. Some are white, some black. They are sweet, very sweet; juicy, very juicy; round, round like a stone, very round.

Xivitl xochiquallo. camoxivitl,

memecatic, movivicomanj xotlanj, cueponjnj, ixia-iaoaltic in jnelhoaio mjmjltic, cequj ololtic: in tlato-qujlia xaltic.

Inin tlanelhoatl: itoca, camotli: cequj iztac, itoca, iztac camotli, poxcauhcamotli: cequj coztic, itoca xo-chicamotli: cequj movitic, itoca: tlapalcamotli. Auh in tlacpac omoteneuh, itoca: camoxalli. Paoaxonj, xo-xouhcaqualonj.

Xicama

xivitl: papatlactic, iaiaoaltic, cueponcaio, xochio-vanj. In jnelhoaio, itoca: xicama, ololtic, patlachtic, cocomotztic, tzopelic, haviac, velic, necutic, xaxaxa-maca, teteinj injc moqua.

Tolcimaqujlitl;

memecatic, movivilananj, cueponjnj chichilpatic in jcueponca, tetlanecti, eleviliztli, icollo, nequjzio, ha-iollo tlapalivi. In jnelhuaio: itoca: Tolcimatl, nexaio-tic: paoaxonj, texio, tetexio. Ichcatolcimatl cenca texio, cujtlatolonton:

njtolcimachqua, njtolcimaquaqua.

Acaxilotl:

tolpatlactli inelhoaio, xoxouhcaquaqualonj, paoa-xonj:

nacaxilotataca, nacaxiloquaqua.

Atzatzamolli

inelhoaio, in atlacueçonan: chachaquachtic, teçon-tic, tliltic: in jiollo, paoaxonj, iuhqujn quauhnexta-malli.

Çacateztli

tlanelhoatl; ololtõtli, paoaxonj, texio, velic, aviac

Xaltomatl, xaltotomatl

icapollo: in xaltomaxivitl, cequj iztac, cequj tliltic: necutzopatic necutzopiltic, aio, aiopipitzictic, ololtic, teloltic, ololpatic:

---

24. *Camotli: Ipomoea Batatas* (L.) Poir (Dressler, *op. cit.*, p. 135).

25. *Pachyrrhizus erosus* (L.) Urban (cf. Chap. VI, § 9, n. 5).

26. *Atzatzamoli:* prob. *Castalia gracilis* Rose (Sahagún, *op. cit.*, p. 323).

27. *Çacateztli:* prob. *Panicum* sp. (*ibid.*, p. 372).

28. *Xaltomatl: Saracha jaltomata* Schlecht., *Physalis mollis* (*ibid.*, p. 368).

I pick, gather, eat the *xaltomatl*. I mash it. I break it up; I juice it in my mouth.

Its root is edible uncooked, and it can be baked on a griddle and cooked in an olla. It is savory.

Coyototomatl [or] coyotomatl[29]

Its fruit, its product, is just like the tomato, the small tomato. Its skin is yellow, very yellow, quite yellow. It is sweet. Its root is somewhat bitter to the throat. A little is drunk as a laxative. In moderation it soothes the intestines. She who suckles drinks this in order to clean, to purify, her milk.

Atlitliliatl

Its fruit is small and black. It is sweet; however, it is a little harsh. Its leaves are used for the bath, in the sweat bath; they relieve the sick.

The tlalxilotl is edible.

Tlalayotli[30]

It is a creeper like the *ayotetontli*. Its fruit can be cooked in an olla; it can be baked on a griddle. But [in an infusion], its root is not good to drink; it is a laxative.

I gather *tlalayotli*.

¶

Fifth paragraph, which telleth of the medicinal herbs and of different herbs.

1

Iztac patli[1]

2

Cuicuitlapile [or] cuitlapile[2]

With just the root, one who has had a relapse is cured. And all [these] are mixed [with it]: *tlatlauhcapatli, aacaxilotic, auatoton, tochtetepon, çacacilin, iztac çaçalic, atepocapatli, uei patli, iztac chichic patli*. They are all cooked together when the patient drinks it [in an infusion]. And if one has drunk it three or four days, then one bathes in the sweat bath.

njxaltomacujcuj, njxaltomaeoa, njxaltotonquaqua: njcpitzinja, njccamapatla, njccamapatzca.

In jnelhoaio in: xoxouhcaqualonj, yoan ixconj, yoan paoaxonj, velic.

Coiototomatl, coiotomatl:

in jcapollo, in jtlaaqujllo, vel iuhquj tomatl: in mjltomatl izoaio, coztic, cocoztic, cozpiltic, tzopelic, achi tozcachichic in jnelhoaio. In achi vel ommj, tlanoqujlonj: in çan vel ipan tecujtlaxcoliecti. In tlachichioalhuja, iehoatl conj, ic chipaoa, ic iectia in jmaio.

Atlitliliatl:

in jcapollo, tliltotonti, necutic, iece achi tetelqujc: in jxiuhio ic nealtilo temazcalco, qujiamanja in cocoxquj.

Tlalxilotl, qualonj.

Tlalaiotli,

movivilananj, iuhqujn aiotetontli: in jtlaaqujllo paoaxonj, ixconj. Auh in jnelhoaio, amo ivanj tlanoqujlonj:

njtlalaioieva.

¶

Injc macuilli parrapho itechpa tlatoa in xivitl patli, yoan nepapan xivitl.

.1.

Iztac patli

.2.

Cujcujtlapile, cujtlapile.

çan tlanelvatl: ic pati in aqujn mocaxanja: auh muchi moneneloa in tlatlauhcapatli, aacaxilotic, avatoton, tochtetepon, çacacilin, iztac çaçalic, atepucapatli, vei patli, iztac chichicpatli, mocentzonja in conj, cocoxquj: auh intla ie iuh eylvitl anoço navilvitl oqujc njman motema.

---

29. *Coyoltomatl: Vitex mollis* H.B.K. (*ibid.*, p. 329).

30. *Tlalayotli: Asclepias linaria, Gonolobus erianthus* D.C. (Dibble and Anderson, *op. cit.*, p. 144, n. 73).

1. *Iztac patli:* various plants represented, probably, according to Sahagún, *op. cit.*, p. 339. According to Santamaría, *op. cit.*, p. 620, "*se usó mucho antiguamente en purgantes y parches que todavía se venden en algunas boticas. Es una apocinácea.*"

2. *Cuicuitlapile:* Possibly *Valerianoides* sp. (Dibble and Anderson, *op. cit.*, p. 143, n. 52).

3

Iztac Çaçalic[3]

It is only a root. Its leaves are green, small and round. It grows in this manner: it only creeps. With it are cured those who pass blood or expel a flux. And it is prepared thus: when roasted and mixed with wrinkled *chía*, then it is ground. The sick one drinks it [in an infusion].

4

Centli ina or cintli ina

The root is white, cylindrical; its foliage is a faded ashen color. It grows like an herb; it grows in the forest. He who has a fever is cured with it. Some drink just it alone, after it has been ground. Some mix it with the small and the slender *iztac patli* herb. It is ground. He who becomes sick drinks it. It is not cooked.

5

Tlatlauhcapatli[4]

Its appearance is red. It is not a large tree [but] just like an herb. Its leaves are also red. It grows there at Tepçolco. It is required by those whose flesh is suppurated. When it is applied, perhaps it is just moistened, or it is ground. It is not mixed [with anything]; just it alone [is used].

6

Tlanoquiloni

It is only a root, small and round like a turnip. It grows just like an herb. It has only one stalk; its leaves are small. It grows there at Tepçolco.

He who has a swollen stomach or a fever has it ground up; he drinks it [in an infusion] to purge the sickness with it. When purged, he drinks an *atole* of raw, ground maize, whereby [the purging] is stopped.

7

Eloxochineloatl

It is just a root like a stick. It is white. It grows just like an herb. Its leaves are green, slender. Its growing place is the forest.

It is required by one who has a fever; they grind it for him to drink, thereby purging him who takes sick. He drinks it alone and only cold. It is also re-

.3.

Iztac çaçalic:

çan tlaneloatl, in ixiuhio xoxoctic iavaltotonti, injc muchioa çan movivilana: ic mopatia in aqujque eztli qujnoquja, in anoço tlaielli quitlaça: auh injc muchichioa in jcequj, yoan moneloa chiãtzotzol: njmã moteci: conj in cocoxquj.

.4.

Centli ina, anoço cintli ina:

tlanelhoatl, iztac, mjmjltic: in jxiuhio cujtlanextic, iuhqujn xivitl ic mochioa quauhtla in muchioa. Ic pati in aqujn motlevia: in cequjn çan mjxcavia in conj, in jquac omotez: cequjn qujneloa in iztac patli tepitoton, yoã iztac patli pitzaoac: moteci, conj, in cocoxquj, amo tzoionj.

.5.

Tlatlauhcapatli,

tlatlauhquj in jtlachieliz, amo vei quavitl, çã iuhqujn xivitl, no tlatlauhquj in jxiuhio: vmpa mochioã tepçolco. Itech monequj in aqujn papalanj inacacaio; aço çan paltic, in contlaliz, anoço mocoxonjz: atle moneloa, çã mjxcavia.

.6.

Tlanoqujlonj:

çan tlanelhoatl, ololtontli, iuhqujn nabos, çan juhqujn xivitl ic mochioa, ça ce in jtlacoio: in jxiuhio, çã tepitoton, vmpa muchioa in tepçolco.

In aqujn itipoçaoa, anoço motlevia cõtexilia, conj, ic oalnoqujvi in cocolli: in ontlanoquj conjtia iollatolli, ic ommotzaqua.

.7.

Elosuchineloatl

çan tlanelhoatl, iuhqujn tlacotl, iztac: injc mochioa çan iuhqujn xivitl, xoxoctic in jxiuhio, mapitzatoton, quauhtla imuchioaia.

Itech monequj in aqujn motlevia, cõtexilia, conj; ic oalnoquja in qujcocoa, çã mjxcavia, yoã çã itztic in conj. No itech monequj in aqujn palanj inacaio, mo-

---

3. *Iztac çaçalic:* desc. in Hernández, *op. cit.,* Vol. III, p. 792.

4. *Tlatlauhcapatli: Geranium carolinianum* (Dibble and Anderson, *op. cit.,* p. 86, n. 9; also p. 142).

quired by one whose flesh is festered. It is ground. He places it there where the flesh is suppurated; either moistened or powdered, he presses it there.

teci oncan contlalia in canjn palanj tonacaio, aço paltic, anoço teuhtic in vncan compachoa.

<table>
<tr><td>8</td><td>.8.</td></tr>
</table>

NAUI IUIPIL

It is perhaps green. It is just a root, small and round, not long. Its skin is ruddy and its center white. Its foliage is like that of the *iztac quilitl*. Its growing place is the forest.

With it they cure those who cough. And it is prepared in this manner: they prepare chili-*atole*, maize soaked in water and ashes, and chili. They boil it all together in an olla. The sick one drinks it. And also it cures one who has inflamed eyes. He grinds it. It is only dropped in the eye with a cotton wad.

NAVI IVIPIL,

anoço xoxoctic, çã tlanelhoatl, ololtontli, amo vei tlatlactic in jeoaio: auh in jiollo iztac: in jqujllo, iuhqujn iztaqujlitl, quauhtla imuchioaia:

ic pati in aqujque tlatlaci. Auh injc muchioa, chillatolli, qujchioa, nextamalli qujchioa, yoã chilli, qujcenpoçonja, conj in cocoxquj. No yoan, ic pati in aqujn mjxtlevia, qujteci, çan cõchipinja ichcatica in jxco.

9

TLALCACAUATL[5]

It is just a root, small and round. Its skin is black and its interior white; its leaves are green, small and round. It grows there at Xaltenco.

He who has a fever requires it. Nothing is mixed in; only it alone [is used], ground up. The sick one drinks it in water. When he has drunk it, he expels the ailment in the urine.

.9.

TLALCACAOATL,

çan tlanelhoatl, ololtontli, in jeoaio tliltic, auh in jtic iztac, in jxiuhio xoxoctic, çan iaoaltotonti: vmpa mochioa in xaltenco.

Itech monequj in aqujn motlevia, atle moneloa, çã mjxcavia: moteci, atl ipan conj, in cocoxquj, in oconjc caxixa in cocolli.

TETZMITL[6]

It grows everywhere in the forest. Its blossoms are yellow. It is small, not tall. He who has blistered his flesh requires it. He drinks [an infusion of] it, or it is placed on his head, so that the head throbs. And if the eyes are ailing, it is applied in drops in the eye. Since it is cold, it drives out the fire.

TETZMJTL:

çan novian in quauhtla mochioa, coztic in jsuchio, çan tepiton, amo quauhtic. Itech monequj in aqujn totonjc inacaio, conj, anoço icpac motlalilia, ic moquatzotzona. Auh intla ixtelolo mococoa, ixco ommochipinja, ca itztic qujqujxtiã tletl.

10

ELOQUILTIC[7]

It grows in the forest. And for this reason it is called *eloquiltic*: it resembles *eloquilitl*. It is small; it is red-centered. Its flower is like that of the Peru tree. He who has a fever requires it. And if it purges him, it is boiled; when he drinks it, what purges him is thereby stopped off.

.10.

ELOQUJLTIC,

quauhtla in mochioa: auh injc mjtoa eeloqujltic, qujnevilia in eloqujlitl, çã tepiton, iollo chichiltic, iuhqujn peru quavitl isuchio. Itech monequj in aqujn tletl itech ca. Auh intla qujnoquja poçonj in conjz ic motzaqua, in qujnoquja.

---

5. *Tlalcacauatl: Arachis hypogaea* Linn. (*ibid.*, p. 86, n. 15).

6. *Tetzmitl: Sedanum sedroideum* Moc. (Sahagún, *op. cit.*, p. 357). See also n. 11, p. 219.

7. *Eloquiltic: Amaranthus* sp. (Hernández, *op. cit.*, Vol. II, p. 583).

11

CHICHIPILTIC

It is just a root, like a stick. The skin is black, its interior white. Its leaves are green, small and slender. It grows like an herb. He who has a fever requires it. It is ground. He drinks it only in water to bring the fever to the surface. And also it cures him whose flesh is festered. Ground or moistened or only as a powder, it is placed thereon.

It grows in Xaltenco.

12

COYOTOMATL[8]

Only its root is required. Its blossom is chalky; it is not required. [The root] is required by one who has a swollen stomach or diarrhea. It is boiled, cooked, when he drinks it. Also with it are cured nipple ailments.

13

TLALCHICHIC

It is just a cylindrical root. It is just like an herb, not tall. Its foliage is ashen. He whose stomach is swollen or who has diarrhea is to drink it. First it is boiled; thereupon it cures.

It grows in Teuhtlalpan.

14

COATLI[9]

It is a large tree. It is serrated. It is set, soaked, in water. He who has a fever or whose urine is stopped drinks its water. It waters the urine.

It grows in the forest of Coyotepec.

15

TZIPIPATLI OR NANACACE

The root is small and thick. The foliage of *nanacace* is like that of *eloquilitl*. Still another kind, *tzipipatli* or *uei patli*, [has] a round root. All are mixed together, boiled. A small child, or one relapsed into sickness, or one who has a fever drinks a *tzipiti* [infusion]. It is the cure for all this.

Nanacace comes from Chillocan, *uei patli* from Tezcatepec.

16

TEÇOMPATLI

It is a root like the *xicama*. It is rough, large. Its foliage is just like that of the *eloquilitl*. It is required

. 11 .

CHICHIPILTIC,

çan tlanelhoatl: iuhqujn tlacotl, eoaio tliltic, in jiollo iztac in jxiuhio xoxoctic, çan pitzatoton: injc muchioa iuhqujn xivitl. Itech monequj in aqujn motlevia, moteci çã atl ipã in conj, ic oalpanvetzi in tletl. No yoã ic pati in aqujn papalani inacaio. õmoteci, aço paltic, anoço çã teuhtic in õcã ommotema:

xaltenco in mochioa.

. 12 .

COIOTOMATL:

çan ie in jnelhoaio monequj, in ixuchio tenextic, amo monequj. Itech monequj in aqujn itipoçaoa, anoço qujnoquja: poçonj, quaqualaca in conj no ic pati in tlachichioalhuja.

. 13 .

TLALCHICHIC,

çan tlanelhoatl. mjmjltic, çan iuhqujn xivitl, amo quauhtic, nextic in jqujllo. In aqujn itipoçaoa, anoço qujnoquja conjz: achtopa poçonj, ic pati:

teuhtlalpã in mochioa.

. 14 .

COATLI,

vei quavitl, motzatzaiana, atlan motema, ciaoa: in jaio conj, in aquin motlevia, in aço omaxixtzacu; qujciaoa in taxix,

coiotepec quauhtla in muchioa.

. 15 .

TZIPIPATLI, ANOÇO NANACACE,

tlanelhoatl, tomactontli nanacace: in jq'llo, iuhqujn eloqujlitl: oc no cẽtlamãtli tzipipatli, anoço vei patli, tlanelhoatl ololtic, mocenneloa, moquaqualatza: conj in tzipiti piltontli, anoce omocaxanj, anoce motlevia: muchi ipaio.

In nanacace chillocã oallauh: in vei patli, tezcatepec.

. 16 .

TEÇOMPATLI,

tlanelhoatl, iuhqujn xicama, teçontic, vepol: auh in jqujllo, çan no iuhqujn eloqujlitl. Itech monequj in

---

8. Cf. § 4, n. 24, *supra.*
9. *Coatli: Eysenhardtia polystachya* (Ortega) Sarg. (Dibble and Anderson, *op. cit.,* p. 150, n. 14).

by him who pants much. It is grated; one drinks the juice. And he whose flesh is swollen places it there with lampblack. Thus he recovers.

It grows at Chillocan

17
NANAUAXIUITL

It is like cotton, only it is small. Its blossom is yellow. He who suffers from pustules or whose flesh is festered spreads it thereon. Thus he recovers. Only all its leaves are ground. When ground, they become like cotton.

18
NECUTIC

It is also only a thick root. It is ground together with [and] added to *xoxocoyoltic*. And also its name is *oquichpatli*. It is required by one who has harmed his genitals, or has expelled semen in his sleep, or they have frightened him [in the act]. It draws out something like pus. And it is drunk with acidulous water or with plain water. *Xoxocoyoltic* is also an eye medicine. It is applied only as a dry powder when the eyes are flesh-filled.

19
COAYIELLI

It is long. Its leaves are like those of *uitzquilitl*, but its root is like grass. It is black. Only its root is taken. It is required by one who has a fever. He drinks it [in an infusion]. And when the flesh is swollen, it is spread thereon. Lampblack is added.

It grows in Chillocan.

TEMEMETLA[10]

Its leaves are wide, thick. It is required by one who has a fever. It is ground or only juiced when he drinks it; and he places it on his head. When the eyes are inflamed, he applies some of it in drops to the eyes. Thus the fever leaves.

TESUCHITL

It is the same. Sometimes [it is used] alone, or it is mixed with *tememetla*.

20
YIAUHTLI[11]

It is small like the *tepecempoalxochitl* herb. One who has chills drinks [an infusion of] it. It is rubbed

aqujn cenca icica, õmjchiquj, conj in jaio. yoã in aqujn poçaoa inacaio; vncan cõteca tlillo, ic pati.

chillocan in mochioa.

.17.
NANAOAXIVITL,

iuhqujn ichcatl çan tepiton, coztic in jcuepõca In aqujn nanaoati, anoço papalanj inacaio: vncan cõpapachoa, ic pati: çan mochi in jqujllo moteci iuhqujn ichcatl mochioa in õmotez

.18.
NECUTIC

çan no tlanelhoatl tomaoac, mocenteci, monamjctia in xoxocoioltic. no yoã itoca oqujchpatli Itech monequj in aqujn omjtlacoconi in anoçe omocochtemjc, in anoço qujmauhtiq̃: in qujqujxtia iuhqujn temalli: auh in õmjz xocoatl ipã, anoço çan atl ipã: no yoã ixpatli in xoxocoioltic, çan coxõquj in õmotemjlia, in ixnacapachivi.

.19.
COAYIELLI,

viac: iuhqujn vitzqujlitl iqujllo: auh in jtzintlan iuhqujn çacatl. tliltic, çanio in jnelhoaio mocuj. Itech monequj in totonquj itech ca coni yoan in poçaoa tonacaio vncã õmoteca tlillo,

chillocã in muchioa.

TEMEMETLA,

papatlactic, tilaoac in jqujllo: itech monequj in motlevia, moteci, anoço çã mopatzca in conj. yoã icpac qujtlalia, in mjxtlevia, cequj ixco conchipinja: ic qujça in tletl.

TESUCHITL,

çan ie no iuhquj: in q'nmã, çan mjxcavia: anoço moneloa in tememetla.

.20.
IIAUHTLI:

çan tepiton, iuhqujn tepecempoalsuchitl; conj in atonavi, atica momaxaqualoa: yoã ic nepochvilo, yoã

---

10. *Tememetla: Echeveria* sp. (?); cf. *ibid.*, p. 152, n. 13.
11. *Yiauhtli: Tagetes lucida* (Sahagún, *op. cit.*, p. 371).

in the hands with water. And with it there is incensing, and there is washing. It is mixed with *iztauhiatl.*

ic nepapaco, moneloa in iztauhiatl.

21

XONECUILPATLI

It is the same as *yauhtli.* Its leaves are required when there is gout. They drink it in water, and it is spread on with lamp black. One feels as if one were bitten by a scorpion. And one who is paralyzed is also cured by it. He rubs himself with it; he bathes himself in it.

.21.

XONECUJLPATLI,

çan no iuhquj in jauhtli, ie in jqujllo monequj: in coacivi atl ipan conj, yoan ic moça tlillo: iuhqujn colotl ic tequa injc qujmati: yoan in aqujn ovelcocototzauh no ic pati, ic moça ic maltia.

22

XOXOUHCAPATLI[12]

It is somewhat like *topoçan;* however, its leaves are greenish. Its leaves are pulverized, ground up. He who has festered flesh or the scabies places it there. Thus he recovers. But it can also be drunk; he who has a fever drinks it.

.22.

XOXOUHCAPATLI:

achi iuhquj in topoçan, iece çã xoxoctic in jqujllo: in jqujllo mocoxonja, moteci, õmotemjlia vncã in aqujn papalanj, inacaio anoço çacaoati, ic pati; tel no vel mj, conj in aqujn atonavi.

23

TZITZICAZTLI[13] OR COLOTZITZICAZTLI

It grows in Malinalco or Quauhnauac. It is a large tree whose blossoms are like those of the Peru herb. It is required when one has gout; he rubs himself with it. Also *coyoxochitl* and *tecomaxochitl* are added, mixed all together. Thereupon he who has gout spreads it on. It is not potable.

.23.

TZITZICAZTLI, ANOÇO COLOTZITZICAZTLI:

malinalco, anoço quauhnaoac in mochioa; vei quavitl, in jsuchio iuhqujn peru xivitl: itech monequj in coacivi ic moxaxaqualoa: no vel monamjctia in coiosuchitl, yoã tecomasuchitl mocenneloa, ic moça, in aqujn coacivi: amo ivanj.

24

TECOMAXOCHITL[14]

It is a thick root. Its leaves are long like those of the *acocotli.* Mixed all together, as already mentioned, it cures one who has the gout.

.24.

TECOMASUCHITL:

tomaoac tlanelhoatl iuhqujn acocotli iqujllo, via: mocẽneloa: ic pati in juh õmjto, in aqujn coacivi.

25

PICIETL[15]

Its leaves are wide, somewhat long; and its blossoms are yellow. It is pounded with a stone, ground, mixed with lime. He who suffers fatigue rubs himself with it, likewise he who has the gout. And it is chewed. In this manner is it chewed: it is only placed in the lips. It intoxicates one, makes one dizzy, possesses one, and destroys hunger and a desire to eat. He who has a swollen stomach places it on the stomach and there in the navel.

.25.

PICIETL,

papatlaoac, achi viac in jqujllo: auh in jsuchio coztic: motetzotzona, moteci, tenextli moneloa: ic moxaxaqualoa in aqujn ciciavi: ioã in coacivi: auh moqua: injc moqua çan tetexipalco ommotlalia: teivintia, teçotlaoa, tetech quj: yoan qujpoloa in apizmjqujliztli, ioã teuciviliztli. In aqujn itipoçaoa, itipã contemjlia yoan vncã in jxico.

---

12. *Xoxouhcapatli:* uncertain; *Datura* sp. ? *Caesalpina crispa?* Cf. Dibble and Anderson, *op. cit.,* p. 143, n. 64.

13. *Tzitzicaztli: Jatropha urens;* cf. § 3, n. 8, *supra.*

14. *Tecomaxochitl: Maximiliana vitifolia? Datura* sp. ? Or *Amphitecna macrophylla,* or *Bignoniácea, Solandra grandiflora,* or *Swartia guttata?* (Dibble and Anderson, *op. cit.,* p. 149, n. 3).

15. *Picietl: Nicotiana rustica* Linn. (Hernández, *op. cit.,* Vol. I, p. 245); *N. tabacum* L. (Dressler, *op. cit.,* p. 138).

26
ITZIETL

It is somewhat tall, slender, straight. And its leaves are like *picietl,* green, hairy, wide. It grows in Xochimilco. It is pounded with a stone, placed inside a tobacco tube, mixed with pine resin. It is smoked.

27
HECAPATLI[16]

Also its name is *quauhxiuitl.* It grows in the forest. It is ground. He who has gone out in the wind or a child who has been struck by lightning drink it. And near him it burns, so that there is incensing. It is mixed together with *quauhyayaual* and *iztauhiatl.*

28
TLAPATL[17]

There are two kinds; the name of still another is *toloatzin.*[18] And *tlapatl* is somewhat tall; its blossoms, its foliage, reach upward. One who has gout or whose flesh is swollen rubs himself with it. Lampblack is mixed in. It is not potable.

29

NANACATL [OR] TEONANACATL[19] is a fever medicine.

30
PEYOTE[20]

It is a fever medicine. It is eaten, it is drunk moderately, just a little.

31
TOLOA[21]

It is also a fever medicine; it is drunk in a weak infusion. And where there is gout, there it is spread on, there one is anointed. It relieves, drives away, banishes [the pain]. It is not inhaled, neither is it breathed in.

32
ÇOÇOYATIC[22]

It is like a little onion. At first this is dropped in the nose. Its roots, leaves, seeds are all ground

.26.
ITZIETL:

achi quauhtic, pipitzaoac, monelactic: auh in jqujllo iuhq'n picietl, xoxoctic, ixtomjo papatlaoac suchimjlco in muchioa: motetzotzona, acaiietl itic motema, moneloa ocotzotl, mochichina.

.27.
HECAPATLI:

yoan itoca quauhxivitl: quauhtla in muchioa: moteci conj in aqujn ehecatl ipan oqujz, anoço ipan otlatlatzin piltzintli yoan itlan tlatla, ic mopopochvia mocẽneloa, quauhiaiaoal, yoan iztauhiatl.

.28.
TLAPATL.

ontlamantli in oc centlamantli, no itoca, toloatzin: auh in tlapatl. achi quauhtic, acopa itzticac in jsuchio, in jqujllo. In aqujn coacivi: anoço popoçaoa inacaio, ic moça, tlilli moneloa, amo ivanj.

.29.

NANACATL, TEUNANACATL atonavizpatli.

.30.
PEIOTL:

atonavizpatli: çan achi, çan tepiton in moqua, in mj.

.31.
TOLOA:

çan no atonavizpatli cencan auhtic in mj: auh in canjn onoc coaciviztli, oncan ommoteca, oncan ommalaoa; qujcevia qujtopeoa, qujquanja: amo mjnecujz: amo no mjhio anaz.

.32.
ÇOÇOIATIC

iuhqujn xonacatõtli. achtopa iehoatl teiacacpa onvetzi: In jtzinteio, in jamatlapal in jxinachio, mochi

16. *Ecapatli: Cassia occidentalis* (Santamaría, *op. cit.,* p. 467; *ecapacle*).

17. Cf. § 1, n. 3, *supra.*

18. *Toloatzin: Datura stramonium* (Santamaría, *op. cit.,* p. 1065; *toloache*).

19. Cf. § 1, n. 5, *supra.*

20. *Ibid.,* n. 2.

21. *Toloa: Datura* sp. (Dibble and Anderson, *op. cit.,* p. 141, n. 21).

22. *Çoçoyatic: Veratrum* sp. ? *Stenanthium frigidum, Zygadenus* or *Schoenocaulon* sp. ? (*Ibid.,* p. 140, n. 19).

together. Only as a powder, or in solution, a very little is dropped in the nose. If much of it is inhaled, if much is dropped in the nose, it causes bleeding.

It grows there at Motlauhxauhcan, at the edge of the forest near Quauhnauac.

It is not potable.

33
Pipitzauac[23]

It is like grass, a little stalky. Only its root is ground. He who is feverish, who feels much heat within his breast, drinks it. It expels the phlegm, causes vomiting, and purges, thereby reducing the fever within a man's body; it draws out the pus by dissolving it [in the urine; and for] women [it does] likewise. Thereafter one is to drink an *atole* of ground maize; then one is to eat.

It grows in the forests of Chalco. Its leaves are useless.

34
Iztac quauitl[24] or uauauhtzin

Its root is like that of *cimatl;* it is just as thick. It is very white, a little sweet to the taste, cooling. It counteracts fever. He who has first purged himself drinks it; it is his drink. And for ailments of men and women,[25] *coanenepilli* is added, to cure, to remove the ailment, [or for] nocturnal emissions. A purulent fluid [and] blood come out. And the root of *iztac quauitl* [is used]. When someone wounds his head it is placed there for him, moistened; thus it cures. And one who has inflamed, swollen eyelids, whose eyes are reddened, applies it there in drops moderately diluted.

And its leaves are dark; the branches are slender, serrated. They are not required.

It grows everywhere in the mountains, in the forest.

35
Coanenepilli[26]

Its root is white; the outer skin is thick. It is a medicine for ailments of men and women. *Iztac quauitl* is added when [an infusion] is drunk. At this time, first a little is eaten; then it is drunk. Its leaves are small and wide; they are just in two parts, a little bit long. They are not useful.

mocenteci, çan teuhtic, anoço paltic: cencã çan aqujton in teiacac õvetzi: Intla mjec mjnecuj, intla mjec teiacac onvetzi: eztli qujqujxtia,

vmpa mochioa: motlauhxauhcan, quauhtenco, quauhnaoac, itlan,

amo ioanj,

.33.
Pipitzaoac,

iuhqujn çacatl: xivitl, achi tlacotic: çanjo in jnelhoaio moteci, conj in aqujn motlevia: ic cenca totonja, in jelpan qujmati, ca qujnoquja in alaoac, qujçotla, yoan icujtlapampa qujça: ic cevi in totonjllotl. Yoan in jitic toqujchnacaio qujqujxtia, qujciaoa temalli; no iehoantin in cioa çatepan iollatolli conjz, çatepan tlaquaz.

vmpa mochioa in chalco, quauhtla: in jamatlapal çan vetzi.

.34.
Iztac quavitl, anoço vavauhtzi:

in jnelhoaio, iuhqujn çimatl ic tomaoac, cenca iztac, achi camanecutic, itztic: qujnamjquj in tletl. Iehoatl conj, in aqujn achto omotlanoqujli, yiauhpovi: yoan toqujchcocol, yoã cioacocolli monamjctia in coanenepilli, ic pati, qujqujxtia in netlacolli, in cochtemjctli: temalatl eztli in qujça. yoan in iztac quavitl inelhoaio: in aq'n qujquatzaiana, vncã motlalilia, paltic: ic pati. yoan in aqujn mjxtlevia in poçaoa in ixquenpal ixchichilivi in tixtelo vncan mochipinja, çan vel ie catic.

Auh in jiamatlapal yiapaltic, mapitzatoton, matzatzaianquj: amo monequj,

çã novian tepepan, quauhtla in mochioa.

.35.
Coanenepilli,

iztac in jnelhoaio: eoaiotilaoac. Iehoatl ipaio in toqujchio, yoan cioacocolli mjxnamjctia in iztac quavitl in jquac ommj: iquac in achtopa, achiton ommoqua: çatepan mj: in jamatlapal patlactotonti, çan moomemana, achiton viviacatotonti: amo monequj,

---

23. *Pipitzauac: Perezia adnata* (*ibid.,* p. 150, n. 11).

24. *Iztac quauitl: Mimosaceae* or *Caesalpiniaceae* fam. ? (*Ibid.,* p. 144, n. 68).

25. Corresponding Spanish text: *"sana el mjembro genjtal assi a los hombres como a las mugeres."*

26. *Coanenepilli: Passiflora jorullensis, P. suberosa* ? (Dibble and Anderson, *op. cit.,* p. 156, n. 9).

It grows there to the east.

36

ILACATZIUHQUI

Its root is like a twisted cord. It is sweet, piquant. Its skin is somewhat black, its interior white. A ground root [is taken] perhaps four times as a purgative. The ailment is expelled from the mouth and from the rectum. Not very much is drunk. Also it lowers the temperature. Its little leaves are green, small, round like those of the *iztaquilitl*. They are of no use. And if one is too lax when he takes the purgative, a turkey broth or *atole* of ground maize will be drunk.

It grows there in the land of the Acolhua, in the deserts, on the plains; but seldom is it seen in the forests, in the mountains.

37

YELLOW-LEAFED MAGUEY

Also its name is *teometl*.[27] The edge of its leaf is yellow, the central part green. It is placed in the fire; when it is cooked, then the juice is pressed out. Yellow chili and ten gourd seeds and the [juice of] small tomatoes are added. The liquid from all this is pressed out. He who suffers a relapse drinks it as medicine. First he eats; then he drinks it. He is not to drink anything thereafter.

It grows everywhere, in the mountains and at one's home.

Later one enters the sweat house.

38

CHAPOLXIUITL[28]

It is a shrub. It has no branches; its leaves only come out from its green trunk. Its leaves and its wood are ground. It is required by him who is pierced by an arrow or has a sliver in the foot. It draws out that which has remained there,[29] and it is a cure for the festering. When, perhaps, a knife cuts one [and the cut festers, the herb] is placed thereon.

Its growing place is everywhere, in the mountains, on the plains.

vmpa mochioa in tlalhujc.

.36.

ILACATZIUHQ'

inenelhoaio: iuhqujn tlamalintli, necutica cococ, achi tliltic in jeoaio, iŋ jiollo iztac. In ce tlanelhoatl: aço nappa moteci, tlanoqujlonj: ic vetzi in cocolli: tecamacpa, yoan tecujtlapampa, amo cenca vel mjec mj, yoan ic cevi in tletl. In jamatlapalton, xoxoctic, iuhquj in jztaqujlitl, mjmjltotonti, çã vetzi. Auh intlacamo cenca motzaqua, injc qujnoquja: totolaiotl, anoço iollatolli ommjz.

Vmpa mochioa in jpan acolhoacatlalli, ixtlaoacan patlachiuhcan: tel çan moveiitta in quauhtla, tepepan.

.37.

IN MACOZTIC METL,

yoan itoca teumetl: in ce imatetencoztic, in jiolloco xoxoctic: tleco maquja: in oicucic, çatepan mopatzca: monamjctia chilcoztli, yoan matlactetl aiovachtli, yoan mjltomatl, mocenpatzca. conj ic pati in aqujn mococolilochtia; achtopa tlaqua, çatepã conj: aocmo tle qujz çatepan

çan novian in mochioa, tepepan, yoan techan:

çatepã temazcalco calaquj.

.38.

CHAPOLXIVITL,

quavitl: amo maie in jamatlapal: çan njman itech qujça in jquauhio maxoxoctic. Moteci in jamatlapal, yoan in jquauhio moteci: itech monequj in aqujn mjnalo, anoço mjhxili: qujqujxtia in tlein oncan õmocaoa yoã palancapatli, in aço aca qujcochiloa, vncan ommotlalia

Çan novian imochiuhian in tepepan, in tlalmaia.

---

27. *Teometl: Agave atrovirens* (Sahagún, *op. cit.*, p. 355).

28. *Chapolxiuitl: Pedilanthus pavonis* Kl. or *P. tilthymaloides* L. (*ibid.*, p. 333).

29. Corresponding Spanish text: *"si a alguno le quedo algun pedaço de flecha en el cuerpo o trompeçando se le quedo algun pedaço estilla de estilla [sic] en el pie o alguna espina hueso puniendole alli lo saca."*

39

Totoncaxiuitl[30]

Its leaves are small, round, green. It grows only slightly upright. It relieves the inflammation, when such as an abscess settles on one. Its foliage, its roots are small and slender, small, not very long. They are ground up; they are placed there on top [of the abscess after being] dissolved in water. With this the abscess breaks up; with this, in some, the inflammation abates.

It grows in the mountains.

40

Uei patli

[The root] is bitter, small and round, white. Underground it is intertwined. Its foliage is small and wide, pointed on the end, green. It is useless, valueless.

And its root is like that of the small tomato. It is ground up. It is required by one who has indigestion, who is constipated; he eats it, or drinks it [with water]. And the small children who have diarrhea drink a little of it, in order to arrest their diarrhea.

It grows in the deserts, on the grassy plains.

41

Ixyayaual[31]

It burns the throat a little. Its leaves are round, small, green; its root blackish on the surface. He who has a feverish body drinks it, and it purifies the urine. Its leaves cure the little children who have sores on the head, or diarrhea, [or] fever. And the root of this *ixyayaual* added to [the leaves of] the *eloquiltic* is a medicine for one who has dysuria, when the abdomen swells. It releases the urine.

It grows all over in the crags.

42

Eeloquiltic[32]

It is stalky, green; its leaves are like those of the *eloquilitl*. It aids digestion, and it is a remedy for fever, and it is a urine medicine.

It grows everywhere in the mountains.

.39.

Totoncaxivitl:

in jamatlapal, iaiaoaltotonti, xoxoctic, çan achi moquetztiuh. ic pati in totonquj, in cana tetech motlalia: in iuhquj tlaxviztli. Iehoatl in jxiuhio, in jnelhoaio çan pitzactotonti, tepiton, amo cenca viac moteci, vncan motlalia pani, çan atic: ic xitinj, cequj ic iloti in totonquj

tepepan in mochioa.

.40.

Vei patli,

chichic, ololtotonti, iztac, çan nenetzolcate in tlalla in jxiuhio papatlactotonti, quavitztoton, xoxoctic çan vetzi atle inecoca:

Auh in inelhoaio in juhquj miltomatotonti moteci itech monequj in aqujn melixvitia, in aocmo vel temo qujqua anoço quj. Auh in pipiltotonti mapitza achiton conj ic motzaqua in japitzal

ixtlaoacan çaçacatla in mochioa

.41.

Ixiaiaoal.

achi tozcacococ iaoaltotonti: in jxiuhio xoxoctic in jnelhoaio ixtliltic In aqujn totonja inacaio conj, yoan qujchipaoa in taxix. In jamatlapal ic mopa in pipiltotonti: in aço quatotomonj, in anoço mapitza, motlevia, yoan in iehoatl in, in jnelhoaio ixiaiaoal: mjxnamjquj in eeloqujltic: ipaio in aqujn maxixtzaqua, in ie itipoçaoa: ic vitomj in taxix.

çan novian mochioa in texcalla.

.42.

Eeloqujltic,

tlacotic, xoxoctic iuhqujn eloqujlitl yiamatlapal, tlatemovia, yoan totonquj inamjc, yoan axixpatli

çã novian tepepan in mochioa.

---

30. *Totoncaxiuitl: Cassia alata* L. (Sahagún, *op. cit.*, p. 360).

31. *Ixyayaoal:* Mountain balm or calamint is suggested for one of several varieties in Hernández, *Hist. Natural* ,Vol. II, pp. 9–10.

32. *Eeloquiltic: Piper* sp. ? *Piperomia* sp. ? *Iresine calea?* See Dibble and Anderson, *op. cit.*, p. 151, n. 7.

Toçancuitlaxcolli[33]

Its leaves are chili-red on the surface; the branches are red. [The leaves] are small and round, with serrated edges. Some are bicolored, one-half chili-red, one-half green. Its root is white. It is red on the surface; it has little nodules; it is like intertwined cords. Its root is lightly ground; they add one small chili to it. It is toasted; then it is cooked.

He who has a flux or a bloody discharge takes it as a purgative; [in an infusion] he drinks it. And when he has drunk it, it subdues the ailment. Often the ailment still flares up; thereafter its remedy is to drink a little . . . , to which wrinkled *chía* or toasted tortillas are added. Then one is to eat something. Its leaves are useless.

It grows everywhere, in the forest, in the crags, in the mountains.

44

Coztomatl[34]

[The root] is very bitter, long, white, small and cylindrical, like that of the *cimatl*. It is yellow on the surface; likewise it is somewhat the same inside. Its leaves are like those of the small tomato; the branches are somewhat ashen. And its tomatoes, when cooked, become very yellow. They are edible, sweet.

Its root cures him who cannot digest what he eats, and drives away the heat which makes one's flesh burn.

It grows everywhere, in the mountains, in the gardens, on the plains.

45

Çacacili[35]

The leaves form right next to the ground; they are long, broad, green like the leaves of the Spanish *omi-xochitl*. They are not thick, only small and thin. It has white flowers; its blossoms are useless. Its roots are a little sweet. When one expels blood from his rectum, it is stopped with this. They add *chía* or wrinkled *chía* to it. It is drunk; an *atole* is made.

When one has eaten, then he drinks it. And he who breaks a foot or a hand — perhaps someone is struck, or someone is hurled to the ground — or there are slivers [in his foot], it is spread on there. Since

Toçancujtlaxcolli:

in jxiuhio ixchichiltic, matlatlauhquj, iaoaltotonti, tentzitziqujltic, cequj chictlapanquj: centlacotl chichiltic, centlacotl xoxoctic. In jnelhoaio iztac, in panj tlatlauhquj, oololtotonti, iuhqujn memecaiotica. Moteci in jnelhoaio çan quexqujchton chilli ceton qujnamjquj, mjcequj, çatepan tzoionj.

In aqujn tlaelli, anoço eztli qujnoquja conj: auh in oconjc qujoalpachoa in cocolli: cenca oc oaltotoca in cocolli, çatepan iamanje: achitonca conjz oiotl, chiẽtzotzol qujnamjqujz, anoço tlaxcaltotopochtli: çatepan tlaquaz. In iamatlapal amo monequj:

novian mochioa in quauhtla in tetexcalla in tepepan.

Coztomatl,

cenca chichic, viviac iztac, mjmjltotonti, iuhqujn cimatl: in panj ixcoztic, çan no ach iuhquj in tlanj: in jamatlapal iuhqujn mjltomatl çan achi manextic. Auh in jtomaio in jquac icuci: cenca coçavia qualonj; necutic.

In jnelhoaio ic pati in aqujn aocmo vel temo qujqua: yoã qujpoloa in tletl, injc totonja tonacaio.

can noujã mochioa tepepan, tlalmilpan ixtlaoacan.

45

Çacacili:

çan njman tlaltitech in mamatlapaltia, viviac patlactotonti, xoxoctic: iuhquj in jamatlapal castillan omjxochitl, amo titilaoac, çan canactotonti, xoxochio iztac in jcueponca: çan vetzi in jnelhoaio achi necutic. Ic motzaqua, in aqujn eztli qujnoquja icujtlapampa: chien anoço chiantzotzol qujnamjquj: mj, atolli mochioa:

iquac in otlaqua çatepan conj. Yoan in aqujn mocxipoztequj, anoço momapoztequj, anoço aca motlavitequj: anoço aca tlaxoa, anoço quexiliviliztli: vncã ommoteca, ca iuhqujn ocotzotl, anoço tzacutli: in

---

33. *Toçancuitlaxcolli:* prob. *Canna indica* L. (Sahagún, *op. cit.,* p. 360).
34. *Coztomatl: Physalis costomatl* Moc. (*ibid.,* p. 329).
35. *Çacacili: Lithospermum* sp. ? (Hernández, *Hist. de las Plantas,* Vol. III, p. 826).

it is like pine resin or glue, when it is spread on where one is ailing, it is as if someone pressed wooden slats on it. With it [pustules] are broken, ripened; and when someone has some sliver embedded in the foot, it draws it out.

It grows in the forest, especially there in the forests of Tecomic [and] Xochimilco; however, it grows everywhere.

46

Iztac palancapatli[36]

It is stalky, green. The leaves are small and slender, chili-red. [The blossoms] are half red, half white. [Both leaves and blossoms] are useless.

Its root is somewhat long; it cannot be [used for] a drink. It has many bunched roots — thick, white, each one long, like tree roots. It is ground up. Where there are abscesses, or they wound someone on the head, there it is applied, powdered or moistened. When already it heals, pine resin powdered for the purpose is added, and feathers.

And he who has a festering or a wound on the head is to eat no fish, nor meat, nor small fish.

It grows everywhere on the mountains.

47

Cototzauhqui xiuitl

Its leaves are like the leaves of the *ahuehuetl*, only small. Its root is stinging to the throat, deadening, burning-sweet. It expels phlegm. He who can no longer spit, whose tongue is as if dried out, who has pains in the chest, who is out of breath drinks a little [of its infusion]. Thereby the phlegm or the pus which has caused the festering within is discharged. Some also pass the ailment from the rectum. It is to be drunk during fasting, in order to cure the sick. Its foliage is useless.

It grows in the mountains.

48

Cococ xiuitl, cococ patli,[37] or uitzocuitlapilxiuitl

It is like a small stalk; only one stands. Perhaps two or three little branches are on top. Its blossom is yellow. [Its foliage] is useless.

Its root is like a radish. It cannot be drunk [in an infusion]. It is required by him who suffers from

jquac ommotecac in canjn mococoa, iuhqujn aca qujquappachoa, ic pitzinj, ic icuci. Yoan qujquixtia in aca itla ic mjxili:

quauhtla in mochioa, cenca vmpan tecomjc, xochimjlco, quauhtla: tel noviã mochioa

.46.

Iztac palancapatli:

tlacotic xoxoctic, amatlapalpitzatoton chichiltic, iztacachichictlapãquj amo tle inecoca.

In jnelhoaio achi ça viac, amo vel mjh: mjec in jnelhoaio centacatl: totomaoac, iztac, viviac: iuhqujn quauhnelhoatl, moteci. In canjn catquj palaxtli, anoço aca qujquatzaiana vncã motlalia coxonquj, anoço paltic: in jquac ie pati, ocotzotl monamjctia, ic mopotoni yoan hivitl.

Auh in aqujn palanj anoço tlaquatzaiantli, amo tle qujquaz xoqujiac: aço nacatl, anoço michi:
novian mochioa, tepetitech.

.47.

Cototzauhquj xivitl:

in jamatlapal, iuhquj in avevetl ixiuhio, çan tepitoton: in jnelhoaio tozcacococ, cocototztic, necutica cococ: alaoac ic vetzi. In aqujn aocmo vel chicha, in juhquj ooac inenepil, ineltzitzica, in cenca hicica: conj, çan tepiton: ic oalhuetzi in alaoac, anoço timalli, in tlein opalan titic; cequjntin no yoan icujtlapampa qujça in cocolli. In jquac mjz: iquac in aiatle moqua, ic pati in cocoxquj: in jxiuhio çan vetzi.

tepepan in mochioa.

.48.

Cococ xivitl, cococ patli, anoço vitzocujtlapilxivitl,

iuhqujn tlacotontli, ça ce moquetza aço ei, anoço vme in icpac imaxalloton: coztic in ixochio, amo tle inecoca.

In inelhoaio iuhqujʃ Rauanos, amo vel mjh iehoatl itech monequj in aqujn omaxixtzacu, anoço omotzin-

---

36. *Iztac palancapatli: Senecio vulneraria* D.C. (Sahagún, *op. cit.,* p. 339).
37. *Cococ patli: Bocconia frutescens* (Dibble and Anderson, *op. cit.,* p. 161, n. 5).

dysuria or has become constipated, whose excrement can no longer come out, who already has a distended abdomen. He inserts it in his rectum. It burns like chili. Not much is required.

It grows everywhere in the mountains.

49
Chichientic[38]

It is an herb. It is somewhat reddish. Its blossom is like the amaranth; its root is also like the radish, small and slender, somewhat sweet. He who has taken a purgative for reasons mentioned above is then to drink it [in an infusion]. It is the proper drink for this, as it is a cooling medicine.

It grows everywhere in the mountains.

50
Cococ xiuitl[39]

It is small and slender, stalk-like, with rather small branches. Its leaves are rounded on the tips; its blossoms are like those of *chía*. Its root is bitter, matted, yellow on the surface.

Ground up, it is required by one who has a fever, whose body becomes very hot. To some extent the ailment passes from one's rectum.

And its foliage is not required.

And he who goes about coughing is helped by it; it lowers the phlegm in the throat, settles it perhaps in the chest.

It grows everywhere in the mountains.

51
Xaltomatl[40]

It is an herb. It is somewhat stalky; its fruit is sweet, edible; its root is just like the radish — thick, somewhat sweet.

For him who has taken a purgative because of his dysuria, they say, it is the proper drink for the ailment. He is not to eat hot food.

It grows everywhere in the fields.

52
Ixnexton

It is an herb; it is a creeper. Its leaves are somewhat hairy, green, small and round, pointed on the tips. They are useless.

tzacu in amo vel qujça inemanavil, yie itipoçaoa: icujtlapampa qujmaca cococ, iuhquj in chilli: amo cenca mjec in tetech monequj:

novian mochioa in tepepan.

.49.
Chichientic

xivitl: achi ixtlatlauhquj, iuhquj in oauhtli ixochio: in jnelhoaio çan no iuhquj in Rauanos pitzatoton: achi nenecutic. In aqujn oqujtlanoqujlique, in jpampa tlacpac omjto: çatepan conjz, yiauhpoviz: ca itztic patli.

Novian mochioa in tepepan.

.50.
Cococ xivitl,

pitzatoton, tlacotic, mopitzatoton, quaiaoaltoton: in jamatlapal, in jxochio, iuhqujn chien: in jnelhoaio cococ paçoltic, ixcoztic,

moteci. Itech monequj: in aqujn motlevia, in cenca mjtonja inacaio: achiton qujça tecujtlapampa in cocolli.

Auh in jxiuhio amo monequj:

yoan in aqujn çan totolcatinemj, ic mopalevia; ic temo in totozcac motlalia alaoac, anoço telpan.

Çan novian tepepã in mochioa.

.51.
Xaltomatl

xivitl: achi tlacotic: in jcapollo necutic, qualonj in jnelhoaio çan no iuhquj in Rauanos, totomaoac, achi necutic.

In aqujn oqujtlanoqujlique. in jpampa ineaxixtetzaqualiz qujtoz, yiauhpoviz in cocoxquj amo totonquj in qujquaz tlaqualli:

çan novian mochioa in milpan.

.52.
Ixnexton

xivitl: çan movilana, achi tomjo: in jamatlapal xoxoctic, iaoaltotonti, quavitztoton, amo tle inecoca.

38. *Chichientic*: prob. *Salvia* sp. (Sahagún, *op. cit.*, p. 334).
39. *Cococ xiuitl*: Papaveraceae — *Bocconia arborea* or *frutescens?* (Dibble and Anderson, *op. cit.*, p. 141, n. 29).
40. *Xaltomatl*: *Saracha jaltomata* Schlecht., *Physalis mollis* (Sahagún, *op. cit.*, p. 368).

Its root is bitter to the taste; kernels of maize are added. It is ground up. It is required by, [and] one gives it in a drink to, a woman who has given birth to a child. Then she enters the sweat bath.

53

TECANALXIUITL[41]

It is green-branched. Its little leaves are somewhat hairy, slender at the base, wide on the tip, long. They are useless.

Its root is white, small and round. It is as if interwoven with the ground. It is sweet like the *xicama*. It is mixed with maize kernels. When one's body is feverish, [an infusion] is drunk. And its leaves are cooked.

It grows everywhere, in the fields, in the mountains.

54

XOXOCOYOLTIC[42]

It is an herb. It is chili-red on the surface. The branches are small and wide; its stem is chili-red; it is as if jointed. Its leaves are useless.

Its root is only a single one, small and round, somewhat red on the surface, white within, bitter. One who has a venereal disease or dysuria places it in the member with a syringe. And it is to be mixed with white wine or the like. Thereby there will be vomiting. And also thereby the liquid of the ailment issues out. The pus is passed through the rectum; some is urinated.

It grows everywhere in the crags.

And one is first to drink a turkey broth and to drink warm ground maize *atole*. Then one is to eat. One is not yet to drink cold water.

55

TLACOXIUITL[43]

All appears like the stalk, which appears green; its leaves extend from it. Its blossoms are yellow, like the roses; its odor is like the *tlacoxiuitl*. Its stem is square.

Its roots are small and slender, interwoven; its foliage spreads out. And its root is ground up while wet.

He who has a fever which comes to the surface in his eyes, in his face, drinks it. In a clear liquid he

---

.53.

TECANALXIVITL:

maxoxoctic, çã xiuhtontli, achi ixtomjo, tzinpitzatoton, quapatlactotonti, viviacatotonti: anotle inecoca.

In jnelhoaio iztac ololtotonti: iuhqujn çoçoticate tlallan, necutic: iuhquj in xicama: tlaolli moneloa. iquac in totonja tonacaio ommjh: auh in jxiuhio mopaoaci.

çan novian mjlpan tepepan in mochioa.

.54.

XOXOCOIOLTIC

xivitl, ixchichiltic, mapatlactotonti, chichiltic in jquauhio, iuhquj in hiixe, amo tle inecoca in jxiuhio.

In jnelhoaio çan centeca ololtontli; in pani achi tlatlauhquj, in jitic iztac, chichic. In aqujn mjtlacoa, anoço maxixtzaqua: xerjncatica qujteca, in jitic tototouh: yoan iztac octli moneloz, anoço çan iuhquj, ic mjçotlaz. Yoa no ic qujça iaoa, in tonetlacol: temalli qujçaz tocujtlapampa, çequj maxixa:

çan novian in mochioa in texcalla,

yoan totolaiotl achtopa conjz: yoã iollatolli iamanquj in conjz: çatepan tlaquaz, aiamo qujz in itztic atl.

.55.

TLACOXIVITL:

mjec in momana, iuhqujn tlacotl ic momana, xoxoctic: çan qujtotocatiuh in jamatlapal, coztic in jxochio, ixqujch in Rosales: tlacoxiuh yiac nauhcampa nacaçe in jquauhio.

In jnelhoaio pitzatoton: tapaçoltontli, motlaça in jxiuhio: Auh in jnelhoaio mopalticateci:

Conjtia in aqujn motlevia in jxco, in jxaiac itech papanvetzi: ixco qujchipinjlia in jtevilotca, cequj

---

41. Read *tacanalxiuitl;* unident.

42. *Xoxocoyoltic: Oxalis angustifolia, O. corniculata* (Sahagún, *op. cit.,* p. 370).

43. *Tlacoxiuitl: Bocconia arborea* according to Santamaría, *op. cit.,* p. 1054 (*tlacojigüite*); equivalent of *tlacoxochitl* or *Bouvardia termifolia* Schl. according to Sahagún, *op. cit.,* p. 361.

drops it in the eyes. Some drink it, thereby cooling the body. The water of the plant is purple, strong smelling. The patient is as if someone had put him in a bath as the fever comes to the surface.

It grows in the forest.

56

Acocoxiuitl[44]

Its leaves begin right at the ground. Its stem is small and slender; then it forms its leaves upward like the *tzayanalquilitl*. They are useless.

Its root is burning, sour. It is ground up. It is required by one who has pus settle in his abdomen, who has the male sickness, who dries up. It goes in his rectum; thus the ailment goes out. Only a little is to be drunk; it is not thickened. Neither is one to eat chili, nor anything hot. And likewise it cools the fever which is within one.

It grows in the mountains.

57

Iceleua

It is a stalk with branches. Its leaves are set on only singly. They are round and small, green, like the foliage of the apricot. Its blossom is like the blossom of the *caxtlatlapan;* it is dark blue. These are useless.

Its root is black, large, like the trunk of a tree. When it is required, it is chopped up, cut, boiled, and [mixed with] gourd seeds, [with] kernels of maize. It is cooked. [The liquid] is made clear. [When] cooked, it becomes like *atole.*

It is required when one who has become sick has a relapse, or if soon [after sickness] a woman sleeps with a man or a man sleeps with her. One drinks it. Twice, thrice, four times is it drunk. And it can be drunk uncooked; just a little. When one begins to sicken, he is given it to drink, so that he may vomit, so that there issues yellow, white, green phlegm.

[One drinks it] whose body burns and who is about to faint, who is as if someone made his heart throb. He is thereafter to drink *atole* of raw, ground maize, or turkey broth.

It grows rarely, near the mountains.

58

Chilpanton[45]

It has stalks. Its foliage is at the base. The interior

conj: ic cevi in jnacaio. In jaaio ixcamopaltic xiuhhiia: iuhq'n aca caltia in cocoxquj injc pãvetzi tletl:

quauhtla in mochioa.

.56.

Acocoxivitl:

çan njmã tlaltitech in peoa in jamatlapal, çan pitzatoton in jquauhio, qujn acopa in mamatlapaltia, iuhquj in tzaianalqujlitl: atle inecoca.

In jnelhoaio, cococ, xoiac, moteci: itech monequj in aqujn ixillan omotlali temalli in toqujchcocol, in ie quãvaquj: icujtlapãpa iauh, ic qujça in cocolli: çã tepiton conjz, amo tetzaoac, amo no moquaz chilli, amo no totonquj. Yoan ca no qujcevia in tletl teitic nemj:

tepepan in mochioa.

.57.

Iceleoa

tlacotl, mamae: çan icel moquetza in jamatlapal iaiaoaltotonti, xoxoctic iuhquj in arvarcoque, ixiuhio: in jxochio iuhquj in caxtlatlapã ixochio, movitic. atle inecoca.

In jnelhoaio, tliltic: vei, iuhqujn quauhtzontetl: in jquac tetech monequj, motetequj, moxoxotla, quaqualaca, yoã aiovachtli, tlaolli: icuci mochipaoa, tzoionj: iuhqujn atolli mochioa.

Itech monequj in aqujn mocaxanja in omococoaia: anoço cioatl iciuhca oqujchcochi, anoço cioacochi: conj, aço vppa, expa, nappa in mjh. Yoã vel mjz in xoxouhquj, çan tepitoton iquac in aqujn qujnpeoa mococoa: conjtia ic mjçotla ic oalqujça coztic, iztac, xoxoctic alaoac.

In cenca totonja inacaio, yoan in juhquj poliviznequj yiollo: in juhquj aca queltzitzquja, iollatolli conjz çatepan, anoço totolaiotl:

çã motlaçochioa in tepetitech.

.58.

Chilpanton,

tlacotic, ihicxe in jxiuhio, itipochinquj, mapitzato-

---

44. *Acocoxiuitl: Arracacia atropurpurea trifida* or *Dahlia coccinea* Cav. (Sahagún, *op. cit.,* p. 319).

45. *Chilpanton: Lobelia laxiflora* H.B.K. or *L. angustifolia* (*ibid.,* p. 334).

is fibrous. The leaves are small and slender. Its blossoms can be smelt; its leaves are odorless. They are useless.

Its root is black on the surface, white within, intertwined, bitter. It is toasted on a griddle. It is required by one who has a nosebleed which cannot be stanched. He puts drops in his nose. And to one who coughs much they give it to drink, that he may vomit, that it may dissolve the phlegm, that it may soften the throat.

It grows everywhere in the mountains.

59
CHICHILQUILTIC[46]

Somewhat chili-red on the surface, it is stalky; its leaves are somewhat long, narrow at the bottom, wide at the top, spaced far apart. Its stalk has joints. Its foliage is not required.

He who has a fever, a fever located internally, while there are chills on the surface of the body, or chills settled in the nerves, drinks [an infusion of] its roots. Thereafter the fever, which is within, comes up to the surface; thereby the nerves are quieted. At this time one is not to eat hot tortillas nor chili. It will abate a little.

It grows everywhere, in the fields, in the mountains.

60
TLATLALAYOTLI[47]

The herb creeps somewhat, about the same [as the *ayotli*].[48] Its leaves are edible.

Its root is just like that of the *tolcimatl*; it is bittersweet. It is ground up. [For] where the flesh is suppurated, it is mixed with pine resin. When the suppuration is already improving, it is applied there; thus it heals. And a little is drunk [powdered].

It grows everywhere, in the fields, in the mountains.

61
TEPEAMALACOTL[49]

It is just like the *amalacotl*, which grows in the water. Its leaves are small and round. It is as if each one of its leaves spread out at the top; they are like

ton: mjhnecuj in jxochio, amo aviac in jamatlapal, çan vetzi.

In jnelhoaio pani tliltic, in tlanj iztac, çan tapaçoltontli, chichic: mjcequj comalco. Itech monequj in aqujn eztli qujça yiacac in amo vel motzaqua yiacac conchipinjlia: yoã in aqujn cenca tlatlaci: conjtia ic oalmjçotla, ic ciaoa in alaoac, ic iamanja in totozquj.

çan noviã mochioa tepepan.

.59.
CHICHILQUJLTIC,

achi ixchichiltic, tlacotic, achi viac in jamatlapal, tzimpitzatoton, quapatlaoac, çan veveca in manj, ihixe in jquauhio, amo monequj in jxiuhio.

In jnelhoaio: conj in aqujn motlevia, in jitic motlalia tletl: in tonacaio itztic in pani, anoce vel itech motlalia in totlalhoaio, in ticececmjquj çatepan oalpanvetzi in tletl in totic onenca: ic cevi in totlalhoaio. Auh in jquac in, amo moquaz in totonquj tlaxcalli, amo no chilli, achi ceviz.

Çan noviã mochioa in mjlpan in tepepan.

.60.
TLATLALAIOTLI

xivitl achi movilana, çan no ach iuhquj in jamatlapal: qualonj.

In jnelhoaio: ça çe iuhqujn tolcimatl necutica chichic: moteci in canjn palanj tonacaio, ocotzotl moneloa: iquac in ie pati palaxtli vncan ommotlalia, ic pati: yoan achiton mjh.

çã novian mochioa, milpan tepepan.

.61.
TEPEAMALACOTL:

vel iuhquj in atlan mochioa in amalacotl, iaoaltotonti in iamatlapal: iuhqujn quaquauhçotica in iamatlapal: iuhqujn texos ic catquj, pitzatoton in jquauhio

---

46. *Chichilquiltic*: prob. *Amaranthus* sp. (*loc. cit.*).

47. *Tlatlalayotli*: same as *tlalayotli* (*Asclepias linaria* or *Gonolubus erianthus* D.C.) in Sahagún, *op. cit.*, pp. 364, 362; *tlalayotli* is *G. pedunculatus* Hemsl. in Hernández, *op. cit.*, Vol. I, p. 165.

48. The corresponding Spanish text and the context of the Nahuatl seem to indicate that *ayotli* is meant.

49. *Tepeamalacotl*: *Solidago* sp. (Sahagún, *op. cit.*, p. 355).

very small tiles. Its stems, fibrous within, emerge right next to the root.

Its root is in segments; they are small and round. It burns. It is a remedy for one who coughs; it removes the phlegm. Four are eaten. But small children are to eat only one.

It grows by the crags.

62

IZTAQUILTIC

It is just like the *iztaquilitl*. It is edible. Its small stalks are red; its leaves green, somewhat ashen. Its leaves are useless.

And its root is somewhat long, single, like a small *cimatl* [root]. It is ground up. One who has scabies drinks it; he drinks it only once. And it is spread over [the affected part].

It grows everywhere, in the fields, in the mountains.

63

TLALMIZQUITL[50]

It is stalky. Its leaves are just like those of the *uei mizquitl*. They are useless.

Its root is yellow, like that of the *cimatl*. Only one forms; some are divided. It is tasty, savory. It is ground up to be drunk during fasting.

It is required by him who has diarrhea, and by him whose body is very hot. It is the proper drink to cool his body. What he is to eat is still to be cool.

It grows all over in the fields, in the mountains.

64

POÇAUIZPATLI

It is a broad-branched herb. Its leaves are like those of the fig tree — small, green, serrated along the edge, small and pointed on the ends. At the beginning it just creeps along the surface of the ground. Its leaves are a little bitter.

Its root is like a radish, yellow on the surface, white in the interior. Its leaves are ground up together with its root.

It is required by one whose body is swollen, or whose body is festered. All is thus placed on, so that it may soothe, so that it may lessen the heat of the inflammation.

It grows everywhere in the mountains.

itipochinquj, çan njman inelhoaiotitech in oalquj-qujça.

In jnelhoaio cuecueiochauhticate, ololtotonti, cococ: ipaio in aqujn tlatlaci, qujtemovia in alaoac, nauhtetl in moqua. Auh in pipiltotõti çan centetl in qujquazque.

texcaltitech in mochioa.

.62.

IZTAQUJLTIC

vel iuhqujn iztaqujlitl: qualonj; chichiltic in jquauhiototon: in jamatlapal xoxoctic, achi ixnextic: amo monequj in jamatlapal.

Auh in jnelhoaio, achi ça viac: ça çe iuhqujn cimatõtli: moteci, conj in aqujn çaçaoati, çan ceppa in conj: yoã panj motequjlia,

çan novian mjlpan tepepan mochioa.

.63.

TLALMJZQUJTL,

tlacotic, in jamatlapal vel iuhquj in vei mjzqujtl. amo tle inecoca

In inelhoaio coztic iuhqujn cimatl: ça çe moquetza, in cequi momaxallotia aujac, velic, moteci, mj. iquac in aiamo tle moqua.

Itech monequj in aqujn mapitza: yoan in aqujn cenca totonja inacaio, yiauh povi ic cevi in jnacaio oc no ceviz in qujquaz.

çan novian mjlpan tepepan in mochioa

.64.

POÇAVIZPATLI,

xivitl mapatlaoac, iuhquj in higos in jamatlapal ic catquj: çan ie tepitotõ, xoxoctic, tentzitziqujltic, quavitztoton: çan njman tlalli ixco in peoa, movilana, achichichic in jamatlapal.

In jnelhoaio iuhqujn Rauanos in pani coztic, in jiolloco iztac: mocenteci in jamatlapal in jnelhoaio.

Itech monequj in aqujn poçaoa in jnacaio: anoce ie palanj in jnacaio ixqujch ic motlalilia; ic cevi, ic iloti in totõquj mopoçaoaia.

Tepepan noviã mochioa.

---

50. *Tlalmizquitl*: prob. *Prosopis* sp. (*ibid.*, p. 362).

Also [it is named] *iztac quauitl.* This one has been mentioned above. As is already told, it counteracts fever.

And sometimes the root of the *iztac quauitl* counteracts ailments of the genitals.[51] At this time they add the blossom of the *matlalin*; its blossom and *uauauhtzin* are ground up together. The water is heated. And he who has [the ailment] named *matlaltotonqui* also drinks it.

As a result, that which is within appears. In two places, in three places, there are dark spots; bruises appear on the body when it is drunk. Because of this they come to the surface in all places. Then they are lanced with an obsidian point. And by one who always has loose bowels, who has diarrhea which can no longer be stopped, whether child or old man, the root of the *iztac quauitl* and *chia* are drunk in hot water.

It grows everywhere in the mountains.

66

TLACOXIUITL[52]

It is like a stalk; only one stands. Its branches stretch far out; likewise its foliage stretches far out. [Its leaves] are small and slender; they are green, its blossoms white. Its foliage is of no use.

Its roots are interwoven; they are white. They are boiled, and not much water [is used], only a little. He who has diarrhea drinks only moderately of it. Then he will drink *atole* of raw, ground maize. And it is a cure for boils; it is spread on the surface. It breaks them, dissolves them.

It grows everywhere, in the gardens, in the mountains.

He who is to drink it is not to eat oily things.

67

TLALCHIPILI[53]

Its leaves are like those of the *chilquilitl.* It is small and stalky, as high as two spans. It is green. Its leaves are not required. It has only one small root,

yoan iztac quavitl, iehoatl in tlacpac ommoteneuh: ca ie omjto in totonquj qujnamjquj.

Auh quenmanjan, toqujchio qujnamjquj in jztac quavitl inelhoaio: in jquac in qujnamjctia matlalin ixuchio, ixochio, yoan vavauhtzin mocenteci, totonja in atl. yoã no iehoatl conj in aqujn itech catquj, in qujtocaiotia matlaltotonquj.

Injc neci in tlatitic nemj: occan, excan cujcheoa, xoxovixtimomana in jtech tonacaio. in jquac mj, ic noviã oalpãvetzi: njman mjtzmjna. yoan in aqujn çan mochipa qujnoquia, in mapitza, in aocmo vel motzaqua, in aço piltontli, anoço tivevein, totonquj atl ipan mj: iehoatl in jnelhoaio iztac quavitl, yoan chien.

Çan novian tepepan in mochioa.

tlacotic: çan ce moquetza, vevecamanj in jma, no vevecamanj in jxiuhio: pitzatoton, xoxoctic: iztac in jxochio, çan amo tle inecoca in jxiuhio.

In jnelhoaio tapaçoltontli, iztac: poçonj, yoan atl, amo cenca mjec, çan tepiton. Conj in aqujn mapitza, çan iamãquj: çatepan iollatolli conjz yoan ipaio in tlaxviztli panj moteca, qujxitinja, qujpitzinja.

Çan novian in mochioa: mjlpan, tepepan:

in aqujn qujz amo qujquaz in chiaoa.

iuhqujn chilqujlitl ixiuhio: tlacotontli, omjztitontli injc quauhtic: xoxoctic, amo monequj in jxiuhio: çan ce in jnelhoaioton, ixcujchectic in panj, auh in

---

51. Corresponding Spanish text: *"tambien es medicinal para la hychaçon o pudremjento del mjembro."* See also *oquichyotl* in Rémi Siméon, *op. cit.*

52. See n. 43, *supra.*

53. *Tlalchipili: Crotalaria* sp. or *Swartia nitida* (Sahagún, *op. cit.*, p. 362).

which is dark green on the surface and livid underneath. It is bitter. It is powdered or ground up while wet.

When it is powdered, it is mixed with pine resin. It is the cure for abscesses. One whose body is inflamed, festered, applies it there.

It grows everywhere, in the mountains, in the fields.

68
ACAXILOTIC

It is an herb. Its branches begin right from its root; several spread out. Perhaps in three places its small stalks form branches, produce foliage. Some of its small leaves are in threes, some in twos, fours [or] fives. The branches are small and slender. These are useless.

Its root is white, a little blue at the ends. It is harsh to the taste. Just a little is ground up, or it is merely soaked. It is required by one who has a relapse, who pants considerably, whose body burns considerably. With this [infusion] he vomits up the ailment; yellow phlegm and pus come out from his rectum. If he has finished [vomiting], only then he drinks an *atole* of raw, ground maize.

It grows in the mountains, in the forest.

69
CHICHILQUILTIC QUAUITL[54]

It is like the *quauhtzontapaçoltontli*. Its leaves are stalky, long. It has branches. Its leaves are small and round, serrated, somewhat chili-red on the surface; they are useless.

Its root is not bitter; it is sweet, savory. It is black on the surface, white inside. It is mixed with maize kernels; ten kernels are ground up together with it.

He who has a fever drinks it. And it cleanses the urine; through the urine it washes out the fever within one. The food which is to be eaten is to be cold.

It grows in the mountains, in the forest.

70
UAUAUHTZIN

It is like the *iztaquilitl*. Likewise the leaves are small and slender, although broad. Its branches are chili-red. Its foliage is somewhat stalky, stinking,

tlanj ixxoxoctic, chichic: mocoxonja anoço mopalticateci:

in jquac mocoxonja ocotzotl moneloa. palaxtli ipaio: iehoatl in totonquj: in opalan tonacaio, vncan ommoteca.

Çan noviã tepepan, milpan in mochioa.

.68.
ACAXILOTIC

xivitl: çan njmã inelhoaiocan im peoa momaxallotia quezquj momana; çan iuhqujnma excã momaxallotia, moxiuhiotia in jquauhiototon: cequj excan cequj occan: navi, macuilli in jamatlapaltoton, mapitzatoton. amo tle inecoca.

In jnelhoaio iztac, achi xiuhiiac, tetelqujc: çan tepiton in moteci, anoçe çan mociaoa in tlanelhoatl Itech monequj in aqujn mococolilochtia, in cenca icica, in cenca totonja inacaio: ic oalmjçotla, yoan icujtlapampa qujça in cocolli, in coztic alaoac, yoan temalli: intla otlamjtoquj ça çatepan iollatolli coni

tepepan, quauhtla in mochioa.

.69.
CHICHILQUJLTIC QUAVITL:

iuhqujn quauhtzontapaçoltontli: In jamatlapal, tlacotic, viac, mamae: in jamatlapal iaoaltotonti, tzitziqujltotonti, achi ixchichiltic, çan vetzi.

In jnelhoaio amo chichic: necutica âviac, in pani tliltic. in tlanj iztac: tlaolli moneloa, matlactetzintli, mocenteci.

In aqujn motlevia conj: yoan qujchipaoa in taxix, qujteaxixaltia in totonquj teiticnemj: oc ceviz in tlaqualli moquaz.

tepepan quauhtla in mochioa.

.70.
VAVAUHTZIN,

iuhquj in iztaqujlitl: çan no mapitzatoton, iece mapatlactoton, ixchichiltic in jquauhio: achi tlacotic in jxiuhio, xoiac, achi matenextic, ixtomjo: Iehoatl in

---

54. *Chichilquiltic quauitl*: corresponding Spanish text refers to "*otra yerua medicinal que se llama Chichilquiltic*," which is identified as perhaps *Amaranthus* sp. in Sahagún, *op. cit.*, p. 334.

somewhat ashen, hairy. Its foliage is ground up. And its roots are small and interwoven; they are yellow on the surface, white underneath. For one whose feet are deadened, benumbed, or who suffers from a chest ailment, this alleviates the ailment.

It grows everywhere in the mountains.

71

IZTAQUILTIC

Also its name is *tepeacocoxochitl*. It is stalky, somewhat long, with branches [and leaves] like the *aueuetl*. Its leaves are green, slick. Its root is not required. Its branch burns the mouth somewhat. It is ground up. This helps one whose urine is stopped. It is drunk many times. It is the proper drink for this.

And for one who vomits blood or phlegm — yellow, white, green — it expels the phlegm; thus it cures. And he who has epilepsy,[55] after it has just begun, drinks it. Thus he recovers, or thus [the sickness] abates somewhat. And it is the remedy for one who spits pus. *Uauauhtzin* is added. He is to take it in a drink; it purges all the ailment. Then he is to drink *atole* of raw, ground maize.

It grows in the forest, in the mountains.

72

QUAUHELOQUILTIC

Also its name is *quauheloxochitl* or *cexochitl*. Its stem is stalky. It is as if it were jointed. Its leaves are green, small and wide, somewhat thick. Its blossom has a scent; it is blue or dark green. Its foliage is useless.

Its root is required. It burns the throat. It is ground up. Not thick but well diluted with water, it is the proper drink for one whose body burns. And when one is not ailing, it can be drunk; it helps the urine when it thickens from fever.

It grows everywhere, in the mountains, in the inaccessible places.

73

UIUITZQUILTIC

It is just like the thistle of Castile, only it is small; the branches are one span long. Also it produces foliage. Its blossom is yellow. Its foliage is useless.

Its root burns somewhat. It is black on the surface, white inside. He who has a relapse drinks [the water in which it is] cooked. He is to take two drinks from

jxiuhio moteci, yoan inelhoaio, çan tapaçoltontli: in panj coztic, in tlanj iztac: in mjmiquj, in cecepoa tocxi, anoço telpan mococoa: iehoatl qujcevia in cocolli,

çan novian mochioa in tepepan.

. 71 .

IZTAQUJLTIC,

yoan itoca tepeacocoxochitl, tlacotl, achi viac mamae, iuhqujn avevetl in jamatlapal, xoxoctic, xipetztic: in jnelhoaio, amo monequj. Iehoatl in jqujllo, achi camacococ; moteci: iehoatl qujnamjquj in aquj iaxix motzaqua, mjecpa mjz, yiauhpoviz.

Yoan in aqujn eztli qujçotla, anoço alaoac, coztic, iztac, xoxoctic: qujqujxtia in alaoac, ic pati. yoan in aqujn mjmjquj, in qujn opeuh conj, ic pati anoço ic achi cevi. Yoan ipaio in aqujn timalli qujchicha monamjquj in oaoauhtzon conjz: mochi qujoalnoquja in cocolli, çatepan iollatolli qujz.

Quauhtla, tepepã in mochioa.

. 72 .

QUAUHELOQUJLTIC

yoan itoca quauheloxochitl, anoço cexochitl, tlacotic in jquauhio iuhquj in hiixe, in jamatlapal xoxoctic, papatlactotonti, achi tilactotonti mînecuj in jxochio, texotic, anoço matlaltic: in jxiuhio çan vetzi.

Iehoatl in jnelhoaio monequj: tozcachichic, moteci, amo tetzaoac, çan vel iecatia: yiauhpovi in aqujn totonja inacaio, yoan vel mj in amo necocolo: qujpalevia in taxix iquac tetzaoa, totonjliztica.

Çan novian quauhtla ovican in mochioa.

. 73 .

VÎVITZQUJLTIC:

vel iuhquj in castillan vitzqujlitl, çan tepiton, cemjztitontli injc maviviac: no moqujiotia, in jxochio coztic: atle inecoca in jxiuhio.

In jnelhoaio achi cocoiac: in panj tliltic, in tlanj iztac. In aqujn mococolilochtia conj tzoionj: oppa mj, in cemolotl: ca iuhquj in camotontli, monelhoa-

---

55. Corresponding Spanish text: *gota coral*.

one root — for it forms a root like a small sweet potato. It is drunk during fasting. In all parts [the fever] leaves the body. And one is not to eat anything with much chili.

It grows in the crags, in the mountains.

74

MEMEYA[56]

It is a small herb, which grows only one [stalk]. Its root is small and round like garlic; only one is its core, a small stick, smooth. Its leaves are only six; they are green, small and wide. Its blossoms are white. [These] are useless.

Its root is not sweet nor bitter; it is just like water. It is yellow on the surface, white inside. One of them cannot be drunk, even if we are mature. One [root] is drunk twice, thrice [in an infusion]. This is required by one whose abdomen is distended, whose abdomen goes rumbling, or whose body is swollen, and by one whose abdomen goes resounding, whether woman or man or child. Its root is ground up, and several gourd seeds are mixed in. Also it can be used alone, in tepid water, or it cures just as it is; for it expels the yellow, white, green phlegm, and the pus. It is to be drunk during fasting. Then one is to drink *atole* of raw, ground maize. There will be eating, [but] nothing will be eaten containing chili.

And also it expels that which is lodged within one; it serves as a purgative for intestinal worms or for [other] worms.

It grows everywhere, in the mountains, in the forest.

75

TETZMITIC[57]

It is just about like the *tetzmetl* which grows in the mountains; the shoot of the *tetzmetl*. Its name is also *quauholli*. Its leaves are green, leathery, small and rounded on the ends. It bleeds. Its branches are chili-red. The sap, which comes from its leaves and its tender tips, is like milk. It is dropped in one's eyes. [If] one has inflamed eyes, the white of the eye reddened, a film spread over the eyes, its sap is dropped there. Thus the eyes are cooled, and [the medicine] removes the small growth which has settled in one's eyes.

And its roots are sweet; many of them are intertwined. It is yellow on the surface, white inside. It

iotia: in jquac mj, iquac in aiamo tle moqua, novian itech qujça in tonacaio: auh amo cenca chillo in qujquaz:

texcalla, tepepã in mochioa.

.74.

MEMEIA

xiuhtontli: çan centetl in mochioa in jnelhoaio ololtontli iuhqujn in axos: çã ce in jiollo tlacotontli, xipetztic, çan chiquacen in jamatlapalton, xoxoctic, patlactotonti: iztac in jxochio, amo tle inecoca.

In jnelhoaio, amo necutic, amo no chichic, çan iuhqujnma atl: in panj ixcoztic, in tlani iztac: amo vel centetl in mj, in manel tivevein. In centetl vppa expa in mj: Iehoatl itech monequj in aqujn itipoçaoa in jiti xaxamacatinemj, anoço ie poçaoa in jnacaio: yoan in aqujn ixillan tetecujcatinemj, aço cioatl, aço toqujchti, aço piltontli: moteci in jnelhoaio, yoan quezqujtetl aiovachtli moneloa: no uel mjxcavia, yamanje in atl anoço çan iuhqui: ic pati. ca qujqujxtia in alaoac, in coztic, in iztac xoxoctic, yoan temalli: iquac mjz in aia tle moqua, çatepan iollatolli õmjz, tlaqualoz: amo chillo in moquaz.

yoan no qujqujxtia in tlein titic ixqujvi monoquja, aço tzoncoame, anoço ocujltin.

çan novian in mochioa in tepepan in quauhtla.

.75.

TETZMJTIC

çan achi vel iuhquj in tetzmetl, tepepan mochioa çan xiuhtetzmetl: yoan itoca quaolli. In jamatlapal xoxoctic, cuetlaxtic quaiaoalton, memeia, chichiltic in jquauhio: in jamatlapal imemeiallo, yoan yiacacelica iuhquj in chichioalaiotl itech qujça, teixco mochipinja: in aqujn mjxtlevia in chichilivi iztacauh, anoço aiavitl teixcomomana: vncã mochipinja in jmemeiallo, ic cevi in tixtelolo, yoan qujqujxtia in teixco motlalia nacatotonti.

Auh in jnelhoaio necutic: mjec in momana, paçoltic, coztic in panj, iztac in tlanj: moxipeoa, iehoatl in

---

56. *Memeya*: Euphorbia sp. (Sahagún, *op. cit.*, p. 342).
57. *Tetzmitic*: Sedanum sedroideum Moc. (*ibid.*, p. 357).

is peeled, and its inside is required for there to be purging. When urine is stopped, [this medicine] releases it. And one whose body is feverish cools his body with it.

It grows everywhere, in the crags, in the mud.

76

TZATZAYANALQUILTIC[58]

It is an herb. Its foliage comes out slender, just on the surface of the ground. Its leaves are just like those of the *tza[ya]nalquilitl*, not very long, just small, serrated, green. Its foliage does not branch out. It is useless.

Its root is single; it is just as if something were threaded like beads. Midway in it there are small constrictions. It is yellow on the surface, white inside. It is ground up.

It is required by one nursing [infants] whose milk is sour. She goes about drinking it [infused] many times; it purifies her milk. And the baby drinks a little of it when it has diarrhea, in order to recover.

It can also be crushed. Its juice, which is extracted, when drunk, cleanses the baby's urine. And those who nurse [an infant] are to eat no avocado, for the baby gets diarrhea; it quickly dies of it.

It grows everywhere, in the forest, in the crags.

77

ICHCAYO

It is an herb. Its leaves sprout out right next to the earth. Each is as long as a small thumb. Its single blades are many; its foliage stands up like the maguey. The blades are ashen, fuzzy; the fuzz is only on the blades. It does not branch. Its foliage is ground up, pulverized.

It is required by one who has pustules or is covered with sores. There they make it cover the pustules where the serous blood flows out, or else the sores. With this they heal. One who has pustules does not eat smelly food such as fish.

It grows everywhere in the mountains.

78

TLALYETL[59]

It is a small herb. It just spreads; it spreads right on the surface of the ground. Its small leaves are green, small and wide; they are as much serrated

---

jiollo monequj, ic tlanoqujlo: in taxixtetzaoa ic vetzi: yoan in aqujn motlevia inacaio ic cevi in tenacaio.

çan novian texcalla teçoqujpan in mochioa.

.76.

TZATZAIANALQUJLTIC,

xivitl çã njman tlalli ixco valpitzaoatiuh in jxiuhio: vel iuhqujn tzanalqujlitl in jamatlapal, amo çẽca viac, çan tepitoton, matzatzaian, xoxoctic: amo moqujio-tianj in jxiuhio, amo tle inecoca.

In jnelhoaio, çan çe iuhqujnma çan itla çoçoticate, tlacotacapitztotonti in panj coztic, in tlanj iztac: mo-teci.

itech monequj in chichioa in oxocox ichichioalaio, mjecpa qujtinemj, qujchipaoa in jchichioalaio: yoan achi conj in piltontli in mapitza, ic pati.

vel no motetzotzona: maqujxtia in jaio in ommj: ic axixchipaoa in pipiltotonti. Auh in chichioa, amo qujquaz in aoacatl: ic mapitza in pipiltotonti, iciuhca ic mjquj.

Novian quauhtla texcalla in mochioa.

.77.

ICHCAIO

xivitl, çan njman no tlaltitech ixoatica in jamatla-pal: cenmacpaltotonti injc viviac, mjec in cẽtacatl ixiuhio iuhqujn metl ic catqui matenextic, totomjo, çan itech onoc in tomio amo moqujiotia: moteci, mo-coxonia in jxiuhio

Itech monequj in aqujn nanaoati, anoço papalanj in inchichic. vncan quitemjlia in jtech nanaoatl in vncan oalqujquiça chiavizatl, anoço palaxtli: ic pati. In aqujn nanaoati, amo qujqua in xoqujac: in iuh michi

Çan novian tepepan in mochioa.

.78.

TLALIETL,

xiuhtontli: çan joca momana: çan njmã no tlallixco in momana yiamatlapalto, xoxoctic, papalactotonti iuhquj in njcan tepaçouh ic matzitziqujltic: in jnel-

---

58. *Tzatzayanalquiltic: Deanea tuberosa* Coult. et N. (Dibble and Anderson, *op. cit.,* p. 143, n. 57).

59. *Tlalyetl: Erigeron scaposus* D. C. (Hernández, *op. cit.,* Vol. I, p. 247); *Cunila* sp. (Sahagún, *op. cit.,* p. 363).

as those of our native *epaçotl*. Its root is just like a small ball of maguey fiber. Its foliage is bitter. And its root [and foliage] are ground up together, pulverized. And only one is its little, pale blossom, only one its little stem. It is required by him who has hemorrhoids. It is placed in the anus, or the penis, or in the crotch, or in the rectum. It is pressed thereon; thus it cures. It is applied many times.

It grows everywhere, on the plains, in the mountains, in the sand, in the forest.

79

Mexiuitl

It is stalky. It burns. Its leaves and its stalk are chili-red on the surface. It has blossoms. Its blossoms and its leaves are like those of the *tlapalhuauhtli*, small and round, pointed at the end, serrated along the edges. All its root and foliage are powdered.

It is required by one who has a swelling of the groin, or else jigger fleas are located on him, wherever they settle. Pine resin is added, wherewith feathers are pasted on.

It grows abundantly there among the maguey or among the trees.

90

Uitzocuitlapilxiuitl

It is somewhat stalky. Its stem, its foliage are chili-red. Only one [stem] stands, and its branches follow, standing out from it. Its foliage, its leaves, consist of only four; they are small and pointed, serrated on the edges, very green. It has blossoms; its blossoms are yellow like the blossoms of the tuna cactus. These are not required; only its root is required. It is black on the surface; its inside is yellow. It burns. It is ground up. It goes into the rectum in order to purge; [or] it removes the pus or the clotted blood in the sicknesses of men, or in some ailment which has settled in the abdomen. And one who has a colic, who can no longer have a bowel movement, with this softens [the matter]; it breaks up, comes out. And it is drunk during fasting in the early morning, and when the food has digested at early evening.

It grows everywhere, in the forest, on the plains.

91

Iztac patli[60]

It is a small herb creeping along the surface of the ground. Its leaves are like those of the *aueuetl*, small

hoaio, çan iuhqujn ichtapaçoltontli: in jxiuhio, cococ: yoan in jnelhoaio mocenteci, mocoxonja auh çã ce in jcueponcaton, ixtlaztaleoaltic: ça ce in jquauhioton. Itech monequj in aquin xochicivi, in tetzintlan anoço tototouh itech motlalia, anoço temaxac, anoço tequexilco: vncã ommopapachoa, ic pati: mjecpa motema.

çan novian ixtlaoacan, tepepan, xalpã, quauhtla in mochioa.

.79.

Mexiuitl,

tlacotic cococ, ixchichiltic in jamatlapal, yoã in jquauhio, xochioa, iuhquj in tlapalhoauhtli ixochio in jamatlapal iaoaltotonti, quavitztoton, tentzitziqujltic: mocoxonja, mochi in jnelhoaio in jxiuhio.

Itech monequj in aqujn quexilivi, anoço itech motlalia qualocatl, vncã motlalilia: in quẽmanjan, ocotzotl monamjctia, ic mopotonja, hivitica:

cenca vncã mochioa in memetla, anoço quaquauhtla.

.90.

Vitzocujtlapilxivitl:

achi tlacotic, chichiltic in jquauhio in jxiuhio, ça çe in moquetza: auh in jmaxallo, çan qujtocatimoquetza: çan navi in jxiuhio, in jamatlapal vitztotonti, tentzitziqujltic, cenca xoxoctic, xochio: coztic in jxochio, iuhquj in nochtli ixochio: amo monequj. Çanjo in jnelhoaio monequj: tliltic in panj, coztic in jiollo, cococ: moteci tecujtlapampa iauh: ic noqujvi, qujqujxtia in temalli, anoço eztli tetzaoa, in jtechpa toqujchcocol, anoço itla cocolli. toxillan motlalia, yoan in aqujn cujtlatecpichavi, in aocmo vel momanavia, ic ciaoa, vitomi, qujça Auh in jquac mjz aiamotle moquaz, oc iovac: yoan iquac in otemoc totlaquac, intla ie ioa

Çan novian quauhtla, ixtlaoacan in mochioa.

.91.

Iztac patli

xiuhtontli, tlalli ixco movilana: iuhqujn avevetl yiamatlapal, pitzatoton in jxochio, iztaleoac: çã no-

---

60. *Iztac patli: Psoralea pentaphylla* L. (Dibble and Anderson, *op. cit.,* p. 86, n. 12).

and slender. Its blossom is pale. Its blossoms are located all over, among its foliage. Its root is white, thick-skinned, bitter. There are many — four, five — and in very many places. It is required by one whose flesh is suppurated, and for white fever. This does not show, since it is a swelling; it only suppurates underneath, not much on the surface. It swells to a large size. With this it is cured; it is just spread on the surface. The water [from the root] of the *iztac quauitl* is appropriate for this ailment.

It grows everywhere here in the mountains.
And the fruit is not to be eaten.

vian motlatlalia in jxochio, in jtlan ixiuhio: in jnelhoaio iztac, eoaiotilaoac, chichic; mjec in momana, navi, macujlli: auh in cana vel mjec. Itech monequj, in aqujn palanj inacaio: yoan iztac totonquj, iehoatl in amo neci injc poçaoa: çan tlanj in palanj, in panj amo cenca, vei injc poçaoa; ic pati, çan panj in moteca. yiauhpouj in iztac quavitl.

Çan novian njcan tepepan in mochioa:
yoan amo moquaz in xochiqualli.

92

QUACHTLACALHUAZTLI[61]

It is a tree, a small tree. The branches are green, broad and small. The leaves stretch far; they are small and round, serrated. Its blossoms are tawny; [these] are not required. And its root, a tree root, is thick, white, very bitter, fibrous. It is ground up or just broken up. It is placed in water, soaked in water.

One who has pustules requires it; he goes about drinking it during fasting. And it also cleanses the urine. And pulverized it is placed there where there are pustules, and thus they heal.

One who suffers from chest ailments [uses this] when he can no longer eat, when that which he eats just sours in his stomach, [when] he can no longer digest chocolate. And also it cures the woman who has a relapse if she has just given birth, or has worsened when she has become sick. And it also cleanses her milk.

And this root, when ground up or soaked, makes the water very blue; it becomes like a fine blue.

Its growing place is the mountains, the forests, the plains.

.92.

QUACHTLACALHOAZTLI:

quavitl, quauhtepiton, maxoxoctic, mapatlactotonti: çan veveca in mamanj yiamatlapal, iaoaltotonti, tzitziqujltic in jxochio, quappachtic: amo monequj. Auh in jnelhoaio: quauhnelhoatl, totomaoac, iztac, cenca chichic, tlalichtic: moteci, anoço çan motzatzaiana, atlan motema, aciaoa.

Itech monequj, conjtinemj in jquac aiatle moqua, in aqujn nanaoati: yoan no qujchipaoa in taxix, yoan mocoxonja vncan ommotema, in canjn catquj nanaoatl, yoan ic pati

in aqujn yielchiqujuh qujcocoa, in aocmo vellaqua, in ça yielpã xocoia in qujqua: aocmo no vel temo in cacaoatl. yoã no ic pati in aqujn mocolilochtia cioatl, intla omjxiuhca; anoço omocaxanj, in omococoaia: auh no qujchipaoa in chichioalaiotl.

Auh in iehoatl inin tlanelhoatl, in jquac moteci, anoço mociaoa; cenca xoxovia in atl, iuhqujn matlali mochioa,

Tepepan quauhtla, ixtlaoacan in jmochioaian.

93

AAUATON[62]

Also [it is called] *tlalcapulin*.[63] It is stalky, small and bushy, red on the surface. And the interior of the tree is very red. Its leaves are rough like the foliage of the apricot tree. And it produces fruit; its fruit is red on the surface when ripe. [This] is not required.

.93.

HAAVATON,

yoan tlalcapuli: tlacotic, tapacoltontli. ixchichiltic. auh in jiollo quavitl cenca chichiltic, chachaquachtic in jamatlapal iuhquj in jxiuhio quavitl arvarcoques: yoã mocapollotia, ixchichiltic in jcapollo, in jquac icuci: amo monequj.

---

61. *Quachtlacalhoaztli: Mentzelia hispida* Willd. ? *Phaseolus* sp. ? (Hernández, *op. cit.,* Vol. III, pp. 955–6).

62. *Aauaton: Pernettia ciliata* (Sahagún, *op. cit.,* p. 335).

63. Corresponding Spanish text refers to *"otro arbusto que se llama haavaton, o tlalcapuli."* In Sahagún, *op. cit.,* p. 362, the latter is identified separately as probably *Rhamnus serrata* or *Karwinskia humboldtiana.*

Its root is also somewhat red on the surface. It is long, thick; perhaps a *vara* or a cubit long. It is harsh to the taste; neither sweet nor bitter. It is as if it contracts, puckers, the tongue. Only the bark of its root is required. Its center is ground up; it is ground, cooked, boiled in water. And one who passes a flux or blood is to drink the medicine tepid, in order to recover.[64]

It grows in the mountains.

94

OLOLIUHQUI

Also its name is *xixicamatic*. It is a small herb. Its leaves are like those of the *miltomatl*; just so long are its leaves. And its blossoms are yellow; they are useless. Its foliage is useless.

And its root is small and round like a turnip. Two [or] three persons may use [one]. It is sweet. During fasting, when it is still night, [an infusion] is to be drunk. One who has started to have a fever settle in his stomach, who already has a swollen abdomen, as if something boils inside him, when already he has a nausea about the heart, is to drink it. Thereby that which was in his breast comes out his rectum; he purges it. It is drunk once. Then one is to eat; one is to drink *atole* of raw, ground maize.

95

IZTAUHYATL[65]

It is small and stalky. The branches are ashen, the foliage slender. It is bitter, just like the wormwood of Castile. Its foliage is ground up or crumbled in the hands. It is the cure for many things; it remedies many things. When some one has much phlegm settle in him, when it seems that it will make him dizzy, he drinks it thickened. And one who has a relapse drinks it; it throws off the fever which is within one. And it cleanses the urine. And one whose head is fevered or whose head blisters is relieved therewith.

And when someone is anguished in his heart, or a humor is oppressive, *iztauhyatl* and *quauhyayaual* are ground up, that is, the center of the stalks; its surface bark is peeled off. Its center is white, somewhat sweet to the taste. One drinks it to recover, boiled; only its water is required. One who coughs also drinks it.

In jnelhoaio çã no achi ixchichiltic, viviac: totomaoac: aço ce vara. anoço cẽmolicpitl inic viac: camatetelqujc, amo necutic, amo no chichic, çan iuhqujn qujoapaoa qujmotzoloa in tonenepil. çan iehoatl in jxipeoallo tlanelhoatl monequj: in jiollo moteci, moteci, poçonj, quaqualaça in atl, yoan in patli: iamanquj in conjz in aqujn tlaelli, anoço eztli qujnoquja: ic pati.

tepepã in mochioa.

.94.

OLOLIUHQUJ,

yoan itoca xixicamatic, xiuhtontli, iuhquj in mjltomatl ixiuhio: çan veveca in cacatquj in jxiuhio, yoan coztic in jxochio: ça çan vetzi in jqujllo atle inecoca.

Auh in jnelhoaio ololtõtli, iuhquj in nabos: in vme ei tlacatl itech monequj necutic, aiatle moqua, oc ioatzinco in vmmjz in aqujn qujn opeuh in jitic omotlali totonquj, in ie itipoçaoa in iuhquj itla quaqualaca in jitic, in ie motlaeltia toiolio: conjz, ic oalqujçaz, icujtlapampa iauh in jelchiqujppan ocatca, capitza ceppa in mj. njman tlaquaz iollatolli in conjz.

.95.

IZTAUHIATL.

tlacototonti, matenextic, pitzaoac in jxiuhio. çã no iuhquj in castillan iztauhiatl chichic: iehoatl moteci in jxiuhio, anoço momaxaqualoa in jxiuhio: mjec tlamantli in jpaio in qujnamjquj. In jquac aca mjec itech motlalia. mjec alaoac in iuhquj qujiolmalacachoa, conj tetzaoac. yoan in aqujn mocaxanja, conj: in totonjllotl titicnemj qujoalpantlaça: yoan qujchipaoa in taxix. yoan in aqujn totonja itzontecon anoço quatotomonj ic mopa.

Auh in iquac aca vel ic mjmjquj in jiollopã in omocentlali alaoac: moteci in iztauhiatl, yoan in quauhiaiaoal iehoatl in jiollo itlacoio: moxixipeoa in ipan jeoaio, ca iztac in jiollo, achi camanecutic, conj; ic pati, moquaqualatza, çan jaio in monequj, no conj in tlatlaci.

---

64. Corresponding Spanish text: *"cozida esta corteça de la rrayz con agua bebenla los que tienen camaras de podre y sanan con ella."*

65. *Iztauhyatl: Artemisia mexicana* Willd. (Dibble and Anderson, *op. cit.,* p. 85, n. 5).

96

THE QUAUHYAYAUAL

It is an herb. It is stalky. Its stem is chili-red on the surface. Its leaves are green, small and round, not thick; also they are somewhat hairy, serrated on the edges. Its foliage is required; it is just mixed with incense. With this there is incensing. But its root is useless.

It grows everywhere in the mountains.

It is to be eaten with chili during meals.

97

MAMAXTLA

It is an edible herb; it can be cooked in an olla. It is green. The branches are small and slender. [These] are not medicine. The root of this is required. It is somewhat long, somewhat thick. It is chili-red, reddish on the surface; inside it is yellow. It is sweet. With it, foot ailments heal.

98

THE XALTOMATL

It has already been mentioned. The root of *mamaxtla* and the root of *xaltomatl* are ground up together. It is also somewhat sweet. It is required by one who suffers a urine ailment; who has yellow urine, who has dysuria. Also a few small kernels of maize may be mixed [with it]. It can be drunk before there is eating, or when there has been eating. It is the proper drink for this, for with it dysuria leaves. It cleanses [the urine].

It grows everywhere, in the fields, in the mountains, on the plains.

99

QUAPOPOLTZIN[66]

It is an herb. It is small and stalky. Its branches are many. It is as if the joints go along it; there where its joints are located, its foliage appears. The branches are green, and there where the branches form, it is yellow. Its little flowers are yellow. Its roots are interlaced; they are neither long nor thick. It burns the throat. It is required by one whose body burns. It is his proper drink; he goes about drinking it. He passes out the heat in the urine.

It grows in the mountains.

.96.

IN QUAUHIAIAOAL:

xivitl tlacotic: ixchichiltic in panj in jtlacoio: xoxoctic in jamatlapal, iaoaltotonti, amo tilaoac, no achi ixtomjo tentzitziqujltic: monequj in jxiuhio çan encienso moneloa ic nepopochvilo: auh in jnelhoaio çan vetzi.

Çan novian tepepan in mochioa:
chillo in moquaz tlaqualli in jquac.

.97.

MAMAXTLA:

xivitl qualonj, paoaxonj, xoxoctic, mapitzatoton: amo patli. Iehoatl in jnelhoaio monequj pitzaton, achi tomactontli; im panj ixchichiltic, ixtlatlactontli: in tlanj catquj coztic, nenecutic: icxicocolli ic pati.

.98.

IN SALTOMATL,

ie omoteneuh: mocenteci in jnelhoaio mamaxtla, yoan inelhoaio saltomatl no achi nenecutic. Itech monequj in aqujn axixcocoia, axixcoçavia, axixtetzaoa: no vel moneloa, quezqujtetontli tlaolli: vel mj in aiamo tlaqualo, anoço otlaqualoc yiauhpoviz. Ca ic qujça in taxixtetzaoaliz qujchipaoa:

çan novian in mochioa mjlpã tepepan, ixtlaoacan.

.99.

QUAPOPULTZIN,

xivitl, tlacotontli: mjec in jmaxallo, iuhquj in hiixetiuh: vncan in jxecã momamana in jxiuhio, maxoxoctic yoan vncã momaxallotia, ixcoztic, coztic in jxochiototon in jnelhoaio tapaçoltontli, amo viac, amo no totomaoac: tozcacococ. Itech monequj in aqujn totonja inacaio: yiauhpovi, qujtinemj: ic caxixa in totonjllotl

tepepan in mochioa.

---

66. *Quapopoltzin: Piqueria trinervia* (Santamaría, *op. cit.*, p. 319 — *cuapopolchi*).

100

TLALAMATL[67]

It is a small, bushy herb. Its small leaves are green. It is as if its little leaves form in threes on top of its little stems. The yellow blossom is also small and slender, also split at the top. It is not required. Its root is white on the surface and like the *tolcimatl* inside. It is long. It is rather seldom eaten. But this is required by one who has been burned or whose body is festered. Moistened, it is placed there many times; thus is heals.

It grows everywhere.

101

XOXOTLATZIN

It is a small herb which creeps along the surface of the ground. It is green, somewhat stinking. It blossoms all over among its branches; [the blossoms] are dark blue. It is ground up. It is required by one on whom a high fever has settled; perhaps he has a swelling or an abscess. It is placed thereon; [the abscess] is encircled. And when the abscess has burst, then, mixed with saltpeter [the *xoxotlatzin*] is inserted there where the abscess has formed a hole, where it has burst. Thus it heals.

It grows everywhere, in the mountains, on the plains.

103

TONALXIUITL[68]

It is ashen. Its foliage only creeps along the surface of the ground. [Its leaves] are brittle, not leathery. Its branches are small and slender; its blossoms are white, yellow in the center. [The foliage] is ground up. It is required by one who has pimples. Moistened, it is placed there where the pimples are.

And its root is useless, of no value. And this one, when someone tastes it, deadens the tongue somewhat.

It grows all the time, in the winter, in the summer. It grows everywhere, on the plains, in the mountains.

104

TLACOXOCHITL[69]

It is a stalk; only one stands. Then, above, it forms branches. Its leaves are green, the branches small and

.100.

TLALAMATL,

xiuhtontli, tapaioltontli; xoxoctic in jamatlapaltoton, iuhqujn tzinquauhiocatotonti, eeimanj, in jamatlapaltoton in jicpac: coztic in jxochio, çan no pitzatoton, çan no icpac in quaxeltic: amo monequj. In jnelhoaio iztac in panj yoan in tlanj: iuhquj in tolcimatl, ça viac; vel achi quĕmanjan moquaqua. Auh iehoatl itech monequj in aqujn omotlati, anoço papalanj in jnacaio; paltic in vncan ommotlalilia, mjecpa; ic pati:

çan novian in mochioa.

.101.

XOXOTLATZIN,

xiuhtontli; tlalli ixco in movilana, xoxoctic achi hiiac: çan novian in jmatitlan moxochiotia, movitic: moteci. Itech monequj in aqujn vevei totonquj itech motlalia: aço poçaoa, anoçe tlaxviztli: vncã ommotlalia, moiaoalochtia: auh in tlaxviztli in oxiti, moneloa çatepan tequjxqujtl: vncã ommaqujlia in vncan ocoion in vncan oxitin tlaxviztli: ic pati.

Çan novian mochioa in tepepan in jxtlaoacan.

.103.

TONALXIVITL:

ixnexton: çan tlalli ixco movilana: in jxiuhio çã tlatlapaca, amo cuetlaxtic: mapitzatoton, iztac in jxochio, iollocoztic: moteci. Itech monequj in aqujn çaçaoati: paltic in jtech motlalilia in vncã ca çaoatl.

Auh in jnelhoaio, çan vetzi atle inecoca: auh in iehoatl in; in aca qujpaloa achi qujcepoa in tonenepil:

çan mochipa mochioa in tonalco, in xopantla: auh çan noviã in mochioa ixtlaoacan, tepepan.

.104.

TLACOXOCHITL:

tlacotl çan ce moquetza, qujn aco in momatia; xoxoctic in jamatlapal, çã mapitzatoton, in jxochio iz-

67. *Tlalamatl: Gonolobus parviflorus* or *Desmodium urbiculare* (Dibble and Anderson, *op. cit.*, p. 157, n. 10).
68. *Tonalxiuitl: Stevia salicifolia* or *Veronica americana* (*ibid.*, p. 152, n. 11).
69. *Tlacoxochitl:* see n. 43, *supra*.

slender, its flowers white, small, dark-purple. These are useless.

And its root is somewhat black on the surface, thick-skinned; it is white in its interior. It is sweet. It is ground up. The foliage of *chilpanton* is added. It is required by one from whose nose blood issues; who cannot stop the dripping from his nose. It is stopped with this. Also it cures one who has much fever, who pants. He is to drink it during fasting or after there has been eating. Also it cleanses stringy matter in the urine.

And it has been told how *chilpanton* [is used].

[*Tlacoxochitl*] grows everywhere in the mountains.

105
OCOPIAZTLI[70] OR TLILPOTONQUI

It is an herb. It forms its foliage right on the surface of the ground; its foliage is like that of a small maguey. Its leaves are green, as much as a span long, serrated on the edges. It has only one base [stem]; its blossom is green, formed like a small fruit, small and round.

And its roots are many, small and slender, black on the surface, and yellow within. Its foliage, its roots are scented. All are ground up together. It is required by one who has contracted a high fever, such as the white fever. Some can be drunk before eating, or when the food has been digested. And the medicine is smeared there where the heat is. On some it breaks [the swelling] open; thus it ripens. On some it just dissolves it. Many times, when it is to be placed on, one is to add the root of the *xalacocotli*,[71] [which is] thick like a tree root; it is somewhat burning. [*Ocopiaztli*] is drunk in white wine or just in water.

And the stems of this *xalacocotli* are hollow within, like the reeds of Castile. It has much foliage which begins to branch just at the surface of the ground. Its branches are serrated, green; its blossoms yellow. Its foliage is useless; only its root [is used], as has been mentioned.

It grows everywhere, in the forest, in the mountains.

106
TOPOÇAN[72]

It is a large tree. Its leaves are small, broad, long, green on the surface but ashen underneath, and

tac, tepitoton, camopalpoiaoac: atle inecoca.

Auh in jnelhoaio, achi ixtliltic im panj: eoaiotila-oac, in jiollo iztac, nenecutic: moteci, monamjctia in jxiuhio chilpanton. Itech monequj in aqujn eztli qujça yiacac, in amo vel motzaqua: iiacac mochipi-nja, ic motzaqua. no ic pati i cenca motlevia, in hi-cica: iquac in aiamo tle moqua, anoçe otlaqualoc: conjz. no qujchipaoa in axixtetzaoaliztli:

auh in chilpantõ, omjto in quenamj.
çan noviã tepepan in mochichioa.

. 105 .
OCOPIAZTLI, ANOÇO TLILPOTONQUJ,

xivitl: njmã tlalli ixco in moxiuhiotia, iuhqujnma metontli ic catquj: in jxiuhio. xoxoctic, vel cemjztitl injc viviac in jamatlapal. tentzitziqujltic, ça çe in jioio: in jxochio xoxoctic, iuhqujn xocototonti injc motlatlalia ololtotonti.

Auh in jnelhoaio mjec çan pitzatoton, tliltic in panj: auh in jitic coztic. in jxiuhio, in jnelhoaio ha-viac: mocenteci. Itech monequj; in aqujn vei toton-quj itech motlalia: in juhquj iztac totonquj: cequj vel mj, iquac in aiamo tlaqualo, anoço iquac motemoc tlaqualli. Auh in canjn catquj totonquj vncã ic mo-xaoa in patli: cequj qujxitinja, ic icuci: cequj çan qujlochtia: mjecpa in ommotlaliz, mjxnamjqujz, in jnelhoaio xalacocotli: tomaoac, iuhqujn quauhnel-hoatl, achi cococ: iztac octli ipan in mj, anoço çã atl.

Auh inin xalacocotli iqujioio, hiticoionquj, iuhquj in castillan acatl: mjec in momana in jxiuhio: çan njmã no tlalliixcopeoa. in momatia: matzatzaianquj, xoxoctic: in jxochio coztic: amo tle inecoca in jxiuhi-io, çan iehoatl in jnelhoaio, in juh omjto.

çan novian mochioa, quauhtla, tepepan.

. 106 .
TOPOÇAN,

vei quavitl; tepitõ in jamatlapal, papatlaoac, vevei: im panj xoxoctic, auh in tlanj ixtenextic, yoã tomjo:

---

70. *Ocopiaztli: Eryngium beecheyanium* Hook (Sahagún, *op. cit.,* p. 347).
71. *Xalacocotli:* prob. *Arracacia atropurpurea* (*ibid.,* p. 368).
72. *Topoçan: Buddleia* L. sp. (Standley, *op. cit.,* Pt. 4, p. 1143).

hairy. They stink a little. Small children, or people already aged, are cured with this when their heads are hot.

And its roots are thick, white; they also stink. They are chopped up, ground up. The root of the *tepexiloxochitlacotl* is added. It is required by one who has the nosebleed. Drops are placed there [in the nostrils]; with this [the bleeding] is stopped.

It grows in the mountains, in the gorges.

And this *xiloxochitlacotl* is hard, firm. [Its stalks] are small and slender, just like the branches of the quince tree. It is not very leafy; its leaves are far apart. They are green, serrated. And its blossoms are chili-red; there are not very many. They smell like flowers. A few, [like] those named *xiloxochitl*,[73] are spread in the manner of corn silk. These are useless; only its root [is useful].

It grows always, in the summer, in the winter; its growing places are the mountains, the forests.

107

QUETZALUEXOTL[74]

It is a large tree. Its leaves are small and slender, pointed, green, bitter. And its foliage and its stalks and its buds are ground up or rubbed in the hands, and ground together with toasted tortillas and a little warm water.

It is required by one who has blood come out of his rectum. He is to drink it when there is fasting or a little while after eating. Thus it is stopped. It is a little better still that its stalks be peeled. Then they are ground up along with the foliage of the [*quetzal*]*uexotl*. Thereby small children and older people are cured when there is fever, [when] the head is hot, when it has pustules. And a little can be drunk; it removes the fever, the ailment which is within one.

It grows everywhere.

108

TLAYAPALONI XIUITL

It spreads matted right on the surface of the ground. Its foliage is chili-red on the bottom, round and small, green on top. Its leaves are also green. They form only at the top. The edges [of the leaf] are serrated as if formed in five parts. It has only one stem. Its blossoms are tawny on the surface. Its foliage is useless.

achi xiuhhiiac: Ic mopa in pipiltotonti, anoço ie veveintin tlaca: in jquac imjcpac motlalia tletl.

Auh in jnelhoaio totomaoac iztac, çã no xiuhiiac motzatzaiana, moteci, monamjquj in jnelhoaio tepexiloxochitlacotl. Itech monequj, in aqujn eztli qujça yiacac: vncã ommochichipinjlia, ic motzaqua:

tepepan, atlauhco in mochioa.

Auh inin xiloxochitlacotl tepitztic, tlaquaoac, çan pitzatoton: vel iuhquj in membrillo itlacoio. amo cenca xiuhio, çã veveca in mamanj ixiuhio, xoxoctic, matzatzaianquj: auh in jxochio chichiltic, amo cẽca mjec in manj; in juhquj xochitl mjnecuj; In jtoca xiloxochitl, çã quezquj in juhquj xilotzontli injc moiaoatica: amo tle inecoca. çan iehoatl in jnelhoaio:

çan mochipa mochioa in xopã, in tonalco: tepepan quauhtla in jmochioaian.

.107.

QUETZALHUEXOTL:

vei quavitl, mapitzatoton, vivitztic, xoxoctic, chichic. Auh iehoatl in jxiuhio, yoan itlacoio, yoã iiacacelica moteci, anoço momaxaqualoa: yoã tlaxcaltotopochtli, mocenteci, achi iamanjc in atl.

Itech monequj, in aqujn eztli icujtlapampa qujça: conjz, iquac in aiamo tlaqualo, anoço oachitonca tlaqualoc ic motzaqua. oc achi cenca qualli in moxixipeoa in jtlacoio: moteci çatepan, yoan in jxiuhio vexotl; ic mopa in pipiltotonti, yoan veveintin tlaca. In jquac motlevia, totonje intzontecon in quatotomonj, yoã achi vel mj: qujqujxtia in totonjllotl, in cocolli titic nemj,

çã novian mochioa.

.108.

TLAIAPALONJ XIVITL:

çan njmã tlalli ixco in oalpotzauhtimomana: in jxiuhio tzinchichiltic, mjmjltotonti: in aco xoxoctic, no xoxoctic in jamatlapal çan icpac in mamanj tentzitzitziqujltic: iuhqujn macujlcã qujztica, çan ce in jqujoio in jxochio ixquappachtic: in jxiuhio amo tle inecoca.

---

73. *Xiloxochitl: Pachira insignis, Calliandra grandiflora,* or *Bombax ellipticum* (Santamaría, *op. cit.,* p. 637 — *jilosúchil;* see also p. 1033 — *tepejilosúchil, Calliandra anomala*).

74. *Quetzalhuexotl: Salix lasiopelis* (Sahagún, *op. cit.,* p. 351).

Its root is thick-skinned, purple on the surface, quite chili-red in its center, thick. Its roots are many. It is chopped, not ground up. It is cooked; it is boiled in water. It should cook in two jar[fuls of water]; one jar[ful] of water should remain [after cooking]. He who can no longer stop his diarrhea, the so-called intestinal flux, is to drink it. Thus it is stopped.

And it is required by one who has been sick, when he suffers a relapse; perhaps [a man] sleeps with a woman, or [a woman] sleeps with a man. It can be drunk after meals. And usually, if the woman has slept with a man or a man has slept with a woman, and the ailment returns to one, he is to drink it during fasting.

And [for] little children who have diarrhea or stomach cramps, the root is to be mixed with five cacao beans. All is ground together. The little child is to drink it; thus [the diarrhea] is stopped.

109

UEI PATLI

It is an herb with long branches resembling sticks. They are matted. [Its leaves] are green, small and somewhat rounded on the botton, pointed on the ends, serrated on the edges, somewhat hairy. Its blossoms are formed like bells. They are purple; many spread blossoming. Its foliage is useless.

Its root is like that of a tree: thick. It has two [or] three forks. It is white outside and in. It is not thick-skinned; it consists completely of center. It is somewhat bitter-sweet. It is ground up. And gourd seeds and cacao beans — several, perhaps ten [or] fifteen — are all ground together [with it].

It is required by one who spits blood. [It is taken] during fasting or after eating; however, when one has digested that which he has eaten, he is then to drink it; he is to drink it three, four, five times. Thus it is stopped.

And one who is sick is not to eat very fat [food]. Also the *uei patli* can be drunk alone; it is to be boiled in water. The ailment will come out the rectum. The food, the tortillas, are to be eaten soft; or eggs [may be eaten].

It grows everywhere in the mountains [but] is quite rare.

110

OLOLIUHQUI OR UEUEI ITZONTECON[75]

It is an herb creeping along the surface of the

In jnelhoaio: eoaiotilaoac, camopaltic in panj: in jiollo vel chichiltic, tomaoac, mjec in jnelhoaio: motzatzaiana, amo moteci: poçonj quaqualaca in atl vme jarro injc tzoionjz ce jarro mocaoaz. Conjz in aqujn aocmo vel motzaqua in japitzal: in mjtoa cujtlaxcolalaoa, ic motzaqua.

Yoan itech monequj in aqujn omococoaia in mococolilochtia, anoço cioacochi anoce oqujchcochi: vel mjz in otlaqualoc. Auh çan ic intla aqujn ooqujchcoch, anoço ocivacoch: aiamo tle qujqua in conjz: yoan in aqujn omococolilochti.

Auh in pipiltotonti in mapitza, anoço mamjna: in tlanelhoatl moneloz macujltetzintli cacaoatl, mocenteciz: conjz in piltontli ic motzaqua.

.109.

VEI PATLI

xivitl, veiac, mamae: motlaconenequj, tapaçoltic, maxoxoctic, achi tziniaoaltotonti in jma, quavitztoton, tentzitziqujltic, achi tomjo: in jxochio iuhqujn campanjllas ic motlatlalia, camopaltic, mjec in cuecuepontoc: amo tle inecoca in jxiuhio.

In jnelhoaio iuhqujn quauhnelhoatl, tomaoac: vme, ei in jmaxallo, in panj iztac, yoan in tlanj: amo eoaiotilaoac çan moiqujtica in jiollo achi camanecuticachichic moteci yoan aiooachtli, yoã cacaoatl quezqujtetl, aço matlactetl, caxtoltetl mocenteci.

Itech monequj in eztli qujchicha iquac in aiamo tle qujqua, anoço otlaqua: ieçe otemoz in oqujqua, çatepã conjz: expa nappa, macujlpa in conjz: ic motzaqua.

Auh in aqujn cocoxquj amo qujquaz in cenca chiaoa. No vel mjz in vei patli çan mjxcaviz, quaqualacaz in atl: icujtlapampa qujçaz in cocolli: in tlaqualli, in tlaxcalli iamanquj in qujquaz, anoço tototletl.

Çan novian in tepepan in mochioa; çan tlaçoneci.

.110.

OLOLIUHQUJ, ANOÇO VEVEI ITZONTECON:

xivitl tlalli ixco movilana, xoxoctic, achi ixcujchec-

---

75. *Ueuei itzontecon: Gomphrena decumbens* Jacq. or *Helenium mexicanum* (Sahagún, *op. cit.*, p. 367).

ground. Its foliage is green, somewhat dark. Its leaves are small and slender at the base; they form in threes. It also intersperses its blossoms; purple are its blossoms, like those of the *caxtlatlapan*. These are useless. Its root is small and round, black on the surface, white inside, herb-sweet. The skin is not thick.

Ground up, it is required by one who becomes very sick; his stomach seems to hurt, and his heart seems faint, and his temples throb, and his nerves tremble, quiver, exceedingly. One is to drink it before eating in order to recover. It sheds the green, white, yellow phlegm; it quiets all the nerves of his body. First the water is to be heated. And [a man with] pus in the penis, and a woman [with the same in the] vulva, and one who has started to have a fever, these are to receive it as a drink. With this, it is extinguished; it removes all his ailments; with this his body cools.

It grows everywhere, in the mountains, on the plains, though it also is rare.

THE OLOLIUHQUI mentioned above is another kind.

111
AITZTOLIN[76]

It grows by the water, on the water's edge. Its green leaves are many, solid, like the reeds of Castile. Its leaves have a sharp edge; they are hard. Its blossom forms a stalk; it is tawny, small, straight and long. Two, three cluster together. It is edible.

And if I shall feel much hunger, I shall relieve it with this when I have nothing to eat. Also [with the blossoms] tortillas can be made; they can be cooked on a griddle.

Its root is small and round, black on its surface, white on its inside. And when it is ground, it is peeled; it becomes red. This is a little sweet. It is required by one whose urine is completely stopped, when he can no longer urinate [and] his stomach really distends. He drinks it during fasting, whenever he desires. Thereby [the urine] drops out; it removes the sand or whatever is clotted within the bladder.

It grows everywhere in the sweet water.

112
COAXOXOUHQUI

Also [it is called] *xoxouhcapatli*. It is an herb. It is just a creeper, a tree-climber. The branches are

tic in jxiuhio, tzitzinpitzaton in jamatlapal, ei qujztica, çan no qujvivicatica in jxochio; camopaltic in jxochio, iuhqujn caxtlatlapan: amo tle inecoca. In jnelhoaio ololtontli: in panj tliltic, in jtic jztac: xoiacanecutic, amo eoaiotilaoac:

moteci. Itech monequj in aqujn cenca qujcocoa in juhquj tetecujca ixilla: yoã in juhquj patzmjquj in jiollo: yoã in jcanaoacã tetecujca. yoan in cenca vivivioca, papatlaca in jtlalhoaio: conjz in jquac aiamo tlaqua: ic pati, ic vetzi in xoxoctic, in jztac, in coztic alaoac qujcevilia in mochi itlalhoaio, in jnacaio: achto totonjaz in atl. yoan temalli in toqujchio, yoan in incioaio cioa, yoan in aqujn atonavi in opeuh, conjtizque: ic cevi, qujqujxtia in ixqujch icocol: ic cevi in jnacaio.

Çan novian in mochioa in tepepan, quauhtla ixtlaoacan: iece çan no tlaçonemj.

IN OLOLIUHQUJ tlacpac omjto, oc centlamantli.

.111.
AITZTOLIN:

atlan, atenco in mochioa; xoxoctic, mjec in momana in jamatlapal, vapactic, iuhquj in castillan acatl yiamatlapal: tene, tetêtec: moqujotia, in jxochio quappachtic, melactotonti: vntetl, etetl çaliuhticate: qualonj.

Auh intla cenca njteuciviz, ic ceviz in atle njqua no vel tlaxcalli mochioa comalco icuci.

In jnelhoaio ololtontli, tliltic in panj, in jitic iztac: auh in jquac moteci moxixipeoa, tlatlavia inin achi necutic. Itech monequj in avel motzaqua yiaxix: in aocmo vel qujça iaxix, vel titilinj in jitic conj iquac in aiamo tlaqua, in quexqujch veliti: ic vetzi qujqujxtia in xalli, anoço in tlein tetzaoa in taxixtecon yitic:

çan novian mochioa in acellopan.

.112.
COAXOXOUHQUJ,

yoan xoxouhcapatli: xivitl, çan movilana, quauhtleconj, maxoxoctic, tziniaoaltotonti, quavitztoton,

76. *Aitztolin: Cyperus* sp. ? (Dibble and Anderson, *op. cit.*, p. 160, n. 28).

green. [The leaves] are small and round at the base, pointed at the tip. It blossoms; its blossom is white. And when already it withers, when it has matured, it closes once again. Within remains its little seed, only one, which is small, black, round.

Its leaves and its seeds are ground together. With these there is bathing, with [water and] lampblack added or alone, for the gout. So it is cured. Or pine resin is mixed in so that it may be spread on and feathers applied there where the gout has settled.

He who is already thin, who already is pale because of the gout, when it has covered him all over, when it is everywhere within his body, is to bathe in it, or it is to be spread on [mixed with pine resin, and] feathers applied. Thus it alleviates. It is drunk during fasting — just its seed alone for gout.

And in olden times, [as well as] today, one used it when he had been sick for a long time; when, as is said, "the doctor had finished," when he could not recover; [then] he drank its seed [in water]. It is said that it cured the patient. He acted of his own volition; he massaged himself when it had taken effect, when already he was drunk from the *coaxoxouhqui*.

And it is also the cure for one whose body is suppurated, who cannot recover. Its seeds and foliage are ground up. It is pressed on there, moistened or in powder.

It grows abundantly in the Totonac region.

113

ACOCOXIUITL

The branches are green, small and slender. It forms a stalk; it is tall. Its blossoms are green without, chili-red in their centers. These are useless.

Its root is thick like a tree root. It forks at its ends. It is somewhat black on its surface, somewhat yellow within. The skin is not very thick. It burns the throat.

Ground, it is required by one who has suffered a relapse after having been cured, when use has been made [of those herbs] first mentioned.

And he is to drink this when he is about to enter the sweat bath, in order that he will no longer feel the [heat of the] sweat bath. Or, when he is to come out, he is also to drink a little of it. And also those who are not sick can drink it, for it aids digestion, it alleviates feverishness. [It is to be drunk] during fasting or when one has eaten.

moxochiotia, iztac in jxochio: auh in jquac ie tlatzivi, in oicucic: oc ceppa mocamapiquj, itic mocaoa in jxinachio, çan centetl tliltontli, ololtontli.

In jamatlapal, yoan in jxinachio mocenteci, ic nealtilo, tlillo, anoço çan mjxcavia: ipampa coaciviztli, ic pati: anoço ocotzotl moneloa, ic mopotonja in canjn omotecac coaciviztli.

In aqujn ie quavaquj, in ie ticeoa in jpãpa coaciviztli, in oqujquẽ in ie novian itic catquj inacaio: ic maltiz, anoço ic mopotonjz, ca ic cevi. Auh in jquac mj aiamo tle moqua; çan mjxcavia in jxinachio in jpampa in coaciviztli:

yoan in ie vecauh in axcã. In aqujn qujnequj in cenca ie vecauh mococoa: in mjtoa oticitlan, in amo vel pati: conj in jxinachio: iuh mjtoa, ca iehoatl qujpatia in cocoxquj: çan monomavia in mopapachoa, in jquac oitech qujz in ie ic ivinti coaxoxouhquj.

Yoan no ipaio in aqujn papalanj inacaio, in amo vel pati: moteci in jxinachio, yoã in jxiuhio, vncan ommopapachoa paltic, anoço teuhtic.

Cenca mochioa in totonacatlalpan.

.113.

ACOCOXIVITL,

maxoxoctic, mapitzatoton, moqujotia, quauhtic in jxochio xoxoctic in panj, in jiolloco chichiltic: amo tle inecoca.

In jnelhoaio tomaoac, iuhquj in quauhnelhoatl, hiiac momamaxallotia: im panj achi ixtliltic, in tlanj achi ixcoztic, amo cenca eoaiotilaoac, tozcacococ:

moteci. Itech monequj in aqujn omocaxanj: in jquac opatiloc in oitech monec in achto ommoteneuh.

auh iehoatl in conjz, in jquac ie temazcalco, calaqujz, injc aocmo qujmatiz temazcalli, anoço iquac ovalqujz, no achitõ conjz: yoan no vel qujzque, in amo cocoxque: ca tlatemovia, qujcevia in totonjlizçotl: iquac in aiatle moqua, anoço otlaqualoc.

It grows everywhere in the forest.

114
TEPETOMATL[77]

It is a small bush. The branches are green, somewhat small and wide. [The leaves] are also somewhat far apart, pointed; they are pointed at the ends. It forms its leaves far apart; then its blossoms also go accompanying them. They are yellow. [Its leaves] are of no use, of no value, nor are its tomatoes edible.

Its root is small and slender. It is hard, for it is really a tree root. It is rough to the taste. It is ground up; a few of its leaves are mixed in. It is required when one's urine is stopped, and one has become constipated; and when one has harmed his manhood, when his abdomen is swollen — he can no longer urinate, he can no longer defecate; when he pants exceedingly, when he no longer eats. The water is to be tepid. It is to be drunk during fasting, when it is still a little dark, or when what one has eaten has been well digested. Thus the ailment comes out one's rectum.

It grows everywhere, in the mountains, in the forest.

115
TLATLACOTIC[78]

It is small and stalky. [The branches] are solid. Many spread out. They are hard. The branches are green, jointed. Where there are joints, there their foliage spreads out. The small, broad leaves are green, pointed on the ends, long. They are useless.

Its roots are intertwined; they are many, small and slender, black on the surface, somewhat yellow within. The skin is not thick. It is savory. Ground, it is required by one who has purged himself by his mouth or from his rectum; who has dysuria and a swollen abdomen, and fever is within him. It is the proper drink for this. The drink is to be given the patient after or before he has eaten. And he is to drink an *atole* of uncooked ground maize when he has finished. And he is not to eat very hot food.

It grows everywhere, in the forest, on the plains, in the mountains.

116
TEXOXOCOYOLI[79]

It is a small herb. It stands upright. Its leaves are far apart, broad and small. They are as if iridescent

Çan novian quauhtla in mochioa.

.114.
TEPETOMATL:

quauhtapaçoltontli, maxoxoctic, achi mapatlactotonti, achi no veveca vivitztic, quavitztoton, çan veveca in moxiuhiotia, njmã no qujvicatiuh in jxochio, coztic, çan vetzi, atle inecoca: in jtomaio amo no qualonj.

In jnelhoaio pitzaton tlaquaoac, ca nel quauhnelhoatl, tetelqujc, moteci, achi moneloa in jamatlapal. Itech monequj in omaxixtzacu, yoan omotzintzacu: yoan in oitlacauh in toqujchio in cenca ie itipoçaoa, aocmo vel moxixa, aocmo vel momanavia: in cenca ie icica, in aocmo tlaqua: iamanjaz in atl, aia tle moqua in ommjz, oc iovatzinco: anoço iquac in oveltemoc in omoqua: ic icujtlapãpa qujça in cocolli:

çan novian tepepan quauhtla in mochioa.

.115.
TLATLACOTIC,

tlacotontli, tlaquaoac: mjec in momana, tepitztic, maxoxoctic, ihixe: in vncã ihixe, vncã momãtiuh in jxiuhio: amatlapalpatlactotonti, xoxoctic, quaviztoton, melactotonti: atle inecoca.

In jnelhoaio tapaçoltic, mjec in momana, pitzatoton: ixtlitliltic in pani, in tlanj achi ixcoztic: amo eoaiotilaoac, âviac, moteci. Itech monequj in aqujn omotlanoqujli in jcamacpa, anoço icujtlapampa in jtechpa neaxixtzatzaqualiztli: yoan in jtipoçaoaliztli, yoan in totonjliztli in titic onenca: yiauhpoviz, catlitoz in cocoxquj, in otlaqualoc, in anoçe aiamo tlaqualo: yoã iollatolli miz, in jquac otlanqui. yoan amo cenca totonquj in qujquaz tlaqualli.

çan noviã mochioa, in quauhtla, ixtlaoacã tepepan.

.116.
TEXOXOCOIOLI:

xiuhtontli, çan moquetztiuh, veveca mamanj in jamatlapal: patlachtotonti, iuhqujnma camopaltica

---

77. *Tepetomatl: Physalis?* (Hernández, *op. cit.*, Vol. III, p. 710). See also p. 109, *supra*.

78. *Tlatlacotic*: unident.; however, see Santamaría, *op. cit.*, p. 248 (*clacacote*).

79. *Texoxocoyoli: Oxalis* sp. (Sahagún, *op. cit.*, p. 357).

[green] with purple. Its blossoms are single, small, chili-red, also a little purple. They are far apart. Its stalks are ground up. Its foliage tastes herb-like, bitter. It is required[80] by one whose body swells. For the swelling to diminish, it is placed there where the body swells.

Its root is single, small and round, blackish on the surface, yellowish underneath. It is wound around like a ball of fiber. It is ground up. It is a little rough to the taste; it deadens the mouth. It is required by one who is a tender woman, who hence becomes very pale, like lime, who is like a tender tree; by one whose sickness has returned; perhaps [a woman] has slept with a man or [a man] has slept with a woman.[81]

When they have ground it up, that which is ground is wrapped in cotton; it is placed there right on the flesh. There it is dampened; the medicine does its work. Then all the ailment comes out — a stinking pus. And the men who did likewise would drop it in the member with either a dropper, a straw, or a syringe. And anyone who has had excessive relations with women does likewise.

This root is mixed with the root of the *chilpanton;* they are ground together. They are required by one whose stomach swells, who has sickened internally. He drinks it [in an infusion] during fasting. The ailment comes out from his rectum or from the genitals.

The characteristics of the *chilpanton* have already been mentioned.

[The *texoxocoyoli*] grows everywhere, in the mountains, in the forests, on the plains.

117

Tlatlanquaye[82]

It is a shrub; it has only one crown which branches much at the top, and it produces much foliage. Its stems are as if jointed; from these also go its leaves. They are wide, striped green, rounded on the base, pointed at the tip. Its blossom is tawny, small and cylindrical. There are its seeds, white, like amaranth seeds. Its leaves and flowers are ground up. They are savory.

moviviltec: çan centetl in ixochio, chichiltontli: no achi camopaltic veveca: In jquauhio moteci, in jxiuhio xoiacacococ. Itech moquj in poçaoa inacaio: ic patzaoa in poçaoaliztli. vncã ommoteca, in canjn poçaoa tonacaio.

In jnelhoaio çan centetl, ololtontli; in panj achi tliltic, in tlanj achi coztic: iuhqujn ichtapaçolli ic qujmjliuhtica moteci, achi camatetelqujc, qujcepoa in tocama. Itech monequj, in aqujn cioatzintli, in cenca ic tenexivi: in ça iuhquj quauhtzintli, in omococolilochti: anoço ooqujchcoch, anoçe ocioacoch.

In oqujcoxonjque ichcatica moqujmjloa in omotez vncã ommotlalilia in vel itech inacaio, vncan ciaoa qujmati in patli njmã qujça in jxqujch cocolli ixpampa: temalli hiiac. Auh in toqujchtin, in oiuh mochiuh: tototouh itic onvetzi, anoço tlapiloltica, çacatica, anoço xerencatica: no iuh mochioa in anoço aca tetech omjtlaco.

Inin tlanelhoatl: monamjquj in jnelhoaio chilpanton, mocenteci: Itech monequj, in aqujn ie itipoçaoa, in otlacocox itic: conj in aiamo tlaqua, icujtlapampa qujça in cocolli, anoço ixpampa.

In chilpanto ie omjto in quenamj.

çã novian mochioa, tepepan quauhtla, ixtlaoacan.

.117.

Tlatlanquaie,

quauhtlacotõtli, çan ce in jicxi, cenca momaxallotia, in jicpac: yoan cenca moxiuhiotia, in jquauhio iuhquj in jhixe, no vncã mamantiuh in jamatlapal, papatlaoac vavanqui xoxoctic, tziniaoaltotõ quavitztoton, in jxochio quappachtic, çan mjmjltotonti: onca ixinachio, iuhquj in oauhtli, iztac: moteci in jamatlapal, yoan in jxochio âviac:

---

80. Read *monequi.*

81. Corresponding Spanish text: *"Esta rrayz molida: es buena para las mugeres que tornaron a rrecayer por aver tenjdo su marido aceso a ellas ante que estuujesen bien sanas. Y tambien para el hombre que torno a rrecayer por tener aceso a su muger ante de estar bien sano. Molido ase de revoluer con vn poco de algodon ase de poner dentro en el mjembro femjnjl o en el vrril. luego por alli purga lo que hazia daño al cuerpo."*

82. *Tlatlanquaye: Iresine calea* (Dibble and Anderson, *op. cit.,* p. 159, n. 19).

It is before eating or after eating that it is drunk. It is boiled and the water [drunk]. It is required by one who purges blood, when much flows from his rectum. He drinks it, in order to stop it. And one who purges from his rectum and vomits, when it cannot be stopped, they quickly give it to drink. Thus it is stopped at both ends.

And one who has a pain in the side which begins in his side and reaches into his heart, as if he would suddenly faint; or who has an ailment settled in the chest, as if he would sleep, [as if] he were about to die of it — [this one] is to drink it; it will quiet him. And one who is sluggish, [who] starts in vain, whose arms become paralyzed, whose mouth becomes twisted, whose arms become paralyzed, [whose] legs wobble — he drinks it. Some bathe themselves in it. The medicine is warm, tepid. At this time it is not to be ground; its leaves and its blossoms are to be cooked. One is to bathe just in the water which comes from it. And he who passes a flux also drinks it. Thus he recovers.

And [as for] its root, only one forms. Thick, it branches much. It is useless.

It grows everywhere, in the forest, in the mountains, in the crags, in temperate lands. Also it is scarce.

And also one who is already suffering from a swelling stomach drinks it in order to recover. Also whatever the ailment, it thereby leaves; and it cleanses the insides.

And one who encounters fever and chills, so that there is pain in the sides, in the chest, in the nerves, as if the heart were seized, beginning in the sides — [this one] is to drink it. It will cast [the sickness] out; thus it will be ended.

118

TONACAXOCHITL

It is well scented. It just creeps; it is a climber of trees, even of tall trees; it climbs up crags. Its leaves are green, small and straight, a little wide. At the same time its blossom goes accompanying them. It is yellow, dark red, small and slender, about a small thumb [long], hollow, a little hairy. Its scent diffuses.

It is ground up; the foliage of the *tlachichinoa xiuitl* is added. The *tonacaxochitl* is cooling. It is drunk so that a fever may leave, and it cleanses the urine. The *tonacaxochitl* can be taken alone; it is added to

aiamo tlaqualo, anoço otlaqualoc in ōmj, moquaqualatza yoan in atl. Itech monequj in aqujn eztli qujnoquja, in cenca totoca in jcujtlapampa: conj, ic motzaqua, yoã in aqujn, qujnoquja icujtlapãpa, yoã mjçotla in amo vel motzaqua: iehoatl conjtivetzi, ic motzaqua necoccampa.

yoan in aqujn quaquauhti: in jxillã peoa, yiollopan valaci: iuhqujnma ōtlapolotivetzi, anoço telchiqujuhpan moteca cocolli, iuhqujn toncochi ic timjqujznequj: conjz, qujiollaliz, yoan in aqujn çan qujpiquj, çan nenpeoa in matzicolivi, in tennecujlivi, in matzicolivi, icxiqujcuecuetza: conj, cequj ic maltia: totonquj, iamãquj in patli: in jquac in, amo moteciz in jamatlapal: tzoionjz, yoã in jxochio, çan aqujça injc maltiz, yoan in aqujn tlailli qujtlaça, no conj, ic pati.

Auh in jnelhoaio ça ce moquetza tomaoac, cenca momaxallotia: amo tle inecoca:
çan novian in quauhtla, in tepepan in texcalla, in iamancatlalpan: çan no tlaçoneçi.

No yoan in aqujn ie itipoçaoacocoltica: conj; ic pati: no ic qujça in tlein cocolli, yoan tlachpana in titic:

yoã in aqujn totonquj, yoan itztiliztli, qujnamjquj: injc quaquauhti. in telpan; in jtic totlalhoaio: in juhquj commapiqui toiollo yoan in toxillan oalpeoa: ommjz, qujtopeoaz, ic poliviz.

. 118 .

TONACAXOCHITL,

vel mjnecuj, çã movilana, quauhtleconj, in manel huei quavitl: texcaltitech movivicoma: in jamatlapal xoxoctic, melactotonti, patlactotōti: çan njmã no qujvicatiuh in jsuchio, coztic tlauhpoiaoac, melactotonti, achi vel cemmapiltotonti, iticoionquj, achi tomjo, moiamanca inecuj:

moteci, mjxnamjctia in jxiuhio tlachichinoa xivitl: ca itztic in tonacasuchitl, mĵ, ic qujça in tletl: yoan qujchipaoa in taxix: vel mjxcavia in tonacaxochitl, qujnamjquj in cacaoatl in mj: in manel amo cocox-

cacao when drunk. Even though one be not sick, just healthy, one may drink it.

It takes root in crags, at the bases of trees. It grows everywhere in temperate places.

119

THE TLACHICHINOA XIUITL[83]

It is quite small. The branches are green, small and slender. Its leaves come in threes; they are small and slender, pointed at the ends. These are ground up. They are required by one who has a fever in the mouth or in the abdomen. It destroys this quickly when drunk. And it is applied where there are festering sores or the itch.

Its root is useless.

It grows everywhere, in the forest, in the crags.

120

TLACOXOCHITL

It is a small herb. It goes standing upright. Its leaves are green; they are divided in two [or] three places. They are somewhat small and wide, serrated at the edges, a little thorny, hairy. Its flowers are rose-colored; they are small and cylindrical. They are useless.

And its roots are thick, small and thick, black on their surfaces, white on the inside, thin-skinned, bitter-sweet. They are ground up. Many times they add to it grains of maize, perhaps fifteen, or ten, and eight cacao beans. They drink this [mixed in water] during fasting or after food is digested, when sick or well. One who is very sick of body, feverish, panting, hence faint of heart, [with this] lessens the fever.

It grows everywhere, in the mountains, in the forests.

121

QUETZALMIZQUITL[84]

It is a small tree, many-branched. Its leaves are green, serrated, like those of the cypress. They are about a span long, as small and slender as blades of wheat. Its blossoms are yellow, drooping. Like the willow, it produces no seeds. Its foliage is required. Ground together are a very little of the tips of *quetzalmizquitl* foliage and the root of the tomato and the root of the yellow tomato.

quj, in çan pactinemj: conj,

Texcalco quavitl itzintlan in monãtia, çan novian in mochioa in tlaiamania.

.119.

IN TLACHICHINOA XIVITL,

çan tepiton xoxoctic, mapitzatoton, ie excan qujz-tica in jamatlapal pitzactotonti, quavitztoton: iehoatl in moteci itech monequj in aqujn icamac nemj toto-njliztli, anoço titic: içiuhca qujpoloa in jquac mj. Auh in canjn catquj palastli, anoço çaoatl: vncan om-motlatlalia:

in jnelhoaio, atle inecoca:
Çan novian quauhtla texcalco in mochioa.

.120.

TLACOXOCHITL,

xiuhtontli: moquetztiuh injc iauh, xoxoctic: in jamatlapal vccan excan xeliuhtica, achi patlactotonti, tentzitziqujltic: achi âoaio tomjo, xochipaltic, in jxo-chio mjmjltotonti, amo tle inecoca.

Auh in jnelhoaio totomaoac, totomactotonti: im panj ixtliltic, in jitic iztac: amo eoaiotilaoac, necuti-cachichic, moteci: mjecpa qujnamjquj in tlaolli, aço caxtoltetl, anoço matlactetl, yoan chicuetetl cacaoatl: iquac in aiamo tlaqualo, anoço otemoc tlaqualli iquac conj in cocoxquj, anoço amo cocoxquj. In aqujn in cenca mococoa inacaio, in totonja, in icica, in ic cenca patzmjquj in toiollo: qujcevia in totonquj.

çan novian mochioa in tepepan, quauhtla.

.121.

QUETZALMJZQUJTL:

quauhtepiton, cenca momamatia, xoxoctic, matza-tzaianquj, iuhquj in avevetl, achi vel cemjztitl inic viviac, injc patlactotonti iuhqujn iamatlapal trigo: in jsuchio coztic, çan tepeuj amo moxinachiotia, in juh-quj vexotl. Iehoatl monequj, in jxiuhio, mocenteci, çan aqujtzin in jxiuhio quetzalmjzqujtl: xiuhiiac, yoã inelhoaio saltomatl, yoan inelhoaio coztomatl.

---

83. *Tlachichinoa xiuitl: Plumbago scandens* L.; *Tournefortia hirsutissima* (Sahagún, *op. cit.*, p. 362). See also Santamaría, *op. cit.*, p. 1056 (*tlachichinoa*).

84. *Quetzalmizquitl: Prosopis* sp. (Sahagún, *op. cit.*, p. 351).

It is required by one who has suffered a relapse, who has sickened; perhaps he has fallen, striking himself, or he has carried something heavy; or [a woman] has slept with a man, or [a man] has slept with a woman. He drinks it three times, four times, [in water]. And it can also be drunk during fasting or after eating. And also it can then be drunk when required by one as the first remedy mentioned above, referring to a relapse.

And this can be drunk in all of three ways: this alone is used; or just as one is to enter the sweat bath — no longer will he feel the heat of the sweat bath; and when he has left the sweat bath, or has eaten a little, he is still to drink a little of the *quetzalmizquitl*.

But its root is not required.

The characteristics of the tomato, of the yellow tomato, of the *quetzalmizquitl* have already been told.

It grows in the hot country, in Huaxtepec.

123

YOALXOCHITL

It is a large tree. Its leaves are green, long, small and wide, pointed at the end. They are rather repulsive to one; they smell mildly of herbs. Its foliage and its buds are ground up.

It is required by one who contracts a high fever, such as the white fever, when the body swells. It is placed there where the body swells, in order to gather [the swelling], which later breaks or dissolves. And a little is to be drunk. And all the abscesses or sores are bathed with it, so that the flesh heals over where the sores were.

Its root is not required. Its blossom is white; like the *acuilloxochitl* it blossoms only at night and remains closed all day long. It has a somewhat unpleasant scent.

The places where it grows are rare. It grows in Hecatepec.

124

COZCAQUAUHXIUITL[85]

It is a small tree. It is green; it forms branches. The leaves are small and broad, small and straight, pointed at the ends. It bears fruit. Just as soon as little round green balls are formed, its seed forms within. [Its leaves] are ground up dry, not wet,

Itech monequj in aqujn omocaxanj, in omococoaia, in aço omotlavitec, anoço itla etic oqujnapalo, anoço ooqujchcoch, anoço ocioacoch: iehoatl conj, expa, nappa: yoan no vel mj in aiamo tlaqualo. anoço otlaqualoc. No yoan iquac vel mjz: in jquac otetech monec achtopa in tlacpac omjto patli in jtechpa necaxanjliztli.

Auh in iehoatl in, in etlamanjxti vel mjz, çan mjxcaviz: anoço çan ipan calacoaz temazcalco, aocmo qujmatiz injc totonquj temazcalli. Auh in jquac ooalqujz temazcalco, anoço oachiton côqua: oc no achi conjz in quetzalmjzqujtl.

Auh in jnelhoaio amo monequj:

in saltomatl, in coztomatl; ie omjto in quenamj in quetzalmjzqujtl.

Totoncatlalpan in mochioa, in vaxtepec.

.123.

IOALXOCHITL:

vei quavitl, in jamatlapal xoxoctic, melactotonti, patlactotonti, quavitztoton: achi tetlaelti, xoiacaiamanquj, in jqujiac: moteci in jxiuhio, yoan in jiacacelica.

Itech monequj, in aqujn itech motlalia vei totonquj; in juhquj iztac totonquj, in poçaoa tonacaio vncã motlalilia in canjn poçaoa tonacaio, ic qujcentlalia, çatepan xitinj, anoçe qujlochtia, yoan achiton mjz, yoã mochi in tlaxviztli, anoço çaoatl: ic nealtilo, ic tetetzolivi in tonacaio, in vncã ocacatca çaoatl.

In jnelhoaio, amo monequj: in jsochio iztac, iuhquj acujllosuchitl; çan ioaltica in cueponj, auh in çemjlhujtl pictica: mjnecuj, achi aviiac.

çan tlaçomanj in canjn mochioa, hecatepec in mochioa.

.124.

COZCAQUAUHXIVITL,

quauhtepiton, xoxoctic, momamatia, amatlapalpatlactotonti, melactotonti, quavitztoton, moxocoiotia: çan njmã iuh motlalia in ololtotonti, xoxoctic, itic motlalia in jxinachio: mocoxonja, amo mopalticateci, moneloa in quauhiaiaoal ixiuhio. iehoatl in jamatla-

---

85. *Cozcaquauhxiuitl: Perezia moschata* Llave (*ibid.,* p. 329).

mixed with the foliage of the *quauhyayaual*: that is, with its leaves and its blossoms.

It is required by one who has received a blow, who has broken a bone, who perhaps has fallen from a roof terrace, who has damaged his bones or his nerves. When [the bones] have been set by hand, then [the break] is washed; perhaps pine resin is mixed in. If the body is feverish, this alone [is used]. If the body is not feverish, pine resin and lampblack with feathers are to be applied as a poultice. It is to be applied two times, three times.

But its root is not needed.

It grows in Chiconauhtla and Tepepulco, and everywhere in the hot lands. And its seed can be sown.

125

Tzopelic xiuitl

It goes upright. The leaves are wide and small, of pointed tip, of green base; their tips are tawny. Its blossoms are cylindrical, round at the tip, brown, useless.

Its roots are small and round, tawny, as if strung on a thread, white on the inside, sweet. Ground up, they are required, they make the proper drink for one who has a urinary obstruction. If he has eaten, or before he eats, he drinks it [in water] to cleanse. He is only to eat warm food or [drink] *atole*.

It grows everywhere, in the crags, in the mountains, on the plains.

126

Tlatlapaltic

It is an herb. Its leaves spread out profusely. They are long, a little wide; they go extending in opposite directions. Then its blossoms go accompanying [the leaves]. Like small, slender rattles, its seeds rest within. They are useless.

Its roots are savory. They are densely matted — many small, slender ones. Outside they are reddish, inside likewise. Ground up, they are required by one who is fevered, who has an internal fever. He is to drink it [in water] during fasting or after eating; it will be his proper drink. He will urinate something like pus. And also at the time the sweat bath is entered, the sick and the healthy drink it. Also one can add it to chocolate, when it is drunk; it improves the chocolate.

It grows everywhere, in the forest, among the trees.

pal, yoan isuchio.

Itech monequj in aqujn omotlavitec, in omopoztec, in anoço tlapanco ooalhuetz in oitlacauh yiomjo, anoço itlalhoaio: in oqujpapachoque in tematica: njman ic maltia, anoçe ocotzotl moneloa: intla totonje in tenacaio, çan mjxcavia: intlacamo totonje tenacaio, ocotzotl yoan tlilli ic nepotonjlo: vppa expa motecaz, hivitica.

Auh in jnelhoaio, amo monequj:

mochioa chicunauhtlan, yoan tepepolco, yoan novian in totoncatlalpan, yoã vel mopixoa in jxinachio.

.125.

Tzopelic xivitl:

moquetztiuh mapatlactotonti, quavitztotõ, tzinxoxoctic, in jquaquauh quappachtic: in jsuchio mjmjltic, qualololtic, camopaltic: atle inecoca.

In jnelhoaio ololtotonti, quappachtic, iuhquj in çoçoticate, in tlanj iztac, necutic, moteci. Itech monequj, yiauhpovi in aqujn axixtetzaoa: intla otlaqua, anoço aiamo tlaqua; conj, ic chipaoa; çan iamanquj in tlaqualli qujquaz, anoço atolli.

çan novian texcalco, tepepan, ixtlaoacã in mochioa.

.126.

Tlatlapaltic,

xivitl. mjec in momana, in jamatlapal, pitzaoacapatlactotonti, nenecoc in mamãtiuh, njmã qujvivicatiuh in jsuchio: mjmjltotonti. iuhqujn aiacachmelactotonti, itic tetemj in jxinachio: amo tle inecoca.

In jnelhoaio aviac, tapaçoltic, mjec pitzatoton: ixtlapaltic in panj, in tlanj çã no iuhquj: moteci, itech monequj in aqujn motlevia, in jtic nemj in totonjliztli: conjz, iquac in aiamo tlaqualo, anoço otlaqualoc, yiauhpoviz: iuhqujn temalli caxixaz. yoan no vel ipan calacoa in temazcalco: in cocoxque yoan in amo cocoxque; conj. no vel qujnamjquj in cacaoatl in mj: qujqualtilia in cacaoatl.

Çan novian in mochioa quauhtla, quavitic.

178

127
METL[86]

It is that which is bored into. From it comes the white wine which they make. This is *tlacametl.* The leaf is thick, green, spiny-edged. It is named "maguey breast." Also it has many thorns.

The white wine is added to many kinds of medicine, as has been told: roots or leaves. One who has suffered a relapse is to drink it. It is to be mixed with one yellow chili and gourd seeds, which are to be shelled. He is to drink it twice, thrice, and is later to take a sweat bath. The pulpy maguey leaf is pounded with a stone, ground, cooked, sometimes put in the fire. The juice of the small maguey, when still tender, is later pressed out when it has been cooked, or it is boiled in an olla, well cooked; salt is mixed in [the water]. With it is healed one who is wounded in the head, or someone who is cut somewhere, or whom they have knifed. It is placed there where the head is wounded, or where he is cut. And the maguey can also be pulverized when dry. Mixed with pine resin, it is applied with feathers as a poultice where there is gout.

And this white wine is added to what is called *chichic patli.* It is boiled, well cooked. It is required by him who goes about ailing in his chest, [or] on his back, who is already wizened. He is to drink it during fasting; he is to drink it once or twice.

And this, the *chichic patli,* comes from the bark of a large tree named *chichic quauitl.* Only the bark is required; the rest is useless. It grows there in the forest; also it is in Chalco.

And with the leaves of this maguey he who is a great coward, if he thinks that they want to whip him, rubs himself on his back, in order no longer to feel the lash. His body is much covered with welts.

128
CIUAPATLI[87]

It is just stalks, of which many extend. Its stalk is about a fathom tall. Its leaves are somewhat ashen, small and wide, pointed at the ends. Its branches are many. Its blossoms are yellow; some are white. It forms seeds like amaranth; they are white.

Its foliage is required. It is not ground; it is just as it were boiled. That which comes from its well-

. 127 .
METL:

iehoatl in mj̃chiqujnj, in jtech qujça iztac octli qujchioa: iehoatl in tlacametl, matilaoac, xoxoctic; in jtenco vitzio, motocaïotia mechichioalli, no vivitzio.

In iztac octli mjec tlamantli in qujnamiquj patli, in iuh omito, in tlanelhoatl, anoço xivitl. In aqujn omocaxanj, conjz ce chilcoztli moneloz, yoã aiovachtli, moxipeoaz. vppa, expa in conjz, yoan çatepan motemaz. In iehoatl metzintamali motetzotzona, moteci, motzoionia: in quenmanjan tleco maquja: in tepitoton metl, in oc celtic, çatepan mopatzca iquac moicucic, anoce moquaqualatza caxic, vel tzoionj, iztatl moneloa: ic pati in aqujn moquatzaiana, anoço aca cana omoxotlac, anoço aca oqujcochilovique: vncã motequjlia, in canjn quatzaianquj anoce in canjn omoxotlac yoã in iehoatl metl, no vel mocoxonja, in jquac ovac, ocotzotl moneloa, ic mopotonja in canjn catquj coaciviztli:

yoan in iehoatl iztac octli qujnamjquj in motocaiotia chichic patli, moquaqualatza, vel tzoionj. Itech monequj in aqujn qujcocotinemj yielchiquiuh, tocujtlapampa, in ie tiquavaquj, conjz, aiamo tlaqualo, çeppa, anoço vppa in conjz.

Auh in iehoatl, in chichic patli, itech qujça, itlaxipevallo in vei quavitl, itoca chichic quavitl, çanjo in jtlaxipeoallo, monequj, in oc cequj, atle inecoca: vmpa mochioa in quauhtla, no oncatquj in chalco.

Ioan in iehoatl metl ima: in aqujn cenca momauhtianj intla qujmati, ca qujmecavitequjzque in jcujtlapampa ic momamatiloa, injc aocmo qujmati in mecatl, cenca cuecuetzoca in jnacaio.

. 128 .
CIOAPATLI,

çan tlacotl: mjec in momana, achi vel cen nequetzalli in jtlacoio, achi ixtenextic: in jxiuhio patlactotonti, quavitztoton, mjec in jma, in jsuchio coztic, cequj iztac: moxinachiotia, iuhqujn oauhtli iztac.

Iehoatl monequj in jxiuhio, amo moteci, çan iuhquj in quaqualaca: qujça in jxiuhio, vel tzoionj: itech

---

86. *Metl:* "generic term for agaves and other plants of similar appearance"; *Agave atrovirens* Karw. is the most important cultivated species (Dressler, *op. cit.,* p. 120).

87. *Ciuapatli: Montanoa tomentosa* (Sahagún, *op. cit.,* p. 327).

cooked foliage is required by the woman when she senses birth pains, when she is about to have a child. First the blood comes out, which shows that the baby is about to follow, about to be forced out. She is to drink it; wherewith she will quickly give birth. Thus she will not suffer much. It is to be drunk only once; but if the baby does not then follow, once again a little is to be drunk. Thus the baby can emerge.

And its roots are small, slender and long; many are black on the surface, yellow inside. It is odorous, bitter, tough, stinking. It is ground up, boiled in water, to be drunk tepid.

It is required by one who passes blood from his rectum. If he has eaten or is yet to eat, he will drink it. But when he will eat food, it is only warm.

It grows everywhere, in the mountains, on the plains; it can also grow among the houses.

129

Nopal[88]

It is green. It is very thick; some of its leaves are two fingers thick. They are like tiles. They are spiny, thorny; the bases are small and slender, the tips small and pointed; they are wide in the middle; they are long. Its blossoms are set on the leaf. Some are yellow, some rose, some white. The fruit named *nochtli* comes from it. It is edible.

The leaves of this *nopal* are peeled, ground up. They give this [in water] as a drink to the woman who cannot give birth, as is already mentioned [regarding] *ciuapatli*. When the baby has extended crosswise, they give this to her as a drink so that she may quickly eject the baby. When this happens to the young woman, that her child extends crosswise, that she gives birth with difficulty, perhaps she endures two days, three days of trying to give birth. Such is a young woman who does not abstain, who still sleeps with the man.[89]

This *nopal* grows everywhere.

130

The chía[90]

Already mentioned is the nature of its foliage, of its seeds, as well as the many things added to it to make it useful to one. For everyone knows *atole* is

monequj in cioatzintli, in ie qujmati iti, in ie mjxiviznequj: achtopa oalqujça in eztli, ic neci ca ie oalotlatoca, ie qujoaltopeoa in piltzintli: conjz, iciuhca ic tlacachioaz, injc amo cēca motolinjz: ça ceppa in mjz. Auh intla njman amo valtotoca piltzintli oc ceppa çan achiton in conjz: ic vel valqujça in piltzintli.

Auh in jnelhoaio çan pitzatoton viviacatotonti, mjec tliltic in panj, in tlanj coztic: âviac, chichic, chicaoac, ihiiac: moteci, quaqualaca; iamãquj in conjz.

Itech monequj in aqujn eztli qujnoquja icujtlapampa; intla otlaqua, anoço aiamo tlaqua in conjz: auh in qujquaz tlaqualli, çan iamanquj;

çan novian tepepan ixtlaoacan, in mochioa: no vel mochioa in techachan.

.129.

Nopalli

xoxoctic, cenca titilaoac, cequj ommapilli injc tilaoac in jma iuhqujn tapalcatl vivitzio, havaio, tzinpitzatoton, quavitztoton itipatlaoac, quauhtic, moxochiotia: in jxochio, cequj coztic, cequj tlaztaleoaltic, cequj iztac: itech qujça in suchiqualli, itoca, nochtli: qualonj.

Iiehoatl yiamatlapal in nopalli: moxipeoa, moteci: conjtia, in aqujn cioatl, in amo vel ic mjxivi in omjto, cioapatli: in tlaixtlapal omotecac in piltzintli: iehoatl conjtia iciuhca, ic qujoaltopeoa in piltzintli. Iehoatl in juh mochioa cioatzintli mjxtlapalmoteca in jconeuh, in aiaxcan mjxivi: aço omjlhujtl, eilhujtl nemj in mjxiviznequj iehoatl in amo motlacaoaltia cioatzintli, oc noma oqujch coqujch.

Inin nopalli novian mochioa.

.130.

In chien

ie omjto, injc iuhquj in jxiuhio, in jxinachio: yoan in jzqujtlamantli qujnamjquj, injc tetech monequj: ca mochi tlacatl qujmati, in atolli muchioa, izqujtl

88. *Nopalli: Opuntia ficus-indica* (L.) Miller, *O. megacantha* Salm-Dyck, *O. streptacantha* Lemaire, *O. amyclaea* Tenore (Dressler, *op. cit.*, p. 140).

89. Corresponding Spanish text: *"Esto acontece por la mayor parte a las mugeres q̃ no se abstienē del varon ante de parir."*

90. *Chía: Salvia hispanica* L. (*S. Chian* La Llave, *S. polystachia* Ort.), in Dressler, *op. cit.*, p. 146. *Hyptis suaveolens* Poit. often goes by the name of *chía* (*ibid.*, p. 134).

made; parched maize kernels are mixed in. The name of the seed alone is *chía*. Its foliage is useless.

And this *chía* is savory. It is ground raw. A little is mixed with opossum tail [and water], just a little, perhaps one-half the length of the little finger, also raw. It is also required [by] the woman who is about to give birth; she drinks it; she will promptly give birth. When it is to be drunk, it is just this alone, in preference to drinking the aforementioned *ciuapatli* or *nopal*. This *chía* is very good; still, few people know of it.

And the root of the *chía* is mixed with the root of the *quetzalhuexotl*. They are ground together; an *atole* is made. The *chía* is raw. It is required by one who spits blood, who cannot stop it, who just coughs constantly, whose blood comes from within. And it also cures a dry cough, and dislodges the flux. He is to drink it two or three times for it to be stopped.

The *chía* is sown. It grows yearly. And this is ground raw; the juice is pressed out. It is to be drunk during fasting, for it clears the chest. Also it is like *atole* when mixed with grains of maize or with toasted tortillas. And with this *chía* the painters apply *chía* oil. With it they varnish things, make them glossy. With it paintings are beautified. And this *chía,* when ground, is moistened with hot water. Then it is wrapped in a rag; with this the beautiful thing is washed. When still wet, it consequently glistens much, appears beautiful, becomes just like crystal; there we can see ourselves.

131

Haacxoyatic[91]

It is a small herb — small and slender, green. Only one small [stalk] stands, a small span high. Its blossoms are small and white; its foliage is just like the leaves of the *iztac quilitl*. This is useless.

Its root is also only one. It rises small and cylindrical, a small span long. Its surface is white. It burns a little. Only the skin of the root is required, and its center is useless. It is required when one has contracted a high fever, when phlegm destroys the heart. It is drunk [in water]; with it the phlegm is quickly expelled from the mouth; with it the heart, the body are soothed. And so the feverishness lessens, disappears.

moneloa, in ça iehoatl ixinachio, in jtoca: chien: in jxiuhio atle inecoca.

Auh in iehoatl chien aviac, xoxouhquj; moteci, achiton moneloa tlaquacujtlapilli, çan vel tepiton; aço ixqujch in cemjxtli tomapilxocoiouh, can no xoxouhquj. No itech monequj conj in ie mjxiviznequj cioatl: çan ic iciuhca mjxiviz. In jquac mjz can mjxcaviz: amo achtopa mjz in omjto cioapatli, anoço nopalli: inin chien, ca cenca qualli, ca amo mjec tlacatl qujmati.

yoan in iehoatl chien inelhoaio: monamjquj in jnelhoaio quetzalhuexotl, mocẽteci, atolli mochioa: xoxouhquj in chien. Itech monequj in aqujn eztli qujchicha in amo vel motzaqua in ça iuhquj totolcatinemj in vel iticpa oalqujça eztli. yoan no ic pati in vaccatlatlaciztli: yoã in tlaelli qujtlaça conjz, vppa, anoço expa, ic motzaqua.

In chien mopixoa: cecexiuhtica mochioa, yoan in iehoatl xoxouhquj moteci, mopatzca: onmjz: iquac in aiamo tle moqua: ca qujchipaoa in toiollo: no iuhquj in atolli in moneloa tlaolli anoço tlaxcaltotopochtli: yoã in iehoatl chien ic tlachiamavia, ic tlatzotlanja in tlacujloque, ic tlaxipetzoa, ic qualneci in tlacujlolli, yoã in iehoatl chien: in jquac omotez, mocuechaoa atotonjltica: çatepã tzotzomatica moqujmjloa, ic mjxpopoa: in tlaqualli, in jquac oc paltic: ic cenca xipetzivi, qualneci, vel iuhqujn tevilotl mochioa vmpa tonneci.

. 131 .

Haacxoiatic,

xiuhtontli çan pitzaton, xoxoctic, çan ceton in moquetza, cemjztitontli, injc quauhtic: in jxochio iztacatontli; in jqujllo vel iuhquj in jamatlapal iztaqujlitl, atle inecoca.

In jnelhoaio, çan no ce moquetza, mjmjltõtli, cemjztitontli injc viac: im panj iztac, achi cocoiac: çan iehoatl monequj in jeoaio tlanelhoatl: auh in jiollo, çan vetzi. Itech monequj, in matlaltotonquj itech motlalia: in alaoac qujpoloa toiollo, ommj: ic iciuhca valhuetzi, in alaoac tocamacpa: ic cevi in toiollo, in tonacaio: auh ic cevi, ic polivi in totonjllotl:

---

91. *Aacxoyatic: Ipomoea capillacea* Don. ? *Polygala verticillata* L. ? (Hernández, *op. cit.*, Vol. I, pp. 34 *sqq.*).

It grows everywhere, in the forest, in the mountains. It is quite rare. And it grows in this manner: the foliage falls from its stalk, but when spring comes, this same little root sprouts once again.

132

MATICEUAC

It is a small herb. Many small, stick-like [branches] appear; they are tough, small and slender. Its leaf is chalky, ashen, hairy, somewhat fibrous on the surface. The Chichimeca can make fire with its stalk. Its blossom is white, shaped like a small spindle whorl; it is scented. Its name is *tlacoxochitl*. Its foliage is not required.

Its roots are many, small and slender, black on the surface, white inside, bitter. They are not ground; they are only hammered, crushed with a stone. Just as the water bubbles, boils, cooks well, the water is removed.

It is required as a cure by one who has the nosebleed, who cannot stop it. Drops are put in his nose once.

It grows everywhere, in the mountains, on the plains.

133

IZTAC PATLI

Also its name is *teçonpatli*. It is a small stalk. It is green, its stalk is tough, its leaves are like those of the *uauhquilitl*, serrated on the edges, wide. It has fruit; its fruit is just like the *tlalayotli*. It is not good. Its blossom is white; its foliage is useless.

Its roots are a little long, some like a small mano, some round and small. The skin is thick, somewhat black on the surface, white undernearth, bitter. Its skin is useless.

Its center is required, to be ground up. It is required by one upon whom a fever has settled, whose body is swollen. It is placed there upon it. Thus it alleviates, it quickly abates the fever.

It grows everywhere, in the mountains, in the forests. Also it is rare. Its growing place is especially in Tequixquiac.

134

OQUICHPATLI

It is a small herb. It creeps along the surface of the ground like the *tianquizpepetla*. Its foliage is green, small and round, like the *chilachtli*; the ends are pointed. Then its leaves go carrying with them

çan novian quauhtla, tepepan in mochioa, çã tlaçonemj. Auh injc mochioa: in cexiuitl, vetztiuh in jquauhio: auh in jquac tlatzmolinj, çan no iehoatl in tlanelhoatontli, oc ceppa ixoa.

. 132 .

MATICEOAC,

xiuhtontli, mjec in momana, iuhqujn tlacotõtli, tlaquaoac, pitzatoton: in jamatlapal maticeoac, matenextic, tomjo, achi ixpochinquj: in jtlacoio, vel ic tlequauhtlaça in chichimeca. In jxochio iztac, malacachtontli, mjnecuj: itoca, tlacosuchitl: in jxiuhio amo monequj:

in jnelhoaio, mjec, pitzatoton: im panj tliltic, in tlanj iztac, chichic: amo moteci, çan motetzotzona, motepapatlachoa: çan iuhquj in apoçonj, quaqualaca, vel tzoionj, aqujça.

Itech monequj ic pati in aqujn eztli yiacac qujça, in amo vel motzaqua: ceppa in jiacac ommochipinjlia.

çan novian tepepã ixtlaoacan in mochioa.

. 133 .

IZTAC PATLI,

yoan itoca teçompatli, tlacotontli, xoxoctic: in jtlacoio, tlaquaoac: in jamatlapal, iuhquj in oauhqujlitl, tentzitziqujltic, papatlaoac: xocoioa in jtlaaqujllo, vel iuhquj in tlalaiotli, amo qualli, in jsuchio, iztac: amo tle inecoca in jxiuhio.

In jnelhoaio veitontii, cequj metlapiltotonti, cequj ololototonti: eoaiotilaoac, in panj achi ixtliltic, in tlanj iztac, chichic, çan vetzi in jeoaio.

Iehoatl monequj in jiollo, moteci: itech monequj, in aqujn totonquj itech motlalia: in jnacaio poçaoa, vncan panj motlalia: ic cevi, ic iciuhca ic iloti in tletl.

Çan novian tepepan, quauhtla in mochioa; çan no tlaçoneci: çenca in imochioaiã tequjxqujac.

. 134 .

OQUJCHPATLI,

xiuhtontli: çan tlali ixco in movilana, iuhquj in tianqujzpepetla: in jxiuhio, xoxoctic, iaoaltotonti, iuhquj in chilachtli, quavitztoton: njmã qujvivicatiuh in jamatlapal, iuhqujnma hivitl, itlan ieietiuh,

—as if they were feathers which went among them
—its white blossoms which lie there as part of them.
These [leaves and blossoms] are swept away by the
wind; they are useless.

[As for] its root, only one rises. It burns much. It
is small and cylindrical, a full span long, yellow on
the surface, very white inside. And the roundness
of this root is like that of a pot support. Ground, it
is required when a man or a woman has harmed the
genitals; when he cannot eject [his semen]. If a man
has mated with a woman and they have frightened
or harmed them [in the act];[92] when he just goes
about coughing; when already his body turns black;
when already he is wizened, when already he loses
flesh; even if he has been sick already one year, or
perhaps already four years, it is required. They administer it in his rectum; it dilutes the ailment. Then
the ailment comes out; it stinks exceedingly. In two
days, three days, five days, the giving off of the ailment ends. And from within his genital comes something like ashen water, [like] sand. It stinks. The
same with the woman: it is expelled when she urinates it. And to one who has ejected semen in his
sleep,[93] man or woman, it is likewise to be given in
his rectum.

And one root is used by two or three persons. One
requires half a finger of it.

It grows profusely on the plains of Tollantzinco.

135

TLAMACAZQUI IPAPA[94]

It is a small stalk; many of them extend a good
fathom tall. They are tough. Its stalk, as well as its
foliage, is like that of the quince tree, ashen on top,
green underneath. Each of its stalks is separate. Its
flowers are large, yellow, [rough] like volcanic rock,
without petals. These are useless.

Its roots are small and slender. There are many,
about a span long; one root is a fist [thick]. Its fuzzy
top is yellow. It burns the throat. The surface is
chili-red; below it is yellow. The skin is thin. And
its center is just like strings of maguey fiber; many
of them extend.

Ground up, it is required by one who has harmed
his genitals or has expelled semen in his sleep, or has

iztac: ixochio pouhtoc, çan ehecatoco: atle inecoca.

In jnelhoaio, çan ce·moquetza: cenca cococ, mjmjltõtli, vel cemjztitl injc viac: im panj ixcoztic, in tlanj
cenca iztac. Auh inin tlanelhoatl, tetevilacachiuhtica:
injc catquj, iuhquj in jtlaiaiaoaliuhtica, moteci. Itech
monequj in toqujchtin, anoço cioatl, in omjtlaco: in
amo vel qujchiuh, intla oqujchtli oitech acia: auh
oqujnmauhtique, anoço oqujmjtlacoque, in ça totolcatinemj, in ie tlileoa inacaio; yoan in ie quavaquj, in
ie itech iauh inacaio: intlanel ie ce xivitl, intlanoço ie
nauhxivitl mococoa: itech monequj, icujtlapampa
qujmaca: qujciaoa in cocolli: ic njman qujça in cocolli, cenca hiiac: omjlhujtl, eilhujtl, macujlilhujtl
tlamj, in cocolli vetzi. yoan in jitic tototouh qujça,
iuhqujn tenexatl, xalli, hiiac: no iuhquj in cioatl, ixpampa vetzi, in caxixa. yoan in aqujn omocochtemjc
toqujchtin, anoço cioatl. çan no icujtlapampa moma-
caz:

auh in ce tlanelhoatl, vme tlacatl, anoço ei tlacatl
itech monequj, cemjxtli in tomapil tetech monequj.
cenca mochioa in tollantzinco ixtlaoacan.

. 135 .

TLAMACAZQUJ IPAPA:

tlacototonti, mjec in momana: vel cen nequetzalli,
injc quauhtic, tlaquaoac, iuhqujn membrillo itlacoio:
çã no iuhquj in jxiuhio: im panj, matenextic, in tlanj
xoxoctic: çã ceceiaca momana in jtlacoio. In jsuchio
vei, coztic; çan iuhquj in teçontic, atle yiamatlapal:
amo tle inecoca.

In jnelhoaio pitzatoto, mjec, achi vel cemjztitl injc
viac: in centacatl vel cemmapichtli, coztic in jquato-
mjo, tozcacococ; im panj ixchichiltic, in tlanj ixcoztic; eoaiocanaoac: auh in jiollo, vel iuhquj in ichtli,
mjec temj:

moteci. Itech monequj, in aqujn omjtlaco, anoço
omocochtemjc: anoço cioatl oqujmjxiuhcaiecoque,

---

92. Corresponding Spanish text: *"es muy prouechosa para el hombre o muger que porque no acabo de espeler la semjente humana o por mjedo o por otra ocasion que se ofrecio y queda cortado o estragado."*

93. Corresponding Spanish text: *"para ãn alguno en soennos acabo de espeler el humor sementino."*

94. *Tlamacazquj ipapa*: Lycopodium dichotomum Jacq. ? (Dibble and Anderson, *op. cit.*, p. 143, n. 49).

had intercourse with a woman [too recently] confined, or has mounted in haste. He drinks it during fasting. Thereupon the ailment quickly comes from his rectum; thus he is cured. It is drunk [in water] only once, very early in the morning. Later, when he is to eat food at midday, he will eat it with chili; the food is warm.

It grows everywhere, in the forest, in the mountains.

136

CICIMATIC[95]

It is an herb; it just creeps. It has much green foliage. Its leaf is broad, divided as if in three parts like the foliage of the *eçoquilitl*. It does not flower. [Its foliage] is useless.

Its root is harsh to the taste, like that of the *quauhtzontetl*. It is very thick; it can be almost as thick as a head, as long as a forearm. The skin is thick, black on the surface, chili-red and white inside. It can be chopped, ground.

It is required by one who suffers an eye ailment; by one who, it is said, has a fleshy growth over the eyes, who is about to become blind from flesh on the eyes. It is dropped in the eyes. As a result, [the flesh] falls; [the drops] remove the flesh.

It grows everywhere in the forest.

137

TZOMPOTON

It is an herb which forms many branches; they are green. Its leaves are long, small and wide, straight. Its blossoms are white. When it has bloomed, its blossoms are like feathers. Right there they are borne away by the wind. [These flowers and branches] are useless.

Its root is bitter. There is just one — small and cylindrical, forked. It is small, one finger thick. On the surface it is white; it is yellow below. It is pounded with a stone, boiled, well cooked.

It is required by one who is about to die of diarrhea, who cannot stop it, who just vomits up the *atole*, the food. He drinks it; thus [the diarrhea] is quickly stopped. Just a little is to be drunk. And if a little child [is sick], it is to drink one or two mouthfuls to stop it.

It grows everywhere, in the mountains, in the forest.

---

95. *Cicimatic: Canavalia villosa* Benth. (*ibid.*, p. 141, n. 25).

anoçe iciuhca otlamama: conj, aiamo tlaqua: ic iciuhca icujtlapampa qujça in cocolli, ic pati: çan ceppa in mj, vel oc ioatzinco, qujn nepantla tonatiuh in tlaquaz: chillo in qujquaz, iamanquj in tlaqualli:

novian mochioa, in quauhtla, tepepan.

.136.

CICIMATIC

xivitl: çan movilana mjec in jxiuhio, xoxoctic: in jamatlapal, patlaoac: iuhqujn excã xeliuhtica, iuhqujn eçoqujlitl in jxiuhio: amo mosuchiotia, atle inecoca.

In jnelhoaio. tetelqujc, iuhqujn quauhtzontetl, cenca tomaoac: achi vel centzõtecomatl injc tomaoac: injc viac cemmolicpitl, eoaiotilaoac im panj tliltic, in tlanj chichiltic, yoan iztac: vel motzatzaiana moteci.

Itech monequj, in aqujn ixtelolo qujcocoa: in mjtoa ixnacapachivi, in ie tlapachiviznequj tixtelolonacatica: vncan mochipinjlia in tixteloloco: ic vetzi, qujqujxtia in nacatl,

çan novian quauhtla in mochioa.

.137.

TZOMPOTON,

xivitl: mjec in momana, xôxoctic, momaxallotia: in jamatlapal pitzaoacapatlactotonti, melactotonti: iztac in jsuchio, in jquac ocuepõ iuhquj hivitl icueponca. çan no vncã hecatoco: atle inecoca.

In jnelhoaio chichic, ça ce, mjmjltontli. momaxallotia, çan tepitoton: cenmapiltontli: im pani iztac, in tlanj ixcoztic, çan motetzotzona, moquaqualatza, vel tzoionj:

Itech monequj in aqujn ic mjqujznequj, amjntli in amo vel motzaqua: in çan oalmocuepa in atolli, in tlaqualli: conj, ic iciuhca motzaqua: çan tepiton in mjz: auh intla piltontli, çã cencamatl, anoço oncamatl in conjz ic motzaqua.

çan novian quauhtla tepepan in mochioa.

CUITLAPATLI

It is an herb, a stalk. Its stalk is hollow; one, two, or three appear. Its leaves are green. They are wide like the saltwort of Castile. Its blossoms are white. A few branch out on top; all bloom. These are not required.

Its root is thick. Bunched, two or three parts extend like radishes. They are white on the surface, yellow beneath. Like the radish, it is thick-skinned; its center is also like that of the radish. It is pulverized dry. It is required by one who has a cyst [on the throat] and a scrofula. These in one place heal, in another place open; they just go on absorbing medicine; they continue opening. When the medicine is put on, it is mixed with pine resin and applied with feathers as a poultice.

And also it cures one who has suppurating genitals — woman or man. And also with it are cured the disease of the groin and hemorrhoids. [Infusions of] this root cannot be drunk.

It grows everywhere, in the forest, in the mountains.

139

OQUICHPATLI

It is like gourd vines, and its name is [also] *ayoxochquiltic.* The herb creeps; it even climbs trees. Its leaves are green on top. Its vine is hairy; underneath it is smooth. Its leaf is divided into three parts. Its blossom is large, yellow; it is like the gourd blossom, shaped like a bell. Later its blossom falls off. It forms fruit like small pears, marked like melons. They are useless.

Its root is small and round, bitter, burning. There is just one small one. Its skin is thin. It is somewhat black on the surface, very white beneath. As it creeps, its root goes establishing itself in many places.

The single root is required by many people. Just scraped or ground, it becomes a suppository. A small grass named *xomalli* is rubbed with it; rubber is mixed in.

It is required by one whose member has been harmed, and by one whose urine is stopped. He inserts it into his body [his member], so that the pus may come out, or so that the urine may fall. And [it is required by] the woman who, it is said, has damaged her vagina; when it is turned, twisted, there where the semen is placed; where the semen is just

CUJTLAPATLI,

xivitl, tlacotl iticoionquj in jtlacoio: in centacatl vme, anoço ei momana, xoxoctic: in jamatlapal, papatlaoac, iuhquj in acelcas castilla, iztac in jsuchio: in jzquj icpac momaxallotia mochi cueponj: amo monequj.

In jnelhoaio tomaoac, in centacatl vme eitemj: iuhquj in Rauanos, im panj iztac, in tlanj ixcoztic: in juhquj Rauanos eoaiotilaoac, çan no iuhquj in jiollo: mocoxonja. Itech monequj in aquj itech catquj coatetl: yoan in toçã potzalli: iehoatl in cecni pati, oc cecnj coionj, çan qujmomacatiuh, cocojontiuh: in jquac motlalilia patli, ocotzotl moneloa, yoan mopotonja

Yoan no ic pati, in aqujn tlapalanaltia cioatl, anoço oqujchtli, yoã no ic pati in quexiliviliztli: yoan xochiciviztli. Inin tlanelhoatl amo vel mj:

çan novian quauhtla tepepan in mochioa.

OQUJCHPATLI,

aiomecatic, yoan itoca aiosuchqujltic, xivitl, çã movilana, vel quauhtleco, xoxoctic: im panj yiamatlapal, yoan imecaio tomjo: in tlanjpa xipetztic, in jamatlapal, excan xeliuhtica, vêvei in jsuchio, coztic: iuhquj in jsuchio aiotli, iuhquj in campanjlla ic motlalia: çatepan valhuetzi in jsuchio, moxocoiotia: ixqujch in perasto: injc mocujcujloa, iuhquj in melo: atle inecoca.

In jnelhoaio ololtontli, chichicacococ, çan centetontli: in jeoaio canactontli, im panj achi ixtliltic, in tlanj cenca iztac: injc movivilana, mjeccan in motlalitiuh in jnelhoaio.

In centetl tlanelhoatl; mjec tlacatl itech monequj, çã mjchiquj, anoço moteci: tlapilolli mochioa, çacatontli ic momamatiloa itoca xomali; moneloa olli

Itech monequj in aqujn omjtlaco. yoã in aqujn omotzacu in jaxix: conaqujlia, itic in jnacaio: ic oalqujça in temalli, anoçe ic vitomj in taxix. Auh in cioatl, in mjtoa oitlacauh icioaio: in omocuep, momalacachiuh, in vncã motlalia in xinachtli, in çan nenpolivi xinachtli. In aqujn iuhquj mochioa y, çan mochipa qujnoqujtinemj: intlacaiac qujpati: nappa in

wasted. She to whom this happens always has a discharge. If nothing cures it, she swells up four times; she also dries up four times. So she dies; she recovers no more. If prompt, they cure her. The root is to be mixed with rubber and the herb *xoxocoyoltic*, which they are to press in her body, as has been said — in her vagina. Thus she can restore her body once again; thus once again she can bear children.

And to him who is already wizened from being sick, they administer it, in his rectum, early in the morning, during fasting. The water will be hot.

When they have given the medicine, he becomes very hot; the sweat exudes. Later [the medicine] enters everywhere — in the nerves, to the head, in the chest. As a result, the green, yellow, white phlegm comes out from the mouth, from the rectum. When the ailment has left, he will drink *atole*. And when he has eaten, or before he has eaten, he is to drink a medicine. The name of the proper drink is *chichic patli* root [cooked in water] — just the scrapings; not thickened. Thereby the fever is ended.

[*Oquichpatli*] grows everywhere in the mountains, especially there at Xochiquauhyocan.

The nature of *xoxocoyoltic* has already been mentioned.

140

CHICHIC PATLI[96]

It is an herb, small and stalky, [with] one root. Many [stalks] spread out, or only one stands up. It forms many branches. Its leaves are green, smooth, small and straight, a little wide. Its foliage is like that of the peach tree. Its stems have knots where its leaves go out; they just go meeting, they extend in opposite directions. They stand following one another, [in this manner] continuing toward the top. Its stalk exudes milk; the interior is pithy. Its flower is white; only one blossoms which is small and straight. It is like a bell. It is useless.

Its root is single. It is a little bitter to the taste. They go in pairs; it is said there is the male, likewise there is the female. And the male root goes in this manner: it is about a fathom in length. Of those already old, some are small, thick. [Those not old are] not thick-skinned; those already old are thick-skinned.[97] When about to shed its skin, it is peeled. It is not drunk. Only its center is ground; it can be drunk [in water].

poçaoa, no nappa in quavaquj, ic mjquj, aocmo vel pati. Intla iciuhca qujpatican; in tlanelhoatl moneloz olli, yoã xoxocoioltic: ic qujpachilhujzque in jnacaio; in omjto icioaio, ic vel oc ceppa qujtlalilia in jnacaio, ic oc ceppa vel mopilhoatia.

yoan in aqujn ie quavaquj in mococoa: icujtlapampa qujmaca, oc ioatzinco, aiamo tle qujqua: totonjz in atl.

In jquac oqujmacaque patli: cenca mjtonja, qujça in totonjliztli: çatepan novian cacalaquj in jtic totlalhoaio. in totzõtecontitech, in telchiqujuhpan ic oalqujça in alaoac, xoxoctic, coztic, iztac, tocamacpa, tocujtlapampa: in jquac ooalhuetz cocolli, atolli conjz. Auh in jquac otlaqua, anoço aiamo tlaqua: conjz patli, yiauhpoviz. itoca, chichic patli inelhoaio: çan mjchiquj, amo tetzaoac. ic oallamj in totonjliztli:

çan novian tepepan in mochioa, cenca onca in xochiquauhiocan.

In xoxocoioltic: ie omjto in quenamj.

.140.

CHICHIC PATLI,

xivitl, tlacotontli: in ce tlanelhoatl, mjec in momana, anoço çan ce moquetza, cẽca momamatia; in jamatlapal xoxoctic, xipetztic, melactotonti, patlactotonti: iuhquj in duraznos ixiuhio: in jquauhio hiixe, vncan momantiuh in jamatlapal: çan mjxnamjctiuh, nenecoc mamantiuh, çan qujtotocaticac: âcopa itztiuh, memeia in jtlacoio, itipochinquj in jsuchio iztac, çan centetl in cueponj, melactontli, iuhquj in campanjlla ic catquj: atle inecoca.

In jnelhoaio çan ce achi camachichic: vntlamantitiuh injc iauh: mjtoa vnca oqujchtli, no vnca cioatl: auh injc iauh oqujchtli tlanelhoatl, achi vel cẽmatl injc viac: in ie vecaoa cequj tepitoton, totomaoac: amo eoaiotilaoac: in ie vecaoatilaoac in jeoaio. In jquac iuhquj, vetzi in jeoaio: moxipeoa, amo mj: çanjo in jiollo moteci, vel mj.

---

96. *Chichic patli: Guayacum arboreum* (*ibid.*, p. 141, n. 27).
97. Corresponding Spanish text: *"si es antigua: tiene la corteça gruessa: y si no, tienela delgada."*

It is required by one whose body is hot, who thinks it burns; perhaps the stomach has become unsettled. One whose stomach has become unsettled drinks it. One chili is added. With this he recovers. And [as for] the root called the female: two roots grow. They are long; they also become just like those mentioned. And the skin of the root is pulverized dry; lamp-black is mixed in. With this are cured the festering, or sores, or fever; with this is encircled whatever there is, so that it breaks open.

It grows everywhere, in the mountains, in the forests; only it occurs rarely.

141

COPAL[98]

It comes from a tree named *tepecopalquauitl*. It issues, it exudes only during the dry season. But when it is summer it cannot set; it is only dissolved. Its liquid is like milk. [It becomes] hard like gum for ink.

In this manner is one cured. If it is to be ground, just a little, as much as a small fingernail, is to be ground. It is placed in water; there it is crumbled with the fingers. It is not thick. And it is drunk only once a day. One who has diarrhea drinks it during fasting, mixed with tepid water; or when he has eaten, mixed with lamp-black. And he who passes from his rectum, or who spits blood, is cured by it; it is not to be mixed with lampblack. And [to treat] one whose body swells, perhaps of a high fever, [the gum] is placed thereon; it is placed on top [of the swellings], in order for them quickly to break open.

It grows in the hot lands, toward Temetztla.

142

COCOPI[99]

It is similar to the maize: just like the maize stalk. The grains of this are parched very hard; they are well carbonized. They add *chia* to it, also parched, and a few kernels of wheat, also parched. They are ground together; *atole* is made; it is topped with chili.

It is required by one who passes blood, or a flux. He drinks it early in the morning. It is to be drunk three times during the day: early in the morning, at midday, once again as [the bells] ring — perhaps at four o'clock.

Itech monequj, in aqujn totonje inacaio, in juhquj tlatla qujmati: anoço omocaxanj: in aqujn omocaxanj, conj, monamjctia ce chilli, ic pati. Auh in cioatl mjtoa tlanelhoatl: vme tentiuh, viviac, çan no iuhquj mochioa in iuh omjto: auh in jeoaio tlanelhoatl, mocoxonja, tlilli moneloa: ic pati in palaxtli, anoço çaoatl, anoço totonquj: ic moiaoalochtia in quexqujch ic catquj, ic pitzinj,

Çan novian in mochioa tepepan, quauhtla: can tlaçomantiuh.

. 141 .

CôCOPALTIC:

quavitl, itech qujça itoca tepecopalquavitl: itech qujça ixica, çan iquac in tonalco: auh in jquac xopan, amo vel motlalia, çan atoco: in jaio, iuhquj in chichioalaiotl, tepitztic: iuhquj in mjzqujcopalli.

Injc tepatilo: çan tepiton intla moteciz, iuhquj in iztitontli moteciz: can atlan motlalia; vncan tomapiltica momamatiloa, amo tetzaoac: auh çan ceppa in mj cemjlhujtl, iamãquj in atl moneloa: iquac in aiamo tlaqualo conj, in aquj mamina, anoço otlaqua tlilli moneloa. yoã in aqujn eztli qujnoquia icujtlapampa, anoço qujchicha: ic pati: amo tlilli moneloz. yoan in aqujn poçaoa inacaio; anoço vei totonquj itech motlalia, panj motequjlia; ic iciuhca qujpitzinja,

mochioa totoncatlalpan. tlalhujc, temetztla.

. 142 .

COCOPI:

itlatla in tonacaiotl, vel iuhquj in toctli: iehoatl in jtlaollo mjcequj, ca cenca tepitztic, vel tecoltic: qujnamjquj in chien, no mjcequj: yoan trigo quezqujtetl, no mjcequj: mocenteci, atolli mochioa: chilli ic mopanja.

Itech monequj, in aqujn eztli qujnoquja, anoço tlaelli: conj, oc iovatzinco: expa in mjz cemjlhujtl: ioatzinco, nepãtla tonatiuh: oc ceppa ei tzilinj, anoço navi horas.

---

98. *Cocopaltic:* desc. in Hernández, *Historia Natural*, Vol. I, p. 182.
99. *Cocopi: Euchleana mexicana* Schr. (Sahagún, *op. cit.*, p. 328).

It grows everywhere in the fields. No one sows it. Some of it grows first, before the maize plants sprout; some of it grows later, as the maize grows.

Here follow, here are mentioned some of the stones which are also medicines.

143

QUIAUHTEOCUITLATL

It is really a stone, though not very hard; it is like porous rock. It is very heavy; mottled black and white. It tastes good — not bitter, not sweet, just like pure water. It is not ground up; it is just abraded on some small stone.

It is required by one on whom lightning has flashed, who is as if possessed, struck dumb. It tastes good. He drinks it in cold water; thus he can see; thus he is revived. And it is the cure for one whose body is as if burning; [the sensation] starts from within. And also [the stone] named *xiuhtomoltetl* can be added. One on whom lightning has flashed is to drink it. Also one who only imagines, who becomes demented, whose heart is congested can drink it; he is thereby relieved. It is to be drunk once or twice.

Those of Xalapa know of the *quiauhteocuitlatl* stone. It occurs in their territory; hence they know of it.

When it thunders, there in the forest, in the mountains — not among the crags — the *quiauhteocuitlatl* stone penetrates into the earth there. It is still very small when it falls; year by year it enlarges, it grows bigger.

And thus it comes to light; thus the inhabitants seek it: a single stalk of grass stands; it is visible on the surface as the grass-stalk of the *quiauhteocuitlatl* stone. When they dig it out, it is very thick — perhaps two spans thick — and two spans long. Some are merely round. And also it is to be drunk [by] those who are in good health, if one's heart flutters [or] when one has a headache.

It occurs in many places — Itztepec, Xalapa, Tlatlauhquitepec.

144

XIUHTOMOLTETL

It is a green stone. It appears very marvelous, mottled green and white; it is beautiful, desirable. It is

---

çan novian mochioa in mjlpan, aiac qujtoca: cequj achto mochioa, in aiamo ixoa toctli: cequj çatepan mochioa. in oiuh mochiuh tonacaiotl.

Nican ollatoqujlia, njcã moteneoa in cequj tetl in no patli.

.143.

QUJAUHTEUCUJTLATL:

vel tetl ieçe amo cenca tepitztic, iuhquj in teçontli: cenca etic, tliltic iztacacujcujltic, velic, amo chichic, amo necutic: çan iuhqujn chipaoacatl: amo moteci, çan mjchiquj, itla itech tetontli.

Itech monequj, in aqujn ipan tlatlatzinj, in juhquj itech qujneoa, in onontic âviac, itztic in atl ipan conj: ic tlachia, ic mozcalia. yoan ipaio in juhquj tlecomonj tonacaio: titic peoa, yõa no vel mjxnamjctia, in jtoca xiuhtomoltetl: conjz in aqujn ipã tlatlatzinj. No vel qujz in aqujn çan qujpiquj iollotlavelilocati; in tlapivia yiollopan alaoac: ic cevi, ceppa, anoço vppa in mjz.

In qujauhteucujtlatl, inic qujmati, in inchan mochioa: iuh qujmati in salapaneca.

In jquac tlatlatzini, in vmpa quauhtla, in tepepan: amo texcaltitlã, çan tlalpan: vncan calactivetzi in qujiauhteucujtlatl, çan oc tepiton in oalhuetzi: in cecexiuhtica, veia, mozcaltia:

auh injc neci, injc qujtemoa chaneque: çacatl, çan ce moquetza in jçacaio qujauhteucujtlatl, panj nezticac. In jquac qujtataca, cenca ie tomaoac, aço omjztitl, injc ie tomaoa, yoan viac, omjztitl; cequj çan ololtic, yõ no vel mjz in çan tipactinemj: intla cuecuechca toiollo, in tiquaivinti:

mieccan in mochioa: Itztepec, salapã, tlatlauhqujtepec.

.144.

XIUHTOMOLTETL:

chalchivitl, cenca maviztic injc neci, xoxoctic, iztac ic mocujcujlo, qualnezquj, teicolti çan no mjchiquj

also abraded against [another] stone. It tastes good. It cannot be ground up. It also counteracts the ailments mentioned above. It is to be drunk alone; it can also be mixed with the *quiauhteocuitlatl*. And also arm bracelets can be made of the *xiuhtomoltetl* [to wear] on account of ailments.

The turquoise comes from afar: Quauhtemalla, Xoconochco.

145

EZTETL, EZTECPATL

It is hard, mottled — some chili-red, some white, some herb green, some green, some yellow, some like gold, some a little black. The [colors] are within. And as if with crystal are [the colors] enveloped; all appear in as many places as they are distributed within, when they have been polished. [The color] is uniform at first; it is not beautiful.

It is required by one who passes blood from his nose or from his rectum. It is placed in his hand, or it is made into a necklace for him.

It occurs in far distant [places].

146

ATL CHIPIN

It is a stone, not very hard, just jagged, rough, like *tepetate*. However hard it is, it is just spongy. It is a scented, cold stone. It can be quickly ground. It can also be quickly scraped when necessary. It is required by one who is fevered, who has a fever within, when he is very sick of heart. Also it cleanses one's urine. Sometimes the water only drains from it; it is placed in water [and] this extract is drunk. And at this time one is to eat not very hot, just warm, food.

This *atl chipin* occurs in the crags; it is there all the time. It has its rock [on which it forms]. Thus does it occur: many [such stones] are laid out on the crags; like small hills are they set on; [like] little cones. They look indeed as if they were drops of dripping water.

They come especially there from Malinalco.

147

QUINAMETLI

These are the bones of the ancient people called giants. They are very thick, savory, heavy. Ground, they are required by one who passes blood, or from whose rectum comes a flux, who cannot find a remedy. He drinks it [in chocolate]. He mixes in

tetitech, velic amo vel moteci: çan no iehoatl qujnamjquj in cocolli in tlacpac omjto: vel mjxcaviz in mjz, no vel mjxnamjctia in qujauhteucujtlatl. yoã no vel nemacuextilo in xiuhtomoltetl, in jpampa cocoliztli:

vecca vallauh xiuhtomolli, quauhtemalla xoconochco.

.145.

EZTETL, EZTECPATL,

tlaquaoac: injc mocujcujlo, cequj chichiltic, cequj iztac, cequj qujltic, cequj xoxoctic, cequj coztic, cequj iuhquj in coztic teucujtlatl, cequj tliltotonti, in jtic catquj: yoan iuhqujn tevilotica qujmjliuhtica: mochi oalneci, in jzqujcã xeliuhtica, in jtic catquj: in jquac omopetlauh: çano cẽtetl in achtopa, amo qualnezquj.

Itech monequj in aqujn eztli qujnoquja in ijacac, anoço icujtlapãpa: imac motlalia, anoço qujmocozcatia.

Veca in mochioa.

.146.

ATL CHIPIN:

tetl, amo cenca tlaquaoac, çan tzatzamoltic, chachaquachtic, iuhquj in tepetlatl macivi in tlaquaoac, çan poxaoac, aviac, itztic tetl iciuhca vel moteci, no vel iciuhca mjchiquj, in jquac monequj. Itech monequj in aqujn motlevia, in totonquj itic nemj: in cenca mococoa in toiollo: no teaxixchipaoa, quẽmanjan çã aqujça, atlan motlalia: iehoatl mj in jaio: auh in jquac in amo cenca totonquj in moquaz, çan iamãquj in tlaqualli.

Inin atl chipin texcalco in mochioa, çan mochipa catquj: oncatquj itepeio: injc mochioa, mjec in texcaltitech momamana, iuhquj in tepetotonti, ic motlatlalia, quavitztoton: vel neci in juhquj valchichipintica.

vmpa cenca oallauh in malinalco.

.147.

QUJNAMETLI:

iehoatl in jmomjo ie huecauh tlaca, tlacaviaque motocaiotia: cenca titilaoac, ãviac, etic, moteci. Itech monequj, in aqujn eztli qujnoquja: anoço tlailli icujtlapampa qujça, in atle vel qujmonamjctia pâtli: iehoatl conj, qujneloa cacaoatl, mjcequj, yoã nextamalli,

roasted grains of cacao and tamales of maize softened with lime; all is ground together. In the way that chocolate is prepared, so also is [this] made.

148

OCELOT FLESH

Its flesh is bitter; it gives off a bad odor. It can be cooked in an olla; it can also be roasted hard; it can also be braised. It is salted. And one who is a widower, whose wife has died long ago, eats it in order that he will not suffer because of his thoughts regarding women; for it quiets his body which suffers much with regard to women.

And one who is possessed, who becomes as if deranged, eats it; thereby he recovers. And he who is fevered is to eat it when [the fever] begins. And the rulers consume a little of its broth, when it is cooked, in order to become courageous, as well as to gain honor. Its skin is burned, well carbonized, and its bones are ground; they are drunk. One who lives in vice, who just pretends to go from side to side, drinks it. When its hide, its bones, and its excrement are burned, they are ground together; then pine resin is mixed in. This is burned next to him who so becomes [vicious]. Thus he is affected by the incense.

149

CONYAYAUAL

They are small and cylindrical [worms]; some are deep black, some smoky black. Their legs are many, like the *petlaçolcoatl*. When it travels it goes straight; it goes along the surface of the ground. And when someone sees it, or someone stamps his feet at it, it quickly forms itself into a circle. No more does it move; also, no more does it puff up. It is as if dead.

It has a head; its mouth is like the mouth of a little serpent; it has little black eyes. The male has small antennae; the female is without its antennae. It only comes out, moves about in the summer, when already it rains. It burns like chili. Perhaps three, four, five, six are ground up [dry]. Pine resin is mixed in to make a poultice with feathers where there is gout. It is only spread on the surface. And for one whose teeth are decayed, it is mixed with lampblack; it is spread on the surface to cure.

It grows everywhere, in the fields, or in the mountains.

mocenteci: in juhquj cacaoatl moquetza, no iuh mochioa.

.148.

OCELOTL INACAIO:

in jnacaio, cococ, toquaiac, vel mopaoaci, no vel tepioaquj, no vel motleoatza, iztaio: qujqua in aqujn icnooqujchtli, in ie vecauh ocioamjc, injc amo cocoiez in jpampa itlalnamjqujliz in jtechpa cioatl: ca qujcevia in tonacaio, in cenca techtolinja itechpa cioatl.

Yoan in aqujn itech qujneoa, in juhquj loco mochioa qujqua ic pati. yoan in aquj̃ atonavi conquaz in jquac peoa. yoã in jaio in jquac icuci achi conjltequj in tlatoque, ic iolchicaoa, ic no maviçoa. In jeoaio motlatia: vel tecolti, yoan in iomjo moteci mj, conj in aqujn otlavelilot, in ça qujpiquj âvic iauh: in otlatlac iieoaio, in jomjo, yoan icujtl: mocenteci, çatepan ocotzotl moneloa, itlan tlatla in aqujn oiuh mochiuh, ic mopopochvia.

.149.

COIAIAOAL,

mjmjltontli: cequjntin vel tliltique, cequjntin ixtlilcujchectique: mjec in imma, in juhquj petlaçolcoatl: in jquac nenemj melaoatiuh, tlalli ixcoiatiuh: auh in jquac aca qujtta, anoço aca qujtlaticujnjlia, içiuhca moiaoallalitivetzi, aocmo molinia, aocmo no mopoçaoa: iuhqujnma omjc.

vnca itzontecon: in jten iuhqujn coatontli iten, in jxtelolotliltotonti: in oqujchtli, quaquauhtone: in cioatl, atle iquaquauh: çan iquac in qujça, in nenemj xopantla: iqua in ie qujavi: cocoiac, iuhqujn chilli; aço ie, navi, macujlli, chiquacen in moteci: ocotzotl moneloa. Iic mopotonja in canjn onoc coaciviztli: çan panj moteca. Auh in aqujn tlanqualo: tlilli moneloa, panj ommoteca; ic pati:

çã novian in nemj mjlpan, anoço tepepan.

Sweat Bath

When wood burns, it is very hot and not smoky; but when just rubbish burns, it has much smoke; also it heats little. But when it is not very hot, not much does it help the sick; it just gives the sick a headache. Those already cured enter there; there their bodies perspire; there their bodies, their nerves are as if relaxed.

Then one who has become pregnant, whose abdomen is already large, also enters there. There the midwives massage them; there they can place the babies straight in order that they will not extend crosswise nor settle face first. Two, three, four times they massage them there. And there those recently confined also bathe themselves; there, having delivered, having given birth, they strengthen their bodies. [The midwives] bathe them once, twice; and there they cleanse their breasts, that their milk will be good, and that they will produce a flow [of milk].

And the sick there restore their bodies, their nerves. Those who are as if faint with sickness are there calmed, strengthened. They are to drink one or another of the medicines, as has been mentioned. And one who perhaps has tripped and fallen, or who has fallen from a roof terrace; or someone has mistreated him — his nerves are shattered, he constantly goes paralyzed — they there make him hot. When he has endured the sweat bath, the body, the nerves are somewhat relaxed. There they manipulate him, they massage him. Once again, as [this] is done, he there becomes strong.

And one who has scabs, [one] whose body is much festered, [one] whose body is not [too] much covered with sores, they there have [such as these] wash. When the humor has come out, then they apply the medicine. And the pustules, their pustules, are there cleansed. The sweat bath is very hot.

¶

Sixth paragraph, in which are told all the different herbs.

Axocopac or Axocopaconi[1]

Its growing place is the forest. It tastes like fruit; its odor is sweet, its scent is dense.

Temazcalli:

in jquac quavitl tlatla, cenca vel totonje, yoan amo pocio: auh in jquac in çan tlaçolli tlatla, cenca pocioa, amo no cenca totonja. Auh in jquac amo cenca totonje: amo cenca qujnpalevia in cocoxque, çan qujntzonteconeoa in cocoxque, vncan calaquj in ie pati; vncan ihiioqujça in innacaio: vncan iuhqujn achi atic in innacaio, in intlalhoaio.

Ça no vncan calaquj in ootzti in ie vei imjti: vncan qujnpachoa in cioa temjxivitianj: vncã vel qujnmelaoacatlalia, in pipiltzitzinti, injc amo ixtlapal motecazque, amo no qujmjxnamjctimotlalizque: vppa, expa, nappa in vncan qujmpachoa. Auh in omjxiuhque no vncã motema, vncan chicaoa in innacaio injc ocaxan injc otlacachiuhque: ceppa, vppa in qujntema, yoã, vncan qujchipavilia in inchichioal; injc qualli iez, in inchichioalaiouh, yoan meiaz.

Auh in iehoantin cocoxque, vncã mjmati in innacaio, in intlalhoaio, in juhquj omjmjcca cocoliztica: vncan acovetzi, chicaoa: conjzque in çaço catleoatl patli in juh omoteneuh, yoan in aqujn aço omotlavitec, anoço otlapanco valhuetz, anoço aca oqujmjcti, in ocototzauh in jtlalhoaio, çan mochipa cepoatinemj: vncan qujtotonjlia: in jquac oqujma temazcalli, ca achi atic in tonacaio, in totlalhoaio: vncan caanjlia, qujpapachilhuja: oc ceppa iuhquj mochioa vncan chicaoa,

yoan in aqujn çaçaoati, in cenca papalanj inacaio, in amo cenca totoncaio inacaio, vmpa qujpaqujlia: in jquac oqujz chiaviztli, çatepan contequjlia patli, yoan in nanaoatl, vmpa mopaqujlia in innanaoauh cenca totonje in temazcalli.

¶

Injc chiquacen parrapho: itechpa mjtoa, in jxqujch nepapan xivitl.

Axocopac, anoço axocopaconj:

quauhtla imochiuhian xoxocovelic in jiaca tzopelic motetzaoaca inecuj.

<hr />

1. *Axocopac: Gualtheria acuminata* Schl. et Cham. (Santamaría, *Dic. de Mejicanismos*, p. 101).

Quauhxiuhtic[2]

It is tender, very tender. It is [a plant] from which water can be extracted. Its water is potable; it calms one, it gladdens one.

Mecaxochitl[3]

Its growing place is the hot lands, at the water's edge. It is like a slender cord, a little rough. It is of pleasing odor, perfumed. Its scent is dense; one's nose is penetrated. It is potable. It cures internal [ailments].

Ayauhtonan[4]

It is blue, exceedingly blue, very blue, like the lovely cotinga. It is like a sapling. [Its leaves] are small and round; it has small branches; it has blossoms. It is edible.

Tlalpoyomatli

[Its leaves are] smoke-[colored], each one smoky, ashen, soft; it is many-flowered. It is [a plant] from which an incense is made. It produces a pleasing odor; it produces a perfume. [Its incense] diffuses, spreads over the whole land.

Yiauhtli[5]

It is herb-green; it has stalks; the branches are stiff, rigid. It is an ejector of humors, a medicine; it expels the flux. One is to drink it in chocolate. [The herb] is to be roasted first. In the same way when one spits blood, [and] in the same way when one is fevered, it helps, it cures one.

Uitzitzilxochitl[6]

It is of pleasing odor, perfumed.

Ocoxochitl[7]

[The branches] are rope-like; some are drooping. It is herb-green, with cherry-like fruit. Its growing place is in the forest. It spreads well over the surface; it spreads perfuming, diffusing [its odor].

Iztauhyatl[8]

It has stalks; they are straight. It is ashen. It has spikelets. It is bitter, very bitter, surpassingly bitter.

Quauhxiuhtic,

ceceltic, cecelpatic, aqujxtilonj; ioanj in jaio, teiamanja, teiolpaqujltia.

Mecasuchitl:

tonaian imochiuhian, atenco: iuhqujn mecapitzaoac, chachaquachpipil, velic, aviac, motetzaoaca inecuj, teiacaxelo: ivanj: tlapatia in titic.

Aiauhtonan.

texotic, texocaltic, tetexotic, xiuhtototic iuhqujn quauhconepil malacachtontli, mamaecapil, cuecueponquj, qualonj.

Tlalpoiomatli:

pochqujo, popochqujo, nexeoac, iaiamanquj, xoxochio, yietlalchioalonj velia, âviaia, molonj, centlalmotoca.

Iiauhtli,

qujltic, tlatlacotic, mamapichtic, mamapichauhquj, aioqujçanj, patli: in tlaelli qujtlaça, conjz, cacaoatl ipan, achtopa mjcequjz: no iuhquj in eztli qujchicha: no iuhquj in atonavi, tlapalevia, tepatia.

Vitzitzilsuchitl

velic, aviac.

Ocoxochitl,

memecatic, cequj chachpactic, qujltic, cacapollo: quauhtla imochiuhia, vel ixtoc, aviaxtoc, molontoc.

Iztauhiatl,

tlatlacotic, memelaoac, nexeoac, mjaoaio, chichic, chichipatic chichipalalatic.

---

2. *Quauhxiuhtic: Elaphrium multiugum, E. odoratum* (Sahagún, Garibay ed., Vol. IV, p. 350).

3. *Mecaxochitl: Vanilla planifolia, V. flagrans* (*ibid.*, p. 342); *Piper* sp. (Hernández, *Hist. de las Plantas*, Vol. III, p. 751).

4. *Cuphea jorullensis* H. B. K. (§ 4, n. 20, *supra*).

5. *Tagetes lucida* (§ 5, n. 11, *supra*).

6. *Uitzitzilxochitl: Loeselia coccinea* Don. (Sahagún, *op. cit.*, p. 337); *Toluifera pereirae* (Klotz.) in Hernández, *op. cit.*, Vol. II, p. 558.

7. *Ocoxochitl*: prob. *Didymea mexicana* Benth. (Sahagún, *op. cit.*, p. 347).

8. *Artemisia mexicana* Willd. (§ 5, n. 65, *supra*).

Itztonquauitl

It is of pleasing odor, perfumed.

Epaçotl[9]

Its spikelets are long and slender. It is edible, [a plant] which serves to improve [food]. It is that which can be made into a sauce; it is sauce-producing.
I put *epaçotl* in the sauce.

Azpan Xiuitl

It has stalks; it is straight; it has stems, spikelets; it is bitter. It is a medicine for rubbing the face, a medicine for softening the face.
I wash my face with *azpan*.

Tlalquequetzal[10]

Its leaves, its branches are ashen, spreading, serrated. It is a cough medicine; it is a medicine for overeating.

Itzcuinpatli[11]

It has stalks, spikelets. It is very bitter.

Itztonquauitl

It is a medicine, [a plant] which may be drunk [in water]. It cures internal [ailments]; it aids one's digestion.

¶

Seventh paragraph, which telleth of still other herbs, which are called grasses.

Çacayaman, çacayamanqui

It is soft, fluffy. Its growing place is at the water's edge; in damp places. It lies shining; it is thick; it lies fluffed.

Çacanoualli[1]

It is the same as *çacayaman;* however, it is rough, strong. It is required[2] everywhere. It is necessary to prepare mud for adobes.
I add *çacanoualli*[3] to the mud.

Tequixquiçacatl

Its growing place is in saltpeter, in ashes, in ashen soil, or in ash heaps. It is coarse, rough, dagger-like. It bites one, it pricks one.

Itztonquavitl,

vevelic, âaviac in jiaca.

Epaçotl,

piaztontli; in jmjiaoaio, qualonj, tlavelililonj, molchioalonj, mololonj:

njquepaçoiotia in molli.

Azpan xivitl,

tlatlacotic, melaoac, qujioio, mjiaoaio, chichic, ixteteçonavilizpatli, ixaapalleoalizpatli;

ic njnjxamja in azpan.

Tlalquequetzal,

nexeoac, xexeltic, tzatzaianquj, in jma, in jxiuhio: tlatlacizpatli, nexvitilizpatli.

Itzcujnpatli,

tlatlacotic, mjiaoaio, chichipalalatic,

Itztonquavitl:

patli, ivanj, tlapatia in titic, tetlatemovilia.

¶

Inic chicome parrapho: itechpa tlatoa, in oc cequj xivitl in moteneoa çacatl.

Çacaiaman, çacaiamanquj,

iamanquj, pâçolpil, atenco, tlaciaoaian imochiuhian, pepetoc, popotzavi, popoçontoc.

Çacanovalli,

can no iehoatl in çacaiaman; ieçe chamaoac, chicaoac: novian nequjzço, moneneccaio, ic çoqujpololonj:
njcçacanaoallotia in çoqujtl.

Tequjxqujçacatl:

tequjxqujpa nexpan, nextlalpan imochiuhian, anoço nextlatilco: chamactic, vapactic, coiolomjtic, tequaqua, tetzotzopotza.

---

9. *Epaçotl: Chenopodium ambrosioides* Linn. (Sahagún, *op. cit.*, p. 335).

10. *Tlalquequetzal:* prob. *Achillea millifolia* L. (*ibid.*, p. 363); *Polypodium lanceolatum* L. (Hernández, *op. cit.*, p. 338).

11. *Itzcuinpatli: Senecio canicida* (Sahagún, *op. cit.*, p. 338).

1. *Çacanoualli: Andropogon* sp. (Sahagún, Garibay ed., Vol. IV, p. 372).

2. *Acad. Hist. MS: nequizyo.*

3. *Ibid.: nicçacanovallotia.*

ÇACAMAMAZTLI

Also its name is *teocalçacatl*. It has stems, it has spikelets; [the spikelets] are like amaranth. Its foliage is slender, long, spreading, embracing. It is material of which houses are made. It fluffs up, spreads out, embraces.

I make myself a hut of *çacamamaztli*, of *teocalçacatl*.

UAUHÇACATL

It has no stems. It is slender. It has spikelets; [these] are like amaranth. For this reason is it called *uauhçacatl*: it has many seeds, much like amaranth. And its special attribute is to cover the plots seeded with amaranth.

XIUHTECUÇACATL

It has stems, leaves, stalks, grass blades. It is ruddy; hence is it called *xiuhtecuçacatl*.

ÇACATETEZTLI[4]

It lies scattered in small clumps. It is a little white. [Its growing place is in the poor lands.][5] Wherever it lies, it is a sign that the land is not good.

ELOÇACATL

It is fresh green, each one fresh green, very fresh green; it is soft.

OCOÇACATL

It is slender, long, blue — turquoise. It can be used for houses.

I begin, I make myself a hut with *ocoçacatl*.

AXALLI

It is small and slender, thin, hollow. Its growing place is in the water, at the water's edge.

CALTOLI[6]

It is triangular, cylindrical, pointed at the end, long, pithy within. It is the real food of animals, especially of horses. Its roots are cord-like, asperous. The name of the asperous places is *acateuitzatl*. It is edible, sweet. Its growing place is in the water.

ITZTOLIN[7]

It is triangular, stalky, cylindrical — like a cylinder. It has blossoms; its blossoms are spreading. Its root

ÇACAMAMAZTLI,

yoan itoca teucalçacatl: qujioio, mjiaoaio, vauhio: in jxiuhio pipiaztic, viviac, chachaiactic, mamalcochauhquj: necaltilonj, popoçonj, chachaiaoa, mamalcochavi;

njcnoxacaltia, in çacamamaztli in teucalçacatl.

VAUHÇACATL:

amo qujllo pipiaztic, mjmjaoaio, vavauhio: injc mjtoa, vauhçacatl: cenca xinachio, cenca vauhio, yoan vel inemac, injc motlapachoa vauhtectli.

XIUHTECUÇACATL:

qujllo, atlapale, tlacoio, çacaio, tlatlactic: injc mjtoa xiuhtecuçacatl.

ÇACATETEZTLI:

chapactontli, tetezpil: [in canin amo q̃lcã tlalpã ymochiuhya] in canjn onoc, inezca ca amo qualli in tlalli.

ELOÇACATL,

çeceltic, cecelpatic, celpatic, iamanquj.

OCOÇACATL,

pitzaoac, viac, texocaltic, ximmaltic, necaltilonj:

ocoçacatl njcnotlapeoaltia, njcnoxacaltia.

HAXALLI,

pitzaton, piaztic. iticoionquj: atlan atenco imochiuhian.

CALTOLI,

excampa nacace, mjmjltic, iacavitztic, viac, itipochinquj, vel intlaqual in iolque, oc cenca iehoantin in cavallos: in jnelhoaio, memecatic, tetecujtztic: in jtetecujtzauhca, itoca, acatevitzatl: qualonj, tzopelic, atlan imochiuhian.

ITZTOLIN,

excampa nacace, tlacotic mjmjltic, mjmjliuhquj, xochio: manquj in jxochio: in jnelhoaio patli: ivanj,

---

4. *Çacateteztli: Panicum* sp. (Sahagún, *loc. cit.*).
5. *Acad. Hist. MS* contains a statement (here in brackets) missing in the *Florentine Codex*.
6. *Caltoli: Cyperus* sp. (Sahagún, *op. cit.*, p. 325).
7. *Itztolin: Cyperus* sp. (Hernández, *op. cit.*, Vol. II, p. 400).

is a medicine; it is to be drunk; one who is fevered drinks it.

TOLPATLACTLI[8]

It is wide, long — each blade is long. It has stems, spikes; it is fuzzy. The name of its fruit [spike] is *tomioli*; when it has become firm, its name is *tolcapotl*. The name of its root is *acaxilotl*; it is edible, it can be cooked in an olla.

TOLMIMILLI[9]

It is long, green, blue, very blue, pithy within. It is like a stone pillar. The tip is slender, the base wide. The base is white. The name of its white base is *aztapili* or *oztopili*.

PETLATOLLI[10]

It is cylindrical, pithy within — a material for mat-making.

I make mats with the [*petla*]*tolli* reed.

NACACE TOLIN[11]

It is the same as the *petlatoli*. However, it is strong, hard, triangular.

TOLIAMAN[12]

Also its name is *atolin*. It is not strong; it can be shredded. It is reducible to many parts.

I make mats of *toliaman*, of *atolin*.

TOLNACOCHTLI

It is slender, small and stubby, solid, compact, tough, pithy within. It is mat-making material, yellow of surface. The surface is yellow, shiny, slippery.

XOMALI OR XOMALLI[13]

It is green, slender, thin — thin in all parts, stringy, compact — very compact, quite tawny.

I pull up rushes.

ATETETZON

It is small and cylindrical, small and stubby. It grows in the water.

ACACAPACQUILITL[14]

It grows in the water. It is hollow; it has stems, blossoms.

conj in aqujn motlevia.

TOLPATLACTLI.

patlaoac, viac, viviac, qujioio, tolcapoio, tomjlollo, tomjiollo: in jtlaaqujllo, itoca tomjoli; in ochicaoac, itoca, tolcapotl, in jnelhoaio itoca, acaxilotl: qualonj, paoaxonj.

TOLMJMJLLI,

viac, xoxoctic, texotic, texocaltic, hitipochinquj, temjmjltic, quapitzaoac, tzintomaoac, tziniztac: in jtzin in iztac, itoca aztapili, anoço oztopili.

PETLATOLLI,

mjmjltic, itipochinquj, petlachioalonj:

njcpetlachioa in tolli

NACACE TOLI;

çan no iehoatl in petlatoli, iece chicaoac, vapaoac, excampa nacace.

TOLIAMAN,

yoan itoca, atoli; amo chicaoac, xaqualtic, papaiacanj:

nicpetlachioa in toliama in atoli.

TOLNACOCHTLI,

piaztontli, tetepontontli, pipinquj, pipictic, tlaquaoac, itipochinquj; petlachioalonj, ixcoztic, ixcoçauhquj, petic alaztic.

XOMALI, ANOÇO XOMALLI,

xoxoctic, piaztic, pitzaoac, pipitzaoac, tlalhoatic, pipictic, pipicpatic, vel coiovatic:

njxomalpi.

ATETETZON,

mjmjltotonti, tetepõtontli, atlan mochioa.

ACACAPACQUJLITL:

atlan in mochioa, iticoionquj, qujllo, xoxochio.

---

8. *Tolpatlactli: Cyperus* sp. (Sahagún, *op. cit.*, p. 359).
9. *Tolmimilli: Cyperus* sp. (*loc. cit.*).
10. *Petlatolli: Cyperus* sp. (*ibid.*, p. 349).
11. *Nacace tolin: Cyperus* sp. (*ibid.*, p. 344).
12. *Toliaman: Cyperus* sp. (*ibid.*, p. 359).
13. *Xomali: Cyperus* sp. (*ibid.*, p. 370)
14. *Acacapacquilitl: Aganippea bellidiflora* D.C. (*ibid.*, p. 319).

AMAMALACOTL[15] OR AMALACOTL[16]

The foot [the stem] is long and slender, [the leaf] round. It is herb-green, the color of herbs.

ACAÇACATL[17]

It resembles reeds. It is slender, thin, leafy, prickly, cutting. It bites one, cuts one, rips one.

ATLACOTL[18]

It is slender; it has blossoms.

ACHILLI[19]

It is cord-like. Its leaves, its stalks are ruddy. They are small and straight.

ACATL[20]

It is hollow, jointed, pithy within, leafy. It has leaves [which are] green. It breaks the flesh, seizes the flesh.

OCOPETLATL[21]

It resembles a hand. The branches are serrated, green, very green, outstretching.

QUAMMAMAXTLA

ÇACATL[22]

It is the common name of grass, of the herbs, when dried; not the stalk.

TETZMOLIN[23]

It is smooth, green. Its leaves, its shoots are fibrous, tough, firm, very firm.

QUAUICHPOLLI

TEQUEQUETZAL[24]

It is like the *tlalquequetzal*. It is serrated. Its leaves, its branches glisten.

AMAMALACOTL, ANOÇO AMALACOTL,

xopiaztic, ixiaiaoaltic, qujltic, qujlpalli.

ACAÇACATL:

macanenequj, pitzaton, piaztic, izvaio, havaio, tetec, tequaqua, tetequj, tetoxoma.

ATLACOTL,

pipiaztic, xoxochio.

ACHILI,

memecatic, tlatlavic in iamatlapal, in jqujllo memelacpil.

ACATL,

iticoionquj, iixe, itipochqujo, izoaio, amatlapale, xoxouhquj; nacapoztequj, nacacuj.

OCOPETLATL,

macpantic, matzatzaianquj, xoxoctic, xoxocaltic, mamaçouhquj.

QUAMMAMAXTLA.

ÇACATL;

icentoca çacatl in xivitl in ovac, in amo tlacotl.

TETZMOLIN,

tzotzotlactic, celtic, in jamatlapal in jqujllo tlalichtic, tlaquaoac, tlaquactic, tlaquacpatic.

QUAVICHPOLLI.

TEQUEQUETZAL:

iuhqujn tlalquequetzal, tzatzaiactic: in jma in jqujllo, cuecueiaoa.

---

15. *Amamalacotl: Hydrocotyle ranunculoides* Linn., *Bryophyllum* sp. (Hernández, *Hist. de las Plantas*, Vol. II, pp. 371–372).

16. *Amalacotl: Solidago paniculata* (Sahagún, *op. cit.*, p. 320).

17. *Acaçacatl: familia de trídeas* (Santamaría, *Dic. de Mejicanismos*, p. 18).

18. *Atlacotl: Aster* sp. (*ibid.*, p. 94).

19. *Achilli: Polygonum acre, P. hydropiper* (Sahagún, *op. cit.*, p. 320).

20. *Acatl: Pragmites communis* Trin. (*ibid.*, p. 319).

21. *Ocopetlatl: Cyathea mexicana* Ch. and Sch. (Santamaría, *op. cit.*, p. 767).

22. *Çacatl:* generic term for a number of *Gramineae* and some of the *Cyperaceae* (*ibid.*, p. 1139: *zacate*).

23. *Tetzmolin: Quercus fusiformis* Smal. (*ibid.*, p. 1039: *tesmol*).

24. *Tequequetzal: Selaginella lepidofila, S. pilifera,* and others, according to Sahagún, *op. cit.*, p. 356: *tetequetzal; Adiantum* suggested as possible for a *tequequetzal* in Hernández, *Hist. de las Plantas*, Vol. II, p. 340 (see also p. 339).

Teyiauhtli

It is *yiauhtli* which grows among the rocks. They say it resembles *yiauhtli*.

Tlalcapoli[25]

Iuintiquilitl

Acocoxiuitl[26]

Tlalyetl[27]

Tonalxiuitl[28]

It is ashen green, hard, tough, small and drooping. It is called *tonalxiuitl* because it becomes green, it blossoms in the summer.

Xoxotla

It is a creeper, light green, ashen green. It is called *xoxotla* because its blossom is chili-red, just like a flame.

Tzompachquilitl
Tetzitzilin or tetzitzili

It is cord-like. It is [a plant] which shoots out; a climber, a creeper, which sends out feelers; a bloomer, a blossomer. Its fruit is very prickly, full of spines. It bites one.

The *tetzitzilin* pricks me.

Nopalocoxochitl

It creeps. It is the same as the *ocoxochitl*.

Memeyal[29]

It is a small herb, oozing, [issuing] a liquid. When it is slightly cut milk comes from it.

Tzacutli[30]

The branches are slender. It has stems. Its root is sticky; this is named *tzacutli*. It is an adhesive.

I glue it.

Tlaltzacutli[31]

¶

Eighth paragraph, which telleth of blossom petals and of stalks.

Teiiauhtli:

intechalpan mochioa yiauhtli: qujtoa, itlatla in jiauhtli.

Tlalcapoli.

Ivintiqujlitl.

Acocoxivitl.

Tlalietl.

Tonalxivitl

cujtlanextic, iollotetl, iollotlapali, chapactõtli: injc mjtoa tonalxivitl, iquac in tonalco, xoxovia, in cueponj.

Xoxotla

movivilananj, ihiztaqujltic, cujtlanextic: injc mjtoa xoxotla, chichiltic, in jxochio velletic.

Tzompachqujlitl.
Tetzitzilin, anoço tetzitzili,

memecatic, motlamjnanj, movicomanj, movivicomanj, moiaiacatlaçanj, xotlanj, cueponjnj, in jcacapollo vel havaio, moca havatl, tequaqua:

nechavavia in tetzitzilin.

Nupalocoxochitl,

movivilana, qujnenevilia in ocoxochitl.

Memeial,

xiuhtontli, memeiallo, aio; in achi mocotona, chichioallaiotl in jtech qujça.

Tzacutli,

mapipitzaoac, qujioio in jnelhoaio, çaçalic: iehoatl in motocaiotia tzacutli, tlaçalolonj: njctzacuvia.

Tlaltzacutli.

¶

Injc chicuei parrapho: itechpa tlatoa suchitl in jxiuhio, in joan quauhio.

25. *Tlalcapoli:* prob. *Rhamnus serrata* or *Karwinskia humboldtiana* (Sahagún, *op. cit.*, p. 362).
26. *Acocoxiuitl: Arracacia atropurpurea trifida* or *Dahlia coccinea* Cav. (§ 5, n. 44, *supra*).
27. *Tlalyetl: Cunila* sp. (Sahagún, *op. cit.*, p. 363); *Erigeron scaposus* D.C. (§ 5, n. 59, *supra*).
28. *Tonalxuitl: Stevia salicifolia* Cav. or *Veronica americana* Swed. (Sahagún, *op. cit.*, p. 359).
29. *Memeyal: Euphorbia* sp. (*ibid.*, p. 342: *memeya*).
30. *Tzacutli: Epidendron pastoris* L.H. (*ibid.*, p. 365).
31. *Tlaltzacutli: Sphaeralcea angustifolia* (Hernández, *op. cit.*, Vol. II, p. 382).

OMIXOCHITL,[1] OR WHITE OMIXOCHITL, OR COLORED OMIXOCHITL

Its foliage is spreading, slender, thin. It has stems, it has stalks; it is fragrant, perfumed. It is pleasing to the soul, satisfying.

TLALIZQUIXOCHITL

It is drooping, creeping. Its blossoms are white. It is fragrant, very fragrant; its odor becomes dense.

TLILXOCHITL[2]

It is cord-like; it is like the *tetzitzili*. Its bean is green, but it is black when dried; wherefore it is called *tlilxochitl*. It is perfumed, fragrant, precious, good, potable; a medicine. Roasted, this is mixed with chocolate.

I add *tlilxochitl* to the chocolate; I drink it with *tlilxochitl* added.

COÇAUHQUI XOCHITL OR COÇAUHQUI YIEXOCHITL

The branches are yellow; its foliage is dark yellow. Its blossoms are fragrant, perfumed. It makes one contented; it is agreeable.

CHALCHIUHYIEXOCHITL

Its stems are long, its blossoms green; wherefore it is called *chalchiuhyiexochitl*.

THE QUAUHYIEXOCHITL is the same.

TZOYAC

It is just an ordinary *yiexochitl*. It is not of pleasing odor. It comes last. It emits a fetid odor.

TONALXOCHITL[3]

It is small and slender. It is called *tonalxochitl* because it grows in dry ground. And when the sun becomes hot it sprouts, becomes verdant, blossoms. But it only blossoms when the sun has set. Its scent is very fragrant, well perfumed. It blooms constantly, glistens, produces a perfume, produces a pleasing odor.

TLALCACALOXOCHITL[4]

It is without foliage. It is right on the ground when in blossom. It is chili-red, just like the *cacalo-*

OMJSUCHITL, AÇO IZTAC OMJSUCHITL, ANOÇO TLAPALOMJSUCHITL;

xexeltic in jqujllo, pipitzaoac, pipiaztic: qujioio, tlacoio, velic, aviac, teiolqujma, teiolpachiviti.

TLALIZQUJSUCHITL;

chachapãquj, vilanquj, iztac in jsuchio, velic, vel patic, motetzaoaca inecuj.

TLILSUCHITL,

memecatic, tetzitziltic, xoxoctic in jexoio: auh in ooac tliltic; ic mjtoa. tlilsuchitl, aviac, velic, tlaçotli, qualli, ivanj, patli, mjcequj; inin cacaoatl moneloa:

njctlilsuchivia in cacaoatl, tlilsuchio njquj.

COÇAUHQUJ SUCHITL, ANOÇO COÇAUHQUJ YIESUCHITL,

macoztic: in jxiuhio, coziaiactic, in jsuchio, velic, aviac, tetlamachti, tzopelic.

CHALCHIUHYIESUCHITL;

viviac, in jtlacoio: xoxoctic in jsuchio: injc mjtoa: chalchiuhyiesuchitl

QUAUHYIESUCHITL: çan ie no iehoatl.

TZOIAC:

çaçan ie yiesuchitl, amo velic; tlatoqujlia, tzoiaia.

TONALSUCHITL:

piaztontli: injc mjtoa tonalsuchitl, tlalhoacpa in mochioa: auh iquac in vel tonaltzitzica ixoa, in celia, in cueponj: auh ça qujn iquac, in oonac tonatiuh, cueponj; vel velic, in jiaca, vel aviac: cuecuepoca, tlatlatzca, aviaia, velia.

TLALCACALOSUCHITL,

amo xiuhio: çan njmã tlallampa in cueponquj: chichiltic, vel iuhquj in cacalosuchitl: çan nentlacatl,

---

1. *Omixochitl: Polianthes tuberosa, P. mexicana* (Sahagún, Garibay ed., Vol. IV, p. 347).

2. *Tlilxochitl: Vanilla planifolia (ibid.,* p. 365).

3. *Tonalxochitl: Pithecoctenium echinatum* Jac. (Santamaría, *op. cit.,* 1071, 1072); *Bletia coccinea* La Llave & Lex. or *Epidendrum vitellinum* Lindl. (Hernández, *op. cit.,* Vol. II, p. 376).

4. *Tlalcacaloxochitl:* prob. *Plumeria acutifolia* (Sahagún, *op. cit.,* p. 362).

xochitl, but useless, without fragrance, without perfume. It disappoints one, constantly disappoints one; one is frustrated, constantly frustrated. Its flower is without perfume.[5]

Totec ixoxochiuh

It is the same as the *tlalcacaloxochitl*.

Texoxoli

Its stems are slender, straight; its blossom is chili-red; [its odor] disappoints one. Its bulb is well joined together; many are its coverings. So it is said of one who covers himself well, who wraps himself: "He is a *texoxoli*."

Nopallacotl

It likewise[6] grows among the *nopal*. Its blossom is rose-colored.

Tolcimatl

Its foliage is the creeping kind. Its blossom is chili-red. It is very delicate, coveted, desirable, constantly desired, constantly required though lacking fragrance.

Caxtlatlapan[7]

Its foliage is cord-like; its leaves are round. Some of its blossoms are white, some chili-red, some blue. They are cylindrical at the base, whorl-shaped at the top. Its tendrils are soft, tender, searching, delicate like greens.

Quaztalxochitl

It does not have thick foliage. Its foliage just emerges from the ground. It has stems. Its blossom is white like maguey fibre; hence it is called, it is given the name *quaztalxochitl*. It glistens; it spreads.

Tlaquili

It is [also] called *teotlaquili*. It is like a spindle whorl; it has branches; it is shady. Its leaves, its butterfly-shaped leaves, are herb-green. Its blossoms are white, yellow, chili-red, pale, striped. Its center is not large. It easily falls to pieces.[8]

Acocoxochitl[9]

Its foliage emerges from the ground. Its foliage, its stems are ruddy. They are hollow. Its blossoms are

acan velic, acan âviac, tenenco, tenenenco, tenencoa, tenenencoa: in suchitl acan aviac.

Totec isusuchiuh:

çan ie no iehoatl in tlalcacalosuchitl.

Texoxoli;

pipiaztic, memelactic in jqujllo: chichiltic in jsuchio; tenenco. In jtzinteio vel nenepantic, vel mjec in jqujmjliuhca. Ic ipan mjtoa, in aqujn mjec qujmololoa, qujmoquentia: ie ontexoxoli.

Nupallacutl;

çan no nupaltitlan in mochioa: in jsuchio tlaztaleoaltic.

Tolcimatl:

in jxiuhio, movilananj: in jcueponca, chichiltic, cecelpatic, teicolti, tetlanecti, eheleviliztli, nenequjztli iece atle ivelica.

Caxtlatlapan,

memecatic, in jxiuhio, in jatlapal, iaiaoaltic in jsuchio: cequj iztac, cequj chichiltic, cequj movitic, tzinmjmjltic, quamalacachtic, aiollotlaquaoac, aiollotlapalivi, aiachi in jcocol, chinequjztli, iuhqujn qujlitl.

Quaztalsuchitl,

amo qujllotilaoac, çan tlallampa in oalqujztimanj iqujllo, qujioio in jsuchio iztac, iuhqujn ichtli ic mjtoa, motocaiotia in quaztalsuchitl: cuecueiaoa, xexelivi.

Tlaqujli:

mitoa, teutlaqujli malacachtic, mamae cecevallo ecauhio in jatlapal, in jpapaloio: qujlpalli, in jsuchio iztac coztic, chichiltic, tlaztaleoaltic, vavavanquj, amo vei in jiollo, aiovi patic.

Acocosuchitl,

tlallampa valeoa in jqujllo in jqujioio tlatlavic iticoionquj, in jsuchio xexeltic, pipitzaoac, mamatzaian-

---

5. *Acad. Hist. MS: acā iiac.*

6. *Ibid.: ça yyo.*

7. *Caxtlatlapan: Ipomoea* sp.; *Convolvulus japala* (Sahagún, *op. cit.*, p. 326).

8. *Acad. Hist. MS: pati.*

9. *Acocoxochitl: Dahlia coccinea* Cav. (Hernández, *Hist. de las Plantas*, Vol. I, p. 24); in the *Acad. Hist. MS* it is *acaxochitl: Lobelia fulgens* Willd., *L. laxiflora* H.B.K. (Hernández, *op. cit.*, pp. 94 *sqq.*).

spreading, slender. The leaves are serrated; they are chili-red, very chili-red.

Cempoalxochitl[10]

Its foliage is jagged; the leaf is serrated. It is yellow.

The female cempoalxochitl is the large one.

The male cempoalxochitl is the small one; there is just a single flower.

The macuilxochitl[11] [variety of] *cempoalxochitl* is the color of yellow ochre. It is pale.

Coçatli

It is quite small. There is just a single flower. It grows in the mountains.

Tecacayactli

It also belongs among the *cempoalxochitl*. It is ruddy.

Nextamalxochitl[12]

It has an ashen stalk. Its blossom is blue.

Chilpan[13]

It is small and stalky. Its blossoms are chili-red; they just stand, following along its stem, each one hanging, resting in order.

Cacalacaxochitl[14]

¶

Ninth paragraph, which telleth of the same blossoms, of [their] somewhat large trees.

The flower garden

It freshens things. It germinates, germinates in all places; it becomes green. It makes things lovely; it makes things lovely in all places. It spreads pleasingly; it extends pleasingly. It spreads blossoming; it blossoms, blossoms constantly; it spreads constantly blossoming, extending its flowers. In the flower garden things spread growing; they spread without stint.

[The plants] stand in water; they spread emerging from the water. They are watered, sprinkled.

qui, chichiltic chilpatzcaltic.

Cempoalsuchitl,

tzitziqujltic in jxiuhio, matzatzaianquj coztic.

Civasuchitl, cempoalsuchitl iehoatl in vevej

Oqujchsuchitl: cempoalsuchitl iehoatl in tepitoton çan ce yix.

Macujlsuchitl, cempoalsuchitl iehoatl in teçonauhquj, iztaleoac.

Coçatli,

çan tepitoton, çan çe ijx tepepan in muchioa.

Tecacaiactli,

çan no cempoalsuchitl itech povi, tlatlauhquj.

Nextamalsuchitl,

nextic in jqujllo, movitic in jsuchio.

Chilpan,

tlacotontli: in jsuchio chichiltic, çan qujtocaticac in jquauhio pipilcac, tecpantoc.

Cacalacasuchitl.

¶

Injc chicunavi parrapho: itechpa tlatoa in çan no iehoatl suchitl, in achi vei quavitl.

In suchitla,

tlacecelia, tlatzmolinj, tlatlatzmolinj, tlaxoxovia, tlavelia, tlavevelia, tlavevelixtoc, tlavevelixtimanj, tlacuecuepontoc, tlacueponj, tlacuecuepoca, tlacuecuepocatoc, tlasuchimamanj, suchitlalpan, tlamochiuhtoc, tlacẽquiztoc,

atl icac, atl qujqujztoc, tlaciaoa, tlaciciaoa,

10. *Cempoalxochitl: Tagetes erecta* L. (Sahagún, *op. cit.,* p. 326).

11. *Macuilxochitl: Tagetes canulata* (*ibid.,* p. 340).

12. *Nextamalxochitl: Ranunculus petiolaris* H.B.K. (*ibid.,* p. 346).

13. *Chilpan:* prob. *Pentstemon campanulatus* (Cav.) Willd. (Hernández, *op. cit.,* Vol. III, p. 832).

14. *Cacalacaxochitl: Plumeria rubra* L., *P. bicolor* R. and P., *P. acutifolia* Poir (Santamaría, *op. cit.,* p. 170); *Crotalaria eriocarpa* Benth. (Hernández, *op. cit.,* Vol. II, p. 658).

It is a very good place, a reedy place,[1] a desirable place, desirable in all places, a sought-for place, a constantly sought place, a coveted place, a joyous place, a desirable place.

BLOSSOMS WHICH GROW ON TREES

The blossoming trees are like stone columns. They are big trees. They are branching, forked in different places, round. They are round trees. The buds swell, burst, blossom; they produce a pleasing odor, a fragrance.

YOLLOXOCHIQUAUITL[2]

Its name is also *yolloxochitl*. It is slender, long, tall —a large tree, like a stone column. It has branches. On its surface its bark, its scales are black, dark, dusky. Its leaves are straight, slender, smooth, shiny.

The name of its blossom is *yolloxochitl*. It is white, thick, cylindrical, like a heart, like a bird's egg. The name of the large one is *tlacayolloxochitl*; it is dark colored. The name of the small one is *itzcuinyolloxochitl*.

This *yolloxochitl* is of pleasing odor, fragrant, aromatic. Its scent is dense. It is leafed; it has leaves, a center, seeds. And it is potable in chocolate. It alleviates the fever; it is a fever medicine. Where there is swelling, when there has been fever, there it is placed; it is rubbed on. It gives things a pleasing odor, makes things fragrant, spreads an aroma; it produces a pleasing odor, a fragrance. It alleviates; it cures. It breaks, bursts, opens [sores].

ELOXOCHITL, ELOXOCHIQUAUITL[3]

It is round, branching, pale, ashen. Its leaves are fuzzy like those of the *topoçan*. Its stems are wide, long. The name of its fruit is *eloxochitl*; it has its husk, its center, its seed, the flower. Its husks are slender, long, yellow—yellow-surfaced, pale; its seeds are small and cylindrical, slender; its center is round, round and small. It is aromatic, pleasing of odor; its aroma, its fragrance, its odor, is dense. It is potable [in chocolate]; just a little [is used]. When much is drunk, it takes effect; it intoxicates, deranges, disturbs one.

I cut flowers; I continue to cut flowers. I inhale then scent.

vel qualcan, vel ieccan, vel tolla, tetlanectican, tetlatlanectican, teicoltican, teihicoltican, icolocan, tetlamachtican, tetlanectican.

QUAVITL SUCHITL ITECH MOCHIOA.

Suchiquavitl, temjmjltic, vei quavitl, mamae, mamaxallo, iaoaltic, quauhiaoalli, totomolivi, xotla, cueponj, velia, aviaia.

IOLLOSUCHIQUAVITL,

yoan itoca iollosuchitl, piaztic, viac, veiac, vei quavitl, temjmjltic mamae: in jpan jeoaio, in jxincaio, catzaoac, iaiactic, iaiauhquj: in jatlapal memelactic, memelaoac, ixtzotzotlaca, ixtzotzotlanj.

In jsuchio itoca iollosuchitl, iztac, tomaoac, mjmjltic: iuhqujn iollotli, iuhqujn totoltetl: in tomaoac itoca tlacaiollosuchitl, tlapalpoiaoac. in çan tepiton, itoca: itzcujniollosuchitl.

Inin iollosuchitl velic, aviac, hiiac, motetzaoaca inecuj, izoaio, amatlapale, iollo, achio. auh ivanj, cacaoatl ipan: qujcevia in totonquj, totoncapatli, in canjn poçaoa in totoncavilo; vncan ommotlalia, ommalaoa, tlaavialia, tlavelilia, hiiaia, velia, âviac, tlacevia, tlapatia: tlatzinj, cueponj, xelivi.

ELOSUCHITL, ELOSUCHIQUAVITL,

malacachtic, mamae, ticeoac, cujtlanextic: in jamatlapal tomjo, iuhqujn topoça: in jqujllo papatlaoac, viviac, in jtlaaqujllo, itoca: elosuchitl: in jzoaio, in jiollo, ie in jachio, iehoatl in suchitl: in jizoaio memelactic, viviac, coztic, ixcoztic, pineoac: in jachio mjmjltotonti, pipitzaoac: in jiollo ololtic, ololcapil, hiiac, velic, tetzaoac, in jiaca, in javiiaca, in jvelica: ioanj, çan pinton: in mjec mj, tetech qujz teivinti, teiolmalacacho, teiolitlaco:

njsuchitequj, njsuchitetequj, njqujnecuj,

---

1. *Acad. Hist. MS* adds *tlaloca.*
2. *Yolloxochitl: Talauma mexicana* Don (Santamaría, *op. cit.,* p. 1135).
3. *Eloxochitl: Magnolia dealbata* Succ. (*ibid.,* p. 470).

It spreads an aroma, produces a pleasing odor, perfumes things, spreads over the whole land. It may be used as an unguent.

It ripens, matures, falls apart; each one falls apart. The seeds scatter down, shower down.

Quauheloxochitl

It is a small tree, a small round tree. It has small branches; they are the same as the stalks of the *quauhcamotli*. Its fruit is small; it is called *quauheloxochitl*. It spreads an aroma; it is of pleasing odor; fragrant.

Cacauaxochitl[4]

It is slender, tall, like a stone column. It spreads an aroma; it is fragrant, the same as the *yolloxochitl*. Its leaves, its foliage, are slender. The name of its flower is *cacauaxochitl*; it is yellow, yellowish, small; the same as the *acuilloxochitl*. Its smell is very dense; it penetrates one's nose. It has cup-like [blossoms]; the name of its cup-like [blossoms] is *poyomatli*; a really pleasing odor is their aroma. The tree, the blossoms, its foliage, all are of pleasing odor, all perfumed, all aromatic.

I cut [the blossoms], spread them out, arrange them, cover them with leaves, thread them, make a flower mat of them, make a bed of flowers with them, spread them over the land.

[The perfume] spreads over the whole land, swirls, constantly swirls, spreads constantly swirling, spreads billowing.

Izquixochitl, izquixochiquauitl[5]

It is a round tree with branches, with smooth, slick foliage. The name of its blossom is *izquixochitl*. It is white like pop-corn; hence it is called *izquixochitl*. It is of pleasing odor, fragrant, aromatic; its odor is dense, strong, harsh. Its fragrance is like that of the *tlacopatli*; it penetrates one's nose. Its leaves and its blossoms are potable in water, in cold, chilled chocolate.

It stands blooming, rustling, spreading its branches. It is raining, scattering, showering down [its blossoms], producing perfume which, as it lies, spreads over the whole land — spreads billowing, spreads swirling.

hiiaia, velia, tlaaviialia, centlalmoteca, oxiiova,

icuci, maci, xelivi, xexelivi, achiotepevi, achiopixavi.

Quauhelosuchitl,

quauhtontli, quauhiaoalton, mamaecapil, qujnenevilia in quauhcamotli iquauhio: çan tepiton in jtlaaqujllo. itoca quauhelosuchitl, hiiac, velic, aviac.

Cacavasuchitl,

piaztic, veiac, temjmjltic, hiiac, aviac, qujnenevilia iollosuchitl: in javazvaio, in jqujllo, pipitzaoac; in jsuchio, itoca: cacaoasuchitl, ixcoztic, ixcoçauhquj: tepiton qujnenevilia in acujllosuchitl, vel tetzaoac in jiaca, teiacaxelo; tecomaio, in jtecomaio, itoca poiomatli, vel velic in jqujiac: in quavitl, in suchitl, in jqujllo: muchi velic, muchi aviac, muchi hiiac.

njctetequj, njcmana, njctlalia, njqujzoaiotia, njcço, njcsuchipetlachioa, njcamasuchichioa, njccentlaloa,

centlalmoteca, molonj, momolonj, momolontoc, momolocatoc.

Izqujsuchitl, izqujsuchiquavitl,

quauhiaoalli, mamae, qujqujllo, xipetztic, tlatztic, in jsuchio, itoca: izqujsuchitl, iztac iuhqujn momochitl: injc mjtoa izqujsuchitl, velic, aviac, hiiac, tetzaoac in jiaca, chicaoac, tlapaltic: in jvelica iuhqujn tlacopatli, teiacaxelo; in jatlapal, yoan in jsuchio, ivanj: atl ipan, cacaoatl ipan, cecec, itztic;

cuecuepocaticac, tlatlatzcaticac, maxexeliuhticac, pipixauhticac, motetepeuhticac, tzetzeliuhticac, âviiaxticac, centlalmotecatoc, momolocatoc, momolontoc.

---

4. *Cacauaxochitl: Lexarza funebris* (Sahagún, *op. cit.*, p. 325).

5. *Izquixochitl: Bourreria formosa, B. huanita, B. littoralis* (Santamaría, *op. cit.*, p. 508).

THE TEOIZQUIXOCHITL is the same as the *izquixochitl*.

TLAPALIZQUIXOCHITL[6]

It is the very same as the *izquixochitl*: however, it is blood-spotted, striped with colors, sprinkled with colors, spotted with blood, striped with color.

CUETLAXXOCHITL[7]

It is a round tree, slender, sparse-branched. Its leaves, its foliage, are long and straight, fuzzy, fuzzy over all, white, rough. It has an exudation, a resin. The name of its flower is *cuetlaxxochitl*. It is very chili-red, exceedingly chili-red, the color of blood — a perfected color, finely colored. It is hardy; it becomes hardy. It is dividing, separating. It is leathery, like chili-red leather; wherefore it is called *cuetlaxxochitl*.

The mountains, the crags, the rocks are its growing places; [there] it stands growing.

TEOCUITLAXOCHITL

Teocuitlaxochitl is the collective name of the tree, of the blossoms. It is a slender tree, a smallish tree. Its trunk, even its scales, is dusky green to chalky pale; its foliage is herb green. Its blossom is a little long, hollow, yellow, very yellow, yellowish, like embers, much like embers: a fine-textured yellow.

It is tender, very tender, flexible, infirm; nothing to be called attention to. It is of good appearance, it looks good; [but] it falls to pieces, fades, withers; its foliage falls to pieces.

TEONACAZTLI, UEI NACAZTLI[8]

They are the proper names of the blossoms. They say one drinks chocolate with [these] blossoms; one adds blossoms to tobacco, etc.

UITZTECOLXOCHITL

The name of the tree and of the blossoms is *uitztecolxochitl*. This tree is just a slender tree, a thin tree. It has branches, curved branches. Its leaves are hairy, thorny; its blossoms are dark brown, for which reason they are called *uitztecolxochitl*. Some [blossoms] are very brown, some chili-red, some white. They are

TEUIZQUJSUCHITL: çan no iehoatl; in izqujsuchitl.

TLAPALIZQUJSUCHITL:

çan vel iehoatl in jzqujsuchitl, ieçe ezcujcujltic, motlatlapalhoaoa, motlatlapalalpichi, meezcujcujlo, motlapalhoaoan.

CUETLAXSUCHITL,

quauhiaoalli, pitzaoac, macaiaoa: in jatlapal, in jqujllo, memelactic, tomjo, totomjo, teteztic, tequaqua, memeiallo, oxio: in jsuchio itoca cuetlaxsuchitl, chichilpatic, chilpatzcaltic, eztic, tlapalqujzquj, vel icucic, ixtlapaltic, ixtlapalivi, xexeltic, momoiactic, cuecuetlaxtic, iuhqujn chichiltic cuetlaxtli: injc mjtoa cuetlaxsuchitl,

tepetla texcalla, têtetla in jmuchiuhia mochiuhticac.

TEUCUJTLASUCHITL;

in quavitl, in suchitl, ca in centoca teucujtlasuchitl, quâpiaztli, vel ipã quauhtontli in jtlac, in maço ixincaio, iaiauhcaqujlticectic pineoac: in jqujllo, qujlpaltic, in jsuchio viacapil, iticoionquj, coztic, cozpatic, cozpiltic, tlesuchtic, tlesuchpatic, vellapalqujzquj, injc coztic,

celic, celpatic, atevivi, aiollotlapalivi, anotzalonj: qualnezquj, qualneci, pati, cuetlavia, vaquj, qujlpati.

TEUNACAZTLI, VEI NACAZTLI:

vel ineixcaviltoca suchitl: qujtoa suchio conj in cacaoatl; xochio in jetl. &c.

VITZTECULSUCHITL:

in quavitl, yoan in suchitl, itoca vitzteculsuchitl. Injn quavitl çan quappiaztli, quappitzaoac, mamae, mamacultic, in jatlapal totomjo avaio: in jcueponca tlapalcamjliaiactic: injc mjtoa, vitzteculsuchitl, in cequj, camopaltic, in cequj chichiltic, in cequj iztac, acan avixquj, acan nequjztli, acan eleviliztli, amo

---

6. *Tlapalizquixochitl: Bourreria* sp. (Sahagún, *op. cit.*, p. 363).

7. *Cuetlaxxochitl: Euphorbia (Poinsettia) pulcherrima* Willd. (Hernández, *op. cit.*, Vol. III, p. 958).

8. *Teonacaztli: Cymbopetalum penduliflorum* (Dunal.) Baill. (Emmart, *Badianus Codex*, p. 315). *Uei nacaztli* is the same as *teonacaztli* according to Emmart, *loc. cit.*; it is *Chiranthodendron pentadactylon* Lan. in Sahagún, *op. cit.*, p. 336.

nowhere pleasing, nowhere required, nowhere desired things; not of pleasing odor, not fragrant, not aromatic. They disappoint one, constantly disappoint one; they are sorry things.

Tzompanquauitl[9]

It is a tree of average size; its round branches are of average size. The name of its leaves, its foliage, its blossoms is *equimixochitl*. [The blossoms are] chili-red, very chili-red. They are not fragrant; they are useless, of no use, not required.[10]

This *tzompanquauitl* is honey-like, sweet; however, it is a little harsh to the taste. It produces a bean.[11] The name of its bean is *equimitl*; it is chili-red like the *ayecotli*. It is propagated in this manner: its bean is planted; and the branch is just broken, cut when transplanted, like the *uexotl*.

Equimitl[12]

It is the same as the *tzompanquauitl*. The name of its fruit is also *equimitl*. Its nature has been told.

Mapilxochitl[13]

It is like the fingers, like the palm of the hand. It has fingers. It is a large tree, like a spindle-whorl; spindle-whorl-like. Its leaves are thick; there are many of them — smooth, shiny.

Macpalxochitl

It is the same as the *mapilxochitl*. [The flower is] like the palm of the hand; it has fingers which are spoon-like, concave, dark.

¶

Tenth paragraph, which telleth of those which are also like, which are of the nature of flowering trees; those like trees which also appear herb-like.

Teoquauhxochitl

[The blossom is] chili-red. The branches are slender. [The blossom is] firm, sturdy, not one which fades, withers. It has no aroma, no fragrance; it is useless. From the surface it is fair; it appears beautiful. It grows on a tree, in the tree crotch; it grows on the *auatl*.

velic, amo aviac, amo hiiac, tenenco, tenenenco, tenenentlamachti.

Tzompanquavitl,

çan vel ipã quavitl, çan qualli in jmama ixiaiaoaltic in jpapaloio, in jqujllo, in jsuchio itoca equjmjsuchitl; chichiltic, chichilpatic, amo aviac, nentlacatl, atle inecoca, atle inequjzço.

Inj tzõpanquavitl necutic, tzopelic, iece achi camaquequexqujc, exoio: in jeio itoca, equjmjtl, chichiltic; iuhqujn aiecotli. Injc moxinachoa: motoca in jeio, yoan çan momatzaiana: motequj in maquja iuhqujn vexotl.

Equjmjtl:

çan no iehoatl in tzõpanquavitl: in jtlaaqujllo çã no itoca equjmjtl: omjto in jeliz.

Mapilsuchitl

iuhqujn mapilli ic ca, iuhqujn macpalli, mamapile, vei quavitl, malacachtic, malacachiuhquj, qujllotilaoac, qujqujllo, xixipetztic, tetzcaltic.

Macpalsuchitl:

çan no iehoatl in mapilsuchitl, iuhqujn macpalli ic ca, mamapile, copichtic, copichauhquj, cujchectic.

¶

Inic matlactli parrapho: itechpa tlatoa, in çan ie no iuhquj in quenamj suchiquavitl, in çan iuhquj quavitl ic neci ça no xiuhio.

Teuquavhxuchitl

chichiltic mapipitzaoac, oapaoac, chicaoac acuetlavianj, âmjqujnj, haiiac, âvelic, nentlacatl: ixcopa qualpol, qualneci, quauhtitech quãmaxac in mochioa: itech im muchioa avatl.

---

9. *Tzompanquauitl: Erythrina americana* (Standley, "Trees and Shrubs," Pt. 5, p. 1666).

10. *Acad. Hist. MS: yneq'zyo.*

11. *Ibid.: exoyo.*

12. *Equimitl: Erythrina mexicana* (Sahagún, *op. cit.*, p. 335).

13. *Mapilxochitl, macpalxochitl: Chiranthodendron pentadactylon* Larr. (*ibid.*, p. 341; Standley, *op. cit.*, Pt. 3, p. 796).

THE QUAUHXOCHITL[1] is the same as the *teoquauhxochitl*.

THE TECOLOTL YIATLIA is the same.

ICÇOTL[2]

[Its trunk is] rough with thick scales. [Its leaves are] tousled; they have a fibre. [The wood is] light, spongy. [The leaves are] outstretched, extended, shading.

The name of its flower, its blossom, is *icçoxochitl*. It is cylindrical, long hanging. Its blossom is extended, outspread. It is not enduring. It spreads, it extends. It falls apart.

The name of its fruit is *icçotzotzoualli*. It is honey-like, very honey-like, sweet, very sweet, fiery, much like an ember.

TOMAZQUITL

It is a round tree, chili-red, ruddy. Its seed, its blossom have no aroma; they are only beautiful. The blossom is spreading.

CACALOXOCHITL[3]

It is of average size. It has leaves, foliage. Its leaves are a little wide, a little broad, straight, fuzzy. [When cut] they have an exudation. Its exudation is white, sticky, adhering, like resin. It is an adhesive, a filler. It has blossoms. The name of its blossoms is *cacaloxochitl*. They are black, dark brown—a dusky brown in color. It is said that the blossom of the *cacalotl* is of pleasing odor, perfumed, sweet. Some are called *chacaltzontli*. They are dark red, spattered blood-color, striped. They are very good, desirable, coveted; they are coveted. Some are called *necuxochitl*. Quite small, they are very sweet, honey-like. They are what one merits. Some are called *uitzitziltentli*. They are chili-red, the color of the roseate spoonbill. They are of pleasing odor, fragrant; they are to be taken to oneself; they are to be proud of. They are taken to oneself.

Some are called *miccaxochitl*, and some are called *tlauancaxochitl*. The tree is tall and the blossoms long, large, without aroma. [The name of] some is *cocoyac*, [of others] *xo[co]yac*. They are ignored, never regarded, stupid. They grow everywhere,

QUAUHSUCHITL, çan ie in teuquauhsuchitl.

TECOLOTL YIATLIA, çan no iehoatl.

ICÇOTL,

chachaquachtic, xincaiotilaoac, papaçoltic, ichio, çonectic, çoneoac, cacaçoltic, cacaçoliuhquj, hecauhtic:

in jsuchio, in jcueponca, itoca: icçosuchitl, mjmjltic viac, tlapiloltic, in jcueponca, xexeltic, momoiactic, amo iollotlapalivi: momoiaoa, xexelivi, pati:

In jsuchiquallo itoca, icçotzotzovalli, necutic, necutzopatic, tzopelic, tzopelpatic, tletic, tlexochpatic.

TOMAZQUJTL,

quauhiaoalli chichiltic, tlatlactic: in jxinachio, in jsuchio, amo iiac: çan qualnezquj, cuecueiochauhtica.

CACALOSUCHITL,

çan ipan qualton: xiuhio, qujllo: in jqujllo mamapichauhquj, mamapichtic, memelactic, tôtomjo, memeiallo, iztac in jmemeiallo, çaçalic, çaçaltic, oxitic, çalolonj, aqujlonj, suchio in jsuchio itoca: cacalosuchitl, tliltic, vitztecoltic, tlapalcamjliaiactic: qujl isuchiuh in cacalotl, velic, aviac tzotzopelic: cequj itoca, chacaltzõtli, tlatlapalpoiaoac, ehezcujcujltic, vavavanquj, vel qualli, nequjztli, icollo, teicolti: cequj itoca necusuchitl: çan tepitoton vel tzopelic, necutic: tetonal: cequj itoca vitzitziltentli, chichiltic, tlauhquecholtic: velic, aviac; tlacujcujlolonj, cenmachonj, mocujlia:

cequj itoca mjccasuchitl; yoan itoca: tlavancasuchitl, veiac in quavitl, yõ viviac, vevei in suchitl, aiiac, cequj cocoiac, xoiac, aiac ica, aquẽmachonj, xolopitli: çan novian in muchioa, çan novian in jxoa, amo tlaçotla, motlaillaça, motlailmaiavi, motequjtlaça.

---

1. *Quauhxochitl: Plumeria rubra* (Santamaría, *Dic. de Mejicanismos*, p. 323 — *cuausúchitl*).

2. *Icçotl: Yucca aloifolia* L. (*ibid.*, p. 622 — *izote*); *Y. elephantipes* Regel (Dressler, "Pre-Columbian Cultivated Plants," p. 150).

3. *Cacaloxochitl: Plumeria rubra, Tigridia pavonia* (Sahagún, Garibay ed., Vol. IV, p. 325).

sprout everywhere; they are not scarce. They shed
filth, scatter filth, shed much.

XILOXOCHITL[4]

Its stalk, its stem, is chili-red, ruddy, slender,
spongy within, hollow. It has foliage; its foliage is
serrated. The branches are serrated, slender; they
have blossoms. The name of its blossom is *xiloxochitl*. This is chili-red, extending, radiating, spreading, like maize silk. It extends, spreads, radiates. It
is cup-like; its cup is a small bowl, small and black.
It has stamens; its stamens are small and black, or
each one small and black, like amaranth.

TECOMAXOCHITL[5]

The name of the tree and of the blossom is *tecomaxochitl,* but it is [also] called *tecomaxochiquauitl*.
This is cord-like; the extremes are cord-like. It is a
creeper, a constant creeper, a climber.

Its blossom is yellow. It is like a belly. It is thin;
it has stamens; it is of pleasing odor, perfumed. It is
potable [in chocolate], much diluted, a very little of
it. When much is drunk, it causes one to die of
thirst; it overexcites the testicles; it is deadly. As a
cure, one is to drink a great amount of wine; it will
soothe one; it will quiet one.

CHICHIUALXOCHITL[6]

It is the same as the *tecomaxochitl*. The base is thin,
the top round, the top cup-like;[7] the top is round like
a breast.

TONACAXOCHITL

It is just like the stalk of the *tecomaxochitl*. It is
one which verily sends out runners, which goes far;
it is a climber, one which sends out its tips, which
shoots out its tips. It has foliage. Its blossom is long,
reed-like, curled at the edges, long at the base, slender
at the bottom. It is chili-red; it is the color of gourd
blossoms. The base is pale. It has no aroma; it is just
an ordinary blossom, merely beautiful. It sends out a
shoot; it sends out shoots; it sends out a runner, it
sends out runners; it climbs, it continues climbing.

ACUILLOXOCHITL

The name of the stalk and of the blossom is *acuilloxochitl*. The stalks are long and thin, straight, slen-

XILOSUCHITL:

in jquauhio, in jtlacoio, chichiltic, tlatlactic, pipiaztic, itipochinquj, iticoionquj, qujllo: in jqujllo tzatzaianquj, matzatzaianquj, pipitzaoac, cueponcaio: in
jcueponca, itoca: xilosuchitl: inin chichiltic, xexeltic,
momoiactic, cuecueiactic, iuhqujn xilotzontli, xexelivi, cuecueiaoa, momoiaoa, tecomaio: in jtecomaio
caxtontli, tliltontli, mjmjiaoaio: in jmjiaoaio, tliltontli, anoço tliltotonti, vauhtic.

TECOMASUCHITL:

in quavitl in joan suchitl: itoca tecomasuchitl tel
mjtoa: tecomasuchiquavitl: inin memecatic, quam-
mecatic, movicomanj, movivicomanj: tlatlecavianj;

coztic in jsuchio, cujtlatecontic: canaoac, mjmjiaoaio, velic, aviac: yoanj cencan auhtic, cencan pinton
im mjec teamjcti, teatetzocomjcti, mjcoanj: injc patiz
mjec in qujz octli, vel mjec; qujceviz, qujiollaliz.

CHICHIOALSUCHITL:

çan ie no iehoatl in tecomasuchitl; tzinpitzaoac,
qualoloitic, quatecontic, quatolontic; iuhqujn chichi-
oalli.

TONACASUCHITL:

çan no iuhquj in jquauhio tecomasuchitl, vel motlamjnanj, vecaianj, movivicomanj, moiaiacatlaçanj,
moiaiacatlamjnanj, qujqujllo: in jsuchio viviac, acatic, tencuepquj, xoviac, tzinpitzaoac, chichiltic, aiopaltic, xoiztaleoac, amo iiac, çaçan ie suchitl, çan qualnezquj, moiacatlaça, moiaiacatlaça, motlamjna, motlatlamjna, movicoma, movivicoma.

ACUJLLOSUCHITL:

in tlacotl, yoã in suchitl, itoca: acujllosuchitl, tlacotl pipiaztic, memelactic, pipitzaoac, malcochtic, ma-

---

4. Prob. *Pachira insignis, Calliandra grandiflora,* or *Bombax ellipticum* (§ 5, n. 73, *supra*).

5. Prob. *Maximiliana vitifolia* or *Swartia guttata* (§ 5, n. 14, *supra*).

6. *Chichiualxochitl: Carica papaya* L. (Sahagún, *op. cit.,* p. 334).

7. *Acad. Hist. MS: quatencõtic.*

der, embracing. It is one which embraces. Its foliage is slender. It has a mother, becomes a mother, can be a mother.

The name of its blossom is *acuilloxochitl* [or] *cuilloxochitl*. It is interspersed white and yellow. It has only a single[8] blossom. It is of strong aroma; its aroma, its perfume, is very powerful. It is like the *tlacopatli*. It tears one's nose, penetrates one's nose. It has a pistil; it has a pistil like the *izquixochitl*. It has an aroma, a perfume, a pleasing odor. Its scent is dense; it insinuates itself; it embraces; it continues embracing, encircling; it continually spreads in circles. [Its blossoms] spread bursting, blossoming; it spreads, stands constantly blossoming. It stands spreading an aroma, raining [blossoms. The branches] each lie bent.

CUILLOXOCHITL

It is the same as what is called *acuilloxochitl*.
I arrange [the blossoms]. I lay them on the ground. I thread them; I string them. I smell them. I rejoice in them. I take pleasure in them.

ATLATZOMPILI[9]

It is of slender stalks. Its blossom is cylindrical, like a cylinder; spiraling, a spiral, like a spiral. It is chilired. Some [blossoms] are the color of the roseate spoonbill. They are not of pleasing odor; they just serve as embellishment. They are good looking, of middling appearance. From their front they are goodly.

I lay blossoms on the ground. I arrange blossoms. I paint, I embellish something with the *atlatzompili*.

TZOMPILINALLI

It is the same as the *atlatzompili*.
THE TZOMPILIN is the same.

TOZTLATZOMPILIN

It is like the *atlatzompili*. It is called *toztlatzompilin* because it is yellow.

QUAUIZQUIXOCHITL

It is a stalk which creeps.

TLACOIZQUIXOCHITL:

This is the white *acuilloxochitl*.

malcochavinj: in jqujllo, pipitzaoac, nane, monantianj, nantilonj:

in jsuchio, itoca Acujllosuchitl, cujllosuchitl iztac, coztic, nepanjuhquj, çan ie iixe, vel hiiac, vel chicaoac in jiaca, in jvelica, tlacopatic; teiacatzaia, teiacaxelo, tomjiollo, tomjlollo, izqujsuchitic, hiiaia velia, aviaia, motetzaoaca inecuj, pipiacivi, mamalcochavi, mamalcochauhtimanj, iavaliuhtimanj, iaiaoaliuhtimanj, xotlatoc, cuepontoc, cuecuepocatoc, cuecuepocaticac, hiiaxticac, tzetzeliuhticac, vivitoliuhtoc.

CUJLLOSUCHITL;

çan no iehoatl itoca, in acujllosuchitl:
njctlalia, njcmana, njcço, njcçoço, njqujnecuj, njcpaquj, njcnotlamachtia.

ATLATZOMPILI:

tlacotl, pipiaztic in jsuchio, mjmjltic, mjmjliuhquj, tlailacatzoltic, tlaillacatzolli, ilacatziuhquj, chichiltic: cequj tlauhquecholtic, amo velic, çã tlaqualnextilonj, qualnezquj, çaçan ie qualnezquj: yixcopa qualpul;

njsuchimana, njsuchitlalia: ic njtlacujloa, ic njtlaqualnextia in atlatzompili.

TZOMPILINALLI:

çã no iehoatl, in, atlatzompilli.
TZOMPILIN, çan no iehoatl.

TOZTLATZOMPILIN:

çan no iuhquj in atlatzompili: injc mjtoa toztlatzompili ca coztic.

QUAVIZQUJSUCHITL:

tlacotl movivilana.

TLACOIZQUJSUCHITL:

iehoatl in iztac, acujllosuchitl.

---

8. *Ibid.: ce.*
9. *Atlatzompili: Malvaviscus drummondii* Torr. (Hernández, *Hist. de las Plantas*, Vol. I, p. 127).

Tlacoxochitl[10]

It is small and slender, somewhat squat, sparse of foliage. Its blossom is chili-red; it has no pleasing odor, no perfume; it is never of pleasing odor, in no wise aromatic.

Uitzitzilxochitl[11]

It is the same as the *tlacoxochitl*.

Yiexochitl

It is of pleasing odor; it is fragrant. The stalks are bushy. It is an annually dormant one; it buds, rejuvenates, grows each year. Its leaves, its foliage, are fuzzy; its stalks, its stems, are also fuzzy. It forms buds. These fatten; they grow fat. It forms buds, sends forth growth, enlarges, grows, forms foliage, has foliage. [The flower buds] grow fat, swell, enlarge, burst, blossom, break, break open, open, open wide, produce an aroma, produce a pleasing odor.

Coztic yiexochitl

It is the same though yellow. It is of pleasing odor, perfumed, precious; it is what one merits; it is one's solace. This one is just like an herb, just like a stalk. But some plant the *tzoyac yiexochitl* in the ashes and cover the roots with ashes. Thus it becomes yellow, thus the blossom turns yellow; thus it produces a pleasing odor, a perfume.

Quauhyiexochitl

It is stalky, long, straight, bushy. The branches are embracing; the foliage is long, the foliage is broad. Its stalks are thick, hollow, pithy within. Its blossoms are long, green. They are green. They lengthen, mature, season.

Chalchiuhxochitl

It is the same as the *quauhyiexochitl*. [It is called *chalchiuhxochitl*] because it is the green one; the green-stone-like, the very green one; turquoise-like. It has an aroma; it produces a pleasing odor. It becomes yellow, it becomes brown.

Chalchiuhyiexochitl

It is the same as the one [just] mentioned. It is like a green stone, very blue, wonderful, admirable, desirable, constantly required, required; ever useful, useful, ever useful.

Tlacosuchitl,

pitzaton, tlalpãton, qujllo caiacton: in jsuchio chichiltic, atle ivelica, atle iiaviiaca, aquen velic, njmã amo hiiac.

Vitzitzilsuchitl:

çan no iehoatl in tlacosuchitl.

Iiesuchitl,

velic, aviac, tlacotl popoçonj: in cecexiuhtica vaqujnj, celianj, mozcalianj, mozcaltianj: in jxiuhio in jqujllo, totomjo, in jquauhio, in jtlanjtz no totomjo: celia, mopochqujiotia, pochqujioa, itzmolinj, valpatlanj; mana, mozcaltia, moqujllotia, qujlloa, pochqujiova, totomolivi, mjmjlivi, xotla, cueponj, tlapanj, tlatzinj, tlapovi, camachaloa, hiiaia, velia.

Coztic yiesuchitl:

çan no iehoatl: ieçe coztic, velic, aviac, tlaçotli, tetonal, teiolqujma inin çan iuhquj xivitl, çan iuhqujn tlacotl. Auh in cequj nexpã in caquja, yoan nextli injc qujtzintlalpachoa; in tzoiac yiesuchitl ic coçavia, ic mocuepa; cocauhquj suchitl, ic velia, aviaia.

Quauhyiesuchitl:

tlatlacotic memelactic, memelaoac, popoçonjnj, mamalacachivinj, qujllo, veveiac, qujllo papatlaoac, totomaoac in jtlacoio, iticoionquj, itipochinquj. In jsuchio viviac, xoxouhqui, xoxoctic, viviaquja, maci, icuci.

Chalchiuhsuchitl:

çan no iehoatl, in quauhyiesuchitl: ipampa in xoxoctic, in chalchiuhtic, in xoxocpatic, ximmaltic: hiiaia, velia, coçeoa, camjlivi.

Chalchiuhyiesuchitl:

çan no iehoatl in omjto, chalchiuhtic, texocaltic, maviztic, maviçauhquj, elevilizio, nenequjztli, nequjztli, nêneconj, neconj, neneconj.

---

10. *Tlacoxochitl: Bouvardia termifolia* Schl. (Sahagún, *op. cit.*, p. 361).

11. *Uitzitzilxochitl: Loeselia coccinea* Don. (*ibid.*, p. 337).

Tzoyac yiexochitl

It is the same as the *yiexochitl*; however, it is fetid, resinous; it emits a fetid odor.

The azcalxochitl[12] is like the *tolin*.

Yopixochitl

[The blossom] is white, striped with colors, extending. It has stamens, it has a pistil; it is like a spindle whorl. Its stalk is like that of the *itztolin*, a small spindle whorl.[13] It grows in the water, as has been said.

Uacalxochitl[14]

Its vines are cord-like. It is an emitter of runners. It has leaves. The foliage is broad; its leaves are like those of the *ayoçonan* — very smooth, soft, nerve-like. Its vines are long. Its leaf is a creeper, a climber, an extender of shoots.

Its blossom is cylindrical, roughened within. In its interior stands still another of its centers; it is round, pointed at the end, resinous.

The skin of this flower is thick. It creeps; it is cord-like, like cords. It binds, it coils.

Teccizuacalxochitl

Its vine is thick. Its leaves are very wide. Its blossom is large, white, long. It has no pleasing odor, no aroma. It is of no use. Whoever smells it, [his] nose roughens; the nose swells.

Since it is nowhere required, they say that the women of the palace claimed it as what they merited — those considered as secluded, those who were Moctezuma's women: wherefore, they say, they were carnally guilty. And the women and those who tended the gardens were stoned.

Tochnacazuacalxochitl

It is of average size, of pleasing odor, fragrant. It is one which can be smelled; it is good, fine.

Tlapaluacalxochitl

It is chili-red, of average size. A precious thing, it is one which can be claimed as what one merits.

I claim it as merited. I appropriate it. I take it to myself.

Tzoiac yiesuchitl;

çan ie iehoatl in jiesuchitl, iece tzoiac oxiio, tzoiaia.

Azcalsuchitl, iuhqujn tolin

Iopisuchitl,

iztac, tlatlapalhoaoanquj, maçouhquj, mjmjiaoaio, tomjollo, malacachtic; in jquauhio iuhqujn itztolin, malacachtontli, atlan in mochioa, omjto.

Vacalsuchitl:

in jquauhio memecatic, motlatlamjnanj, amatlapale: quillo papatlaoac in jatlapal iuhqujn, aioçona, tetzcaltic, iamanquj, tlatlalhoaio, viviac in jquauhio: in jatlapal movilananj, movicomanj, moiacatlaçanj:

in jsuchio mjmjltic, ititzaianquj: in jitic hicac, in oc ceppa yiollo, ololtic iacavitztic, oxio.

Inin suchitl in jeoaio tilaoac, movilana, mecatic, memecatic, memecati, mjcuja.

Teccizoacalsuchitl:

tomaoac in jquauhio, cenca patlaoac in jatlapal: in jsuchio tomaoac, iztac, viac, amo velic amo hiia, amo ineconj: in aqujn qujnecuj, iacachachaquachivi, iacatomaoa.

Injc acan monequj: qujl qujmotonaltica, in tecpan cioa, in cacaltzacutoca; in jcioaoan catca motecuçoma: quil ic tlalticpac tlamatque; ic tetzotzonaloque, in qujnpiaia in suchitla, yoan in cioa.

Tochnacazoacalsuchitl,

çan qualton, velic, aviac, hineconj, qualli, iectli.

Tlapalhoacalsuchitl;

chichiltic, çan qualton, tlaçotli, tetonaltilonj;

njcnotonaltia, njcnotechtia, njcnomaca.

---

12. *Azcalxochitl: Amaryllis formossisima* (Santamaría, *op. cit.*, p. 88 — *ascasúchil*).

13. *Acad. Hist.* MS reads, after *malacachtontli, atlā yoā atēco ȳ mochiva Atzatzamolxochitl. atlā ȳ mochiva omito.*

14. *Uacalxochitl: Phyllodendrum affine* Hemsl. (Santamaría, *op. cit.*, p. 601 — *huacalsóchil*).

CHILQUALLI

UITZPALXOCHITL

OÇOMACUITLAPILXOCHITL

NOPALXOCHITL[15]

It is chili-red, the color of the roseate spoonbill, the color of the gourd blossoms. It is prickly, useless — an ordinary flower, with no aroma.

TETZILACAXOCHITL

It is the same as the *toztlatzompili*.

UEUEXOCHITL

It creeps, is fuzzy.

OMIXOCHITL[16]

It has slender stalks; it has foliage, blossoms. Its blossom is white. [It is like] a small spindle whorl on top; the base is slender, a little long; therefore it is named *omixochitl*. It is of pleasing odor, fragrant, sweet; a precious thing, useful.

TLAPALOMIXOCHITL

It is the same. However, it is chili-red, dark colored, striped with color, color-striped. It becomes dark colored.

TLILXOCHITL

It is cord-like, like cords, slender. Its vine is like the *tetzitzilin*; it is a climber, one which sends out shoots. It has a bean. Its bean is green; when dry, it is black. It is glistening; within, it is resinous. It is of pleasing odor, fragrant — a precious thing, wonderful, marvelous. It is of pleasing odor, perfect, superb. It is potable in chocolate. It creeps, constantly creeps, travels, sends out a shoot, forms foliage, produces a bean, forms a bean.

MECAXOCHITL

It is an herb. Its place of occurrence, its sprouting place, its growing place, is in the water, at the water's edge. Its foliage is like cords. It has stems. Its stems are like cords, slender, each slender. The branches are firm; they extend bristling. It is of very pleasing odor, very fragrant.

CHILQUALLI.

VITZPALSUCHITL.

OÇOMACUJTLAPILSUCHITL

NUPALSUCHITL:

chichiltic, tlauhquecholtic, aiopaltic, aoaio, nentlacatl, çaçan ie suchitl, amo hiiac.

TETZILACASUCHITL:

çan no iehoatl in toztlatzompili.

VEVESUCHITL:

movivilana, tomjo.

OMJSUCHITL:

tlacotl, pipitzaoac qujioio suchio: in jsuchio iztac quamalacachton, tzimpitzaoac viiacatontli: injc motocaiotia omjsuchitl, velic, aviac, tzopelic, tlaçotli, neconj.

TLAPALOMJSUCHITL:

ça no iehoatl iece chichiltic, tlappoiaoac, motlapalhoaoan, motlapalhoavana, motlappoiava.

TLILSUCHITL,

mecatic, memecatic, pipitzaoac: in jquauhio iuhqujn tetzitzilin, movicomanj, moiacatlaçanj, exoio, in jexoio xoxoctic: in ooac tliltic, tzotzotlactic, itioxio, velic, aviac, tlaçotli, maviztic, maviçauhquj, velic, vel tzontic, vel tzõpatic, yvanj: cacaoatl ipan, movilana, movivilana, vtlatoca, moiacatlaça, moqujllotia, mexoiotia, exoioa.

MECASUCHITL:

xivitl, atlan atenco imanja, yixoacan, yixoaia: in jqujllo memelactic, qujioio: in jqujioio iuhqujn mecatl, pitzaoac, pipitzaoac, mapichtic, poçontimanj, cenca velic, vel aviac.

---

15. *Nopalxochitl*: flower of the *nopal*; see Sahagún, *op. cit.*, p. 346, *nochtli, nopalli, nochxochitl*. According to Hernández, *op. cit.*, Vol. III, p. 932, it may be *Nopalxochia phyllantoides* D.C. or *Epiphyllum (Phyllocactus) Ackermanii*.

16. *Omixochitl: Polianthes tuberosa, P. mexicana* (Sahagún, *op. cit.*, p. 347).

Coatzontecomaxochitl[17]

It is like the head of a serpent; that is the way it is by nature.

Acaxochitl[18]

It is spreading, like the *tolpatlactli*. The name of its blossom is *acaxochitl*; it is chili-red. It is forked. It spreads. It becomes chili-red.

Quauhacaxochitl

Quauhiztexochitl, quauhiztixochitl

It is an herb. Its leaves are green; its blossom is blue. It is curved, like an eagle talon. It is green, blue, the color of the lovely cotinga. It curves, becomes green, is blue, turns very blue, becomes very blue; it is very blue.

Tzacuxochitl xiuitl[19]

Its foliage is like that of the *tzacutli*. It is tall. [Its blossoms] are chili-red, rose, dark blue. It is tender, very tender. It is coveted; one is made to desire it. It gladdens one, refreshes one. It becomes verdant. It is hardy; it becomes hardy. It stands, it grows in the crags. And in the tree crotches, on the trees it takes hold, forms buds, blossoms, stands blossoming, stands constantly blossoming, stands glistening.

Iuixochitl

It is a small stalk, a stalk. It is dark, bushy. Its blossom is like a feather; it blossoms, it swirls up.

The tlapaliuixochitl is the same as the *iuixochitl*; however, it is chili-red.

The iztac iuixochitl is the same as the *iuixochitl*; however, it is white, like a white feather.

Oloxochitl

It is an herb, small and bushy. The name of its blossom is *oloxochitl*. Each is rather white, ball-like, harsh, rough. It has no pleasing odor, no aroma. It pricks one to no purpose.

Mocuepani xochitl

It is a stalk. Its leaves, its foliage, are serrated. It has blossoms. The name of its blossoms is *mocuepani xochitl*. It is one which nods its head, one which raises its head; hence it is called *mocuepani xochitl*.

Coatzontecomasuchitl:

iuhqujn coatl itzontecon ic ca, çan njman iuh ixoac iuh tlacat.

Acasuchitl

tolpatlactic, xexeltic: in jcueponca itoca acasuchitl, chichiltic, maxeltic, maxelivi, chichilivi.

Quauhacasuchitl.

Quauhiztesuchitl, quaviztisuchitl,

xivitl, xoxoctic in jatlapal: texoti in jcueponca, coltic: iuhqujn quauhtli izti ic ca: xoxoctic, texotic, xiuhtototic, colivi, xoxovia, texoti, texocalivi, texocaltia, texocalti.

Tzacusuchitl xivitl

iuhqujn tzacutli ixiuhio, memelacpil, chichiltic, tlaztaleoaltic, movitic, celic, celpatic, teicolti, tetlanecti, tecelti, tececelti, celia: iollotlapaltic, iollotlapalivi: texcalpan in hicac, in mochioa, yoã quãmaxac, quauhtitech in celia, itzmolinj, cueponj, cueponticac, cuecueponticac, tlatlatzcaticac.

Hivisuchitl:

tlacotontli, tlacotl catzactic, paçoltic: in jcueponca iuhqujn hivitl; cueponj, molonj.

Tlapalihujsuchitl: çan ie iehoatl in hivisuchitl, iece chichiltic.

Iztac hivisuchitl: çan ie iehoatl in hivisuchitl, iece iztac: iuhqujn iztac hivitl.

Olosuchitl:

xivitl, pacoltontli in jcuepõca, itoca olosuchitl, tetetztontli, ololpil teçontic, tequaqua, havelic, ahiiac, tenenquaqua.

Mocuepanj suchitl:

tlacotl, tzatzaianquj in jxiuhio in jqujllo, cueponcaio: in jcueponca, itoca: mocuepanj suchitl, tolovanj, aquetzanj: injc mjtoa mocuepanj suchitl. In jquac oalqujça tonatiuh, ivicpa itztica, ompa ivicpa quech-

---

17. *Coatzontecomaxochitl: Stanhopea tigrina* (Santamaría, *op. cit.,* p. 320 — *cuasontecomasúchil*).
18. *Acaxochitl: Lobelia fulgens, L. laxiflora* (Hernández, *op. cit.,* Vol. I, pp. 94 *sqq.*).
19. *Tzacuxochitl: Bletia coccinea* Ll. and Lex., *B. campanulata* Ll. and Lex. (*ibid.,* Vol. II, p. 376).

When the sun comes up, it is looking toward it, it is twisting its neck there toward it. As the sun goes higher [it raises its head somewhat].[20] At midday the blossom is also straight up. When the sun turns, it also nods a little; it always[21] goes accompanying the sun. When the sun goes down, it also stands nodding there. It nods its head; it raises its head.

XALACOCOTLI[22]

It is a stalk, hollow, spongy within. The name of its bloom, its blossom, is *acocoxochitl*. It is chili-red, brown, yellow; it is fuzzy, developed, round — rounded. Its petals are straight, wide, tender; they disintegrate.

OCELOXOCHITL[23]

It is an herb. Its leaves, its foliage, are straight, long. The name of its blossom is *oceloxochitl*. It is open, cut like a butterfly, yellow; some are chili-red. It is called *oceloxochitl* for the reason that the yellow ones are sprinkled with red, the chili-red ones are sprinkled with yellow. They are painted in various colors, varicolored, variously colored.

QUAZTALXOCHITL

It is a small stalk of [few] leaves, of little foliage. It is cylindrical, hollow. It has flowers. Its flowers are outspread, extended, thick, white. They constantly extend; they extend, spread out, radiate.

POYOMAXOCHITL

This is the cup of the *cacauaxochitl*. They say that it makes one falter, that it deranges one, provokes one. It makes one falter, it deranges one, it provokes one.

TLALPOYOMATLI

It is an herb, aromatic, of pleasing odor, fragrant; pleasing, like the *poyomatli*, something like the *poyomatli*. It produces a pleasing odor; it gives off an aroma.

TEOTLAQUILLI

It has a stalk. It has branches — forked branches, bifurcated, forking, forked. It has foliage; it has thick leaves. It has thick roots. Today it is just called *tlaquilli*.

XALACOCOTLI:

tlacotl, iticoionquj, itipochqujio; in jxotlaca in jcueponca, itoca: acocosuchitl, chichiltic, camopaltic, coztic, tomjollo, manquj, iaoaltic, iavaliuhquj: in jsuchiatlapallo, memelactic, papatlactic, aiollo tlapalivi, patinj.

OCELOSUCHITL:

xivitl, in jatlapal in jqujllo memelactic, memelaoac, in jcueponca, itoca: ocelosuchitl, çouhquj, tlapapalotectli, coztic, cequj chichiltic: injc mjtoa; ocelosuchitl, in coztic motlatlapalalpichi: in chichiltic, motetecoçauhalpichi, mocujcujcujlo, cujcujcujltic, cujcujliuhquj.

QUAZTALSUCHITL:

tlacotontli: in jatlapal, in jxiuhio çan quezquj, mjmjltic, iticoionquj, xuchio: in jsuchio momoiactic, xexeltic, chamaoac, iztac, xexelivi, xelivi, moiaoa, cuecueiaoa.

POIOMASUCHITL:

iehoatl in jtecomaio cacaoasuchitl: qujtoa teiolcuep, teiolmalacachoa, teiollochololti: teiolcuepa, teiolmalacachoa, teiollochololtia.

TLALPOIOMATLI:

xivitl, hiiac, velic, haviac, âvixtic, poiomatic, itlatla in poiomatli, velia, hiiaia.

TEUTLAQUJLI:

tlacotl, mamae, maxallo, mamatzocollo, mamaxaltic, mamaxaliuhquj, qujqujllo, qujllotilaoac, nelhoaio tomaoac, in axcan çan mjtoa, tlaqujlli.

necujlotica, in ie oalpanvetzi tonatiuh: [No achi haquetza] in nepantla tonatiuh, no tlamelauhtimanj in suchitl: in ommonecujloa tonatiuh no achi toloa: çaçan qujvicatiuh in tonatiuh; in oncalaquj tonatiuh, no vmpa toloticac: toloa aquetza.

---

20. *Acad. Hist. MS* includes passage (in brackets) missing in *Florentine Codex*.
21. *Acad. Hist. MS*: ça cē.
22. *Xalacocotli: Arracacia atropurpurea* (Sahagún, *op. cit.*, p. 368).
23. *Oceloxochitl: Tigridia pavonia* (*ibid.*, p. 346).

And hence is it called *teotlaquilli*: its blossom opens in the dark. It does not open with the other flowers; it tarries. They say [other flowers] continue to sleep; it is not night when they wake up. And all the flowers are awakened from sleep; the sun is awaited by them. When it comes up, then they meet it; they greet it. It is said that they picked the flowers then, when all had opened, when the sun had come up. But this one, they say, at this time was allowed to continue to sleep; when later it was already dark, its blossom opened.

Today it is said: "The sun goes in; it enters the house"; for it used to be said: "The god enters." [24] And when somewhere it became dark, when the sun set on someone, he used to say: *"Niteotlaquilia."*

And [as to] this flower, the *teotlaquilli*, it is at night, when the sun has set, that its opening is. It is chili-red, violet, the color of gourd blossoms, striped with yellow, striped blood-red.

Tlalizquixochitl

It is a small herb, small on the ground; it is a creeper. It is a dark ashen color; chalky. Its blossom is white, striped blood-red, striped with colors. It is reed-like, a little long, tender, very tender. It is not hardy; it is delicate. It easily disintegrates. It is perfect, superb, pleasing, very pleasing, exceedingly pleasing. It blossoms, glistens, lies glistening, spreads glistening, lies blossoming. It produces a pleasing odor; it diffuses [its odor].

Ocoxochitl

It is an herb, drooping, bushy, small on the ground, straight, fragrant.

Quetzalocoxochitl

It is the same. It has the same kind of pleasing odor. However, it is like cords. It is one which sends out runners. It creeps, it sends out runners. It lies sending out shoots.

Quiyoxochitl

It is the blossom of the maguey. It is like a cluster, yellow, fuzzy-centered. It is honey-like; it exudes. The different birds suck it.

Nopalxochitl, nochxochitl

It is chili-red, brown. It is thorny, worthless, useless. It pricks one to no purpose. It forms thorns.

Auh injc mjtoa teutlaqujli: in jquac cuepon jvac suchime, amo teoan cuepon, tlavecauh: qujl cochtlamelauh, amo iovac in jçac: auh in jxqujch suchime, cochiçaloc, chialoc in tonatiuh: in jquac oalqujz njman qujnamjque, qujtlapaloque: qujl vncan qujcujque in suchime, in mochi cueponj, in jquac oalqujça tonatiuh. Auh inin qujl iquac cõmocavili in cochtlamelauh in qujn ie ioac cueponj.

In axcan mjtoa: onaquj, calaquj tonatiuh: ca mjtoaia, teutlaqujlli. Auh in aqujn cana ipan iova, in jpan calaquj tonatiuh: qujtoaia. Niteutlaqujlia.

Auh inin suchitl teutlaqujli: ipan ioac, ipan oncalac in tonatiuh: in jcueponca i; chichiltic, camopaltic, aiopaltic, cozoaváquj, ezvavanquj.

Tlalizqujsuchitl:

xiuhtontli, tlalpanton, movivilananj, cujtlanextic, ticeoac, iztac in jsuchio, ehezoavanquj, tlatlapalvavanquj, acatic, viviacapipil celic, celpatic, aiollotlapalivi, chinequjztli, vel pati, vel tzontic, vel tzompatic, avixtic, avixtzõtic, avixcaltic, avialtic, cueponj, cuecuepoca, cuecuepocatoc, cuecuepocatimanj, cuepontoc, velia, molonj.

Ocosuchitl:

xivitl, chachapactic, paçoltic, tlalpanton, ixmemelactic, haviac.

Quetzalocusuchitl:

çan no iehoatl, çan no ivi in velic: iece memecatic, motlamjnanj; movivilana motlamjna, moiacatlaztoc.

Qujiosuchitl:

isuchio in metl, oocholteuhca, coztic, tomjojollo, necuio, meia: qujchichina in nepapan tototl.

Nupalsuchitl, nochsuchitl:

chichiltic, camopaltic, avaio, nẽtlacatl, nenqujzquj, tenenquaqua: havaiova.

---

24. *Acad. Hist. MS: teutl aqui.*

Cempoalxochitl[25]

It is a stalk. It is green. The leaves are serrated; its foliage is spreading, outspread. Its blossom is given the name *cempoalxochitl*. The branches are spreading; it stands blossoming, extends blossoming. There are many kinds.

The female cempoalxochitl is large.

Macuilxochitl [variety of] cempoalxochitl

It is white, roughened, rough, yellow, pale. It becomes ruffled; it becomes round.

The male cempoalxochitl has only a single flower, with thin petals.

All the flowers

They begin to blossom in this manner: first they become fat; they fatten. Then they form a droplet. Then they swell; then they blossom; they burst. Then they open; they produce pistils, they form pistils. Then they are fully in bloom; they fill out. At this time they produce a pleasing odor, a fragrance, an aroma. At this time they are required, desired, coveted, needed. They are cherished, wonderful, meriting wonder, considered wonderful. They fade, shed petals, drop petals, darken, wither. They become verdigris-colored, turn verdigris-colored; they become blotched, dry; they drop. Pertaining to the blossoming of the flower are the fattening, the petals, the calyx, the pistil, the pistils, the seed, the seed of the flower, the ovary, the receptacle, the stamen of the flower, the stamens.

¶

Eleventh paragraph, which telleth how the flowers are offered.

I offer flowers.[1] I sow flower [seeds]. I plant flowers. I assemble flowers. I pick flowers. I pick different flowers. I remove flowers. I seek flowers. I offer flowers. I arrange flowers. I thread a flower. I string flowers. I make flowers. I form them to be extending, uneven, rounded, round bouquets of flowers.

I make a flower necklace, a flower garland, a paper of flowers, a bouquet, a flower shield, hand flowers. I thread them. I string them. I provide them with grass. I provide them with leaves. I make a pendant of them. I smell something. I smell them. I cause

Cempoalsuchitl:

tlacotl, xoxoctic, matzatzaianquj: in jqujllo maxexeltic, maxexeliuhquj: in jcueponca, qujtocaiotia: cempoalsuchitl, mamaxexeliuhticac, cuecueponticac, cuecuepontimanj: mjec tlamantli

In cempoalsuchitl, cioasuchitl: vevei

Cempoalsuchitl: macujlsuchitl:

teteztic, teçonauhquj, teçontic, coztic, iztaleoac: teçonavi, ololivi.

Cempoalsuchitl oqujchsuchitl çan ce yix, amo suchiamatlapaltilaoac.

In jxqujch suchitl,

injc peoa cueponj: achtopa pochqujova, mopochqujotia: njmã chipinj, njman totomolivi, njman cueponj, tlatzinj; njmã xotla motomjollotia, tomjlolloa, njmã maci, chicaoa: iquac velia, âviaia, iiaia: iquac in monequj, in neco, in elevilo, in nêneco: tlaçoti, maviztic, maviztililonj, mavizmacho: tlatzivi, mosuchiamatlapallaça, mosuchiamatlapaltepeoa, tlileoa, cujtlacochivi, qujlpaltia, qujlpalti: cuetlavia, vaquja, motepeoa. In jtech ca in suchitl, in cueponcaiotl: pochqujotl, suchiamatlapalli, suchizoatl, tecomaiotl, tomjoli, tomjlolli, achtli, achiotl, iollotli, suchitl itzin, mjavaiotl, mjmjaoatl.

¶

Injc matlactli oce parrapho: itechpa tlatoa, in suchitl, in quenjn mosuchimana.

Nisuchimana, njsuchipixoa njsuchitoca, njsuchitlacujcujlia, njsuchitequj, njsuchitetequj, njsuchieoa, njsuchitemoa: njsuchimana, njsuchitlalia, njsuchiço, njsuchiçoço: njsuchichioa: njctlalia suchitl, manquj, teçonauhquj, ololiuhquj, ololtic, suchiecaceoaztli:

njcchioa suchicozcatl, icpacsuchitl, suchiamatl, tlatlanecutli, chimalsuchitl, macsuchitl: njcço, njcçoço, njcçacaiotia, njqujzoaiotia, njctlapiloltia njtlanecuj, njqujnecuj, njtetlanecujltia, njqujnecujltia, njtesuchimaca, njcsuchimaca, njcsuchitia, njtesuchitia, njtesu-

---

25. *Cempoalxochitl: Tagetes erecta* L. (Hernández, *op. cit.*, Vol. II, p. 645).

1. *Acad. Hist. MS: nixochiaquia.*

one to smell something. I cause him to smell. I offer flowers to one. I offer him flowers. I provide him flowers. I provide one with flowers. I provide one with a flower necklace. I provide him a flower necklace. I place a garland on one. I provide him a garland. I clothe one in flowers. I clothe him in flowers. I cover one with flowers. I continue to cover one with flowers. I cover him with flowers. I continue to cover him with flowers. I destroy one with flowers. I destroy him with flowers. I injure one with flowers. I injure him with flowers.

"I destroy one with flowers;[2] I destroy him with flowers; I injure one with flowers": [this] is said when I thus beguile or incite someone with drink, with food, with flowers, with tobacco, with capes, with gold. When I incite just with words, when I am beguiling him, it is said: "I caress him with flowers.[3] I seduce one. I extend one a lengthy discourse. I induce him with words."

I provide one with flowers. I make flowers, or I give them to one that someone will observe a feast day. Or I merely continue to give one flowers; I continue to place them in one's hand, I continue to offer them to one's hands. Or I provide one with a necklace, or I provide one with a garland of flowers.

¶

Twelfth paragraph, which telleth of the nature of trees.

Teopochotl[1]

It grows in the east. It is a little thick, fat, quite smooth, very smooth. . . . , polished, just like what is called the paschal candle — bending at the top, rather white at the top.

And behold the good, the evil which there is in it.

One who is very puny eats or drinks of its seed or of its exudation in order to expand, to become big, fleshy, to grow big. For this reason those of experience feed their animals [of this], so that they may fatten, so that they may grow large.[2]

And [as to] the evil which is in it: the one who hates people gives it to one to eat; he gives it to one to drink in water, in wine; he causes one to swallow it in food. But in no wise is it noticeable. That which

chicozcatia, njcsuchicozcatia, njteicpacsuchitia, njqujcpacsuchitia, njtesuchiapana, njcsuchiapana, njtesuchipachoa, njtesuchipapachoa, njcsuchipachoa, njcsuchipapachoa, njtesuchipoloa, njcsuchipoloa, njtesuchimjctia, njcsuchimjctia,

njtesuchipoloa, njcsuchipoloa, njtesuchimjctia: ipā mjtoa in aca ic njctlapololtia, anoço njcioleoa atica, tlaqualtica, suchitica, yietica, tilmatica, teucujtlatica; in çan tlatoltica njcioleoa, njctlapololtia: mjtoa, njctesuchitzotzona, njctesuchivia, hecamecatl njctequjlia, njccoconavia.

Nitesuchitia, njcchioa in suchitl, anoço njctemaca injc aca ilhujtlaz, aço çaçan njctemamaca, temac njctlatlalia, temac njcmamana in suchitl, aço njctecozcatia, anoço njcteicpacsuchitia.

¶

Injc matlactli omume parrapho: itechpa tlatoa in quenjnamj yieliz quavitl.

Teupochotl,

tonaian muchioa, tomactontli, nanatztic, vel xixipetztic, xixipetzpatic, xicatatztic tetzcaltic: vel iuhquj in mjtoa. cirio pasqual, quavivichton, quatetezton.

Auh izca in jtech ca in qualli, in aqualli.

In aqujn cēca auhtic qujqua, anoço quj in jxinachio, anoço imemeiallo, ic tomaoa, ic veiia, ic monacaiotia, ic motoma: ic ipampa in tlaiximatinj, in iniolcaoan qujnqualtia, injc tomaoa, injc veiia.

Auh in amo qualli itech ca: in tecocolianj, qujtequaltia, qujteitia atl ipan, octli ipan, tlaqualli ipan qujtetololtia: çan njman amo machiztli: in qualtilonj, in jtilonj, niman motoma in jnacaio, poçaoa:

---

2. *Ibid.*: a marginal gloss in Sahagún's hand reads *atraer cō dadivas o dones.*

3. *Ibid.*: a marginal gloss in Sahagún's hand reads *atraer cō palabras, o enlabiar.*

1. *Teopochotl*: prob. *Ceiba* sp. or *Bombax* sp.

2. *Acad. Hist. MS: veueya.*

is given as food, that which is given as drink then enlarges his body; it swells; it becomes in no place unblemished. Indeed, he becomes what is called a glutton — very fat, exceedingly fat, lazy, lumpy with flesh, round, an old clod of flesh with two eyes, heavy, very sluggish, a mass of leavened dough, big-headed; with ears like droplets, cylindrical eyelids, contracted eyes, fat cheeks, heavy cheeks, quivering cheeks, *tamal*-like nose, quivering nose, round nose; with thick lips, double chin, multiple chins; with flabby body, with hands like entrails; with filthy fingers, dirt-covered thighs, dirt-covered calves; with thick-soled feet.

He verily enlarges; he becomes quite big. He has a great appetite — eats excessively. He becomes in no place unblemished; he becomes revolting; he just lies stretched out panting, breathing heavily. He has a great thirst, a great hunger; he eats three times, four times a day. All around he stores [food] for himself, and it is no little amount that he eats. He literally tramples upon the food.

And thus does he die: his body falls apart; his hands, his feet burst. And since his medicating, his remedying, is yet in vain, he continually purges himself.

I cause him to swell. I swell. I enlarge. I become big.

Maguey:[3] that which pertains to maguey

It has branches, leaves. It is spiny. It has maguey tips, a center, haunches, a maguey crown, a maguey root, a stem. It has an exudation, maguey syrup, unfermented maguey juice. It is juicy, fibrous, drooping, hanging. It has tapering leaves. It is green. It has a maguey bud, offshoots — an offshoot which can be planted, pressed in, transplanted, set out. It has dried magueys.

Tlacametl[4]

It is large, high. The leaves are thick, wide.

The ocelometl is varicolored — variously colored.

The nexmetl is an ashen maguey,[5] ash-colored, ashen, like the lovely cotinga.

The macocol has curved tips.

The mexoxoctli is green, dark green.

aoccan tlacanezquj mochioa: vel iehoatl mochioa, in mjtoa tlacaçolcujtlapol, cujtlatolpol, cujtlatoxacpol, cujtlananapol, nacatica tlamomotlalpol, tlacamjmjlli, xocopaticapol, eticapol, etipatic, xocotexpol, quatecompol, nacazchichipichtic, ixquatolmjmjlpol, ixtzotzoltic, camatalapol, cantetepol, çan viviiocpol, iacatatamalpol, iacaviiocpol, iacaololpol, texipaltotomacpol, quechnacapol, quechnanacapol, tlactzotzolpol, macujcujtlaxcollocapol, mapilcujcujtlanexpol, metztlatlalqujmjlpol, cotztlatlalqujmjlpol, xocpaltitilacpol:

vel tomaoa, vel veiia, vellaelivi, vel tlacaçoltia, aoccan tlacanezquj mochioa, tetlaelti mochioa: ça vetztoc, icicatoc, neneciuhtoc, tequjamjquj, tequjteucivi: expa nappa in tlaqua cemjlhujtl: auh moiovallacavia; auh amo çan quexqujch in qujqua, nelli mach in qujquequeça tlaqualli.

Auh injc mjquj xixitinj in jnacaio, cujcujtlatzaianj in jma in jcxi: auh in oc nen ipaio in jpaleviloca motlanoqujlitinemj

Nicpochovia, njnopochovia, ninotomava, njnoveilia.

Metl: in jtech ca metl

mamae, amatlapale, vitzio, mechichioalo, iollo, tzintamalle, metzonteio, menelhoaio, qujioio, meiallo, necujo, nequaio, aio, ichio, chapactic, chapanquj, macopiltic, xoxoctic, mecovaio, pipilhoa, pilhoa, teconj, pacholonj, aqujlonj, tlalilonj, meçoio.

Tlacametl,

vei, vecapan; matilaoac, mapatlaoac.

Ocelometl, cujcujltic, mocujcujlo

Nexmetl, menextic, nextic, nexeoac, xiuhtototic.

Macôcol, chichioalcocoltic.

Mexoxoctli, xoxoctic, yiapaltic.

---

3. *Metl:* generic name for agave; cf. § 5, n. 86, *supra.*

4. *Tlacametl: Agave potatorum, A. salmiana, A. atrovirens* (Sahagún, Garibay ed., Vol. IV, p. 361).

5. *Acad. Hist. MS: menextli;* hence not an adjective but an alternative name.

THE XILOMETL has slender leaves.

THE TZILACAYOMETL is varicolored, spattered with white.

THE UITZITZILMETL is of average small size; it is moderately small, blue.

THE ACAMETL has slender leaves, long leaves, a slender center.

TEMETL

It is of average size. The leaves are small and thick. It has a rather high base.

CUEÇALMETL

It is also called *teometl*. It is striped with white. It is small; the leaves are yellow.

PATIMETL OR PATAYAMETL

It is the maguey from which potable maguey syrup comes. It is the kind from which maguey syrup can be made, from which wine is made. The maguey fibre comes from it, the kind which can be dressed, spun; from which capes are made; which can be twisted, dyed, darkened. From the maguey comes the spine, the one which serves to pierce, to puncture. It is pointed, pointed on the end, black.

I plant the maguey. I transplant the maguey. I set out the maguey. I sow the maguey. I press the maguey in. The maguey takes hold, takes root, buds, sets a node, grows, sends out fresh leaves, enlarges, matures, forms a stalk.

I break up the plant. I break up the maguey. I pierce the center. I pierce the stalk. I clean the surface. I scrape it. I remove the maguey syrup. I remove the maguey syrup from each one. I heat the maguey syrup. I make wine. I scrape the maguey leaf. I dress the maguey leaf to extract the fibre.

NOPAL[6]

It is green; it is green, herb-green. It has branches, leaves, forked branches. It is smooth; it is juicy; it has tunas; it is stringy, net-like. It has an excretion.

COZNOCHNOPALLI

TLATOCNOPALLI

ANOCHNOPALLI

XILOMETL, mapitzaoac.

TZILACAIOMETL, mocujcujcujlo, moztacatzitzicujtz.

VITZITZILMETL: çan qualton, çã vel ipanton, texotic.

ACAMETL, mapipitzaoac, maviviac iollopitzaoac.

TEMETL,

çan qualton, matilacpil tetzonvecapanton.

CUEÇALMETL

yoan mjtoa teumetl, iztacatica vavanquj, tepiton, macoçauhquj.

PATIMETL, ANOÇO PATAIAMETL:

in metl itech qujça in necutli ivanj, necutlatilonj, octlalilonj: itech qujça in ichtli, cimalonj, tzaoalonj, tilmachioalonj malinalonj, palonj, iapalonj in metl itech qujça in vitztli, tlatzoponjlonj, tlaçovanj, vitztic, iacavitztic, tliltic.

Nimeteca njmeaquja, njmetlalia, njmepixoa, njmepachoa: in metl tlaana, monelhoaiotia, celia, ce yix qujoalquetza, mozcaltia, papatlaca, tlatlacoiauh, maci qujioti:

njtlatlapana, njmetlapana; njtlaiolloixili, njtlaqujoxili, njtlaixochpana, njtlachiquj, njnecueoa, njnenecueoa, njnecutlatia: noctlalia, njtlachichilia, njtlacima.

NUPALLI

xoxouhquj, xoxoctic, qujltic, mamae, amatlapale, mamaxaltic, alaoac, aio, nochio, ichio, matlaio, iacacujtle.

COZNUCHNUPALLI

TLATOCNUPALLI:

ANUCHNUPALLI

---

6. *Nopalli:* generic term for tuna-producing *Cactaceae* (Santamaría, *Dic. de Mejicanismos,* p. 761 — *nopal*); see also Dressler, "Pre-Columbian Cultivated Plants," p. 140.

Xoconochnopalli[7]

The TENOPALLI is light blue, ashen, thick.

Tecolonochnopalli

The TLANEXNOPALLI is ashen. It is a creeper; it just creeps.

The ÇACANOCHNOPALLI[8] is thick-leafed, sturdy.

The NOPAL PATCH is a place of many thorns, a thorny place, a nopal forest.

Tziuactli

Its name is *tziuactli*. It is like a small maguey, and its stems are a little drooping. It has leaves, slender leaves. It has spines, it has stems, it has a silk. It is edible; it can be cooked in an olla. Its silk is sweet; it can be baked on a griddle. Its stems are slender, long, rough, scabrous. It forms a stem, becomes rough, extends, shoots out.

The TZIUACTLI PATCH is a place of danger, a difficult place.

Nequametl[9]

It is small, full of thorns, blue, a flowerer, a bloomer, a blossomer. It produces thorns; it blooms, it blossoms.

The NEQUAMETL PATCH is in the mountains, on the mountain, in the crags, on the crags.

Teocomitl[10]

It is round. It has coarse thorns, sticky thorns. It is edible; it can be set in ashes. It is called *teocomitl* because if its spine is thrust in someone's foot, it can no more come out unless it is cut out, because it is sticky. His foot enlarges, swells.

The TEOCOMITL PATCH is a difficult place, a place of danger, a frightful place.

Netzoli

It is constricted, like a twisted cord, full of thorns. It has branches.

The NETZOLI PATCH is a place which bites one.

Xoconochnupalli,

TENOPALLI texotic, cujtlanextic, tilaoac,

Tecolonuchnupalli:

TLANEXNUPALLI, cujtlanextic, movivilananj, çan movilana:

ÇACANUCHNUPALLI, matilactic, chicaoac.

IN NUPALIA havatla, havaiocan, nupalquauhtla.

Tzivactli

itoca, tzivactli in juhquj metontli yoan in jqujioio, chapactontli, mamae, mapipitzaoac, vitzio, qujioio, xiloio; qualonj, paoaxonj: in jxiloio necutic, ixconj: in jqujioio, piaztic, viac, chachaquachtic, tetecujtztic, qujioti, chachaquachivi; mana motlamjna.

IN TZIVACTLA tlaovican, ovican.

Nequametl,

tepiton moca havatl, texotic, suchiovanj, mosuchiotianj, cueponjnj, avaiova, mosuchiotia, cueponj.

NEQUAMETLA tepetla, tepepa, texcalla, texalpan.

Teucomjtl;

ololtic, haoaio chamaoac, haoaio çaçalic, qualonj, nexquetzalonj. Injc mjtoa teucomjtl: in aqujn ic mjxili ivitzio, aoc vel qujça intlacamo motequj: ipampa ca çaçalic, tomaoa, poçaoa in jicxi.

TEUCONTLA ovican, tlaovican temauhtican.

Netzoli;

cocomotztic, tlamalintic, moca havatl, mamae.

NETZOLLA: tequaquaia.

---

7. *Xoconochnopalli*: prob. *Opuntia imbricata* (Santamaría, *op. cit.*, p. 640 — *joconostle*).

8. *Çacanochnopalli*: prob. *Opuntia megarhiza* Rose (*ibid.*, p. 952 — *sacanochtli*).

9. *Nequametl*: *Agavis mexicana* (Sahagún, *op. cit.*, p. 345).

10. *Teocomitl*: *Mammillaria tetracantha* Salm-Dyck (*M. dolichocentra* Lehm.) in Hernández, *op. cit.*, Vol. III, p. 942; *Ferocactus* sp. (Standley, "Trees and Shrubs," Pt. 4, p. 940).

TEONOCHTLI

Now it is called *uei nochtli*. It is green, herb-green, long, slender. It is a moistener; it is cooling, a cooler. It cools things.

TEMEMETLA

It is drooping, somewhat squat, tender, broad. It is potable, [a drink] which is constantly fresh, cooling. It freshens, it cures.

TETZMITL OR TETZMETL[11]

It has a continuous exudation. It has blossoms. It is a medicine.

TLACHINOLTETZMITL[12]

It is the same as the *tetzmitl*; however, it is quite small. The foliage is ruddy. Its constant exudation is an eye medicine.

THE TLAPALTETZMITL is the same as the *tlachinoltetzmitl.*

TEXIOTL[13]

It has scales, many scales. It is a medicine, potable; from it water can be extracted. It is cooling; it is a means of cooling. It cools things; it cures, it cools one.

THE TEXIUTL is the same.[14]

ATZOMIATL OR ATZOYATL[15]

It has an aroma, a sickening smell. It has a blossom, it has blossoms; it has foliage, thick foliage; it is shady. It is like spindle whorls;[16] it is spindle-whorl-like.

THE ATZOMIATL PATCH

It spreads stinking; it stinks continuously. It spreads shading, it spreads ever shading, it spreads giving shade.

TETZMOLI OR AUATETZMOLI[17]

It is a little drooping, matted, strong, nerve-like, tough, compact, very compact. It knocks the skin off of one; it scratches one.

THE TETZMOLI PATCH, the *auatetzmoli* patch, is a place which knocks the skin off of one, which scratches one.

TEUNUCHTLI:

axcan mjtoa vei nuchtli, xoxoctic, qujltic, viac, piaztic, nepalonj, itztic, tlacevilonj, tlacevia.

TEMEMETLA;

chapactontli, tlalpanton, celic, papatlactic, ivanj, tlacecelianj, itztic, tlacecelia, tlapatia.

TETZMJTL, ANOÇO TETZMETL,

memeiallo, suchio, patli.

TLACHINOLTETZMJTL:

çan ie no ie in tetzmjtl: iece çan tepiton, qujllo, tlatlavic: in jmemeiallo ixpatli.

TLAPALTETZMJTL: çan ie no iehoatl, in tlachinoltetzmjtl.

TEXIOTL,

xincaio, xixincaio: patli, ivanj, aqujxtilonj, itztic tlacevilonj, tlacevia, tlapatia, tececec,

ÇAN IE NO ie in texivtl

ATZOMJATL, ANOÇO ATZOIATL,

hiiac, cocoiac, suchio, susuchio, qujqujllo, qujllotilaoac, ceceoallo, mamalacachti, mamalacachiuhquj.

ATZOMJATLA

tlaiaxtoc, tlaiiaxtimanj, ceoatoc, ceceoatoc, tlatlacecextoc.

TETZMOLI, ANOÇO AOATETZMOLI:

chapactontli, paçoltic, chicaoac, tlalhoatic, pipinquj, pipictic, pipicpatic, tetoxon, tevaçon.

TETZMOLLA, avatetzmolla, tetotoxonca, tevaçoncan.

---

11. *Tetzmitl: Sedum dendroideum* Moc. y Sessé (Hernández, *Hist. de las Plantas,* Vol. I, p. 140).
12. *Tlachinoltetzmitl:* prob. *Kohleria deppeana* or *Croton draco* Schw. (Sahagún, *op. cit.,* p. 362).
13. *Texiotl: Sedum dendroideum* (Santamaría, *op. cit.,* p. 1041 — *texiote*).
14. *Acad. Hist. MS* adds another heading, *texochitl,* with no text.
15. *Atzomiatl: Compositae? Mirabilis jalapa? Castilleja canescens?* (Hernández, *op. cit.,* Vol. I, p. 194 *sqq.*).
16. *Acad. Hist. MS: mamalacachtic.*
17. *Tetzmoli: Quercus* sp. (Santamaría, *op. cit.,* p. 41 — *aguatezmolli, encina común*).

Tlacopopotl or tepopotl[18]

It is dry, dark-stalked. It is a medicine [plant] from which water can be extracted; it is potable. Its root is bitter. It is a cough medicine, an aid to digestion. It aids the digestion, it cures.

The chimalacatl[19] has blossoms; it is hollow.

The uitzocuitlapilli[20] has slender blossoms; it is hollow, bitter.

The nopallacotl is slender; it has a blossom, it has blossoms.

Tenextlacotl or tetlacotl

It is hard, resilient, strong, tough. It is a writing medium, a covering medium. Its berries are brown, and they are a medicine for dandruff.

Yiamolli[21]

It has berries, it has foliage. Its berries are also a medicine for dandruff.

Tlacopopotl, anoço tepuputl

vavaztic, quauhiocatzaoac, patli, aqujxtilonj, ivanj: in jnelhoaio chichic: tlatlacizpatli, tlatemovianj, tlatemovia, tlapatia.

Chimalacatl: suchio, iticoionquj.

Vitzocujtlapilli, suchiopiaztic, iticoionquj, chichic.

Nupallacotl; pipiaztic, suchio xosuchio.

Tenextlacotl, anoço tetlacotl

tepitztic, oltic, chicaoac, tlaquaoac, tlacujllotilonj, tlatlapacholonj; camopaltic: in jcapollo: yoan quatequjxqujicivizpatli.

Iiamoli,

cacapollo, qujqujllo: in jcapollo, çan no quatequjxqujicivizpatli.

---

18. *Tlacopopotl: Arundinella hispida* (Sahagún, *op. cit.*, p. 361).

19. *Chimalacatl: Verbesina crocota* Cav. ? *Helianthus annuus?* (Hernández, *op. cit.*, pp. 99 *sq*).

20. *Uitzocuitlapilli: Aporocactus flagelliformis* (L.) Lemaire (*ibid.*, Vol. III, p. 936).

21. *Yiamolli: Phytolacca octandra, P. decandra, P. rugosa, P. longispica* (*ibid.*, Vol. I, p. 277).

ILLUSTRATIONS

quando quiere picar yllevanta
se en alto, yarrojese sobre lo
que quiere picar. y quando pica
tambien ella muere. porque e
cha de vn golpe toda su ponço
ña y conella la vida.

¶Parrapho septimo de
otras culebras mostruosas
enst ser y en sus propie da
des.

auh acan velittv. in canjn o
noc: auh notle in qujqua, cñ
iquac noci in teqria. injquac
tzthoponja. auh in aqujn quj
thoponja: çan njmã mjctive
ti. anno vel ce ora in mjqrj,
çan vel athitvnca: auh inje
tequa. ahtvpa paltanj, vel
tlacpac, vel aco iniauh: auh
çan ipan valtemo in aqujn
in noço tlein qujqua. Auh in
icpatlanj: in manoçe ic oal
temo. cenca ioltica : in quex
qujch icremj, injc paltanti
nenj. Auh injquac tequa: nj
mã noiquac mjqrj, qujl ipã
pa: çan njmã mochi tlamj in
itengualac, injztlac, canel
noço iehoatl injtolca, inca
njn teltoponja, aocmo athi
contvca in teltoponjlonj: auh
no vncan veltzi in in cooatvn
tli:

¶Injc chicome parrapho in
techpa tlatva cooame, yew
intin : auh cecë tlamähtli inte
ca.

1. Ocelutl. 2. Iztac ocelotl. 3. Tlatlauhqui ocelutl. 4. Tlacaxolutl. 5. Tzoniztac. 6. Cuitlachtli. 7. Maçamiztli. 8. Cuitlamiztli. 9, 10. Coyotl. 11. Ocotochtli. 12. Oztoua. 13. Mapachitli. 14. Peçotli.

— *After Paso y Troncoso*

15. Coyametl. 16. Techalutl. 17. Tlaltechalutl. 18. Mothotli. 19. Motoyauitl. 20, 21. Tlaquatl. 22. Citli. 23. Tochtli. 24. Coçama. 25. Epatl. 26. Oçomatli. 27. Capturing monkeys. 28, 29. Maçatl. 30. Iztac maçatl. 31, 32. Maçatl. 33. Chichi. 34. Tevih. 35. Xoloitzcuintli. 36. Tlalchichi. 37. Aitzcuintli. 38. Toçan. 39, 40. Quimichin. 41. Chachauatl.

42. Quetzaltototl (Chapter 2). 43. Tzinitzcan. 44. Tlauhquechol. 45. Xiuhquechol. 46, 47. Çaquan. 48, 49. Ayoquan. 50. Chalchiuhtototl. 51. Xioapalquechol. 52. Xochitenacatl. 53. Quappachtototl. 54. Elototl. 55. Toznene. 56. Toztli. 57. Alo. 58. Cocho. 59. Quiliton. 60. Tlalacueçali. 61, 62. Vitzitzili. 63. **Totozcatleton** 64. Yollotototl. 65. Popocales. 66. Tecuçiltototl. 67. Ixmatlatototl. 68. Canauhtli. 69. Concanauhtli. 70, 71. Canauhtli. 72. Tlalalacatl. 73. Tocuilcoyotl. 74. Xomotl. 75. Teçoloctli. 76. Atotolin. 77. Quachilton. 78. Vexocanauhtli. 79. Açolin. 80. Atzitzicuilotl.

81. Acuicuialotl. 82 (a) Aztatl, (b) axoquen, (c) quauhtotoli. 83. Atotolin. 84. Capturing the atotolin. 85. Eating the atotolin. 86. Acoiotl. 87. Hunting the acitli. 88. Tenitztli. 89. Quapetlauac. 90. Quatezcatl. 91. Tolcomoctli. 92. Acuitlachtli.

— *After Paso y Troncoso*

93. Acuitlachtli in the spring. 94. Capturing the acuitlachtli. 95. Couixin. 96. Icxixoxouhqui. 97. Quetzalteçolocton. 98. Metzcanauhtli. 99. Quacoztli. 100. Hecatototl. 101. Amanacoche. 102. Atapalcatl. 103. Tzitziua. 104. Xalquani. 105. Yacapitzauac. 106. Tzoniaiauhqui. 107. Çolcanauhtli. 108. Chilcanauhtli. 109. Achalalactli. 110. Yacapatlauac. 111. Pipitztli. 112. Oactli. 113. Acachichictli. 114. Quauhtli. 115. Itzquauhtli. 116. Iztac quauhtli. 117. Ioualquauhtli. 118. Tlacoquauhtli. 119. Aquauhtli.

120. Itzquauhtli. 121. Aitzquauhtli. 122. Mixcoaquauhtli. 123. Cozcaquauhtli. 124. Oactli. 125. Tzopilotl. 126. Tecolotl. 127. Çacatecolotl. 128. Cacalotl. 129. Acacalotl. 130. Pipixcan. 131. Tlhotli. 132. Tlohquauhtli. 133–135. Quauhtlotli. 136. Coztlhotli. 137. Hecatlhotli. 138. Aiauhtlhotli. 139. Iztac tlhotli.

— *After Paso y Troncoso*

140, 141. Itztlhotli. 142, 143. Necuilictli. 144. Tetzompa. 145. Impaling the prey. 146. Xochitototl. 147. Aiacachtototl. 148. Tachitovia. 149. Quauhtotopotli. 150. Poxaquatl. 151. Vitlalotl. 152. Chiquatli. 153. Tapalcatzotzonquì. 154. Chichtli. 155. Tlalchiquatli. 156 Chiltotopil. 157. Molotl. 158. Quachichil. 159. Cocotli. 160. Çolin. 161, 162. Ouaton. 163–165. Vilotl.

166. Tlacavilotl. 167. Cuitlacochin. 168. Çentzontlatole. 169. Miauatototl. 170, 171. Turkeys. 172. Turkey with brood. 173. Turkey hens. 174, 175. Feathers. 176. Eyes. 177, 178. Head. 179. Neck. 180. Intestines. 181. Canauhtli (Chapter 3).

182, 183. Canauhtli. 184. Atapalcatl. 185. Atoncuepotli. 186. Ateponaztli. 187. Hunting birds. 188. Michi. 189. Tlacamichi. 190. Chimalmichi. 191. Totomichi. 192. Vitzitzilmichi. 193 (a) Papalomichi, (b) ocelomichi. 194. Quauhxouili. 195. Tecuicitli. 196. Chacali. 197. Ayotl.

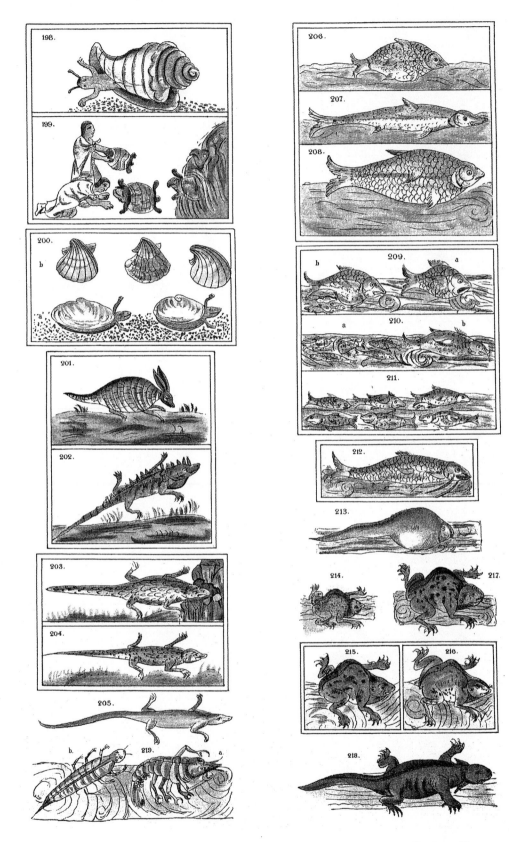

198. Tecciztli. 199. Catching turtles. 200. Tapachtli. 201. Ayotochtli. 202. Quauhcuetzpali. 203. Texixincoyotl. 204. Tecouixi. 205. Milquaxoch. 206. Topotli. 207. Amilotl. 208. Xouili. 209–211. Unidentified small fish. 212. Tentzonmichi. 213. Atepocatl. 214. Cueyatl. 215, 216. Tecalatl. 217. Çoquicueyatl. 218. Axolotl. 219 (a) Acocili, (b) aneneztli.

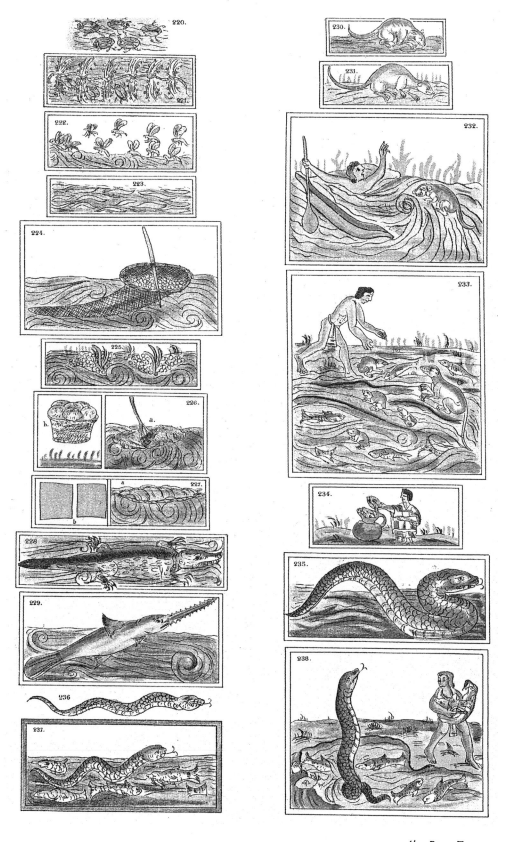

220. Axaxayacatl. 221. Catching the axaxayacatl. 222. Amoiotl. 223. Ocuiliztac. 224. Michpili. 225. Amilotetl. 226. Izcauitl. 227. Tecuitlatl. 228. Acuetzpali (Chapter 4). 229. Acipaquitli. 230. Aitzcuintli. 231. Acoyotl. 232, 233. Habits of the acoyotl. 234. Capture of the acoyotl. 235, 236. Acoatl. 237. Acoatl capturing fish. 238. Acoatl capturing people.

239. Capturing the acoatl. 240. Acoatl. 241. Citlalaxolotl. 242. Cacatl. 243. Tamaçoli. 244. Milcalatl. 245, 246. Tecutlacoçauhqui (Chapter 5). 247. Capturing the tecutlacoçauhqui with club and powdered tobacco. 248. Iztac coatl. 249. Tleuacoatl.

250. Chiauitl. 251. Treatment for chiauitl bite. 252–254. Olcoatl. 255. Maquizcoatl. 256–258. Maça-coatl. 259. Tetzauhcoatl. 260. Tlapapalcoatl. 261. Coapetlatl.

262. Coapetlatl. 263. Break-up of coapetlatl. 264. Coapetlatl. 265. Chimalcoatl. 266. Citlalcoatl. 267. Metlapilcoatl. 268. Aueiactli. 269. Palancacoatl. 270. Hecacoatl. 271. Tzoalcoatl. 272, 273. Cincoatl.

274. Cincoatl. 275. Mecacoatl. 276, 277. Quetzalcoatl. 278. Xicalcoatl. 279. Miauacoatl. 280. Petz-coatl. 281. Coatatapaiolli. 282, 283. Petlaçolcoatl. 284. Colotl. 285. Tequani tocatl.

— *After Paso y Troncoso*

286, 287. Treatment of spider bites. 288. Tocamaxaqualli. 289. Texcan. 290. Caltatapach. 291. Pinauiztli. 292. Azcatl. 293. Ant bite. 294. Tlatlauhqui azcatl. 295. Icel azcatl. 296. Quauhazcatl. 297. Cuitlaazcatl.

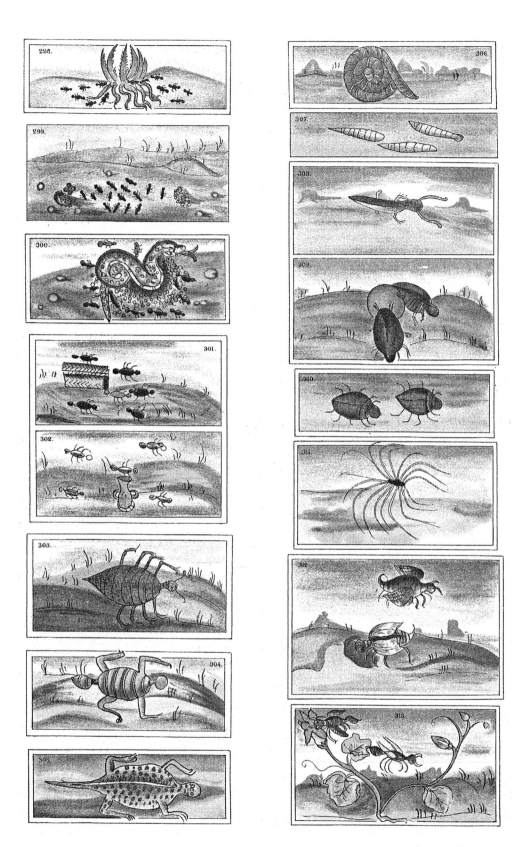

298. Tlilazcatl. 299. Tzicatl. 300. Tzicanantli. 301, 302. Tlalxiquipilli. 303. Tlalacatl. 304, 305. Tapaxi. 306. Conyayaoal. 307. Tlalomitl. 308. Ueuetlaneuhqui. 309. Tecuitlaololo. 310. Pinacatl. 311. Tzontli ima. 312. Xicotli. 313. Pipioli.

314. Mimiauatl. 315. Papalotl. 316. Xicalpapalotl. 317. Tlilpapalotl. 318. Tlecocozpapalotl. 319. Iztac papalotl. 320. Chian papalotl. 321. Texopapalotl. 322. Xochipapalotl. 323. Uappapalotl. 324–326. Chapoli.

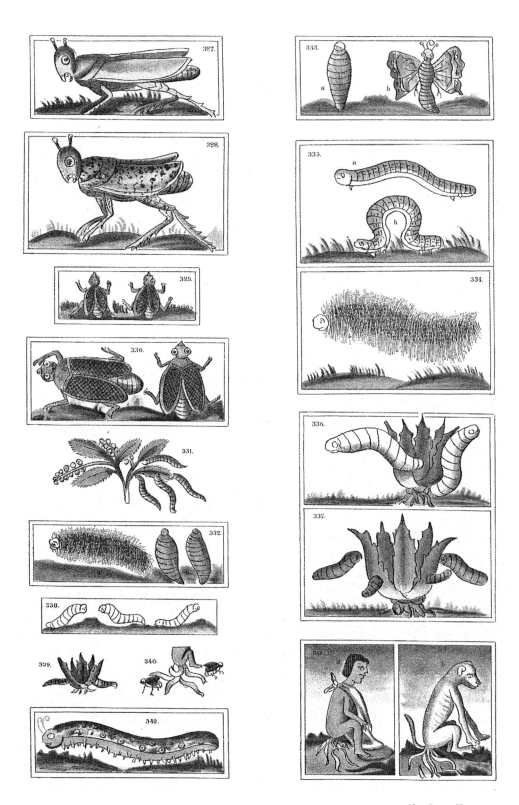

327. Acachapoli. 328. Çolacachapoli. 329, 330. Çacatecuilichtli. 331. Capolocuili. 332, 333. Auatecolotl. 334. Paçotl. 335. Tetatamachiuhqui. 336, 337. Mcocuili. 338. Chichilocuili. 339. Metzonocuili.
340. Tzinocuili. 341. Tzoncoatl. 342. Chiancuetla.

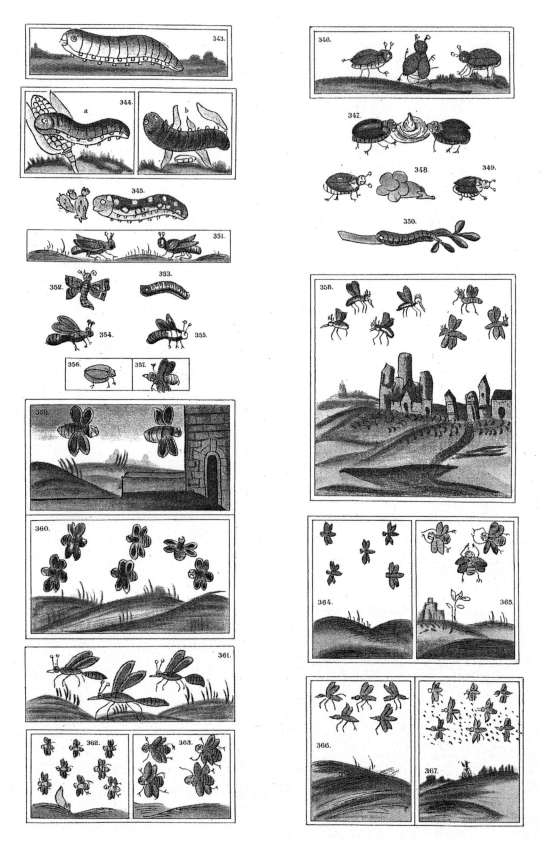

343. Nextecuili. 344 (a) Cinocuili, (b) tlaçolocuili. 345. Citlalocuili. 346. Temoli. 347. Cuitlatemoli. 348. Ayoxochquiltemoli. 349. Quauhtemoli. 350. Quauhocuili. 351–355. Icpitl. 356. Mayatl. 357. Tecmilotl. 358. Çayoli. 359. Miccaçayoli. 360. Xopan çayoli. 361. Tzonuatzalton. 362. Chilton. 363. Cuitlaçayoli. 364. Çayolton. 365. Xiuhçayoli. 366. Moyotl. 367. Xalmoyotl.

368. Forest. 369. Mountainous forest. 370. Forest animals. 371. Wood-gathering. 372. Wild beasts.
373, 374. Tlatzcan. 375. Oyametl. 376. Ayauhquauitl. 377. Ocotl. 378. Ilin. 379. Aueuetl.

— *After Paso y Troncoso*

380. Pochotl. 381. Auaquauitl. 382. Auatetzmoli. 383. Tepetomatl. 384. Pocquauitl. 385. Uexotl. 386. Quetzalhuexotl. 387. Icçotl. 388. Tlacuilolquauitl. 389. Tlacalhuazquauitl. 390 (a) Uitzquauitl, (b) quappotzalli, (c) quauhcayactli. 391. Tree planting. 392. Tree. 393. Tree trunk. 394, 395. Tree shape. 396. Branch.

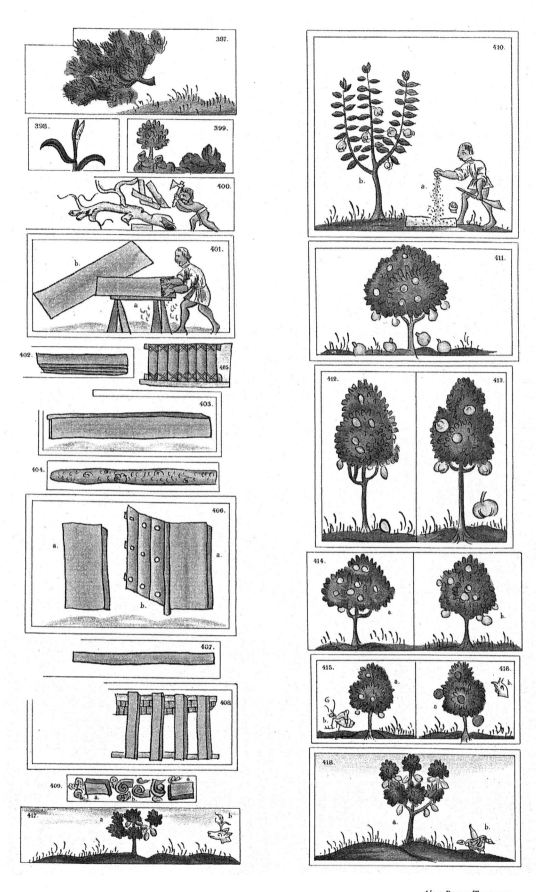

397. Tree top. 398. Tender shoot. 399. Tree bark. 400. Wood chopping. 401. Wood for sieve rims. 402. Small beams. 403. Beams. 404. Plank. 405. Binding wall beams. 406. Wooden door. 407. Joist. 408. Pillars. 409. Wood fragments. 410. Tree planting. 411. Tzapotl. 412. Cochiztzapotl. 413. Tlacaçoltzapotl. 414. Atzapotl. 415. Xicotzapotl. 416. Totolcuitlatzapotl. 417. Maçaxocotl. 418. Atoyaxocotl.

— *After Paso y Troncoso*

419. Xalxocotl. 420. Teonacaztli. 421, 422. Uaxi. 423. Mizquitl. 424. Quetzalmizquitl. 425. Capoli. 426. Elocapoli. 427. Tlaolcapoli. 428. Quauhcamotli. 429. Nopalli. 430. Iztac nochnopalli. 431. Coznochnopalli.

432–439. Nopalli. 440. Quauhcamotli. 441. Camotli. 442. Xicamoxiuitl. 443. Cimatl. 444. Tolcimatl. 445. Cacapxon. 446. Acaxilotl. 447 (a) Çacateztli. 448 (c) Atzatzamolli. 449. Coatl xoxouhqui (Chapter 7). 450, 451. Tlapatl. 452 (a) Tzitzintlapatl, (b) mixitl. 453 (a) Nanacatl, (b) tochtetepon. 454. Atlepatli. 455. Haquiztli. 456 (a) Tenxoxoli, (b) quimichpatli.

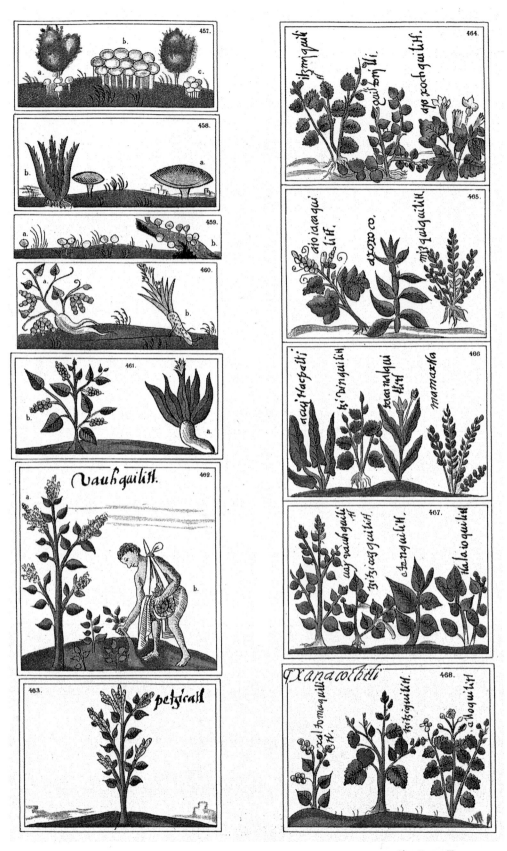

457 (a) Nanacatl, (b) tzontecomananacatl, (c) xelhoaznanacatl. 458 (a) Chimalnanacatl, (b) menanacatl. 459 (a) Çacananacatl, (b) quauhnanacatl. 460 (a) Cimatl, (b) hamolli. 461 (a) Tecpatli, (b) yiamoli. 462. Vauhquilitl. 463. Petzicatl. 464 (a) Itzmiquilitl, (b) quiltonilli, (c) ayoxochquilitl. 465 (a) Ayoyacaquilitl, (b) axoxoco, (c) mizquiquilitl. 466 (a) Acuitlacpalli, (b) tziuinquilitl, (c) tacanalquilitl, (d) mamaxtla. 467 (a) Uei uauhquilitl, (b) tzitzicazquilitl, (c) etenquilitl, (d) tlalayoquilitl. 468 (a) Xaltomaquilitl, (b) tzitziquilitl, (c) eloquilitl.

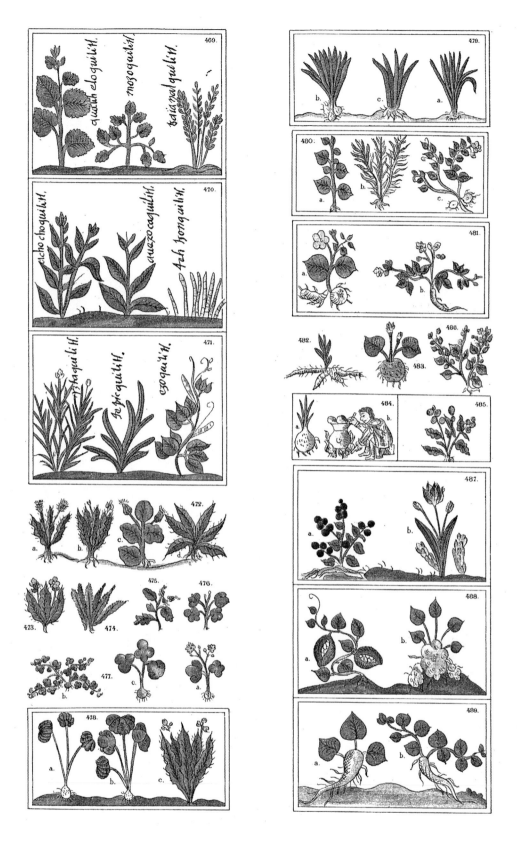

469 (a) Quauheloquilitl, (b) moçoquilitl, (c) tzayanalquilitl. 470 (a) Achochoquilitl, (b) auexoca-quilitl, (c) tehtzonquilitl. 471 (a) Iztaquilitl, (b) tepicquilitl, (c) eçoquilitl. 472 (a) Uitzquilitl, (b) qua-uitzquilitl, (c) chichicaquilitl, (d) coyocuexi. 473. Popoyauh. 474. Mexixin. 475. Xoxocoyoli. 476. Xoxo-coyolpapatla. 477 (a) Xoxocoyolcuecuepoc, (b) xoxocoyolhuiuila, (c) miccaxoxocoyoli. 478 (a, b) Quauh-xoxocoyoli, (c) quanacaquilitl. 479 (a) Xonacatl, (b) tepexonacatl, (c) maxten. 480 (a) Papaloquilitl, (b) ayauhtona, (c) xiuitl xochiquallo. 481 (a) Xicama, (b) tolcimaquilitl. 482. Acaxilotl. 483. Atzatza-molli. 484. Çacateztli. 485. Xaltomatl. 486. Coyototomatl. 487 (a) Atlitliliatl, (b) tlalxilotl. 488 (a) Tlal-ayotli, (b) iztac patli. 489 (a) Cuicuitlapile, (b) iztac çaçalic.

490. Centli ina. 491. Tlatlauhcapatli. 492. Tlanoquiloni. 493. Eloxochineluatl. 494. Naui iuipil.
495. Tlalcacauatl. 496. Tetzmitl. 497. Eloquiltic. 498. Chichipiltic. 499. Coyotomatl.

— *After Paso y Troncoso*

500. Tlalchichic. 501. Coatli. 502, 503. Tzipipatli. 504. Nanauaxiuitl. 505. Necutic. 506. Coayielli. 507 (a) Tememetla, (b) texochitl. 508 (a) Yiauhtli, (b) xonecuilpatli. 509. Xoxouhcapatli. 510. Tzitzicaztli. 511. Tecomaxochitl. 512. Picietl.

— *After Paso y Troncoso*

513. Itzietl. 514. Hecapatli. 515. Tlapatl. 516. Nanacatl. 517. Peyotl. 518. Toloa. 519. Çoçoyatic. 520. Pipitzauac. 521. Iztac quauitl. 522. Coanenepilli. 523. Ilacatziuhqui. 524. Macoztic metl. 525. Chapolxiuitl. 526. Totonacaxiuitl. 527. Uei patli. 528. Ixyayaual. 529. Eeloquiltic. 530. Toçancuitlaxcolli. 531. Coztomatl.

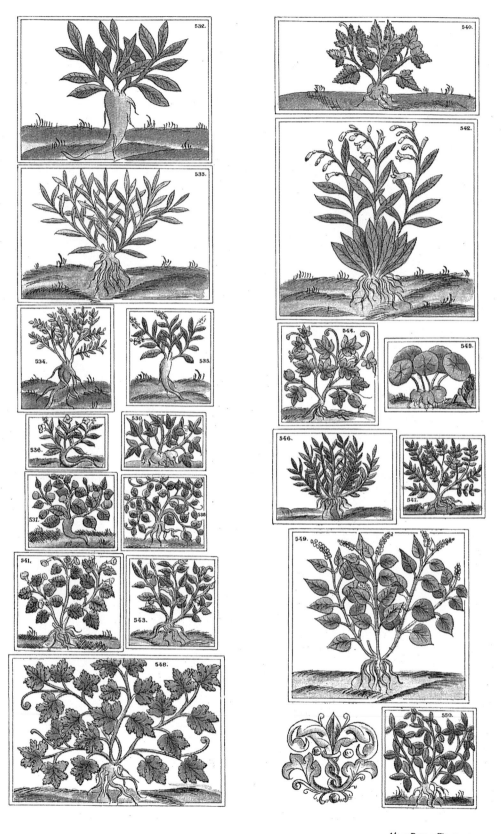

532. Çacacili. 533. Iztac palancapatli. 534. Cototzauhqui xiuitl. 535. Chichientic. 536. Cococ xiuitl. 537. Xaltomatl. 538. Ixnexton. 539. Tecanalxiuitl. 540. Xoxocoyoltic. 541. Iceleua tlacotl. 542. Chilpanton. 543. Chichilquiltic. 544. Tlatlalayotli. 545. Tepeamalacotl. 546. Iztaquiltic. 547. Tlalmizquitl. 548. Poçauizpatli. 549. Uauauhtzin. 550. Tlacoxiuitl.

— *After Paso y Troncoso*

551. Tlalchipili. 552. Acaxilotic. 553. Chichilquiltic quauitl. 554. Uauauhtzin. 555. Iztaquiltic 556. Memeya. 557. Tetzmitic. 558. Tzatzayanalquiltic. 559. Ichcayo. 560. Tlalyetl. 561. Mexiuitl 562. Uitzocuitlapilxiuitl. 563. Iztac patli. 564. Quachtlacalhuaztli. 565. Haauaton. 566. Ololiuhqui. 567. Iztauhyatl. 568. Quauhyayaual. 569. Mamaxtla. 570. Xaltomatl. 571. Quapopultzin.

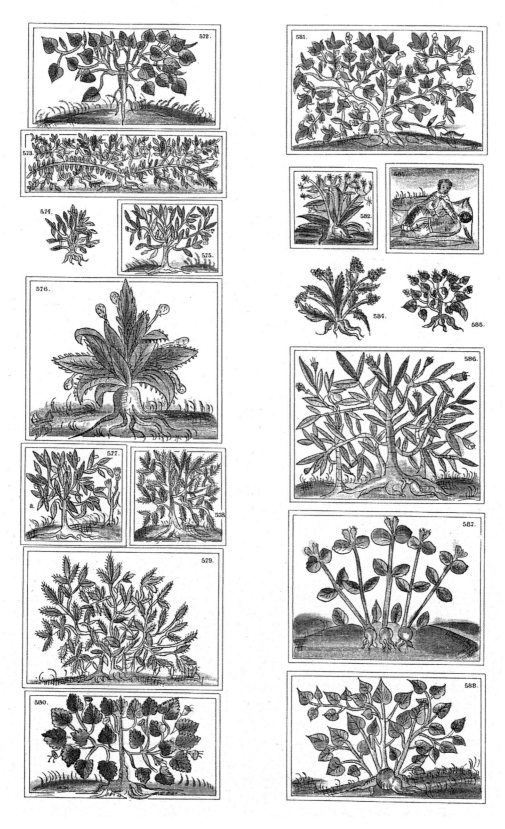

— After Paso y Troncoso

572. Tlalamatl. 573. Xoxotlatzin. 574. Tonalxiuitl. 575. Tlacoxochitl. 576. Ocopiaztli. 577. Topo-çan. 578. Quetzalhuexotl. 579. Tlayapaloni xiuitl. 580. Uei patli. 581. Ololiuhqui. 582. Aitztolin. 583. Use of coaxoxouhqui. 584. Acocoxiuitl. 585. Tepetomatl. 586. Tlatlacotic. 587. Texoxocoioli. 588. Tlatlanquaie.

— *After Paso y Troncoso*

589. Use of tlatlanquaie. 590. Tonacaxochitl. 591. Tlacoxochitl. 592. Quetzalmizquitl. 593. Youalxo-chitl. 594 (a) Cozcaquauhxiuitl, (b) tzopelic xiuitl. 595. Tlatlapaltic. 596. Metl. 597. Use of metl. 598. Ciuapatli. 599. Nopalli. 600. Use of nopalli. 601. Chía.

602. Use of chía. 603. Haacxoyatic. 604. Maticeuac. 605. Iztac patli. 606. Oquichpatli. 607. Tlamacazqui ipapa. 608. Cicimatic. 609. Tzompoton. 610. Cuitlapatli. 611. Oquichpatli. 612. Use of oquichpatli. 613. Chichic patli. 614 (a) Cocopaltic, (b) cocopi. 615. Quiauhteocuitlatl.

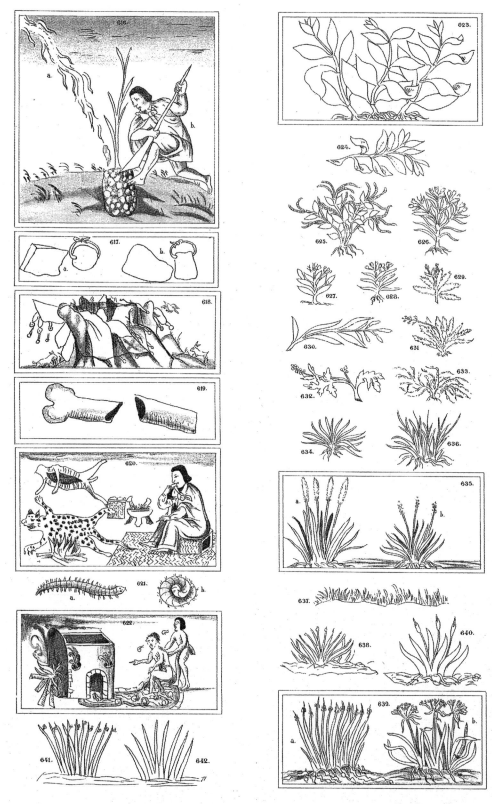

616. Lightning flash and the quiauhteocuitlatl. 617 (a) Xiuhtomoltetl, (b) eztetl. 618. Atl chipin. 619. Quinametli. 620. Flesh of the ocelotl. 621. Coyayaual. 622. Temazcalli. 623, 624. Axocopac. 625. Mecaxuchitl. 626. Ayauhtonan. 627. Tlalpoyomatli. 628. Yiauhtli. 629. Epaçotl. 630. Azpan xiuitl. 631. Tlalquequetzal. 632. Itzcuinpatli. 633. Çacayaman. 634. Tequixquiçacatl. 635 (a) Uauhçacatl, (b) çacamamaztli. 636. Xiuhtecuçacatl. 637. Çacateteztli. 638. Haxalli. 639 (a) Caltoli, (b) itztolin. 640. Tolpatlactli. 641. Tolmimilli. 642. Petlatolli.

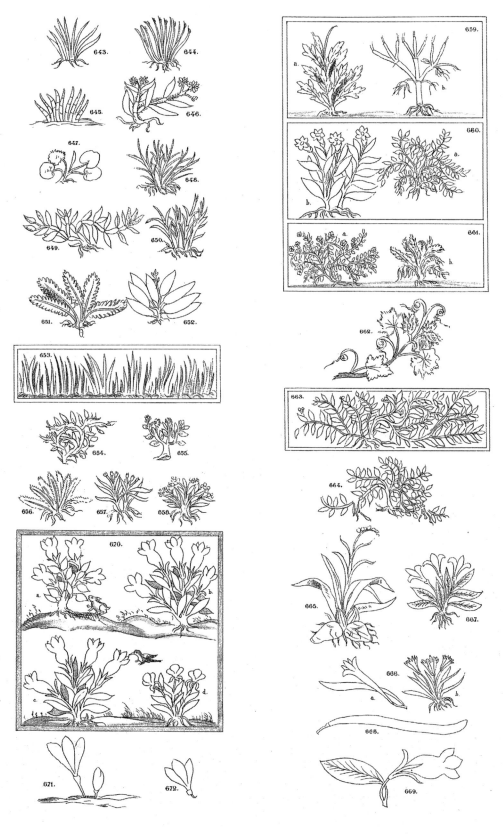

643. Toliaman. 644. Tolnacochtli. 645. Atetetzon. 646. Xomali. 647. Amamalacotl. 648. Atlacotl. 649. Achili. 650. Acatl. 651. Ocopetlatl. 652. Quammamaxtla. 653. Çacatl. 654. Tetzmolin. 655. Quauichpolli. 656. Tequequetzal. 657. Teyiauhtli. 658. Tlalcapoli. 659 (a) Ivintiquilitl, (b) acocoxiuitl. 660 (a) Tlalyetl, (b) tonalxiuitl. 661 (a) Xoxotla, (b) tzompachquilitl. 662. Tetzitzilin. 663. Nopalocoxochitl. 664. Memeyal. 665. Tzacutli. 666. Omixochitl. 667. Tlalizquixochitl. 668. Tlilxuchitl. 669. Coçauhqui xochitl. 670 (a) Chalchiuhyiexochitl, (b) quauhyiexochitl, (c) tzoyac, (d) tonalxochitl. 671. Tlalcacaloxochitl. 672. Totec ixoxochiuh.

673 (a) Texoxoli, (b) nopallacotl, (c) tolcimatl. 674. Caxtlatlapan. 675. Quaztalxochitl. 676. Tlaquili. 677 (a) Acocoxochitl, (b) cempoalxochitl, (c) ciuaxochitl, (d) oquichxochitl. 678 (a) Macuilxochitl, (b) coçatli, (c) tecacayactli, (d) nextamalxochitl, (e) chilpan. 679. Gardens. 680. Xochiquauitl. 681. Iolloxochiquauitl. 682. Eloxochitl. 683. Quauheloxochitl. 684. Cacauaxochitl.

— *After Paso y Troncoso*

685 (a) Izquixochitl, (b) teoizquixochitl, (c) tlapalizquixochitl, (d) cuetlaxxochitl. 686. Teocuitlaxochitl. 687. Teonacaztli. 688. Uitztecolxochitl. 689. Tzompanquauitl. 690. Mapilxochitl. 691. Icçotl.
692. Cacaloxochitl. 693. Xiloxochitl. 694. Chichiualxochitl.

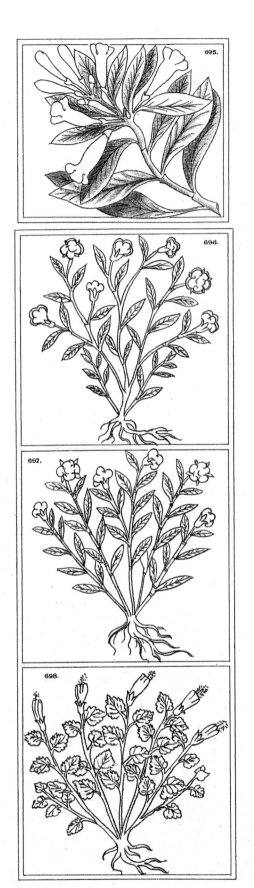

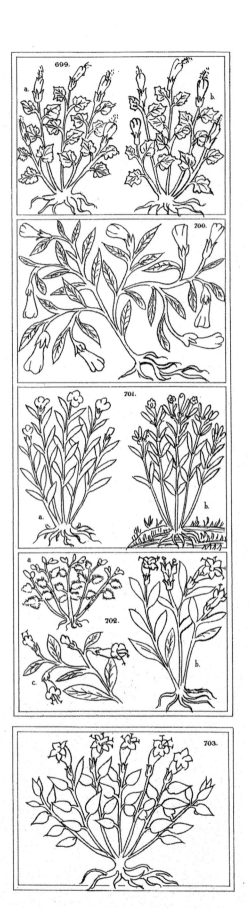

695. Tonacaxochitl. 696. Acuilloxochitl. 697. Cuilloxochitl. 698. Atlatzompili. 699 (a) Tzompilin, (b) toztlatzompilin. 700. Quauizquixochitl. 701 (a) Tlacoizquixochitl, (b) tlacoxochitl. 702 (a) Uitzitzil-xochitl, (b) yiexochitl, (c) coztic yiexochitl. 703. Quauhyiexochitl.

704. Chalchiuhxochitl. 705. Chalchiuhyiexochitl. 706. Tzoyac yiexochitl. 707. Azcalxochitl. 708. Io-
pixochitl. 709. Uacalxochitl. 710. Teccizuacalxochitl. 711 (a) Tochnacazuacalxochitl, (b) tlapalhuacalxo-
chitl. 712. Chilqualli. 713 (a) Oçomacuitlapilxochitl, (b) nopalxochitl. 714 (a) Tetzilacaxochitl, (b) ueue-
xochitl.

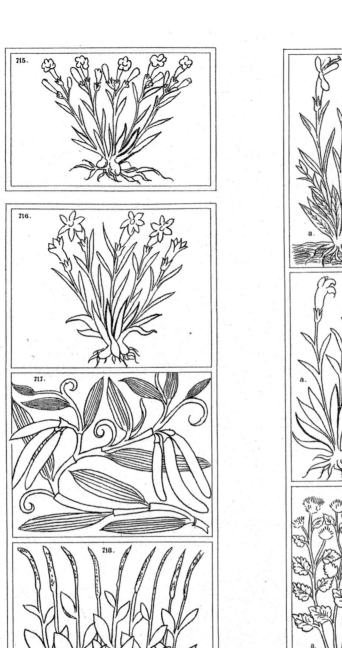

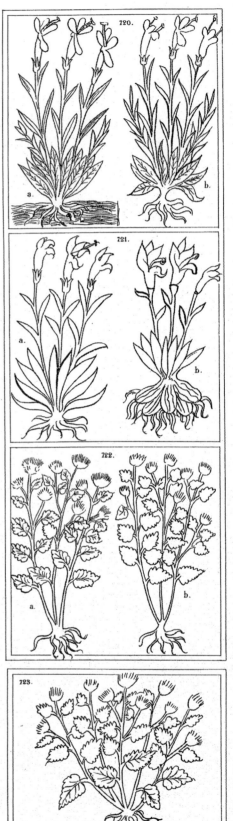

715. Omixochitl. 716. Tlapalomixochitl. 717. Tlilxochitl. 718. Mecaxochitl. 719. Coatzontecomaxochitl. 720 (a) Acaxochitl, (b) quauhacaxochitl. 721 (a) Quauhiztexochitl, (b) tzacuxochitl xiuitl.
722 (a) Hiuixochitl, (b) tlapalihuixochitl. 723. Iztac hiuixochitl.

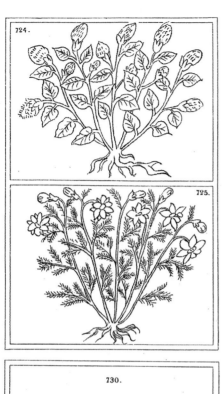

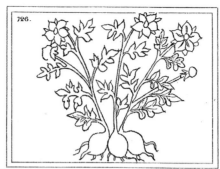

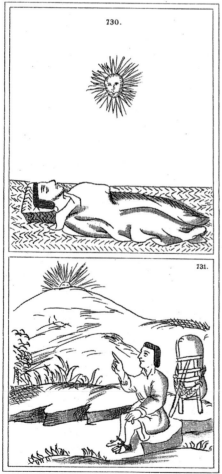

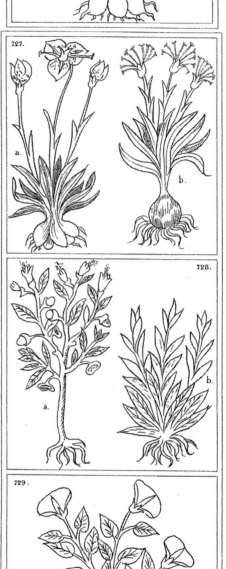

724. Oloxochitl. 725. Mocuepani xochitl. 726. Xalacocotli. 727 (a) Oceloxochitl, (b) quaztalxochitl. 728 (a) Poyomaxochitl, (b) tlalpoyomatli. 729. Teotlaquili. 730, 731. Sunrise and sunset (see teotlaquili).

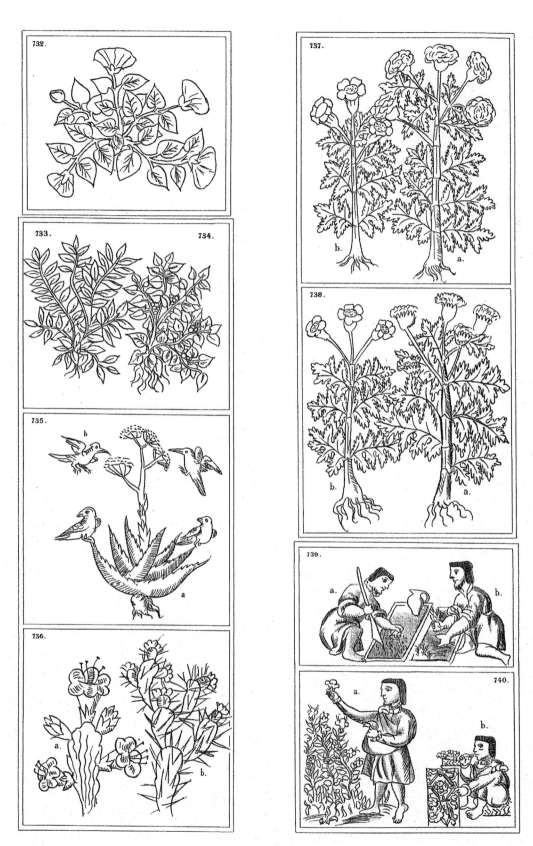

— *After Paso y Troncoso*

732. Tlalizquixochitl. 733. Ocoxochitl. 734. Quetzalocoxochitl. 735. Quiioxochitl. 736. Nopalxochitl. 737, 738. Flowers. 739. Planting flowers. 740. Picking flowers.

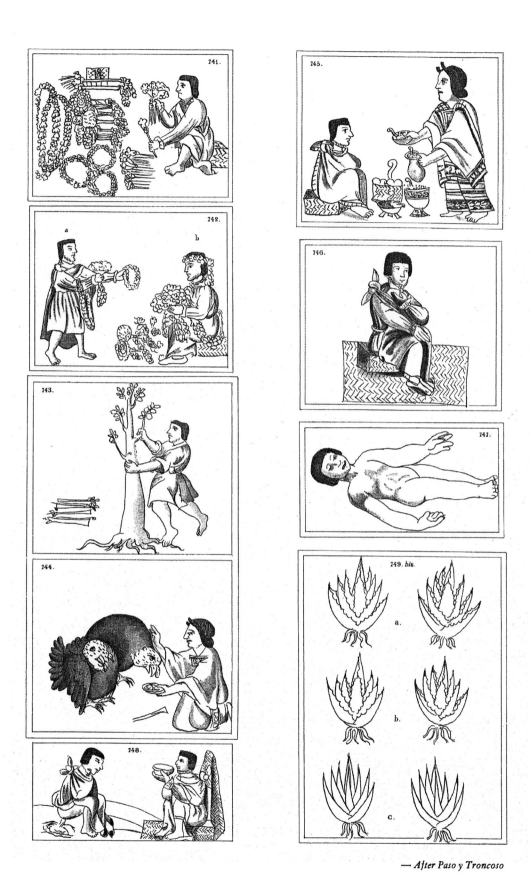

— *After Paso y Troncoso*

741. Stringing and arranging flowers. 742. Flower garlands. 743. Teopochotl. 744. Fattening turkeys. 745–748. Feeding one teopochotl seed. 749 bis. Metl.

749. Metl. 750. Planting and harvesting the metl. 751. Nopalli. 752. Tziuactli. 753. Nequametl.

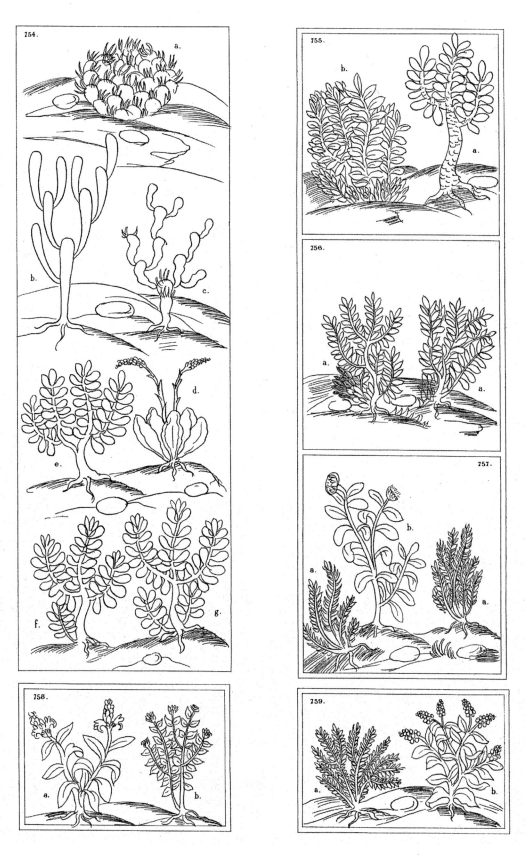

754 (a) Teocomitl, (b) teonochtli, (c) netzoli, (d) tememetla, (e) tetzmitl, (f) tlachinoltetzmitl, (g) tlapaltetzmitl. 755 (a) Texiotl, (b) atzomiatl. 756. Tetzmoli. 757 (a) Tlacopopotl, (b) chimalacatl. 758 (a) Uitzocuitlapilli, (b) nopallacotl. 759 (a) Tenextlacotl, (b) yiamoli.

— *After Paso y Troncoso*

760. Locating precious stones. 761. Seashells. 762. Breaking up the "mother." 763, 764. Quetzal-itztli. 765 (a) Quetzalchalchiuitl, (b) chalchiuitl. 766, 767. Xiuitl. 768. Xiuhtomolli. 769. Tlapalteoxiuitl. 770, 771. Epiollotli.

— *After Paso y Troncoso*

772. Teuilotl. 773–775. Apoçonalli. 776. Quetzalitzepiollotli. 777. Tlilayotic chalchiuitl. 778. Itztli. 779. Tolteca itztli. 780. Xiuhmatlalitztli. 781. Teotetl. 782. Eztetl. 783. Working of the mirror-stone. 784. Tecpatl. 785. Xoxouhqui tecpatl. 786. Uitzitziltetl.

— *After Paso y Troncoso*

787. Tapachtli. 788. Working of shells. 789. Tecçiztli. 790 (a) Quetzalatzcalli, (b) chalchiuhatzcalli, (c) uitzitzilatzcalli. 791 (a) Cili, (b) çulcili, (c) chipoli. 792. Unidentified shell (?). 793. Gold working (Chapter 9). 794. Temetztli. 795. Amochitl. 796. Copper working. 797. Use of teoxalli (Chapter 10). 798. Temetztlalli. 799. Hapetztli. 800. Tezcatlalli. 801. Tecpaxalli.

802–803. Nocheztli. 804. Tlaquauac tlapalli. 805. Tlapalnextli. 806, 807. Xochipalli. 808. Matlalin. 809. Çacatlaxcalli. 810. Achiotl. 811. Uitzquauitl. 812. Nacazcolotl. 813. Tezuatl. 814. Tlacevilli. 815 (a) Texotli, (b) tecoçauitl. 816. Tlilli.

817. Tlalxocotl. 818. Tetlilli. 819. Tlauitl. 820. Tiçatl. 821. Tetiçatl. 822. Yiapalli. 823. Camopalli. 824. Quiltic. 825. Uitztecolli. 826. Quappachtli. 827, 828. Tlapalli. 829. Teoatl (Chapter 12). 830. Origin of sea water. 831. Chicuhnauatl.

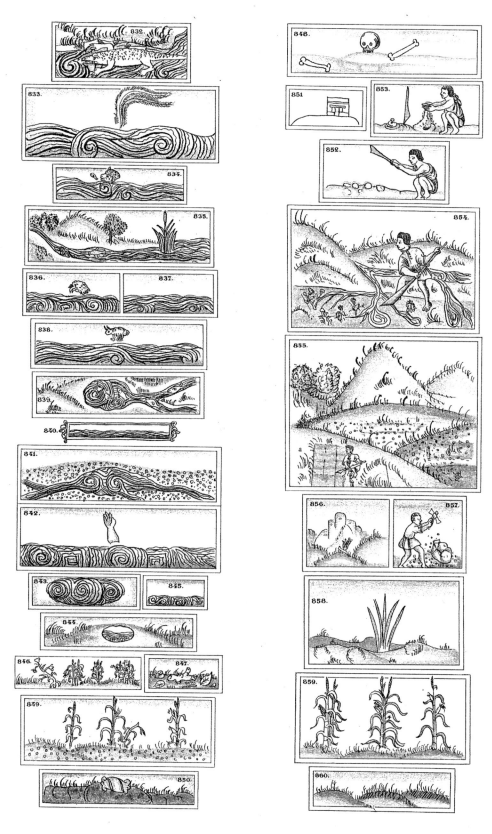

832. Amacozatl. 833. Quetzalatl. 834. Tequanatl. 835. Tollan atl. 836. Totolatl. 837. Tetzauatl. 838. Pinauizatl. 839. Ameialli. 840. Apitzactli. 841. Xalatl. 842. Amaitl. 843. Amanalli. 844. Ayoluaztli. 845. Axoxouilli. 846. Atoctli. 847. Quauhtlalli. 848. Miccatlalli. 849. Xalalli. 850. Teçoquitl. 851. Callalli. 852. Tlaluitectli. 853. Tlalauiiac. 854. Atlalli. 855. Tepetlalli. 856. Tetlalli. 857. Techiiauitl. 858. Tlalcocomoctli. 859. Chiauhtlalli. 860. Tlalçolli.

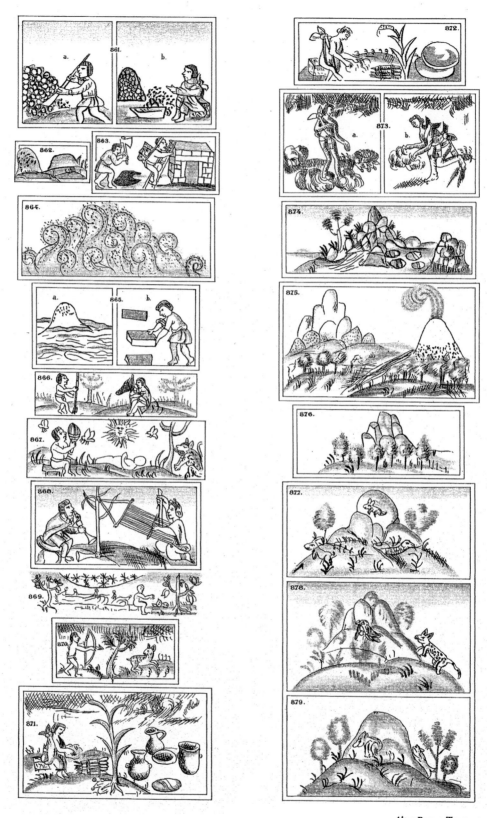

— *After Paso y Troncoso*

861. Teçontlalli. 862. Nextlalilli. 863. Tlapantlalli. 864. Teuhtli. 865. Atiçatl. 866. Mexicatlalli. 867. Totonacatlalli. 868. Michuacatlalli. 869. Anauacatlalli. 870. Chichimecatlalli. 871. Contlalli. 872. Comallalli. 873. Çoquitl. 874. Tepetl. 875. Popocatepetl. 876. Matlalquaie. 877–879. Unidentified landscapes.

880. Unidentified landscape. 881–883. Roads. 884. Teocalli. 885–887. Tecpancalli.

— *After Paso y Troncoso*

888. Tecpancalli. 889. Tlatocacalli. 890. Tecpilcalli. 891. Tlaçocalli. 892. Calpixcacalli. 893. Çaçan ie calli. 894. Puchtecacalli. 895. Nelli calli.

896. Maceualcalli. 897. Tecoyocalli. 898. Icnocalli. 899. Colotic calli. 900. Totecuio ichan. 901. Xacalli. 902. Çaça ie xacalli. 903. Xacaltapayolli. 904. Tlapeoalli. 905. Tecoyoxacalli. 906. Tlapixcacalli. 907. Quauhxacalli. 908. Xacaltetzoyotl. 909. Quauhxacalli. 910. Xacalmimilli.

911. Uapalxacalli. 912, 913. Tlallancalli. 914. Calnepanolli. 915. House construction. 916. Calhuiui-
laxtli. 917. Calyaualli. 918, 919. Chantli. 920, 921. Temazcalli. 922. Oztotl.

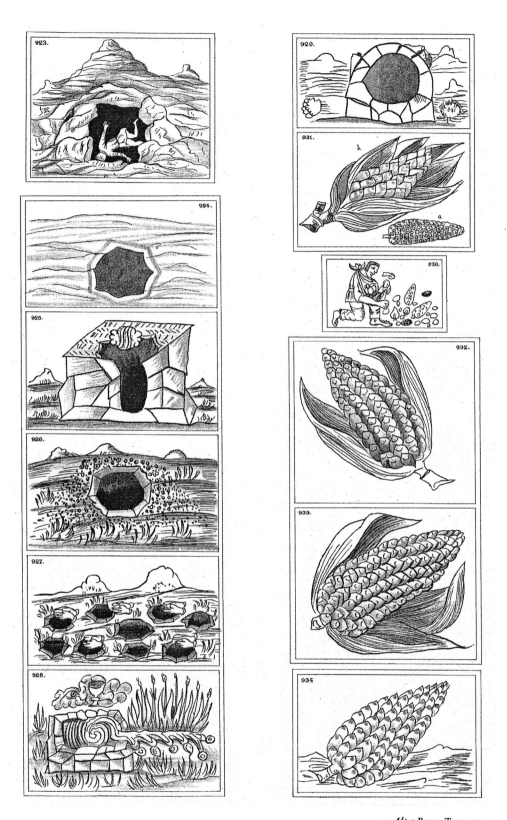

— *After Paso y Troncoso*

923. Oztotl.   924. Tlaloztotl.   925. Tepetlaoztotl.   926. Xaloztotl.   927. Oztoxaxaqualli.   928. Aoztotl. 929. Oztotl.   930–934. Cintli (Chapter 13).

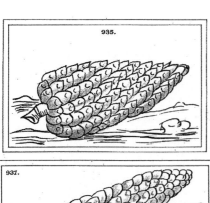

935.

936.

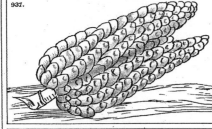

937.

939.

938.

939.

941.

940.

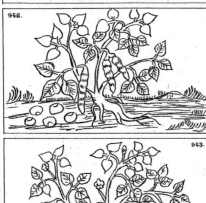

942.

943.

944.

945.

— *After Paso y Troncoso*

935–939. Cintli. 940. Aiecotli. 941–945. Etl.

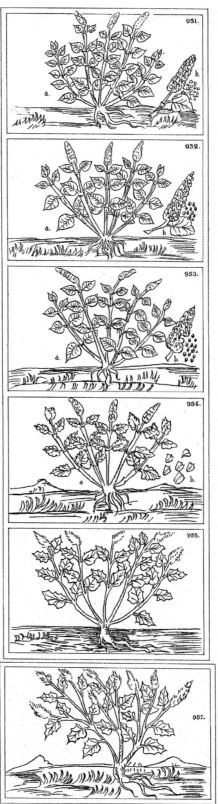

946–950. Etl. 951–957. Uauhtli.

— *After Paso y Troncoso*

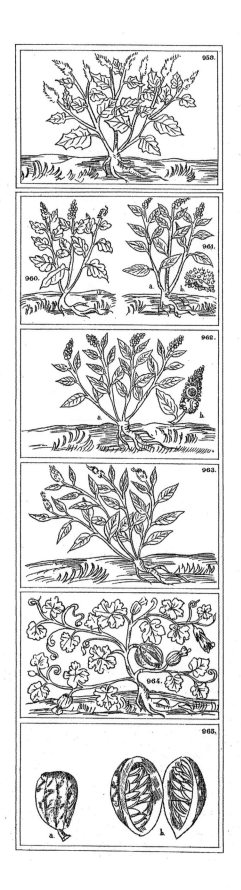

ᶜEsta rrelacion arriba puesta delas
yeruas medicinales, y delas otras
cosas medicinales arriba contenjdas
dieron los medicos del Hatelulco sã
tiago viejos y muy espimentados
enlas cosas dela medicina, y que to
do ellos curan publicamente, los nom
bres delos quales y del escriuano que
lo escriujo se siguen. Yporque nosa
ben escriujr rogaron alescriuano q̃
pusiese sus nombres.

/ Gaspar mathias | Pedro desãtiago
vecino delaconcecion veci. de san Ines.

/ franco symon ? Miguel damjan ?
veci. de sa.to toribio? ve. des.toto
                       ribio

/ felipe hernandez ? Pedro deraque
v.º desancta Ana | na. v.º delacõcep.ⁿ

/ Miguel garcia ? Miguel motolinja
v.º desanto toribio v.º desata Ines.

— *After Paso y Troncoso*

958–962. Uauhtli. 963. Petzicatl. 964. Ayotli. 965. Tzilacayotli.

Eighth Chapter, which telleth of all the precious stones.

FIRST PARAGRAPH, which telleth of all the different precious stones, and how they may be sought.

The different kinds of precious stones — as they occur, as they are encountered — are by no means good, fresh and green; the desirable, the coveted, the longed-for, the wanted. For there is the so-called mother. It is only a common stone, an ordinary stone; one not honored nor desirable; not regarded. Wherever it is, it is passed by; it is bypassed or just cast aside where one dwells.

But this, the so-called mother of the precious stone, is not the whole thing. It is only where it is placed: perhaps well within, or on its side;[1] not all, only a little, a bit, a small part, a fragment there wherever it is sprinkled, located.

And those of experience, the advised, these look for it. In this manner [they see,][2] they know where it is: they can see that it is breathing, [smoking],[3] giving off vapor. Early, at early dawn, when [the sun] comes up, they find where to place themselves, where to stand; they face the sun. And when the sun has already come up, they are truly very attentive in looking. They look with diligence; they no longer blink; they look well. Wherever they can see that something like a little smoke [column] stands, that one of them is giving off vapor, this one is the precious stone. Perhaps it is a coarse stone; perhaps it is a common stone, or something smooth, or something round. They take it up; they carry it away. And if they are not successful, if it is only barren where the little [column of] smoke stands, thus they know that the precious stone is there in the earth.

Then they dig. There they see, there they find the precious stone, perhaps already well formed, perhaps already burnished. Perhaps they see something buried there either in stone, or in a stone bowl, or in a stone chest; perhaps it is filled with precious stones. This they claim there.

Inic chicuei capitulo: itechpa tlatoa, in jxqujch tlaçotetl.

INJC CE PARRAPHO itechpa tlatoa in jxqujch nepapan tlaçotetl, yoan in quenjn vel motemoa.

In jzquj tlamantli tlaçotetl, amo njman iuh qujzquj, in juh itto in qualli, in celic, in tetlanecti, in jcolli, in eleviliztli, in nequjztli, ca vncã, mjtoa, inã çan tlaeltetl, çaçan ie tetl, amo mavizio, amo no neconj, atle ipan itto: in canjn ca çan ipã qujqujxoa, çan papanavilo, anoçe cana techan nemj, çan tlaxooatinemoa.

Auh inin mjtoa inan in tlaçotetl, amo no motqujtica, çan canjn qujmotlalili: aço vel iitic, anoço ca itlacapan, amo no quexqujch, çan quexqujchton, çan qualton, çan achiton, çan tepitõ in canjn in qujmotzicujnjli, in qujmotlalili.

Auh in tlaiximatinjme, in nonotzaleque iehoantin qujtta: injc qujximati, in canjn ca, vel qujtta: ca mjhiotitica, maiauhiotitica: oc ioac, vellavizcalpan in qujça, in contemoa, in canjn motlalia in canjn, moquetza, qujxnamjquj in tonatiuh, auh in ie oalquiça tonatiuh, cenca imjx intequjuh, nelli mach in tlachia, vel mjxpetzoa, aoc õmjxcueionja, vellachia: in canjn iuhquj poctontli moquetza, vel qujtta, in catleoatl maiauhiotitica, iehoatl o, in tlaçotli: aço techachaquachtli, aço tlailtetl, anoço itla texixipetztli aço itla teololli, conana qujvica. Auh intlacatle ipã aci: in canjn poctontli moquetza, intla çan tlalnemjuhian, ic qujmati ca vncã tlallan ca in tlaçotli in tetl:

njmã tlatataca vncã qujtta, vncã qujpantilia, aço ie tlaiecchioalli, aço ie tlapetlaoalli in tlaçotetl, aço vncã tlatoctli in qujtta, anoço tetl, anoço tecaxic; anoço tepetlacalco in ca, in noço temj in tlaçotetl; vncan in tlacnopilhuja i,

---

1. *Acad. Hist. MS,* after *vel iitic,* reads *ano cana ytlacapã.*
2. *Ibid.:* following *qujtta, Auh ynic quitta* is added.
3. *Ibid.: mopocyotitica* is added.

And thus do they know that this precious stone is there: [the herbs] always grow fresh; they grow green. They say this is the breath of the green stone, and its breath is very fresh; it is an announcer of its qualities. In this manner is seen, is taken the green stone.

And how is it with the turquoise? It comes out of a mine. From within, it is removed: the fine turquoise, the even, the smoked; and that called turquoise or ruby; and then the amber, the rock crystal, the obsidian; and then the flint, the mirror stone, the jet, the bloodstone. All are from mines.

And then the seashells, the pearls come from the seashore; they appear on the edge of the ocean. The opals are removed from the ocean sand, and they appear in the rivers of Totonacapan.

And the precious stone, the mother of the green stone, when the experienced seek it, in order to polish it, it is said, "They work, they break up its mother." And when they have found [the green stone], they fashion it, they cut it. And then they work it with abrasive sand; they grind it. To polish it further, to make it glisten, they rub it with a fine cane; they make it shine.

¶

SECOND PARAGRAPH, which telleth of the emerald-green jade, which sometimes looks like a stone.

EMERALD-GREEN JADE[1]

The name of this comes from *quetzalli* [quetzal feather] and *itztli* [obsidian], because its appearance is like a green quetzal feather. And its body is as transparent and as dense[2] as obsidian. It is precious, esteemed, valuable; it is worthy of being cherished; it merits storing; it is desirable, worthy of envy; it merits esteem and is praiseworthy.

It is one's lot, the lot of the rulers, of the old ones. And the good emerald-green jade — not the imitation — the genuine [jade] attracts moisture; it attracts things when rubbed. And when some little piece of rubbish is at hand, it fastens on to it, it sucks it, it draws it. It attracts moisture, becomes wet, has dew. It draws things, sucks things, attracts things. It becomes green. It glistens, glistens constantly; it shines; it gives light, gives constant light, gives rays.

Auh no yoan injc qujximati injn tlaçotetl, vncã ca: muchipa tlacelia, tlacecelia, qujlmach inin chalchivitl ihiio; auh in jhiio cenca cecec, tlacamaoanj: ivin in motta, in mana chalchivitl:

auh quẽ ca xivitl, ca oztoio, itlan vitz, itzalan vetztinemj in teuxivitl, in vel icucic, in vel popoca: njmã ie iehoatl, in mjtoa: xivitl anoço tlapalteuxivitl: auh njmã ie iehoatl, in apoçonalli, in tevillotl, in jtztli: auh njmã ie iehoatl, in tecpatl, in tezcatl, in teutetl, in eztetl: ca muchi oztoio, ca tepeio:

auh njman ie iehoatl in tapachtli, in epiollotli, ca teuatenco vitz: ca ilhujcaatenco neci in vitzitziltetl, ca ilhujcaaxalli itlan vetztinemj, yoan totonacapan, atoiac in neci.

Auh in tlaçotli tetl, in chalchivitl inan; in jquac qujtta, tlaiximatinj, injc qujpetlaoa: mjtoa, qujquaquavi, qujtlatlapatza in jnan: auh in oqujttac qujvellalia, qujxima: auh njmã qujteuxalhuja, qujchiquj, injc iequene qujpetlaoa, injc cuecueioca, qujquetzalotlavia, qujiottovia.

¶

INJC VME PARRAPHO: itechpa tlatoa, in quetzalitztli, in quenjnamj ic tlachia in juhquj tetl.

QUETZALITZTLI:

inin itoca itech qujztica in quetzalli, yoan itztli: ipampa in jtlachializ iuhqujn quetzalli, xoxoctic: auh in jnacaio, injc atic, auh inj ticeoac iuhqujn itztli, tlaçotli, maviztic, patio, pialonj, tlatilonj, neconj, elevilonj, maviçolonj, auh maviztililonj,

tetonal intonal in tlatoque in veveintin. Auh in qualli quetzalitztli, in amo çan itlatla, in nelli vel iehoatl: mjtonjanj, tlaihioananj; in mochichiquj: auh in ommottitia itla tlaçoltontli, conana, compaloa, contilinja: mjtonja palti, aoachiova, tlatilinja, tlapaloa, tlaihiioana, xoxovia, petlanj, pepetlanj, pepetlaca, ontona, ontotona motonameiotia, mavizioa, mavizti, tlaçoti, tlaçotlalo, patiioa.

---

1. William F. Foshag: "Mineralogical Studies on Guatemalan Jade," *Smithsonian Miscellaneous Collections,* Vol. 135, No. 5 (Washington, 1957), p. 8.

2. *Acad. Hist. MS: tetzavac.*

It is honored, esteemed; it is precious, beloved by all, valuable.

QUETZALCHALCHIUITL[3]

The name of this comes from *quetzalli* [quetzal feather], then from *chalchiuitl* [green stone], because its appearance is like the quetzal feather, so green, so herb-green is it. And its body is as dense as the green stone. Also it is an attracter of moisture. It attracts, it exudes moisture. It is perfect, fine, well-textured; it has iridescent colors; it is shaded, flint-like, easy to work. It has blotches.

They are formed in this manner: they are round, reed-like, like a navel, like a tomato, triangular, cut in triangles, formed into triangles, thin, formed into squares. They are polished, ground, worked with abrasive sand, glued with bat excrement, rubbed with a fine cane, made to shine. They glisten, they are transparent; there light appears.

GREEN STONE[4]

Its name comes from nowhere. Its appearance is herb-green, like the amaranth herb. Also it is one which attracts moisture. It is precious, good looking, noble.[5] It is really the property of the noblemen. During past times, when someone wore it, even though in any manner, if[6] his necklace or his bracelet were of green stone, this showed that he was a nobleman, a beloved prince; wherefore he was rendered honor, beloved by all.

TURQUOISE

The name of this turquoise comes from the herb which lies sprouting; because its appearance is [not highly colored,][7] not very herb-green, just a little dull; as if it were not highly estimable. It is really a little dark-surfaced.

And this is not in one piece. It is just broken up in little pieces like sand, small and flat, small and wide,[8] not hard, just soft. It is required for use in adorning; it is just set on, glued on, for which there is gluing of the surface.

I glue turquoise. I affix turquoise. I affix turquoise to the beam, to the image. I search for turquoise. I excavate turquoise. I remove turquoise.

QUETZALCHALCHIVITL:

inin itoca, itech qujça in quetzalli, njmã ie chalchivitl: ipampa ca in jtlachializ, iuhqujn quetzalli, injc xoxoctic, injc qujltic. Auh in jnacaio, injc tetzaoac iuhqujn chalchivitl: no mjtonjanj, in ommahaiovia mjtonjtiqujça: cenqujztica, macitica, vel icucic, chictlapanquj, ceio, hecauhio, tecpaio, tecelicaio, tlacivice

injc tlatlalili, ololtic, acatic, xictic, tomatic, chiqujnalca tlachiqujnaltectli, tlachiqujnallalilli, tlacanaoalli, tlaxãtlaxcalteuhtlalili, mopetlaoa, mjchiquj, moteuxalhuja, motzinacancujtlavia, moquetzalotlavia, moiottovia, cuecueioca, naltona, vmpa tonneci.

CHALCHIVITL

acampa qujça in jtoca: inin itlachieliz qujltic, iuhqujn vauhqujlitl. no mjtonjanj, tlaçotli, qualneci, tecpieli: vel intlatquj in pipilti: In oc ie nepa, in aca in manel çan quenamj qujquemj, intlae chalchivitl icozquj, inoce imacuex, ic neci ca pilli, ca tecpiltzintli, ic maviztililo, tlaçotlalo.

XIVITL:

inin xivitl itech qujça in jtoca xivitl, in ixoatoc: ipampa in jtlachializ amo cenca qujltic, çan achi mjcquj: iuhqujn amo cenca mavizio, çan nel achi ixtlileoac.

Auh inin xivitl, amo cẽqujzquj, çan cacaiacaticac, iuhqujn xalli, patlachtontli, patlachpipil, amo tlaquaoac, çan poxaoac. Injc monequj, injc tlaqualnextilo, çan momana, moçaloa, çã ic tlaixtzaqualo:

njxiuhçaloa, njxiuhtzaqua: njcxiuhtzaqua in vapalli, in teixiptla: njxiuhtemoa, njxiuhtataca, njxiuhqujxtia.

---

3. Jade of fine, green, uniform coloring "that is found among Olmec pieces" (Foshag, *loc. cit.*).

4. *Chalchiuitl*: "undoubtedly the common jade of green and white color" (*loc. cit.*).

5. *Acad. Hist. MS: tecpilli.*

6. *Ibid.: ỹtla ye.*

7. *Ibid.:* following *jtlachializ, amo cẽca tlãpaltic* is added.

8. Some of these are "almost certainly amazonstone" (Foshag, *op. cit.*, p. 28).

THIRD PARAGRAPH, which telleth of still other stones which appear like turquoise.

FINE TURQUOISE

The name of this comes from *teotl* [god] and *xiuitl* [turquoise], which merely means that it is the property, the lot, of the god; and it means that it is much esteemed, because it does not appear anywhere very often.[1] It seldom appears anywhere. This fine turquoise is much esteemed. When in it, when on it [something] is seen, it is not much esteemed. And when it appears some distance away, it is quite pale, like the lovely cotinga, verily as if smoking.

Some of these are flat. Some are round;[2] their name is *xiuhtomolli*. They are called *xiuhtomolli* because one side is round, swollen, but the other side is flat, just as if broken in half. Some are quite smooth, some roughened, some pitted, some like volcanic rock. It becomes flat, it becomes round, it becomes pale. It smokes. The fine turquoise smokes. It becomes rough, it becomes perforated, it becomes pale.

RUBY

The name of this comes from *tlapalli* [red] and *teoxiuitl* [fine turquoise], because it is the same as the fine turquoise. However, it is so constituted as to be colored chili-red.[3] Thus it is truly very wonderful, marvelous; in short, it is very rare. It is rose-colored, blood-speckled, esteemed, rare; it is guarded as precious.

PEARL

The name of this comes from *eptli* [oyster] and *yollotli* [heart], because its appearance is just like the appearance of the oyster. And it is from "heart" because it is round. It is white, translucent; it is translucent, ever translucent, crystalline, like crystal, clear; it is clear, very clear; it is cherished. Some are large, some small. They are really longed for, really craved, really envied, ever desirable, a sought-after thing. They can be made into necklaces, they can be made into bracelets; they are made into bracelets. They can make things beautiful. They are round, flat, translucent, ever translucent. They render things wonderful, are considered crystals, make things attractive.

INJC EI PARRAPHO: itechpa tlatoa, in oc cequj tetl, inique xiuhneçi.

TEUXIUJTL:

inin itoca itech qujça in teutl, ioan in xiujtl, çan qujtoznequj iiaxca, itonal in teutl, ioan, q.n. cenca mavizio; ipampa acan cenca neçi, canin çan quēman in neçi: injn teuxiujtl cenca mavizio, in jtlā in jtech motta amo cenca mavizio: auh in achi veca neçi, vel ticeoac, iuhqujn xiuhtototl, nelli iuhqujn popoca.

Injn cequj patlachtic, cequj ololtic, itoca xiuhtomolli: inic xiuhtomolli, ca centlacotl in ololtic in tomoltic: auh in oc centlapal patlachtic, iuhqujnma çã ic tlapanquj, cequj vel xipetztic, cequj chachaltic, cequj côcoioctic, cequj teçontic, patlachiuj, ololivi, ticeoa, popoca, teoxiuhpopoca, chachaquachiuj, qujqujçavi, teteçavi.

TLAPALTEOXIUJTL:

injn itoca, itech qujzquj in tlapalli, ioan in teoxivitl: ipampa ca çan ie vel iehoatl in teuxiujtl, in qujmotlatlalili, ic mopopoiauh chichiltic, ic cenca nelli mavizio, maviztic: ça cenca iequene tlaçonemj, motlapalpoiava, meezcuicujloa, mavizioa, tlaçoneçi tlaçopialo.

EPIOLLOTLI:

inin itoca itech qujça in eptli, ioan iollotli: ipāpa in iuhquj itlachializ eptli, ca çan no iuhquj in itlachializ: auh in jtechcopa iollotli, ca ipāpa in ololtic, iztac naltic, naltona, nanaltona, teviltic, tevilotic, chipavac, chipactic, chipacpatic, tlaçotli, cequj chamavac, cequj piçiltic, vel tetlanecti vel icollo, vel icolli, nenequjztli, temolonj, necozcatilonj, nemacuextilonj, nemacuextilo, tlaqualnextilonj, ololtic, patlachtic, naltona, nanaltona, tlamaviziotia, tevilotl momati tlatlanexiotia.

---

1. *Acad. Hist. MS:* following *neçi, ça* is added.

2. *Ibid.:* following *ololtic, ȳ ololtic* is added.

3. *Ibid.:* the passage following *teuxiujtl* reads: *ça ye quimotlatlalili yc mopoyauh.*

Rock crystal

The name of the rock crystal comes from nowhere. It is mined. Some are white. Some are the color of gourd blossoms. The violet ones are called, are given the name "amethyst."

This rock crystal is pierced. It is translucent. It is translucent, very transparent, clear. It is clear, very clear, exceedingly clear. Some are shaded, [some are] dense. They are cherished, esteemed, wonderful. They are precious, esteemed, venerated.

Amber

Its name is from *atl* [water] and *poçonalli* [bubble], because during olden times they esteemed it for the reason that those of experience said that it was the bubbles of sea water. At dawn, when the sun rises, it appears just like foam which the sun's rays penetrate. Hence they gave it the name "water-bubble"; hence they esteemed it.

This amber is a stone. It is mined, excavated, extracted. It is quite clear, translucent. It compares well with the rock crystal.

The names of this amber are three, which are taken from, which come from its appearance.

The name of one kind is yellow amber; this is just like a stone. It is as if it were embers. When examined with care, it is as if little sparks continually fly from it, as if a flame stood within it. Its flame appears like a torch, a candle, very marvelous. And it is so very marvelous that when it is placed together with a torch, with a candle, it sucks the fire; it also shines; it burns.

The name of the second kind is quetzal amber, because its appearance is green like the quetzal feather quill. Something like a quetzal feather quill spreads continually flying from it.

The name of the third kind is white amber. It is named white amber because its color is not very yellow; it is just a little pale, just pale, just yellow.

All these ambers are ones which attract things.

Quetzalitzepyollotli

The name of this comes from *quetzalitztli* [emerald green jade] and *epyollotli* [pearl], because it looks a little green. It is only its name of esteem; it is not really that it is just like the emerald-green jade, for it is white.[4] When turned, one side appears green, the

Tevilotl:

in tevilotl acan quizquj in jtoca, tepeio, oztoio: cequj iztac, cequj aiopaltic, camopaltic, mitoa motocaiotia tlapalteviotl.

Injn tevilotl xapotquj, nalqujzquj, naltona vel atic, chipavac, chipactic, chipacaltic, chipacpatic, cequj çeio, hecauhio, tetzavac, tláçotli, maviztic, mavizio, tláçoti mavizioa, maviztililo.

Apoçonalli:

atl itech onca, ioan poçonalli in jtoca: ipampa in oc ie vecauh, inic conmaviziotique, tlaiximatinjme, qujtoque, ca tevatl ipopoçonallo: in tlavizcalpan, in jquac valqujça tonatiuh, in apopoçoqujllotl vel iuhqujn inic neçi ca qujmjna in tonatiuh, ic contocaiotique. Apoçonalli ic conmaviziotique.

injn apoçonalli ca tetl, ca oztoio, ca tepeio ca motataca, ca moqujxtia vel chipavac nalqujzquj, vel qujnenevilia in tevilotl,

etlamantli in jtoca injn apoçonalli, itech mana, itech qujça in itlachializ.

Inic centlamantli, itoca coztic apoçonalli, injn vel iuhqujn tetl; iuhqujnma tletlexochio in mocemjtta, iuhqujnma tlemoiototonti, itech tzitzicujca; iuhqujnma tlecueçallotl iitic icac, iuhqujnma ocutl, candela itlecueçallo ic neçi, vellamaviçoltic: auh inic cenca tlamaviçoltic, in jquac netloc moquetza ocutl candela, compaloa in tletl no tlanextia, no tlatla.

Injc vntlamantli: in jtoca, quetzalapoçonalli: ipampa in jtlachializ xoxoxoctic, iuhqujnma quequetzalomio, iuhq'n quetzalomjtl, itech tzitzicujcatoc.

Injc etlamantli: itoca iztac apoçonalli; ipampa motocaiotia iztac apoçonalli, ca amo cenca coztic, çan achi iztalevac, çan pinevac, çan camavac in jtlapallo.

Inin mochi apoçonalli; tlaihiioananj.

Quetzalitzepiollotli:

injn itoca, itech qujztica in quetzalitztli, ioan epiollotli: ipampa in achi xoxoctic ic tlachia, çan imaviztoca, amo ma nelli: in ma vel iuhquj quetzalitztli, ca iztac, in mocueptinemj: injc neçi i centlapal xoxoctic, xiuhtototic: ic cenca nelli mavizio, tlamaviçolli, xoxo-

---

4. *Ibid.*: following *iztac, ça* is added.

color of the lovely cotinga. Thus it is really very marvelous, a marvel. It is green, verdant; it becomes green. It gives off rays; it is luminous.

TLILAYOTIC CHALCHIUITL[5]

It is a precious stone. Its name comes from *tlilayotl* [black water] and *-tic*, which means "like." This green stone is named "like black water" because it is really not very black; also it is not very green, not even herb-green; it is just a little matte, like something placed in black water. It is esteemed, precious, valuable.

I pay the price for it. I buy it at a high [price]. I pay a high price for it. A high price is paid.

¶

FOURTH PARAGRAPH, which telleth of still other stones; of how they appear.

IZTAC CHALCHIUITL[1]

The name of this comes from *iztac* [white] and *chalchiuitl*. It is a stone. And it is named *iztac chalchiuitl* because some [pieces] are really white, just like bird's eggs. But in some places a little herb-green, green, or blue is placed. And some of the *chalchiuitl* are just white-spotted, or bespattered with green. It becomes white, it is sprinkled with light blue; it is dappled with light blue; it is dappled with herb-green; it is bespattered with light blue; it is sprinkled with herb-green.

MIXTECATETL

Also its name is *texoxoctli*, and its name is *ocelotetl*. Some have white, some black, some green placed in them. It is not esteemed; it is an ordinary stone. It is the last of the green stones; it is the last, it comes after. It is not esteemed; no one considers it. It is unheeded, unregarded.

ITZTETL, ITZTLI

It takes its name from itself. It is excavated from mines. The names of the nodules are *itztetl* and *itztli*. *Itztetl* is also the name of that with which there is scraping. But the proper name of the flake is *itztli*. And of this *itztli*, the name of one [flake] is razor; this is broad. The name of one is scraper; the edge of this one is thick, the back rounded. The name of one

via, xoxoxovia, xoxoctia, motonameiotia, tonameioa.

TLILAIOTIC CHALCHIUJTL:

tlaçotli tetl, itech qujça in jtoca tlilaiotl, ioan, tic, q.n, iuhquj. Inin chalchivitl, ipampa in motocaiotia tlilaiotic: amo cenca vel tliltic, amo no cenca xoxoctic, in ma qujltic: çan achiuhq'n tlaceviltic, iuhqujnma tlilaiotitlan tlaaqujlli, maviztic, tlaçotli patio,

nicpatiotia, nicveicacoa, njcveicapatiotia, veicapatiova.

¶

INJC NAVI PARRAPHO: itechpa tlatoa, in oc cequj tetl, in quenamj ic tlachia.

IZTAC CHALCHIVITL:

injn itech qujça in jtoca iztac, ioan chalchivitl ca tetl: auh inic motocaiotia iztac chalchiujtl, ca in cequj vel iztac, vel iuhqujn totoltetl; auh çan can achichi qujmotlalili in qujltic, in xoxoctic, in anoço texotic; auh in cequj çan iztacacujcujltic in chalchiuitl, anoço çan qujmotzitzicujchili in xoxouhquj. Iztaia motexoalpichia, texopoiaoa, qujlpoiaoa, motexotzitzicujtza, moqujlalpichia.

MIXTECATETL:

ioan itoca texoxoctli, ioan itoca oçelotetl: cequj iztac, cequj tliltic, cequj xoxoctic in qujmotlatlalili, amo mavizio çaçan ie tetl, qujtzacuja chalchivitl, tlatzacuja, tlatoqujlia: amo maviziova, aiac ica, aonaitto, atle ipã itto.

ITZTETL, ITZTLI

mjxcaujtica, in jtoca oztoio, tepeio, motataca in çan oc tetl: itoca itztetl, ioan itztli injc tlachico, no itoca itztetl: auh in ie tlaievalli ineixcaviltoca itztli: auh injn itztli, cequj itoca neximalitztli: iehoatl in patlavac, cequj itoca tlapanevalli, iehoatl in tētilaoac tepotzmjmjltic, cequj itoca vitzauhquj, iehoatl in centlapal cenca iacaujtztic ic teitzmjno, cequj itoca itz-

---

5. *Tlilayotic chalchiuitl:* Foshag (op. cit., p. 8) suggests jade mineral chloromelanite.

1. Classed as jasper in corresponding Spanish text. Foshag (*op. cit.,* p. 9) suggests either "the white forms of jade with little green coloration" or "those mixtures of jadeite and albite in which albite predominates."

is awl; this one is very pointed on one end; with it one is bled. The name of one is obsidian core; this is thick, no longer very sharp-edged. Here originates the *itztetl*, the scraper. The flaked obsidian is double-edged, sharp, sharp on both edges. It cuts things, saws, pierces.

[The name of one is black obsidian.][2] The name of one is white obsidian. It is not very black; it is somewhat white; its thin places are where it appears white, like rock crystal. A yellow one named *itzcuin-itztli* is as if tawny-striped. The name of one is green obsidian; it is somewhat blue.

TOLTECA ITZTLI

This is blue, somewhat matte, somewhat green, blue-brown. It was really the property, the possession, the lot of those who were Toltecs, who came [here] to live. (Today this can be seen.) They were perhaps their ear-rings, perhaps their bowls, or whatever they were. They really used it, for which reason it is named *tolteca itztli*. It appears beautiful; it is held in regard; it is desired.

I shatter an obsidian nodule; I flake the obsidian.

MATLALITZTLI

The name of this comes from *matlalin* [blue] and *itztli* [obsidian] because it is just like the blue coloring, an intense blue; blue, light blue, blue-brown, blue-tinted. And its body is just like obsidian, a little transparent, but also a little dense. It is a very marvelous thing, a really precious thing. It seldom comes, it appears rarely; it is difficult to find; it is only seen in places. It becomes blue. It becomes green.

XIUHMATLALITZTLI[3]

Its name comes from *xiuitl* [turquoise] and *matla-lin* [blue], and *itztli* [obsidian]. It is the stone which surpasses all the other precious stones, so wonderful is its appearance. Wherever it is when seen, it is like water which is about to form a droplet; and furthermore, it appears as if blue, just like the lovely cotinga. And [this droplet] is [like] the smoke which comes from the end of [burning] green wood; from it a small flame stands out like [the color of] the lovely cotinga. And at night it shines out on both sides a finger in length. It excels in wonder, it excels in preciousness.

tapalcatl, iehoatl in titilaoac, aocmo cenca tene: njcan qujça in itztetl in tlachiconj. In tlaevalli itztli, necoc tene, tenatic, tetenatic, tlatequj, tlaxotla, tlatzoponja:

cequj itoca iztac itztli, amo cenca tliltic, achi iztac in jcanaoaia, oncan in neçi in jztac, in iuhquj tevilotl. Cequj coztic: qujtocaiotia itzcujnitztli, iuhqujn quappachtli ic vavanquj. Cequj itoca xoxouhquj itztli, achi mamatlaltic.

TOLTECA ITZTLI:

ie ehoatl in mamatlaltic, in achi tlaceviltic, in achi xoxoxoctic, tetexocamjltic, vel intlatquj catca, vel imaxca catca, vel intonal catca in aqujque nemjco tolteca (ca itto in axcan) in at innacoch catca, in at incax catca, in at anoço tlein catca: vel qujtitlanja ic motocaiotia tolteca, itztli qualneçi, maviçulti, neco,

njtztetlapa, njqueva, in jtztli.

MATLALITZTLI:

injn itoca itech qujça in matlali, ioan itztli: ipãpa in jtlachializ, vel iuhqujn matlali, mamatlaltic, matlaltic, tetexotic, texocamjltic, texopoiavac: auh in jnacaio vel iuhquj̃ itztli injc achi atic: auh in noce ic achi tetzaoac, vellamaviçolli, vellaçotli, tlaçonemj, tlaçoneçi çan tevneçi, çan canjn itto, mamatlaltia, xoxoxovia.

XIUHMATLALITZTLI:

itech qujça in jtoca xivitl, ioan matlali, ioã itztli; ca in tetl qujcempanavi in tlaçotli tetl, injc mavizio itlachializ: in canjn ca, in motta, iuhqujn atl ma ie chipinjz: auh no cuele iuhqujn matlali ic neçi, vel iuhquj xiuhtototl: auh ie vel ie on in poctli qujvaliacantiuh, xoxouhquj quavitl, itech in iuhquj xiuhtototl, valmoquetza, tlecueçallotontli: auh in ioaltica, necoc cenmapilli injc tlanextia tlacempanavi, maviztic, tlacenpanavi tlaçotli.

---

2. *Acad. Hist. MS:* the passage begins with *cequi itoca tliltic itztli.*

3. Corresponding Spanish text: "*segunda [segun la?] relaci[on] de la letra es safiro.*"

JET

Its name comes from *teotl* [god] and *tetl* [stone], because nowhere does a stone appear as black as this stone. That is to say, it is precious, rare, like the special attribute of a god. It is black, very black, completely black; black, the color of bitumen; completely black, perfect in its blackness.

BLOODSTONE

The name "bloodstone" comes from *eztli* [blood] and *tetl* [stone], because the stone is mottled like blood; as if it were dried blood, mottled [with blood] no longer fresh. Some [pieces] are bespattered, some so striped; some have it just placed [in veins], some are half so colored; [some] are intermixed with blood color, with rose color, sprinkled with color, bespattered with color, dotted with blood color, half-blood-colored. They are bespattered with color, rose-colored, touched with color, dotted with blood color.

And its name is bloodstone because, they say, it lessens, it arrests the menses, or perhaps quiets the pain of a blow when much blood comes out. It quiets the pain; it soothes, stops off, cures.

¶

FIFTH PARAGRAPH, which telleth of still another kind of stone. It is a stone [of which] mirrors are made, [a stone] which is converted [into a mirror].

MIRROR STONE

Its name comes from nowhere. This can be excavated in mines; it can be broken off. Of these mirror stones, one is white, one black. The white one — this is a good one to look into: the mirror, the clear, transparent one. They named it the mirror of the noblemen, the mirror of the ruler.

The black one — this one is not good. It is not to look into; it does not make one appear good. It is one (so they say) which contends with one's face. When someone uses such a mirror, from it is to be seen a distorted mouth, swollen eyelids, thick lips, a large mouth. They say it is an ugly mirror, a mirror which contends with one's face.

Of these mirrors, one is round; one is long: they call it *acaltezcatl*. [These mirror stones] can be excavated in mines, can be polished, can be worked.

I make a mirror. I work it. I shatter it. I form it.[1] I grind it. I polish it with sand. I work it with fine

1. *Acad. Hist. MS: nicvellalia.*

TEUTETL:

itech qujzquj in jtoca teutl, ioan tetl; ipampa aoccan centetl neçi, iuhqujn tetl injc tliltic, qujtoznequj çan tlaçoca, çan tlaçonemj: iuhqujnma ineixcaujl teutl, tliltic, tlilpatic, çemacic tliltic, caputztic, chapoputic, vel cemaçic tliltic, vel açic in tlillan.

EZTETL:

in eztetl itech qujça in jtoca eztli, ioan tetl: ipampa injc mocujcujlo in tetl, iuhquj̄ eztli; iuhquinma ezquavacquj, in aocmo tlapaltic ic mocujcujlo, cequj qujmotzitzicujchili, cequj ic vavanquj, cequj çan qujmotlatlalili, cequj ic tlapanquj, ezcujcujltic, tlapalpoiavac, tlapalalpichilli, motlapaltzitzicujtz, meezchapanj, eztlapanquj, motlapaltzitzicujtza, motlapalpoiaoa, motlapalvilteq', meezchapanja:

ioan ipampa in jtoca eztetl, qujl qujlochtia, quelleltia in ezvitomjliztli, in at noço viteccatl in cenca ezqujça quellelcehuja, tlaellecevia, tlacevia, tlatzaqua, tlapatia.

¶

INIC MACUJLLI, PARRAPHO: itechpa tlatoa, oc centlamantli tetl: in mochioa tezcatl, in mocuepa ca tetl.

TEZCATL:

acan qujzquj in jtoca, injn tepeio, oztoio, tataconj, tlapanonj: injn tezcatl çequj iztac, cequj tliltic, in jztac iehoatl in qualli in tlachia, in nettonj in chipavac, atic, qujtocaiotia tecpiltezcatl, tlatocatezcatl,

in tliltic, iehoatl in amo qualli, in amo tlachia, in amo tequalnexti çan (qujtoa) teixavanj, in aqujn ic motezcavia, in ompa õmotta camatalapol,, ixquatolmjmjlpol, tenxipaltotomacpol, camaxacalpol: qujtoa tlaeltezcatl, teixavanj tezcatl.

Injn tezcatl, cequj iavaltic, cequj xopiltic: qujlhuja acaltezcatl, tepeio, oztoio, tataconj, petlavalonj, quaquaovanj,

nitezcachiva, njcquaquavi njctzicueva njcvallalia, njqujchiquj, njcxalhuja, njcteuxalhuja, njctzinacan-

abrasive sand. I apply to it a glue of bat excrement. I prepare it. I polish it with a fine cane. I make it shiny. I regard myself in the mirror. I appear from there in my looking-mirror; from it I admire myself.

cujtlavia, njccencava, njcquetzalotlavia, njciotovia, njnotezcavia, nontlachiantezcac, ompa nonneçi, ompa nonnotta.

FLINT[2]

The name of this comes from nowhere. It is round, flat, triangular, irregular. It is slick, slick in all parts; it is asperous; it is rough, scabrous, concave, dented, hollowed out, bored. It has holes through it; it is pierced in places. Nowhere does it appear [big],[3] even though long. [One] is white; one yellow, not really yellow, just blended, just a little light yellow blended. One is shaded tawny. One is green, one transparent, one dense, one shaded. This [flint] has fire. When it is struck, sparks come out from it, [which] burn, burn things, set things afire, cause things to ignite; [which] make ablaze, set flaming.

TECPATL:

injn acan qujzquj in jtoca, ololtic, patlachtic, chiqujnaltic: acan cenqujzquj. xipetztic, xixipetztic, tetecujtztic, châchaquachtic, côcomotztic, vacaltic, patztic, comultic, côcoioctic, qujqujztic, qujqujçauhquj, acan neçi, in ma vepantli iztac, cequj coztic: amo vel coztic, çan poiavac, çan achi çacatlaxcalpoiavac, cequj quappachtica mehecauhioti, cequj xoxoxoctic, cequj atic, cequj tetzavac, cequj ceio hecauhio, injn tleio in movitequj, tlexochtli itech valqujça, tlatla, tlatlatia, tlatlecavia, tlatlecujtia, tleiova, tleti.

GREEN FLINT[4]

It resembles the green stone a little. The experienced lapidary names it *tecelic*. It is bespattered green, or layered [green], or so blended. Also it is beautiful, fresh, good.

XOXOUHQUJ TECPATL:

achi mochalchiuhnenequj, iehoatl in qujtocaiotia tlatecquj, in tlaiximatinj tecelic, qujmotzitzicujchili, xoxoctic: anoço qujmotlatlalili, anoço ic mopoiauh, no qualnezquj celic, qualli.

FINE CRYSTAL

This is the well-formed crystal, the bracelet, the necklace; that is to say, the *chopilotetl*.[5] That which is very clear is also called *chopilotl*, that is to say, really transparent, much like the *chopilotl*.

CHOPILOTL:

iehoatl in tevilotl ie tlaiectlalili, in ie macuextli, in ie cozcatl; in iuh mjtoa chopilotetl, in tlein cenca chipavac: no mjtoa chopilotl, in iuhquj mjtoa vel naltic, vel chopilotic.

TEPOCHTLI

It is white, really white, very white, clear, very clear; just soft; [sometimes] shaded.

TEPUCHTLI:

iztac, vel iztac, iztacpatic, chipactic, chipaccaltic; çan poxavac, çeio, hecauhio.

AITZTLI OR ACHALCHIUITL[6]

It is white, clear, smooth, fine-textured, a little green.

AITZTLI ANOÇO ACHALCHIVITL,

iztac, chipavac, tetzcaltic, cuechtic, achi xoxoxvic.

OPAL[7]

Its name comes from *uitzitzilin* [hummingbird] and *tetl* [stone], because its appearance is like the feathers of the humming bird, the one called *tozcatleton*. Its appearance is like many fireflies; it radi-

VITZITZILTETL:

in jtoca itech qujça in vitzitzili, ioan tetl: ipampa in itlachieliz, iuhqujnma vitzitzilin iiviio, in mjtoa totozcatleton. In itlachieliz iuhqujnma centzontli icpitl, itech moiava xoxotla, iuhqujn tlatla, itech cen-

---

2. Foshag (*op. cit.*, p. 26) refers to *tecpatl* as jasper.

3. *Acad. Hist. MS* adds *vei* after *neçi*.

4. Green jasper (Foshag, *loc. cit.*).

5. *Acad. Hist. MS: chopilotētetl*.

6. Corresponding Spanish text: "*piedra marmor . . . es la manera de marmor de españa.*"

7. Foshag (*op. cit.*, p. 48) "its occurrence suggests the operculum of a conch."

ates, glows; it is as if it burns. Colors come constantly from it; they are constantly coming—chili-red, green, the color of the lovely cotinga, the color of the roseate spoonbill, purple, red, herb-green, etc. However,[8] there is no black on it.

This is small and cylindrical, like the lone ant, constricted. It is of average size, small. There is its home — there it appears on the seashore, in the ocean sand, when it is found. And it appears there in the rivers of Totonacapan, in the gorges. But it appears only at night.

It is glowing like a small firefly, or is burning like a small candle. If it just appears intermittently, it is the firefly. If, on the other hand, if it just continues burning, this is the opal. It is clear, transparent, translucent, very precious, esteemed, wonderful, marvelous. It glows, shines, appears beautiful; it appears clear; it is rare.

SEASHELL[9]

The name of this comes from nowhere. It is bone; what is named *tapachtli* is the shell of a creature which is edible. It is hard, strong, firm, tough. The name of all is *atzcalli;* these are the shells of the water-dwelling creatures. And of these, one is chili-red. One is white; its name is *ayopalli*. One from which the color comes constantly they name *quetzalatzcalli* or *chalchiuhatzcalli*. Its appearance is just like the opal. Some they name *uitzitzilatzcalli*. One is vermilion; this is called *tapachtli*. This seashell resembles a crystal; it is also translucent; it is also transparent, smooth, slick, ever slick, rough; it is rough, perforated.

I cut the seashell. I make it into a bracelet. I form it into a necklace. I prepare it. I form it into a work of art. I provide myself a bracelet of it. I provide myself a necklace of it. I use it; I make use of it; I exalt it.

ATZCALLI[10]

It is the name of the shell, of all that come from the water, that live in the water, such as the *tecciztli*,[11] the *chipolin,* the *cilin,* the *tapachtli,* the *tecuiciztli,* etc.

SEASHELL[12]

It is white. One is large, one is small. It is spiraled,

quįça ca itech cenqujztica in tlapalli, in chichiltic, in xoxoctic, in xiuhtototl, in tlauhquechol, in camopalli, in tlavitl, in qujltic. etc. çan tetl atle itech ca tliltic:

injn mjmjltontli, iuhqujn icel azcatl tacapitztontli, çan qualton, çan tepiton; ompa ichan, ompa neçi in teuatenco, ilhujcaaxaltitlan, in motta, ioan ompa in totonacapan atoiac, texcalapan in neçi: auh çan iovaltica in neçi.

iuhqujn icpiton xotlatica; anoçe iuhqujn candelaton tlatlatica, intla çan valneneçi ca icpitl: auh intla çan ie ca intla çan ie tlatlatica, ca iehoatl in vitzitziltetl, chipavac, atic, naltic, vellaçotli, maviztic, maviço tlamaviçoltic, xoxotla, pepetlaca qualneci, chipaoacaneci, atca neçi.

TAPACHTLI:

injn acan qujzquj in jtoca, ca omjtl, ca itapalcaio in jtoca tapachtli, in ioioli, in qualonj, tepitztic, chicavac, tlâpaltic, tlaquavac, çan ie mochi itoca Atzcalli: injn itapalcaio, atlan nemj iolque: auh injn cequj chichiltic, cequj iztac: itoca aiopalli, cequj itech cenqujzca ca in tlapalli, iehoatl qujtocaiotia, quetzalatzcalli, anoço chalchiuhatzcalli: in jtlachializ vel iuhqujn vitzitziltetl: cequjntin qujtocaiotia vitzitzilatzcalli, auh cequj tlatlactic, iehoatl in mjtoa tapachtli. Injn tapachtli motevilonenequj, no naltic, no atic, tetzcaltic, xipetztic, xixipetztic, teçontic, chachaquachtic, qujqujztic.

In tapachtli nictequj, njcmacuexchiva, njccozcatlalia, njccozcachiva, njqujmati, njctoltecatlalia, njcnomacuextia, njcnocozcatia, njcnemjtia, njctitlanj, njctimaloa.

ATZCALLI:

ie mochi itoca in atlã vitz, in atlan nemj itapalcaio: in iuhquj tecuçiztli, in iuhquj chipoli, in iuhquj çili, in iuh tapachtli, in iuhquj tecujçiztli. etc.

TECÇIZTLI

iztac, cequj vei, cequj tepiton ilacatztic, maviçauh-

---

8. Acad. Hist. MS: *tel* (instead of *tetl*).

9. *Tapachtli: Spondylus* sp. (Ignacio Ancona H. and Rafael Martín del Campo, "Malacología precortesiana," p. 12).

10. *Atzcalli: Unio* sp., *Anodonta* sp. (*loc. cit.*).

11. *Acad. Hist. MS: tecciztli.*

12. *Tecciztli: Strombus gigas* (Ancona H. and Martín del Campo, *op. cit.,* p. 14).

marvelous. It is that which can be blown, which resounds.

I blow the seashell. I improve, I polish the seashell.

COLORED SEASHELL

It is rose, brown, pale, rosy. It becomes brown, it becomes pale.

TAPACHTLI has been mentioned.

AYOPALLI

It is the same as the *atzcalli*. It is a blend of gourd-blossom color; it is gourd-blossom-colored. It is made gourd-blossom color. The gourd-blossom color comes out. It becomes brown.

QUETZALATZCALLI, OR CHALCHIUHATZCALLI, OR UITZITZILATZCALLI

On the surface it is like something revolting, like [the stone] called *tepepeçoctli*: rough, perforated, ashen; like a rotten bone. But in its interior it is smooth, slick. It is really wonderful, marvelous, for from it the color comes constantly: the chili-red, the yellow, the lovely cotinga [color], the roseate spoonbill [color], the herb-green, the gourd-blossom [color], the brown, the dense color, the blended. It spreads out therefrom. Its appearance is sometimes like the rainbow, sometimes like the radiations of a firefly. It is of different painting, of different colors, of intricate designs, intricate.

SMALL SEASHELL[13]

It is tiny, just like[14] the spiral seashell. It is small and very smooth, very white.

ÇOLCILIN

Its name comes from *çolin* [quail] and *cilin* [small sea shell], because it is bespattered with a tawny color, varicolored, colored like a quail. It is bespattered, varicolored, colored like a quail.

CHIPOLIN[15]

It is a little large, completely white, clear, esteemed, good, beautiful, goodly.

quj, pitzaloni, caqujztinj:

njcpitza in tecçiztli, njciectia, njcpetlaoa in tecçiztli.

TLAPALTECCIZTLI:

tlapalpoiavac tlapalcamjltic, iztalevac, tlapalpoiavac, tlapalcamjlivi, iztaleva.

TAPACHTLI omito.

AIOPALLI:

çan no atzcalli, aiopalpoiavac, aiopaltic, aiopalti, aiopalquiça, tlapalcamjlivi.

QUETZALATZCALLI, ANOÇO CHALCHIUHATZCALLI, ANOÇO VITZITZILATZCALLI:

in panj iuhqujn tetlaelli, iuhqujn qujlhuja tepopoçoctli chachaquachtic, qujqujztic, nextic, iuhqujnma omjpalan: auh in jitic tetzcaltic, xipetztic, vel maviztic tlamaviçoltic, ca itech cenqujzca ca in tlapalli in chichiltic, in coztic, in xiuhtototl, in tlauhquechol, in qujltic, in aiopaltic, in camjltic, in tetzaoac tlapalli, in poiavac, vel ompa cenqujztoc, in jtlachializ: in quemã iuhqujnma aiauhcoçamalotl, in queman iuhqujnma icpitl moiava, nepapan tlacujlolli, nepapan tlapallo, vellamomoxoltic, vel moxtic.

CILI,

piciltontli, vel iuhquj injca tecçiztli in jlacatztic, tetzcaltontli iztacapil

ÇULCILI:

itech qujça in jtoca culi, ioan çili: ipampa ca quappachtica motzitzicujtz, mocujcujlo, moçolcujcujlo, motzitzicujtza, mocujcujloa, moçolcujcujloa.

CHIPOLI:

achi vejtontli çan vel cemjztac, chipavac, mavizio, qualton, qualnezquj, qualtepil.

---

13. *Cili:* listed under *gastropoda* in *loc. cit.*
14. *Acad. Hist. MS: ynic ca.*
15. *Chipolin:* listed under *gastropoda* in Ancona H. and Martín del Campo, *loc. cit.*

Ninth Chapter, which telleth of all the metals which are in the earth.

GOLD

Gold occurs in the earth; it rests in the earth. It appears, it is seen in this manner: where it is, there is its mother. When its mother appears, when she rains her water (as they say), her urine stains deeply.[1] Where it is yellow on the surface, where it is discolored as if glistening green, she stains deeply so that it appears. But especially is its mother within the earth or the mountain, where the gold lies, where it is. But it is not that it abounds; it is not heaped up; it just forms veins in the earth, in the mountain. It is that which can be excavated, can be washed, can be cast. All is the same — the gold, the copper, the lead.

And where the gold falls separately there into the river, the river [carries, bears the gold].[2] Thus, for this reason, when the Spaniards had not come, the Mexicans, those of Anahuac,[3] the experienced, did not mine the gold, the silver. They just took the river sand; they panned it. They found the gold where it settled as big as grains of maize. Then they took there that which was like sand. Later they melted it, cast it; they prepared, they formed necklaces, bracelets, ear pendants, lip plugs, etc.

The name of this gold, the yellow, the white [silver] — its name comes from *teotl* [god] and *cuitlatl* [excrement], because it is wonderful, yellow, good, fine, precious. It is the wealth, the riches, the lot, the possession, the property of the rulers, our lords.

It derives from [the fact that] sometimes, in some places, there appears in the dawn something like a little bit of diarrhea. They named it "the excrement of the sun"; it was very yellow, very wonderful, resting like an ember, like molten gold. So it appears that [the name] gold is taken from this. It is not from God. It is said that this is the sun, for the only God, the true God, was not yet known; for many gods were worshipped. And "sun" was really the name of

COZTIC TEUCUJTLATL:

in coztic teucujtlatl, ca tlallan in mochiva, tlallan in onoc. Injc neci, inic motta in campa ca, ca onca inan: iquac in neçi in jnan in qujavi, in jaio (in qujtoa) iiaxix cenca chiava, canjn ixcoztic, canjn xoxoxoctic: iuhqujn xoxotla, cenca chiava injc neci: auh in mache inan ca tlalli, anoço tepetl itic in onoc, in ca coztic teocujtlatl: auh amo ma çan temj, in ma ololiuhtica; çan qujmotlamjavalti in tlalli, in tepetl, tataconj, paconj pitzalonj. Ie mochi iuhquj, in jztac teucujtlatl, in tepuztli, in temetztli;

auh in canjn atoiapan, ompa vetztica iiovi teucujtlatl, in atoiatl: ic ipampa in aiamo valvi Españoles, in mexica, in aoacã in tlaiximatinj, amo qujtatacaia in coztic, in jztac teucujtlatl, çan atoiaxalli qujcuja, qujquauhxicalhuja; oncã qujttaia in coztic teucujtlatl, in cana vetztivitz in juhquj, ixqujch in tlaolli: njman ie oncan qujcuja, in iuhquj xalli, çatepan catiliaia, qujpitzaia, qujmatia, qujtlaliaia in cozcatl, in macuextli, in nacochtli, in tentetl, etc.

Injn teucujtlatl in coztic, in jztac in jtoca: itech qujça in jtoca teutl, ioan cuitlatl: ipampa in maviztic, in coztic, in qualli, in iectli, in tlaçotli, in necujltonolli, in netlamachtilli, intonal, imaxca, inneixcavil in tlatoque, in totecujiovan:

itech qujzquj, in quẽman cana neçi tlavizcalpan. iuhqujnma apitzaltontli, qujtocaiotia tonatiuh icujtl, cenca coztic, cenca maviztic, iuhqujn tlexochtli manj, iuhqujnma coztic teucujtlatl, tlaatililli; ic neçi itech tlaantli, y, in coztic teucujtlatl, amo iehoatl in jpalnemoanj, in jtechcopa mjtoa, ie in tonatiuh: ca in aiamo iximacho in jcel teutl, in nelli teutl, in ca mjequjntin teteu neteutiloia. Auh in tonatiuh: çan vel itoca catca teutl, nepantla teutl, mjtoaia valqujça teutl, njzteutl:

---

1. Corresponding Spanish text: *"ay señales donde ay mjnas de oro porque la madre se parece sobre la tierra, y es esta señal que ellos seria* [sic; *ello se cria*] *debaxo de tierra, specialmente se parece esta señal quando llueue."*

2. *Acad. Hist. MS* adds *quitqui catoctia teucuitlatl.*

3. *Ibid.: anavaca.*

a god. It was said, "The god comes up; the god is in the middle;[4] here is the god; the god leans on his side; the god enters." *Teotlac* is still said today; it means "the god [the sun] has entered, has set."

The advised took this excrement of the sun, for they said it was pustule medicine. They said it was pustule medicine. One ate it when the pustules had not yet developed; they said the pustules would not develop. But when pustules had developed, they said they were thereby cured. They said it recalled the fable of the sun, who, they said, was Nanauatzin ["little pustules"]. They said that for this reason pustule medicine, his excrement, sometimes appeared on earth.

This — gold, silver — is perfection, the leader of all. It leads all riches on earth. It is that which is sought, that which is desirable, that which is cherished, that which deserves being guarded, that which deserves being stored. [This] for the reason that it is the instrument of torment, because it is a deadly thing. It excites one; one is provided solace; it provides restitution. It is (truly it is said) a deceiver. It is one's lot, the property of the lords,[5] the property of the ruler.

I excavate gold. I pulverize sand. I wash sand. I blow sand. I wash gold. I purify sand. I make something clean. I cast gold. I melt something. I form, I prepare the gold. I cast, hammer, make gold bowls, gold cups, gold eagle vessels, gold jars for water.

I make, I cast, I prepare the gold necklace, the gold bracelet, the gold ear pendant, the pendant, the drop ear-ring. I hammer the gold leaf. I gild something. I give something a gold wash. I rub something [with gold]. I spray gold. Thus I make things beautiful; thus I make things give off rays.

LEAD

Its name comes from *tetl* [stone] and *metztli* [moon], because sometimes it is seen, it appears, at night like *atole* resting [on the ground]. They say it is the excrement of the moon, white, but a little dark; its name is taken from this. And this is also in mines like gold. And its mother is also there, like veins zigzagging in the earth.

And this is that which can be washed, can be cast, can be liquefied; that which melts. It is dark, black, heavy, very heavy, weighty, very weighty.

onmotzcaloa teutl, oncalaquj teutl: teutlac noma mjtoa in axcan, qujtoznequj onac, oncalac in teutl,

injn tonatiuh icujtl, in nonotzaloque qujcujque ca qujl nanavapatli, qujlmach nanaoapatli, in aiamo nanaoati qujqua, qujl amo nanaoatiz: auh in nanavati qujl ic pati, qujtoaia, qujlnamjquja in jçaçanjllo tonatiuh, ca qujl nanaoaton catca: qujl ipampa in nanaoapatli icujtl, in njcan tlalticpac quēman neçi.

Injn teucujtlatl in coztic, iztac, icemaçica, iceniac qujceniacantica, necujltonolli in tlalticpac temolonj, neconj, elevilonj, tlaçotlalonj, pialonj, tlatilonj: ipampa tlaihiyovilonj, ipāpa mjcoanj, teioleuh, teiol itzcalo, tetlacuepili (nel mjtoa) teca mocaiaoanj, tetonal, tecutlatlqujtl, tlatocatlatqujtl,

njteucujtlatataca, njxalteçi, njxalpaca, njxalpitza, njteucujtlapaca, njxaliectia, njtlachipava, njteucujtlapitza, njtlaatilia, njctlalia, njqujmati in teucujtlatl, njcpitza, njctzotzona, njcchiva teucujtlacaxitl, teucujtlatecomatl, teucujtlaquauhcaxitl, teocujtlaapilolli,

njcchioa, njcpitza, njqujmati in teucujtlacozcatl, in teucujtlamacuextli, in teucujtlanacochtli, in pipilolli, in cuecueiochtli: njctzotzona in teucujtlaamatl, njtlateucujtlavia, njtlateucujtlaaltia, njtlaoça, teucujtlatl njctzicujnja ic njtlaqualnextia, ic njtlatonameiotia.

TEMETZTLI:

in jtoca tetl, ioan metztli itech ōca: ipampa in quēman itto ioaltica neçi, iuhqujn atolli manj, qujl icujtl in metztli, iztac tel achi cujchevac, itech tlaqujxtilli in jtoca: auh injn no tepeio, oztoio, in iuhquj teucujtlatl: auh no onca inan, in iuhquj tlamjiavalli tlallan iaiaticac:

auh injn paconj, pitzalonj, atililonj, atianj, catzavac, tliltic, etic, eticpatic, cujtlaxocotl, cujtlaxocopatic:

---

4. *Ibid.: nepantla teutl* follows *valquiça teutl*.
5. Read *tecutlatquitl*.

I wash lead. I remove lead. I purify lead. I search for lead. I melt the lead. I form, I prepare it.

Mica[6]

The name *metzcuitlatl* comes from *metztli* [moon] and *cuitlatl* [excrement]. They say it is the excrement of the moon. It is dark, brown, shiny, very thin. It is like papers which are together. It is a delicate thing, trembling, soft, buoyant, light. It can be broken up; it is resistant; it is something which can be reduced to fragments in the hands.

Tin

Its name comes from *atl* [water] and *mochitl*: it means foam. It really means vapor, such as the vapor of water.[7] So it is referred to as white, the somewhat silver-like, somewhat hard, that which appears somewhat beautiful. There are its mines, its fissures. Like gold, there is also its mother.

Copper

There are also its mines; it is from mines, from fissures. And there is also its mother. Like gold, it forms veins in the rocks, the crags, the *tepetate*. When taken, it is still just earth; its name is "copper earth." [The copper] is washed, heated, liquefied, cast; stretched, extended.

Some of the copper[8] is red; it is called, it is given the name "chili-red copper." Here in New Spain, there used to exist, there used to be, only the chili-red. The Castilian copper is the yellow, the black.

I cast copper. I liquefy copper. I spread it. I alloy it. I solder it. I add tin to it. I harden it.

njtemetzpaca, njtemetztlaça, njtemetzchipava, njtemetztemoa, njcatilia in temetztli, njctlalia, njqujmati.

Metzcujtlatl:

in metzcujtlatl itech qujça in jtoca metztli, ioan cujtlatl, qujl icujtl in metztli, catzavac, camjltic, pêpepetlaca, cenca canaoac: iuhqujn amatl nenepanjuhtica, chinequjztli, hatevivi, haiollotlapalivi, ecauhtic, aco vetzquj, patinj, momapatlanj, maxaqualolonj.

Amochitl:

in jtoca itech qujça in atl, ioan mochitl: qujtoznequj apopoçoqujllotl, vel qujtoznequj apochqujotl, iuhqujnma ipochqujotl atl: ic motocaioti in iztac, in achi moztacteucujtlanenequj, in achi tlaquavac, in no achi qualneçi, vnca itepeio, ioztoio, itecochio; in iuhquj teucujtlatl, no iuhquj no onca inan.

Tepuztli:

no vnca itepeio, ioztoio, tepeio, oztoio, tecochio: auh no vnca inan in tetl, in texcalli, in tepetlatl qujmotlamiiavalti; in iuhquj teucujtlatl. in mocuj çan oc tlalli, itoca tepuztlalli, mopaca, mototonja, matilia, mopitza, moteca, motoiava:

In tepuztlalli cequj tlatlavic, mjtoa, motocaiotia chichiltic tepuztli, in njcan nueva españa: çan iio in nenca, in catca chichiltic, castillan tepuztli in coztic, in tliltic:

njtepuzpitza, nitepuçatilia, njctoiava, njctlanellotia, njctzictilia, njcamochivia, njctlaquava.

---

6. Cf. desc. in Hernández, *Historia Natural*, Vol. II, p. 405; also in his *Rervm Medicarvm Novae Hispaniae Thesavrvs sev Plantarvm Animalivm Mineralivm Mexicanorvm Historia* (ed. Nardo Antonio Reccho; Rome, Vitalis Mascardi, 1651), pp. 336, 895.

7. *Acad. Hist. MS: ypochquio ȳ atl.*

8. *Ibid.: tepuztli.*

Tenth Chapter, which telleth of the really fine stones.

TEOXALLI
Emery[1]

It is now called *uei xalli*. [It is of] the mountains, the crags. It is white, yellow, ashen, ruddy, mixed black and green. It is a grinder; it is that which wears away, which thins things. Some are like volcanic rock, rough, fragmented; some are fine, quite minute. They grind, abrade, thin, wear things away.

I treat things with *teoxalli*. I abrade things. I harden.

TEMETZTLALLI
Pulverized lead

This is the earth from which the gold, or the lead, or the tin comes. It is green, like flint, like limestone, like sand. It is useful, desirable, necessary; it is washable, liquefiable. It is heavy, very heavy; it is weighty, very weighty.

I excavate *temetztlalli*. I gather *temetztlalli*. I pulverize *temetztlalli*. I heat *temetztlalli*. I fire *temetztlalli*.

TEMETZTLALLI
A kind of black pyrite

It is like iron pyrites. It shines; it is like sand, like fine sand.

I apply *temetztlalli* to something.

IRON PYRITE
Pyrite

It is the same as *temetztlalli*; however, it is nothing but sand. It is black. It shines. It is a means of drying things; thus it is a medium for drying paintings.

I gather iron pyrite. I carry iron pyrite upon my back. I sell iron pyrite. I apply iron pyrite to something.

MIRROR STONE EARTH
Pulverized mirror stone

It is the same as iron pyrite earth, as *temetztlalli*. It is black; it is like sand. It shines.

I apply mirror stone earth to something.

Inic matlactli capitulo: itechpa tlatoa tetl, vel ixpitzavac.

TEUXALLI:
Esmeril

axcan mjtoa vei xalli tetl, tepetl, texcalli, iztac, tecoçauhtic, nexeoac, tlatlavic, tlilaiotic, tlaquaquanj, tlatlamjanj, tlacanaoanj: cequj teçontic, chachaquachtic, papaiaxtic; cequj cuechtic, vel pitzavac, tlaquaqua, tlâchiquj, tlacanaoa, tlatlamja:

njtlateoxalhuja, njtlachiquj, njtlaquava.

TEMETZTLALLI:
Plomo molido

iehoatl in jtech qujça in teucujtlatl, in aço temetztli, anoço amuchitl, tlalli, xoxoxoctic, tecpatetic, tenextetic, xaltic, moneccaio, nequjzio, neconj, paconj, atililonj, etic, eticpatic, cujtlaxocotl, cujtlaxocopatic;

njtemetztlaltataca, njtemetztlalcuj, njtemetztlalteçi, njtemetztlallatia, njtemetztlallatilia.

TEMETZTLALLI:
Vna manera de margaxita negra

iuhqujn apetztli pêpepetlaca, xaltic, xalpitzactic.

njtlatemetztlalhuja.

HAPETZTLI:
Margaxita

çan vel no iuhquj in temetztlalli, iece çan vel molhuj xalli, tliltic, pêpepetlaca tlaoatzalonj, ic vatzalonj in tlacujlolli.

Nâpetzcuj, napetzmama, nâpetznamaca, njtlaapetzvia.

TEZCATLALLI:
Piedra de espejos molida

çan vel no iuhquj in âpetztlalli, in temetztlalli tliltic, xaltic, pepetlaca,

njtlatezcatlalhuja.

---

1. In the *Florentine Codex*, each Nahuatl paragraph is preceded by a Spanish heading or explanation. In the format devised for this publication, it appears to be preferable to begin with the Nahuatl heading here and in following chapters.

TEZCATETLILLI
A kind of black coloring

It is the same as mirror stone earth. It is something manufactured, something made into a ball. It is like iron pyrite. It shines, shines constantly.

I apply *tezcatetlilli* to something.

FLINT SAND
Flint emery

It is crushed, pulverized, ground. It is flint. It is fragmented, broken up, fine, much ground, very fine, completely ground, all ground like *pinole;* powdery. It is a medium for cleaning, for polishing, for thinning, for scouring. It is a polisher of things, a smoother of things.

I polish something. I smooth something. I dress something.

TEZCATETLILLI,
Cierta manera de tinta negra

çan ie iehoatl in tezcatlalli tlachioalli, tlamaholli, âpetztic, pepetlaca, pêpepetlaca:

njtlatezcatetlilhuja.

TECPAXALLI,
Esmeril de pedernales

tlatetzotzontli, tlatextililli, tlatextli tecpatl, papaiaxtic, papaiaca, cuechtic, cuecuechtic, cuechpatic, cuechtzontic, cuechtzonpatic, pinoltic, teuhtic, tlaiectilonj, tlapetlaoalonj, tlacanaoalonj, tlachichiconj, tlapetlavanj, tlaiottovianj.

Nitlapetlaoa, njtlaiottovia, njtlacencava.

Eleventh Chapter, which telleth of all the different colors.

Fɪʀsᴛ ᴘᴀʀᴀɢʀᴀᴘʜ, which telleth how all the colors are made.

Cᴏᴄʜɪɴᴇᴀʟ

Its name comes from *nochtli* [opuntia] and *eztli* [blood], because it is formed on the *nopal* and is like blood, like a blood blister. This cochineal is an insect; it is a worm. The cochineal *nopal* is the breeding place of this cochineal. It lives, it hatches on the *nopal* like a little fly, a little insect. Then it grows; then it develops; then it increases in size. It fattens, it increases much in size, it thickens, it becomes round. Then it envelops itself in fat. When the worms are distended, they come to rest just like blood blisters. Then they cover themselves with a web. Then they die; they fall; also they are heaped together, swept up. With a broom they are heaped together.

This color is not yet refined. It is of quite dark surface, still like dried blood — round, small and round, a little spongy, a little dry. It is a coloring medium, a chili-red coloring medium, a chili-red colorer.

I dye. I make something cochineal-colored. I apply cochineal.[1] I paint things with colors. I apply colors. I blend colors. I thicken colors. I make something chili-red. I become chili-red. I bring out the color.

Tʟᴀǫᴜᴀᴜᴀᴄ ᴛʟᴀᴘᴀʟʟɪ

Its name comes from *tlaquauac* [dry] and *tlapalli* [color], because it is very good, firm, vivid — a vivid color; a real chili-red, very much like blood, like fresh blood.

Tᴏʀᴛɪʟʟᴀ-ʟɪᴋᴇ ᴄᴀᴋᴇ

And this is the same kind of cochineal. Its name is *nocheztlaxcalli.*

I make tortillas of cochineal. I beat out tortillas of cochineal. I form cochineal into tortillas.

Tʟᴀᴘᴀʟɴᴇxᴛʟɪ

Its name is[2] from *tlapalli* [color] and *nextli* [ashes], because this same cochineal is a preparation, just a

Injc matlactli oce capitulo: itechpa tlatoa, in jxqujch nepapan tlapalli.

Iɴᴊᴄ ᴄᴇ ᴘᴀʀʀᴀᴘʜᴏ itechpa tlatoa, in jsq'ch tlapalli in quenjn mochioa.

Nᴏᴄʜᴇᴢᴛʟɪ:

nochtli itech qujça in jtoca, ioan eztli, iehica nopaltitech in muchiva: auh iuhqujn eztli, iuhqujn eztecocoli, inin nocheztli ca ioioli ca ocujli, in nocheznupalli, in ie imochioaia nocheztli in nopaltitech ioli, tlacati, in iuhquj çaioltoton, in ioiolitoton: njman ie movapava, njman ie mozcaltia, niman ie chamava mopochqujotia, cenca chamava, tôtomava, tolonavi; njman ie mopochqujoqujmjloa, in oimellelaçic in ocujlti, vel iuhqujn eztecocolli motlalia; njman motocatzaoalqujmiloa, njman mjquj valvetzi, noçe mololoa, mozqujzvia popotica mololoa.

Injn tlapalli aiamo chipavac, çan ixtlilectic, çan oc iuhqujn ezvaquj, ololtic, ololtontli, pâpatzpil, vavacalpil, tlapalonj, tlachichililonj, tlachichiloanj.

Nitlapa. njtlanochezvia, njtlanochezaquja, njtlapallacujloa, njtlatlapalaquj, njtlatlatlapalpoiava, njtlatlapaltilava, njtlachichiloa, njchichilivi, njtlapalqujça.

Tʟᴀǫᴜᴀᴠᴀᴄ ᴛʟᴀᴘᴀʟʟɪ:

itech qujça in jtoca tlaquavac, ioan tlapalli: ipampa ca cenca qualli chicavac, ixtlapaltic, ixtlapalivi vel chichiltic, vel eztic; iuhqujn xoxouhquj eztli,

Tʟᴀᴛʟᴀxᴄᴀʟᴏʟʟɪ.

Auh injn, ca çan ie iehoatl in nocheztli tlamantli, itoca nocheztlaxcalli:

njnocheztlaxcalchiva, njnocheztlaxcalmana, njnocheztlaxcaloa.

Tʟᴀᴘᴀʟɴᴇxᴛʟɪ:

in jtoca itech onca tlapalli, ioan nextli: ipampa ca çan ie iehoatl, in nocheztli, tlachivalli, çan tlanello, ce-

---

1. *Acad. Hist. MS* adds *nitlapalchiva.*
2. *Ibid.:* ōca.

mixture. Some has chalk, some has flour, some is a mixture [of both].

The inferior cochineal, which comes from a tuna, an edible *nopal*, is also named *tlapalnextli*. Its cochineal, of a kind of fruit-producing *nopal*, is made into cakes.

It is named *tlapalnextli* because it is uncolored; it is not like blood, but is ash colored, ashen, chalky.

I apply *tlapalnextli* to something. I apply color to something. I blend something. I shade something.

Fine yellow[3]

The name of this comes from *xochitl* [flower] and *tlapalli* [color]; it is as if to say "flower which dyes." This *xochipalli* occurs in the hot lands. It is a dyeing medium, a medium for coloring, for beautifying, for making things radiant, for giving luster.

I make something a fine yellow. I apply a fine yellow to something. I color it a fine yellow.[4]

Blue

Its name comes from nowhere. It is the blossom of an herb, a blossom. This *matlalin* is blue and a little herb-green. It is very sound, firm, good, of good appearance, fresh green. It is fresh green, very fresh green. It colors solidly; it is solid-colored.

I make the blue color. I make something blue.[5] I blue something. I blend the blue. I apply blue to something.

Light yellow[6]

Its name comes from *çacatl* [grass] and *tlaxcalli* [tortilla], because [the plant] climbs like grass. Yellow comes from it. It is long, it is slender. From it comes light yellow. It is a tortilla in the sense that it is formed like a tortilla, like a round tortilla — wide, round, big, thin. The hot lands are the places where it grows. It is yellow — yellow; it is yellow, very yellow, extremely yellow.

I make something light yellow. I color something light yellow. I make something yellow. I yellow something.

quj tiçaio, cequj texio, cequj tlaixnamjctilli,

in çacan nocheztli, in nochtli, in qualonj, nopalli, itech qujça, no tlapalnextli motocaiotia, inochezio, nochio nopalli tlamātli, tlatlaxcalolli.

Injc motocaiotia tlapalnextli; amo ixtlapalivi, amo eztic, çan nexevac, nexectic, ticevac.

Nitlatlapalnexvia, njtlatlapalaquja, njtlapoiava, njtlacevallotia.

Xochipalli:

injn itoca itech qujça xochitl, ioan tlapalli; iuhqujn qujtoznequj, xochitl, tlapalonj. Injn xochipalli tonaian muchiva, tlapalonj, tlacujlolonj, tlaqualnextilonj, tlatonameiotilonj, tlacueponaltilonj.

Nitlaxochipalhuja, njtlaxochipalaquja, njcxochipalhuja.

Matlali:

acan qujzquj in jtoca, xivitl ixochio, xochitl: inin matlali texotic, ioan achi qujltic, cenca ixtlapalivi, ixchicactic, qualli, qualnezquj, celic, celtic, celpatic, ixtlapalivi, ixtlapaltic:

njmatlalchiva, njtlamatlalchiva, njtlamatlallotia, njtlamatlalpoiava, njtlamatlalaquja.

Çacatlaxcalli:

çacatl, ioan tlaxcalli, itech qujztica in jtoca: ipampa iuhqujn çacatl movivicoma, in jtech qujça coztic, memelactic, pipitzavac, in jtech qujça çacatlaxcalli. Injc tlaxcalli, ca tlatlaxcaltilli, iuhqujn iavale tlaxcalli, patlavac iavale, vej, canaoac, tonaian in jmochiuhian, coztic, coçauhquj, coçauic, cozpatic, cozpiltic.

Nitlaçacatlaxcalhuja, njtlaçacatlaxcallotia, njtlacoçalhuja, njtlacoztilia.

---

3. *Xochipalli:* "*Yerba cuya hoja se parece a la artemisa, y sirve para teñir las telas de amarillo, rojo o anaranjado*" (Santamaría, *Dic. de Mejicanismos*, p. 987 — *suchipal*, citing Robelo).

4. *Acad. Hist. MS: nicxochipalchiva.*

5. *Ibid.: nitlamatlalvia.*

6. *Çacatlaxcalli:* prob. *Cuscuta tinctorea* Mart.; *Con el nombre de "zacatlascal" se designa a* C. americana *L., a* C. odontolepis *Eng., y con el de "zacatlaxcale" a* C. americana (Hernández, *Hist. de las Plantas*, Vol. II, p. 394).

LIGHT RED[7]

Its name comes from nowhere. Its growing place is in the hot lands. The blossoms which it produces are ground up. It is like vermilion, ruddyish.[8]

I make light red. I make something light red. I apply light red to something. It appears light red. It becomes vermilion.

¶

SECOND PARAGRAPH, which telleth of still other colors, so that it is seen how coloring is done.

UITZQUAUITL[1]

Its name comes from *uitztli* [thorn] and *quauitl* [tree]. This is a big tree. And a color is made from its wood, its trunk, with which to dye. Its peculiarity is that it is that which can be cut, split, steeped; it is for steeping; water can be extracted. It is only a little dark, a little blackish. Later they make it clear with alum; and besides they mix it with other things. It becomes chili-red, very chili-red, chili-like, vivid chili-colored, very chili-like. It is a dyeing, not a painting medium.

I make something the *uitzquauitl* color. I dye things with the *uitzquauitl* color. I apply the *uitzquauitl* color to something. I make something the color of *uitzquauitl*. I cut the *uitzquauitl* [tree]. I gather *uitzquauitl* [wood]. I sell *uitzquauitl* [wood].

NACAZCOLOTL[2]

It is the fruit of a large tree which grows in the hot lands. Its name comes from *nacaztli* [ear] and *colotl* [hook]; that is to say, it is like a small ear, a small hook, a small miter. It is small and twisted, small and slender, small and straight; a little vermilion; dark. The not very good has maize flour, well-ground maize flour; the very good, the best, which one leaves in turpentine unguent, in much turpentine unguent, is sticky. It is sticky, very sticky; sticky. It is a medium for dyeing things black, for dyeing *uitztecolli*.[3] It is a solvent for *uitztecolli*, for *yapalli*. It is a medium for painting, a medium for writing.[4]

I dye something. I make something dark green. I dye something dark green. I dye with *uitztecolli*. I

ACHIOTL, ANOÇO ACHIOTETL:

acan qujzquj in jtoca, tlatotoian imochiuhia. Xochitl in mochiva moteçi, ixtlatlauhquj, ixtlatlactic:

nachiochiva. njtlaachiochiva, njtlachioaquja, achioneci, tlatlavia.

¶

INJC VME PARRAPHO: oc centlamantli tlapalli itechpa tlatoa, iuh motta in quenin tlapalo.

VITZQUAUJTL:

vitztli, ioan quaujtl: itech qujça in jtoca injn vei quavitl: auh vel iehoatl in jnacaio, in jtlac, in tlapalli mochiva injc tlapalo, tetzotzonalonj, tzatzaianalonj, çiavalonj, çiavanj maqujxtianj in çan mjxcavia, çan oc achi cujchevac, achi ixtlilevac: qujn qujtlachialtia in tlalxocotl: ioan in oc cequj qujneloa chichiltic, chichilpatic, chiltic, chilpatzcaltic, chilpatic, tlapalonj: amo tlacuilolonj.

Nitlavitzquavia, vitzquauhtica njtlapa, njtlaujtzquauhaquja, njtlavitzquauhiotia, njvitzquauhtequj, nivitzquauhcuj, njvitzquauhnamaca.

NACAZCOLOTL:

tonaian in muchivaia, vei quaujtl itlaaqujllo in jtoca itech qujztica nacaztli, ioan colotl, qujtoznequj iuhqujn nacaztontli, colochtontli, copiltontli, ilacatzpil, melactontli, melaoacatontli, tlatlacpil, cujchevac: i çan ipan qualli texio, tetexio, i cenca qualli in jiac in tlâcaoa ôxio, ôoxio, çaçalic, çaçaltic, çaçalpâtic, çaçaltic, tlatlilpalonj, tlavitztecolpalonj, ipaloca in vitztecolli, in iapalli. tlacujlolonj, letrachioalonj

Nitlapa, njtlaiapa, njtlaiapalpa, njvitztecolpa, njvitztecolchiva, njtlaujtztecolaquja, njtlavitztecoltilia.

7. *Achiotl: Bixa orellana* L. (Santamaría, *op. cit.*, p. 28).

8. *Acad. Hist. MS: tlatlactic.*

1. *Uitzquauitl: Caesalpinia echinata* (Sahagún, Garibay ed., Vol. IV, p. 367).

2. *Nacazcolotl: Caesalpinia coriacea, C. coriaria* (Santamaría, *op. cit.*, p. 749 — *nacascolote*).

3. *Acad. Hist. MS* adds *tlayapaloni.*

4. *Ibid.: tlatolicuiloloni* is added.

make the *uitztecolli* color. I apply the *uitztecolli* color. I make something the *uitztecolli* color.

Tezuatl[5]

It is a shrub which grows in the hot lands. This *tezuatl* is converted into color. Cochineal is crushed; it is added to the *tezuatl*. It is provided with alum, with copperas. To purify it, it is boiled. From it comes the dried color or a good colored water. With it rabbit hair is tinted; with it there is tinting.

I use the *tezuatl* color. I dye something with dried color.

Tlaceuilli[6]

It is an herb. Its growing place is in the hot lands. It is pounded with a stone. The juice is squeezed out. It is wrung dry. [The juice] is placed in a bowl. There it becomes thick; there the *tlaceuilli* gathers. This color is dark blue, gleaming, greenish. It is a dyeing medium, a medium for painting black, for painting in colors.

I squeeze juice from the *tlaceuilli*. I make the *tlaceuilli* color.

Light blue[7]

The name, *texotli*, comes from nowhere. *Texotli* is blue. It is blue, very blue, green — a little brown; a little brown; thick.

Tecoçauitl[8]

Its name comes from *tetl* [stone] and *coçauhqui* [yellow]; that is, it is a yellow stone; yellow in the form of a stone. It is ground up. It is a dyeing medium, a painting medium, a means of making things especially brilliant.[9]

I make something yellow. I wash something in yellow. I make something the yellow color.

Black

It is the smoke of pine pitchwood, the lampblack of pine pitchwood. It is a medium for blackening, for dyeing, for tracing lines, for blending with black. It is powdery, finely powdered, pulverized. It is that which admits water, which blots, which stains.

Tezvatl:

quauhxivitl tlatotoiã muchiva: injn tezvatl tlapalli mocuepa, mopitzinja in nocheztli, monamjctia in tezvatl motlalxocovia, motlaliiacavia ic chipava, moquaqualatza, vncan qujça in tlaquavac tlapalli, anoço qualli tlapalatl ic tochomjpalo, ic tlapalo:

njtlatezvavia, njtlaquavactlapalpa.

Tlacevilli:

xivitl tlatotoian imuchiuhia, motetzotzona, mopatzca, motetzavacapatzca, caxic motlatlalia, vncan tetzava vncan mocuj in tlaceujlli. Injn tlapalli movitic, xoxotlanj, tlapalonj, tlillacujlolonj, tlapallacujlolonj:

njtlacevilpatzca, njtlacevilchiva.

Texotli:

in texotli acan qujzquj in jtoca: in texotli xoxoctic, xôxovic, xoxoxovic, xoxouhquj; achi ixcamjltic, ixcamjliuhquj tetzavac.

Tecoçavitl:

in jtoca itech qujztica tetl, ioan coçauhquj. q. n. tetl coztic, coztic tetl moteci, tlapalonj: tlacujlolonj tlaquauhnextilonj:

njtlatecoçavia, njtlatecoçauhaltia, njtlatecoçauhiotia.

Tlilli

ocutl ipocio, ocotl icalcujchio, tlatlilhujlonj, tlatlilpalonj, tlatlilanjlonj, tlatlilpoiavalonj, cuechtic, cuecuechtic, cuecuechiuhquj, hatlamatinj, hatlamavanj, hatlacauhquj.

---

5. *Tezuatl: Miconia laevigata* (L.) D.C. (Standley, "Trees and Shrubs," Pt. 4, p. 1068).

6. *Tlaceuilli:* Hernández (*Hist. Natural*, Vol. II, p. 112) describes the extraction of blue coloring (*mouitli* or *tlaceuilli*) from leaves of the *xiuhquilitl pitzauac* (*Indigofera añil*, in Sahagún, *op. cit.*, p. 369). See also corresponding Spanish text.

7. *Texotli:* according to corresponding Spanish text, a dye made of *matlalin* leaves; according to Hernández (*op. cit.*, p. 407), "una especie de tierra . . . que se tritura, se mete en sacos, y echándole agua encima se deja colar su parte más fina, la cual secada se conforma en pastillas azules."

8. *Tecoçauitl:* "cierta especie de ocre o tierra amarilla" (*ibid.*, p. 410).

9. *Acad. Hist. MS: tlaqualnextiloni.*

I dye something black. I blacken something. I blend something with black. I make black lines on something. I blacken something. I darken something.

COPPERAS

Its name comes from *tlalli* [earth] and *iyac* [stinking], because it is an earth; it is *tepetate*; it is tufaceous.

¶

THIRD PARAGRAPH, which telleth of that of which colors [are made]; that which improves colors.

ALUM

Its name is said [from] *tlalli* [earth] and *xocotl* [sour fruit], because it is an earth like *tepetate*, like saltpeter; and as for *xocotl*, it is sour, very sour. It causes one to salivate; it deaden's one's teeth; it puts one's teeth on edge; it makes one acid. It is white, white of surface; a medium for refining colors, for cleaning the surface of something, for improving something.

I use alum on something. I clean the surface of something. I improve the surface of something.

TETLILLI OR TEZCATETLILLI

Its name comes from *tetl* [rock] and *tlilli* [black], because it is a hard rock, and black, very black; and from *tezcatl* [mirror], because it glistens.

I make something black. I make something glistening black. I glisten.

RED OCHRE[1]

Its name comes from nowhere. It is a rock; it is *tepetate*; it is like *tepetate*. It is ruddy. It is mined. It is necessary, required, useful. It is a medium for beautifying, for reddening.

I redden something. I make something red. I anoint something with ochre.

CHALK

With it women spin. It is white, cylindrical, round. This is mud; this is a watered chalk. Then it is fired in an oven to refine. It becomes chalk.

I apply chalk to myself. I apply chalk to something. I place white on something.

Nitlatlilpa, njtlatlilhuja, njtlatlilpoiava, njtlatlilanja, njtlatlillotia, njtlacatzava.

TLALIIAC:

in jtoca itech qujça in tlalli, ioan iiac: ipampa ca tlalli, ca tepetlatl cacaiacatica.

¶

INJC EI PARRAPHO: itechpa tlatoa, injc mochiva qujqualtilia in tlapalli.

TLALXOCOTL:

in jtoca itech mjtoa tlalli, ioan xocotl: ipampa ca tlalli, tetepetlatic, tetequjxqujtic: auh injc xocotl, ca xococ, xocopatic, teiztlacmealti, tetlanmjmjcti, tetlâcecepouh, texôxocoli, iztac, ixiztac, tlatlapalchipavalonj, tlaixchipavalonj, tlaiectilonj.

Nitlatlalxocovia, njtlaixchipava, njtlaixiectia.

TETLILLI: ANOÇO TEZCATETLILLI,

in jtoca itech qujztica tetl, ioan tlilli: ipampa ca tetl tlaquavac, auh tliltic, tlilpatic: auh injc itech vnca tezcatl; ipampa pepetlaca.

Nitlatetlilhuja, njtlatezcatetlilhuja, njpepetlaca

TLAVITL:

acan qujzquj in jtoca, tetl, tepetlatl, tepetlatlalli, tepetlatic, tlatlaujc, tepeio, oztoio, moneccaio, monequj, neconj, tlaqualnextilonj, tlatlaujlonj,

njtlatlavia, njtlatlauhiotia, tlauhtica njtlaoça.

TIÇATL:

injc tzaoa civa, iztac, mjmjltic, ololtic: injn çoqujtl, ca iehoatl in atiçatl: njman moxca texcalco ic chipava, tiçati.

Ninotiçavia, njtlatiçavia, njtlaztallalia.

---

1. *Tlauitl:* "*almagre fabril*"; "*una especie de tierra amarilla que puesta al fuego toma al punto un color rojo*" (Hernández, *op. cit.*, p. 409).

LIMESTONE

Its name comes from *tetl* [rock] and *tiçatl* [chalk], because it is a rock. It is ground, fired, pulverized. With it things are painted.

I apply limestone to something.

THE XICALTETL[2]

It occurs only in the gorges, there in the reeds. It is just gathered and later ground up, well pulverized. And when the earthen vessel is to be made matte, then [the powder] is mixed with blue coloring from Michoacan, called *texotlalli*; then it is mixed with *chia* oil. With it one glues. With it the earthen vessel or gourd is made matte.

CHIMALTIÇATL[3]

It comes from Uaxtepec. It is broken off like a cliff rock. And when it is to be painted on, it is fired; it becomes very soft. Then it is ground up; it is mixed with glue. With it things are painted; they are varnished white.

HERE ARE MENTIONED the colors which are only manufactured.

DARK GREEN

Its name comes from *yauhtli* [wormwood] or *yayauhqui* [dark] and *tlapalli* [color]. It is just something made, mixed; a composite, thoroughly mixed.

It is [a color] made in this manner: they add blue to yellow. Blue is poured into, blue is joined with yellow. It is not very green; neither is it yellow. The yellow which thus appears is very dark.

I make a dark green color. I manufacture a dark green color. I mix, I pour together, I thoroughly mix blue and yellow. I make something dark green. I color something dark green. I blend dark green. With dark green I give things luster, I shade something.

BROWN

It is a dark color, a medium for beautifying things, for giving them brilliance, for giving them luster, for painting, for coloring. To make this, cochineal and alum are brought together; they are mixed together; they are poured together.

TETIÇATL:

in jtoca, tetl, itech qujça, ioan tiçatl: ipampa ca tetl, moteci, mjcequj, mocuechoa, ic tlacujlolo.

Nitlatetiçavia.

IN XICALTETL:

çan atlauhco in muchioa, vmpa in tollã çan mopepena: auh çatepan moteci uel mocuechoa: auh in jquac ie ic mjqujliz in tecomatl; njman ic moneloa in mjchoacaiotl texotli, motocaiotia texotlalli, njman ic moneloa in chiamatl, ic çaçalia, ic mjquj in tecomatl, anoco xicalli.

IN CHIMALTIÇATL:

vmpa qujça in oaxtepec, iuhqujn texcalli motlapana: auh in jquac ie ic tlacujloloz moxca, cenca iamanquj muchioa: njman moteci, tzacutli moneloa, ic tlacujlolo, ic tlatiçavilo.

NICAN MJTOA, i çan tlachioalli tlapalli.

IIAPPALLI:

in jtoca, itech qujztica iiauhtli, anoço iaiauhquj, ioan tlapalli, iuhqujn qujtoznequj iaiactic, iiauhtic tlapalli, çan tlachivalli, tlanelolli, tlanamjctilli, tlanelolli.

Injc tlachioalli, çacatlaxcalli texotli qujnamjquj, texotli momjnaltia, texotli monamjctia in çacatlaxcalli: amo cenca xoxoctic, amo no coztic, cencan poiavac in coztic itech neci.

Niiappalchioa, njiappallalia, texotli, çacatlaxcalli njcneloa, njcmjnaltia, njcneneloa, njtlaiiappalhuja, njtlaiiappalaquja, njtlaiiappalpoiaoa, iiappaltica njtlacueponaltia, njtlacevallotia.

CAMOPALLI:

tlapalpoiavac, tlaqualnextilonj, tlacueponaltilonj, tlatlanexiotilonj, tlâcujlolonj, tlapallacujlolonj. Injc mochioa, y, nocheztli, tlalxocotl monamjquj, moneloa, momjnaltia.

---

2. *Acad. Hist.* MS lists *xicaltetl* and *chimaltetl* with no descriptions.

3. Corresponding Spanish text: *"son como hyeso de castilla."* According to Hernández, *op. cit.,* p. 405, *"Quemado proporciona una especie de yeso, así como un tinte blanco."*

I make a brown color. I dissolve the brown color. I paint, I dye brown.

HERB-GREEN

Its name comes from *quilitl* [herb] and *-tic*, that is, like an herb. It is a little green, a little dark yellow; quite a little. To make this, blue [and] yellow are brought together.

I apply the herb-green color. I apply the herb-green to something. I blend something with herb-green.

UITZTECOLLI

Its name comes from *uitztli* [thorn] and *tecolli* [charcoal], as if to say carbonized, brownish brazilwood. To make it, two things are mixed together: brazilwood and copperas. Thus it becomes black, dark brown.[4]

I make the *uitztecolli*. I apply the *uitztecolli* to something. I dye something with *uitztecolli*.

TAWNY

Its name comes from *quauitl* [tree] and *pachtli* [Spanish moss], because the Spanish moss is of a tree which is also called *quappachtli*. It is ground up; it is soaked. Thence issues the color. The name of that from which it comes is *quappachtli*, or the *quauhtepoztli* tree. It is somewhat dark yellow—dark brown. To improve this, the *nacazcolotl* herb is mixed with it as well as with a little mud called *palli*.

HERE ARE MENTIONED the principal colors; the names of the true colors.

Tlapalli is the collective term for all the different colors — the clear, the good, the fine, the precious, the wonderful.

I paint with the different colors. I make different paintings. I beautify them. With intricate designs I make them. Painted like earrings — painted like earrings I make them. I paint varicolored paintings.

Very white — exceedingly white. I whiten something. I make something white. I make something exceedingly white.

Black has been mentioned. Yellow has been mentioned. Chili-red has been mentioned. Green has been mentioned.

Nicamopalchioa, njcamopalpatla, njcamopallacujloa, njcamopalpa.

QUJLTIC:

in jtoca, itech qujztica in qujlitl, ioan tic, qujtoznequj: iuhqujn qujlitl, achi xoxouhquj, achi ixcoziaiauhquj cencan achi. Injc muchiva, y, in texotli, çacatlaxcalli monamjctia.

Nitlaqujlaquja, njtlaqujltiçaaquja, njtlaqujltiçapoiava.

VITZTECOLLI:

in jtoca vitztli itech qujztica, ioan tecolli: iuhqujn qujtoznequj vitzquavitl, tecoltic, camjltic. Injc muchioa vntlamantli in monêneloa vitztecolli ioan tlaliyac: ic muchiva in tliltic, tlapalcamjlpoiaoac.

njvitztecolchioa, njtlavitztecolaquja, njtlaujtztecolpa.

QUAPPACHTLI:

in jtoca, itech qujztica quavitl, ioan pachtli: iehica ca in jpachio quavitl, in no itto ca quappachtli, ca moteçi, mopaltilia: vncan qujça in tlapalli, in jtoca quappachtli, anoço iehoatl in quauhtepuztli, itech qujça achi ixcoziaiactic, ixcamjliaiactic. Injc qualtia, y, nacazcolotl moneloa, ioan achi çoqujtl, in jtoca palli.

NICAN MJTOA, in tlapalli, tlaiacatia: in nelli tlapalli in jtoca

Tlapalli: icentoca in jxqujch nepapan tlapalli, chipavac, qualli, iectli, tlaçotli, maviztic.

Ninepapantlacujloa, nepapan tlacujloli njcchiva, njcqualnextia, tlamomoxoltic njcchiva, cujcujlchampotic, cujcujlchampochtic njcchiva, niqujcujloa.

Iztacpaltic, aztapiltic, njtlaztalia, njtlaiztalia, njcaztapiltilia.

Tliltic, omjto. Coztic, omjto. Chichiltic, omjto. Xuxuctic, omjto.

---

4. *Acad. Hist.* MS differs in this passage: *Inic mochiva. yetlamantli ȳ monêneloa. chichiltic yoā texotli yoā tlilli yc mochiva ȳ tliltic tlapalca-milpoyavac* — to make it, three things are mixed together: chili-red and *texotli* [blue] and lampblack. Thus it becomes black, dark brown.

Twelfth Chapter, in which are mentioned, are named, the different kinds of water and the different kinds of earth.

FIRST PARAGRAPH, in which is told the nature of the sea and the rivers.

The first paragraph tells of that called water; of that called *teuatl*.

It is called *teuatl* [sea], not that it is a god; it only means wonderful, a great marvel. And its name is *ilhuicaatl*. The people of old, the people here of New Spain, thought and took as truth that the heavens were just like a house; it stood resting in every direction, and it extended reaching to the water. It was as if the water walls were joined to it. And hence they called it "water which reaches the heavens," because it stretched extending to the heavens. But now, because of the true Faith, it is only called *uei atl* [great water].

It is great. It terrifies, it frightens one. It is that which is irresistible; a great marvel; foaming, glistening, with waves; bitter — very bitter, most bitter; very salty. It has man-eating animals, animal life. It is that which surges. It stirs; it stretches ill-smelling, restless.

I live on the sea. I become a part of the sea. I cross over the sea. I die in the sea. I live on the sea.

ATOYATL

Its name comes from *atl* [water] and *totoca* [it runs]; as if to say "running water."

The people here in New Spain, the people of old, said: "These [rivers] come — they flow — there from Tlalocan; they are the property of, they issue from the goddess named Chalchiuhtli icue."

And they said that the mountains were only magic places, with earth, with rock on the surface; that they were only like ollas or like houses; that they were filled with the water which was there. If sometime it were necessary, the mountains would dissolve; the whole world would flood. And hence the people called their settlements *altepetl*. They said, "This mountain of water, this river, springs from there, the womb of the mountain. For from there Chalchiuitl icue sends it — offers it."

Injc matlactli omome, capitulo: ipan mjtoa, moteneva in nepapan atl, ioan in nepapan tlalli.

INJC CE PARRAPHO: ipan mjtoa, in quenamj in ilhujcaatl, in atoiaatl.

Injc ce, parrapho: qujtoa, qujteneva in atl: iehoatl in mjtoa teuatl:

injc mjtoa teuatl, camo teutl, çan qujtoznequj maviztic vei tlamaujçolli, ioan itoca ilhujcaatl, in ie vecauhtlaca, in njcan nueva españa tlaca, momatia, ioan iuhquj neltocaia, ca in ilhujcatl, çan iuhqujnma calli, noviiampa tlacçaticac: auh itech acitoc in atl, iuhqujnma acaltechtli, itech motlatzoa: auh ic qujtocaiotique ilhujcaatl, iehica ca itech acitimanj in ilhujcatl. Auh in axcan ī ipampa tlaneltoqujliztli, çan mjtoa vei atl,

vei temauhti, teiçavi, aixnamjqujliztli, tlamaviçolli, popoçoqujllo, cuecueio, atlamjmjlollo, chichic, chichipatic, chichipalalatic, itztonquavitl, tequaio, ioioliio, molinjanj, ioltimanj, xoxoqujuhtimanj, âtlacamanj.

Teuapan njnemj, ilhujcaatl njcviltequj, vei atl njcpanavia, vei atlan njmjquj, ilhujcaapan njnemj.

ATOIATL:

in jtoca, itech qujztica in atl, ioan totoca, iuhqujn qujtoznequj, atl totocanj:

in njcan nueva españa tlaca, in ie vecauh tlaca qujtoaia. Injn ca vmpa vallauh, vmpa valeva in tlalocan, ca iiaxca, ca itech qujça in teutl, in jtoca, chalchiuhtli icue:

ioan qujtoaia, ca in tepetl çan navalca, çan panj in tlallo, in teio, ca çan iuhqujn comitl, noce iuhqujn calli, ca tentica in atl, vmpa ca, intla quēmān monequjz xitinjz in tepetl, ca apachiviz icemanavac: auh ic contocaiotique, injn necentlaliliztlaca, altepetl qujtoaia, injn altepetl, injn Atoiatl ca ompa oaleva in jtic tepetl ca vmpa qujvaliva, qujvalmacava in chalchivitl icue.

247

But the truth, the right, is that thus our Lord hath willed.

For the sea enters within the land; its water passages, its ducts stand; they extend. It goes in all directions within the land in the mountains. Wheresoever it finds large spaces [or] small ones, there it makes its first beginning, perhaps somewhere[1] on the plains, perhaps on the mountains. Or else little rivulets join together. This is the big water. This is called a river.

And the sea water is bitter, but this is no longer bitter. On rocks, on land it improves. Especially when it comes out of the sand, there it becomes sweet, there it improves.

The river is [water] which flows, wells up, gushes. It is a runner; a former of rapids, of swift currents; a glider. It is that which crashes, which groans. It has man-eating animals. It is irresistible; it frightens people; it drowns people. It is that which is swift of current. It has fish; it has serpents. It wells up, it gushes, it forms rapids, it crashes.

¶

SECOND PARAGRAPH, which telleth of the divisions into which are divided [waters] such as rivers and seas.

CHICUNAUATL

Its name is in *chicunaui* [nine] and *atl* [water], because it gushes, it flows out in nine places. They become one; they join together. Hence is it called "nine waters," "ominous waters." Tolocan is there.

AMACOZATL

It is here in the hot lands. It has man-eating animals; it frightens one. It is in the Couixca country.

QUETZALATL

Its name is from saying *quetzalli* [precious feather] and *atl* [water]; because it is clear, dark green, gourd-green. It is here from Cuextlan.[2] It is very green, extremely green, smoky green, dark green, gourd-green; transparent. It becomes gourd-blue, gourd-green.

I pass over, I cross over on the dark green river. I cross the river.

TEQUANATL

Its name comes from *tequani* [man-eater] and *atl* [water], because it has many man-eating animals.

Auh in nelli, in melaoac, ca iuhquj monequjltia in tot⁰.

ca tlallan calaquj in ilhujcaatl, ihicac ohonoc, icocoio, ipiazio noviian iauh in tlallan, in tepepan, in canjn tlacoiava qujtta iiovica, oncan moceniacatia, aço ma ixtlaoacã, aço tepetitech: auh anoçe çan apitzactotonti, monenepanoa, iehoatl vey atl, iehoatl in motocaiotia atoiatl:

auh in ilhujcaatl, ca chichic, auh injn aocmo chichic, tetitech tlalli, itech velia, oc cenca in xaltitlan qujça oncan aviiaia, vncan velia,

in atoiatl meianj, molonjnj, motompitzoanj, totocanj, çolonjnj, motlaloanj, mopetzcoanj, xaxamacanj, qujqujnacanj, tequaio, aixnamjqujliztli, temamauhti, teatocti, atocoanj, mjchio, covaio, molonj, motompitzoa, çolonj, xaxamaca.

¶

INJC VME PARRAPHO: itechpa tlatoa, in jtlatlamantiliz, injc moxexeloa, in iuhquj atoiatl, ioan vei atl.

CHICUHNAVATL:

in jtoca, itech ca in chicunavi, ioan atl: ipãpa chicunauhcan in molonj, in meia, mocematilia, monenepanoa: ic mjtoa chicunavatl, tetzavatl, vncan icac toloca.

AMACOZATL:

njcan in icac tlatotoian, tequaio, temamauhti: covixcatlalli ipan in jcac.

QUETZALATL

in jtoca, itech mjtotica quetzalli ioan atl: ipampa chipavac matlaltic. matlalaiotic: njcan Cuextlampa, xopalevac, xopalectic, texoapoctic, matlaltic, matlalaiotic, nalqujzquj, texoaiotia, matlalaiotia.

njqujxtia, njcpanavia, quetzalapan njpano.

TEQUANATL:

in jtoca, itech qujztica in tequanj, ioã atl. ipampa cenca tequaio.

In fear I pass over, in fear I cross over the river of man-eating animals. In fear I travel in, [I travel] on the river of man-eating animals.

TOLLAN ATL

Its name is from the city of Tollan and *atl* [water], because it passes within the city of Tollan. It is a little dark, a little black; it is rocky, with slippery rocks; an engulfer of things, a carrier of trees, of rocks.

I drown; it carries me off, it drowns me; it is winding.

NEXATL

Its name comes from *nextli* [ashes] and *atl* [water], because it is thick, chalky; like ashes is the color. It becomes ashen; it becomes chalky.

TOTOLATL

Its name comes from *totolin* [bird] and *atl* [water], because, it is said, there was the drinking place of the wild birds, those still in the cacti, in the palms. It is rapid-flowing.

TETZAUATL

Its name comes from *tetzauitl* [omen] and *atl* [water], because it flows only at times, and it terrifies people greatly. It is black; it has many man-eating animals, many serpents. It is an ominous river which passes, which flows.

PINAUIZATL

It is a stream of little flow. Its name is said from *pinauiztli* [shame] and *atl* [water], because when no one crosses over it, when no one passes over it, it continues to run. But when crossed, when passed, it diminishes, lessens, dries up. Gradually this becomes a spring; it is ashamed; it lessens; it abates.

AMEYALLI

Its name comes from *atl* [water] and *meya* [it flows]. This is really the name of its attribute. It comes forth from within the earth. Perhaps it runs, or perhaps it just rests. It is potable, good tasting, savory, life-giving, our sustenance, our soul, our freshness. It is bitter, salty, stinking. It sickens one; it makes one sick; it is deadly; it harms one.

It flows, it wells up, it runs, it forms rapids, it gushes. It becomes good tasting; it becomes savory. It becomes bitter, salty, stinking. It is drunk.

Nicmauhcaqujxtia, njcmauhcapanavia: in tequanatl, njmauhcaqujça in tequanac, in tequanapa.

TOLLAN ATL:

in jtoca itech ca in altepetl tollan, ioan atl; ipampa ca iitic in qujzticac in altepetl tollan, achi cujchevac, achi tlilevac, têteio, tealacio, tlaatoctianj, qujvicanj in quavitl, in tetl:

Natoco, nechvica, nechatoctia, cocoliuhticac.

NEXATL:

in jtoca, itech qujztica nextli, ioan atl: ipampa tetzavac, tiçevac, iuhqujn nextli, tlapalli nexeva, ticeva.

TOTOLATL:

in jtoca, itech qujztica totoli, ioan atl: ipampa qujlmach vncan imatliian catca, in quauhtotolme in oc tzivactla, nequametla, xaxamacaticac.

TETZAVATL:

in jtoca itech qujztica tetzavitl, ioan atl: ipampa çan iqujn in qujztiuh: ioan cenca temamauhti, tliltic, cenca tequaio, covaio, tetzavatl, qujça molinj.

PINAVIZATL:

apitzactli, in jtoca, itech mjtoa in pinaviztli, ioan atl: ipampa in jquac aiac ipan qujça, in aiac qujpanavia totocaticac: auh in jquac ipan qujxova, in panavilo, caxava, canava, vaquj; çan iuh nenti in achichiacpã muchiva, pinava, canava, iloti.

AMEIALLI:

in jtoca itech qujztica in atl, ioan meia: iehoatl vel ineixcaviltoca, in tlallãpa valqujztica, in at totoca, in at noço çan manj, ivanj, velic, aviiac. Nemovanj, tonenca, toiolca, tocelica, chichic, poiec, hijac, tecoco, tecocolizcujti, mjcoanj, teiolitlaco,

meia, molonj, totoca, çolonj, motompitzoa, velia, aviaia, chichiia, poieia, hijaia, iva.

249

APITZACTLI

Its name comes from *atl* [water] and *pitzauac* [thin]; that is, a river which is narrow. It is a thin river, narrow; thick; deadly; a former of rapids; deep. It forms rapids. It shoots; it drowns one. It kills one.

XALATL

Its name is from *xalli* [sand] and *atl* [water]. That is, water emerges from the sand; the spring is in the sand. It is good tasting, very healthful, good, precious; something desirable; one's lot.

AMAITL

Its name comes from *atl* [water] and *maitl* [arm]. This is an arm of the sea which is extending among the mountains, which is becoming narrow as it extends.

AMANALLI

Its name comes from *atl* [water] and *tlamanalli* [something flat placed on the ground], or *mani* [it lies flat]. It is water which is just flat, which does not run. It has reeds; it has fish; it has substance; beetles lie spread [on it]; it lies flat; it lies flat and outspread.

AMANALLI

It is the name of water just lying flat; something flat placed on the ground: either rainwater or a pond. It lies sparkling, it lies glistening; it lies glistening; it lies shining.

ACUECUEXATL is [a spring] which is here at Coyoacan, in the vicinity of Mexico.

[THE SPRING AT] CHAPULTEPEC

Its name comes from *chapulin* [locust] and *atl* [water], because water flows, wells up from the base of Chapultepetl. It is good tasting, good, precious, potable. With it the Mexican nation, the Tenochca nation endures. It provides drink, refreshment to the Mexican nation.

ATLACOMOLLI

Its name comes from *atl* [water] and *comoltic* [pitted]. That is, it is something excavated down below, deep, very deep. From it all take water; there all Mexicans drink.

I make a well; I dig a well.

AYOLUAZTLI

It is the name of the characteristics of very deep wells. It is very deep. The deep darkness sparkles.

APITZACTLI:

itech qujztica in jtoca atl, ioan pitzavac, qujtoznequj, pitzaoaticac atoiatl, acanactli, pitzavac, tilavac. mjcoanj, çolonjnj, vecatla, çolonj, motlamjna, teatocti, temjctia.

XALATL:

in jtoca itech ca xalli, ioan atl: qujtoznequj atl xaltitlan valqujça, xalpan ca ameialli, veltic vel patic, qualli tlaçotli, tlaçotlalonj, tetonal.

AMAITL:

in jtoca itech qujça in atl, ioan maitl: iehoatl in ilhujcaatl, ima in tepetla iaticac, anoço in valpitzavaticac.

AMANALLI:

itech qujztica in jtoca atl, ioan tlamanalli, anoço manj: iehoatl in çan manj atl, in amo otlatoca, tollo, mjchio, nacaio, tlalactimanj, manj, mantimanj.

AMANALLI:

itoca in çan manj atl, in tlamanalli, in aço qujavatl, in aço tlaqujlatl, pepeiontimanj, cuecueiontimanj, cuecueiocatimanj, mocueiotitimanj.

ACUECUEXATL: njcan coiovacan catquj, mexico inavac.

CHAPOLTEPETL:

in jtoca itech qujça in chapoli, ioan atl: ipãpa ca chapultepetl itzintlan in meia, in molonj, velic, aviiac, qualli tlaçotli, ivanj: ic manj in mexicaiotl, in tenochcaiotl, ic ioltimanj catlitia, qujceliltia in mexicaiotl.

ATLACOMOLLI:

in jtoca itech qujça in atl, ioan comoltic, qujtoznequj tlatatactli, tlanj, vecatlan centlanj: vncan atlacujva, oncan atliva mextica.

Natlacomollalia, natlacomoltataca.

AIOLVAZTLI:

ineixcaviltoca in atlacomolli, cenca vecatlan in centlanj, mjxtecomac valcueionj.

I form a well; I dig a well; I take water from the well.

AXOXOUILLI

Its name is from *atl* [water] and *xoxouhqui* [green]. This is a cavern of water which is just flat; the very deep one; the green one. It lies green.

¶

THIRD PARAGRAPH, which telleth of the nature of the soils.

ATOCTLI

Its name comes from *atl* [water] and *totoca* [it runs]; that is, water-borne yellow soil, water-borne sand. It is soft, porous, very porous, good, good smelling. It is that which is fertile, esteemed, well considered: it is food-producing.

QUAUHTLALLI

Its name comes from *quauitl* [wood] and *tlalli* [earth]. It is rotten wood or oak leaves; humus; or silt with [rotten] wood. It is black or yellow. It is a fertile place.

TLALCOZTLI

It is named from *tlalli* [earth] and *coztic* [yellow], because yellow soil is good, fine, fertile, fruitful, esteemed.

XALATOCTLI

This is sand borne by the water. It is very loose. Borne by the water, it is porous, very porous.

TLAÇOLLALI

This is humus which turns into soil. It is [soil] which is fertile.

TLALCOUALLI

Its name comes from *tlalli* [earth] and *tlacoualli* [something bought]. It is the name which characterizes land which is sold, which is bought.
I sell land; I buy land.

MICCATLALLI

It is named from *micqui* [dead person] and *tlalli* [earth]. This was the name of land of one who had died. And it is the name of the body of the dead, which has decayed, which has become dust.

XALALLI

It is [so] called from *xalli* [sand] and *tlalli* [earth], because it is sandy, of fine sand. It is not fertile; it is

Naiolvaztlalia, naiolvaztataca, aiolvazco, natlacuj.

AXOXOVILLI:

in jtoca itech ca in atl, ioan xoxouhquj: iehoatl in aoztotl, in çan manj i cenca vecatlan, xoxoctic, xoxovixtimanj.

¶

INJC EI PARRAPHO: itechpa tlatoa, in quenamj iieliz tlalli.

ATOCTLI:

in jtoca itech qujztica in atl, ioan totoca, qujtoznequj, valatococ tlalcoztli, xalatoctli, iamanquj, cuechtic, cuecuechtic, velic, aviiac. Tlamochivanj, temachtli, temachilonj, qualonj.

QUAUHTLALLI:

in jtoca itech qujztica in quaujtl, ioan tlalli: iehoatl in palanj quavitl, anoço avazvatl, in quauhtlaçolli, in anoço tepetlalli, in quauhio, cujchevac, anoço coztic tlamochivaia.

TLALCOZTLI:

itech mjtotica tlalli ioan coztic: ipampa ixcoztic, qualli, iectli, tlamochioanj, tlaaqujllo, temachtli.

XALATOCTLI:

iehoatl in valatoco xalli, cuecuechtic, atoco cuechivi, cuecuechivi.

TLÂÇOLLALI

iehoatl in tlaçolli palanj, in tlalli mocuepa, tlamochivanj.

TLALCOVALLI:

in jtoca itech qujça in tlalli, ioan tlacovalli: iehoatl in ineixcaviltoca, in tlanamactli tlalli, in tlacovalli:

njtlalnamaca, njtlalcova.

MICCATLALLI:

itech mjtotica mjcquj, ioan tlalli: iehoatl itoca in omjc, in jtlal catca, ioan itoca in mjccanacatl in opalan, in otlaltic.

XALALLI:

itech mjtotica in jtoca xalli ioan tlalli: ipampa in xallo, in xalpitzavacaio, amo tlamochivanj, çan tla-

just a producer of maize stalks. It produces straight, slender maize stalks. It is not esteemed, not of much substance. It does not germinate much; it has no substance.

TEÇOQUITL

Its name comes from *tetl* [rock] and *çoquitl* [mud], because it is firm, gummy, hard; dark, blackish, bitumen-like. It becomes hard, it becomes firm; it hardens.

CALLALLI

Its name comes from *calli* [house] and *tlalli* [earth]. This is the land upon which a house has rested, and also the surrounding houses. It is fertile; it germinates.

TLALMANTLI

Its name comes from *tlalli* [earth] and *manqui* [level]; that is to say, land neither hilly nor hollowed. Houses are there.

TLALUITECTLI

This is land which is worked, worked down, packed.

I beat the land. I work the land down with blows. I work the land with blows.

TLALAUIYAC

This is the land which is good, which produces, which is mellow.

I fertilize it. I add humus to it. I make it mellow. I make it good.

METLALLI

This is earth spread with maguey plants; provided with maguey plants, with maguey roots. It is made replete with maguey plants.

ATLALLI

Its name is [so] called from *atl* [water] and *tlalli* [earth]. This is the irrigated field. It is a watered garden, one which can be irrigated; it is irrigable; [land] which becomes wet, becomes mud. It is good, fine, precious; a source of food; esteemed; a place of fertility. It is a fertile place; it has substance. It is [a place] to be planted to maize, to be planted to beans, to be harvested. There is harvesting, there is eating.

I work the irrigated land. I form myself an irrigated garden. I work the irrigable land. I eat on irrigated land.

ovatinj tlaovatlamelaoaltia, amo cenca temachtli, amo cenca nacaio, amo cenca vntlaca, amo nacaio.

TEÇOQUJTL:

itech qujztica in itoca tetl, ioan çoqujtl: ipampa ca tlaquavac, tzictic, tepitztic, cujchevac, tlilevac, chapopotic, tepitzavi, tlaquava, tlaquactia.

CALLALLI:

itech qujztica in itoca calli, ioan tlalli: iehoatl in calli ipan manj tlalli, ioã in qujiavalotoc calli, tlamochivanj, ontlaca.

TLALMANTLI:

itech qujztica in jtoca tlalli, ioan manquj q. n. tlalli amo tliltic, amo no comoltic, calli vncã manca.

TLALVITECTLI:

iehoatl in tlalli in tlachiuhtli, tlatlalilli, in tlatepitztlalilli.

Nitlalhujtequj, njtlalvitectlalia, njtlalhujtecchiva.

TLALAVIIAC:

iehoatl in tlein qualli tlalli, in tlamochioaia tlalaviaia:

njtlacujtlavia, njtlatlaçollalhuja, njcaviialia, njcvelilia.

METLALLI:

iehoatl in tlalli meiotoc, meio, menelhoaio, meiova.

ATLALLI:

itech mjtoa in jtoca atl, ioan tlalli: iehoatl in tlalli mavilianj, matequjanj in tlaavililli atequjlonj avililonj apacholonj, paltinj, çoqujtinj qualli, iectli, tlaçotli, qualonj. temachtli, tlamochiuhia, tlamochivaia, nacaio, toconj etlaxonj, pixconj, pixcoia, tlaqualoia,

natlalchiva, njnatlalmjltia, atlalli njcchiva, atlalpan njtlaqua.

TEPETLALLI

This is the top soil of a mountain, the upland, the slope. It is also called *ximmilli*. It is dry, clayey, ashen, sandy soil, ordinary soil, rain-sown. It is the growing place of mature maize, of amaranth, of beans. It is the sprouting place of the tuna, the *nopal*, the maguey; of the American cherry; of trees. Trees form shoots, herbs sprout, grass sprouts. It becomes grassy; there are maguey plants. The maguey spreads; grass spreads; trees spread. The grasses thicken, trees thicken. The *nopal* develops; the *nopal* spreads.

TETLALLI

This is pulverized, like *pinole*. It comes from the rocks, the crushed rocks. They scatter, they spread whatsoever kind of rock. It is pulverized, it becomes pulverized, it is made pulverized. It is made like *pinole;* it is made very fine.

TETLALLI

It is land on the mountain — rocky, gravelly, loose-graveled. It is very rocky, gravelly, rough, dry, dry deep down; a productive place, the growing place of *tecintli* maize. It is dry deep down; it is dry. It hardens; it becomes wet; it produces.

TECHIYAUITL

It is just the same as *tetlalli*. Hence it is called *techiyauitl*, because when it gets water, it does not dry off quickly; it just lies moist, it lies completely workable, it lies wet. It becomes moist; it becomes workable; it becomes wet.

TLALTZACUTLI

It is just the same as clayey soil, because it is sticky, viscous, gluey. It is sticky, it is gluey.

TLALCOCOMOCTLI

It is that land which is not wetted. It lies spongy, it lies uneven. It is like reed land, ashen land, ashen mounds. It becomes uneven; it becomes spongy.

TOLLALLI

It is reedy land, or the rotting of the very reeds; the reed, the small reed converted into soil. It becomes reedy, full of small reeds, grassy. It produces; it becomes fertile; it has true substance.

CHIAUHTLALLI

Its name is [so] called from *chiaua* [it becomes soggy] and *tlalli* [land]. This always lies wet, al-

TEPETLALLI:

iehoatl in jnacaiotepetl, in tlacpactli, in tlamjmjlolli, no itoca ximmjlli, vaquj teçoqujtl, nextlalli, xallalli, çaça ie tlalli qujiauhtoconj, çintli, vauhtli, etl, mochiuhia, nochtli, nopalli, metl, capoli quavitl iixvaia, quauhixva, xiujxva, çacaixva, çacaiova, meiova, meiotoc; çacaiotoc, quauhiotoc, çacapachivi, quappachivi, nopalloa nopallotoc.

TETLALLI:

iehoatl in cuechtic, in pinoltic, tetl itech qujça: in tetzotzonquj qujtlaça, qujpixoa. in anoço tlein tetl, cuechtic, cuechivi, cuechtia, pinolti, pipinolti.

TETLALLI:

in tepepan tlalli in teio, in texallo, papaiaxtic, têteio, texallo, tequaqua vacquj, elvaquj, tlamochiuhia, tecintli imochiuhia. Elvaquj, vaquj, tepitzavi, çiava, tlamochiva.

TECHIIAVITL:

çan ie no iehoatl in tetlalli, injc mjtoa techiiavitl: ipampa in jquac atl qujtta amo içiuhca vaquj, ca çan paltitoc, ça cenchiavatoc, ciavatoc, palti, chiava, çiiava.

TLALTZACUTLI:

çan ie no ie in teçoqujtl; ipampa ca çaçalic, çacaltic, tzacutic, çaçalia, tzacutia.

TLALCOCOMOCTLI:

in tlein tlalli in amo paltic, in papatziuhtimanj, in cocomocatimanj in iuh tollalli, nextlalli, nextlatilli, cocomoca, papatzivi:

TOLLALLI,

in tollo tlalli, in anoço vel iehoatll tolin opalan, in otlaltic tollo, xomallo, tolloa, xomalloa, çacaiova, tlamochiuhia monacaiotia, vel nacatl.

CHIAUHTLALLI:

itech mjtoa in jtoca chiava, ioan tlalli iehoatl in çan mochipa çiavatimanj, in macivi amo tlaavililli,

253

though unirrigated.[3] It has substance; it is food-producing. When it rains heavily, [the maize] perishes. But when the rain is not heavy, it brings joy, it brings contentment. There is rejoicing therefrom.

I work the workable land; on the workable land I eat.

TLALÇOLLI

It is called *tlalçolli*, bad soil, because nothing can be grown there. It is the growing place of nothing —useless, productive of nothing. It is worked in vain; it fails. It is worn out land; it becomes worn out land.

¶

FOURTH PARAGRAPH, which telleth of still other characteristics of useless lands.

NITROUS SOIL

It is salty, bitter, corrosive, that which is leached [of its salt]; unwanted, undesirable. It is waste, disregarded. It becomes salty, it becomes bitter; it corrodes, it is leached. It is abandoned; it lies useless.

SALT LAND

It is salty, bitter — that which is leached. Nothing can be grown on it.

NANTLALLI

The water extends on top; it does not soak in; it does not reach below. As it is wet it just forms a thin film, goes on the surface; [as it is wet][4] the water [just] spreads out.

TLALIZTALLI

Its name comes from *tlalli* [earth] and *tlaiztalli* [something white]; that is to say, white earth. It is not very white; only whitish. Its characteristics are just the same as those of *nantlalli*.

TENEXTLALLI: this is limestone [land] — bad, undesirable.

TLALTENEXTLI

This is to say, it is not limestone but soil, [as for] adobes: the black, the white. It is baked, fired. When it has been cooked, it is beaten, pulverized, mixed with lime. Thus it becomes sticky.

TEÇONTLALLI

Its name comes from *teçontli* [porous volcanic rock] and *tlalli* [earth]. This is pulverized *teçontli*.

nacaio qualonj in jquac tlaielqujavi, mjquj, polivi, auh in jquac amo totoca qujiavitl, qujpactia, qujtlamachtia, itlocpa aviia.

Chiiauhtlalli njcchiva, chiiauhtlalpan njtlaqua.

TLALÇOLLI:

injc mjtoa tlalçolli amo qualli tlalli: ipampa in amo tle vel mochiva vncan in atle imuchiuhia, nenqujzquj, atle inecoca. Nenqujça, nenpolivi, tlalçolti, tlalçoltia.

¶

INJC NAVI PARRAPHO: itechpa tlatoa, oc centlamãtli in jieliz tlalli, amo monequj.

TEQUJXQUJTLALLI:

poiec, chichic, tlaquaquanj, tlapaltilianj, âneconj, aelevilonj, atle imonecca, aiac ica, poieia, chichiia, tlaquaqua tlapatilia, atle ipã itto, nenqujztimanj.

IZTATLALLI,

poiec, chichic, tlapatilianj, atle vel itech mochiva

NANTLALLI:

in atl ipan moteca amo elaquj, amo tlanj açi injc palti, çan peiava. iixco quiça, momana in atl

TLALIZTALLI:

itech qujztica in jtoca tlalli, ioan tlaiztalilli, qujtoznequj iztac tlalli, amo cenca iztac, çan iztalevac, çã ie no iuhquj in iieliz nantlalli.

TENEXTLALLI: iehoatl in tenextli, in amo qualli, in amo ihiio.

TLALTENEXTLI:

qujtoznequj amo tenextli, çan tlalli in xamjtl, in tliltic, in jztac moxca, motlatia: in jquac oiccucic, movitequj, mocuechoa, moneloa in tenextli, ic çaçalia.

TEÇONTLALLI:

teçontli, ioan tlalli: itech qujztica in jtoca, iehoatl in cuechtic teçontli, piciltic, papaiaxtic, tequaqua, tla-

---

3. Corresponding Spanish text: *"tierras que son humedas, de su natural: por ser uaxas."*
4. *Acad. Hist. MS,* after *quiça,* adds *inic palti ça.*

It is made into fragments, broken up, roughened, sticky. It hardens. It is mixed with lime; thus it becomes sticky, thus it becomes adhesive; thus it hardens.

I gather powdered *teçontli*; I sell powdered *teçontli*; I add powdered *teçontli* to something.

çaçalilli, tlatepitzo, moneloa in tenextli, ic tzacutia, ic tzictia, ic tepitzavi.

Niteçontlalcuj, niteçontlalnamaca, njtlateçõtlalhuja.

Axixtlalli

This is land which has been urinated upon, which is greasy. Its characteristics are just the same as[5] those of nitrous land.

He makes urinated soil. He made urinated soil. I put urinated soil on something.

Axixtlalli:

iehoatl in axixio tlalli, in chiavac: çan ie no iuhquj in jieliz tequjxqujtlalli,

axixtlaltia, axixtlalti, njtlaaxixtlalhuja.

Nextlalilli

Wheresoever ashes are heaped together, like a small mountain, this is the *nextlalillli*. It is useless, full of grama grass, black, mountain-like.

Nextlalilli:

in canjn mocentlalia nextli: in iuhquj tepetontli, iehoatl nextlalilli atle imonecca, tequjxqujçacaio, tliltic, tepetic.

Tecpatlalli

This is flaked, pulverized flint. It is abrasive, like sand.

Tecpatlalli:

iehoatl in pitzavac, in cuechtic tecpatl, tequaqua, xaltic.

Tlapantlalli

This is what houses are roofed with — the earth which rests as the terrace; that which serves for roofing.

I raise up the terrace earth. I gather the terrace earth. I take off the roof; I remove the terrace earth. I provide the roof. I smooth the terrace.

Tlapantlalli:

iehoatl injc motlapachoa calli, in tlapanco onoc tlalli, tlatlapacholonj:

njtlapantlallecavia, njtlapantlalcuj, njtlatzontlapoa, njtlapantlallaça, njtlatlapachoa, njtlapanchichiva.

Teuhtlalli

Its name comes from *teuhtli* [dust] and *tlalli* [earth]. This is the top soil and the upland; that is, dry land.

Teuhtlalli:

teuhtli, ioan tlalli, itech qujça in jtoca, iehoatl in tepetlalli, ioan ximmjlli, q. n. vaquj tlalli.

Teuhtli

From nowhere does its name come. This is earth which is very fine — that which swirls up, which sweeps up. It blackens things; it soils things. It swirls up, it sweeps up; it blackens things.

I make things dirty.

Teuhtli:

acan qujzquj in jtoca, iehoatl in tlalli; i cenca auhtic molonjnj, haco qujçanj, tlacatzavanj, tlatzoiotianj molonj, haco qujça tlacatzava

njlatzoiotia.

Atiçatl

Its name comes from *atl* [water] and *tiçatl* [chalk]. It is white, spongy, light, fluffy, airy. Nothing can be done with it; only adobes are made, and it turns into chalk. It is molded; it is molded into adobe bricks. Adobe bricks are made.

Atiçatl:

in jtoca itech qujça in atl, ioan tiçatl, iztac, çonectic haietic, aco vetzquj, hecauhtic: atle vel itech mochiva, çan ixqujch xamjtl, mochiva, ioan tiçatl mocuepa, mocopina, moxancopina, moxanchiva,

---

5. *Ibid.: ach iuhqui* instead of *iuhquj.*

I mold it. I remove adobe bricks. I mold adobe bricks. I lay adobe bricks.

MEXICATLALLI[6]

It is the City of Mexico and the land which belongs to it — all which pertains to the Mexican nation, to the Mexicans who live on it. It is a good place, a favorable place.

TOTONACATLALLI

It is the land on which live the Totonaca. It is hot, a hot place, a productive place, a rich place, a land of flowers, a place of flowers, a land of fruits. It is a place of quick death; it is not a place to grow old in. It is a place of sweating, a place of flies, a place of wild beasts.

MICHOACATLALLI

On it live the Michoaca. It is an esteemed place — salubrious, a place to grow old in, a cool place, in some places warm. The people of Michoacan are prudent, able; they are weavers of designs.

MIXTECATLALLI

This is the land on which dwell the Mixteca — all the Pinome, the Chontals, the Nonoalca. Those of the land of the Mixteca are experienced; they have knowledge; they have knowledge of green stones.

ANAUACATLALLI

This lies by [and] near the sea; it is a land of wealth, of riches.

CHICHIMECATLALLI

On this dwell the Chichimeca. It is a place of misery, pain, suffering, fatigue, poverty, torment. It is a place of dry rocks, of failure; a place of lamentations; a place of death from thirst; a place of starvation. It is a place of much hunger, of much death. It is to the north.

¶

FIFTH PARAGRAPH, which telleth of a kind of earth of which are made ollas and water jars.

CONTLALLI

[Its name] comes from *comitl* [olla] and *tlalli* [earth], because [with it ollas][1] are made; bowls, basins, etc. *Teçoquitl* is sticky, gummy; it is provided

njtlacopina njxamana, njxancopina, njxãtlaça.

MEXICATLALLI:

iehoatl in altepetl mexico, ioan in jtlallo, in ixqujch ic ca mexicaiotl, in jpan onoque mexica, qualcan, ieccã.

TOTONACATLALLI:

in tlalli in jpan onoque totonaque, totonquj, tlatotonjaia, tlamochioaia, necujltonoloia, xochitlalpa xochitla, xochiqualla: içiuhca mjcovaia, âvecaoaloia, teitonjca, çaiolla, tequanjtla.

MICHVACATLALLI:

in jpan onoque mjchvaque, nêmachoia, techicauhca, vêcaoaloia, tlaceceiaia, cana tlatotoian: mjmatinj, mozcalianj, tlâmachchiuhque, in mjchoaca tlaca.

MIXTECATLALLI:

iehoatl in ipan onoque mjxteca: in ie ixqujch cenpinotl, in chôchon, nonoale, in mjxteca tlalli, tlaiximatinj, tlaiximati, chalchiuhiximati.

ANAOACATLALLI:

iehoatl in jlhujcaatl, itlan, inaoac, onoc, necujltonoloia, netlamachtiloia.

CHICHIMECATLALLI;

iehoatl in chichimeca ipan onoque, netolinjloia, in toneuhca, in chichinatzca, iciavia, ompa onqujça, tetolinjca, tetl oaoacca, atle iqujztoca, choqujztli iieoaia, amjcovaia, teoçiovaia, apiztla, mjctla, mjctlampa.

¶

INJC MACUJLLI PARRAPHO: itechpa tlatoa, centlamantli tlalli, muchiva comjtl, ioan apilolli.

CONTLALLI:

comjtl itech qujztica, ioan tlalli: ipampa [comitl] muchioa caxitl, apaztli. Etc. teçoqujtl. çaçalic, tzacutic, tolcapuio, tlaxaqualolli, tlatolcapuiotilli.

6. *Ibid.*: a marginal note in Sahagún's hand, headed *provincias*, reads: *las calidades de las pvincias primeramẽte desta pvincia mexicana.*
1. *Ibid.*: *ipampa* is followed by *comitl*, here in brackets.

with reed stem fibres.[2] It is that which is kneaded, which is tempered with reed stem fibres.

I make ollas. I make water jars. I make large water jars. I make bowls, pots, basins. Whatsoever I make, I make of clay.

COMALLALLI

It is the same as *teçoquitl*. It is that which may be beaten, which may be thinned.

I knead it, I temper it with reed stem fibres. I beat it, I thin it out. I make griddles, I fire griddles. I fire things in an oven. I cool the oven.

CAXTLALLI is the same as *teçoquitl*.

I make bowls.[3] I make things with molds. I mold things.

IZTATLALLI is very salty, exceedingly bitter, exceedingly salty.

I heap up alkaline soil. I leach the alkaline soil. I make brine, I make salt.

TLALCOZTLI is a medium which stains things yellow, which serves as a wash.

I apply yellow earth to things. I apply a wash to something.

TLALCHICHILLI is chili-red earth, spongy, dark, dark-surfaced.

I make something chili-red. I apply a wash to something.

CAXTLAUITL is the same as *tlalchichilli*.

I make something chili-red. I apply *caxtlauitl* to something.

CLAY

It is moist, wet, thick, hard, firm. It is water and earth mixed together, moistened.

I apply clay to something. I cover something with clay. I apply clay to something. Also it means, I besmirch something, I snare something. I prepare clay for ollas. I trample clay. [I][4] extract clay.

AÇOQUITL[5]

[Its name] comes from *atl* [water] and *çoquitl* [mud]. This is mud which is by the water. It is watery, soft.

I take up mud. I spatter something with mud. I extract mud.

Niconchiva, napilolchiva, njtzotzocolchiva, njcaxchiva, njteconchiva, napazchiva: in çaço tlein njcchiva, njçoqujchiva.

COMALLALLI:

çan ie no iê in teçoqujtl tzotzonalonj, canaoalonj.

njcxaqualoa, njctolcapoiotia, njctzotzona, njccanaoa, njcomalchiva, njcomalixca, njtlatexcaltema, njtexcalcevia.

CAXTLALLI: çan ie no ie in teçoqujtl, njcachiva, njtlacopinalchiva, njtlacopina.

IZTATLALLI: poielpatic, chichipalalatic, itztonquavitl,

njztatlalololova, njztatlalapachova, njztaiochiva, njztatlatia.

TLALCOZTLI: tlacoçalhujlonj, tlaoçalonj,

njtlatlalcozvia, njtlaoça.

TLALCHICHILLI; tlalli chichiltic, poxavac, ixtlilevac, ixtliltic:

njtlachichiloa, njtlaoça

CAXTLAUJTL: çan no iuhqui in tlalchichilli, njtlachichiloa, njtlacaxtlavia.

ÇOQUJTL:

paltic, atic, tetzavac, tepitztic, tlaquactic, atl, tlalli, neneliuhquj, paltic;

njtlaçoqujvia, njtlaçoqujiotia, njtlaçoqujvia: no qujtoznequj njtlapinavia, njtlatzovia, njçoqujpoloa, njçoqujquequeça, no çoqujqujqujça.

AÇOQUITL:

itech quiztica atl, ioan çoquitl: iehoatl in atlan ca çoqujtl, in atic, atoltic,

njçoqujana, nitlaaçoqujchapanja, naçoqujquixtia.

---

2. Corresponding Spanish text: *"amasanlo con aquellos pelos de los tallos de las espadañas."*

3. *Acad. Hist. MS:* nicaxchiva.

4. *Ibid.:* niçoq̃q̃q̃ça.

5. Corresponding Spanish text: *"Ay vn cieno en los camjnos de las canoas que se llama Açoqujtl cõ que hazen muchas cosas [con] ello trasponen el mayz y con ello tanbien hazẽ tlapancos y son buenos tlapancos."*

PALLI

Its name comes from nowhere. It is just the same as clay. It exists only in places; it is scarce. It is black, dark. It colors the face. It is [mixed] with *quauhtepoztli*, with *uixachin*.

I dye something. I dye something with clay. I blacken something. I dye something black.

TLALTZACUTLI is sticky, gummy; a medium for gluing.

I dig up *tlaltzacutli*. I knead *tlaltzacutli*. I apply *tlaltzacutli* to something.

¶

SIXTH PARAGRAPH, which telleth of, which mentions, the eminences of the land.

MOUNTAIN

That is to say, "being hilled up." It is high, pointed, pointed on top, pointed at the summit, towering; wide, cylindrical, round; a round mountain, low, low-ridged; rocky, with many rocks; craggy, with many crags; rough with rocks; of earth; with trees; grassy; with herbs; with shrubs; with water; dry; white; jagged; with a sloping plain, with gorges, with caves; precipitous, having gorges; canyon land, precipitous land with boulders.

I climb the mountain; I scale the mountain. I live on the mountain. I am born on the mountain. No one becomes a mountain — no one turns himself into a mountain. The mountain crumbles.

HERE ARE TOLD the names of several designated mountains.

POPOCATEPETL

It is here[1] [by] Chalco [and] Iztac ciuatl. It has [a smoke outlet].[2] It is sandy. It smokes. It becomes white.

IZTAC TEPETL OR IZTAC CIUATL

It is here by Chalco. Its name is Iztac tepetl because it is icy, white, with icy water. It is cold, extremely cold, very cold, exceedingly cold. It becomes white. From afar it is white. It is beautiful.

POYAUHTECATL

It is by Auilizapan, on the borders of the hot lands. It is high.

PALLI:

acan qujzquj in itoca çan ie iê in çoqujtl, çan can ca, çan tlaço ca, tliltic, ixtlilevac, ixtlapalivi, quauhtepuzio, vixachio.

njtlapa, njtlaçoqujpa, njtlaiapa, njtlaiapalpa.

TLALTZACUTLI: çaçalic, tzacutic, tlaçalolonj,

njtlaltzacutataca, njtlaltzacuxaqualoa, njtlatlaltzacuvia.

¶

INJC CHIQUACEN PARRAPHO: qujtoa, qujteneva, in jvecapanjviliz tlalli.

TEPETL:

qujtoznequj tepeuhtica, vecapan, vitztic, quavitztic quavitzauhquj, panqujzquj, patlachtic, mjmjltic, ololtic, tepeololli, pachtic, cujtlapachtic, teio, têteio, texcallo, tetexcallo, techâchaquachio, tlallo, quauhio, çacaio, xiuhio, tlacoio, aio, vacquj, ticevac, tlachichiqujllo, tlamjmjlollo, atlauhio, oztoio, tepexio, atlauhio, tlalatlauhio, tlaltepexio, tepetlaio:

njtepetleco, tepetl njctlecavia, tepepan njnemj, njtepetlâcati aiac tepeti, aiac tepetl mocuepa, tepetl xitinj.

NICAN MJTOA: in jtoca, in quezqujteme, tocaieque tetepe.

POPOCATEPETL:

njcan chalco iztac çivatl, callo, xallo popoca, iztaia

IZTAC TEPETL, ANOÇO IZTAC ÇIVATL:

njcan chalco, in ca ipampa in jtoca, iztac tepetl, ca ceio iztac, ceaio, itztic, itzcapatic, itzcaltic, itzcalpatic, iztaia, iztaztica, chipaoatica.

POIAUHTECATL:

avilizapan in ca, totoncatlaltenco, vecapan.

---

1. After *njcan*, *Acad. Hist.* MS adds ȳ *ca*.
2. *Ibid.*: *tlecallo* in place of *callo*.

Matlalcueye

It is by Tlaxcalla. It is a principal one, large, big, huge. It is radiating, outspread, going far out, rough, uneven, with ravines, with gorges.

Uixachtecatl

It is here by Itztapalapan. It is of medium, average size.

Yaualyuhqui

It is here by Cuitlauac. Its summit is round. It is hollowed out; it is dished. It is extending, spreading.

Quetzaltepetl

Another mountain which is near
Santa Clara Coatitlan[3]

It is wooded; it spreads green.

Chiquimolin

Another mountain which is near Motlauhxauhcan

It is by Motlauhxauhcan. It is wooded, heavily forested.

Tonan

Another mountain which is near Coyoacan

It is the mountain of Coyoacan. It is large, high; it lies reaching outward. It is outward-reaching, towering.

Tonan

Another mountain which is in the district of Texcoco

It is on Acolhua land. It is of medium, average size.

Quauhtepetl

Another mountain which is near Tenayocan
It is here at Tenayocan.

Tenayo:

Another mountain which is near Tenayocan

This is what the one called Tenayocan is [also] called.

Teucalhuiyac

Another mountain which is near Teucalhuiyacan

It is here at Corpus Christi; the name of the place is San Lorenzo. It is completely of *tepetate*. It is low; it lies reaching outward. It is peopled; it is dwelt upon.

Matlalquaie:

tlaxcallan in ca, tachcauh, vei, veipol, veitepul, tepeuhtica, toiauhtica, veca tlacçatica, xixipuchtic, xixiqujpiltic, vacaltic, vacaliuhquj.

Vixachtecatl:

njcan itztapalapan in ca, çan qualton, çan ipan.

Iaoaliuhquj:

njcan cujtlavac in ca, quaiavaltic, quacomoltic, quacaxtic, chapantica, toxauhtica.

Quetzaltepetl:

Otro monte que es cabe sancta clara coatitlã.

quauhio, xoxovixtica.

Chiqujmoli:

Otro monte que esta cabe motlauhxauhcan.

motlauhxauhcã in ca, quauhio, quauhiovacaio.

Tonan:

Otro monte que esta cabe coyoacan.

coiovacan tepetl, vei, vecapan, vilantoc, vilanticac, quauhtic.

Tonan:

Otro monte que esta en los termjnos de tet[z]cuco.

acolhoacan tlalli, ipan in ca, çan qualton, çan qualli.

Quauhtepetl:

Otro monte que esta cabe tenayocan.
njcan ca tenaiocan.

Tenaio:

Otro monte que esta cabe tenayocan.

iehoatl in tlatocaiotia, in mjtoa tenaioca

Teucalhujiac:

Otro monte que esta cabe Teucalhujacan.

njcan corpus xp̄i. itocaiocan Sanct lorenço tepetlatl motqujtica, pachtic, vilantoc, tlacaio, itech onovac.

---

3. Headings or explanations in Spanish appear between paragraphs in the Nahuatl text. The Spanish text discusses *"las ydolatrias principales antiguas, que se hazian, y aun hazen."*

Chapultepetl

*Another well-known mountain whence issues the
former spring of Mexico*

It is here at Atlacuiuayan. The name of the place
is San Miguel. It is watered, wooded, very rocky,
craggy; it has [a formation like] a tail. It provides
drink; it establishes, it provides development, growth,
to the Mexican nation, to the realm of Tenochtitlan,
to all the city.

Petlacaltepetl

*Another mountain which is toward San Pedro,
which is called Xaloztoc, near Santa Clara*

It is wide, like a basket. Hence it is named Petla-
caltepetl. It is wooded, high, outreaching, watered.

Acontepetl

*Another mountain which is in
the Mixteca province*

It is in Mixtlan, a Mixteca mountain. It is very
large, high, big — huge.

Coatepetl

Another mountain which is among the Chichimeca

It is here in Chichimeca land. It is large, high. It is
radiating, spreading in various directions, going far
out.

Chicunauhtecatl

*Another mountain which is near Tolocan;
at its foot originates the Tolocan River*

It is here at Tolocan. It is very large. It is icy.

Coliuhqui

*Another mountain which is near
the province of Michoacan*

Here it is between Mexican land and Michoacan
land. It is wooded; it has wild beasts.

Tepepul

Another mountain which is near Tepepulco

It is in the land of Acolhuacan. This is the famed
curved mountain[4] at Tepepulco.

Spur

Extended mountain

This is next to a large mountain; it proceeds more
or less out of it. Thus [the mountain] towers above

Chapultepetl:

*Otro monte bien conozido de dõde mana la fuẽte
de mexico que solia ser.*

njcan atlacujvaian catquj, itocaiocan San miguel,
aio, quauhio, têteio, texcallo, cujtlapile, catlilia, quj-
manjltia, qujceliltia, qujtzmolinaltia in mexicaiotl,
tenochcaiotl muchi in civdad.

Petlacaltepetl:

*Otro monte que esta hazia Sanct P.⁰ que se llama
Saloztoc iunto a sancta clara.*

patlachtic iuhqujn tanatl: ic motocaioti petlacalte-
petl, quauhio, vecapan, vilantoc, aio.

Acontepetl:

*Otro monte que esta cabe en la provincia
de los mixtecas.*

mjxtlan in ca, mjxteca tepetl, cenca vei, vecapan,
vei, veitepol.

Coatepetl:

Otro monte que esta entre los chichimecas.

njcan chichimeca tlalli ipan in ca, vei, vecapã, tete-
peuhtica, totoxauhtica, veca tlacçaticac.

Chicunauhtecatl:

*Otro monte que esta iunto a tulocan
del pie del nace el rio de Tulocan.*

njcan tolocan in ca, cenca vei, ceiotica.

Coliuhquj:

*Otro monte que esta cabe en
la projncia de mjchoacã.*

njcan mexicatlalli, ioan mjchoacatlalli itzalã in ca,
quauhio, tequaio.

Tepepul:

Otro monte que esta cabe Tepepulco

acolhoaca tlalli ipan in ca, iehoatl in tlateiotia col-
tepetl tepepulco.

Tepemaitl:

Monte continuado

iehoatl in jtloc ca, vei tepetl in achi qujtoqujlia ic
panqujztica, ioan iehoatl qujtoznequj, in jtech çaliuh-

---

4. *Acad. Hist. MS: tlatẽyotia altepetl.*

it. And this means that which is adhering to the large mountain which also is towering above it, or else lies reaching outward.

SLOPING PLAIN

Hillock

It slopes downward. It is rounded — rounding.

PEAK

Sharp-pointed mountain

It is like an arrow point. This rises from the shoulder of a mountain which is sloping downward to a deep gorge.

HILL

Another mountain or hillock

It is hilly, large, high; small and low, small and round; cylindrical.

CLIFF

Another mountain; a cliff

Wherever it is next to a mountain, it is towering, it looms high; it forms a cliff. It becomes precipitous.

SUMMIT

Summit of a mountain

It is the top of the mountain. It becomes wide, spacious. It becomes wide, it becomes narrow, slender; it contracts; it decreases in size. It is high. It becomes cold, windy.[5] It is stone-dry, sterile.

HILLSIDE

Mountain slope

It is a mountain somewhat on its side, or tilted somewhat on its shoulder. It is hollowed; it is flat. It just stands tilted, sloping downward.

NARROWS

Narrow passage between two mountains

There is the mountain's short cut.
I go along the narrows, I come upon the narrows. That is, I travel the short cut, I take a short cut through the hillside, through the side of the mountain.

UPLAND VALE

Mountain promontory[6] or brow

It is hollowed. It is there where the side of a mountain, or a hillside, or a sloping plain is hollowed out.

tica vei tepetl, in no panqujztica, in noce vilantoc.

TLAMJMJLOLLI:

Collado.

temotoc, mjmjltic, mjmjliuhqui.

TLACHICHIQUJLLI:

Monte agudo.

chichiqujltic, iehoatl in jquechpan oaleoa tepetl, in oaltemoticac in jpan atlauhtli.

TLATILLI

Otro monte o colado otero

tiltic, vei, vecapan pachtontli, ololtontli, mjmjltic.

TLAXIXIPUCHTLI:

Otro monte. Risco

in cana tepetitech ca, in panvetztica, in panqujztica, xixipuchauhtica, xixipuchavi.

TEPETICPAC:

Cũbre de monte

in jicpac tepetl, tlapatlava, tlaveiia, tlatlalpatlaoa, tlatzolivi, tlapitzaoa, tlatitichavi, tlatepitonjvi, vecapan, ceoaia, iehecaatla, tetl oaoacca, atle iqujztoca.

TLAELPAN:

ladera de mõte

in achi itlacapan tepetl, anoço achi iquechtlan, peiaoac, comoltic, pechtic, çan icac, peiaoaticac, temoticac.

TLATOZCATL:

Gargãta entre dos montes.

vncan in jelhujltecaiopan tepetl, tlatozcatl njctoca, tlatozcatl njcnamjquj. q. n. ixtlapal njqujça, ixtlapal njiauh, in jelpan, in jtlacapan tepetl.

TLACOPACTLI:

… de monte o sobrecejo

comoltic, vncan in canjn tlacomoliuhtica, in jtlacapan, in anoço iquechtlan tepetl, anoço tlamjmjlolli.

---

5. *Ibid.:* yehecayotla.
6. Questionable: illeg. in Spanish text.

WOODED PLAIN

Tree-covered mountain plain

That is to say, it is a flat surface between mountains or at the top; or a break in the land. It is wooded; it is a forest. It lies well; it lies on the surface of the slope.

UPLAND PLAIN

High plain

That is to say, it is flat on the mountain, or on either side of a sloping plain. It is wooded, grassy, rocky, sandy.

CRAG

Sharp pointed mountain crag

It stands looming, high. It looms high; it stands towering; it stands smooth; it is smooth. It is smooth. It stands upright, ashen, chili-red. It is rough. It is like a warrior's hairdress. It is jagged.

CAVE

Narrow cave

It is narrow, penetrating, perforated, dark. It is spacious, enlarged. It is extensive, profound, deep. It is the home of wild beasts, of the coyote, of the serpent — a frightful place, made into a hole: perforated.

VALLEY

Valley with sloping plains or mountains on both sides

On both sides is a mountain. It is a dangerous place, a difficult place.

PASS

Another cut on both sides

It narrows; it is a narrow place, rocky, of many crags, with many boulders.

DESERT

Trackless desert, unpeopled, and full of desert trees

It lies shimmering, it lies shimmering mightily; it lies glowing, misty. It is unirrigated.[7] The *tziuactli*, the *nequametl*, the *netzolli* spread.

I go along the desert. I come upon the desert. I trot, I hurry; I become numb.

DESERT WASTE

Rough, harsh land like that of Totonacapan

Now it is called *uei tlalli*, which means it is very expansive. It lies glowing.

QUAUHIXTLAOATL:

llanora de monte poblada de arboles

qujtoznequj, iixtepetl itzalan, anoço iicpac, anoço tlalpetlaia, quauhio, quauhtla, vel manj, ixtlactitimanj.

TLAPECHTLI:

llanora en lo alto

qujtoznequj in jpan tepetl, anoço necoc tlamjmjlolli, pechiuhtimanj, quauhio, çacaio, têteio, xallo.

TEXCALLI:

Risco de monte agudo ē lo alto

panqujzticac, panqujztica, panvetzticac, xipetziuhticac, xipetztic, xipetziuhquj, moquetzticac, nenexeoaticac, chichileoaticac, chachaquachtic, tzôtzocoltic, vivitztic.

OZTOTL:

Cueua angosta

tzoltic, qujqujztic, coionticac, tlatlaioaticac, tlacoiaoa, tlapatlaoa, coiaoac, veca, vecatla, tequanj, coiotl, covatl ichan, temamauhtican, coionquj, coiocpul.

TEPETZALAN:

Valle que de ambas partes tiene cuesta o monte.

necoc tepetl, tlaovican, ovican.

TLACAMAC:

Otra tajada de ambas partes.

tlatzolivi, tlatzoliuhia, techâchaquachtla, têtexcalla, teôololla.

IXTLAOATL:

Desierto sin camjno sin habitacion llena de arboles de desierto.

cueiontimanj, cuecueiocatimanj, popocatimanj, aiauhtimanj, amomatoca tzioaciotoc, nequameiotoc, netzollotoc,

ixtlaoatl njctoca, ixtlaoatl njcnamjquj, nocxiquauhti, njnocxiana, njquappitzavi.

TEUTLALLI:

Tierra aspera y fragosa como la de totonacapā.

axcan mjtoa vei tlalli, qujtoznequj: cenca vei popocatimanj,

7. *Acad. Hist. MS: amo motocacama.*

I go along the desert waste; I come upon the desert waste.

GRASSY PLAIN
Land of many high, cold regions, uncultivated and treeless

It is a plain where the grass lies as a covering. Nowhere are there gardens, nowhere are there houses. It lies worthless, wasting. There are rabbits, serpents, wild beasts, wild animals.

FOREST PLAIN
Highlands with many trees and wild beasts

It is a plain with trees, wild beasts, wild animals; with coyotes, with serpents.

GORGE
Deep, rough gorge

It is deep: a difficult, dangerous place. There is fear.

PRECIPICE
Deep, dangerous abyss

It is deep — a difficult, a dangerous place, a deathly place. It is dark, it is light. It is an abyss.

¶

SEVENTH PARAGRAPH, which telleth of the kinds of rocks which are worked.

METLATETL
Stones from which metates are made

It is black, dark, hard; it is hard, very hard; it is ground. It is solid, round, wide; asperous, scabrous, unpleasing, blemished. It is [material] which can be fashioned well, worked, pecked, smoothed, abraded, sculptured.

I work a metate. I work a mano. I hammer out a metate.

IZTAC TETL
Another kind of Tenayuca stone

Iztac tetl is white, spongy, buoyant, light, weightless, flinty, airy. It is made cool; it is made airy.

IZTAC TETL
Another kind of Tenayuca stone

It is also called Tenayuca stone. It is whitish; some is a little chili-red on the surface, some white on the surface. It is wide, thick, thin.

teutlalli njctoca, teutlalli njcnamjquj.

ÇACAJXTLAOATL:
Tierra de muchos paramos ynculta y sin arboles.

ixtlaoatl, çacapachiuhtimanj, acan ca mjlli, acan ca calli. Nenqujztimanj, nēpoliuhtimanj, tochio, covaio, tequaio, tequanjo.

QUAUHIXTLAOATL:
Montañas de muchos arboles y bestias fieras.

ixtlaoatl, quauhio, tequaio, tequanjo, coioio, coaio.

ATLAUHTLI:
Barranca profunda y aspera

vecatlan, ovican, tlaovican, temamauhtica.

TEPEXITL:
Sima profunda vscura peligrosa.

vecatlan, ovican tlaovican, mjcovaia, tlatlaioaticac, tlanezticac, centlanj.

¶

INJC CHICOME PARRAPHO: itechpa tlatoa, centlamantli tetl mochioanj.

METLATETL:
Piedras de que se hazē los metates

tliltic, tlilevac tlaquavac, tlaquactic, tlaquacpatic, cuechtic, picquj, ololtic, patlachtic, tetecujtztic, côcomotztic, âcemelle, acan tlacanezquj, tlaiectlalilli, tlaxintli, tlaquaquauhtli, tlaxipetzolli, tlachichictli, tlacuicuitl.

Nimetlaxima, njmetlapilxima, nimetlatzotzona.

IZTAC TETL:
Otra manera de piedras tenayocas.

in jztac tetl, iztac, poxaoac, êcauhtic, çonectic, âietic, tecpaio, êcauhio, moceiotia, mecauhiotia.

IZTAC TETL:
Otra manera de Piedras tenayocas.

no itoca tenaiocatetl in jztaleoac, cequj achi ixchichiltic, cequj ixiztac, patlactic, tilavac, canaoac.

Itztapaltetl

Another kind of slate stone

It is dark, thin, wide, large; it is small; quite cold. I break *itztapaltetl*. I use *itztapaltetl*. I remove *itztapaltetl*.

Teçontli

Another kind of black pumice stone

It is black, chili-red, rough; it has holes. It is broken up, pulverized.

Tlayeltetl

Another kind of pebble

It is yellow on the surface, and its name is yellow stone. It is small; it is striped yellow.

Tetlayelli

Another kind of pebble

It is a rock which is nowhere regarded: a wretched round, twisted [stone], scabrous, asperous, pitted, full of holes.

Tetlaquactli

Another kind of pebble

It is the same as *tlayeltetl* — like *itztapaltetl*. It is round.

Metlatetl is round, hard, hard.

Tenextetl

Another kind of limestone

It is [a rock] which may be broken up; which is broken up, which is burned. It is like *tepetate*, like *cacalotetl;* hard.

I break up *tenextetl*, I burn *tenextetl*, I pulverize *tenextetl*.

Tenextetl

Another kind of burned limestone

This also means limestone which is not[1] pulverized, which is yet whole. It is white — very white; it is burning to the mouth — very burning, exceedingly burning.

Tlaquauac tetl

Another kind of coarse black stone

This means the same as *tetlaquactli*.

Cacalotetl

Another kind of stone which is not worked

It is clear, fine, smooth, very smooth: that which is to be burned to make lime.

Itztapaltetl:

Otra manera de piedras Pirraças

tlileoac, canaoac, patlachtic, vei, tepiton: vel itztic. Nitztapallapana, njtztapaloa, njtztapalqujxtia.

Teçontli:

Otra manera de piedra pomjze negra.

tliltic, chichiltic, chachaquachtic, côcoioctic, papaiaxtic, cuechtic.

Tlaieltetl:

Otra manera de Gujjarros

ixcoztic, ioan itoca tecoztli, çan qualton coztic ic oaoanquj.

Tetlaielli:

Otra manera de Gujjarros

in tetl acan motlacaitta, in ololpol, necujlpol, cocomotzpol, tetecujtzpul, xixipuchtic, qujqujztic.

Tetlaquactli:

Otra manera de Gujjarros

çan no ie in tlaieltetl, in jtztapaltetic, ololtic,

In metlatetl, ololtic, tlaquaoac, tepitztic.

Tenextetl:

Otra manera de piedra de cal

tlapanalonj, tlapanonj, tlatilonj, tepetlatic, cacalotetic: tlaquaoac.

Nitenextlapana, njtenextlatia, njtenexmolonja.

Tenextetl:

Otra manera de piedra de cal cozida.

no iehoatl qujtoznequj, in amo molonquj tenextli in oc maçitica iztac, iztacpatic, cococ, cocopatic, cocopalalatic.

Tlaquaoac tetl:

Otra manera de piedras recias negras.

çan no iehoatl qujtoznequj, in tetlaquactli.

Cacalotetl:

Otra manera de piedras q̃ no se labrã.

chipaoac, cuechtic, tetzcaltic, tetzcalpatic, tenextlatilonj,

---

1. *Ibid.:* ayamo.

264

I burn *cacalotetl* to make lime.

TEXCATETL
Another kind of stone which is not worked

It is the same as *tetlaquactli*. It is solid, hard, very hard, very tough. It is like a long pottery water jar.

ATOYATETL
Another kind of cobble stone

It is a rock lying in the river — round, roundish; large; small, minute.
I gather river rocks.

ATLAN TETL
Another kind of pebble

It is the same as *atoyatetl*.

TEPOXACTLI
Another kind of stone which is not worked

It is somewhat yellow. Some are green on the surface. They are broken up, like tamales of dried kernels of maize: round, wide, long, small, thick, thin.

XALNENETL
Another kind of stone which is not worked

It is somewhat green on the surface. It is broken up, fragmented.
I break up *xalnenetl*. I work *xalnenetl*.

XALTETL
Another kind of pebble

It is also a name for *xalnenetl*.

XALTETL
Another kind of cobble stone

It is coarse sand — coarse, round, spongy, airy.

I collect *xaltetl*. I gather *xaltetl*.

TECOZTLI
Another kind of good building stone

It is hard, yellow, round, wide, soft.

TEPETLATL
Another kind of rough stone

It is whitish, porous. It is porous.
I break up *tepetlatl*. I dig up *tepetlatl*.

njctenextlatia in cacalotetl.

TEXCALTETL:
Otra manera de piedras q̃ no se labran.

çan no ie in tetlaquactli, chicaoac, tepitztic, tepitzpatic, tlaquacpatic, tzôtzocoltic.

ATOIATETL:
Otra manera de piedras gujjas

iehoatl in atoiac onoc tetl, ololtic, ololauhquj, vei, tepiton, piciltic,
Natoiatenechicoa.

ATLAN TETL:
Otra manera de gujjas

çan no ie in atoiatetl.

TEPOXACTLI:
Otra manera de piedras que no se labrã.

achi coztic, cequj ixxoxoctic, papaiaxtic, tlaoltamaltic, ololtic, patlachtic, veiac, tepiton, tilaoac, canaoac.

XALNENETL:
Otra manera de piedras que no se labran.

achi ixxoxoctic, papaiaxtic, câcaiactic.

Nixalnenetlapana, njxalnenexima.

XALTETL:
Otra manera de piedras gujjas.

no itoca in xalnenetl.

XALTETL:
Otra manera de piedras gujjas

in xalli tomaoac, chamaoac, ololtic, çonectic, êcauhtic.
Nixaltepepena, njxaltenechicoa.

TECOZTLI:
Otra manera de piedras buenas para edificar.

tlaquaoac, coztic, ololtic, patlachtic, patztic.

TEPETLATL:
Otra manera de piedra Tosca

iztaleoac, poxaoac, poxactic.
Nitepetlatlapana njtepetlatataca.

Tecacayatli:
Another kind of clumsy stone

These are small rocks; they are fragmented.

Tepitzactli
Another kind of clumsy stone

These are tiny rocks.[2]
I gather up *tepitzactli*.

Tepopoçoctli
Another kind of clumsy stone

It is whitish, chalky, spongy, light; not heavy; honeycombed. It is honeycombed.

¶

Eighth paragraph, which telleth of the different kinds of roads of all sorts.

Road

[With] this [term] alone are named collectively all the sorts of [ways] for traveling, for walking, [whether] they are descending, are ascending, take short cuts, go direct, become narrows, are straight, are direct, are direct roads, are winding.

I come down the road. I follow the road; I walk it. I go half way along the road. I go beyond on it. I double back on it. I travel the road. I widen it, I narrow it. I go straight along it. I take a curve in it. I double back on it; I double back and forth on it. I travel the short cut. I travel straight along it. I narrow it. I make one lose his way; I make one wander from the road.

Main road
Wide roads made like paved highroads, with all their characteristics

It is wide, broad—one which widens, which broadens, which is spacious. It is clean, smooth, slick; very stony, full of holes. It is full of holes. It is pitted. It has gullies,[1] a gorge, crags; it is precipitous, with many breaks.

It has a log crossing, a wooden bridge. It has plants, trees. It is muddy; it has muddy places; it is abundant with mud, thick mud. It is watery, in the water, in much water. It is craggy, sandy, rough. It becomes rough. It is a rough place. It hardens; it is a hard

Tecacaiatli:
Otra manera de cargajo

iehoatl in tetl, tepitoton, cacaiacatica.

Tepitzactli:
Otra manera de cargajo.

iehoatl in tepitoton tetl.
Nitepitzacnechicoa.

Tepopoçoctli:
Otra manera de cargajo.

iztaleoac, ticeoac, çonectic, acovetzquj, aietic, qujqujztic, quĵqujçauhquj.

¶

Injc chicuei parrapho: itech tlatoa, in jtlatlamantiliz in çaço quenamj vtli.

Vtli,

çan ie mocemjtoa, in çaço quenamj toconj, nenemoanj temoticac, tlêcoticac. Tlaxtlapalhuja, tlaviltequj, tlatozcavia, melaoaticac, ixtlapal icac, ixtlapal vtli, cuecueliuhticac,

nôtemoa, njctoca in vtli, njcnênemj, njctlâcovia, njcnachcavia, njcxolochoa; nôquetza njcpatlaoa, njcpitzava, njcmelaoa, njccoloa, njccueloa, njccuecueloa, njqujxtlapalquetza, njctlamelauhcaquetza, njctzoloa, njteûtlaxilia, njteixcuepa.

Vchpantli
Camjnos anchos hechos como calçadas cõ todas sus calidades.

patlaoac, coiaoac tlapatlaoa, tlacoiaoa, tlaveiia, chipaoac, tetzcaltic, ixtlactic, teteio, côcomoltic, côcomoliuhquj, tlaacã tlâtlalacallo, atlauhio, tepexio, cotonquj, cocotonquj,

quappaio, quappanavazio, xiuhio, quauhio, çoqujo, çoqujtla, moca çoqujtl, çoqujchachaquachtli, aio, atlan, âatlã, texallo, xallo, vapavac, tlaoapaoa, tlaoapaoaticac, tlatepitzavi, tlatepitzauhticac, tlaoapavaia, tlatepitzauhia, techachaquachio, quappachiuhquj, te-

---

2. *Ibid.*: ỹ çaço *tleī tetl* is added.

1. *Ibid.*: *tlaaccã*.

place; it becomes rough. It is a hardened place, a rocky road, choked with trees, full of stones; an old road, an old main road; a new road, a new main road.

I travel the road, I travel the main road. I widen it, broaden it, narrow it — make it narrow. I sweep the road, I clean it up, I improve it.[2]

I take it straight ahead; I go directly along it; I go straight on it. I clear it of weeds. I go down it, I go up it; I travel directly along it. I follow its curve, I follow its curves. I double back on it. I follow the winding road. I break off [my journey] along it. I regard the smoothed [road].[3]

I remove trees from the road. I clean the road. I improve the road. I weed the road. I go along the road. I go on the main road. I encounter the road, the main road. I place myself on the main road. I fill the main road with dirt. I fill the main road with sheep. I herd them, I bring them to the main road. I join the main road. I come to join it. I join it there. I depart from it.

TRAIL

Narrow roads, with all their characteristics

It is slender. It is slender, thin, straight; a straight thing, long, very long, like an arrow. It is curved; it is many-curved, bending, winding, zigzagging, meandering. It is meandering, many-curved. It is curved, long, straight; it is completely good, fine. It is good, fine. It is bad. It is full of wild beasts, a place of fear, a place of fright. It is ascending, it is ascending in different places; it is ever meandering; it is choked with weeds, choked with trees, full of rocks. It lies full of rocks. It lies choked with weeds. It lies choked with trees.

I follow the trail. I encounter the trail. I join the trail. I travel the trail. I sweep the trail.

SHORT CUT

Its name is short cut, that which is just straight, which does not wind. Either the main road or the trail, where there is a good place, curves there. But the short cut just goes straight; it even passes where there is a difficult place. Perhaps somewhere it joins the main road or the trail, perhaps not. Nevertheless, it at once reaches where it is going.

tenquj, v̂çolli, vchpançolli, iãcujc vtli, iancujc vchpantli.

nûquetza, nuchpanquetza njcpatlaoa, njccoiava, njctzoloa, njcpitzaoa, nj́cochpana, njctlacujcujlia, njciectia,

njctlamelauhcaque, njctlamelaoaltia, njcmelaoa, njcxivichpana, njctemovia, njctlêcauja, njqujxtlapalquetza, njccoloa, njccocoloa, njccueloa, njccuecueloa, njcpoztequj, njcmjchiucaitta,

njcquauhtlaça, njctlacujcujlia, njciectia, njcxiuhpopoa, vchpantli njctoca, ochpanco njiauh, v̂tli, vchpantli njcnamjquj, njnochpantema, njcochpantema in tlalli, njqujmuchpantema in ichcame, vchpantli njqujntoctia, njqujnnamjctia, vchpantli njcnepanoa, njqualnepanoa, noconnepanoa, njcmaxaloa.

V̂PITZACTLI;

Camjnos angustos con todas sus calidades.

pitzaoac, pitzactic, piaztic, melaoac, tlamelauhquj, melactic, melacpatic, mjtic, coltic, cocoltic, cueltic, cuecueltic, cuecuetztic, cuecuetziuhquj, cuecuetziuhticac, cocoliuhticac, coliuhticac, melaoaticac, melactiticac acan quenamj, qualli, iectli, qualtiticac, iectiticac, âqualtiticac, tequanioticac, temamauhtican, teîiçavican, tlêcoticac, tletlecoticac, cuecuecuetziuhticac, xiuppachiuhticac, quappachiuhticac, tetenticac tetentoc, xiuhpachiuhtoc, quappachiuhtoc.

V̂pitzactli njctoca, vpitzactli njcnamjquj, v̂pitzactli njcnamjctia. nôpitzacquetza, nopitzacochpana.

IXTLAPAL VTLI:

itoca ixtlapal vtli, in çan onmelaoaticac, in amo tlatlacoloa, in aço vchpantli, in anoço v̂pitzactli, in campa qualcan vmpa tlacoloa: auh in ixtlapal vtli, çan ontlameaoa in manel ovican oncan qujça, aço cana connepanoa in vchpantli anoço v̂pitzactli: acanoçomo, aço ie njman vmpa âçi, in canjn tlamattiuh,

---

2. *Ibid.: nictlamelavhcaquetza.*
3. *Ibid.: nicmichiuhcaitta.*

"Short cut" means that it is straight: straight, good, fine; a good place, a fine place. It is good, it is fine; it is a difficult place, rough, a dangerous place.

SECRET ROAD

Secret road or short cut

Its name is secret road, the one which few people know, which not all people are aware of, which few people go along. It is good, fine; a good place, a fine place. It is where one is harmed, a place of harm. It is known as a safe place; it is a difficult place, a dangerous place. One is frightened. It is a place of fear.

There are trees, crags, gorges, rivers, precipitous places, places of precipitous land, various places of precipitous land, various precipitous places, gorges, various gorges. It is a place of wild animals, a place of wild beasts, full of wild beasts. It is a place where one is put to death by stealth; a place where one is put to death in the jaws of the wild beast of the land of the dead.

I take the secret road. I follow along, I encounter the secret road. He goes following along, he goes joining that which is bad, the corner, the darkness, the secret road. He goes to seek, to find, that which is bad.

FOOTPATH

Little-used road, with all its characteristics

It means the very seldom traveled trail, small and narrow. It is small and narrow, full of weeds, meandering, not very attractive. It troubles one. It is a forest, a dangerous place. It brings one into the crags; it traps one in a tangle of trees; it loses one, places one in peril, causes one to lose the way.

I go along the path. I encounter the path. I travel the path. I descend the path. I steal. By guile I kill one who goes along the path.

OQUETZALLI

It means the new road. It is clean, a cleaned place, very smooth. It is smoothed, decorated, arrayed, new, a road which is the privilege of the rulers. It is preciously good, a preciously good place, completely clean, made good, smoothed. Nothing lies cast away.

OLD ROAD

It is a road which one no longer travels, a dangerous place, impassable, full of stones, choked with trees. It is pitted with gullies, a difficult place.

ixtlapalotli qujtoznequj melaoaticac, melaoac, qualli iectli, qualcan ieccan, qualtiticac, iectiticac, ovican ovititicac, tlaovican.

ICHTACA VTLI:

Camjno secreto o ataxo.

itoca ichtaca vtli, in amo mjiec tlacatl qujmati, in amo muchi tlacatl qujximati: anoço in amo mjiec tlacatl qujtoca, qualli, iectli, qualcan ieccan, tetlacavi, tetlacavican, tlacacotlamachoia, ovican, tlaovican, temauhtica, temamauhtican,

quauhtla, texcalla, atlauhtla, atoiatla, tepexitla, tlaltepexitla, tlatlaltepexitla, têtepexitla, atlauhtla, aatlauhtla, tequanjtla, tequantla, tequaio, teichtacamjctiloian, temjctiloian, mjctlan tequanj icamac.

Ninochtacaᵛtia, ichtaca vtli njctoca, njcnamjquj, ichtaca vtli qujtocatinemj, qujnamjctinemj in tlatlacole, xomolli, tlaioalli, ichtaca vtli, qujtemotinemj, qujmottititinemj in tlatlacole.

ICXIVTLI:

Camjno poco vsado cõ todas sus calidades.

qujtoznequj icenca çan quenman toco vtontli, pitzactontli, pitzaton, xiuhio, cuecuetziuhquj: amo cenca nezquj, teixpolo, quauhtla, ovican, texcalco tecalaquj, tequavixmatlatili tepolo, teovicanaquj, teixcuep.

Icxiuhtli njctoca, icxiuhtli njcnamjquj, njcxiuquetza, njcxivtemoa, njchtequj njteichtacamjctique qujtocatinemj in jcxivtli,

ᵛQUETZALLI:

qujtoznequj, iancujc vtli, chipaoac, tlachipaoaia, tetzcaltic, tetzcaliuhticac, tlacencaoalli, tlachichioalli, iancujc, tlatocavtli, itonal, tlaçoqualli, tlaçoqualcã; acan quenamj chipaoaticac, qualtiticac, tetzcaliuhticac atle vetztoc,

ᵛÇOLLI:

in aocac qujtoca vtli, tlaovican amo toconj, tetenquj quappachiuhquj, tlaacan tlâtlallancallo, ovican

I go along the old road. I encounter the old road. I lose my way.

The old people also gave the name *coatl* to the road, the main road, etc. Thus they said: "Can it be that it is a little danger, a little serpent of our lord?" Or they said: "How hast thou come? Can it be that it is the serpent, the road of stumbling?" Thus they named the road "serpent," because it is long and winding. And they called the road *tequatoc*, since there is stumbling, there is the running of thorns into the feet.

¶

Ninth paragraph, which telleth of the various manners of houses, [and] their classifications.

Teocalli

Palaces of the gods made like massive towers, which they climbed by means of steps leading from bottom to top. On the summit of this tower was a building like a small chapel where there was the image of the idol to which it was dedicated, over an altar which they called momoztli

It means house of the god. In idolatrous times it was named *teocalli*. It is high, just an artificial mountain with levels, with steps. Some have one hundred steps, etc. And on its summit there stood two small houses, or just one; there the image of the demon, the devil, was guarded. This *teocalli* has levels, a landing, a stairway, a junction; it has a house, a house standing; it has a parapet, a column; it has columns.

I erect a *teocalli*. I build a *teocalli*. I climb up the *teocalli*. I dedicate a *teocalli*. I consecrate a *teocalli*.

Teocalli

It means the house, not the artificial mountain; [the house] just standing on the ground. There is, or there are, the images of the devils. Or the reed chest of one's image or the property of the god is there; it is guarded there. It is big, high, roomy, long, wide, stretched out, long and straight, a long room, a row of rooms.

It has a portal, corners, an entrance, a covering to the entrance, a stone column, a column, a door bar, a façade, a frontispiece, a wooden enclosure. It is roofed with thin slabs, with planks; it is uncovered; it is protected, with a parapet, with conduits. It is high, very high, very good, surpassingly good. It is a place to show, a place to exhibit.

v̂çolli njctoca, v̂çolli njcnamjquj ninjxcuepa.

In vtli in vchpantli Etc. no qujtocaiotia coatl in vevetque, in iuh qujtoa Cujx tlaca icac in jovitzin, in jcoatzin totecujo: anoço qujtoa quen otioalmovicac cuix tlaca icac in coatl, in vtli ca tequatoc. ic qujtocaiotia coatl in vtli, ipãpa viac, ioan cuecueltic: auh ic qujtoa, tequatoc in vtli ca neteputlamjlo, nêxiliva.

¶

Injc chicunavi parrapho: itechpa tlatoa, in queninamj icacalli, ixexeloloca

Teucalli:

Casas reales de los dioses echas a manera de torres macizas a las quales subē por vnas gradas hechas de baxo hasta arriba en lo alto desta torre: estaua vna [sic] edificio como capilleta dōde estaua la ymagē del ydolo a quien ella [era?] dedicada sobre vn altar q̃ los llamauā momuztli.

qujtoznequj teutl ical, in tlateutoqujlizpa in teucalli: motocaiotiaia vecapan çan tlatepetlalilli tlatlamaio, tlamamatlaio, cequj macujlpoalli in jtlamamatlaio Etc. auh iicpac, in vmpa icaca vntetl caltotonti, anoço çan centetl, in vncan mopiaia iixiptla in tzitzimjtl, in coleletli, Diablo: injn teucalli, tlatlamaio, apetlaio, tlamamatlaio, tlatlanquaio, callo, calloticac mjxioio, tlaquetzallo, tlatlaquetzallo.

Niteucalquetza, njteucalchioa, njctlecavia in teucalli, niteucalchalia, njteucalmamali.

Teucalli

q. n: in calli in amo tlatepetlalilli, i çan tlalpan icac, in oncan onoc, anoço onoque in jmjxiptlaoa diablome: anoço in oncan onoc, in vncan mopia ipetlacallo in teixiptla, in anoço in teutlatqujtl, vei, vecapan, coiaoac, tlaveca, tlapatlaoa, vilanquj, melactic, calmelactic, calmecatl

calixacaio, xomollo, qujiaoatenio, tlatempechio, tlaquetzalteio, tlaquetzallo, tlâxillo, calixquaio, ixquamole, quauhtepaio, calquauhio, tlaxamanjllo, tlapechoapallo, apechio, tlapachiuhquj, atenaio, apipilhoazio, vecapa, ixachicapa, qualpul, qualtepul, temachtli, temachpol,

It is very big, surpassingly big; very large, surpassingly large; strong, sturdy — a house sturdy in all its parts. It is beautiful, really good, a product of care, a thing made with care, formed with skill, fashioned with skill, one's lot.

Tecpancalli

Palaces where the lords lived. They were city buildings where audiences were held and the lords and judges met to determine public lawsuits

It means the house of the ruler, or the government house, where the ruler is, where he lives, or where the rulers or the townsmen, the householders, assemble. It is a good place, a fine place, a palace; a place of honor, a place of dignity. There is honor, a state of honor.

It is a fearful place, a place of fear, of glory. There is glory, there are glories, things are made glorious. There is bragging, there is boasting; there are haughtiness, presumption, pride, arrogance. There is self-praise, there is a state of gaudiness. There is much gaudiness, there is much arrogance — a state of arrogance. It is a place where one is intoxicated, flattered, perverted. There is a condition of knowledge; there is knowledge.[1] It is a center of knowledge, of wisdom.

It is not just an ordinary place; it is in some way good, fine. It is something embellished, a product of care, made with caution, a product of caution, a deliberated thing, made with deliberation; well made, the product of carved stone, of sculptured stone, plastered, plastered in all places: a plastered house; a red house. It is a red house, an obsidian serpent house. It is an obsidian serpent house, a painted house. It is a painted house — painted.

It is wonderful, of diverse striped colors, of intricate design, intricate. It stands constantly shining, wonderful, a marvel. It is the house of artisanship, a product of skill: formed with skill. It has a deep footing, a deep foundation; a deep foundation, a wide foundation. The lower wall is high. . . . It has sides. It has resplendent stones, hard stones. It is burnished, encrusted with mosaic, smoothed, thick-walled, wide-walled, thin-walled, straight-walled, smoothed. It is a smooth-rubbed [structure]; it stands scraped, roughened, unsmooth, pitted, uneven, irregular, rough. It is [a structure] which has an entrance, vaulted, with

veipul, veitepul, ixachipul, ixachitepul, chicaoac, chicactic, calchichicactli, qualnezquj, vel ipan qualli, tlanematcaujlli tlanematcachioalli, tlatoltecatlalilli, tlatoltecachioalli, tetonal.

Tecpancalli:

Casas reales donde habitauan los señores eran casas del pueblo donde se hazia audiencia y concurrian los señores y Juezes a determjnar las causas publicas.

qujtoznequj, in tlatoanj ical anoço altepecalli, in vncan ca in vncan nemj tlatoanj, anoço in vncan mocentlalia tlatoque, in anoço altepeoaque, in chaneque, qualcan, ieccan tlatocan, maujziocan, tlamaviziocan, tlamavizmamanj, mavizpa,

mauhcaiocan, mauhcapan, timalpan, netimaloloia, netitimaloloia, tlatimaloloia, neixpatlaoaloia, neçôçoaloloia, nepoaloia, atlamachoia, neixacocujoaia, nechamaoaloia, nepancoloia, topalpan, topalla, chamatla, chamapa, teivintican, teatlamachtican, teitonjcan, nemachpa, nemachoia, nemachovaia, nezcaliloia,

â çan cana queçinamjcan çan quecinamjcan, qualli, iectli, tlacencaoalli, tlanematcavilli, tlaivianchioalli, tlaivianvilli, tlaiolicavilli, tlaiolicachioalli, tlaiecchioalli, tetlâcujlolli, tetlacujlollo, tlâqujlli, tlâtlaqujlli, tlaqujlcalli, tlauhcalli, tlauhcali, itzcoacalli, itzcoacali, tlacuilolcalli, tlacujlolcali, tlacujlolli,

maviztic, tlatlapalpoalli, tlamomoxoltic, moxtic, tôtônaticac, maviztic tlamaviçolli, toltecacalli, tlatoltecavilli, tlatoltecatlalilli, veca tlatlalantli, vecatlan tetzone, veca tetzone, tetzonpatlaoac, tetzontilaoac, tetzovecapan, caltetzonvecapa, calanauhio, tlâmaio, tepepetlacio, tetlaquacio, tlachichicio, tlaxiuhçalolli, tetzcaltic, tepantilaoac, tepanpatlaoac, tepanpitzaoac, tepanmelaoac, tetzcaltic, tlachictli, ichicticac, chachaquachtic, chachaquachiuhquj, xixipuchtic, comotztic, cocomotztic, cocomotzauhquj, qujiaoateio, vitoliuhcaio, quauhteio, tzaccaio, puchqujaoaio, pupuchqujaoaio,

---

1. *Ibid.*: *nemachyoca.*

270

cross beams, with a covering; with an opening — with openings.

It stands constantly shining, it rests constantly shining. It stands ever resplendent, smoothed in all places. It is high, very high, enormously high; large, very large; good, very good. It is a suitable product, matched,[2] finished, agreeable, well considered; one which gladdens men, which pleases the soul. It is extended, roomy; it has a portal, a servants' hall — servants' halls, [rooms] pertaining to women, [rooms] pertaining to men. It is provided with a place of detention, an audience room, an eating place, a sleeping place. It is a populated place, a place surrounded by trees. It is a courtyard; it is provided with a walled enclosure,[3] it has a walled enclosure. It is low, a little low, squat, a small house; it is of average size, of ordinary size, pleasing.

TLATOCACALLI
House where the lord usually lived

This is the house of the ruler or of him who is esteemed. It means a good, fine, cherished, proper house.

HOUSE OF NOBLES
Palaces of important persons

It means the cherished, good, proper, beautiful house. Not high nor roomy, it is ordinarily agreeable. It is a place where there is deliberation, thinking.

TLAÇOCALLI
Sumptuous houses with many buildings

It is the house set, placed among many.

TLAPANCALLI
Flat-roofed house

It means not a hut, [but] a wooden house, the beams covered with planks; a house covered with wood, having a flat roof; flat,[4] with earth above,[5] with a parapet, with a conduit. It is open, unfriendly, an unsheltered house, nowhere peaceful, nowhere relaxing; a wild beast. It is called a wild beast because it becomes very cold.

tôtônaticac, tôtônatimanj, tlâtlanezticac, têtetzcaliuhticac, vecapan, ixachicapan, ixachicapãpul, vei, veitepul, veipul, qualpol, qualtepol, tlapanjtilli, tlapontilli, tlapanjtilli, ipan tlaqualittalli, tlanemjlilli, tlaiollocacopavilli, teiolqujma, vilanquj, coiaoac, calixaio, tlecopaio, tlêtlecopaio, çioapan, oqujchpan, tetlaliloiaio, tecutlatoloia, itequaia, cochioaia, ieieloaia, quauhtlaiaoaloca, itoalco, itvallo, tepancallo, tepancale, pachtic, pachtontli, pachpil, caltepiton, ipan qualli, ipan qualto, tlauelittalli.

TLATOCACALLI:
Casas del señor do[nde] el biuja ordinariamente.

iehoatl in jcal tlatoanj, anoço in aqujn maviztic. qujtoznequj, qualli, iectli, tlaçotli, mjmati calli.

TECPILCALLI:
Palacios de personas principales.

qujtoznequj, tlaçotli, qualli, mjmatquj, qualnezquj calli, amo vecapan, amo no coiaoac, çan vel ipan tlaqualittalli teicnjuh nemachoia, nematia.

TLAÇOCALLI:
Casas sumtuosas de muchos edificios.

in calli mjec ic tlaquetzalli, in mjec ipan actica.

TLAPANCALLI:
Casa de açotea.

qujtoznequj, amo xacalli, tlaquauhtentlli, vapaltzacquj, quauhpixollo, tlapanio, tlachiuhquj, pantlallo, atenaio, apipilhoazio, coiaoac, acan teicnjuh, calceceoazco, acã tetlacama, acan tetlacamatca, tequanj, injc mjtoa tequani, ipampa cenca tlaceceiaia.

---

2. *Ibid.:* *tlapôtilli.*

3. *Ibid.:* *yhitvallo* is added after *itvallo.*

4. *Ibid.:* *tlapachiuhqui.*

5. *Ibid.:* *tlapātlallo.*

CALPIXCACALLI
Strong house to keep the lords' property

It is the house of the steward, or where the property of the ruler or of the city is guarded. Each one is big, high, sturdy, strong, very strong. It is a trusted [place], much trusted. Things are heated; things are cooled. There is a gradual warming. It means the property is there. There is drinking, eating there.

ORDINARY HOUSE
Common houses

It means the not very good house, never presentable, never agreeable, disdained — a navel, that which can be ignored. It is disregarded. The little fireside is hot, warm.

POCHTECACALLI
Merchants' houses

It is good, very good, sumptuous. From its façade it is very good, attractive, beautiful.

NELLI CALLI
Well-made house

It means the good, fine, sturdy, cherished house. It is rugged.

MACEUALCALLI
Houses of the commoners

It means the house of the poor. It is a little squat, low, crude, unfit, unfinished; small and not finished; a humble house. It is of meager walls, a little good, a little sturdy. It has a little fireside. It stands disorganized, without eaves, without walls — a house exposed to the elements. It is cold, chilly. Water flows through; it spurts up in places. The wind swirls about; the wind blows through.

TECOYOCALLI
Small house like a pigsty

It means pigsty. It is a small house, small, not high, nor roomy, nor good.

HUMBLE HOUSE
Humble house

It means the unpretentious house, or the house of the humble, or the house of the poor. The humble home means [that of] one become indigent, a commoner, or the home of the humble or the poor.

CALPIXCACALLI:
Casa fuerte para guardar las cosas de los señores.

in jcal calpixquj, anoço in vncan mopia itlatquj tlatoanj; anoço altepetl, vevei, vevecapan, chicaoac, chicactic, chicacpatic, temachtli, temachpol, tlatotonja, tlaiamanja, totonjxticac: qujtoznequj vmpa ca tlatqujtl, atlioa, tlaqualo, in vncan.

ÇAÇAN IE CALLI:
Casas communes.

qujtoznequj, amo cenca qualli, calli, aquen nezquj, aquen onnezquj, xictic, xictli, nexictilonj, atle ipan motta tentletzin, totonquj, iamanquj.

PUCHTECACALLI:
Casas de mercaderes.

qualteul, qualtepul, topalpul, iixcopa qualpul, qualnezcapul, qualnezquj.

NELLI CALLI:
Casa bien hecha.

qujtoznequj, qualli, iectli, chicaoac, tlaçotli calli, colotic.

MACEOALCALLI:
Casas de Villanos.

qujtoznequj, motolinja ical, pachtontli, pachpul, âmjhimati, aompa êeoa, aiuh tlanquj, aiuh tlancatzintli, icnocalli, icnoiopantzin, qualtetzin, chicactzintli, tentletzin, cacaoacaticac, âtzonjpilhoace, aiatename, calceceoaztli, itztic, cecec atl qujqujzticac, atl memexticac, êecatl motetevilacachoa, êecatl qujqujztoc.

TECOIOCALLI:
Casa pequeña como pucilga.

qujtoznequj, caltepipitzotl, caltontli tepiton amo vecapan, amo no coiaoac, amo no qualli.

ICNOCALLI:
Casa humilde.

qujtoznequj, amo topalcalli, anoço mocnomati ical, anoço motolinja ical Mocnocha. q. n, mocnotlacauh, momaceoal, anoço mocnomatinj icha anoço motolinja.

272

COLOTIC CALLI
Hut or hovel

It means it is unpretentious, a lowly house.

HOUSE OF OUR LORD
Secluded sanctuary

It means there where the revered image of Our Lord is, or where prayers are offered, or where there is contentment. As is said, in Temitztla or Anauac there are really the houses of Our Lord.

XACALLI
Straw house

It is the house covered with grass, straw-covered, covered with straw; covered, whitened with chalk; a wide hut, a pointed hut, a sharp-pointed hut, a cylindrical hut. It is painted, a painted thing, bound with thongs. It is provided with a wooden enclosure, a reinforcing plank — reinforcing planks. It is a hut of wood, with a wooden roof.

ORDINARY HUT
Another kind of hut

It is not chalk-whitened. It is a reed hut or a grass hut, etc., mud-plastered, with chinks filled.

TLAPEUALLI
Straw-covered entry

It means a hut of just one side, which somewhere is just against the house; just one, just one side. *Tlapeualli* also means that with which the deer, the coyote, the wild beast is taken. It is also called *quauhtlapeualli*.

XACALTAPAYOLLI
Pointed structure of straw

It is whatsoever kind of round hut.

TLAPIXCACALLI
Hut in which the harvest watchers or maize field guards hide

The guardian of the fields sleeps there. It is small and low: a small passageway, small and narrow.

TECOYOXACALLI
Another kind of hut with peaked roof

It means a small hut. It is small, small and narrow; a small passageway.

COLOTIC CALLI:
Choça o cabaña.

q. n. amo topal amo no tlei, chaviztli calli.

TOTECUJO ICHAN:
Hermita.

q. n, in vncan onoc iixiptlatzin totecujo, anoço in vncan tlatlauhtilo, anoço in canjn vnca necujltonolli, in iuh mjtoa in temetztla, in anoço in anaoac, vel ichan in totecujo.

XACALLI:
Casa paxiza.

in calli: in çacatl ic tlapachiuhquj, tlatzontli, tlatzomalli, tlatlapacholli, teteçauhquj, xâcalpatlachtli, xacalhujtzolli, xacalnetzolli, xacalmjmjlli cujlloio, tlacujllotilli, tlamecacujalli, quauhtepaio, elquauhio êelquauhio, xacalquauhio, tzonioquauhio.

ÇAÇA IE XACALLI:
Otra manera de choça.

in amo teteçauhquj, tolxacalli, aco çacaxacalli. et. ixpeche, ixtzacaio.

TLÂPEOALLI:
Portal cubierta com paxa.

q. n. in xacalli in çaçecotl, in çan cana caltech manj ça çe ça çecotl, no qujtoznequj, tlapeoalli, injc maci maçatl, coiotl, tequanj, no mjtoa quauhtlapeoalli.

XACALTAPAIOLLI:
Chapitel de paxa.

in çaco tlein xacalli ololtic.

TLAPIXCACALLI:
Cauaña donde se ascūden los meseguerros o guardas de los mayzales.

in mjllapixque vncan cochi, pachtontli, qujqujztontli, tzoltontli.

TECOIOXACALLI:
Otra manera de choça puntiaguda.

qujtoznequj, xacaltontli tepiton, tzolpil, qujqujzpil.

XACALTETZOYOTL
Another kind of hut

QUAUHXACALLI
Plank house

Its name is "wooden hut." The walls of the hut are made of wood, either pieces, or beams, or poles, or sticks.

XACALMIMILLI
Another kind of poor house

Its walls are either of stone, of adobe, or of wood. [Its roof,] however, is just cylindrical, like a stone pillar.

QUAUHXACALLI
Another kind of plank house

Its understructure is either a [masonry] wall or wood; its roof is of beams.

UAPALXACALLI
Another kind of plank house

Its understructure, its walls are either a [masonry] wall or wood, but its roof is of beams; they are flat, unsteady.

TLALLANCALLI
Another kind of plank house

It means its understructure, its walls, are either a [masonry] wall or wood, but its roof is of beams; they are flat, unsteady.

TLALLANCALLI
Underground hand-dug cave

It means a house which stands in the ground. Nowhere does it become light; like a dark night, it is terrifying. There is hiding, there is torment. It is a place of misery, a house of weeping, a house of death, a house of the dead, a home for wild beasts. There is glorification, there is torment, there is suffering, there is pain.

CALNEPANOLLI
House with shading [upper story]

It means a house set in two parts; one stands below, one stands above it. It is sturdy. The footing is deep, the footing of stone and mortar is deep, well sunken into the earth; it stands well provided with a house foundation. It is a house with sturdy foundation, a house with wide foundation, thick-walled, sturdy-walled, thin-walled. It frightens one. Frail, it stands rumbling, trembling.

XACALTETZOIOTL
Otra manera de choça

QUAUHXACALLI:
Casa de tablas.

itoca quauhxacalli, in xacalli quavitl, aço tlatlapantli, aço oapalli, anoço quauhacatl, anoço tlacotl, in jtepaio muchioa.

XACALMJMJLLI:
Otra manera de casa pobre.

aço tetl, aço xamjtl, anoço quavitl, in jtepaio; ieçe çan mjmjltic, temjmjltic.

QUAUHXACALLI:
Otra manera de casa de tablas.

aço tepanjtl, anoço quavitl in jicxi, vapalli in jtlapachiuhca.

VAPALXACALLI:
Otra manera de casa de tablas.

aço tepanjtl, anoço quavitl in icxi, in jtepaio auh oapalli in jtlapachiuhca pepechtic, vixaltic.

TLALLANCALLI:
Otra manera de casa de tablas.

qujtoznequj aço tepanjtl, anoço quavitl, in jicxi, in jtepaio: auh oapalli in jtlapachiuhca, pepechtic, vixaltic.

TLALLANCALLI:
Cueua hecha a mano debaxo de tierra.

qujtoznequj, tlallan in jcac calli acan tlaneçi, mjxtecomac, temauhtica, netlatiloia, tlaihiioviloia, tetolinican, choqujztli ichan, mjqujztli ichan, mjcquj ichan, tequanj ichan, tetlamachtiloia, tetlaihiioviltiloia, tetlaçiaviltiloia, teellelaxitica.

CALNEPANOLLI,
Casa con sombrado.

q.n. ontemanj, calli, centetl tlanj icac, centetl tlacpac icac, chicaoac, vecatla tlatlalantli, vecatlan tlatetoctli, vellatemotlalpan in icac, vel caltetzoio, caltetzonchicaoac, caltetzonpatlaoac, tepanpatlaoac, tepanchicaoac, tepancanaoac, temauhti, âtevivi, cuecuetlacaticac, vivixcaticac.

274

I erect one house on another. I form one house on another for myself. I place one house on another. I form houses in two parts for myself.

CALHUIUILAXTLI
Houses extending one after another

It means many houses which are as just one. They are crowded, grouped together.
I bring houses together. I string houses out.

CALYAUALLI
Round house without corners

It means a round house. Nowhere does it have corners; it is a cornerless house.
I make a round house, I erect a round house. I make a house round.

CHANTLI
House in general

It means "house," in the speech of small children and the vain. It can only be said by one owning property. So it is said: "My house. Where is your house? The house of the ruler, the ruler's house."
Also they say it of the cave, the forest, the grassy place, in the water, the hole. So it is said: the home of the wild beast, of the coyote, is in the cave; the forest is the home of the rabbit, of the deer; the home of the fish is in the water; the home of the serpent, of the mouse, is in the hole.

TEMAZCALLI
House where they bathe

It is low, squat, provided with outlets, with a navel-like opening, with channels. It is wet. There is bathing, there are washing, cleansing, the holding of vigils.
I bathe myself. I wash myself. I cleanse myself. I hold vigil.

TEMAZCALLI
Underground cave for roasting meat

Also it means the oven where meat is cooked, where it is baked. [The meat] is called *tlatemalli*. And tortillas are cooked there.

¶

TENTH PARAGRAPH, which telleth of the kinds of caves, whatever kind they are.

Nicalnepanolquetza, njnocalnepanoltia, njcalnepanoa, njnocâcalnepanoltia.

CALHUJVILAXTLI.
Casas continuadas vnas con otras.

q.n. mjec calli, ça cenmanj, ololiuhtimanj, tepeuhtimanj.
Ninocalvivilaxtia, njcalhujvilana.

CALIAOALLI:
Casa redonda sin esqujnas.

qujtoznequj, calli iaoaltic, acampa nace, acalnacazio.
Nicaliaoalchioa, njcaliaoalquetza, njcaliaoaloa.

CHANTLI,
Casa generalmente.

qujtoznequj, calli pipiltotontin, ioan in âavillatoa intlatol, çan neaxcatiliztica in vel mjtoa; in iuh mjtoa nochan, can muchan, ichan in tlatoanj, tlatoanj ichan.

No itechcopa tlatoa in oztotl, quauhtla, çacatla, atlan, tlacoioctli; in iuh mjtoa, in tequanj, in coiotl, oztoc ichan in tochin, in maçatl, quauhtla ichan, in michi atlan ichan, in coatl, in qujmjchi tlacoiocco ichan.

TEMAZCALLI:
Casa donde se bañan

pachtontli, pachpil nacoche, xique, acallo, avio, nealtiloia, nepapacoia, nechipaoaloia, netotoçoloia.

Ninotema, njnopapaca, njnochipaoa, njnototoçoa.

TEMAZCALLI,
Cueua para asal carne debaxo de tierra.

no iehoatl qujtoznequj, in texcalli, in vncan icuçi, in vncan motema nacatl, in mjtoa tlatemalli, ioan in vncan icuçi tlaxcalli.

¶

INJC MATLACTLI PARRAPHO: itechpa tlatoa, in jtlatlamantiliz in oztotl, in çaço quenamj ic caca.

Cave

Naturally formed underground cave

It is hollowed. It stands hollowed, hollowed transversely, hollowed straight ahead,[1] hollowed downward into the interior of the earth. It is an abyss; it stands dark; it becomes dark, dark as night.

Cave

Cavern

[The cave of] the mountain, of the crags is extensive. It becomes long, deep; it widens, extends, narrows. It is a constricted place, a narrowed place, one of hollowed out places. It forms hollowed out places. There are roughened places; there are asperous places. It is frightening, a fearful place, a place of death. It is called a place of death because there is dying. It is a place of darkness; it darkens; it stands ever dark. It stands wide-mouthed; it is wide-mouthed. It is wide-mouthed; it is narrow-mouthed. It has mouths which pass through [to the other side].

I place myself in the cave. I enter the cave.

Tlaloztotl

Cave formed underground

It means just the earth hollowed out. It is that which falls in, caves in, fills with earth, fills with mud.

Tepetlaoztotl

Cave between two [rocks of] tufa, or perforated in various parts

That called *tepetlaoztotl* is the hollowed out *tepetate*. It is white, ashen; it stands darkened.

Xaloztotl

Cave from which sand is removed

The sandy *tepetate* which is hollowed out is called "sand cave." [The sand,] in small particles, is scattered, lies scattered; it becomes broken up. It is a place of magic, a supernatural place, a lurking place, a hiding place, a crouching place, a spying place.

Oztoxaxaqualli

Cave like a labyrinth; or cave which has many ways or many compartments

It means many caves all together, all in one system. Here in the cave I make holes, I make passages, I open the mouths [of the cave].

Oztotl:

Cueua debaxo de tierra naturalmēte hecha

coionquj, coionticac, ixtlapal coionquj, tlamelauhca coionquj, tlanjpa tlallampa coionquj, centlanj, tlatlaioaticac, tlaioa, mjxtecomac.

Oztotl:

Sima

tepetl, texcalli, veca, tlaveca, vecatlan, tlacoiaoa, tlapatlaoa, tlatzolivi, tlatzoliuhia, tlapitzaoaia, tlaxixipuchauhia, tlaxixipuchavi, tlachachaquachiuhia, tlatetecujtzauhia, temauhtica, temamauhtican, mjctlan: ic mjtoa mjctlan, ca mjcovaia, tlaioaia, tlaioa, tlâtlaiovaticac, tencoiaoaticac, tencoiavac, camacoiaoac, tentzoltic, tenqujqujztic.

Ninoztotema, oztoc njcalaquj.

Tlaloztotl,

Cueua hecha debaxo de tierra.

qujtoznequj, çã tlalli in coionquj, pachivinj, activetzinj, tlaltemjnj, çoqujtemjnj.

Tepetlaoztotl:

Cueua entre dos toscas o vna agujerada por diuersas partes.

iehoatl in mjtoa, tepetlaoztotl, in tepetlatl coionquj, ticeoac nexeoac, pocheoaticac.

Xaloztotl,

Cueua donde sacan arena

in xaltepetlatl coionquj, mjtoa xaloztotl tlacacaiacaticac, tlapipixauhticac, tlapipixauhtoc, tlapapaiaxivi, naoalloca, tlanaoalloca, netlatiloia, neinaialoia, nepacholoia, netepachiviloia.

Oztoxaxaqualli,

Cueua como laberintho o cueua que tiene muchos caminos o muchas apartamjētos

q.n. mjec oztotl, çan cemonoc, motqujticac njmjz motztoc tlacocoioca, tlaqujqujçavi, tlatenco ionj.

---

1. *Acad. Hist. MS:* after *tlamelauhca coionqui, acopa coyōqui* is added.

AOZTOTL

Deep source of water, like a cave

It is where in the water or in the mud it is very deep: an abyss. It is dark, dark as night, a fearful place, a terrifying place. It is agitating — a frightful thing, a place of ill fortune, without end.

It also means a water cavern in the crags; water in the crags.

OZTOTL

*The cave of Hell, which they call
by the names here noted*

It also means place of the dead. As the saying relates: "Our mothers, our fathers have gone; they have gone to rest in the water,[2] in the cave, the place of no openings, the place of no smoke hole, the place of the dead."

AOZTOTL:

Manãtial de agua profũdo como cueua.

in canjn atlan, anoço çoqujtitlan, in cenca vecatlan, centlanj, tlatlaiovaticac, mjxtecomac, temamauhtican, teiiçavican, tecuecuechqujtica, tecuecuechmjctica, tetonallazcan acan tlanquj.

Atexcaloztotl atexcalco, no qujtoznequj.

OZTOTL:

*La cueua del infierno que la llamã
por estos nõbres aquj puestos.*

no qujtoznequj mjctlã in iuh qujtoa tlatolli. Oiaque in tonaoan, in totaoan, in atlan oztoc, omotecato in apuchqujiaoaiocan, in atlecallocan in mjctlan.

Thirteenth Chapter, which telleth of all the kinds of sustenance.

FIRST PARAGRAPH, which telleth of maize, of whatever sort.

CINTLI OR CENTLI[1]
Ears of maize

That named ear of dried maize has grains of dried maize; it has a cob. It is the grains of dried maize; it is the cob. The top end is filled; the top smutty. It is thick-cobbed, much cobbed,[2] slender-cobbed. [The cob] forms first; it is the first formed: thick, slender, long. The straight ear of dried maize is thin of flesh, or thin-fleshed; a maize ball-reject; a ball-reject, a pyrite-reject, a sand-reject, a rotten ear of dried maize. It has husks — husks. It has dried husks, maize silk, tassels at the top. It is a cluster, cluster-like. It is storable. It can be made into a cluster, shelled, harvested, husked. It is huskable.

I harvest. I break it off at the base.[3] I pick the ear of dried maize. I cluster. I make a cluster. I form something cluster-like. I remove the green maize stalk.[4] I husk it. I take the ear from the stalk. I pick it. I pick the ear. I husk it. I remove the maize silk. I shell it. I shell the upper end. I shell the lower end, I shell it.

The white maize ear — that of the irrigated lands, that of the fields, that of the Chinampas, that of Chalco, that of Uexotzinco, that of the Tlateputzca, that of the Tlalhuica, that from the east, that of the Matlatzinca, of the Maçaua, of Michoacan, of the Totonaca, of Anauac — is small; it is hard, like a copper bell — hard, like fruit pits; it is clear; it is like a seashell, very white; it is like a crystal. It is an ear of metal, a green stone, a bracelet — precious, our flesh, our bones. It is soft, spongy, porous, light, extended, thick-hulled.

WHITE TENDER MAIZE STALK

Also its name is *olotzintli*.[5] It is first white, first

INJC CE PARRAPHO: intechpa tlatoa, in çaço quenamj in tonacaiotl.

ÇINTLI: ANOÇO CENTLI,
Espicas de mayz.

in motocaiotia cintli, tlaollo: oloio, tlaulli, vlotl, quatenquj, quâpopoiotl olotomaoac, olopatic, olopitzaoac, achcatlan, achcatlantic, tomaoac, pitzaoac, viac, cinmelactli, nacaiototochtli, anoço nacaiototochtic, cintapaiolli molqujtl, molqujtapaiolli, molqujpetztli, molqujxalli, çinpala, izoaio, izoatl, totomochio, xilotzoio, quamjiaoaio, ocholli, ocholteutl, tlalilonj, ochololonj, oialonj, pixconj, izoacujoanj, izoaiotlaxonj:

njpixca, njtlatzinpoztequj, njçincuj, nochoa, nocholoa, njtlaocholteuhtlalia, njtlavaiotlaça, njtlazoacuj, njtlatzicueoa, njtlaquechcuj: njtlacotona, njtlaxipeoa, njtlaxilotzontlaça, njtlaoia, njtlaquaoia, njtlatzinoia: njcoia

in iztac cintli, amjlpanecaiotl, ximmjlpanecaiutl, chinanpanecaiotl, chalcauitl, vexutzincaiotl, tlateputzcaiutl, tlalhujcaiotl, tonaiancaiutl, matlatzincaiotl, maçaoacaiutl, mjchoacaiutl, totonacaiotl, anaoacaiotl, atic, tepitztic, coioltic, tlaquactic, xocoiollotic, naltic, tecciztic, iztacpatic, chopilotic, çintepuztli, chalchiujtl, maqujztli, tlaçotli, tonacaiotl tomjo, poxaoac, poxactic, çonectic, açotic, cacaçoltic, eoaiotilaoac,

IZTAC, XIUHTOCTLI,

ioan itoca olotzintli, iztac achtic, achpiltic, achca-

---

1. *Cintli: Zea Mays* L. (Dressler, "Pre-Columbian Cultivated Plants," p. 150).
2. *Acad. Hist. MS:* olopantic.
3. *Ibid.:* nitlacinpoztequi.
4. *Ibid.:* nitlazvayotlaça.
5. *Ibid.:* olocintli.

tender, first reddened, like gourd seeds. It is something to be broken up. It is of two bodies, with slender cobs. They say it is [its] nature.

I cause it to have a slender cob. I cause it to form first. I make it like a gourd seed. I cause it to have a slender cob. I make the cob slender. It is broken up. It is cracked. It increases, multiplies.

YELLOW MAIZE EAR
Yellow ears of maize

It is hardened, hard, transparent; it glistens; it is clear.

REDDISH MAIZE EAR OR RUDDY MAIZE EAR
Bright reddish ears of maize

It is red, even-colored, soft, hard.

TAWNY MAIZE EAR OR TAN MAIZE EAR
Tawny ears of maize

It is tawny, of an even, tawny color; tawny in appearance. It becomes tawny, it becomes brown.

FLOWER MAIZE EAR

It is a white maize ear striped with color, varicolored; mottled, blotched, speckled with blood color. It is varicolored, unevenly varicolored, spattered with color, sprinkled with blood color.

COLORED MAIZE EAR
Colored ears of maize

Of that called colored maize, the husks of some are chili-red,[6] the maize ears white, but the interiors of [the grains] are ruddy. The husks of some are white; the maize ear is chili-red.

Its husk is dark blue. It is wonderful, marvelous, coveted, desirable — a coveted thing.

I honor it. I desire it. I venerate it, esteem it. I consider it with respect. I prize it.

BLACK MAIZE OR BLACK MAIZE EAR
Black ears of maize

It is black, dark, dark, brown, a black blend. Its maize silk is chili-red, soft, spongy, very spongy, not lasting, edible. It becomes black, it becomes brown. The hardened black maize ear is first, like gourd seeds, the first formed, hard; hard, small, a little white, a pyrite-reject.

tlauhtic, aiovachtic motlapananj, ontlaca olopitzaoac, dize la natura.

njcolopitzaoa, njcachcatlanoa, njcaiooachtilia, njcolopitzaoa, nolopitzaoa, motlapana, mjxtlapana, mjequja, tlapivia.

COZTIC ÇINTLI:
Espicas de mayz amarillas.

tlaquaoac, tepitztic, naltic, cuecueioca naltona.

TLATLAUHCACINTLI: ANOÇO TLATLAUHQUJ CINTLI,
Espicas de mayz bermejas

tlatlactic, icucic, poxaoac, tepitztic.

QUAPPACHCINTLI: ANOÇO QUAPPALCINTLI,
Espicas de mayz leonadas.

quappachtic, quappachicucic, quappachnezquj, quappachtia, canjlivi.

XOCHIÇINTLI:

Xochiçentli iztac cintli tlapaloaoanquj, tlapalcujcujltic, êezcujcujltic, êezcujcujliuhqui, êezcujcujltic, mocujcujloa, mocujcujcujloa, motlapalchachapatza, mezalpichia.

TLAPALCINTLI:
Espicas de mayz coloradas.

in moteneoa tlapalcintli, in cequj izoaio, chichiltic, iztac in çintli: auh ie tlatlauhquj in iiolloio, in cequj izoaio iztac, ie chichiltic in çintli,

moujtic in izvaio, maviztic, maviçauhquj, teiculti, tetlanecti, eleviliztli.

Nicmaviçoa, njquelevia, njcmaviztilia, njctlaçotla, tleoia ipan njcmati, njcmavizmati.

IAVITL, ANOÇO IAUHÇINTLI,
Espicas de mayz negro.

tliltic, tliliaiactic, iaiauhquj, camjltic, tlilpoiavac, chichiltic in jxilotzoio: poxavac, poxactia, poxacpatic, âvecaoanj, quaqualonj, tlilivi, camjlivi, tlaquaoac, iauhçintli, achtic, aiovachtic, achcatlantic, tepitztic, tlaquaoac, çan qualli, çan iztac, molqujpetzpa.

---

6. *Ibid.*: çan follows *chichiltic.*

The black pinto [maize ear], or the fly-specked [maize ear], or the fly maize ear

Varicolored ears of maize

Also it is named *cuitlacintli*. Its kernels are "pintoed" black. They are big, thick, long, large. Its kernels are soft. The white maize ear changes, the fly maize ear changes; it takes on a design.

Tender maize stalk

Maize stalks sprouted green, small, and medium-sized

It is brown, it is purple, it is a little ruddy on the surface, it is a little chili-red. Also they name it *otocintli*. It becomes red, it becomes brown.

Tender maize stalk

Varicolored young maize stalks

Yet also the chili-red tender maize stalk is called *xiuhtoctli*. It is interspersed with black which is really a little green — not especially black.

Double maize ear

Maize ears appearing in pairs

It is the divided maize ear, a maize ear coming out double. It is wide, an ear consisting of two.

Nubbin

Small ears of maize which are shoots of [large] ears

It emerges from another [ear]. It is like one's mouth. It is small. It is that which causes impotence, which smuts things; that which is prized above all others, a destroyer. It is highly esteemed, prized above all others. It causes impotence, spreads impotence; it causes things to be smutted.

I tear off a nubbin. I lift off a nubbin. I split off the nubbin. I make, I produce a nubbin.

Smut

Ears of maize which appear malformed

It is black, dark, like a *tamal*, like mud, appearing like mud. The green maize ear, the ripened maize ear become smutted. Smut forms. It becomes smutted.

Maize fungus

Ears of maize which appear malformed

It is white, thin, paper-like. It forms mushroom-like fungus.

Iauhcacalquj, anoço çaiolcacalquj, anoço çaiolcintli;

Espicas de mayz por diuersas colores.

ioã qujtocaiotia cujtlaçintli, iztaccacalqui in itlaollo cequi iztac, cequj iavitl câcalquj, vei tomavac, quauhtic, chamaoac in jtlaollo, poxaoac, in jztac çintli mocuepa in çaiolcintli mocuepa motlamachia.

Xiuhtoctli:

Pies de mayz nacidos verdes peq̃ños y medianas.

camjltic, camopaltic, achi ixtlatlauhquj, achi chichiltic: ioan qujtocaiotia otôcintli, tlatlavia, camjlivi.

Xiuhtoctli,

Pies de mayz yerua y de diuersas colores.

oc no mjtoa xiuhtoctli, in chichiltic xiuhtoctli, ic mocâcal in iavitl, çan nel achi xoxoxoctic, amo cenca vel iavitl.

Tzatzapalli:

Espicas de mayz que nacen de dos en dos.

in cintli maxaltic, omoloqujzquj, patlachtic omolomanquj.

Cacamatl:

Mazorquillas de mayz que son hijos de las maçorcas

tetech qujzquj, tecacamaio, çan qualton: tlamjctianj, tlapopoiotilianj, moieoatilianj, tepopoloanj, moieoatoca, moieoatilia, tlamjctia, tlamjmjctia, tlapopoiotilia:

njccamatzaiana, njccacamaaquetzaltia, njccacamatzicueoa: njcacamaiova, njcacamati.

Cujtlacochi:

Mazorca de mayz q̃ nacē disformes.

tliltic, catzaoac, tamaltic, çoqujtic, çoqujnezquj, cujtlacochti in elotl, in çintli, cujtlacochioa, cujtlacochivi.

Cinnanacatl:

Mazorcas de mayz q̃ nacē disformes

iztac, canaoac amatic, nanacati.

281

Rotten ear of maize

The green maize ear, the dried maize ear: that which rots, develops fungus, becomes moldy at harvest.

VOLUNTEER MAIZE

Maize which appears anywhere

It is the unplanted maize grain, the grain of maize which has fallen somewhere, which sprouts. Its name is *cinuechtli*.

CINCOZCATL

Ears of maize strung together

It is the ears of dried maize tied singly together by means of their husks, forming a necklace.

I form a necklace of maize ears for him. I make a necklace of maize ears for him. I provide one with a necklace of maize ears. I provide him with a necklace of maize ears.

DARNEL GRASS

False maize which looks like maize but is not

It used to be called *cinteococopi*. It is strong, vigorous, obstinate, sturdy. It is that which crowds out, which overcomes; it is a destroyer, which kills off vegetation. It kills off vegetation; it destroys, crowds out, overcomes.

EAR OF DRIED MAIZE

*Maize from various provinces, in the ear
and in various forms*

It is our sustenance, product of the fields, of the dry lands, of Matlatzinco, of the Maçaua. The kernels are slender, small, hard; they are hard like a bell, like fruit pits. They say it is that which breaks up, rots, powders. It is that which breaks up. It rots, it powders.

The dried maize ear — the maize of the irrigated lands, of the fertile lands, of the *chinampas*, of Chalco, of the Tlateputzcatl, or the Tlalhuica, of the east, of Michoacan, of the Totonaca, of Anauac — is large, a large maize ear. Its kernels are thick, fat, long, the first. They are soft — soft, feather-like, long, spongy.

And [the kernels] of the black maize are not those which break up. They say that they are those which do not rot, those which do not powder. They form ahead of time. They are those which do not break up, do not crack. They do not rot; they do not powder.

CIMPALA

Mazorca de mayz podrida.

elotl cintli, pixqujtl palanj, nanacati, poxcavi.

CINVECHTLI:

Mayz que se nace por ay.

in amo tlatoctli tlaolli: in çaçan can ovetz tlaolli, in jxoa: itoca cinvechtli.

CINCOZCATL:

Saltales de maçorcas de mayz

cintli tlanenetechilpilli in jca iizoaio, cozcatl mochioa,

njcçincozcatlalia, njcçincozcachioa, njteçincozcatia, njccincozcatia.

CINCOCOPI:

Mayz falso que parece mayz y no lo es.

mjtoaia cinteococopi, iollotlapalivi, iollochicaoac, iollotetl, chicaoac, moieoatocanj, moieoatilianj, tlapopoloanj, tlaximmjctianj, tlaximmjctia, tlapopoloa, moieoatoca, moieoatilia.

CINTLI:

*Mayz de diuersas proujncias en mazorca
y de diuersas maneras.*

in toncacaiotl, in ximmjlpanecaiotl, in tlaloacpanecaiotl, in matlatzincaiotl, in maçaoacaiotl, çam pitzavac, piçiltic in tlaolli, tlaquaoac, tlaquactic, coioltic, xocoiollotic, qujtoa: motlapananj, çioatinj, teutinj, motlapananj, cioati teuti.

In cintli: in tonacaiotl, in amjlpancaiotl, in tlalcozpanecaiotl, in chinanpanecaiotl, in chalcaiotl, in tlateputzcaiotl, in tlalvicaiotl, in tonaiancaiotl, in mjchoacaiotl, in totonacaiotl, in anaoacaiotl vevei, vei çintli in jtlaollo tomaoac, chamaoac, veveiac, achtic, poxaoac, poxactic, îvitic, patlachtic, çonectic,

ioan in iavitl amo motlapananj, qujtoa: âcioatinj, âteutinj, çan ie itemja in temj: amo motlapana, âmjxtlapana, âçioati, âteuti.

282

SECOND PARAGRAPH, which telleth of whatever kind of seed which is considered.

Maize in the ear selected for planting

The best seed is selected. The perfect, the glossy maize is carefully chosen. The spoiled, the rotten, the shrunken falls away; the very best is chosen. It is shelled, placed in water. Two days, three days it swells in the water. It is planted in worked soil or in similar places.

First a hole is made. The land is sought where there is moisture. The grains of maize[1] are tossed in. If there is no moisture, it is watered. At the same time it is covered over with soil, and the soil which is placed on it is pulverized. Then it is gathering moisture; then it swells; then the grain of maize bursts; then it takes root. Then it sprouts; then it pushes up; then it reaches the surface; then it gathers moisture; it really flies.[2] Then it forks, it lies dividing; it spreads out, it is spreading out. And they say it is pleasing. At this time it is hilled, the hollow is filled in, the crown is covered, the earth is well heaped up.

Also at this time beans are sown[3] or cast. They say that at this time this [maize] once again begins to grow, also begins to branch out. Then it reaches outward; then it spreads out; then it becomes succulent.[4] Once again at this time it is hilled. Then the corn silk develops; then the corn tassels form. At this time, once again it is hilled; it is, they say,[5] the hatching of the green maize ear. Then an embryonic ear forms. Then the green maize ear begins to form; the green maize ear shines, glistens, spreads glistening. Its maize silk spreads blanketing the green maize ear; its maize silk spreads blanketing it. [The maize silk] spreads becoming coveted — spreads becoming desired. Then, it is said, the maize silk dries up, withers away.

[The kernels] spread forming little droplets; it is said that they spread taking form. Then [the kernels] form milk; they spread forming milk. Then the surface [of the kernels] becomes evened. Then it becomes the *nixtamal* flower; now it is called *chichipelotl*. Then [the milk] thickens, at which time

INJC VME PARRAPHO: itechpa tlatoa, in çaço quenamj ic motta xinachtli.

Mayz en maçorca escogido para sembrar.

Mopepena in xinachtli; vel mocenqujxtia, in acan quenamj, in vel tetzcaltic tonacaiotl: vetzi in xoiauhquj, in palanquj, in piçiltic; vel motzonana, moia, atlan motema: omjlhujtl, eilhujtl, atlan temj: auh in tlaelimjcpa, anoço çan iuhcan in motoca.

achtopa motacaxtlalia in tlalli, ommotta, vnmana in çiaoac, õmotema in tlalli: intlaca çiaoac matoca, çan vel ipan in tlalli ic motlapachoa: auh cuechtic in tlalli ipan motema. Nimã ie ic mjtonjtica, njman ie poxcavi, njman ie iollotlatzinj, njman ie monelhuaiotia; njman ie iacaomjti, njman ie oallaxiponoa, njman ie oalpanvetzi, njman mjtonja, vel patlanj, njman xolloti, xollotoc, njman ie moiaoa, moiaoatica: ioan qujtoa, maviltitica oncan, y, motlalhuja, motacaxpoloa, vel moquechpotzoa, vel motlaltepevia:

no vncan jn metlaça, anoço motlapixavia: qujl oncan oc ceppa peoa, y, in mana, vncan peoa in no mamaxalloa: njman moteteoana, njman ie iaoalivi, njman ie ovanenecuioa: oc ceppa vncan, y, motlalhuja, njman ie tzopilivi, njman ie mjiaoati: oc ceppa vncan motlalhuja, in qujl moxilotlapana: njman ie nenepilqujça, njman xiloti, cueponj, tlatlatzca, tlatlatzcatoc in xilotl, itzon qujquequẽtoc in xilotl, itzon qujquequentoc teicoltitoc, tetlanectitoc: njman ie ic mjtoa tzommjctoc, chichinavi,

mjtonjtoc, mjtoa tlacattoc: njma ie chichiqujlivi, chichiqujliuhtoc: njman ie ic mjxteca, njman ie ic nextamalxochitia: njman mjtoa, chichipelotl, njman ie tetzaoa: vncan mjtoa, elotl: njman njcan vmpeoa, tlaquaoa, coçavia: njman mjtoa, çintli.

---

1. *Acad. Hist. MS: tlaolli.*
2. *Ibid.: mitoa valpatlani for mjtonia, vel patlanj.*
3. *Ibid.: hi for jn.*
4. *Ibid.: ouanenecoyoa.*
5. *Ibid.: hi for in.*

it is called *elotl*. Then, at this time, it begins to harden; it turns yellow, whereupon[6] it is called *cintli*.

¶

THIRD PARAGRAPH, which telleth of the different beans.

LARGE BLACK BEAN[1]
Large black beans like broad beans

It is large, big, long and flat. It has an eye. It is black, like charcoal; very black, gourd-colored, vari-colored, striped, colored like the quail, white, whitish, pale. It is like bean foliage; it is sturdy, tall, slender. It does not require water; it is compatible with the sun. It is that which suffers from rain. It is that which sheds its blossoms. The pod is thick.

I sow the large black bean. I plant the large black bean. It germinates, it sets a node. It sends out its first leaves. It forms bean foliage. It produces bean foliage. It sends out runners. It spreads, sending out runners. It forms a bud; it has blossoms; it bursts, breaks open. It forms a nascent pod; the nascent pods form, spreading. It forms a green bean. Green beans form spreading, spread forming. The green beans ripen; they spread ripening. They spread drying.

I harvest it. I take beans. I gather beans. I thresh beans. I clean beans. I winnow, I expose them to the wind. I cook beans in an olla. I eat the large black beans.

YELLOW BEAN
Brown or red beans

It is yellow; it has an eye; it is round, round like a stone. It is considered so big that they name it "yellow bean ball." It is long. It makes one vomit. It can be cooked in an olla; it can be baked. It is tasty, savory, pleasing, very pleasing; it is edible in moderation. It causes flatulence in one — it distends one's stomach. Grains of maize can be added.

RED BEAN
Red beans

It is round, like a round stone; chili-red, blood colored, red; small, tasty, pleasing. It is that which can be ground, that which can be broken up.

WHITE BEAN
White beans

It is small, round like a seashell, very white, polished, highly polished. It becomes white.

¶

INJC EI PARRAPHO: itechpa tlatoa, in nepapan etl.

AIECOTLI:
Frisoles negros grandes como auas.

chamaoac, vei, patlachtilaoac, ixe, tliltic, tecultic, tlilpatic, aiopaltic, cujcujltic, vaoanquj, çulcujcujltic, iztac, iztaleoac, pineoac eçoqujllo, oapaoac, quauhio, memelactic: amo anequjnj, tonalli inamjc, qujiauhti-ca cocolizcujnj, moxochiotepeoanj, exotomaoac.

Naiecotlaça, naiecotoca, oalhujtonj: ce iix qujoal-quetza, papatlacatoc: eçoqujlloa, meçoqujllotia, moia-catlaça, moiacatlaztoc, tatapachivi, xochio, xotla, cue-ponj, mjchpiltia, mjchpiltitoc, exoti, exottoc, mexo-iotitoc, exotl, coçavia, coçaujztoc, vactoc;

njcpixca, neana necujcuj, nevitequj, neiectia, njtla-êcamotla, njtlaêcaquetza, nepaoaçi, naiecoqua.

ECOZTLI;
Frisoles castañas o rrojos

coztic, ixe, ololtic, teololtic: injc qujveicateneoa. qujtoa: ecoztapaiolli ça viac, teiçotlalti, paoaxonj, hi-ceconj, velic, âviiac, veltic, velpatic, çan ipan in qua-lonj, teîiote teîtipoçaouh, tlatlaoiotilonj.

ECHICHILLI,
Frisoles colorados

ololtic, teololtic, chichiltic, eztic, tlapaltic, pitzaoac, velic, âvixtic, texonj, tlatlapatzalonj.

IZTAC ETL:
Frisoles blancos

pitzaoac, ololtic, tecçiztic, aztapiltic, tetzcaltic, tetz-calpatic, iztaia.

---

6. *Ibid.*: nican.
1. *Ayecotli: Phaseolus* sp. (Dressler, "Pre-Columbian Cultivated Plants," p. 142).

PALETL
Purple beans

It is violet, dark blue, large; like a round stone. It is in two parts.

AQUILETL
Red beans

It is purple, small, hard.

SAND BEAN
Whitish beans

It is whitish. Its appearance is like coarse sand; it is spongy, resembling black maize; it is light. It can be scattered by the wind.

QUAIL BEAN
Quail-colored beans

Also it is named *itzcuinetl*. It is white, spattered with black; it is small like a round stone.

MOTTLED BEAN
Speckled beans

It is broad, varicolored, mottled with white, mottled with black, varicolored. It can be scattered by the wind.

SMALL BEAN
Small beans

It is small, disordered: a disordered bean resembling the black maize.

MOUSE BEAN
Mouse beans; they are black and small

Also its name is black bean. It is tiny; it is like a round stone, like charcoal, like carbon.

QUAUECO

It is a producer of runners, a climber. Its pod is thick, its bean fat. It is variously colored.

¶

FOURTH PARAGRAPH, which telleth of *chia*.

CHIEN OR CHIAN[1]
A seed which is like flaxseed, from which comes an oil like linseed oil

White *chia* resembles the ear of white maize. It is hard, juicy, oily.[2] It is in twos. It is that which can be broken up, that which fills out. It is tasty, savory. It is that of which *pinole* is made; it is potable.

PALETL:
Frisoles morados

camjltic, movîtic, chamaoac, teololtic, ontlaca.

AQUJLETL:
Frisoles de color encarnado.

camopaltic, pitzaoac, tepitztic.

XALETL:
Frisoles blanquecinos

ticevac in jtlachializ: iuhqujn xaltetl, poxaoac, iavitl momati, âcouetzquj êcauhtic.

ÇOLETL:
Frisoles pintadas de color de codornjz

ioan qujtocaiotia, itzcujnetl iztac, motlilchachapatz, pitzaoac, teololtic.

ECUJCUJLLI:
Frisoles jaspeados

patlachtic, mocujcujlo, iztacacujcujltic, tlilcujcujltic, tlapalcujcujltic, hecauhtic.

EPITZACTLI:
Frisoles menudos

pitzaoac, tlanênel, enênel iauitl momati.

QUJMJCHETL:
Frisoles de Ratones son negros y menudos

ioan itoca tliletl, piçiltic, teololtic, tetecoltic, teconaltic.

QUAVECO:

moiacatlaçanj, movicomanj, tomaoac, in jexoio, chamaoac in jeio nepapã tlapaltic.

¶

INJC NAVI PARRAPHO: itechpa tlatoa, in chian.

CHIEN: ANOÇO CHIAN
Vna semilla que es como linaça y sale della olio como de la linaça

iztac chien, iztac cintli, momati tepitztic, aio, chiavacaaio vntlaca, motlapananj, mopoçaoanj, velic, aviac, pinololonj, ioanj:

---

1. *Chien: Salvia hispanica* L. (Dressler, *op. cit.,* p. 146).
2. *Acad. Hist. MS: chiavacayo.*

I make *pinole*. I make it into *pinole*. I sow *pinole*. I produce *pinole*.

BLACK CHÍA
A kind of black chía

Also its name is *ayauhchien*. It resembles black maize. It is that which does not break up, does not swell up, does not rot, does not powder.

CHIENTZOTZOL, CHIENTZOTZOLLI
A kind of white, rather round chía, like chili seeds, or almost

Its growing place is the hot lands. It is like a spindle whorl, hard. It is that which fills out, which is broken up. It is broken up; it breaks up.

Thus is the *chía* sown, thus is it seeded: it is only sown and covered over with the soil, just thinly, just smoothed over with the foot.[3] It forms a shoot, develops, grows, becomes like a spindle whorl, produces a shell, forms a shell,[4] colors, ripens, matures.

The white *chía* is that which is uprooted, which can be rubbed in the hands.

I uproot *chía*. I rub *chía* in my hands.

AYAUHCHIEN

It is that which can only be rattled because its shells are just hollowed out.

¶

FIFTH PARAGRAPH, which telleth of a kind of edible amaranth.[1]

COCOTL
Amaranth which is like Spanish goosefoot

Also its name is *nexuauhtli*. Its foliage is herb-green. It is leafed. It has butterfly-like leaves; it has leaves. It has branches; it has a top. The name of its spikelets is *uauhtzontli*;[2] the name of its seeds is *uauhtli*. They are sand-like, like spindle whorls, small and round, whitish.

FLOWER AMARANTH
A kind of red amaranth

It is red, flower-colored.

njpinoloa, njcpinoloa, njpinolpixoa, njpinolchioa.

TLILTIC CHIEN:
Vna manera de chia negra.

ioan itoca: aiauhchien, iavitl momati, âtlapanjnj, âmo poçaoanj âcioatinj, âteutinj.

CHIENTZOTZOL: CHIENTZOTZOLLI.
Vna manera de chia blanca y redonda como granos de chilli o casi.

tonaian imochiuhia, malacachtic, tepitztic, mopoçaoanj, motlapananj, motlapana, tlapanj.

Injc mopixoa: injc motoca chien, çan ommopixoa: auh in tlalli ic motlapachoa çan auhtic, çan vnmocxitlapachoa, achichilacachti, mooapaoa, mozcaltia, malacachivi, mocuechtia, cuechioa, moxaoa, coçavia, icuçi,

in iztac chian pioanj, matelolonj:

njchienpi, njchienmatiloa.

IN AIAUHCHIAN:

çan tzetzelolonj: ipampa çan camacoiõquj in jicacallo.

¶

INJC MACUJLLI PARRAPHO: itechpa tlatoa, centlamantli oauhtli, qualonj.

COCOTL:
Vnus bledos que son como cenizos o cenilcos de españa

ioan itoca nexoauhtli, qujltic in jxiuhio, qujllo, papaloio, amatlapale, mamaie, tzone in jmjiaoaio, itoca vauhtontli, in jxinachio itoca oauhtli: xaltic, mamalacachtic, iaiaoaltotonti, ticeoac.

XOCHIOAUHTLI:
Vna manera destos bledos colorados.

tlatlactic, xochitic.

---

3. *Ibid.*: õmocxipachoa.
4. *Ibid.*: after *cuechioa, xochiyoa* is added.
1. *Uauhtli: Amaranthus leucocarpus* S. Wats. (Dressler, *op. cit.*, p. 121).
2. *Acad. Hist. MS: vauhtzontli.*

COLORED AMARANTH
A kind of delicate red amaranth

It is chili-red colored.

BIRD AMARANTH
Another kind of amaranth. It is white —
at least the seeds

Its seed is white. It is just like a spindle whorl. It is not long lasting; it is a rapid grower. All of this can be cooked in an olla. Its tops, its foliage are edible.

YACACOLLI
Another kind of amaranth

Some of its seeds are chili-red, some black.
YACATZOTL. It is chili-red.

LARGE AMARANTH
Another kind of very red, very good amaranth

Also it is called the real amaranth. It is bitter, very bitter, exceedingly bitter.

ITZTONQUAUITL

This is all cookable in an olla: edible. Its foliage, when still small, can be very well drained of the water.

FISH AMARANTH
Amaranth, or its seeds, which are like fish roe

Also its name is *chicalotl*. It is yellow, round, rounded, quite like a round stone, hard. It is sand-like, hard. It is that from which amaranth seed dough is made.
I make amaranth seed dough.

BIRD AMARANTH
Chicken amaranth

It is likewise white. Its stalks are of average size; there are two.

MIRROR-STONE AMARANTH
Amaranth with very black seeds

Its seeds are black; they glisten.

PETZICATL
A plant whose seeds the chickens eat

When still small, after it germinates, its name is *quiltontli*; the name of its seed is *petzicatl*. And when it has grown, when it already has spikelets, its name

TLAPALOAUHTLI:
Vna manera destos bledos colorados finos.

chichiltic, tlapaltic.

TOTOLOAUHTLI:
Otra manera de bledos son blancos a
lo menos la semilla

iztac in jtlaaqujllo, vel malacachtic: amo vecaoanj, îciuhca mochioanj. Injn mochi paoaxonj, qualonj, in jtzõ in jqujllo.

IACACOLLI:
Otra manera de bledos.

cequj chichiltic, cequj tliltic in jtlaaqujllo.
IACATZOTL: chichiltic.

VEI OAUHTLI:
Vna manera de bledos muy colorados y muy buenos.

ioan mjtoa teuoauhtli, chichic, chichipatic, chichipalalatic,

ITZTONQUAVITL.

Injn mochi paoaxonj, qualonj, in jqujllo in oc tepitoton, cenca vel maqujxtia.

MICHIOAUHTLI:
Bledos o semjlla dellos como hoeuos de peces.

ioan itoca chicalotl, coztic, ololtic, ololiuhquj, vel teololtic, tlaquaoac, xaltic, tepitztic, tzoalolonj

njtzoaloa.

TOTOLOAUHTLI:
bledos de gallinas.

çan no iuhquj iztac, çan qualton in jquauhio, ontlaca.

TEZCAOAUHTLI:
Vnus bledos cuya semilla es muy negra.

tliltic in jxinachio, pepetlaca.

PETZICATL:
Vna ierua cuya semilla comen las galinas.

in oc tepitoton, in qujn jxoa: itoca qujltonjli, in jxinachio itoca petzicatl, ioan in oveix, in ie tzone: no itoca petzicatl. Injn mochi amo qualonj [in iquillo]

is also *petzicatl*. All this is not edible, [neither its foliage][3] nor its spikelet. Only the *quiltontli* is edible. And its seed is that which can be ground; it can be made into something sweet, it can be made into amaranth seed dough.

I make amaranth seed dough.

And its chaff is mixed with tamales of maize softened with lime. Tamales are made, tortillas are made.

I sow amaranth. I plant amaranth. It sprouts. Its crown lengthens. It is transplanted. I transplant amaranth. It takes root, forms branches, becomes round like a spindle whorl. The spikelets emerge; it becomes like the *iztauhyatl* herb. [The seed] becomes like coarse sand; it enlarges, swells, ripens.

I thresh amaranth. I rub it in my hands. I rub amaranth in my hands. I cleanse amaranth. I make amaranth seed dough. I eat amaranth seed dough.

¶

Sixth paragraph, which telleth of the gourds[1] presently edible.

Gour or yecayotli
Native edible squashes

It is cylindrical, long, rounded. The *tamalayotli* gourd has ridges; it is cacao-bean-like. It has gourd seeds; it has entrails. It is flower-like, sweet, pale, tasting of ashes, tasteless, stemmed, juicy, stringy, prickly. It has blossoms, gourd blossoms. It is edible uncooked, harming no one. It can be cooked in an olla. It is edible in moderation; it causes one's stomach to swell.

Tzilacayotli
Another kind of smooth, dappled squash

It is round, varicolored, colored like the quail, exuding milk. It is a weeper.

The name of the center of the *yecayotli* is gourd seed. It is white, long, pointed on both ends, having an eye.

The center of the *tzilacayotli* is black, small and round; yet again, earlier, its center, this gourd seed, is white. It is really[2] savory, pleasing, very pleasing, exceedingly pleasing, oily, juicy. It stains things.

I parch gourd seeds. I eat gourd seeds. I plant gourd seeds. I make gourd tamales. They sprout, burst, burst open, shoot out. The gourd [vine] be-

amo no in jtzon: çan iio in qujltonjli qualonj: auh in jxinachio texonj, tzopelililonj, tzoalolonj:

njtzoaloa.

Auh in jpolocaio, nextamalli moneloa, motamaloa, motlaxcaloa.

Nioauhpixoa, njoauhteca, ixoa, xoviiaquja, maquja, njoaoaquja, tlaana, momatia, momalacachoa, tzonqujça, iztauhiatia, texalivi, tomaoa, poxaoa, icuçi,

njoauhpoztequj njtlamateloa, njoauhmateloa, njoauhiectia, njtzoaloa, njtzovalqua.

¶

Injc chicuace parrapho: itechpa tlatoa in aiotli axcan qualonj.

Aiotli: anoço iecaiotli
Calabaças destas tierras que se comen

mjmjltic, patlachtic, cujtlapatlachtic tamalaiotli cuecueio cacaoaio aioachio, cujtlaxcole, xochitic necutic, iztaleoac, nexcococ, acecec, tzinquauhio, aio, mecaio, aioçonaio, cueponcaio, aioxochqujllo, xoxouhcaqualonj, aquẽ techiuh, paoaxonj, çan vel ipã in qualonj teîtipoçauh.

Tzilacaiotli:
Otra manera de calabaças lisas y pintadas.

ololtic, cujcujltic, çolcujcujltic, memeiallo chôchocanj.

In iecaiotli iiollo, itoca aiovachtli, iztac, patlachtic, necoc iaque, ixe

in tzilacaiotli, iiollo tliltic, iaoaltotonti: in oc ceppa nepa iiollo, inin aiovachtli, iztac vel âviiac, âvixti, âvixpatic, âvixcaltic, chiaoac, aio, tlachiaoa:

naiovachîcequj, naioachqua. Naiotoca, naiotamaloa, ixoa, vitonj, oalhujtonj, valpatlanj, maioçonantia, movilana, motlamjna, maioxochqujllotia, mjmj-

---

3. *Ibid.: in iquillo* is added.

1. *Ayatli: Cucurbita* sp. (Dressler, *op. cit.*, p. 130).

2. *Acad. Hist. MS: velic.*

comes prickly,[3] creeps, forms runners, produces gourd blossoms; they become cylindrical. The gourd blossom opens; the gourd blossom is yellow, very yellow, intensely yellow, like an ember, fuzzy in the center, hairy within. The gourd forms a small fruit. It drops [to the ground], grows larger, forms a rind. I break the gourd open. I remove the gourd seeds. I eat the gourd seeds.

[*End of Book XI*]

livi: in aioxochqujlitl cueponj, in aioxochqujlitl coztic, cozpatic, cozpiltic, tlexochtic, tomilollo, tomjollo; in aiotli chipinj, vetzi, chicaoa, quaxicaltia; naiotlapana, naiovachqujxtia, naiovachqua.

---

3. *Ibid.: mayoçonayotia.*

INDEX OF NAHUATL TERMS